Antitrust and Competition Policy

Business Economics

Series Editor: Scott E. Masten
Professor of Business Economics and Public Policy
University of Michigan, Ann Arbor, USA

1. Mergers and Corporate Governance
   J. Harold Mulherin

2. Antitrust and Competition Policy
   Andrew N. Kleit

Future titles will include:

Franchise Contracting and Organization
Francine Lafontaine

Wherever possible, the articles in these volumes have been reproduced as originally published using facsimile reproduction, inclusive of footnotes and pagination to facilitate ease of reference.

For a list of all Edward Elgar published titles visit our site on the World Wide Web at
www.e-elgar.com

Antitrust and Competition Policy

Edited by

Andrew N. Kleit

Professor of Energy and Environmental Economics
Pennsylvania State University, USA

BUSINESS ECONOMICS

An Elgar Reference Collection
Cheltenham, UK • Northampton, MA, USA

Published by
Edward Elgar Publishing Limited
Glensanda House
Montpellier Parade
Cheltenham
Glos GL50 1UA
UK

Edward Elgar Publishing, Inc.
136 West Street
Suite 202
Northampton
Massachusetts 01060
USA

A catalogue record for this book is available from the British Library

ISBN 1 84376 319 2

Printed and bound in Great Britain by MPG Books Ltd, Bodmin, Cornwall

Contents

Acknowledgements

The editor and publishers wish to thank the authors and the following publishers who have kindly given permission for the use of copyright material.

American Economic Association for articles: Oliver E. Williamson (1968), 'Economies as an Antitrust Defense: The Welfare Tradeoffs', *American Economic Review*, **58** (1), March, 18–36; Franklin M. Fisher and John J. McGowan (1983), 'On the Misuse of Accounting Rates of Return to Infer Monopoly Profits', *American Economic Review*, **73** (1), March, 82–97; Paul A. David (1985), 'Clio and the Economics of QWERTY', *American Economic Review, Papers and Proceedings*, **75** (2), May, 332–7; Michael L. Katz and Carl Shapiro (1985), 'Network Externalities, Competition, and Compatibility', *American Economic Review*, **75** (3), June, 424–40; Philippe Aghion and Patrick Bolton (1987), 'Contracts as a Barrier to Entry', *American Economic Review*, **77** (3), June, 388–401; Janusz A. Ordover, Garth Saloner and Steven C. Salop (1990), 'Equilibrium Vertical Foreclosure', *American Economic Review*, **80** (1), March, 127–42; David Reiffen (1992), 'Equilibrium Vertical Foreclosure: Comment', *American Economic Review*, **82** (3), June, 694–7.

Blackwell Publishing Ltd for article: Steven C. Salop and David T. Scheffman (1987), 'Cost-Raising Strategies', *Journal of Industrial Economics*, **XXXVI** (1), September, 19–34.

Brookings Institution for article: Robert D. Willig (1991), 'Merger Analysis, Industrial Organization Theory, and Merger Guidelines', *Brookings Papers on Economic Activity (Microeconomics)*, 281–312, references.

Center for Law and Economic Studies, Columbia Law School, and Harold Demsetz for excerpt: Harold Demsetz (1974), 'Two Systems of Belief About Monopoly', in Harvey J. Goldschmid, H. Michael Mann and J. Fred Weston (eds), *Industrial Concentration: The New Learning*, 164–84.

Elsevier for articles: Paul Milgrom and John Roberts (1982), 'Predation, Reputation, and Entry Deterrence', *Journal of Economic Theory*, **27** (2), August, 280–312; Jonathan B. Baker and Timothy F. Bresnahan (1988), 'Estimating the Residual Demand Curve Facing a Single Firm', *International Journal of Industrial Organization*, **6** (3), 283–300.

Federal Legal Publications, Inc. for articles: Kenneth G. Elzinga and Thomas F. Hogarty (1973), 'The Problem of Geographic Market Delineation in Antimerger Suits', *Antitrust Bulletin*, **XVIII** (1), Spring, 45–81; Timothy J. Brennan (1988), 'Understanding "Raising Rivals' Costs"', *Antitrust Bulletin*, **XXXIII**, Spring, 95–113; Timothy J. Brennan (1995), 'Is the Theory Behind *U.S. v. AT&T* Applicable Today?', *Antitrust Bulletin*, **XL**, Fall, 455–82.

Barry C. Harris and Joseph J. Simons for their own article: (1989), 'Focusing Market Definition: How Much Substitution is Necessary?', *Research in Law and Economics*, **12**, 207–26.

Journal of Law and Economics and the University of Chicago for articles: John S. McGee (1958), 'Predatory Price Cutting: The Standard Oil (N.J.) Case', *Journal of Law and Economics*, **I**, October, 137–69; Lester G. Telser (1960), 'Why Should Manufacturers Want Fair Trade?', *Journal of Law and Economics*, **III**, October, 86–105; George A. Hay and Daniel Kelley (1974), 'An Empirical Survey of Price Fixing Conspiracies', *Journal of Law and Economics*, **17** (1), April, 13–38; William J. Baumol and Janusz A. Ordover (1985), 'Use of Antitrust to Subvert Competition', *Journal of Law and Economics*, **XXVIII** (2), May, 247–65; Benjamin Klein and Kevin M. Murphy (1988), 'Vertical Restraints as Contract Enforcement Mechanisms', *Journal of Law and Economics*, **XXXI** (2), October, 265–97; S.J. Liebowitz and Stephen E. Margolis (1990), 'The Fable of the Keys', *Journal of Law and Economics*, **XXXIII** (1), April, 1–25; Malcolm B. Coate, Richard S. Higgins and Fred S. McChesney (1990), 'Bureaucracy and Politics in FTC Merger Challenges', *Journal of Law and Economics*, **XXXIII** (2), October, 463–82; David A. Butz and Andrew N. Kleit (2001), 'Are Vertical Restraints Pro- or Anticompetitive? Lessons from *Interstate Circuit*', *Journal of Law and Economics*, **XLIV** (1), April, 131–59.

Oxford University Press for articles: Gregory J. Werden and Luke M. Froeb (1994), 'The Effects of Mergers in Differentiated Products Industries: Logit Demand and Merger Policy', *Journal of Law, Economics, and Organization*, **10** (2), October, 407–26; Malcolm B. Coate, Andrew N. Kleit and Rene Bustamante (1995), 'Fight, Fold or Settle?: Modelling the Reaction to FTC Merger Challenges', *Economic Inquiry*, **XXXIII** (4), October, 537–51.

RAND Corporation for article: Thomas E. Cooper (1986), 'Most-Favored-Customer Pricing and Tacit Collusion', *Rand Journal of Economics*, **17** (3), Autumn, 377–88.

Simon and Schuster, Inc. for excerpt: Robert H. Bork (1978), 'Injury to Competition: The Law's Basic Theories', in *The Antitrust Paradox: A Policy at War with Itself*, Chapter 7, 134–60, references.

University of Chicago Press for article: George J. Stigler (1964), 'A Theory of Oligopoly', *Journal of Political Economy*, **72** (1), February, 44–61.

Every effort has been made to trace all the copyright holders but if any have been inadvertently overlooked the publishers will be pleased to make the necessary arrangement at the first opportunity.

In addition the publishers wish to thank the Marshall Library of Economics, Cambridge University, the Library of the University of Warwick and the Library of Indiana University at Bloomington, USA for their assistance in obtaining these articles.

Introduction

Andrew N. Kleit

I. Introduction

At the beginning, and at the end, antitrust and competition policy is about litigation. One party seeks either to stop another party from doing something or to collect damages from that party for previous actions. Each side presents its arguments to a decision-maker, such as an agency or a court. Each party competes with the other for the decision-maker's favor, throwing in whatever theory and facts they believe pertinent.

Driving the antitrust litigation process to a very large, and perhaps surprising, degree is the underlying economic literature. In the end, most antitrust decisions depend on the economic theory, well developed or not, that is employed by the decision-maker. Given this competition for litigation success, the economic literature has responded with evolving theories about what constitutes competitive and anticompetitive behavior.

While the US Sherman Antitrust Act dates from 1890, this volume picks up the story around 1970. By the 1960s, outside of the University of Chicago, a near-consensus had emerged in antitrust thinking. That consensus, however, which seemed to imply that a very large portion of firms' actions were anticompetitive, was deeply flawed.

The readings in this volume have been chosen to provide a sense of both the history and the current state of thinking about antitrust. Part I opens with two articles that exposed some of the flaws in the 1960s view on monopoly. The next two parts deal with cooperation between competitors. Part II examines economic thinking with respect to mergers. Mergers may represent the archetypical antitrust problems with their potential for both anti- and pro-competitive outcomes. Part III considers the economics of collusion. Despite broad agreement among industrial organization economists that collusion harms consumers and the economy in general – though there is much to gain from a reading of Telser (1994) – remarkably little empirical evidence is available on explicit collusion to support the *per se* rule on collusion in the United States.

Parts IV–VI contain selections on three specific sets of practices that have been frequent targets of antitrust scrutiny. Part IV samples the literature on vertical restraints. Part V covers predatory pricing, and Part VI examines perspectives on exclusionary behavior. A good deal of effort has been put into these theories, but their robustness and empirical relevance have also been questioned.

Part VII follows up the related issue of network externalities. Like the literature on exclusionary behavior, the empirical relevance of network externality concerns has been the subject of a great deal of controversy – controversies that have played out, and perhaps even reached their apex, in the *Microsoft* case. Indeed, the mixed outcome of that case mirrors in many ways the advances, and the challenges, facing the economic literature in this area.

Finally, Part VIII contains chapters examining the role of bureaucracy and politics in antitrust enforcement. Ultimately, enforcement policy is the result of a political process. As these chapters illustrate, even though economic principles do not always guide politicians and civil servants, government actors, and firms' responses to their actions, can nevertheless be examined through the lens of economics. I conclude this introduction with some thoughts on the direction of antitrust research and policy.

Selecting the articles for this volume was not a simple task. Decisions were based on how the articles changed the way economists or policy-makers viewed important antitrust issues. Unfortunately, it was not possible to include several law review articles of great importance. Many of those articles, and other important works from the economics literature, are cited in this introduction and in the chapters themselves.

II. The Articles

Monopolization

The volume begins with Harold Demsetz's (1974) classic assault on the 1960s consensus view on monopoly, 'Two Systems of Belief About Monopoly' (reprinted here as Chapter 1). At that time, a long chain of influential studies had apparently shown that concentrated markets had higher profits. Demsetz asked two fundamental questions: first, do the accounting profits in these studies have anything to do with economic profits? Second, even if accounting measures indicate the existence of economic profits, are excess profits the result of superior efficiency or market power? The answer to the second question, he argued, depended on which theoretical lens one used: did monopoly power cause high profits, or are high profits the result of greater efficiency, which also results in concentrated markets?

The influence of Demsetz's arguments quickly began to appear in economic analyses of antitrust cases (see e.g. Schmalensee, 1979). Nowhere was that influence more evident than in Franklin Fisher and John McGowan's analysis of the Department of Justice's suit against IBM, published as 'On the Misuse of Accounting Rates of Return to Infer Monopoly Profits' (Chapter 2). Their analysis of the relationship between accounting rates of return and economic profits (or the lack thereof), applied to the seminal case of the 1960s, contributed what many regard as the last nail in the coffin of the 1960s paradigm.[1]

Mergers

Merger regulation is the meat-and-potatoes of antitrust enforcement at the Federal level. Prior to the publication of the 1982 Department of Justice Merger Guidelines, however, the absence of a roadmap for executing merger policy left both courts and agencies without a systematic framework for assessing merger decisions.[2] This began to change with Oliver Williamson's 1968 article, 'Economies as an Antitrust Defense: The Welfare Tradeoffs' (reprinted here as Chapter 3), which laid out for perhaps the first time the important tradeoffs in the merger review process. Arguing that society should allow mergers that increased net welfare by creating efficiencies, Williamson set out the modern framework for a 'rule-of-reason' merger policy that contrasted with a line of Supreme Court decisions in which efficiencies could actually count against the defendants in a merger proceeding. His approach began the process that led to the establishment of a 'cut-off' threshold in concentration levels for merger enforcement.

Kenneth Elzinga and Thomas Hogarty, in 'The Problem of Geographic Market Delineation in Antimerger Suits' (Chapter 4), make what may have been the first attempt to propose a systematic version of market definition. The article is, in large part, a response to arbitrary market definitions proposed by the Department of Justice for beer merger cases in the 1960s. The Elzinga–Hogarty proposal of 'little in, little out' markets based on trade flows, though not directly responsive to the hypothetical price rise later postulated by the modern Merger Guidelines, has remained highly useful in such areas as hospital mergers, where accurate data on where consumers come from and where they seek service is often available.

The existence of a high market share in a well-defined antitrust market is not enough to find a merger anticompetitive. A complete theory of anticompetitive behavior also needs a 'competitive effects' component, that is a description of how the firms in the market will actually raise prices. In addition, it requires an explanation of how the resulting price increase will not be defeated by new entry. Robert Willig, in an article that offered a preview of the 1992 Merger Guideline revisions ('Merger Analysis, Industrial Organization Theory, and Merger Guidelines', Chapter 5), advanced the intellectual basis for the Merger Guidelines by integrating pricing and entry effects into the earlier framework to create a more comprehensive foundation for merger policy.

Among the other questions left open by the Merger Guidelines was how to determine whether a price increase would be profitable for a given monopolist. Barry Harris and Joseph Simons tackled this issue in 'Focusing Market Definition: How Much Substitution is Necessary?' (Chapter 6). If market power is the ability to profitably raise prices above competitive levels, what determines whether a price increase is profitable? Harris and Simons showed that market power depends, in large part, on the elasticities of demand and on marginal cost. This spawned a very large line of follow-up work.

Jonathan Baker and Timothy Bresnahan, in 'Estimating the Residual Demand Curve Facing a Single Firm' (Chapter 7), address the empirical estimation of demand elasticities. Econometrics requires data, and industry data were very scarce when Baker and Bresnahan wrote their piece. Today, with the widespread availability of scanner data for consumer products, extensions of the Baker–Bresnahan approach have been applied to a wide variety of mergers. A recent example is the Federal Trade Commission's (FTC) successful action blocking the Staples/Office Depot merger, in which Baker–Bresnahan played a starring role.[3]

Even with the critical market elasticities known, by just how much would a given merger raise prices, and how large do efficiencies have to be to offset that rise? Gregory Werden and Luke Froeb, in their 1994 article, 'The Effects of Mergers in Differentiated Products Industries: Logit Demand and Merger Policy' (reprinted here as Chapter 8), analyze these questions in the context of a differentiated product market. Using a logit model to simulate the impact of mergers in differentiated products markets, Werden and Froeb find that it often takes only a relatively small amount of efficiency gains to offset the anticompetitive effects of a merger. The article represents perhaps the first attempt to see how prices might actually change as a result of a merger or, as the authors suggest, to shed 'a little light in a very dark place'.

Collusion

Mergers are one method for firms to control the output of their rivals. Collusion represents another method to reach the same goal. While the potential for collusion is a central part of antitrust enforcement, surprisingly few articles have greatly influenced the thinking of scholars and enforcers about antitrust. One important exception was George Stigler's 'A Theory of Oligopoly' (Chapter 9), which posed collusion as a problem of information. Posing the problem for cartels as one of acquiring the information necessary to police collusion and stop cheating, Stigler sought to identify the factors likely to facilitate successful collusion. The factors Stigler identified, including the extent of a good's homogeneity and the size of contracts between sellers and buyers in the industry, are still crucial parts of the enforcement strategy against collusion.

In a review of Department of Justice conspiracy cases, George Hay and Daniel Kelley, in 'An Empirical Survey of Price Fixing Conspiracies' (Chapter 10), look for patterns in the data regarding which firms are likely to explicitly collude. The expectation in the economic literature up to that time was that explicit collusion would exist in industries with large numbers of competitors, with tacit collusion being sufficient in highly concentrated markets. Hay and Kelley, however, found that explicit collusion was more likely in highly concentrated markets, suggesting that markets are more prone to competition than was believed at the time.

Thomas E. Cooper's 'Most-Favored-Customer Pricing and Tacit Collusion' (reproduced here as Chapter 11) extended the Stigler framework into a more game-theoretic setting.[4] In particular, Cooper notes that facilitating devices, by changing the nature of the competitive game, can discourage cheating on cartels and therefore make them more stable and likely. Cooper also allows, however, that facilitating devices can have efficiency rationales and therefore need to be evaluated on a case-by-case basis.

Vertical Restraints

Firms engage in a variety of contractual relationships with suppliers and customers. By their nature, these agreements restrict the ability of the contracting parties to behave in certain ways. Since the 1911 *Dr. Miles*[5] decision, the antitrust attitude toward vertical restrictions has been generally hostile. Perhaps the most 'obviously' anticompetitive vertical price restraint is minimum retail price maintenance (RPM). Often called 'vertical price fixing' by its opponents, a minimum RPM contract is a constraint placed on a downstream firm not to lower the price of a relevant good below a certain level. Since the first focus of antitrust is to stop prices from rising above competitive levels, the anticompetitive effects of RPM would seem quite intuitive.

The first modern attempt in the economic literature to defend RPM was Lester Telser's (1960) piece, 'Why Should Manufacturers Want Fair Trade?' (Chapter 12). Telser explains that upstream firms may use RPM to assure downstream firms higher margins, which the downstream firm then converts into investments into special point of sales services for the product. Despite the article's explicit attention to RPM's use as a collusive device, Telser's 'special services' argument remained for many years the cornerstone of efficiency theories of resale price maintenance.

Benjamin Klein and Kevin Murphy offer additional insights into the potential efficiencies of vertical restraints in 'Vertical Restraints as Contract Enforcement Mechanisms' (Chapter 13). In addition to supplying the equilibrium analysis missing from Telser's argument, Klein and Murphy (drawing on Klein and Leffler (1981)) model vertical restraints as a self-enforcing contract in which the upstream firm assures downstream firms' compliance through the threat of termination. Their analysis extends the efficiency properties of vertical restraints beyond Telser's special services setting to almost any vertical relation with noncontractible dimensions.

Predatory Pricing

One of the legacies of the Standard Oil litigation from the beginning of the twentieth century was the widespread belief that predatory pricing was a large threat to the competitive system. This belief helped support antitrust policies that condemned 'bigness' for its own sake and led agencies and courts to discourage, rather than encourage, efficiency in the economy. But whereas predatory pricing was once thought to be endemic in the marketplace, today the argument is whether predatory pricing exists at all.

John McGee, in 'Predatory Price Cutting: The Standard Oil (N.J.) Case' (Chapter 14), began the academic attack on predation by undertaking what was then a novel idea: he went back and read about the Standard Oil case. It turned out to be a simple and effective approach. What McGee found was that Standard Oil, while a very clever monopolist, was by no means a predator. Indeed, it seemed the chance to gain Standard Oil's attention, and the merger premium that went along with it, was quite lucrative.

Robert Bork, in a chapter from his classic book, *The Antitrust Paradox* (reprinted here as Chapter 15), continued the attack on the underpinnings of price predation by outlining the economic task facing a would-be predator. Among other things, the predator must not only lower the price, but must also increase its own output to meet both the higher demand at that price and the lower supply from its rivals. Once the prey is driven out of business, barriers to entry must also exist that preclude the original and future entrants from re-entering the market once the predator raises its price. But since barriers to entry are likely to be barriers to exit, if new entry is unlikely to happen, inducing exit will be difficult as well. Indeed, under Bork's theory, it is difficult to see how predation could ever be profitable at all.

The modern theory of predation began with Paul Milgrom and John Roberts's 'Predation, Reputation, and Entry Deterrence' (Chapter 16). Milgrom and Roberts showed that, if there is even a small probability that instead of being profit maximizing a dominant firm 'enjoys' predation, a 'pooling equilibrium' may exist where profit-maximizing firms mimic the 'irrational' firm and engage in predation. In effect, the profit-maximizing firm pretends to be irrational and is thereby able to deter entry into its market.[6]

Exclusionary Behavior

Even if firms find predatory pricing rational under some circumstances, instances of pure predatory pricing seem likely to be rare. The same may, or may not, be true of other exclusionary tactics, however. In 'Cost-Raising Strategies' (Chapter 17), Steven Salop and David Scheffman argue that one way firms might seek to disadvantage rivals is to interfere in input markets in a way that raises the price of a strategic input. The theory has proven popular, and the phrase 'raising rivals' costs', though often ill-defined, has attached itself to many an antitrust matter.

Timothy Brennan was among those critical of Salop and Scheffman's argument. In 'Understanding "Raising Rivals' Costs"' (Chapter 18), Brennan contends that the phrase reflects nothing more than the old theory of monopolization cast in a new light. Specifically, he argued that the scenarios outlined by Salop and Scheffman are best observed as straightforward monopolization, and that raising rivals' cost arguments *themselves* can be used for anticompetitive purposes. Brennan is also skeptical of much of the empirical evidence cited for this theory.

Janusz Ordover, Garth Saloner, and Salop, in 'Equilibrium Vertical Foreclosure' (Chapter 19), present the now standard model of vertical foreclosure. In a model consisting of two independent upstream firms and two independent downstream firms, Ordover *et al.* show that vertical merger of one pair of firms creates higher input prices for the remaining independent upstream firm and higher prices for consumers. The model would thus seem to provide an economic rationale for antitrust scrutiny of vertical mergers.

Or does it? David Reiffen, in 'Equilibrium Vertical Foreclosure: Comment' (Chapter 20), suggests a number of difficulties with the Ordover *et al.* model. The structure of the competitive game, for example, seems to change before and after the vertical merger. More broadly, Reiffen challenges proponents of vertical foreclosure to demonstrate the robustness of their models. Are these models simply highly complex and fragile theoretical constructions, or can they truly be applied in real cases of antitrust litigation?

One of the central features of the economics of exclusionary practices is the ability of cooperating parties to impose externalities on other firms through their agreements. In Philippe Aghion and Patrick Bolton's 'Contracts as a Barrier to Entry' (Chapter 21) an entrant is sometimes deterred from entering and serving the monopolist's customer, despite being more efficient, by a long-term contract with large liquidated damages. Although the customer limits its ability to switch to the entrant, it gets a better price than it would have otherwise when entry does occur. While others have pointed out limitations of the model – including the unenforceability of excessive liquidated damages in English and American common law – Aghion and Bolton's analysis is notable for overcoming the Chicago School critique of exclusionary claims.

The literature on exclusionary behavior relies, in large part, on references to famous historical antitrust cases. Yet most of the allegations of anticompetitive exclusion in these cases have now been rebutted.[7] In perhaps the most 'obvious' case, *U.S. v. Interstate Circuit* 306 U.S. 208 (1939), the government successfully prohibited the movie theater chain Interstate Circuit from imposing minimum prices on its competitive rivals. In what may be the last article in this vein (as the supply of unrefuted historical exclusion cases has dwindled rapidly), David Butz and Andrew Kleit, in 'Are Vertical Restraints Pro- or Anti-competitive? Lessons from *Interstate Circuit*' (Chapter 22), undercut the logic of the anticompetitive theories underlying the *Interstate Circuit* case and trace Interstate Circuit's behavior to prevent free-riding on its promotional activities.

Network Externalities

As the economy becomes more and more information based, there is a greater interest in the economics of network externalities. The theory of network externalities, as laid out in Michael Katz and Carl Shapiro's 'Network Externalities, Competition, and Compatibility' (Chapter 23),[8] implies that standardization of network products can lead to large market inefficiencies. When consumers are 'locked in' to a standard, it can be difficult for a better product with a different standard to break into the market. The incumbent technology has 'excess inertia,' and consumers have insufficient incentives to learn about the new standard.

The article that first captured scholars' and enforcers' imagination in this area was Paul David's 'Clio and the Economics of QWERTY' (Chapter 24). David relates the story of the QWERTY keyboard, and how it achieved dominance in the typewriter area, even though the competing Dvorak keyboard is more efficient. Through this story, he has motivated the network externalities story to a far greater audience than is generally available to authors of scholarly economic literature. Ironically, the facts on which the notion of network externalities was popularized are subject to question, as Stan Liebowitz and Stephen Margolis show in their detailed investigation, 'The Fable of the Keys' (Chapter 25). Indeed, after considering the effect of such factors as heterogeneous products and large purchases, Liebowitz and Margolis, in this and a series of subsequent articles, have contended that the problem of network externalities has only limited relevance.

Antitrust, Regulation, and Bureaucracy

How is antitrust actually enforced? While antitrust is supposed to be about protecting market efficiency, firms may act in plenty of ways in the antitrust system to have the opposite impact. William Baumol and Ordover describe some of these methods in 'The Use of Antitrust to Subvert Competition' (Chapter 26). In particular, claims by competing firms against one another have the flavor of trying to protect competitors rather than competition. This is one of the aspects that make assertions of exclusionary behavior so difficult to evaluate.

Antitrust does not live in a vacuum with other forms of government intervention. Following up on Brennan (1987), Timothy Brennan explains in 'Is the Theory Behind *U.S. v. AT&T* Applicable Today?' (Chapter 27) the rationale for antitrust scrutiny of a firm that is regulated at one level of production and unregulated at another, an issue that is crucial to the competitive restructuring of the electricity and telephone industries. The level of policy success seems to depend on how complicated the relevant product is. For electricity, this approach appears to be viable. For telephone and communications products, which have a myriad of product and product attributes, this policy regime has had mixed results, at best.

Given all of the theory about ways to evaluate the competitive impact of mergers, how do the Federal antitrust agencies perform this duty? Malcolm Coate, Richard Higgins, and Fred McChesney present evidence from the US Federal Trade Commission in 'Bureaucracy and Politics in FTC Merger Challenges' (Chapter 28). Using internal FTC data, the authors find that merger decisions are, in large part, focused on criteria laid out in the Merger Guidelines. When disagreements about those criteria arise between the FTC's legal and economic staff, the lawyers' views had about two to three times the influence of the economists' views.

Perhaps not surprisingly, congressional oversight also played a role in FTC merger decisions.

Once the agency has decided to seek to block a merger transaction, the parties can fight the agency and go to court, fold and thereby give up the merger, or try to cut a deal. In 'Fight, Fold or Settle?: Modelling the Reaction to FTC Merger Challenges' (Chapter 29), Coate, Kleit, and Rene Bustamante find that the competitive merits of a merger transaction have very little impact on firms' responses to agency action. Rather, it is the financial nature of the deal that largely determines firms' actions. If a merger has a large conglomerate portion, the firms will settle with the agency to allow the uncontroversial portion of the deal to be consummated. Thus, in these matters, the agencies appear to have powers more akin to those of a regulatory agency than a prosecutor.

III. Conclusion

Antitrust continues to be an active intellectual field. At this point, scholars and practitioners agree about what constitutes market power and how to go about evaluating the competitive impacts of mergers. Greater discord exists in the area of exclusionary conduct. One can see these theories clashing in the *Microsoft* case.

Of course, there are many other unanswered questions in antitrust. With respect to mergers, there still is no agreed-upon methodology for determining whether and when the threat of entry is sufficient to stop anticompetitive activity or for measuring merger-specific efficiencies. For monopolization cases, there remains no consensus on how to determine the relevant market definition. It remains to be seen if antitrust enforcement can successfully work together with the regulatory regimes in telecommunications and electricity to foster robust competition. Finally, it is unclear if the increasing internationalization of competition policy will result in more policy harmonization, or even if such harmonization is desirable. These are just some of the issues challenges that await future antitrust scholars.

Notes

I thank, without implication, Tim Brennan, Malcolm Coate, Scott Masten, Jim Meehan, Jon Nelson, Tom Ross, Margaret Sanderson, and Ralph Winter, for their assistance.

1. Landes and Posner (1981), in a lengthy law review piece not reprinted here, offer one of the first systematic efforts to measure market power other than through accounting profits.
2. Having contemplated pre-Merger Guidelines case memoranda as an economist at two competition agencies, I can personally attest to the extent of the influence of the Guidelines on enforcement practice. Werden (1983) discusses how the Merger Guidelines dramatically changed the way merger enforcement was applied.
3. *FTC v. Staples, Inc.* 970 F. Supp. 1066 (1997).
4. See also Salop (1986).
5. *Dr. Miles Medical v. John D. Park and Sons*, 220 U.S. 373 (1911).
6. The Milgrom and Roberts theory is tested, at least indirectly, in Burns (1986).
7. See Lopatka and Kleit (1995, pp. 1260–61) for a literature review.
8. See the similar work by Farrell and Saloner (1985).

References

Brennan, T. (1987), 'Why Regulated Firms Should Be Kept Out of Unregulated Markets: Understanding the Divestiture in U.S. v. AT&T,' *Antitrust Bulletin*, **32**, 741–93.

Burns, M. (1986), 'Predatory Pricing and the Acquisition Cost of Competitors,' *Journal of Political Economy*, **94**, 266–96.

Cooper, T.E. (1986), 'Most-Favored-Customer Pricing and Tacit Collusion,' *Rand Journal of Economics*, **17**, 377–88.

Farrell, J. and G. Saloner (1985), 'Standardization, Compatibility, and Innovation,' *Rand Journal of Economics*, **16**, 70–83.

Klein, B. and K.B. Leffler (1981), 'The Role of Market Forces in Assuring Contractual Performance,' *Journal of Political Economy*, **89**, 615–41.

Landes, W. and R. Posner (1981), 'Market Power in Antitrust Cases,' *Harvard Law Review*, **94**, 937–96.

Lopatka, J.E. and A.N. Kleit (1995), 'The Mystery of *Lorain Journal* and the Quest for Foreclosure,' *Texas Law Review*, **73**, 1255–306.

Salop, S. C. (1986), 'Practices that (Credibly) Facilitate Oligopoly Co-ordination,' in Stiglitz, Joseph E. and Mathewson, G. Frank (eds), *New Developments in the Analysis of Market Structure*, Cambridge, MA: MIT Press, pp. 265–90.

Schmalensee, R. (1979), 'On the Use of Economic Models in Antitrust: The ReaLemon Case,' *University of Pennsylvania Law Review*, **127**, 994–1050.

Telser, L.G. (1994), 'The Usefulness of Core Theory in Economics,' *Journal of Economic Perspectives*, **8**, 151–64.

Werden, G.J. (1983), 'Market Delineation and the Justice Department's Merger Guidelines,' *Duke Law Journal*, **3**, 514–79.

Part I
Monopolization

[1]

Two Systems of Belief About Monopoly

Harold Demsetz*

I

The old adage "seeing is believing" contains a double measure of truth, for there also is much merit in the notion that "believing is seeing." Facts must be placed into a system of belief before they yield to interpretation. The same astronomical observations in the Copernican theory convey an entirely different image of the universe in the Ptolemaic theory, and phenomena assume new meaning when we shift from the Newtonian system to the Einsteinian system. Economic facts also require a system of belief before they can be interpreted. There is an impression that economists share a common system of belief about monopoly and competition into which the facts about concentration and profits, whatever they may be, can be fitted neatly. But this is not so, and the illusion of unanimity is now being shattered.

This disillusionment stems partly from the fact that students of monopoly and competition now are being asked to respond to policy alternatives of greater significance than those posed since the decade of the thirties. The renewed attempt to link monopoly to inflation via some type of "cost-push" inflation theory has thrust the monopoly problem into policy areas usually reserved to Keynesians and Monetarists. But more important has been the continuing attempt to incorporate the monopoly model, as that term often is understood or misunderstood, into legislation that would bring about a radical restructuring of industry. Such legislation was recommended by President Johnson's antitrust task force, and, in much stronger form, currently is sought by Senator Hart. These legislative programs already have brought the debate among economists before the public and have forced closer questioning of our beliefs and evidence about the operation of the economic system.

In addition, there recently have been factual findings that are difficult to explain with the accepted doctrine about the relationship between competition and industry structure. These new findings must, at the least, stimulate a reexamination of doctrine and, possibly, a revolution in doctrine. All of this should make the workday of the economist more interesting and that of the policymaker more hesitant.

Two competing theories about monopoly are heading for a showdown. Our understanding of the operation of the economic system depends largely on which of these two systems of belief is adopted. The currently most familiar belief conceives of monopoly power as producible by a firm or an industry without any substantial aid from the government. I shall call this the "self-

* Professor of Economics, The University of California at Los Angeles, and Senior Research Fellow, The Hoover Institution. For further biographical information, see Appendix D.

sufficiency" theory. A second belief, which may be named the "interventionism" theory, sees monopoly power as a derivative of governmental interventions. These two views refer to a difference in belief about the source of *most* monopoly power, not to every instance of monopoly power.

It is true that the government's agreement to provide protection from would-be competitors is secured at least partly through the activities of firms, and therefore, that the interventionism theory of monopoly is a variant of the self-sufficiency theory. Nonetheless it is useful to preserve the substantive distinction of these competing views when we deal with the problem of how we can best cope with monopoly power. Should we try to reduce the degree of government intervention, or should we seek to restructure industries and to modify the competitive tactics used by firms? Those who hold to the belief of self-sufficient monopoly will answer this question by seeking more intervention, while those who see the source of monopoly in government intervention will seek to reduce the role of government in our economy.

This brief description suggests a clearer distinction of these competing beliefs than actually exists. Proponents of either view might see one source of monopoly in explicit agreements to collude, and both groups might consider it desirable to make such agreements illegal. The existence of such agreements might be interpreted as a self-sufficient source of monopoly; or alternatively, the legality of such agreements might be seen as government intervention to help enforce the agreements. Setting aside such problems about specific practices, a correct difference in emphasis is nonetheless captured by this description. The belief in a self-sufficient source of monopoly generates a view of the unregulated economy as one that is monopoly prone, while the belief that government intervention is the prime source of monopoly sees the unregulated economy as essentially competitive. The self-sufficiency theory suggests that political intervention is required; market concentration is seen as an important inhibitor of competition from within the industry, and large capital requirements, intensive advertising, and "predatory" pricing are viewed as important obstacles to competition from outside the industry. The belief that monopoly arises because of government intervention considers these to be relatively unimportant sources of monopoly so long as the government does not use its coercive powers to create and police legal barriers to competition; this viewpoint suggests that the regulation of transport, the imposition of tariffs, the various agricultural programs, the enforcement of licensure, the control of prices, and the legal restrictions imposed on entry and on the use of competitive tactics are the origins of more serious monopoly problems.

II

The intellectual origin of the interventionist theory of monopoly can be traced at least to Adam Smith's attack on mercantilism. In several chapters of *The Wealth of Nations,* Smith explored inefficiencies caused by governmental measures to protect and subsidize industries. This view of the nature of the monopoly problem dominated the thinking of economists until the first quarter of the twentieth century — after which it became quiescent, only to be resurrected recently in work dealing with the economic theory of political behavior. The quiescent period began after an important restructuring of industry had taken place, brought about partly because transport cost had fallen rapidly (thereby making it feasible for larger firms to sell across obsolete geographic market boundaries), and partly because the laws of incorporation had been revised in ways that facilitated the massing of large amounts of capital at low cost through public stock subscription.

Coincidentally with this restructuring, the economic theory of monopoly became increasingly explicit as to its assumptions and narrow as to its applications. The theory contrasted two industry structures and the prices that could be deduced from each: an atomistic structure comprised of an extremely large number of firms, and a monopoly structure containing but one firm. The atomistic structure denied any firm the power to control price. The one-firm structure conveyed complete control over price to the single firm. Increasingly these two structures were interpreted as descriptions of counterparts in real markets. I believe this interpretation errs seriously, but, in any case, the search for the source of monopoly power began to shift from government protection to industry structure.

Although markets had become more concentrated at the turn of the century (but, in general, not since then), only a very few were so dominated by one firm that they could be thought to resemble closely the one-firm industry assumed in the monopoly model. Nonetheless, the system of belief had so shifted that many economists came to view many actual industrial structures as near-enough approximations to the single-firm structure of monopoly theory. There was a growing expectation that monopoly was significantly correlated with market concentration, and this expectation soon hardened into a market concentration doctrine.

No serious theoretical basis yet exists for this doctrine, notwithstanding Weiss's efforts to demonstrate the existence of such a basis. Weiss does marshal enough "theories" of oligopoly to make a very convincing case. But the case he makes is mine.

The essence of monopoly power is the ability to prevent an expansion of capacity when price exceeds unit cost; yet not one of the oligopoly theories he described deals with the problem posed for colluding oligopolists by potential and actual entry; not one tells us how price can be maintained above a competitive level even *if* oligopolists should succeed in eliminating competition among existing firms. These models thus share a seldom recognized characteristic of the basic monopoly model from which they derive; the monopoly model *assumes* that monopoly power exists, it does not explain *how* monopoly power is acquired and maintained; the theory then proceeds to show how such power will be exercised.

The structure of an industry is determined largely by the degree to which scale economies prevail, or by the comparative efficiencies of firms; but no good theoretical link has been forged between the structure of the industry and the degree to which competitive pricing prevails, because no good explanation has been provided for how present and potential rivals are kept from competing without some governmentally provided restrictions on competitive activities.

What these descriptions of oligopoly behavior attempt to explain is: how oligopolists will act *if* there is no concern about entry. Even at this much more restricted game, these descriptions, with the exception of Stigler's, can hardly be dignified as theories. One theory assumes that each oligopolist believes that his rivals will not change their outputs no matter what he does; another assumes that rivals will keep their prices unchanged no matter what; others reach no definite equilibrium price or fail to explain how the equilibrium price is established. Stigler's theory of oligopoly is the only one that assumes sensible behavior on the part of oligopolists; but even his theory, which is worked out much better than the others, neglects the problems posed by open entry and by the need to discipline firms that compete.

Note that I have been discussing the absence of a well-worked-out theory supporting the link between industry structure and *monopoly power*. The testing of the market concentration doctrine has relied extensively on a search for a correlation between industry structure and *profit rates*. This implies that there is good reason to expect collusion among oligopolists to record higher profit rates as these are measured by accountants. There are, of course, many problems in the use of accounting data as approximations for economic concepts; but even if these measurement problems are set aside, there remain serious theoretical problems which I will discuss later.

Confirmation of the market concentration doctrine was offered first in the work of Professor Joe Bain[1] who, in 1951, published his famous study of the relationship between market concentration and profit rates in 42 selected industries. He found that profit rates were higher for industries in which the largest eight firms accounted for at least 70 percent of industry value added. Table 7 summarizes his results.

Continuing through the decades of the fifties and sixties with the work of Bain and others, there was growing acceptance of the market concentration doctrine. Soon it became the dominant view of economists working in this area. It was taught in economics departments throughout the land at the time that most persons at this conference were attending college. Its influence spread beyond the narrow confines of professional economics and filtered into the world of politics and antitrust law. It has become part of the conventional wisdom of intellectuals and policymakers. "Oligopoly," "shared monopoly," "conscious parallelism in pricing," and "barriers to entry," not yet household words, have become establishment clichés.

When a profession accepts a new system of belief, research is guided by that belief to rationalize observed phenomena in ways that confirm it. The belief in a self-sufficient theory of monopoly power offers no exception. Several studies followed quickly on Bain's and, although a few produced contrary results, most found confirmation of the new paradigm. A weak but gen-

1. Joe S. Bain, "Relation of Profit-Rate to Industry Concentration: American Manufacturing, 1936-1940," *Quarterly Journal of Economics*, 65 (August 1951), p. 293.

TABLE 7
Average of Industry Average-Profit Rates Within Concentration Deciles, 42 Selected Industries, 1936-1940

Value Added, Supplied by 8 Largest Firms	Average of Industry Average-Profit Rates	Number of Industries
90-100.0%	12.7%	8
80- 89.9	9.8	11
70- 79.9	16.3	3
60- 69.9	5.8	5
50- 59.9	5.8	4
40- 49.9	8.6	2
30- 39.9	6.3	5
20- 29.9	10.4	2
10- 19.9	17.0	1
0- 9.9	9.1	1

Source: Joe S. Bain, "Relation of Profit-Rate to Industry Concentration: American Manufacturing, 1936-1940," *Quarterly Journal of Economics, 65* (August 1951), p. 293.

erally persistent correlation between market concentration and profit rates is a fairly accurate description of these findings. Alternative explanations for these data generally were ignored because the market concentration doctrine had won the imagination of investigators and had given direction to their thoughts, much as Ptolemaic astronomy provided the signposts for the study of heavenly bodies during the four hundred years surrounding the life of Christ.

How did concentrated markets remain concentrated if they yielded above-average profits and were not protected by the government? Why did Bain observe lower profit rates for the smaller firms relative to the larger ones that occupied the same concentrated industries? What distortion is implied when industry profits are measured primarily by the profits of the larger firms in the industry? Why did nine industries with concentration ratios between 50 and 70 percent have lower profit rates than the eleven less concentrated industries contained in Bain's sample? (See Table 7). These matters generally were set aside during the period when most of the confirmatory studies were produced, although some attention was given by Bain (and his student H. Michael Mann) to the problem of why a positive relationship between concentration and profit rates should be resilient in the face of entry threats. It was decided — largely by intuition, not analysis — that the use of advertising and capital, as well as the existence of economies of scale, created what Bain called barriers to the entry of resources from outside the industry. No clear rationale was given as to why the use of particular kinds of inputs should create such barriers when these same inputs are available to firms both inside and outside the industry.

But Bain and Mann did find a stronger correlation between concentration and profits for those industries that used these inputs very intensely.

By 1960, then, collected evidence indicated a weak but generally positive correlation between concentration and profit rates. One large study covering a different time span, by George J. Stigler,[2] did not support these findings nor did a few smaller studies. Nonetheless, the balance of evidence, when measured by a number of studies, clearly favored the market concentration doctrine. In addition, there was the smaller amount of work indicating a potential explanation for this relationship in the intensive use of advertising and capital. Those who believed in the self-sufficient source of monopoly power had found confirmation.

During the middle sixties, development less clearly favored the belief in self-sufficient monopoly. It is true that Stigler[3] did construct a formal rationale for the market concentration doctrine in 1964, and Comanor and Wilson[4] in 1967 presented statistical evidence that higher profit rates were associated with more intensive use of advertising. But both studies really gave less support to the market concentration doctrine than might be supposed. Comanor and Wilson found that after account was taken of advertising expenditures and capital requirements, there no longer existed any correlation between market concentration and profit rates; and Stigler's theoretical analysis indicated that it takes relatively few firms to reduce significantly the gains from a collusive arrangement. Moreover, Stigler's study took no account of the role that entry would play in making such arrangements even less profitable.

Largely unnoticed, there appeared several studies during the late fifties and the decade of the sixties that provided cumulating evidence in favor of the belief that government intervention is a major source of monopoly power. It had always been recognized that tariffs, oil import quotas, the agricultural program, and the legal support of unions constructed impediments to the free flow of resources and created higher returns for small segments of the economy at greater cost to the more dispersed masses. But it generally was believed that government regulation of industry as provided for in the Act to Regulate Commerce, the Maritime Act, the Federal Communications Act, the Air Transport Act, etc., worked to the advantage of consumers. These studies provided arguments and evidence that this was not the case, and that, in general, this type of regulation protected the regulated industries from competition at the expense of consumers. Even at the local level, regulations such as those limiting entry into the taxi business and into housing through zoning requirements were shown to be protective devices creating serious impediments to the efficient use of resources.

2. George J. Stigler, *Capital and Rates of Return in Manufacturing* (Princeton Univ. Press 1963).

3. George J. Stigler, "A Theory of Oligopoly," *Journal of Political Economy*, 72 (February 1964), p. 44.

4. W. S. Comanor and T. A. Wilson, "Advertising, Market Structure, and Performance," *Review of Economics and Statistics*, 49 (November 1967), p. 423.

These studies offered support for the belief that government intervention plays a substantial role in the creation of monopoly power, but they did not undermine the evidence that had been accumulating in favor of the belief in self-sufficient monopoly power, nor did they lead many economists to doubt the market concentration doctrine. The way of looking at economic phenomena remained fairly fixed by the belief in self-sufficient monopoly power. But, beginning with the present decade, new evidence raised doubts about the main statistical supports and theoretical conjectures of the market concentration doctrine.

Yale Brozen[5] attempted to find evidence that would substantiate the rationalization used by President Johnson's Task Force on Antitrust Policy in its call for a Concentrated Industries Act for the purpose of reducing market concentration. The task force based its recommendation on its belief that there existed a large body of evidence showing a *persistent* relationship between concentration and high rates of return. The task force report stated that:

> It is the persistence of high profits over extended time periods and over whole industries . . . that suggest[s] artificial restraints on output and the absence of fully effective competition. The correlation of evidence of this kind with very high levels of concentration appears to be significant.[6]

Brozen found that none of the studies supporting the market concentration doctrine had looked at the question of the persistence over time of the correlation between profit and concentration; their results were based essentially on observations of a cross-section of industries during a given time interval. He examined the question of persistence directly by carrying forward in time three studies that supported the market concentration doctrine. (These were the basic study by Bain, a follow-up study by Mann, and a second, smaller study by Stigler that had found a correlation between profit and concentration for a group of 17 highly concentrated industries.) Brozen found no confirmation of the persistence in these correlations. The correlations degenerated within a few years, and high and low profit rates tended to converge toward a common level.

Why should the period used by Bain, 1936-1940, support the market concentration doctrine when subsequent time periods did not? Brozen[7] answered this puzzle by enlarging the sample used by Bain from 42 to 80 industries, and, in some industries, Brozen also increased the number of firms used to measure profit rates. Bain had used only 42 out of the 340 industries for which census data were available. The information in which Bain was interested was available for only 149 of these, because he relied on profit data

5. Yale Brozen, "The Antitrust Task Force Deconcentration Recommendation," *Journal of Law and Economics,* 13 (October 1970), p. 279.

6. White House Task Force on Antitrust Policy, "Report 1," in *Role of the Giant Corporations* (1968), p. 883.

7. Yale Brozen, "Bain's Concentration and Rates of Return Revisited," *Journal of Law and Economics,* 14 (October 1971), p. 351.

reported by the Securities and Exchange Commission. Another group of industries was omitted because Bain felt that the market definitions used by the census were inaccurate. Brozen was able to enlarge this sample by using information not earlier available to Bain. The enlarged sample, examined for the same time period studied by Bain, failed to reveal any significant correlation between concentration and profits. Apparently Bain's findings were not representative of the population from which he selected his industries.

The undermining of the evidence favoring the market concentration doctrine continued with a recent article by Stanley Ornstein.[8] Ornstein found profit rates to be related significantly to industry and firm growth rates, and to the minimum efficient scale of production, but *not* to market concentration. Meanwhile, other studies have revealed a high degree of temporal instability in correlations between profit rates and market concentration, and some of these correlations are negative.

These new studies constitute a fundamental challenge to the empirical work underlying the market concentration doctrine. Doubts have been raised as to whether there exists a positive correlation between profit rates and concentration, and the proposition that any such relationship holds persistently through time seems to be discredited.

Weiss has provided us with a tabulation of most of the empirical studies bearing on the market concentration doctrine [Table 11]. His detailed critical review of these, however, is limited to those studies whose results are inconsistent with the market concentration doctrine. These he dismisses in some cases because their methodology was poor, because the time period covered was inflationary, or because regional industries were treated as if they had national markets. But almost all of the studies in support of the market concentration doctrine either have methodological problems, or are very heavily influenced by deflationary periods, or treat regional industries as national. If the criteria that Weiss adopts to criticize nonconfirmatory studies are applied to all studies, we are left with very little acceptable evidence about the relationship between profit rates and concentration.

Apparently, we now confront the proposition that successful collusion is practiced only during noninflationary periods by firms that advertise or use capital intensely — unless, of course, market concentration should be less than 70 percent! The theories to which Weiss has appealed tell us very little about oligopoly behavior, and they certainly do not tell us that collusion fails to work when the Consumer Price Index turns upward or when the 8-firm concentration ratio dips below 70 percent.

Brozen's study is selected for special criticism by Weiss. He contends that it was improper for Brozen to classify a few industries as concentrated or unconcentrated. For example, Weiss charges that Brozen was incorrect to include beet and cane sugar among his concentrated industries, because they compete on the same market and "their combined 8-firm concentration ratio was probably less than 70." The reader might suppose from Weiss's discussion that

8. Stanley Ornstein, "Concentration and Profits," *Journal of Business*, 45 (October 1972), p. 519.

these problems were not discussed by Brozen, but the appendix to Brozen's paper [see n. 7 *supra*] discusses the very industries referred to by Weiss, and I recommend a reading of that appendix for those who are curious about why Brozen constructed the sample as he did. For example, Brozen writes:

> Bain excluded the sugar industries (beet and cane) on the ground that the separation of close substitutes "would tend seriously to overstate the true concentration for the theoretical industry within which the outputs in question fell." If we assume that no cane suger refiner produced beet sugar and take the proportion of the output of the leading eight cane sugar refiners of total refined sugar (beet and cane) sales, thus obtaining the lower limit of the possible sugar refining concentration ratio, it exceeds 70 percent and puts the sugar industry in Bain's more concentrated groups.

Brozen did not specially select his sample as seems to be implied by Weiss, but chose to use the complete Federal Trade Commission sample that had been used by the commission to conduct one of the studies quoted by Weiss as support for the market concentration doctrine. Brozen merely shifted the time period to that examined by Bain.

We have already seen that Weiss is simply wrong in saying that the combined 8-firm concentration ratio for the sugar industry was less than 70 percent. Weiss also removed several industries because of their regional character, but it is not proper to exclude an industry from the unconcentrated category merely because it is regional. An accepted procedure is to require regional industries to exhibit very low national concentration measures before they are allowed to enter the unconcentrated category. A national 4-firm concentration ratio less than 20 percent has been found acceptable to other investigators. If we use this criterion, Weiss should not have removed the bread and bakery products industry from the unconcentrated category, nor should he have removed nonalcoholic beverages or malt liquors. The cement industry profits in 1939 and 1940 were below the average for the unconcentrated group, where the industry was placed in Brozen's sample. If it were removed from this category, as Weiss suggests, and placed instead in the concentrated industries category, as was done in Mann's study, the results would have turned out even more favorable to a rejection of Bain's findings. For alcoholic beverages, a strong case can be made that the market was national in scope; for example, most of the beer sold by the top brewers was sold nationwide from single plants. Finally, I am not sure how blast furnace products should be handled, since it is difficult to discover the extent of competition between pig iron producers and integrated steel mills.

Weiss's techniques, of course, can be applied to studies favoring the market concentration doctrine. For example, Bain was not so careful as Weiss implies. Bain did not eliminate all industries with regional characteristics. He used cement and also cast iron pipe. He didn't use the locomotive industry, although it clearly is highly concentrated and manufactures a single product. It earned only 1.7 percent, and its inclusion in Bain's sample would have lowered the concentrated industries' rate of return.

But even after Weiss recasts the FTC sample, he gets a 2.2 percent difference in return between concentrated and nonconcentrated industries for one year — no small reduction from the 4.4 percent difference found by Bain. And in the other year there is no significant difference. The guts of Brozen's study hold their shape very well even when operated on by Weiss.

We have seen that the theoretical basis for the market concentration doctrine is weak at best, and that the empirical work is not clear cut as to results. The situation is much worse when we turn to the notion of self-created barriers to entry. The lack of a theoretical justification for identifying certain types of expenditures as "barriers to entry" is even more glaring than is the lack of a theoretical basis for the market concentration doctrine. The costliness of producing commodities does, of course, limit the amounts that will be made available at particular prices; in this sense cost does create a "barrier" to production, but no pejorative interpretation can be given to such a "barrier to entry." Indeed, it would be wasteful to produce additional units when the cost of doing so exceeds the value of these units to prospective purchasers. Cost, whether incurred to acquire labor or capital or to inform prospective buyers, sets proper limits on the production and marketing of commodities.

What does it mean to say that advertising expenditures and capital outlays constitute barriers to entry? One meaning is that firms must make such expenditures if they are to produce and communicate about the commodities they hope to sell. Such expenditures are no more barriers than are expenditures on labor and material. A second meaning is that existing firms are more efficient in the employment of such inputs than are firms not yet in the industry. If this is so, the existing firms deserve applause, not divestiture. A third meaning is that existing firms have an *undesirable* advantage in the use of these inputs. Since all firms can borrow in the capital markets and can purchase advertising campaigns, it is difficult to see wherein the unfair advantage lies. If large firms are better risks to lenders and, therefore, if they can borrow at lower rates (internally or externally) than can small or new firms, then this element of superiority for the large-scale, older firm is properly recognized by capital markets. Similarly, if buyers have more confidence in, and are more knowledgeable about, well-established products, then this also is a real efficiency not to be denied to firms that have invested in building substantial reputations. Nor should buyers who do not desire to bear the risk of consuming and the cost of searching for *possibly* equally good but less well-known alternatives be denied the advantage of trading with older, larger firms.

Objections based on problems of accounting methods have been raised about the notion that advertising creates a barrier to entry. There is a suspicion that the empirical correlation between advertising intensity and profit rate is an accounting artifact brought about by the fact that accountants treat advertising as a current expense even though the returns from advertising may be earned over several years. Critics have argued that it is this accounting artifact and not barriers to entry that produces this correlation. Two studies have attempted to take into consideration the investment-like quality of advertising. Weiss[9] adjusted Comanor and Wilson's study by introducing a depreciation rate for advertising, but he found that this did not significantly reduce the correlation between profit rates and advertising that had been uncovered by Comanor and Wilson. A doctoral dissertation by H. Bloch[10] using different methods and data, however, concluded that the correlation between these variables disappears when the accounting data are corrected to allow for the investmentlike quality of advertising.

When Weiss modified the Comanor and Wilson study, he applied a uniform advertising depreciation rate to all industries. This is likely to result in a bias if advertising depreciation rates actually differ among industries. R. Ayanian, in a dissertation now being completed at UCLA, has estimated depreciation rates for various industries and found that they do differ. When he uses the different depreciation rates applicable to different industries, he finds no correlation between profit rates and advertising intensity.

The current popularity of "barriers to entry" is puzzling. It is said that existing firms have created a preference for their products through the use of advertising and, therefore, that new competitors need to advertise even more intensely if they are to attract customers. But the firms now in the industry once needed to attract customers away from the established products of other industries, to an unknown new product, so it is not at all clear that new entrants suffer a disadvantage as compared with those who showed the way. Furthermore, the inputs most likely to create a differential advantage for existing firms are those that might make it more difficult for new firms to learn the source of strength enjoyed by old firms. Old firms may have developed particular trade secrets or ways of organizing that are relatively difficult for new firms to learn about. But the use of advertising and large amounts of capital are there for everyone to see and duplicate. Even the particular type of sales pitch used by successful firms can be imitated with relative ease. The use of advertising and capital would seem to me to be the least likely candidates for the role of barriers to entry. One grandfather's clause is worth a very, very large advertising budget.

In summary then, we can conclude that the theoretical support of the market concentration doctrine, including its barriers-to-entry variant, is weak or nonexistent. On the empirical side, it is clear that more studies reveal a positive correlation between profits and concentration than do not. There are enough of those that fail to show such a correlation, however, that the policymaker ought not suppose that conclusive evidence of this statistical relationship exists. What is needed is a thoroughgoing fresh look at the data and methodology. But even if this should reveal a positive correlation, there would still remain a serious problem for policy, for what can be inferred from a positive correlation?

9. L. Weiss, "Advertising, Profits, and Corporate Taxes," *Review of Economics and Statistics*, 51 (November 1969), p. 421.

10. H. Bloch, "Advertising, Competition, and Market Performance" (unpublished Ph.D. thesis, Univ. of Chicago 1971).

III

That any meaning can be given to persistent correlations between profit and concentration is attributable to the fact that accounting measures are necessarily poor approximations to the theoretical concepts they represent. The most important imperfection is their weakness in attaching appropriate values to those assets that are likely to be associated with the preservation of monopoly or the attainment of superior efficiency. If proper economic values were given on these assets, then all firms, whether monopolies or competitive, could be expected to yield the same rate of return. Thus, the trucking industry obtains a grandfather's clause to block entry. This increases the value of the licenses to operate, but accountants are unlikely to value these licenses at anything like their market value; if they were so valued, the rate of return recorded by trucking firms would be no different than that recorded by free-entry industries. A correct evaluation of assets would capitalize monopoly profits into the value of the assets which shield the firms from competition. Similarly, an explicit or implicit agreement to collude, if successful, is an undervalued asset to companies. Hence it is possible to look at accounting returns and form some guess as to the degree of monopoly that is present.

Unfortunately, it is not only sources of monopoly that are undervalued by accountants but also sources of efficiency. For example, General Motors has made a decision to push ahead with a rotary-engine car. No element of monopoly is present in that decision, since Ford and Chrysler also could have adopted the same course of action. But they did not. Let us suppose that GM's decision turns out to be correct, and that it gains both profit and market share, which it holds for many years because of the difficulty of quickly imitating that decision, the uncertainty among all firms as to whether the rotary engine will continue to be successful, and the tendency of consumers in this industry to rate experience highly. Accounting procedures are essentially backward-looking, but the uncertain value of such a decision rests in the future. Hence, for many years GM may record high profits and high market share even though monopoly is absent.

It might be supposed that management wages would reflect the value of a correct decision, but they will do so only imperfectly and with long lags. Indeed, if the full value of such decisions accrued to management, there would be no reason for GM stock to appreciate. Part of the reason that salaries will not capture the full value of such decisions is because some of the reward accrues to shareholders who had a role in selecting a productive (or lucky) team. Another reason is that it is difficult to forecast how long the decision will remain the correct decision. The better the decision turns out in retrospect, the more undervalued (relatively) will have been the management. Finally, the goodness of the decision may not reflect the ability of one man but the ability of an entire management team. No one member of such a team can hope to obtain a salary elsewhere that reflects his value as a member of this team; hence there is no reason for the market to push such salaries to the point where all the gain from the correct decision is exhausted in wages; nor should the market do so, since it is the firm itself, as a team, that has created this value. Similar problems arise in the case of monopoly profits. Since management is "responsible" for the decisions that create monopoly, it might be expected that the monopoly gains will be fully absorbed in managerial salary.

Higher accounting profit rates can arise either for reasons of monopoly or for superior efficiency, because accountants simply cannot appropriately value the assets or the decisions that may give rise to the profits. (Similarly, incorrect or unwise decisions will produce lower accounting profit rates.) Sometimes there will be an element of both efficiency and monopoly. Patent and copyright privileges may deliver to innovative firms some protection from competition and also may lead to higher concentration. To the extent that accounting procedures undervalue such legal protection, there will exist a positive correlation between profit and concentration. But this is cause for alarm only if we believe that the proper workings of the incentive system do not require such protection against easy imitation.

One difference in the implications of the source of high returns should be noted. If firms succeed in colluding to raise price, this may give rise to an increase in accounting profits because this agreement is undervalued by accountants. But these profits and the undervaluing of the agreement will be short-lived if firms cannot control competition in other directions. There will be great incentives to improve product quality and services in order to sell more at the collusive price. Such competition will raise cost towards price and dissipate the profitability of the agreement. This will not be the case if the cause of the higher profits is superior efficiency; there is no reason for a superior firm to dissipate its gains in such a fashion.

We do not yet understand the permanence that can be attached to either source of high accounting rates of return. Collusive agreements, even when enforced by government, do not last forever. The competition for government protection that sometimes creates new monopoly also may do away with old monopoly. Similarly, basic decisions having nothing to do with monopoly sometimes turn out well but other times turn out poorly. The Ford Motor Company acquired a dominant profitable position in the automobile industry by virtue of Henry Ford's decision to produce a standard model with mass-production techniques; but after several years of this, the same decision-maker lost share and profits to GM. In some cases, the effects of monopoly or of superior decisions may be felt for many years, and, in part, this could explain any persistence in high accounting rates of return.

A phenomenon that is likely to generate fairly persistent differences in accounting rates of returns is the fact that some products are more efficiently produced by firms possessing a large share of the market, while in other industries large market shares are not necessary for efficiency. Those firms that first act on the belief that large scale is an advantage, and that invest in the marketing and production techniques prerequisite to executing the move to large scale, will possess a competitively secured advantage in timing and in obtaining early consumer acceptance that will be difficult to overcome in a short time period. The market may not have grown large enough to accommodate more than a handful of such firms. These firms can produce at lower unit cost than smaller firms. They are superior in this respect, and they command an economic rent for achieving primacy. This rent will be measured as profit by accountants. Even though such firms can achieve generally low unit cost, at the margin their capacity may be strained and price will be high enough to allow smaller, higher unit cost firms to accommodate that part of the market not easily serviced by the larger firms. If and when the market grows enough to accommodate additional large firms, such firms will form, perhaps by merger of the smaller firms.

If industries are *persistently* concentrated, the fundamental reason will be the prevalence of large scale advantages. Such firms will record higher profits because the market has not yet grown sufficiently; in order to bring smaller, less efficient firms into production, price will need to be high enough to cover their unit cost, and this means that price will need to be high enough for *accounting* profits to be recorded by the large firms in these industries. Of course, these industries will be the highly concentrated ones.

Since most of the earlier studies of the relationship between profit and concentration relied heavily on the rate of return of only larger firms, it is difficult to know whether monopoly or superior efficiency accounts for the positive correlations frequently found. Does the market concentration doctrine, *unaided by this "efficient structure"* explanation, adequately explain the pattern of profit rates and market concentration? Do higher profits in concentrated industries reflect only monopoly? Or are they in whole or part brought about by the efficiency of large firms in these industries? [11] Some light can be shed on these questions by examining profit–concentration correlations after taking account of firm size. Firms of each size class should have profit rates that increase with concentration if collusion is more successful in concentrated markets. The absence of such correlations for most size classes of firms would be difficult to reconcile with the market concentration doctrine.

Table 8 tabulates the correlation between profit rates and concentration for firms in five different size categories and for each of five years.[12] Each entry shows the size of the correlation (which can vary from −1, for a perfect inverse relationship, to +1 for a perfect direct relationship) and indicates the level of significance that can be attached to the measured correlation. The most important information in Table 8 is that after the size of the firm is taken into account, *no* significant correlation between profit rate and market con-

11. Earlier empirical work exploring this problem can be found in H. Demsetz, "The Market Concentration Doctrine" (AEI-Hoover Policy Studies, August 1973), and H. Demsetz, "Industry Structure, Market Rivalry, and Public Policy," *Journal of Law and Economics,* 16 (April 1973), p. 1.

12. Four size classes were used when this paper was originally presented. At that time the largest class size was $50 million and up, but L. Weiss objected that the three smaller classes did not contain large enough firms. In response to this point, a fifth class size has been added. No cell in Tables 2 and 3 has less than 63 industries represented, and most have over 90.

TABLE 8
Correlations Between Rate of Return and Concentration by Asset Size of Firms

Asset Size ($000)	No. of Industries:	94	116	116	116	76
	Year:	1958 [a]	1963	1966	1967	1970
$0-500		.29 [b]	−.19 [c]	−.09	−.01	−.38 [b]
500-5,000		.11	−.00	−.06	−.07	−.01
5,000-50,000		.14	.11	.04	−.05	−.00
50,000-100,000		−.01	.01	.09	.10	−.03
100,000 and up		.03	.16	.16	.16	.28 [c]
All asset sizes		.28 [b]	.35 [b]	.28 [b]	.19 [c]	.27 [c]

Note: Concentration is based on 4-digit census industries weighted by employment to match IRS profit data. The 1958 data were not yet complete, with 14 industries stlll to be tabulated.

a. Sample coverage for 1958 is small, and the data for 1958 must be interpreted with caution.

b. Significant at 1 percent confidence level.

c. Significant at 5 percent confidence level.

centration is apparent even though the correlations which ignore firm size are positive. It would appear that most, if not all, of the positive correlations between profit rates and concentration uncovered by some earlier studies can be attributed to variations in the size of firms, not the degree to which markets are concentrated. This general pattern of profit rate/concentration correlations cannot be explained by recognized oligopoly or monopoly theory. Indeed, it could be argued, with no more casualness than other arguments surrounding the market concentration doctrine, that the positive correlations should be strongest for moderate- and small-sized firms, since the large firms need to adhere more to the collusive agreement than do moderate-sized firms.

The strongest positive correlations tend to be found in the largest class size; and even though these fail to meet the standard tests of statistical significance, there no doubt will be attempts to link this fact to market power. One such explanation deserves attention. In effect, it is a compromise explanation. Larger firms in concentrated industries have lower cost because there are scale economies in these industries or because of some inherent superiority of the larger firms in these industries. Nonetheless they succeed in colluding so that *their* profit rates are relatively high. The prices they set in this collusion are not so high as to yield high profits for less efficient, more moderately sized smaller firms. Hence we observe a stronger positive correlation between profit rates and market concentration for the largest firms than for other firms.

In this rationalization of the data, the cost of production to moderate-sized firms in concentrated markets apparently sets the upper limit to the prices that are (can be?) set through the collusion of large firms; otherwise, firms of moderate size would exhibit higher profits in concentrated industries than in unconcentrated. Presumably, this limit to profits is effective because higher profits would lead new firms, possibly large new firms, and existing smaller firms to merge or expand capacity in the industry. All of this, of course, implies that existing large firms possess superior characteristics that are difficult to imitate. Their methods of organizing production, of providing service, and of establishing buyer confidence must yield lower cost than can be obtained by newer or smaller firms.

This compromise explanation hardly can justify a call for deconcentration, because considerable economies of large-scale production or other advantages of existing large firms would then be lost with no compensation in the form of lower prices. If the sizes of all firms are limited by deconcentration policies to be no larger than moderate-sized firms in their industries, then it will be the costs of the moderate-sized firms that determine prices. But that is how price is constrained without deconcentration if we accept this rationalization of these data. Since persistent market concentration seems to be associated with economies of scale or other forms of superior performance by existing larger firms in concentrated industries, a move to deconcentrate such industries is very *likely* to increase, not decrease, cost even *if* it were true that collusion is more successful in these industries. Embracing the market concentration doctrine through legislation is thus very likely to penalize the success and superior performance upon which depends the progress and wealth of this nation.

Table 8 reveals that most of the correlation between accounting profit rates and concentration can be attributed to firm size, not market concentration. The remaining correlation might only reflect accounting artifacts or special sources of efficiency other than size. There is a suspicion that the accounting treatment accorded advertising expenditures tends to exaggerate the rates of return recorded by those firms that advertise intensely, because accountants fail to treat advertising as a long-lived asset.

It might well be the case that some of the correlations in Table 8 reflect variations in advertising intensity and not variations in market concentration. It is possible to examine what happens to the correlations shown in Table 8 when variations in advertising intensity are taken into account. Table 9 recasts Table 8 after the effect of variations in advertising intensity are removed from the data. The entries in Table 9 thus isolate to a finer degree than Table 8 the relationship between accounting profit rates and concentration for given size classes of firms. The effect of taking account of advertising intensity is to weaken substantially the correlations between profit rates and concentration.

A closer look at Table 9 is rewarding. For firms with asset sizes larger than $1 million, the correlations prevalent in Table 8 all but disappear. Moreover, the correlations which ignore asset sizes turn out to be insignificant in 1967 and 1970 where before they were significant, and the correlations for 1963 and 1966 are weakened. Only the correlation for 1958 is strengthened, but oddly enough only the smallest firms reveal a significant positive relationship between profit rates and concentration for that year; this hardly can constitute strong evidence of collusion among large firms. The years 1958, 1967, and

TABLE 9
Correlations Between Rate of Return and Concentration by Asset Size of Firms

Asset Size ($000)	1958 [a]	1963	1966	1967	1970
$0-500	.29 [b]	—.18 [c]	—.11	.00	—.41 [b]
500-5000	.12	—.03	—.05	—.11	—.08
5000-50,000	.17	.02	—.03	—.14	—.12
50,000-100,000	—.01	—.07	.04	.04	—.11
100,000 and up	.04	.06	.06	.06	.11
All asset sizes	.36 [b]	.29 [b]	.21 [c]	.09	.08

Note: All data identical to data underlying Table 8, but correlations between profit and concentration are partial correlations derived by taking account of the partial correlation between profit rates and advertising sales ratios.

a. Sample coverage for 1958 is small, and the data for 1958 must be interpreted cautiously.

b. Significant at 1 percent confidence level.

c. Significant at 5 percent confidence level.

1970 no longer yield evidence confirming the market concentration doctrine. The year 1966 yields weak evidence on an overall basis, but not for firms smaller than $50 million in asset size. Only 1963 retains a very significant overall correlation, but even here the smaller firms do not provide confirming data. It happens that 1963 is the year chosen by Weiss to correlate "profit margins" with concentration and advertising intensity. But 1963 appears to be a very atypical year with respect to this correlation, a fact to which I called attention in earlier work.[13] Table 9 does not offer convincing evidence for the market concentration doctrine. This is especially true since the correlations presented in that table are based on "one-tailed" tests of significance. Such tests seek to ascertain the probability that a positive correlation between profits and concentration exists. In view of the severe problems of securing dependable accounting data and the very weak theory underlying the market concentration doctrine, it might be wiser to ascertain whether the correlations differ significantly from zero in either a positive or a negative direction. Such a two-tailed test would cut (approximately in half) the remaining significance of the correlations shown in Table 9.

The role played by advertising in producing the results of Table 9 is still difficult to interpret. In some yet-to-be-described way, advertising might be associated with "barriers to entry." However, much of the correlation between profit rates and concentration found in earlier studies may be due to the inappropriate accounting treatment accorded to advertising; evidence for this exists in other studies referred to above. On the other hand, a true source

13. See Demsetz, "The Market Concentration Doctrine," *supra* n. 11, at 16.

of superior efficiency may exist in the use of advertising by large firms in concentrated industries.

IV

Let us now complete the circle, returning to discuss the relative merits of the "self-sufficiency" and "interventionist" views of the monopoly problem. The evidence that has been cumulating in recent years must raise doubts about the importance of self-sufficient sources of monopoly and must increase our estimate of the importance of government intervention to protect industries from competition. It is possible, I think, to give good reasons for believing that this new evidence is indicative of the underlying truth.

The key to sustained monopoly power is the ability of an industry to restrict or retard the expansion and utilization of productive capacity. Government can offer to industry much greater powers of coercion to accomplish this end than can be supplied by the industry itself. Most of the resources supplied by the Department of Agriculture at taxpayer expense have been used to subsidize the policing of output restrictions that never could have been obtained without such aid. Moreover, an industry attempting to restrict capacity by its own efforts would need to rely on much less effective techniques than are available when the laws of the land can be marshaled toward this end. For example, if existing firms attempt to block entry by "predatory" pricing, they must all suffer reductions in their profits. The techniques available to firms without the aid of government are not very specific to penalizing only entrants. But the use of CAB or FCC to restrict competitive entry through the use of licensure or certificates of convenience and necessity specifically penalizes prospective entrants. An investment by an industry to obtain government aid to monopolize is likely to yield much more control than the investment of the same sum without the aid of governmental techniques. Some would argue that without government aid such an investment would generally be unprofitable.

More important than this, however, is the greater ease of securing the funds for such an investment if the restrictions are to be achieved through the government. In the absence of government cooperation there are important incentives for not contributing to an effort to restrict output. First, such an effort might very well run afoul of the antitrust laws. Secondly, to the extent that the agreement to restrict output is likely to succeed, a firm would find it profitable to remain outside the agreement; the firm could then expand its output to take full advantage of any higher prices brought about through the private efforts of other firms. These factors, which undermine the success of efforts to collude, are not as important if restrictions are to be achieved through the good offices of the government.

The government and the courts have been careful to protect the constitutional right of petition. If the firms in an industry cooperate in an in-house *attempt* to restrict output, they are in violation of the antitrust laws; but if they cooperate to obtain the aid of the White House and the Congress in building tariff barriers or in increasing agricultural support prices, they are not in violation of the antitrust laws. The basic conflict between the fundamental right of collective petition and the illegality of attempting to collude has been decided in favor of the right to petition.

The Noerr case in 1961[14] dealt explicitly with this conflict. In that case the Court of Appeals for the Third Circuit had held that no violation of the Sherman Act can be predicated upon mere attempts to influence the passage or enforcement of laws even if two or more persons associate in an attempt to persuade the legislature or the executive to take particular action that would produce a restraint or a monopoly. (There was some backing away from this decision in a later case, but this tended to emphasize the illegality of restricting one's competitors from easy access to the judicial or legislative machinery.) The antitrust laws are not violated by agreements to petition the government to restrict competition — but are violated when such agreements do not involve the government, even if those agreements fail to achieve their ends. The legal route of monopoly runs through Washington and the state capitals.

More important than the legality of a collusive agreement, perhaps, is the greater difficulty that would confront a firm which seeks to take advantage of an agreement secured and acted upon by other firms when this agreement works through the law. If such an agreement were to operate outside the law, a firm not joining in the agreement could hope to expand its output in response to the higher price brought about by the output restrictions which other firms imposed on themselves. The propensity to stay out of such an agreement or to secretly break its terms constitutes a serious impediment to collusion outside the law. But if the government is brought into the collusive agreement, then higher powers of coercion can be brought into play to make sure that firms in the industry do not undermine the agreement. How else can individual farmers be prevented from increasing output when prices rise? How else can individual owners of oil-rich land be prevented from increasing crude oil output when oil prices rise or when imports are restricted? In one case the discipline is obtained through the federal government's agricultural program, and in the other through the prorationing programs of state governments.

For these reasons and others, including the statistical evidence that has come to light recently, it is quite plausible to believe that government intervention constitutes the main threat to a competitive economy. It is important that this threat be recognized, because our belief on this score governs how we deploy resources to ensure that competition will flourish. What is called for is a redirection of our efforts. Government intervention that has created and sustained monopoly should be our primary target.

How such a redirection can be brought about is hardly the province of the economist. I doubt that monstrosities such as the agricultural program can be modified significantly until basic changes in the political makeup of this nation continue for several more years. But I see no basic political beliefs of the

14. Eastern R.R. Presidents Conference v. Noerr Motor Freight, Inc., 365 U.S. 127 (1961).

voters of this nation that predispose them to rejoice when the FCC protects established networks and movie theaters from the competition of pay TV. Nor are there obvious cheers from the electorate when the ICC exercises its control over minimum freight rates, or when it prevents truckers and railroads from competing with each other. John Q. Public does not rise to salute when the SEC cooperates with the attempts of the NYSE to protect itself from competition within and without, nor does he exude great pleasure at the efforts of the CAB to keep airlines from setting lower fares. These regulatory actions have benefited special interests in situations where the typical citizen suffers no great illusion as to where his interest lies.

If we can not do away with such regulation, let us at least make it easier for the Justice Department (or some other agency not beholden to any particular industry) to ask whether the decisions of our regulatory tribunals are in the public interest, and, when it feels that they are not, to bring the issue before the courts of this land. I commend the Justice Department for recent moves that it has made on the question of fixed commissions on our organized exchanges. This is a welcome indirect challenge of the authority of the SEC as the sole arbiter of the public interest in the operation of capital markets. But it should be made easier for some agency to question the merits of regulatory decisions and to represent consumer interests in affairs of these industries.

I do not suggest that we abandon the search for private conspiracy, but I do think that it is time to pay much less attention to the structure of industry and virtually no attention to the notion of nongovernmental barriers to entry. A commitment to the machinery of competitive organization requires that we generally accept the consequences of effective competition. For antitrust, this means that market share and profits can be expected to shift in favor of successful rivals.

Unfortunately, our antitrust laws are being used to protect competitors and penalize efficiency. Competitive pricing policies, effective advertising campaigns, and the efficient management of resources are as likely to run afoul of antitrust as are attempts to collude. To an increasing extent, the *United States Steel* [15] and *Alcoa*[16] cases typify the reasoning in contemporary antitrust cases.

The United States Steel Corporation escaped dissolution by refraining from competitive pricing, thus escaping any charge that it used its power to make life difficult for smaller rivals, but Alcoa was found to violate antitrust laws because it behaved competitively. Alcoa had claimed that it never excluded competitors, but Judge Learned Hand clearly described the source of illegality in his reply: "[W]e can think of no more effective exclusion than progressively to embrace each new opportunity as it opened, and to face every newcomer with new capacity already geared into a great organization having the advantage of experience, trade connections, and the elite of personnel." [17]

15. United States v. United States Steel Corp., 251 U.S. 417 (1920).

16. United States v. Aluminum Company of America, 148 F.2d 416 (2nd Cir. 1945).

17. *Id.* at 431.

Those who seek freedom, productivity, and protection through market competition must believe that there is a steady stream of competition that disciplines even those who best their rivals on a given day or during a given decade. The history of market economies provides overwhelming evidence that this belief is based on experience. A public policy based on this belief should cease to be alarmed when effective competition *actually* shifts market share and profits, and certainly should not interfere with competitive processes in *anticipation* of such consequences. Such a cool and unconcerned posture must contemplate the possibility of a modicum of monopoly power for short periods of time in some instances, but this is a small cost to bear in order to avoid the attempt to tune finely the operation of competitive forces. The inadequacies of attempted fine-tuning are readily revealed in contemporary antitrust and in the substitution of regulatory restrictionism and favoritism for market rivalry.

Present trends in antitrust make it difficult to refrain from asking whether present practices encourage more competition than they inhibit. The answer cannot be given yet with any certainty, but there are numerous instances where judicial "cartelization" seems to have taken place. Given these uncertainties, it would seem wise to redirect our efforts to the task of reducing governmentally protected monopolies.

[2]

On the Misuse of Accounting Rates of Return to Infer Monopoly Profits

By FRANKLIN M. FISHER AND JOHN J. MCGOWAN*

Accounting rates of return are frequently used as indices of monopoly power and market performance by economists and lawyers.[1] Such a procedure is valid only to the extent that profits are indeed monopoly profits, accounting profits are in fact economic profits, and the accounting rate of return equals the economic rate of return.

The large volume of research investigating the profits-concentration relationship uniformly relies on accounting rates of return, such as the ratio of reported profits to total assets or to stockholders' equity as the measure of profitability to be related to concentration.[2] Many users of accounting rates of return seem well aware that profits as reported by accountants may not be consistent from firm to firm or industry to industry and may not correspond to economists' definitions of profits. Likewise, they recognize that accountants' statements of assets, hence also stockholders' equity, may fail to correspond to economically acceptable definitions, because accounting practices do not provide for the capitalization of certain activities such as research and development and do not incorporate allowances for inflation. This is to say they are well aware of certain measurement problems which arise in using available accounting information to measure profitability. They seem, however, totally unaware of a much deeper conceptual problem, namely, that accounting rates of return, even if properly and consistently measured, provide almost no information about economic rates of return.[3]

The economic rate of return on an investment is, of course, that discount rate that equates the present value of its expected net revenue stream to its initial outlay. Putting aside the measurement problems referred to above, it is clear that it is the economic rate of return that is equalized within an industry in long-run industry competitive equilibrium and (after adjustment for risk) equalized everywhere in a competitive economy in long-run equilibrium. It is an economic rate of return (after risk adjustment) above the cost of capital that promotes expansion under competition and is produced by output restriction under monopoly. Thus, the economic rate of return is the only correct measure of the profit rate for purposes of economic analysis.[4] Accounting rates of return are useful only insofar as they yield information as to economic rates of return.[5]

*Fisher is professor of economics, Massachusetts Institute of Technology. McGowan was Vice-President, Charles River Associates. He died on April 7, 1982. This paper is based on work done for Fisher's testimony as a witness for IBM in *U.S. v. IBM* (69 Civ. 200, U.S. District Court, Southern District of New York). We are indebted to Larry Brownstein, Steven Hendrick, and especially Karen Larson and Leah Hutten for computational and programming assistance. Any errors are our responsibility.

[1]Aside from *U.S. v. IBM*, see, for example, Joseph Cooper, p. 15; the various industry studies in Walter Adams; and the discussion in Philip Areeda and Donald Turner, Vol. II, pp. 331–41.

[2]See the comprehensive reviews of this literature by Leonard Weiss and more recently by F. M. Scherer, pp. 267–95. Additional accounting problems raised by attempting to measure profitability by line of business are discussed extensively in George Benston.

[3]A referee suggests that even the crudest accounting information tells us IBM is more profitable than American Motors (AMC), but we disagree. Surely accounting information tells us IBM generates more dollars of profits per dollar of assets than does AMC but, as the examples below demonstrate, that information alone does not tell us which firm is more profitable in the sense of having a higher economic rate of return.

[4]This is literally true only if the cost of capital is first subtracted. In what follows below, we follow the usual empirical practice of measuring all rates of return before such subtraction.

[5]The existence of a uniquely defined economic rate of return—which we now assume for the theoretical analysis below and which occurs in all the examples—is

Now, it should be obvious that only by the merest happenstance will the accounting rate of return on a given investment, taken as the ratio of net revenue to book value in a particular year,[6] be equal to the economic rate of return that makes the present value of the entire net revenue stream equal to the initial capital cost. Indeed, as we shall see below, accounting rates of return on individual investments generally vary all over the lot. Hence, only if such fluctuations are somehow averaged out by a firm's investment behavior over time will its accounting rate of return even be roughly constant—let alone approximate the economic rate of return.[7]

It is easy to show that such averaging requires that the firm grow exponentially, investing in the same mix of investment types each year—an investment type being defined by a time shape of net revenues. Even in such an unrealistically favorable case, the accounting rate of return will generally depend on the rate of growth, equalling the economic rate of return only by accident. Furthermore, the relationship between the accounting and economic rates of return depends on the time shape of net revenues.

guaranteed only if the net revenue stream stemming from an investment has any negative terms occurring before the positive ones. If the economic rate of return fails to be unique, then, while present value calculations using the cost of capital remain the correct method for analyzing profitability, profitability cannot be summarized correctly by *any* rate of return, including accounting rates of return.

[6]Throughout this paper we work with accounting rates of return defined as ratios of profits to book values of capital. Similar (but not identical in detail) results apply to accounting rates of return on stockholders' equity. The precise relations involved can, in principle, be inferred from the results given below. (Such results do apply directly to accounting rates of return on stockholders' equity even in detail if we consider the firms being analyzed to hold neither debt nor retained earnings.)

[7]For discussion purposes—and in our examples below—we assume that the firm achieves the same economic rate of return on all its investments, and thus speak of "the" economic rate of return for the firm without worrying about differences between average and marginal rates. This is, of course, the most favorable case for the accounting rate of return for the firm as a whole.

Hence, only by accident will accounting rates of return be in one-to-one correspondence with economic rates of return. We show by example below that the effects involved cannot be assumed to be small—indeed, they can be large enough to account for the entire interfirm variation in accounting rates of return among the largest firms in the United States.

The plan of the paper is as follows. Section I summarizes the theoretical results which are proved and elucidated in the Appendix. These results establish the relationships among the various rates of return, time shapes, and rates of growth, and demonstrate in principle that accounting rates of return are not informative. The balance of the paper analyzes a series of relatively simple examples to show that the theoretical effects are not so small that they can be neglected in practice. Indeed, they are very large. A ranking of firms by accounting rates of return can easily invert a ranking by economic rates of return.

Before proceeding, we note that some of the theoretical results given below are not new. Ezra Solomon wrote a number of articles culminating in one dealing with the case of exponential growth in 1970. Thomas Stauffer published various theorems a year later (1971) and also attempted to make adjustments to accounting rates of return to correct for alternative cash flow profiles in testimony for the FTC in the Ready to Eat Cereal Litigation.[8] J. Leslie Livingstone and Gerald Salamon (1971) have also studied and attempted to determine a relationship between the accounting and internal rates of return. Yet, perhaps because Solomon's focus was on the correct concepts of rate of return and cost of capital for rate regulation, or perhaps because none of the studies cited makes clear just how large the effects involved can be, the importance of these matters for more general industrial organization research appears to have gone largely unnoticed. It is our hope that the self-contained discussion of the present paper and, especially, the mag-

[8]The proofs given below are different from Stauffer's proofs, and, we think, more suitable for our present purposes than his where the propositions coincide

nitudes of the effects exhibited in the examples below will remedy this.

I. Summary of Theoretical Results

The main theoretical results, which are proved and elucidated in the Appendix, are as follows:

(a) Unless depreciation schedules are chosen in a particular way, so that the value of the investment is calculated as the present value at the economic rate of return of the stream of benefits remaining in it[9]—a choice which is exceptionally unlikely to be made—the accounting rate of return on a particular investment will differ from year to year, and will not in general equal the economic rate of return on that investment in any year.

(b) The accounting rate of return for the firm as a whole will be an average of the accounting rates of return for individual investments made in the past. The weights in that average will consist of the book value of those different investments which in turn depend on the depreciation schedule adopted, and, particularly, on the amount and timing of such investments.

(c) Unless the proportion of investments with a given time shape remains fixed every year, and unless the firm simply grows exponentially, increasing investments in each and every type of asset[10] by the same proportion for every year, the accounting rate of return to the firm as a whole cannot even be expected to be constant, let alone be equal to the economic rate of return.

(d) Even where the firm does operate in such an unrealistic manner—the case most favorable to the accounting rate of return—the accounting rate of return will vary with the rate of growth of the firm, and will not generally equal the economic rate of return.

(e) The only reliable inferences concerning the economic rate of return that can be drawn (and only in such an unrealistically favorable case) from examination of the accounting rate of return stem from the fact that the accounting rate of return and the economic rate of return will be on the same side of the firm's exponential growth rate. If the accounting rate of return is higher than the growth rate, then the economic rate of return is also higher than the growth rate. If the accounting rate of return is lower than the growth rate, then the economic rate of return is lower than the growth rate. If the accounting rate of return equals the growth rate, and in this case *alone*, the economic rate of return is guaranteed to be equal to the accounting rate of return.[11]

(f) Even in the unrealistically favorable exponential growth case, the accounting rate of return depends *crucially* on the time shape of benefits, and the effect of growth on the accounting rate of return also depends on that time shape. In particular, it is not true that rapidly growing firms tend to understate their profits and slowly growing firms tend to overstate them. The effect can go the other way.[12]

(g) All these results apply both to before- and after-tax rates of return.

II. The Likely Size of the Effects

We now show by example that differences between the accounting and economic rates of return can be quite large indeed. For the sake of economy we examine only differences in after-tax rates of return. We as-

[9]Such a "natural" depreciation formula—which we shall term "economic depreciation"—was first suggested by Harold Hotelling in 1925. It is somewhat misleading, however, to say that the fundamental conceptual problems discussed in the present paper are basically matters of depreciation accounting. Rather, there exists a particular form of depreciation which will correct those problems which stem from a fundamental difference between the economic and accounting rates of return. These problems arise even where machines never wear out. An example is given in Fisher (1979).

[10]Two assets are said to be of the same "type" if they yield the same time shape of benefits.

[11]It is worth pointing out that these results apply to accounting rates of return on total assets, not directly to accounting rates of return on stockholders' equity. Further, they apply to accounting rates of return on beginning-of-year, not end-of-year or yearly average assets. As the examples below show, the problem of making inferences from accounting rates of return on end-of-year (or average) assets is even worse—if possible—than when beginning-of-year assets are used.

[12]Compare Cooper, pp. 132–33.

TABLE 1—AFTER-TAX ACCOUNTING RATES OF RETURN[a]
(Percent for the Q-Profile; Six-Year Life; No Delay)

Year	Gross Profits (Cash Flow Before-Tax)	Depreciation	After-Tax Profits	Beginning-of-Year Assets: Net	Beginning-of-Year Assets: Accounting Rate of Return	End-of-Year Assets: Net	End-of-Year Assets: Accounting Rate of Return
1	23.3	28.6	(5.3)	100.0	(5.3)	71.4	(7.4)
2	44.1	23.8	11.2	71.4	15.7	47.6	23.5
3	51.9	19.0	18.1	47.6	38.0	28.6	63.3
4	40.5	14.3	14.4	28.6	50.3	14.3	100.7
5	20.2	9.5	5.9	14.3	41.3	4.8	122.9
6	7.8	4.8	1.7	4.8	35.4	0	Infinite

[a]Tax rate: 45 percent; After-tax economic rate of return: 15 percent; Sum-of-the-years' digits depreciation.

sume a corporate tax rate of 45 percent, and (for most examples) fix the after-tax economic rate of return at 15 percent while varying growth rates and depreciation methods and the time shape of benefits.[13] Enormous variations in the accounting rates of return are readily generated.

A. *The "Q-Profile"*

We start with an investment whose benefits begin immediately and last for six years, and follow the time shape exhibited in column 2 of Table 1. For convenience we refer to this shape as the Q-profile.[14] The figures in column 2 are scaled to produce an after-tax economic rate of return of 15 percent on an initial investment of $100 when sum-of-the-years' digits depreciation over a six-year life is used. The remainder of the table shows the calculation of the corresponding accounting rate of return each year.

Plainly, the after-tax accounting rates of return vary substantially. They never equal the after-tax economic rate of return (15 percent), and exceed it in every year with positive net profits. Real-life firms do not generally exhibit such variation in their accounting rates of return because the averaging effects of growth, as it were, attribute profits from past investment to the book value of investments whose profit results are yet to come, rather than to the declining book value of such past investment.

While such an averaging effect tends to stabilize the accounting rate of return, it becomes a hodgepodge devoid of information about the economic rate of return. This point is illustrated by Table 2, which presents asymptotic accounting rates of return assuming constant exponential growth for three different versions of the Q-profile, each with the same tax rate (45 percent) and after-tax economic rate of return (15 percent).[15] The first version (the case of Table 1)

[13]Fifteen percent was roughly the average *accounting* rate of return in U.S. manufacturing corporations in 1978 (*Economic Report of the President*, 1979, pp. 279–91). If accounting and economic rates of return tended to coincide, 15 percent would be a reasonable choice for the economic rate of return. Since the rates do not generally coincide, the choice is immaterial. Choosing a lower economic rate of return would reduce the range of accounting rates of return in the results below (for the *same* examples), but would not affect the conclusions.

With a fixed capital investment, a given time shape of gross profits before depreciation and taxes results in different after-tax economic rates of return for different depreciation methods. To fix the after-tax economic rate of return for a given time shape, therefore, we adjust the height of the gross profit benefit stream proportionally to produce the desired after-tax economic rate of return.

[14]This shape was (erroneously) suggested during *U.S. v. IBM* as being typical of IBM's experience. We use it for convenience.

[15]In this context, exponential growth takes place by repeated investment in the same type of project; i.e., all investments have the same time-shape of benefits. This is obviously an unrealistic assumption, but one which is more likely to produce equality between accounting and economic rates of return than more realistic assumptions.

TABLE 2—ASYMPTOTIC ACCOUNTING RATES OF RETURN (%) ON THREE VERSIONS OF THE Q-PROFILE[a]

	Six-Year Life (No Delay)			Seven-Year Life (One-Year Delay)			Eight-Year Life (Two-Year Delay)		
Growth Rate	Straight Line	Declining Balance	Sum-of-Years' Digits	Straight Line	Declining Balance	Sum-of-Years' Digits	Straight Line	Declining Balance	Sum-of-Years' Digits
A. Beginning-of-Year Assets									
0	15.2	17.8	18.1	18.1	21.3	22.0	21.0	24.7	25.9
5	15.2	16.9	17.0	17.0	19.1	19.4	18.9	21.1	21.7
10	15.1	15.9	15.9	16.0	17.0	17.1	16.9	17.9	18.1
15	15.0	15.0	15.0	15.0	15.0	15.0	15.0	15.0	15.0
20	14.8	14.1	14.1	14.0	13.2	13.1	13.3	12.4	12.3
25	14.7	13.3	13.3	13.1	11.5	11.4	11.7	10.1	9.9
30	14.5	12.5	12.6	12.2	10.0	9.9	10.3	8.0	7.8
B. End-of-Year Assets									
0	15.2	17.8	18.1	18.1	21.3	22.0	21.0	24.7	25.9
5	14.5	16.1	16.2	16.2	18.1	18.5	18.0	20.1	20.7
10	13.7	14.5	14.5	14.6	15.4	15.5	15.3	16.3	16.5
15	13.0	13.0	13.0	13.0	13.0	13.0	13.0	13.0	13.0
20	12.4	11.8	11.8	11.7	11.0	10.9	11.1	10.3	10.2
25	11.7	10.6	10.7	10.5	9.2	9.2	9.4	8.1	7.9
30	11.1	9.6	9.7	9.4	7.7	7.6	7.9	6.2	6.0

[a]See Table 1.

has no delay between investment and the beginning of the benefit stream, and depreciation is taken over the resulting six-year life. The second version has a seven-year life including a one-year's delay between investment and initial return. The third has an eight-year life including a two-year delay between investment and initial return. Except for the lag at the beginning and differences in scale, the gross benefit stream is the same in each case. Panel A of the table gives accounting rates of return on beginning-of-year assets; Panel B gives those on end-of-year assets.

Several things are apparent from Table 2. First, the accounting rates of return only equal the economic rate of return of 15 percent when the growth rate is also 15 percent and when the accounting rate of return is measured on beginning-of-year assets. Otherwise, the accounting rates vary from seven points below to almost eleven points above the economic rate of return.

Second, it is not true (as is sometimes stated) that more rapid depreciation, other things equal, tends to understate accounting rates of return. In this example, when the rate of growth is below 15 percent, declining balance and sum-of-the-years' digits depreciation produces a higher accounting rate of return than straightline depreciation for given growth rates, time profiles, and economic rates of return. The effect is reversed when the growth rate exceeds the economic rate of return of 15 percent. This illustrates a general proposition: more rapid depreciation *increases* the accounting rate of return (measured on beginning-of-year assets) when the growth is less than the economic rate of return, and *decreases* the accounting rate of return when the growth rate exceeds the economic rate of return.[16] Since this is the only point about depreciation which we wish to demonstrate, we provide only results for sum-of-the-years' digits depreciation in the rest of this paper.[17]

In all the examples in Table 2, firms growing at rates greater than the economic rate of

[16]By Theorem 1, the changeover point is also where the growth rate equals the accounting rate of return on beginning-of-year assets.

[17]There is one additional point about depreciation which we shall not bother to exemplify. Since the depreciation method chosen affects the time shape of the after-tax benefit stream, the relationship of after-tax accounting rates to the growth rate is particularly sensitive to the depreciation method. It can even happen that faster growth increases accounting rates of return for one choice of depreciation method and decreases them for another—all for the same pre-tax benefit time shape and the same after-tax economic rate of return. This makes adjustments for growth even harder to make than appears from the examples below.

TABLE 3—ASYMPTOTIC ACCOUNTING RATES OF RETURN (%) ON FOUR VERSIONS OF THE Q-PROFILE[a]

Growth Rate	Ten-Year Life (No Delay, Last Year Spread)	Six-Year Life (No Delay)	Seven-Year Life (One-Year Delay)	Eight-Year Life (Two-Year Delay)
A. Beginning-of-Year Assets				
0	13.9	18.1	22.0	25.9
5	14.5	17.0	19.4	21.7
10	14.8	15.9	17.1	18.1
15	15.0	15.0	15.0	15.0
20	15.1	14.1	13.1	12.3
25	15.1	13.3	11.4	9.9
30	15.0	12.6	9.9	7.8
B. End-of-Year Assets				
0	13.9	18.1	22.0	25.9
5	13.8	16.2	18.5	20.7
10	13.5	14.5	15.5	16.5
15	13.0	13.0	13.0	13.0
20	12.6	11.8	10.9	10.2
25	12.0	10.7	9.2	7.9
30	11.5	9.7	7.6	6.0

[a]See Table 1.

return of 15 percent have accounting rates of return on beginning-of-year assets less than the economic rate of return, while those growing at rates less than the economic rate of return all have accounting rates of return on beginning-of-year assets greater than the economic rate of return.[18] Contrary to what might be expected, this qualitative relationship provides no practical basis for adjusting accounting rates of return so that they will accurately reflect economic rates of return.

Table 2, for example, shows that firms which use sum-of-the-years' digits depreciation and grow at 5 percent have accounting rates of return on beginning-of-year assets which range from 17.0 to 21.7 percent. Thus, even for firms with the same growth rate and depreciation method, the required adjustment varies from 2 to 6.7 percentage points depending upon the time profile. Clearly, the time profile, depreciation method, and growth rate must all be known before accounting rates of return can be adjusted to reflect economic rates of return.

In the foregoing examples, for a given time shape, faster-growing firms have lower accounting rates of return than slower-growing ones with the same economic rate of return. We have seen that even if this were a universal phenomenon, it would not provide a way to adjust accounting rates of return to reflect economic rates of return, since different firms will generally have different time shapes and therefore require different adjustments. The difficulties are even worse in practice, because the accounting rate of return can actually *rise* with the growth rate, causing *slower*-growing firms to have their economic rates of return *under*stated. Thus, even the strong assumption that firms have the same time profile is insufficient to permit adjustment of accounting rates of return; the specific profile must also be known in order to make inferences about the ranking of economic rates of return.

We demonstrate this phenomenon by taking the original Q-profile (six-year life and no delay) and spreading the last year's gross profits out evenly over five years (years 6–10) instead of having them all in year 6. Table 3 shows that this small change in the profile produces an increasing relationship between the growth rate and the accounting rate of return. The original results for sum-of-the-year's digits depreciation are reproduced for ease of comparison.

[18]So simple a relationship does not hold if the accounting rate of return is based on end-of-year assets.

Focusing on the first column (10-Year Life), we see that the accounting rate of return on beginning-of-year assets actually begins by rising with the growth rate, reaching the value of the economic rate of return (as it must) at a 15 percent growth rate, and then going slightly above it before falling back again. (It is a special feature of this particular example that these values are all close to the economic rate of return of 15 percent.) The behavior of the accounting rate of return on end-of-year assets is different. This magnitude falls with the growth rate (in this example), but it exhibits still another phenomenon. As opposed to the previous example, where the accounting rates of return on both beginning- and end-of-year assets were above the economic rate of return of 15 percent for low growth rates and below it for large ones, here the accounting rate of return on end-of-year assets starts *and finishes* below the economic rate of return of 15 percent. There is *no* rate of growth for which the accounting rate of return on end-of-year assets equals the economic rate of 15 percent.

The impossibility of making inferences about relative profit rates should be obvious even within the confines of these examples, all of which represent only relatively slight variations on the same profile. *Every one of the firms exhibited in Table 3 has the same underlying after-tax economic rate of return. Yet their after-tax accounting rates of return on end-of-year assets vary from* 6.0 *to* 25.9 *percent.*[19]

Further, it is impossible to infer anything about relative profitability by attempting to adjust for growth rates. For example, each row of Table 3 involves firms with the same growth rate, so that there is nothing to adjust for in comparing them; yet, except for the special row corresponding to the point where the growth rate is equal to the true after-tax economic rate of return, the after-tax accounting rates of return continue to vary. For the row corresponding to 5 percent growth, for example, after-tax accounting rates of return vary between 13.8 and 20.7 percent. For the row corresponding to 25 percent, they vary between 7.9 and 12.0 percent. Further, it is not correct to say that slow-growing firms have accounting rates of return that overstate their economic rate, while fast-growing firms have accounting rates of return that understate them. Continuing to use accounting rates of return on end-of-year assets, the firm just introduced (10-Year Life) has an accounting rate of return which understates its economic rate of return at all levels of growth. If one uses beginning-of-year assets, it has accounting rates of return which tend to understate its economic rate of return at low rates of growth and (slightly) overstate it at higher ones.

[19]Here and later, the results for beginning-of-year assets are similar.

Table 4—Before-Tax Benefit Streams from an Investment of $100[a]

Year	*X* Firm ($)	*Y* Firm ($)
1	90.2	107.0
2	27.1	10.7
3	18.0	10.7
4	9.0	10.7
5	9.0	10.7
6	9.0	10.7

[a]See Table 1.

Moreover, the phenomenon of accounting rates of return increasing with the growth rate can be considerably more marked if we use other profiles. Table 4 shows the before-tax benefit stream (corresponding to an initial investment of $100, an economic rate of return of 15 percent, and sum-of-the-years' digits depreciation over a six-year life) for two other profiles (*X* firm and *Y* firm). Table 5 shows the after-tax accounting rates of return for these firms when they grow exponentially at various rates. The after-tax accounting rates of return on beginning-of-year assets rise rather rapidly with the growth rate. The after-tax accounting rate of return on end-of-year assets also rises with the growth rate. However, as was also the case for the variation on the *Q*-profile examined earlier, it does not rise by enough to get to the economic rate of return of 15 percent.

TABLE 5—ASYMPTOTIC ACCOUNTING RATES OF RETURN (%) FOR X-FIRMS AND Y-FIRMS[a]

Growth Rate	Beginning-of-Year Assets		End-of-Year Assets	
	X Firm	Y Firm	X Firm	Y Firm
0	12.9	12.5	12.9	12.5
5	13.6	13.3	13.0	12.7
10	14.3	14.2	13.0	12.9
15	15.0	15.0	13.0	13.0
20	15.7	15.8	13.0	13.2
25	16.3	16.6	13.0	13.3
30	16.9	17.3	13.0	13.3

[a]See Table 1.

III. Conclusions

That the accounting rate of return—after tax as well as before tax—is a misleading measure of the economic rate of return is evident from examining cases of single projects such as in Table 1. The cases shown in later tables are unduly *favorable* to the accounting rate of return in that they mask its behavior by averaging. That averaging effect is achieved by the quite unrealistic assumption that investment by the firm always brings in the same time shape of returns, and that the firm grows each year by increasing its investments at the same percentage rate. Even on such favorable terms, it is impossible to infer either the magnitude or direction of differences in economic rates of return from differences in accounting rates of return. This is because such inferences require not only correction for growth rates, but *also* knowledge of the time shapes of returns.

The level and behavior of the accounting rate of return are both sensitive to the type of time shape used. Even within the Q-profile example, the rates vary depending on when the time shape begins and how the last few years are spread out. There is every reason to suppose that firms differ in the time shapes of their investments, and that a particular firm's investments will also differ among themselves. Thus, comparisons of accounting rates of return to make inferences about monopoly profits is a baseless procedure.

This conclusion can be most dramatically demonstrated by juxtaposing accounting rates of return for firms with different time shapes and *different* economic rates of return. When this is done, it is easy to see that firms with *higher* accounting rates of return can have *lower* economic rates of return. Table 6 gives after-tax economic rates of return and after-tax accounting rates of return on end-of-year assets for three growth rates (0, 5, and 10 percent), and for each of the six time shapes already discussed as well as two other "one-hoss shay" time shapes.[20] For *each* growth rate, the examples are chosen so that the eight firms represented are ranked in *ascending* order of economic rates of return and in *descending* order of accounting rates of return—a complete reversal even with growth rates constant.

Examination of Table 6 shows again that no inference about relative after-tax economic rates of return is possible from after-tax accounting rates of return. For example, the lowest after-tax economic rate of return in the table is that for the Q-profile with an eight-year life at a zero growth rate. For that firm, the after-tax economic rate of return is 13 percent. Yet, its after-tax accounting rate

[20]The one-hoss shay time shapes have a constant return (no lag) for four and six years, respectively, and zero returns thereafter.

TABLE 6—AFTER-TAX ECONOMIC RATES OF RETURN (E) AND ASYMPTOTIC ACCOUNTING RATES OF RETURN ON END-OF-YEAR ASSETS (A) FOR EIGHT TIME SHAPES[a]

	Growth Rate					
	0 Percent		5 Percent		10 Percent	
Growth Rate	E	A	E	A	E	A
Q-Profile						
8-Year Life (2-year delay)	13.0	21.6	16.0	22.6	17.8	21.2
7-Year Life (1-year delay)	14.0	20.2	17.0	21.6	18.8	20.9
One-Hoss Shay						
6-Year Life (no delay)	15.0	20.0	18.1	21.4	19.7	20.7
4-Year Life (no delay)	16.0	19.8	19.0	21.3	20.0	20.289
Q-Profile						
6-Year Life (no delay)	16.1	19.6	19.05	21.2	20.05	20.287
10-Year Life (no delay; last year spread)	18.0	16.9	20.0	18.5	22.0	19.8
X Firm	19.0	16.2	21.0	17.8	23.0	19.2
Y Firm	19.2	15.8	21.2	17.4	23.2	18.9

[a]Tax rate: 45 percent; Sum-of-the-years' digits depreciation.

of return on end-of-year assets is 21.6 percent, the second *highest* accounting rate of return in the table, and a value well above that of 15.8 percent for the Y firm at zero growth, corresponding to a 19.2 percent economic rate of return. The 21.6 percent accounting rate of return so encountered is even above the 18.9 percent figure obtained for the Y firm at 10 percent growth—a figure which corresponds to an economic rate of return of 23.2 percent, the highest in the table, and more than 10 percentage points above the economic rate of return of 13 percent for the Q-profile with an eight-year life at zero growth. Similar examples of reversals occur throughout the table.

Nor can one eliminate these effects by correcting somehow for differences in rates of growth. The table as constructed exhibits a reversal of the ordering of economic and accounting rates of return with the rate of growth held constant. Rate of growth effects have thus *already* been removed from each pair of columns to an extent beyond that which one could hope to achieve in practice. Moreover, it is not true that faster-growing firms should have their accounting rates of return adjusted upwards relative to slower growing ones. Consider the comparison between the Q-profile with a ten-year life at zero growth and the Q-profile with an eight-year life at 5 percent growth. The faster-growing firm has an accounting rate of return (22.6 percent) already greater than that of the slower-growing firm (16.9 percent), but its economic rate of return (16.0 percent) is *below* that of the slower-growing firm (18.0 percent). Adjusting the faster-growing firm's accounting rate of return *upwards* relative to that of the slower-growing one will make things *worse*, not better.

As all of this makes clear, there is no way in which one can look at accounting rates of return and infer anything about relative economic profitability or, a fortiori, about the presence or absence of monopoly profits. The economic rate of return is difficult—perhaps impossible—to compute for entire firms. Doing so requires information about both the past and the future which outside observers do not have, if it exists at all.[21] Yet it is the economic rate of return which is the magnitude of interest for economic propositions. Economists (and others) who believe that analysis of accounting rates of return will tell them much (if they can only overcome the various definitional problems which separate economists and accountants) are deluding themselves. The literature which supposedly relates concentration and economic profit rates does no such thing, and examination of absolute or relative accounting rates of return to draw conclusions about monopoly profits is a totally misleading enterprise.

Appendix
I: Before-Tax Analysis

A. *The Accounting Rate of Return on Individual Investments*

We begin our analysis of the problem by considering the before-tax accounting and economic rates of return on a single investment. Later we shall consider the firm as being made up of a series of such investments which may be (but need not always be) of the same type. The after-tax case is treated below and shown to be isomorphic, although more complex.

An investment may be thought of for heuristic purposes as a "machine" costing one dollar. If this is invested at time 0, the firm experiences a stream of net benefits as a result. Such benefits include all changes in revenues and costs (other than the initial capital cost) which accrue to the firm as a result of making the investment. The flow of such benefits at time θ is denoted by $f(\theta)$.[22]

[21] If one made the strong assumption that the same time shape of returns held for all investments made by a given firm throughout its life, then it might be possible to recover that time shape by regression of gross returns on a distributed lag of past investment. We are indebted to Zvi Griliches for this suggestion.

[22] The time origin is arbitrary. The flow of benefits is assumed to depend on the age of the machine only. Thus an investment at time t brings in benefits of $f(\theta - t)$ at time $\theta \geqslant t$. Time dependence of the benefit stream can be handled below by thinking of it as equivalent to investment in different kinds of machines at different times.

The economic rate of return on a machine, r, is that discount rate which makes the discounted value of the benefit stream equal to the capital costs of the investment. In other words, r satisfies

$$\text{(A1)} \qquad \int_0^{\infty} f(\theta)\, exp(-r\theta)\, d\theta = 1.$$

We assume that the integral in (A1) is monotonically decreasing in r so that (A1) has a unique positive solution. This will be true if the negative portion of the net benefit stream (if any) precedes the positive portion. This is the usual case.[23]

Now the firm adopts a depreciation schedule for this machine. Let $V(\theta)$ denote the book value of the machine as of time θ. Then $-V'(\theta)$ is the rate of depreciation at θ, where the prime denotes differentiation. Plainly, $V(0)=1$, and it makes sense to suppose that $V(\infty)=0$, although this latter condition is not really needed.

Accounting profits attributable to this machine at time θ will be equal to net benefits less depreciation. We can think of the accounting rate of return for this machine as the accounting rate of return which the firm would have if this were its only asset. Denoting that rate by $b(\theta)$,

$$\text{(A2)} \qquad b(\theta) = (f(\theta) + V'(\theta))/V(\theta).$$

The first question which comes immediately to mind is that of when $b(\theta) = r$ for all θ within the life of the machine. We prove this will occur if and only if the depreciation schedule adopted by the firm always values the machine as the discounted value of the future benefit stream, discounting at the economic rate of return, r (see Hotelling).

THEOREM 1: *$b(\theta) \equiv r$ if and only if*

$$\text{(A3)} \qquad V(\theta) = \int_{\theta}^{\infty} f(u)\, exp(-r(u-\theta))\, du.$$

[23] If (A1) has more than one solution, then the economic rate of return is ill-defined and there is even less point in considering whether the accounting rate of return yields information about it.

PROOF:

(a) Suppose (A3) holds. Differentiating with respect to θ, we obtain

$$(A4) \qquad V'(\theta) = -f(\theta) + rV(\theta),$$

which when substituted in equation (A2) yields $b(\theta) = r$.

(b) Suppose $b(\theta) \equiv r$. Then, from (A2),

$$(A5) \qquad V'(\theta) \equiv rV(\theta) - f(\theta).$$

This is a linear differential equation with an additive forcing function $(-f(\theta))$. Its solution is therefore in the form

$$(A6) \qquad V(\theta) = C\,exp(r\theta) + z(\theta),$$

where $z(\theta)$ is any particular solution of (A5) and C is a constant to be determined by the initial conditions. However, by part (a) of the proof, the integral on the right-hand side of (A3) is a particular solution of (A5). Hence $z(\theta)$ can be taken as that integral. Do this and note that $z(0) = 1$ by (A1), the definition of the economic rate of return. Since we have $V(0) = 1$, setting $\theta = 0$ in (A6) yields $C = 0$, and the theorem is proved.

Thus even where the firm has a single simple investment with no ambiguity about marginal vs. economic rates of return, the accounting rate of return will not equal the economic rate of return except for a particular choice of a depreciation schedule—which choice we may term "economic depreciation."

The reason for this is not hard to find. The book value of the firm's assets reflects the investment expenditures made in the past less the depreciation already taken on them. The benefits for which such investments were made are at least partly in the future. Yet the accounting rate of return takes gross profits before depreciation as the benefit flow which happens to be currently occurring. Unless depreciation is chosen so as to reflect the change in *future* benefits in the appropriate way, there is no reason to suppose that such a calculation should equal the economic rate of return, and Theorem 1 shows that the two will generally not be equal.

Will firms tend to adopt an "economic depreciation" schedule yielding book value as in equation (A3)? This is pathologically unlikely. Except in the simple "Santa Claus" case of $f(\theta) = k\,exp(-\lambda\theta)$ which corresponds to exponential depreciation or other similarly special cases corresponding to straightline or other standard depreciation methods, the benefit stream from investment when plugged into (A3) will not yield depreciation schedules anything like those used by real-life firms to optimize after-tax profits given IRS rules or those schedules used for nontax purposes. Real investments will almost invariably have complicated time shapes for their benefit streams. Further, even relatively simple shapes yield economic depreciation schedules which are quite far from actual ones. To see this, one need only observe that if $V(\theta)$ satisfies equation (A3), there is no reason that $V'(\theta)$ must always be negative. Indeed, if the time stream of benefits starts low and then has a hump a few years out, taking economic depreciation would require writing up the value of assets for the first few years. Yet there is nothing bizarre about such an example.

We must, therefore, with pathologically unlikely exceptions, expect that the accounting rate of return on a particular machine, $a(\theta)$, will generally not equal the economic rate of return r. (How far off it can be is demonstrated by examples.) This should make us suspect that the same thing will generally be true of the firm as a whole, and we now go on to explore that question.

B. *The Accounting Rate of Return for the Firm as an Average*

It is fairly plain that the best hope for an accounting rate of return equal to the economic rate of return will occur if all investments made by the firm are exactly alike, since otherwise (as shown below), changes in the mix of investment types will change the accounting rate. So we begin by considering the case in which all machines are like the machine above.

It now becomes necessary to distinguish calendar time, denoted by t, from the age of a machine, denoted by θ. We let $I(t)$ be the value of investment made at t (equals the number of machines purchased). Let $K(t)$ denote the book value of the firm's assets at t and $\pi(t)$ the value of its accounting profits at t. Then,

$$\text{(A7)} \quad K(t) = \int_{-\infty}^{t} I(u)V(t-u)\,du = \int_{0}^{\infty} I(t-\theta)V(\theta)\,d\theta,$$

where $\theta = t - u$. Similarly,

$$\text{(A8)} \quad \pi(t) = \int_{-\infty}^{t} I(u)\{f(t-u)+V'(t-u)\}\,du = \int_{0}^{\infty} I(t-\theta)\{f(\theta)+V'(\theta)\}\,d\theta = \int_{0}^{\infty} I(t-\theta)V(\theta)b(\theta)\,d\theta,$$

using (A2).

Hence, letting $a(t)$ be the firm's accounting rate of return at t:

$$\text{(A9)} \quad a(t) \equiv \pi(t)/K(t) = \left[\int_0^\infty \{I(t-\theta)V(\theta)\}b(\theta)\,d\theta\right] \Big/ \left[\int_0^\infty \{I(t-\theta)V(\theta)\}d\theta\right];$$

so that we have proved

LEMMA 1: *At any time t, the accounting rate of return for the firm as a whole is a weighted average of the individual accounting rates for its individual past investments, the weights being the book values of those past investments.*

It should be obvious that this result would also be true if machines were not always of one type.

We now ask whether such an average will equal the economic rate of return. First consider whether the average can even be independent of t. This can happen in two ways. First, $b(\theta)$ might be independent of θ. We know from Theorem 1 that this will happen for $b(\theta) \equiv r$ only for the cases of economic depreciation already discussed which we rule out. It is easy to show that $b(\theta) \equiv q \neq r$ is impossible.[24]

The other way in which $a(t)$ might be independent of t would be if the relative weights in the average did not change over time.[25]

$$\text{(A10)} \quad \frac{I(t_1-\theta)V(\theta)}{I(t_2-\theta)V(\theta)} = k,$$

whence

$$\text{(A11)} \quad \frac{I'(t_1-\theta)}{I(t_1-\theta)} = \frac{I'(t_2-\theta)}{I(t_2-\theta)},$$

for all (t_1, t_2). Evidently it must then be the case that

$$\text{(A12)} \quad I(t) = M\,exp(gt)$$

for some constant growth rate g.

The remainder of our investigation will concern the case of exponential growth with the scale factor, M, set equal to unity. This case is the most favorable to accounting rates of return approximating economic rates of return, since in its absence accounting rates of return will not even be constant, even though the economic rate of return is well defined and constant.

C. *The Effect of the Growth Rate in Exponential Growth*

We are now dealing with a case in which the accounting rate of return is (at least

[24] To see this, observe that a proof essentially the same as that of Theorem 1 would show that $b(\theta) \equiv q$ if and only if

$$\text{(a)} \quad V(\theta) = C\,exp(q\theta) + z(\theta),$$

where

$$\text{(b)} \quad z(\theta) = \int_\theta^\infty f(u)\,exp(-q(u-\theta))\,du,$$

but $V(0) = 1$ so that $C = 1 - z(0) \neq 0$ if $q \neq r$. Then (A4) yields $V(\infty) = \pm\infty$ depending on $q \gtrless r$ and this is not possible.

[25] For a *given* distribution of $b(\theta)$ there might be other possibilities, but these would be even more special than the case of economic depreciation already discussed. The statement in the text is true if $a(t)$ is to be constant despite unknown variations in $b(\theta)$ with θ.

asymptotically) constant and given as

$$\text{(A13)}\quad a=\frac{\int_0^\infty\{exp(g(t-\theta))V(\theta)\}b(\theta)\,d\theta}{\int_0^\infty\{exp(g(t-\theta))V(\theta)\}\,d\theta}$$

where a denotes the (asymptotic) constant value. This is still a weighted average of the accounting rates of return on individual investments. Plainly, the growth rate g affects the weights. Since the accounting rates of return on individual investments will almost always not be constant in view of Theorem 1, changes in the weights will usually affect the average.

The present section studies such effects and asks, in particular, what inferences can be drawn concerning the economic rate of return r, from knowledge of the accounting rate of return a, and the growth rate g, without information on the time shape of benefits, $f(\cdot)$, since the latter information is plainly never available from the books of the firm—even assuming it is known in detail to the firm's forecasters.

The first thing to say in this regard is that while (as we shall show) there exist values of g for which $a=r$, these values will be the exception. One cannot expect accounting and economic rates of return to coincide even in the most favorable case of exponential growth and a single investment type except by the merest accident. What information *can* be gleaned from the accounting rate of return is analyzed in this section.

It will be convenient to set up the problem a little differently from the analyses above. Let $\pi^*(t)$ denote the gross profits of the firm before depreciation. Let $\delta(t)$ denote total depreciation taken at time t. Let $K^*(t)$ denote the *undepreciated* value of the firm's capital stock. Let $D(t)$ denote the total depreciation already taken on that stock. Finally, let $a^*=\pi^*(t)/K^*(t)$, so that a^* is the accounting rate of return which would be observed if there were no depreciation. The following relationships hold:

$$\text{(A14)}\quad a=\frac{\pi^*(t)-\delta(t)}{K^*(t)-D(t)},$$

$$\text{(A15)}\quad \pi^*(t)\equiv\int_{-\infty}^t exp(gu)f(t-u)\,du$$

$$=\int_0^\infty exp(g(t-\theta))f(\theta)\,d\theta$$

$$=exp(gt)\int_0^\infty exp(-g\theta)f(\theta)\,d\theta$$

$$=exp(gt)\pi^*(0),$$

$$\text{(A16)}\quad K^*(t)\equiv\int_{-\infty}^t exp(gu)\,du$$

$$=exp(gt)/g$$

$$\text{(A17)}\quad \delta(t)=\int_{-\infty}^t exp(gu)V'(t-u)\,du$$

$$=\int_0^\infty exp(g(t-\theta))V'(\theta)\,d\theta$$

$$=exp(gt)\delta(0),$$

$$\text{(A18)}\quad D(t)=\int_{-\infty}^t \delta(u)\,du$$

$$=\int_{-\infty}^t exp(gu)\delta(0)\,du$$

$$=\delta(0)exp(gt)/g.$$

Evidently, we have proved:

LEMMA 2: $\delta(t)/D(t)=g$.

We now study the effects of g on a^*.

LEMMA 3: (a) *If $g=r$, then $a^*=r=g$.*

(b) $d\log a^*/d\log g<1$.

(c) *a^* and r are always on the same side of g. That is, $a^*<g\leftrightarrow r<g$; $a^*=g\leftrightarrow r=g$; $a^*>g\leftrightarrow r>g$.*

PROOF:

(a) Using equations (A15) and (A16),

$$\text{(A19)}\quad a^*=g\pi^*(0)$$

$$\equiv g\int_0^\infty exp(-g\theta)f(\theta)\,d\theta.$$

If $g = r$, then $\pi^*(0) = 1$ by the definition of the economic rate of return (A1), whence $a^* = g = r$.

(b) From (A19),

$$\text{(A20)} \qquad \log a^* = \log g + \log \pi^*(0),$$

but examination of $\pi^*(0)$ shows that it is necessarily decreasing in g since it is the discounted integral of future benefits from a single machine discounted at the rate g. Thus $d \log a^* / d \log g < 1$.

(c) These statements follow directly from (a) and (b).

Using Lemmas 2 and 3, we can now proceed to the main result of this section for the magnitude of interest, the accounting rate of return a, itself.

THEOREM 2: *a and r are always on the same side of g. That is,*

$$a < g \leftrightarrow r < g; \qquad a = g \leftrightarrow r = g;$$
$$a > g \leftrightarrow r > g.$$

PROOF:

By definition, $\pi^*(t) = a^* K^*(t)$. By Lemma 2, $\delta(t) = gD(t)$. Substituting in (A14)

$$\text{(A21)} \qquad a = \frac{a^* K^*(t) - gD(t)}{K^*(t) - D(t)} \gtreqless g,$$

accordingly as $a^* \gtreqless g$. The desired result now follows from Lemma 3.

A diagram may be illuminating here. In Figure 1, the growth rate is measured on the horizontal axis and rates of return on the vertical axis. The 45° line indicates where growth rates and rates of return are equal. Theorem 2 states that the accounting rate of return must be above the 45° line to the left of the dashed line at $g = r$; it must pass through H, the point of intersection of the dashed line and the 45° line; and it must be below the 45° line to the right of the dashed line.

Can we say more than this? The answer is in the negative without information on the time shape of benefits $f(\cdot)$. In particular, it is

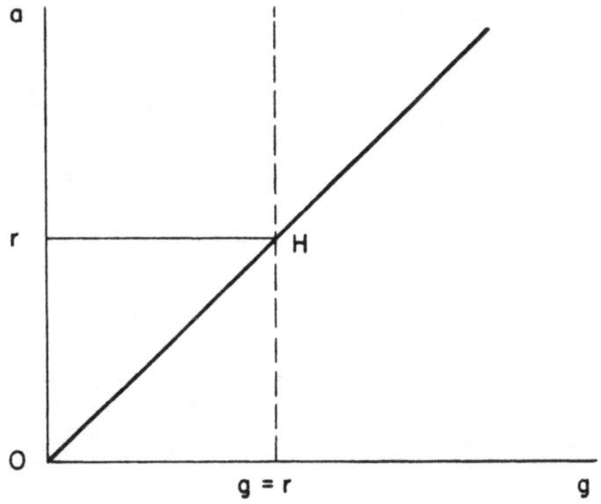

FIGURE 1

not the case that the direction of change of a with respect to g is signed. Nor is it true that r must lie between a and g. These facts are exemplified in the text.

II. After-Tax Analysis

These same results apply to the analysis of the relationship between the after-tax economic rate of return and the after-tax accounting rate of return. This is obvious if the depreciation schedule used is not that used for tax purposes; in that case, the effect of taxes is just to change the benefit profile with the analysis the same as before, given the new benefit profile $f(\cdot)$. Moreover, the same thing is true if tax depreciation is used. To see this, let α be the tax rate $0 < \alpha < 1$ (assumed constant for simplicity). Let r' denote the after-tax economic rate of return. Then r' satisfies

$$\text{(A22)} \qquad \int_0^\infty \{(1-\alpha)f(\theta) + \alpha d(\theta)\} \times \exp(-r'\theta)\, d\theta = 1,$$

where $d(\theta)$ denotes depreciation on an asset of age θ and $f(\theta)$ denotes its *before*-tax benefits, as before.

This reflects the fact that the choice of a depreciation schedule, $d(\cdot)$, affects after-tax returns. Define

$$\text{(A23)} \quad f^*(\theta) \equiv \{(1-\alpha)f(\theta)+\alpha d(\theta)\}.$$

We now show that the analysis of the before-tax case applies directly to the after-tax case with $f^*(\cdot)$, the after-tax benefit schedule, replacing $f(\cdot)$, the before-tax benefit schedule.[26]

To see this, observe that the denominator of the accounting rate-of-return (whether total capitalization or stockholder's equity) will be the same before and after taxes. The numerator in the after-tax case, after-tax profits less depreciation, will be:

(A24)

$$\int_{-\infty}^{t}(1-\alpha)\{f(t-\theta)-d(t-\theta)\}I(\theta)\,d\theta,$$

$$=\int_{-\infty}^{t}\{(1-\alpha)f(t-\theta)+\alpha d(t-\theta)\}I(\theta)\,d\theta$$

$$-\int_{-\infty}^{t}d(t-\theta)I(\theta)\,d\theta,$$

$$=\int_{-\infty}^{t}f^*(t-\theta)I(\theta)\,d\theta-\int_{-\infty}^{t}d(\theta)I(\theta)\,d\theta.$$

But this is the *same* numerator as would be encountered in the before-tax analysis for a firm with the same depreciation schedule, but *before*-tax benefits $f^*(\cdot)$. For such a firm, r' would be the before-tax economic rate of return. Hence analysis of the after-tax case is identical to that of the before-tax case with an appropriate adjusted definition of the benefit schedule. All previous results apply to it.[27]

[26]A word about the treatment of inflation seems appropriate here. In the before-tax analysis it does not matter whether we work in real or nominal dollars (so long as we are consistent). In the after-tax case, however, the fact that depreciation which is deductible for tax purposes must be in nominal terms appears to raise some difficulty. That difficulty is only apparent however. Suppose that we begin by working in real terms. The nominal nature of the depreciation deduction plus the effects of inflation affect the depreciation schedule measured in real terms. We show, however, that any after-tax case with *any* depreciation schedule is isomorphic to a before-tax case. The effects being considered will, of course, influence *what* that before-tax case is, but they will not alter the existence of such a case. Hence, while the nominal nature of depreciation (like any other factor affecting the depreciation schedule) will affect what the numerical value of the real after-tax accounting rate of return is, it will not change our results.

[27]It is interesting (and revealing of the full unity of the before- and after-tax analyses) to note what happens in the case of "economic depreciation" examined above. In that case, it turns out that the (pathologically unlikely) choice of an economic depreciation schedule involves the *same* depreciation schedule whether economic depreciation is chosen before or after tax. Assets are valued at the present value of all remaining benefits either before or after tax; it makes no difference. Further, that choice of depreciation schedule makes the after-tax economic rate of return r' relate to the before-tax economic rate of return r, in the natural (but—except with this depreciation schedule—not inevitable) way: $r'=r(1-\alpha)$. To show these things, return to the differential equation (equation (A5)) from which we derived the formula for economic depreciation in the before-tax case.

$$\text{(a)} \quad V'(\theta)=rV(\theta)-f(\theta).$$

Consideration of the before-tax analysis shows that if and only if $V(\cdot)$ satisfies this and $V(0)=1$, then

$$\text{(b)} \quad V(\theta)=\int_{\theta}^{\infty}f(u)\exp(-r(u-\theta))\,du$$

the present value of future benefits. Now, choose $V(\cdot)$ and hence $d(\cdot)$ to satisfy (b) and therefore (a). Then

$$\text{(c)} \quad (1-\alpha)V'(\theta)=r(1-\alpha)V(\theta)-(1-\alpha)f(\theta),$$

$$\text{(d)} \quad V'(\theta)=r(1-\alpha)V(\theta)$$

$$-\{(1-\alpha)f(\theta)+\alpha d(\theta)\}=r(1-\alpha)V(\theta)-f^*(\theta),$$

since $d(\theta)\equiv -V'(\theta)$. But this is in the same form as (a). Hence, as in (A6):

(e)

$$V(\theta)=\int_{\theta}^{\infty}f^*(u)\exp(-r'(u-\theta))\,du+C\exp(r'\theta),$$

with $r'\equiv r(1-\alpha)$. Here, C is a constant of integration; however $C=0$, since (b) shows that $V(\infty)$ is finite. Since $V(0)=1$, we have

$$\text{(f)} \quad 1=\int_{0}^{\infty}f^*(u)\exp(-r'u)\,du,$$

which shows that r' is the after-tax economic rate of return. From (b) and (e) with $C=0$, $V(\theta)$ is both the before- and the after-tax present value of the remaining benefit stream at θ, whence economic depreciation is the same in both cases. See Paul Samuelson.

Thus, in after-tax analysis as in before-tax analysis, there is no reason to believe that differences in the accounting rate of return correspond to differences in economic rates of return. Our computer examples show the effects can be very large; the belief that they are small enough in practice to make accounting rates useful for analytic purposes rests on nothing but wishful thinking.

REFERENCES

Adams, Walter, *The Structure of American Industry*, New York: Macmillan, 1970.

Areeda, Philip and Turner, Donald F., *Antitrust Law: An Analysis of Antitrust Principles and Their Application*, Boston: Little, Brown and Co., 1978.

Benston, George J., "The FTC's Line of Business Program: A Benefit-Cost Analysis," in Harvey Goldschmid, ed., *Business Disclosure: Government's Need to Know*, New York: McGraw-Hill, 1979, 58–118.

Cooper, Joseph D., *Proceedings of the Second Seminar on Economics of Pharmaceutical Innovation*, Washington: American University, 1976.

Fisher, Franklin M., "Diagnosing Monopoly," *Quarterly Review of Economics and Business*, Summer 1979, *19*, 7–33.

Hotelling, Harold, "A General Mathematical Theory of Depreciation," *Journal of the American Statistical Association*, September 1925, *20*, 340–53.

Livingstone, J. Leslie and Salamon, Gerald L., "Relationship Between the Accounting and the Internal Rate of Return Measures: A Synthesis and Analysis," in J. Leslie Livingstone and Thomas J. Burns, eds., *Income Theory and Rate of Return*, Columbus: Ohio State University, 1971, 161–78.

Samuelson, Paul A., "Tax Deductibility of Economic Depreciation to Insure Investment Valuations," *Journal of Political Economy*, December 1964, *72*, 604–06.

Scherer, F. M., *Industrial Market Structure and Economic Performance*, Chicago: Rand McNally, 1980.

Solomon, Ezra, "Alternative Rate of Return Concepts and Their Implications for Utility Regulation," *Bell Journal of Economics*, Spring 1970, *1*, 65–81.

Stauffer, Thomas R., "The Measurement of Corporate Rates of Return: A Generalized Formulation," *Bell Journal of Economics*, Autumn 1971, *2*, 434–69.

Weiss, Leonard W., "The Concentration-Profits Relationship and Antitrust," in Harvey J. Goldschmid et al., *Industrial Concentration: The New Learning*, Boston, Little, Brown and Co., 1974.

U.S. Council of Economic Advisers, *Economic Report of the President*, Washington: USGPO, 1979.

Part II
Mergers

[3]

ECONOMIES AS AN ANTITRUST DEFENSE: THE WELFARE TRADEOFFS

By OLIVER E. WILLIAMSON*

Suppose that a merger (or other combination) is proposed that yields economies but at the same time increases market power. Can the courts and antitrust agencies safely rely, in these circumstances, on a literal reading of the law which prohibits mergers "where in any line of commerce or any section of the country, the effect of such acquisition may be substantially to lessen competition, or to tend to create a monopoly,"[1] or does this run the risk of serious economic loss? In the usual merger where both effects are insubstantial this problem is absent.[2] But in the occasional case where efficiency and market power consequences exist, can economies be dismissed on the grounds that market power effects invariably dominate? If they cannot, then a rational treatment of the merger question requires that an effort be made to

* The author is associate professor of economics at the University of Pennsylvania.

[1] Public Law 899, Sec. 7, 38 Stat. 731, as amended; 15 U.S.C. 18.

[2] Donald Dewey has observed in this connection that most mergers "have virtually nothing to do with either the creation of market power or the realization of scale economies" [9, p. 257]. Jesse Markham agrees that since 1930 monopolization has not been a principal merger objective, but finds that "some mergers have undoubtedly come about as adjustments to major innovations . . . : the first great wave of mergers followed a period of rapid railroad building, and the wave of the 1920s came with the rise of the motor car and motor truck transportation and a new advertising medium, the home radio" [22, pp. 181–82]. It might be useful briefly to summarize some of the ways in which efficiencies might result from combination. These would include miscalculation, shifts in demand, technological developments, displacement of ineffective managements, and mixtures thereof.

As an example of miscalculation consider two firms that have entered a market at an efficient plant scale but have incorrectly estimated the volume necessary to support an efficient distribution system. Combination here could lead to efficiencies but might also have some market power effects (reducing competition between the two but possibly enhancing their competitive position with respect to their rivals). A significant, persistent decline in demand might produce a condition of excess capacity in which combination would permit economies but would also have market power consequences. As discussed in Section III, an increase in demand might induce a change from job shop to assembly line type operations with vertical integration consequences. Technological developments may similarly provide opportunities for a significant reorganization of resources into more efficient configurations—the electronic digital computer being a recent example. Finally, merger may be the most expeditious way of displacing an inefficient by a more efficient management—but the benefits here may only be of a short-run variety. A manifestly inefficient management would, hopefully, be displaced by other means if, by reason of the market power consequences of a combination, the merger route were closed.

A merger can, of course, produce diseconomies as well. What I have previously characterized as the "control loss" phenomenon appears to be an increasing function of firm size [31]. See also Parts 7 and 8, Section II, infra.

establish the allocative implications of the scale economy and market power effects associated with the merger.

The initial indication of the Supreme Court's view on this question came on the occasion of the first merger case to come before it under the 1950 amendment to Section 7 of the Clayton Act. In a unanimous opinion, the Court took the position in *Brown Shoe* that not only were efficiencies no defense, but a showing that a merger resulted in efficiencies could be used affirmatively in attacking the merger since small rivals could be disadvantaged thereby [6, p. 374]. Opportunities to reconsider this position have presented themselves since, *Procter & Gamble* being the most recent.

Justice Douglas, in delivering the opinion of the Court, observed that Procter & Gamble "would be able to use its volume discounts to advantage in advertising Clorox," and went on to state that "economies cannot be used as a defense to illegality. Congress was aware that some mergers which lessen competition may also result in economies but it struck the balance in favor of protecting competition" [10, pp. 1230–31]. Although reference to congressional intent may relieve the Court of the responsibility for making tradeoff valuations, this does not fully dispose of the issue. What tradeoff calculus did Congress employ that produced this result?

In a concurring opinion to the Clorox decision, Justice Harlan provides the first hint that efficiencies may deserve greater standing. At least with respect to conglomerate or product-extension mergers "where the case against the merger rests on the probability [as contrasted, apparently, with a certainty] of increased market power, the merging companies may attempt to prove that there are countervailing economies reasonably probable which should be weighed against the adverse effects" [10, pp. 1240–41]. But inasmuch as the economies in Clorox were in his opinion merely pecuniary rather than real, which distinction is of course appropriate, he concluded that Procter's efficiency defense was defective [10, p. 1243].

Even if Justice Harlan's position were the prevailing one, it is clear that economies would be an acceptable antitrust defense for only a restricted set of structural conditions. Since the relevant economic theory, although widely available, has never been developed explicitly on this issue, such a result is not unexpected. Indeed, lacking a basis for evaluating net effects, for the Court to hold that the anticompetitive consequences of a merger outweigh any immediate efficiency advantages is only to be expected. An institution acting as a caretaker for the enterprise system does not easily exchange what it regards as long-term competitive consequences for short-term efficiency gains.

The merits of the Supreme Court's position on mergers are at the heart of the recent Bork and Bowman v. Blake and Jones debate [2, 3, 4, 5]. Although this dialogue deals directly with the critical issues, its failure to produce a consensus is at least partly due to the fact that essential aspects of the relevant economic model were not supplied. Lacking a tradeoff relation, Bork is forced to assert that "Economic analysis does away with the need to measure efficiencies directly. It is enough to know in what sorts of transactions efficiencies are likely to be present and in what sorts anticompetitive effects are likely to be present. The law can then develop objective criteria, such as market shares, to divide transactions [into those predominantly one type or other]" [5, p. 411]. But this obviously leaves the mixed cases, which are the hard ones, unresolved. Blake and Jones, by contrast, conclude that "claims of economic efficiency will not justify a course of conduct conferring excessive market power. The objective of maintaining a system of self-policing markets requires that all such claims be rejected" [3, p. 427]. But what are the standards for "excessive" market power and "self-policing" markets? And are these really absolute or do they reflect an implicit tradeoff calculation? And if it is the latter, should we (if we can) make this tradeoff explicit?

Indeed, there is no way in which the tradeoff issue can be avoided. To disallow tradeoffs altogether merely reflects a particularly severe a priori judgment as to net benefits. Moreover, it is doubtful that a goal hierarchy scheme of the sort proposed by Carl Kaysen and Donald Turner has acceptable properties. As they formulate the problem, higher level goals strictly dominate lower level goals, so that only when the latter are available without sacrifice in the former is lower level goal pursuit allowed [16, pp. 44–45]. Inasmuch as they rank efficiency and progressiveness above reductions in market power, an absolute defense would appear to obtain when, for any structural condition present or prospective, it could be shown either that economies have not yet been exhausted or that discreteness conditions (indivisibilities) would not efficiently permit a separation [16, pp. 44–46, 58, 78]. But this may be to construe their intentions too narrowly; for it is with antitrust actions that result in *substantial* efficiency losses [16, pp. 44, 133] and involve *too great* a sacrifice in performance [16, p. 58] that they are especially concerned. Although these distinctions are important, they are not ones for which goal hierarchy analysis is well suited to deal. Tradeoff analysis, by contrast, is designed to cope with precisely these types of issues.

The relevant partial equilibrium model with which to characterize the tradeoffs between efficiency and price effects together with a representative set of indifference relations are developed in Section I of this paper. A variety of essential qualifications to this naive model are then

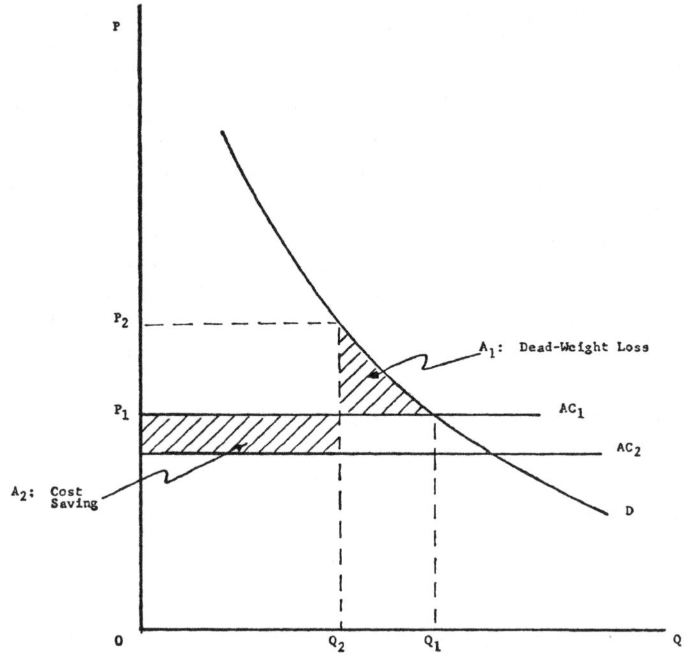

FIGURE 1.

presented in Section II. Extensions of the argument, which is developed initially in horizontal merger terms, to deal with questions of dissolution as well as vertical and conglomerate mergers, are given in Section III. The conclusions follow in Section IV.

I. *The Naive Tradeoff Model*

The effects on resource allocation of a merger that yields economies but extends market power can be investigated in a partial equilibrium context with the help of Figure 1. The horizontal line labeled AC_1 represents the level of average costs of the two (or more) firms before combination, while AC_2 shows the level of average costs after the merger. The price before the merger is given by P_1 and is equal to $k(AC_1)$, where k is an index of pre-merger market power and is greater than or equal to unity. The price after the merger is given by P_2 and is assumed to exceed P_1 (if it were less than P_1 the economic effects of the merger would be strictly positive).[3]

[3] This is a simple but basic point. It reveals that market power is only a necessary and not a sufficient condition for undesirable price effects to exist. It would be wholly irrational to regard an increase in the price to average cost ratio ($P_2/AC_2>P_1/AC_1$) as grounds for opposing a merger if, at the same time, the post-merger price were less than the pre-merger level ($P_2<P_1$).

The net welfare effects of the merger are given (approximately) by the two shaded areas in the Figure. The area designated A_1 is the familiar dead-weight loss that would result if price were increased from P_1 to P_2, assuming that costs remain constant. But since average costs are actually reduced by the merger, the area designated A_2, which represents cost savings, must also be taken into account. The net allocative effect is given by the difference, $A_2 - A_1$, of these two areas.[4]

The area A_2 is given by $(AC_2 - AC_1)Q_2$, or $[\Delta(AC)]Q_2$, while A_1 is given approximately by $\frac{1}{2}(P_2 - P_1)(Q_1 - Q_2)$, or $\frac{1}{2}(\Delta P)(\Delta Q)$. The net economic effect will be positive if the following inequality holds:

$$[\Delta(AC)]Q_2 - 1/2(\Delta P)(\Delta Q) > 0. \tag{1}$$

Dividing through by Q_2 and substituting for $\Delta Q/Q$ the expression $\eta(\Delta P/P)$, where η is the elasticity of demand, we obtain:

$$\Delta(AC) - 1/2(\Delta P)\eta \frac{\Delta P}{P} > 0. \tag{2}$$

Finally, dividing through by $P_1 = k(AC_1)$ we have as our criterion:

$$\frac{\Delta(AC)}{AC} - \frac{k}{2}\eta\left(\frac{\Delta P}{P}\right)^2 > 0. \tag{3}$$

If this inequality holds, the net allocative effect of the merger is positive. If the difference is equal to zero the merger is neutral. If the inequality is reversed the merger is negative.

In words, the inequality shown in (3) says that if the decimal fraction reduction in average costs exceeds the square of the decimal fraction increase in price multiplied by one-half k times the elasticity of demand, the allocative effect of the merger is positive. Setting k equal to one (which it will be if the pre-merger market power is negligible), the cost reductions necessary to offset price increases for various values of the elasticity of demand are shown in Table 1.

For example, if price were to increase by 20 per cent, then running across the row $[(\Delta P/P) \times 100] = 20$ we observe that if η is 2 a cost reduction of 4 per cent will be sufficient to offset the price increase, while if η is 1 only a 2 per cent cost decrease is needed to neutralize the price effect, and if η is $\frac{1}{2}$, a cost reduction of 1 per cent is sufficient. More generally it is evident that a relatively modest cost reduction is usually

[4] My use of dead-weight loss is somewhat restrictive. Inefficiency is also a dead-weight loss. For convenience of exposition, however, I refer to the Marshallian triangle as the dead-weight loss and compare this to the cost saving (efficiency) aspects of a merger. Estimating the value of consumers' surplus by the Marshallian triangle follows the common (and broadly defensible) practice of suppressing the income effects associated with a price change. The net social benefit associated with a particular cost-price configuration is defined as total revenue plus consumers' surplus less social cost, where social and private costs are assumed to be identical (externalities and producers' surplus are both assumed to be zero).

TABLE 1—PERCENTAGE COST REDUCTIONS [(Δ(AC)/AC)×100] SUFFICIENT TO OFFSET PERCENTAGE PRICE INCREASES (ΔP/P×100) FOR SELECTED VALUES OF η

η / [(ΔP/P)×100]	2	1	1/2
5	.25	.12	.06
10	1.00	.50	.25
20	4.00	2.00	1.00
30	9.00	4.50	2.25

sufficient to offset relatively large price increases even if the elasticity of demand is as high as 2, which is probably a reasonable upper bound. Indeed, if a reduction in average costs on the order of 5 to 10 per cent is available through merger, the merger must give rise to price increases in excess of 20 per cent if $\eta \cong 2$, and in excess of 40 per cent if $\eta \cong \frac{1}{2}$, for the net allocative effects to be negative. Moreover, it should be noted, if the merger reduces average costs by x per cent and the post-merger price increases by y per cent, the post-merger price to average cost differential slightly exceeds $x+y$ per cent. Thus, expressing price with respect to the post-merger level of average costs yields an even greater differential than is reflected by the relations stated above. The naive model thus supports the following proposition: a merger which yields non-trivial real economies must produce substantial market power and result in relatively large price increases for the net allocative effects to be negative.

II. *Qualifications*

Our partial equilibrium analysis suffers from a defect common to all partial equilibrium constructions. By isolating one sector from the rest of the economy it fails to examine interactions between sectors. Certain economic effects may therefore go undetected, and occasionally behavior which appears to yield net economic benefits in a partial equilibrium analysis will result in net losses when investigated in a general equilibrium context. Such a condition has been shown to exist in an economy in which monopoly exists in many sectors. Thus, whereas partial equilibrium analysis indicates that an increase in the monopoly price in any one sector invariably yields a loss, viewed more generally such an isolated price increase may actually lead to a desirable reallocation of resources.[5] Conceivably, therefore, a merger that has monopoly power and cost-saving consequences could yield benefits in *both* respects —although it is probably rare that operational content can be supplied

[5] This is the familiar "second-best" argument. For a discussion of second-best qualifications in treating the monopoly problem, and references to this literature, see Ferguson [11, pp. 16–17, 49–51].

to this qualification. But were there no other considerations, such bias as our partial equilibrium construction produces would be to underestimate the net economic gains of combination.

This does not, however, exhaust the range of qualifications. Among the other factors that can or should be taken into account are inference and enforcement expense, timing, incipiency, weighting, income distribution, extra-economic political objectives, technological progress, and the effects of monopoly power on managerial discretion.

A. *Inference and Enforcement Expense*

The relevant effects are those which take the form of real rather than pecuniary economies. Also, since evaluating a claim that economies exist will itself absorb real resources, it seems reasonable to impose a requirement that the net gain exceed some threshold value before such a defense will even be entertained. This, in conjunction with qualifications B through D below, would appear to meet Donald Turner's point that if economies are to be invoked as a defense "the law might well require clear and convincing evidence that the particular merger would produce substantial economies that could not be achieved in other ways" [27, p. 1328]. As the tools for assessing economies are progressively refined (and the incentive to make such improvements is obvious once an efficiency defense—even in principle—is granted), this threshold level should be reduced accordingly.

Operationally it may be essential to express the value of the threshold as a function of the ease with which economies can be established. Economies that have a highly speculative aspect should be required to reach a higher minimum level than those which are more objectively specified. (Thus if economies in both production and distribution expenses are claimed, and if the former are better specified than the latter, distribution economies would have to reach a higher threshold than would production economies to be admissible.) Since the ease with which exaggerated claims are detected varies directly with the degree of distortion attempted, and since evidence of distortion seriously debilitates a defense, adjusting the threshold in this way will tend to protect the enforcement agencies against grievously inflated efficiency claims.

Bork, apparently, would resist the argument that the defendants should bear the burden of proof on efficiencies since many efficiencies may be difficult to establish [5, p. 410]. But if efficiencies are to be a defense at all, it is clear that the companies—which are, presumably, sensitive to the relevant economies in proposing the merger in the first place—must be prepared to make the case for them in court. They have the data and these must be supplied. Otherwise the mixed case which involves both scale economy and market power effects can only be handled arbitrarily—and this is satisfactory to no one.

B. *Timing*

Significant economies will ordinarily be realized eventually through internal expansion if not by merger. Growth of demand can facilitate this internal adjustment process; the necessity for part of the industry to be displaced in order that efficient size be achieved is relieved in a growing market. Thus, although a merger may have net positive effects immediately (cost savings exceed the dead-weight loss), when allowance is made for the possibility of internal expansion these effects can become negative eventually (the cost savings persist, but these could be realized anyway, and the dead-weight loss could be avoided by prohibiting the merger).

Designating the dead-weight loss effects of the merger by $L(t)$ and the cost savings by $S(t)$, the argument would be that the value of $S(t)$ falls while $L(t)$ persists over time. Thus, taking the discounted value of net benefits (V) we have:

$$V = \int_0^T [S(t) - L(t)]e^{-rt}dt, \tag{4}$$

and if initially $S(t)/L(t) > 1$, but eventually $S(t)/L(t) < 1$, this can easily become negative. Consider, for example, the case where $S(t) = \overline{S}$ for a period of length T' and then becomes zero, while $L(t) = \overline{L}$ indefinitely. Using a social discount rate of 10 per cent, what initial combinations of $\overline{S}/\overline{L}$ and T' would leave us just indifferent over the allocative effects of a merger? For $\overline{S}/\overline{L}$ of 3, indifference occurs at a value of T' of 4 years; any value of T' less than 4 years would reveal that the scale economies can be realized by internal expansion in a sufficiently short interval that the merger should be disallowed, while any value of T' that exceeds 4 years would show that net gains are available by approving the merger. For $\overline{S}/\overline{L}$ of 2, the corresponding value of T' is 7 years, while for $\overline{S}/\overline{L}$ of 1.5, the value of T' increases to 11 years. The necessary qualifications to our earlier results are thus obvious: only if $\overline{S}/\overline{L}$ is relatively large, or T' reasonably long, should a merger which results in eventual net losses be approved.

By contrast with a growing market, to force economies to be realized by internal expansion in a static market is generally without merit. The market power effects will occur here anyway, and the internal expansion route merely delays and may upset the market adjustment.

The above results are merely illustrative. More generally, equation (4) calls attention to the importance of considering the shape of the time stream of benefits and costs that a merger produces. Thus it is not sufficient to justify a merger on the basis of merely potential economies. Not only is it relevant to consider whether the merger would produce net benefits, but whether the timing is such as to maximize these gains. If a merger is proposed that promises potential economies, but these will not be realized for some time, it may be better to delay the combination. Such might be the case in circumstances where the existing plant has not exhausted its useful life and has limited value in other uses; in this situation investment in the new facilities may not be economical immediately. For the merger to occur much earlier than the indicated economies will be realized would permit whatever market power effects as the merger produces to take effect at an earlier time than is clearly most beneficial.

Plausible as this last argument may appear, it raises a serious question of how extensive a "management" function the enforcement agencies should play in merger matters. It is an easy step from the suggestion that a proposed merger should be delayed until maximum net gains are realized to the proposition that the enforcement agencies should "arrange" optimal firm pairings. Both of these, however, are much more ambitious tasks than merely testing whether the net gain associated with a proposed combination is positive. Subject possibly to occasional exceptions where the social net benefit calculus identifies a distinctly superior timing or combination from that which has been proposed privately (and assuming that the change can be implemented), the simple requirement that discounted net gains be positive is probably a sufficient test. Otherwise, mergers are too complex to postpone casually; and the enforcement agencies are not designed (nor should they be redesigned) to function in a brokerage capacity.

C. *Incipiency*

It is likewise vital to consider not merely the market power effects of any single merger taken in isolation, but whether the merger is representative of a trend. If a series of such mergers can reasonably be expected, the judgment of whether to permit any given combination should properly be cast in an industry context—in which case the anticipated economy and market power effects throughout the industry should be examined. Since, if economies are available by combining one pair of firms they will often be available more generally, this may frequently be an important consideration. The notion of incipiency thus has special relevance in administering the law on mergers where economies are claimed.

This proposition might usefully be contrasted with that of Bork and Bowman [2, p. 594]:

> The difficulty with stopping a trend toward a more concentrated condition at a very early stage is that the existence of the trend is prima facie evidence that greater concentration is socially desirable. The trend indicates that there are emerging efficiencies or economies of scale—whether due to engineering and production developments or to

new control and management techniques—which make larger size more efficient. This increased efficiency is valuable to the society at large, for it means that fewer of our available resources are being used to accomplish the same amount of production and distribution. By striking at such trends in their very earliest stages the concept of incipiency prevents the realization of those very efficiencies that competition is supposed to encourage.

Their evaluation of the social desirability of a trend suggests a certain insensitivity to the relevant scale economy-market power tradeoff considerations, and they appear to read the significance of a trend somewhat too loosely. That a trend necessarily implies emerging efficiencies is incorrect: it may also indicate an emerging awareness that market power advantages might be realized through a series of combinations.[6] Moreover, whereas they seem to suggest that to disallow a merger is to prevent the realization of scale economies altogether, ordinarily it is not a question of whether economies will be realized but when and with what market power effects. Thus, while Bork and Bowman may be correct in charging that scale economy justifications have not been given sufficient weight in the recent enforcement of the merger law, they are also guilty of a certain heavy-handedness in their own treatment of the incipiency question.

D. *Weighting*

The economies that a merger produces are usually limited strictly to the combining firms. But the market power effects of a merger may sometimes result in a price increase across a wider class of firms. Where this occurs, a weighting factor should be introduced into expression (3) to reflect this condition. The criterion becomes:

$$\left(\frac{Q_2}{Q_T}\right)\frac{\Delta(AC)}{AC} - \frac{k}{2}\eta\left(\frac{\Delta P}{P}\right)^2 > 0, \tag{3'}$$

where Q_2 is the output of the merging firms and Q_T is the total quantity of industry sales for which the price increase becomes effective.

E. *Income Distribution*

An additional qualification to our analysis involves income distribution effects. The rectangle in Figure 1 bounded by P_2 and P_1 at the top and bottom respectively and O and Q_2 on the sides represents a loss of consumers' surplus (gain in monopoly profits) that the merger produces. On the resource allocation criteria for judging welfare effects advanced above, the distribution of these profits becomes a matter of indifference.

[6] This is George Stigler's point in his treatment of "Monopoly and Oligopoly by Merger" [24]. Bork concedes this possibility in his response to Blake and Jones [5, p. 412]; but his principal emphasis, which is probably correct, is that a trend signals emerging economies.

For specific welfare valuations, however, we might not always wish to regard consumer and producer interests symmetrically—although since, arguably, antitrust is an activity better suited to promote allocative efficiency than income distribution objectives (the latter falling more clearly within the province of taxation, expenditure, and transfer payment activities), such income distribution adjustments might routinely be suppressed. If they are not, the tradeoff between efficiency gains and distributive losses needs explicitly to be expressed. Thus, while economies would remain a defense, any undesirable income distribution effects associated with market power would be counted against the merger rather than enter neutrally as the naive model implies.

Inasmuch as the income redistribution which occurs is usually large relative to the size of the dead-weight loss, attaching even a slight weight to income distribution effects can sometimes influence the overall valuation significantly. Thus, expressing the dead-weight loss ($L=\frac{1}{2}\ (\Delta P)\ (\Delta Q)$) as a ratio of the income distribution effect ($I=(\Delta P)Q$), and substituting into this ratio the expression for the elasticity of demand (η), the fraction $L/I=\frac{1}{2}\ (\Delta P/P)\ \eta$ obtains. It is therefore obvious that, except where the elasticity of demand is "high," the dead-weight loss as a fraction of the income distribution effect is relatively small—certainly less than unity. Hence if, as is probably common, the income redistribution which results when market power is increased is regarded unfavorably, an appropriate weighting of this factor will, at least occasionally, upset a net valuation which on resource allocation grounds is positive.

Note in this connection that the transfer involved could be regarded unfavorably not merely because it redistributes income in an undesirable way (increases the degree of inequality in the size distribution of income), but also because it produces social discontent. This latter has serious efficiency implications that the above analysis does not take explicitly into account. This same point also appears to have gone unnoticed in the entire Bork and Bowman v. Blake and Jones exchange [2] [3] [4] [5]. Distinguishing social from private costs in this respect may, however, be the most fundamental reason for treating claims of private efficiency gains skeptically.

F. *Political Considerations*

Combinations which involve firms that are already very large in absolute terms might be resisted on grounds that these raise extra-economic problems of political significance. There is not, however, any obvious way in which to integrate these into the analysis. Rather, although the political implications of control over wealth are a matter for serious concern, these are separable from the economic problems posed by control over markets; a different calculus is required to deal with each. The necessary political judgment, ideally, is one for Congress to make. Possibly, as Carl Kaysen has suggested, this would take the form of a prohibition against expansion by merger of the largest 50 or 100 corporations [17, p. 37].

The issue here reaches beyond the social discontent matter raised above. Thus, whereas social discontent can be reduced, in principle at least, to efficiency-equivalent (net value product) terms, the political implications of the control over wealth involve a judgment of how the quality of life in a democracy is affected by size disparities. The latter is less easily (or even appropriately) expressed in efficiency terms. The issue is nevertheless important, and failure to deal with it may be unresponsive to the position taken by Blake and Jones. Inasmuch as several of the counterexamples that they pose in their critique of Bork and Bowman appear deliberately to have been selected from the giant firm universe [5, pp. 425–27], possibly it is mergers within this subset that concern them most. Should economies be allowed as a defense, therefore, the rule proposed by Kaysen would limit such a defense in a way which would presumably relieve this aspect of their concern.

G. *Technological Progress; and*
H. *Managerial Discretion*

The highly conjectural nature of qualifications G and H makes it unclear at this time what weight ought to be assigned to them. It is at least arguable that the prevailing uncertainties are too great to give any effect to these two factors at this time. They are, nevertheless, potentially of such significance that to dismiss them may run the risk of serious error. In consideration of this potential importance, additional research which would permit us better to evaluate their actual significance would seem warranted. The manner in which each would influence the estimate of net effects is sketched out below.

Consider technological progress first. Such increases in market power that result in predictable effects on technological progress should, if they can easily, be taken into account. The present evidence, while hardly abundant, suggests that, as a general rule, the research and development expenditures of the four largest firms in an industry are neither as large proportionately nor as productive as those of their immediately smaller rivals.[7] But this fails to answer the question of what

[7] With respect to size, Mansfield found that the ratio of innovations to firm size reached a maximum at about the sixth largest firm for the petroleum and coal industries, and at a much lower rank for steel [20, p. 566]. Elsewhere Mansfield reports that the largest firms in petroleum, drugs, and glass spent somewhat less on R&D, relative to sales, than did somewhat smaller firms; in chemicals they spent somewhat more; in steel they spent less, but the difference was not statistically significant [21, p. 334]. Scherer concludes from his study of patent behavior in a group of 448 firms selected from the Fortune list of the largest 500 industrial corporations in 1955 that "the evidence does not support the hypothesis that corporate bigness is especially favorable to high inventive output" [23, p. 1114]. Turning to productivity, Mansfield con-

market structures most enhance progressiveness. The evidence on this latter is somewhat mixed.[8] It seems unlikely, however, that subsequent investigation will upset the basic proposition that progressiveness is promoted by at least some elements of competition at virtually every stage of an industry's development—if for no other reason than that competition tends to assure that variety in research approaches will be employed. Local or regional monopolies may provide partial exceptions (since here the requisite variety will be available nationally, although the rate at which innovations are implemented may nevertheless lag if competitive pressures are lacking), but monopoly, or near-monopoly, would not seem to be the perfect instrument for technical progress in industries for which the relevant market is national.

Lacking additional evidence, it would not seem injudicious to assume that mergers between relatively small-sized firms rarely have negative (and may frequently have positive) effects on progressiveness, whatever the condition of concentration. This judgment probably holds for most mergers involving lower-middle sized firms as well. Thus it is mainly in the relatively large firms, particularly those in moderately to highly concentrated national markets (which, of course, are also ones where market power effects may be important), that the effects of a merger on technological progress deserve special attention.

Whether the effects be positive or negative, the necessary extension to the model is identical. Assume therefore that a merger is proposed involving a large firm in a concentrated industry, and that while it yields economies it also predictably decreases the rate of progressiveness. Holding constant for the moment the effects on price, how large a change in the rate of technical progress would be required to offset the available economy of scale advantage? To obtain a crude estimate of this, let θ be the ratio of the immediate post-merger to pre-merger average costs (so that $1-\theta$ is the immediate decimal fraction reduction in average costs), g_1 be the rate of productivity increase in the absence of the merger and g_2 the rate if the merger is approved (where $g_1 \geq g_2$), $Q(t)$ be the output in period t, and let r be the social discount rate. Then the merger will have neutral effects if the discounted value of costs under

cludes that "in most industries, the productivity of an R&D program of given scale seems to be lower in the largest firms than in somewhat smaller firms" [21, p. 338]. Comanor found that diseconomies of scale in the pharmaceutical industry were encountered at even moderate firm sizes [8, p. 190]. For a recent review of this literature, see Johnson [15, pp. 169–71].

[8] Hamburg [13, Ch. 4] and Horowitz [14, pp. 330–01] report a positive correlation between R&D expenditures and industrial concentration. Scherer finds a much weaker but slightly positive association [23, pp. 1119–21]. Kendrick concludes from an examination of Terleckyj' data that there is no significant correlation between productivity changes and industrial concentration [18, p. 179]. Stigler found in an earlier study "hints that industries with lower concentration had higher rates of technological progress" [26, p. 278], while I, using Mansfield's data, found a negative correlation between the proportion of innovations introduced by the four largest firms and industrial concentration [30].

each condition is the same. This requires that the equality given below should hold:

$$\int_0^\infty [(AC)Q(t)e^{-g_1 t}]e^{-rt}dt = \int_0^\infty [\theta(AC)Q(t)e^{-g_2 t}]e^{-rt}dt \tag{5}$$

Assuming that output increases exponentially at the rate α, the critical value of g_2 is given by:

$$g_2 = \theta g_1 - (1 - \theta)(r - \alpha) \tag{6}$$

If, for example, the values of θ, g_1, and $r-\alpha$ were .90, .03, and .07 respectively, the critical value of g_2 would be .02. Were g_2 to fall below this value, an indicated economy of 10 per cent would not be sufficient to offset the cumulative productivity loss associated with the merger, to say nothing of the market power effects that the merger produces. If indeed the selected values of g_1 and $r-\alpha$ are at all representative, a predictable decrease in the rate of productivity advance by one-third or more would thus be sufficient to disallow a merger for which an efficiency advantage as large as 10 per cent could be expected.[9]

Consider now the managerial discretion argument. Here the direction of the effect is not so much a matter for dispute as is its quantitative significance. The argument is that market power provides a firm with the opportunity to pursue a variety of other-than-profit objectives. Although this is an "old" argument, its persistence at least suggests the possibility that it may not be without merit.[10] Whether qualitatively there is anything to it turns essentially on the behavioral proposition that where competition in the product market presents no significant threat to survival, the resources of the firm are absorbed in part as corporate consumption activities by those members of the firm who are knowledgeable of discretionary opportunities, powerfully situated, and disposed to be assertive [29, 32]. Its quantitative significance rests on a judgment over whether the conspicuous evidence is sufficiently strong.[11]

If indeed a predictable relaxation in the least-cost posture of a firm which has acquired market power through merger can be made, the

[9] If the beneficial economies of scale are available only to the combining firms, while the negative progressiveness effects are felt throughout the industry, the above results underestimate the extent of economies necessary to produce indifference.

[10] As Arthur Hadley observed in 1897, "The tendency of monopoly to retard the introduction of industrial improvement is . . . a more serious thing than its tendency to allow unfair rates. This aspect of the matter has hardly received proper attention. We have been so accustomed to think of competition as a regulator of prices that we have lost sight of its equally important function as a stimulus to efficiency. Wherever competition is absent, there is a disposition to rest content with old methods, not to say slack ones. In spite of notable exceptions this is clearly the rule" [12, p. 383].

[11] This presently is the weakest part of the argument. For a recent survey of the data, see [19].

estimated cost savings that appear in equation (4) should be adjusted accordingly. Economies which are available in theory but, by reason of market power, are not sustainable are inadmissible.

III. *Extensions*

Although the foregoing analysis has been concerned exclusively with horizontal mergers, the argument applies generally to problems in which market power-efficiency tradeoffs exist. Dissolution, vertical mergers, and conglomerate mergers can all be treated within this general framework.

A. *Dissolution*

The argument here is perfectly straightforward. It is simply not sufficient in a monopolization case for which dissolution is the indicated relief that (1) a persistent monopoly condition ($P_1 > AC_1$) exist, and (2) a reduction in price following dissolution ($P_2 < P_1$) be expected. It is necessary in addition that the gains realized by the price reduction be sufficient to offset any losses in economies that result. The relevant test is that shown in equation (3)—modified, as may be necessary, by the qualifications discussed in Section II above.

B. *Vertical Mergers*

It is important to note in dealing with vertical mergers that the conventional analysis of vertical integration, which takes a historical definition of an industry as given, often leads to incorrect results. The logical boundaries of a firm are not necessarily those which have been inherited but rather are defined by the condition that the firm be unable to arrange a transaction internally more cheaply than the market.[12] This is not something which is given once-for-all but depends both on technology and the extent of the market. Thus what may be regarded as "vertical integration" under a historical definition of an industry might, in many instances, more accurately be characterized as a reorganization into a more efficient configuration. For example, as technology evolves processes that are more fully automated or as demand for a commodity increases sufficiently to warrant continuous processing techniques, combinatorial economies may result by serially linking activities within a single firm that had previously been done in separate specialty firms.[13] A transformation of this sort accomplished in part

[12] As Ronald Coase has pointed out, "a firm will tend to expand until the costs of organizing an extra transaction within the firm become equal to the costs of carrying out the same transaction by means of an exchange on the open market or the costs of organizing in another firm" [7, p. 341].

[13] Stigler argues that increasing the extent of the market will often lead to dis-integration of manufacturing processes since now the market will be sufficient to support a specialized firm [25, pp. 188–90]. Although this may often occur, there is also the countervailing tendency

through vertical mergers is probably common in the production of commodities which shift from sequential job shop to continuous assembly line type operations.

That vertical integration can produce real economies is a result of the fact that the market does not perform its exchanges costlessly. Going to the market involves search costs, contracting costs, misinformation costs, delay costs, transfer costs, interface costs, etc.,[14] and these must be balanced against the costs of organizing a transaction internally. Where the former exceed the latter, "vertical integration" is indicated. But of course this is vertical integration in only an apparent sense: in fact it represents a rationalization of the firm into an optimum economic unit.

The historical organization of an industry can ordinarily be presumed to reflect adequately basic efficiencies where significant market or technological developments have been lacking. And even where such recent changes have occurred, an efficiency defense is not automatic. Furthermore, if an efficiency defense can be supplied, any market power consequences that a vertical merger produces need also to be considered.[15] Again the basic tradeoff calculation is that given by equation (3)—modified as necessary by the qualifications discussed in Section II.

C. *Conglomerate Mergers*

The principal ways in which conglomerate mergers can produce efficiencies have been given previously by M. A. Adelman [1, pp. 241–42] and Turner [27, pp. 1323–39, 1358–61]. The ways in which conglomerate mergers may produce market power are also discussed by Turner. All that remains, essentially, is to deal with the tradeoff question. Again the rules for estimating net benefits are substantially those given above.

IV. *Conclusions*

Most mergers produce neither significant price nor efficiency consequences, and where this is true the analysis of this paper has limited relevance. Where both occur, however, and if without merger the transition to an efficient industrial configuration is apt to be both painful and delayed, an efficiency defense deserves consideration. This does not of

to maintain or extend integration where coordination among the parts in the face of market uncertainties is critical—as it often is where assembly line operations are employed. See Coase [7, p. 337].

[14] Coase discusses some of these [7, pp. 336–37]. (For an early example in which the costs going to the market were examined in a common law proceeding, see *Hadley* v. *Baxendale.*) In addition, if suppliers possess market power, going to the market may involve pecuniary expenses that could be avoided by integrating backward into supply activities.

[15] Stigler identifies barriers to entry that take the form of increased capital and/or knowledge requirements as potential anticompetitive consequences of a vertical merger [25, p. 191].

course mean that the mere existence of economies is sufficient to justify a merger. But since a relatively large percentage increase in price is usually required to offset the benefits that result from a 5 to 10 per cent reduction in average costs, the existence of economies of this magnitude is sufficiently important to give the antitrust authorities pause before disallowing such a merger. There are, as indicated in Section II, a variety of qualifications that may upset this general conclusion in any particular case, but absent these and the result clearly holds.

It might be objected that the courts do not possess the expertise to make the types of judgments described. This is typically true. But that does not mean that an analysis of these effects should be not performed by the Antitrust Division or Federal Trade Commission before deciding to challenge a merger. The enforcement agencies can obtain, at reasonable cost, the necessary expertise to make these evaluations.[16] Only after they are convinced that such economies as may exist are not sufficient to justify a merger should a case go forward. Although possibly this extends the responsibility of the enforcement agencies beyond those that are clearly intended, the alternative is scarcely acceptable. For if neither the courts nor the enforcement agencies are sensitive to these considerations, the system fails to meet a basic test of economic rationality. And without this the whole enforcement system lacks for defensible standards and becomes suspect.

Once economies are admitted as a defense, the tools for assessing these effects can be expected progressively to be refined. Since such refinements will permit both the courts and the enforcement agencies to make more precise evaluations, the threshold value under which an economies defense will be allowed can be reduced accordingly. Thus even if initially only a few mergers for which mixed effects are present are able to pass an appropriately qualified tradeoff test because of high threshold requirements, this proportion can be expected to increase as research results and analytical aids for evaluating scale economies accumulate. As an interim gain, solemn references to early oratory might finally be displaced in favor of analysis in the continuing dialogue on antitrust enforcement.

[16] That the enforcement agencies are sensitive to scale economy considerations is evidenced by the recent Federal Trade Commission merger guidelines "Enforcement Policy with Respect to Mergers in the Food Distribution Industries," issued January 3, 1967. See especially pages 6–9.

Justice Brennan observed in the Philadelphia National Bank merger that "a merger the effect of which 'may be substantially to lessen competition' is not saved because, on some ultimate reckoning of social or economic debits and credits, it may be deemed beneficial. . . . [Such] is beyond the ordinary limits of judicial competence" [28, p. 371]. My point is that, at least with respect to efficiencies, such reckoning need not and indeed should not be beyond the competence of the antitrust agencies. It is here that the first critical decision of whether to file suit is made.

References

1. M. A. Adelman, "The Antimerger Act, 1950–60," *Am. Econ. Rev., Proc.*, May 1961, *51*, 236–44.
2. H. M. Blake and W. K. Jones, "In Defense of Antitrust," *Columbia Law Rev.*, March 1965, *65*, 377–400.
3. ———, "Toward a Three-Dimensional Antitrust Policy," *Columbia Law Rev.*, March 1965, *65*, 422–66.
4. R. H. Bork and W. S. Bowman, "The Crisis in Antitrust," *Columbia Law Rev.*, March 1965, *65*, 363–76.
5. R. H. Bork, "Contrasts in Antitrust Theory: I," *Columbia Law Rev.* March 1965, *65*, 401–16.
6. *Brown Shoe v. United States*, 370 U.S. 294 (1962).
7. R. H. Coase, "The Nature of the Firm," *Economica*, N.S., IV, 1937, 386–485. Reprinted in G. J. Stigler and K. E. Boulding, eds., *Readings in Price Theory*, Homewood, Ill., 1952, pp. 331–51.
8. W. S. Comanor, "Research and Technical Change in the Pharmaceutical Industry," *Rev. Econ. and Stat.*, May 1965, *47*, 182–90.
9. D. Dewey, "Mergers and Cartels: Some Reservations about Policy," *Am. Econ. Rev., Proc.*, May 1961, *51*, 255–62.
10. *Federal Trade Commission v. Procter & Gamble Co.*, 87 S. Ct. 1224 (1967).
11. C. E. Ferguson, *A Macroeconomic Theory of Workable Competition*. Durham, N. C., 1964.
12. A. T. Hadley, "The Good and Evil of Industrial Combination," *Atlantic Monthly*, March 1897, *79*, 377–85.
13. D. Hamburg, *R & D: Essays on the Economics of Research and Development*. New York 1966.
14. I. Horowitz, "Firm Size and Research Activity," *So. Econ. Jour.*, Jan. 1962, *28*, 298–301.
15. R. E. Johnson, "Technical Progress and Innovation," *Oxford Econ. Papers*, July 1966, *18*, 158–76.
16. C. Kaysen and D. F. Turner, *Antitrust Policy: An Economic and Legal Analysis*. Cambridge, Mass., 1959.
17. C. Kaysen, "The Present War on Bigness: I," in *The Impact of Antitrust on Economic Growth*, Fourth National Industrial Conference Board Conference on Antitrust in an Expanding Economy, New York 1965, pp. 31–38.
18. J. W. Kendrick, *Productivity Trends in the United States*. Princeton, N. J., 1961.
19. H. Leibenstein, "Allocative Efficiency versus 'X-Efficiency'," *Am. Econ. Rev.*, June 1966, *56*, 392–415.
20. E. Mansfield, "Size of Firms, Market Structure, and Innovation," *Jour. Pol. Econ.*, Dec. 1963, *71*, 556–76.
21. ———, "Industrial Research and Development Expenditures: Determinants, Prospects, and Relation to Size of Firm and Inventive Output," *Jour. Pol. Econ.*, Aug. 1964, *72*, 319–40.
22. J. W. Markham, "Survey of the Evidence and Findings on Mergers,"

in *Business Concentration and Price Policy*, Princeton, N. J., 1955, pp. 141–82.
23. F. M. SCHERER, "Firm Size, Market Structure, Opportunity, and the Output of Patented Inventions," *Am. Econ. Rev.*, Dec. 1965, *55*, 1097–1125.
24. G. J. STIGLER, "Monopoly and Oligopoly by Merger," *Am. Econ. Rev., Proc.*, May 1950, *40*, 23–24, reprinted in R. B. Heflebower and G. W. Stocking, eds., *Readings in Industrial Organization*, Homewood, Ill., 1958, pp. 69–80
25. ———, "The Division of Labor is Limited by the Extent of the Market," *Jour. Pol. Econ.*, June 1951, *59*, 185–93.
26. ———, "Industrial Organization and Economic Progress," in L. D. White, ed., *The State of the Social Sciences*, Chicago 1956, pp. 269–82.
27. D. F. TURNER, "Conglomerate Mergers and Section 7 of the Clayton Act," *Harvard Law Review*, May 1965, *78*, 1313–95.
28. *United States v. Philadelphia Nat'l Bank*, 374 U.S. 312 (1963).
29. O. E. WILLIAMSON, *The Economics of Discretionary Behavior: Managerial Objectives in a Theory of the Firm.* Englewood Cliffs, N. J. 1964.
30. ———, "Innovation and Market Structure," *Jour. Pol. Econ.*, Feb. 1965, *73*, 67–73.
31. ———, "Hierarchical Control and Optimum Firm Size," *Jour. Pol. Econ.*, April 1967, *75*, 123–38.
32. ———, "A Dynamic-Stochastic Theory of Managerial Behavior," in A. Phillips and O. E. Williamson, eds., *Prices: Issues in Theory, Practice and Public Policy*, Philadelphia (forthcoming).

[4]

THE PROBLEM OF GEOGRAPHIC MARKET DELINEATION IN ANTIMERGER SUITS

by

KENNETH G. ELZINGA*

and

THOMAS F. HOGARTY†

I. INTRODUCTION

In common parlance the term *market* refers to one of three phenomena: (1) sellers of a particular product, where the focus is on the supply side of the market; (2) a particular group of buyers, where the focus is on the demand side of the market; (3) a particular place of exchange, such as the Seventh Avenue ladies' garment district in New York or the Bromfield Street stamp market in Boston.

While the term market has various expressional uses, the concept of a *relevant market* is of particular importance in antitrust enforcement due to the emphasis on structural standards in Section 7 enforcement.[1] Indeed, determination of the relevant market is a key threshold issue in an antimerger case since the outcome of many cases seems to hinge largely on

---

* Associate Professor of Economics, University of Virginia. In 1970–71, Special Economic Assistant to the Assistant Attorney General, Antitrust Division. The paper does not necessarily reflect the views of the Antitrust Division.

† Assistant Professor of Economics, Virginia Polytechnic Institute and State University.

AUTHORS' NOTE: The authors are grateful for the helpful comments of Arthur Andersen, Stanley Boyle, Robert Larner, and James W. Meehan, Jr. All remaining errors are the sole responsibility of the authors. A preliminary version of this paper was presented by the senior author at the Southern Economic Association meetings (Miami, Fla., November 1971).

[1] 64 Stat. 1125 (1950); cf. *Brown Shoe Co.* v. *United States,* 370 U.S. 294, 343 (1962) and *United States* v. *Philadelphia National Bank,* 374 U.S. 321, 363 (1963); Dept. of Justice, *Merger Guidelines* (mimeo, May 30, 1968), pp. 2-3, 7-10.

which of the proffered markets the court ultimately accepts as the appropriate one for determining whether Section 7 has been violated.[2]

The delineation of the relevant market has two dimensions: specifying the appropriate product line and delineating the correct geographic market area.[3] Conceptually these two dimensions are related since each involves a sorting out of close substitutes from those less desirable. For example, the cross-elasticity of demand between two potable liquids may be low because they are poor substitutes in consumption or because one, even though acceptable as a substitute, is unavailable (except at considerable expense) due to transportation costs, information costs, or legal barriers.[4] The question of product market boundaries, e.g., whether tin cans are readily substitutable for glass bottles, has received considerable attention in antitrust literature, but the issue of geographic market delineation has received little, though conceptually both are of equal importance and both must be specified if economic analysis is to be used in predicting the likelihood of a merger being anticompetitive.

The nature of this paper can be illustrated by a prominent antimerger case: the Government's successful suit against the merger of Pabst Brewing Company with the Blatz Brewing Company.[5] During the litigation, both parties agreed that the relevant line of commerce was beer. But the parties

---

[2] Thus in a horizontal merger, the plaintiff will claim a relevant market in which the merging firms have a significant market share; the respondents will argue that the relevant market actually is so broad that the combined firm has small market shares, or else that the markets are so narrow that the merging firms are not in fact competitors.

[3] The statutory language is "line of commerce" and "section of the country" respectively.

[4] For further elaboration, see Stephen Mann and Thomas M. Lewyn, "Comment: The Relevant Market Under Section 7 of the Clayton Act: Two New Cases—Two Different Views," 47 *Virginia Law Review* 1014 at 1015-16 (1961).

[5] *United States* v. *Pabst Brewing Company*, 233 F. Supp. 475 (1964); 384 U.S. 546 (1966); 296 F. Supp. 994 (1969).

disagreed on the scope of the market for beer, with the Government arguing that the merger must be considered in light of a one-state market for beer, namely Wisconsin; a three-state market for beer consisting of Wisconsin, Michigan, and Illinois; and a national market for beer as well.[6] The respondents argued that the market for beer was national in scope. Query: Why could the Government not argue that the market for beer was the city of Milwaukee? And why could the respondents not argue that the market for beer was the entire Western hemisphere? An evaluation of the law and economics of this type of question is the topic of this paper.

II. Economic Theory of Market Areas

Alfred Marshall emphasized that the delineation of a geographic market did not involve looking for a place or geographic location, but rather for the buyers and sellers who were "in such free intercourse with one another that the prices of the same goods tend to equality easily and quickly."[7] A market encompasses the primary demand and supply forces that determine a product's price and the geographic market area is the area that encompasses these buyers and sellers.[8]

---

[6] This "shotgun approach" of the Government is disconcerting to economists but rather common in law. A farmer was being sued for cracking a hog-scalding cauldron which he had borrowed. The farmer's lawyer said that his client's defense rested on three theories: (1) the cauldron was in fact returned in perfect condition; (2) failing that, the cauldron was already cracked when borrowed; (3) failing that, the cauldron was never borrowed in the first place!

[7] Marshall quoting Cournot in Alfred Marshall, *Principles of Economics,* Book V (London: Macmillan, 1920), p. 324; see generally pp. 324-29.

[8] Neglect of either the demand or supply element can be misleading in geographic market delineation. For example, the primary *demand* for diamonds in Cook County may be located in the city of Chicago. But the geographic market area for diamonds is much broader than Chicago since the supply side of the market encompasses much more than that city, as evidenced by the high elasticity of supply to Chicago. If the price of diamonds were somehow to be low in Chicago, relative to that in other cities, none would be supplied in Chicago. If the price of diamonds were relatively high in Chicago, the supply to that great city would be huge. Obviously, diamonds in

Because of this emphasis on demand and supply forces, Marshall could argue:

> Thus the more nearly perfect a market is, the stronger is the tendency for the same price to be paid for the same thing at the same time in all parts of the market: but, of course, if the market is large, allowance must be made for the expense of delivering the goods to different purchasers; each of whom must be supposed to pay in addition to the market price a special charge on account of delivery.[9]

Consequently, the economic conception of a market would seem to suggest that exhibiting (adjusted) price uniformity is the means of delineating geographic market areas.[10] But actually price data are of little use in geographic market delineation—at least for antimerger enforcement—for two reasons, one practical, the other conceptual.

Chicago are not marketed independently of what is happening in other geographic areas and consequently the Windy City is not a unique geographic market area for diamonds. An emphasis on the location of *supply* elements alone can be just as misleading as emphasizing only demand.

[9] *Ibid.*, p. 325. More recent work in economics would probably cite "transaction costs" as the permissible price differential between areas within the same geographic market area. Transactions costs include transportation costs as well as information cost associated with learning of product availability at other locations.

[10] The antitrust lawyer who consults price theory textbooks for clarification of the geographic market area or for a guide to actual geographic market delineation will find little more than what has already been stated. Economic analysis, with notable exceptions, generally neglects distance and firm-customer dispersion (i.e., "space"); indeed, much of price theory assumes a spaceless world with transactions accomplished costlessly at a point. For a brief explanation of this neglect of space see Harry Richardson, *Regional Economics* (New York: Praeger, 1969), pp. 1-5. Much of spatial (or regional) economic analysis is concerned with the optimum location of a firm. Since this is a long-run problem, it has limited application in antimerger cases in general and geographic market delineation problems in particular. To the authors' knowledge the only time classical location theory has been used in an antimerger case is by Warren Smith in *United States* v. *Philadelphia National Bank, Transcript of Record,* vol. 1, pp. 391-98.

The practical difficulty is determining, in two geographic territories, "the price" at which the product sells in each area, as well as "the transportation rate" between the two areas. One need only consider a few of the court-designated relevant product lines—shoes, metal cans and glass bottles, commercial banking, beer, and grocery retailing—to realize that assigning "a price" to these products is a complex task. Moreover there is seldom "a transportation rate" for a product between two geographic territories.[11]

The use of price uniformity in geographic market delineation also has its conceptual pitfalls. While it is true that the existence of uniform prices is consistent with a single geographic market area and differing prices may indicate separate geographic market areas, uniform and differing prices are also consistent with other market configurations. For example, two distinct geographic market areas could conceivably exhibit the same price—but do so because of coincidental demand-supply equilibria, not because market forces extended beyond either of the areas. An examination of price data only could erroneously indicate a geographic market area that was in fact too broad.

A monopolist might discriminate in price among customers in its selling territory. Using a price uniformity criterion, one might falsely conclude that the differentials indicated separate geographic market areas, whereas differentials actually resulted from discriminatory prices charged within the geographic market area. Since antitrust problems occur in markets that, presumably, are not highly competitive, this is a particularly telling point against the uniformity criterion—

---

[11] The ICC Traffic Bureau keeps copious statistics on freight rates but they are generally on an individual carrier basis, between specific points for specific quantities of a particular commodity. The ICC's annual *Motor Carrier Commodity Statistics* and *Freight Commodity Statistics of Class I Railroads* do not enable computation of average ton-mile rates. In addition, freight carrier associations are usually reluctant to divulge average rates. See also Walter Isard, *Location and Space-Economy* (Cambridge: MIT Press, 1956), pp. 81-90.

it is premised on the existence of competitive markets. In a market controlled by a discriminating monopolist, the sales made at the same price compose only a portion of the actual geographic market area.[12]

The Marshallian conception of a geographic market area is its most useful as a predictor and explainer of prices in markets ascertained, *ex ante,* to be competitive, i.e., where "prices of the same goods [can] tend to equality easily and quickly." Indeed, in its most pristine form the Marshallian conception reduces to a theory of price determination between perfectly competitive markets located at a number of points, the points being separated by empty space over which goods may be transported if any price differential exceeds the shipping costs. In such form, the conception has little use in antitrust problems. But in more rough and ready form, the Marshallian conception of a geographic market area is useful in showing that the primary demand and supply forces must *both* be considered in market delineation, and that it is the territory encompassing these forces that comprises the geographic market area.

There is a body of literature in economics concerned with the territory (or "market area" [13]) of spatially dispersed producers in which each will be able to charge a lower price than its rivals. The analysis is short-run, since producers' locations are assumed to be fixed, and the literature seeks to delineate the shape of the territory in which a firm will have a price-cost advantage relative to that of distant producers.

---

[12] As Peter Steiner indicated: To define the market according to the price behavior exhibited destroys any possibility of using the market so defined to say anything about price behavior, and it prejudges predictions. An empirically useful market definition must be independent of the alternative theoretical models of market structure if we wish to test or to apply these theories. See "Markets and Industries," *International Encyclopedia of the Social Sciences* (New York: Macmillan and The Free Press, 1968), 9:577.

[13] "Market area" is the parlance of this branch of economics. This term, which refers to a marketing territory for a single firm, is not to be confused with "geographic market area," which refers to an entire market.

Note what this implies: each spatially dispersed firm might have a unique, discrete territory in which all customers will buy from it (or what in common parlance might be called a "local monopoly" [14]). The exact size and shape of this boundary between two spatially dispersed producers is one of the major issues considered by this analysis. Without detailing the various proofs,[15] the theory shows that the territory will be discrete, the shape being a function of: (1) the firm's costs and prices, with lower costs and prices meaning a larger territory for a firm; (2) the transportation rates facing a firm, with discriminatively low rates, rates that do not increase with the distance shipped, enlarging the territory of a firm.

Businessmen would quickly indicate that they do not view their marketing territory as being in any way discrete—and it seldom, if ever, is the case that a firm faces a territory of any geometric shape that it can consider "its own." The theory of a firm's "market area" offers insight into the manner in which transport costs and production costs enlarge or narrow the area in which a firm might economically sell. But the existence of differentiated products, the avoidance of f.o.b. pricing, and the willingness of many firms to absorb freight in shipping to distant locations all work to destroy neat, discrete "market area" boundaries. The high degree of overlap and cross-shipping found among spatially dispersed producers tends to obviate the usefulness of this liter-

---

[14] Though the local "monopolist" may make no monopoly profits. The returns to a producer from locational advantage is a differential rent, not profit.

[15] Two standard sources are: Frank A. Fetter, "The Economic Law of Market Areas," 39 *Quarterly Journal of Economics* 520 (1924); and C. D. Hyson and W. P. Hyson, "The Economic Law of Market Areas," 64 *Quarterly Journal of Economics* 319 (1950). Good surveys are Melvin L. Greenhut, "The Size and Shape of the Market Area of a Firm," 19 *Southern Economic Journal* 37 (1952); Robert E. Looney, "Antitrust and Mergers: An Economic Analysis of Some Recent Court Decisions" (Ph.D. diss., Univ. of Cal., Davis, 1969), pp. 60-76; and R. G. Bressler and R. A. King, *Markets, Prices, and Interregional Trade* (New York: Wiley, 1970), Parts II-V.

ature for antitrust purposes.[16] Moreover, there have been few empirical attempts, apart from a judicial setting, to measure geographic market areas from an economic standpoint.[17]

III. Current Legal Theories of Geographic Market Delineation

The following is an economic dissection of the process of geographic market delineation in two Section 7 cases. Both are antitrust division cases, and in that sense are not representative of all Section 7 suits; however, they do constitute the most important Supreme Court cases in which the Court has given its imprimatur to the Government's theories of geographic market delineation.[18] Presumably this imprimatur now applies to Federal Trade Commission and private suits as well.

Pabst–Blatz

The Pabst Brewing Company–Blatz Brewing Company merger of 1958 prompted a Government Section 7 suit a year later in which the issue of geographic market delineation was

---

[16] A conclusion also reached by Looney, *ibid.*, pp. 75 and 85; G. E. Hale and Rosemary D. Hale, "Delineating the Geographic Market: A Problem in Antimerger Cases," 61 *Northwestern University Law Review* 538, 551 (1966).

[17] Other attempts to delineate geographic markets include: Robert A. Eisenbeis, "A Study of the Delineation of Geographic Markets for Business Loans" (Ph.D. diss., University of Wisconsin, 1971); Paul M. Horvitz, "Price Uniformity and Banking Markets," paper delivered at the Appalachian Finance Association, Georgetown University, April, 1968; Arnold H. Lozowick, Peter O. Steiner, and Roger Miller, "Law and Quantitative Multivariate Analysis: An Encounter," 66 *Michigan Law Review* 1641 (June 1968); Lloyd Saville, "The Market for Castings in Baltimore: Market Scope in a Customer Centered Industry," 6 *Journal of Industrial Economics* 134 (February 1958); H. O. Stekler, "A Note on the Size of a Market," 9 *Journal of Industrial Economics* 251 (July 1961); Leonard Weiss, "The Geographic Size of Markets in Manufacturing," 54 *Review of Economics and Statistics* 245 (1972).

[18] Legal issues relating to geographic market delineation in other Section 7 suits are discussed in Hale and Hale, *op. cit.*, and Mann and Lewyn, *op. cit.* See also the *Merger Guidelines, op. cit.*, pp. 6-7.

seminal.[19] The Government charged that the merger would violate Section 7 in the sale of beer in the United States, in the three-state area of Wisconsin, Illinois, and Michigan, and in the state of Wisconsin alone. There was no dispute that beer was the relevant line of commerce and that the United States was an appropriate geographic market area. But the respondents disputed the Government's claim that any market smaller than the United States could also be considered a geographic market area for beer.

The Government's theory in support of Wisconsin can be generalized as follows.[20] First, assume, *arguendo,* that Wisconsin is a geographic market area for the stipulated line of commerce of beer. Then, after ascertaining that the merging firms are competitors in the sale of beer in Wisconsin and that the amount of commerce involved is appreciable,[21] see if the market shares meet or exceed the Section 7 standard. In this case the merging companies clearly violated a Section 7 standard for the state of Wisconsin.[22] The final question then becomes: is the hypothetical area, namely Wisconsin, in fact a relevant geographic market area? Under this approach, the seminal question becomes that of geographic market delineation. The Government's theory is rather eclectic, but a sorting of the demand and supply factors yields these elements:

DEMAND

1. *The Peculiar Demand Element:* If a particular region shows an unusual demand characteristic for the product, this is an indicator of a geographic market area. In this case, Wisconsin, largely because it was the leading state

---

[19] *United States* v. *Pabst.*

[20] We use the term theory in its legal sense; economists might substitute "strategy." We confine our discussion to the proposed Wisconsin geographic market area since this represents the narrowest application of the Government's theory.

[21] U.S. Senate, *Report on Celler-Kefauver Amendment,* S. Rep. No. 1775, 81st Cong., 2d Sess., p. 6. See also *Brown Shoe Co.* v. *United States,* 370 U.S. 294, 320 (1962).

[22] In Wisconsin, Pabst was the largest seller prior to the merger; Blatz ranked third and fourth. Combined, they possessed about 25 per cent of the beer sales in Wisconsin.

in terms of per capita beer consumption, was singled out as a geographic market area.[23]

SUPPLY

1. *The Little In From Outside (LIFO) Element*: If only a small proportion of the product consumed in the hypothetical geographic market area is "imported" into the area from outside, this is an indicator of a unique geographic market area. In this case, almost 80 per cent of the beer consumed in Wisconsin was brewed there with 10 per cent coming from outstate breweries just over the state border.[24] The LIFO element is sufficiently important to be diagrammed (see Figure 1). Presumably as the ratio presented approaches unity, the LIFO element more strongly supports the hypothetical geographic market area.

Figure 1. LIFO—"Little In From Outside" Theory (Beer Example)

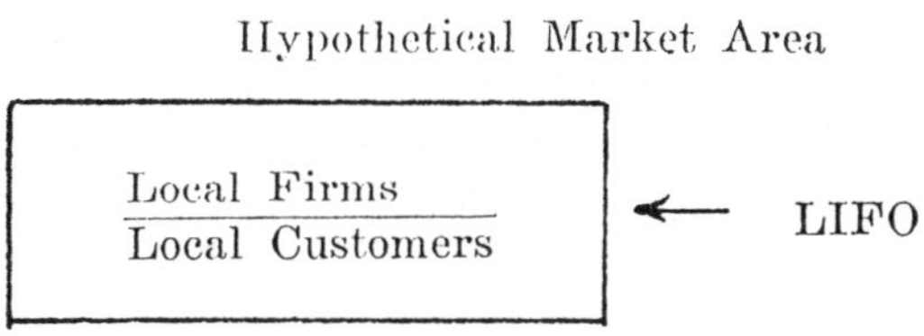

1. Given a hypothetical market area, determine the total beer consumption of the local customers.
2. Then determine the amount of locally produced beer* that is consumed locally.
3. If the ratio (2)/(1) approaches unity, meaning "little beer comes in from outside," this allegedly supports the area as a geographic market area.
4. Note that this theory does not consider the flow of beer out of the hypothetical area.

* "Local" simply means a plant location within the hypothetical market area and does not, of course, connote a "local" as opposed to a "premium" beer.

[23] In U.S. Supreme Court, *Brief for the U.S.,* October term, 1965, pp. 4, 11-12.

[24] U.S. Supreme Court, *Jurisdictional Statement for the U.S.,* October term, 1965, pp. 6, 19-21, 25; *Brief for the U.S.,* pp. 5-6, 36. The LIFO element received its strongest judicial support from Justice Harlan, 384 U.S. at 559.

2. *The Transportation Cost Element*: If transportation costs are high, i.e., if the product has a high transport-to-value ratio, then this is an indicator of a more localized market. Here the Government maintained that beer had a high transport-to-value ratio and this insulated Wisconsin from the competition of brewers in other areas.[25]

3. *The Local Distribution Element*: If the product is distributed locally, this indicates a smaller geographic market area. Since the terminal distribution of beer is completed by local wholesalers and retailers, this allegedly supports a state geographic market area.[26]

4. *The Legal Restriction Element*: If an area, such as a state or city, has unique laws affecting the flow of the product into or out of that area, this is a factor limiting the geographic market to that area. In this case, states have distinctive laws regarding the taxation, labeling, advertising, capping, etc. of beer. This allegedly affected the ability of beer to move into Wisconsin from areas outside of the state.[27]

DEMAND AND SUPPLY

1. *The Price Element*: If prices are set on a region-by-region basis, and vary from region to region, this is an indicator that the regions are separate geographic market areas. In *Pabst,* the Government argued that f.o.b. beer prices, excluding all taxes, varied from state to state. Therefore a single state, Wisconsin, could be a separate market.[28]

2. *The Industry Recognition Element*: If businessmen in the industry consider an area to be a separate market, this supports that area as an economic geographic market area. In *Pabst,* the Government originally planned to have many industry witnesses, then decided to rely largely on statisti-

[25] U.S. Supreme Court, *Brief for the U.S.,* pp. 15, 42-43. The transportation element might be the cause of the LIFO element.

[26] *Ibid.,* pp. 5-7.

[27] *Ibid.,* p. 7.

[28] *Ibid.,* p. 7 and p. 38.

cal evidence. But this element was still offered in support of Wisconsin as a geographic market area.[29]

3. *The Turnover Element*: If there is little turnover among the leading producers in the hypothetical geographic market area, this supports the case that the geographic market area is an economic one. The Government argued that the stability in market shares in Wisconsin was evidence of its being a "private preserve."[30]

Philadelphia National Bank–Girard

The Government's successful suit against the merger of Philadelphia National Bank (hereafter PNB) with Girard Trust Corn Exchange Bank (hereafter Girard), like *Pabst,* has important implications for the delineation of the geographic market area—for in both cases the Supreme Court had to deal specifically and substantively with the issue.[31] In *PNB,* the Government argued that commercial banking is a localized industry much affected by state branching laws. The Government relied heavily on data which, it was contended, showed the Philadelphia four-county area to be the relevant geographic market area. The merging banks claimed several market areas, for various banking services, all of which encompassed a broader territory than the four-county area.[32] The defendants' view was supported largely by the testimony of bankers.[33]

The district court held that the geographic market area was wider than the four-county area (though the court did not

---

[29] *Ibid.*, pp. 5–7.

[30] *Ibid.*, pp. 36–37.

[31] *United States* v. *Philadelphia National Bank,* 201 F. Supp. 348 (1962), 374 U.S. 321 (1963).

[32] The banks suggested: (1) 5 Penna. counties + 3 N. J. counties; (2) group (1) + another N. J. and Delaware county + New York; (3) the northeastern U.S.

[33] For example, see testimonies of J. McDowell, S. J. Galfand, A. T. Mason, H. J. Horan, and S. Weinrott, *United States* v. *PNB, Transcript of Record,* vol. II, pp. 1763-67, 1920-29, 1792-1819, 1964-69, and 1819-48 respectively.

definitely conclude how much wider). But the four-county area prevailed at the Supreme Court.

The demand and supply elements of the Government's theory can be viewed similarly to the earlier *Pabst* exposition. The case begins with a hypothetical geographic market area consisting of the four-county area;[34] it is then demonstrated that PNB and Girard operate in this area, do substantial business there, and that the effect of their combination is likely to lessen competition substantially, as evidenced by the sizable market shares in the relevant market area that the combined banks will possess. In addition to the four-county area, another critical premise that the Government had to demonstrate was that commercial banking was the relevant market.

DEMAND

1. *The Transportation Cost Element*: The Government used no "peculiar demand" arguments akin to *Pabst;* however, the transportation cost element appeared, not on the supply side as in *Pabst,* but on the demand side. Even though the product may not be expensive to ship, if the customers are expensive to "transport," this supports a more localized market. In this case, a certain "locked-in" character of demand into the four-county area was alleged since it would be too costly for most bank customers to shop beyond their immediate area.[35]

SUPPLY

1. *The Little Out From Inside (LOFI) Element*: If the firms in a hypothetical geographic market area receive little of their business from customers outside of the geographic market area, this is an indicator of the propriety of defining that area as a market. Note that this argument differs from the LIFO element found in *Pabst-Blatz.* In the beer

[34] Chosen because Pennsylvania law prohibits branching beyond counties contiguous to the home office county. PNB operates in the permissible counties: Philadelphia, Delaware, Bucks, and Montgomery; Girard is in all but Bucks.

[35] *United States* v. *PNB, Plaintiff's Proposed Findings of Fact and Conclusions of Law,* July 1963, pp. 42-44.

case, the Government began with the local consumers: Wisconsin was considered a separate market because Wisconsin consumers purchased (or "imported") little beer from outside the state. But in *PNB-Girard,* the Government began with the banks: the four-county area was supported because little business done by the banks was "exported," i.e., transacted with customers outside the four counties. Extensive data were presented showing that the bulk of PNB and Girard's deposits, loans and services were from and to customers in the four-county area. For example, a geographical distribution was compiled showing the amount and percentage of commercial and industrial loans, loans to individuals, time and savings deposits, demand deposits, etc., *by location of customer* in and outside the four-county area for PNB, Girard, and the combined PNB-Girard.[36] Figure 2 shows a hypothetical illustration

Figure 2. LOFI—"Little Out From Inside" Theory (Beer Example)

Hypothetical Market Area

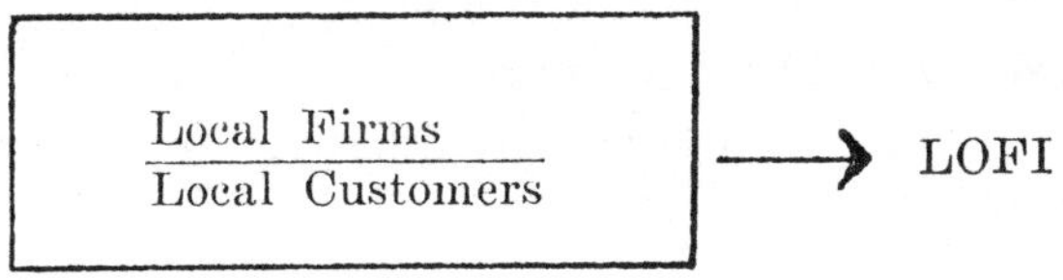

1. Given a hypothetical market area, determine the sales of local brewers to customers in the area.
2. Then determine the total sales of the local brewers, i.e., sales to customers both inside and outside the hypothetical market area.
3. If the ratio (1)/(2) approaches unity, meaning little beer goes out from inside, this allegedly supports the area as a geographic market area.
4. Note that this theory does not consider the flow of beer into the hypothetical area.

---

[36] See Ex. D-63, D-60, D-66, D-30. An excellent summary of these data is found in *United States* v. *PNB, Plaintiff's Proposed Findings of Fact,* pp. 47-67.

of the LOFI element. A high ratio presumably indicates an economic geographic market area.

In this case, the evidence varied according to the nature of the specific commercial banking product but it did show that a substantial part of PNB and Girard's business was generated "at home." The Government concluded:

> The market area of a commercial bank can be determined by analyzing the geographic areas in which its business originates and the percentage of business from those various areas.[37]

2. *The Local Distribution Element* was not specifically used.

3. *The Legal Restriction Element*: Paralleling *Pabst,* the Government relied on a legal restriction to supply argument, in this case the legal barriers to branching which restricted the banks to the Government's proposed four-county area.[38]

DEMAND AND SUPPLY

1. *The Price Element*: The Government made no attempt to show price differentials between banks in and outside of the four-county area.[39]

2. *The Turnover Element*: No data were presented on the turnover among the area's leading banks.[40]

---

37 *Ibid.,* p. 47. See also the testimony of Government witness Prof. Oscar Goodman, *Transcript of Record,* vol. II, p. 1059.

38 *Jurisdictional Statement of the Department of Justice,* March 21, 1962, p. 18; also testimony of Prof. Oscar Goodman, *op. cit.,* p. 1151.

39 GX-115 shows a 1959 PNB study comparing its service charges with those of other banks in the four-county area.

40 The Government also promoted the views of two other regulatory agencies which evaluated the merger. The FRB and the FDIC

A Critique of the Elements

Conceptually there are problems with almost every element in the Government's theory of geographic market delineation. Consider first the peculiar demand element.

In *Pabst,* the Government stressed the keen propensity of Wisconsinites to consume beer. While the existence of a unique demand function is relevant in determining the line of commerce, the element has little or no relevance in geographic market delineation, since a very high or very low demand for a product in a particular area will not delineate that area as a market unless supply is also restricted into or out of that area.[41] If the demand for beer in a Roman Catholic section of a city is higher than that in a Baptist section, so long as beer can move freely between the two sections, the market mechanism will supply more in one section than the other but beer prices will tend toward equality in each part of the city.[42]

---

both consider the four-county geographic market area as appropriate (see *Jurisdictional Statement,* p. 17; Goodman, p. 1059). But this should not be accorded great weight in the Government's eclectic geographic market delineation theory since the Government's use of these evaluations is quite selective, i.e., used when supportive of the Government's geographic market area.

41 Moreover, interstate differences in per capita beer consumption need not reflect unique demand curves in each state. An interesting fact is that the price of beer in Wisconsin is among the lowest in the nation. For a detailed analysis, see Thomas F. Hogarty and Kenneth G. Elzinga, "The Demand for Beer," 54 *Review of Economics and Statistics* 195 (1972).

42 With imagination, one can usually generate some consumer characteristic that will make any geographic area appear unique—by a peculiar demand standard the little town of Holland, Michigan, with its largely Dutch populace, might be a geographic market area for beer, or the German section of Chicago might qualify. Or the same element might be used in trying to broaden the geographic market area for beer, by arguing that the United States displays peculiar demand patterns relative to bordering countries. The difficulties of sorting out substantive demand differences between areas is not insignificant and, as mentioned above, without restrictions on the supply side, there is no analytical reason why demand differences should distinguish an area as a market.

Related to the peculiar demand element is a possible reference to the source of that peculiarity. For example, in *Pabst* the Government also argued that since large promotional costs are associated with entering a new territory, these costs erect a barrier that delineates that territory as an economic geographic market area.[43] However, the matter of product differentiation and brand allegiance, while possibly manifesting a barrier to entry, is not relevant in delineating the geographic market area since, unlike transportation costs, sellers both inside and outside the territory must face the same problem (and costs) of maintaining brand allegiance. Only in the event that local sellers possessed a sales advantage, solely because of locality and apart from any promotional or quality distinctions, would this factor be relevant. There is no evidence that beer consumers possess this character of local nepotism.

The LIFO and LOFI elements, as used in beer, banking, and elsewhere, are also weak pegs upon which to hang a geographic market area since either element, used separately, overlooks an important component in the other. The LIFO element in *Pabst* stressed the production area for Wisconsin-consumed beer. What was not considered important by the Government and the Court was the demand for Wisconsin-produced beer.[44] The record indicated that over 75 per cent of the beer produced in Wisconsin was exported for consumption outside of that state,[45] and it is incorrect to overlook this substantial supply going outside of the hypothetical geographic market area. The fact that an overwhelming percentage of Detroit residents purchase automobiles made in Detroit does not localize the geographic market area for

---

[43] *United States* v. *Pabst, Brief for the U.S.*, pp. 16-17, 38-40.

[44] For an *in extremum* view that beer shipments out of Wisconsin should be neglected in geographic market delineation, see *United States* v. *Pabst, Motion for Leave to File and Brief Amicus Curiae* of Brewers' Association of America, March 1965, pp. 28-29.

[45] *United States* v. *Pabst*, PX 6009 and 8017 and *Answer of Pabst Brewing Company to Post-trial Brief of the U.S.*, January 1968, pp. 45-47.

Detroit-produced automobiles to that city. Likewise the shipment of substantial quantities of beer from Wisconsin affects the price of beer outside of Wisconsin and, therefore, obviates the case for a Wisconsin geographic market area. As Professor Morris Adelman indicated in his testimony in *Pabst-Blatz:*

> Q. . . . even if no beer is shipped into Wisconsin from out of the state, what would be a determining factor as to the market area encompassing Wisconsin?
>
> A. Well, you have to look at what happens to the beer which is brewed in this state, and in round numbers something like four-fifths of the beer goes outside the state, which means that out-of-state is the dog, and Wisconsin, if I may use that expression, is the tail.
>
> The price of beer, the availability of the beer which is sold in this state, is determined overwhelmingly by the competition of brewers outside the state and the preferences of consumers outside the state.
>
> . . . The question is where are the suppliers and where are the buyers. And if they are overwhelmingly outside, then the market is composed overwhelmingly of those buyers and sellers outside.[46]

There are three problems with the LOFI test as used in *PNB,* one practical the other two analytical. Practically, there is no way of deciding what constitutes an amount or proportion of business with customers outside of the hypothetical geographic market area that is more than "a little." In *PNB,* a Government witness-expert economist, Professor Oscar Goodman, found that the amount and the percentage of business originating in the four-county area for the two banks was "overwhelming." On the other hand, Dr. W. Carlton Harris, witness-expert economist for the banks, found, from examining the Government exhibits, that a "substantial" amount of PNB-Girard deposit business and loans is generated from outside the four-county area.[47]

---

46 *Ibid., Trial Transcript,* pp. 2002-3.

47 *United States* v. *PNB, op. cit., Trial Transcript,* vol II, pp. 1059

Moreover, at least as used in *PNB,* the LOFI test does not consider the customer mix of other rival businesses within the hypothetical geographic market area. If all banks in the four-county area had approximately the same small percentage of customers from "outside," the PNB-Girard statistics do give a portrayal of customer location for these other banks. But clearly if other banks in the four-county area drew significant percentages of their customers from outside the four-county area, this means that a reliance on the PNB-Girard statistics to show the LOFI element would be misleading. No evidence on the customer location of the other four-county area banks was offered.

But even assuming (or demonstrating) that all the banks in the four-county area found their customers to be predominantly from that area, this does not conceptually demonstrate or support the four-county area as an economic geographic market area. The logical flaw in the Government's use of LOFI in geographic market delineation is its failure to consider the possibility of customers inside the four-county area who purchase commercial banking services outside the four-county area. Dr. John Gaffey, an economist with the Department of Justice, testified that no evidence was introduced on the amount of deposits originating in the four-county area but held by banks outside this area nor was there evidence on how many banks outside the four-county area solicit loan and deposit business in the four-county area.[48] Although Dr. Gaffey did not believe such evidence was important,[49] such evidence is clearly relevant. Even though PNB and Girard secure most of their business "locally," if, for example, 75 per cent of the citizens in the four-county area do their banking outside the area, this "outside supply" will affect the prices charged by both PNB and Girard. Consequently PNB and Girard would be affected by the actions of banks outside the four-county area; therefore the geographic market area would be wider than the four counties. Dr. Harris was ques-

48 *Ibid.*, vol. I, pp. 91-92, 98, 102.

49 *Ibid.*, vol. I, pp. 91-92.

tioned on this point and his answer is consistent with an economic view of a market area:

Q. . . . If 60 percent, say, of a bank's leading business should be drawn from the four-county area, does it necessarily follow that 60 percent of the loan business generated in the four counties goes to the banks in that area?

A. Oh, no . . . The bank derives 60 percent of its business . . . from the four-county area, but we do not know . . . how many businesses and customers located in the four-county area go outside the four-county area to obtain their financial accommodations. There is not a necessary relationship.[50]

Whether customers in the four-county area did go outside is not indicated in the case. But a vice-president of PNB did plausibly argue that:

> . . . anybody that is, say, on the periphery or the outskirts of the four-county area may find an alternate choice closer in the [banks' proposed geographic market area of] ten counties than in other locations within the four counties.[51]

The LOFI element ignores what LIFO stresses and vice versa. The state of Wisconsin, as a separate geographic market area, never would have survived the LOFI test used in *PNB-Girard*. No data are available to show whether the four-county area would have survived a LIFO test. In any event, the use of neither test by itself will satisfy the economist who is concerned that the geographic market area encompasses both the dominant demand and supply forces. The LIFO element overlooks the possibility of substantial supply flowing outside of the hypothetical geographic market area; the LOFI element overlooks the possibility of substantial demand going outside the hypothetical area.

---

50 *Ibid.*, vol. II, p. 1373.

51 *Ibid.*, vol. II, p. 1329.

The use of the transportation cost element in *Pabst* was rather oblique. While the Government stressed the high transportation cost of beer, it admitted that the "record in this case contains no direct evidence of such costs . . ." [52] The Government did at least convince the Court that if "beer is subject to high transportation costs [this would] be highly persuasive evidence supporting the local market theory." [53] But would it? While most economists probably agree that transportation costs are pertinent to geographic market delineation, the use of these costs is also not without operational and conceptual difficulties.[54]

Quite apart from the operational problem of measuring transportation costs, it is not even clear what the existence of a "high" transportation rate demonstrates. Any evidence on the freight rate for shipping beer should not have been useful in supporting a Wisconsin geographic market area, no matter how "high" the rate appeared, since other data, showing the huge quantities of beer shipped from Wisconsin, refute any charge that the rate is "too high" to insulate Wisconsin. Presumably if the price of beer in Wisconsin were somehow raised as a result of the Pabst-Blatz merger, out-of-state brewers could ship beer into Wisconsin with approximately the same facility Wisconsin brewers shipped out. The use of the transportation cost element is rebutted, at least prima facie, if there are substantial shipments into or out of the hypothetical geographic market area.[55]

---

52 *United States* v. *Pabst, Brief for the U.S.*, p. 42.

53 *United States* v. *Pabst,* 384 U.S. at 559. Cf. G. E. Hale and Rosemary D. Hale, *op. cit.*, p. 544 (especially n. 44).

54 At the authors' request, Mr. Norman Domrose, traffic manager for the Pabst Brewing Company, kindly supplied data on transport rates for beer prevailing during the late 1950s. These rates vary by mode of transport, cities of origin and destination, size (weight) of shipment; moreover, these rates are revised fairly often within a given year. Interestingly enough, excise taxes on beer were typically a far greater proportion of delivered price than were transportation costs.

55 Even in the absence of substantial shipments in or out of a hypothetical geographic market area, a high transportation rate does

The local distribution element, as used in *Pabst-Blatz,* was expressed by the Brewer's Association of America who argued that "... all brewers, whether they be national, regional, or local, compete, in the final analysis, at the local level."[56] The fact that beer distribution is local might be relevant in a merger between beer distributors but size of distributors is not critical in delineating a market area where the issue is competitive effects at the production level.[57]

The legal restriction element is one that is relevant in an economic determination of a geographic market area. If beer produced in Illinois could not move into Wisconsin because of state-imposed sanctions, this supports Wisconsin as a geographic market area. However, both within and between states, these sanctions seldom bar product movements. For example, in *Pabst,* the Government argued that the state sanctions were significant; brewing companies responded that they were more akin to a nuisance since brewers were not barred from any states and major decisions concerning product ingredients, choice of distributor, and a broad range of advertis-

---

not necessarily insulate or determine a geographic market area. For example, if the f.o.b. price of beer (including taxes) were $2.70 per case in Atlanta and $2.80 per case in Detroit, with freight costs between the two cities equal to 11 cents per case, one might find very few or no beer shipments between Atlanta and Detroit. This fact does not necessarily mean, in the context of a Section 7 suit, that any allegedly anticompetitive merger in the Detroit area is insulated from supply factors in Atlanta. If any attempt to raise the Detroit price above $2.81 will attract beer shipments from Atlanta, then in predicting the price effects of a merger in Detroit, Atlanta suppliers must be considered. Under such circumstances, the geographic market area, even in the absence of significant shipments between Atlanta and Detroit, should be drawn to include Atlanta. For a detailed analysis of present government theories in this context, see Richard A. Posner, "Oligopoly and Antitrust," 21 *Stanford Law Review* 1562, 1600 (1969).

[56] *United States* v. *Pabst, Motion for Leave to File and Brief Amicus Curiae* of Brewers' Association of America, March, 1965, p. 13.

[57] The Supreme Court dealt with this element, and seemingly rejected it, in *United States* v. *Grinnell Corp.,* 384 U.S. 563, 575-76 (1966).

ing-packaging decisions remained within managerial discretion.[58]

Perhaps the key factor in determining the emphasis to be placed on this element is whether the unique state requirements, whatever they may be, apply uniformly to producers within and outside the state. That is, if Wisconsin were to require expensive capping and labeling only of outstate brewers, then the legal restriction element must be given weight in geographic market delineation. But in brewing, since all producers must comply in the same fashion to the individual state requirements of labeling, capping, etc., this lessens the case for the legal element supporting any state as a distinct market area.

In general, the legal restriction element must meet two conditions before singling out some area *X* as an appropriate geographic market area for some product *x*. First, the product *x* cannot be imported into *X* except under costly or prohibitive conditions. Second, customers in *X* cannot readily go outside and consume or return with product *x*. If both of these conditions hold, then *X* becomes a unique geographical market area for product *x*.

In brewing, the first condition does not hold, at least at the state level, since the evidence shows large quantities of beer traveling across state lines. If the United States had a prohibitive tariff on beer, then this legal restriction element would be one factor limiting the geographic market area for beer to, at least, the United States. Since the first condition is not met in brewing, the mobility of beer customers is not germane in geographic market delineation.

In commercial banking, the first condition is often met—at the state level, at least—and in many states there are legal supply restrictions operating on an intrastate basis, such as in

---

[58] *Answer of Pabst Brewing Company . . . , op. cit.*, p. 53. See also *United States* v. *Joseph Schlitz*, 253 F. Supp. 129 (1966), affd. 385 U.S. 37 (1966), *Trial Transcript*, Serial No. 16, testimony of John Flanigan, p. 597.

Pennsylvania. However, it is not at all clear that the state sanctions which restrict supply (by limiting branching alternatives) are sufficient to limit a geographic market area to these boundaries due to the mobility of (at least some) bank customers.[59]

---

[59] Consider two examples. Assume bank customers are spread uniformly over three adjacent counties, A (Western), B (Midland), C (Eastern), with home banks home officed in each county. With a state branching law similar to Pennsylvania's, this means that A banks can branch into B (but not C), B banks can branch into A and C, and C banks can branch into B (but not A). In the absence of other barriers to entry, banks in A cannot raise their prices without drawing new supply-competition from banks officed in B—consequently any geographic market area encompassing A must include B as well. But since banks in B face C banks on the supply side, market forces in B are affected by forces in C, and consequently county A is not independent of C.

Now consider a case where branching outside a bank's home office county is prohibited. Is each county then a separate geographic market area? This depends upon the second condition mentioned earlier, that of consumer mobility. If bank customers are rather uniformly distributed over the three-county area, and are mobile without cost over some distance, say one-fourth of a county, a strong increase in demand in eastern C will have price-quantity implications for banks in B, which means B and C are in the same geographic market area. The increased demand in eastern C will, in the short run, cause shortages and upward price pressure there—attracting more banking efforts by banks in C. But the rising prices (and shortages or queuing) will also cause some customers to decrease the quantity of banking services demanded there and to "go West." While this group may go only part-way across the county (since it is costless), if this group is sizable enough to cause a shortage in the more westward segment of the county, bank customers there will find it in their interest to themselves move west. This entails a progression of customers shifting their business west. Since customers near the border of C can costlessly go over that border, the impact of a sizable demand increase in C can be felt in B, theoretically even in A, depending upon the size of the demand increase and the mobility of bank customers. The theoretical underpinnings of this progression argument can be found in Edward H. Chamberlin, *The Theory of Monopolistic Competition,* 5th ed. (Cambridge: Harvard University Press, 1947), p. 103. Greenhut refers to this as "chain oligopoly" where (using a different example than ours) "A is linked to B and C; B is linked to A and D; C is linked to A and E; and D is linked to B and F in many such combinations, with price effects spreading through the chain." See M. L. Greenhut, *Microeconomics and the Space Economy* (Chicago: Scott, Foresman, 1963), p. 107, and Looney, *op. cit.,* pp. 82–83.

With regard to the second condition, the evidence on customer mobility for commercial banking services varies according to the banking service being sought. Obviously, the search for a $250,000 loan normally covers a larger geographic territory than the search for a home mortgage loan. There seems little doubt that for many banking services, customers do not range widely in their search of alternatives.[60] For example, Girard's suburban offices had 72 per cent of their deposits originate within a two-mile radius of the office; for their Philadelphia offices, 80 per cent of the deposits originated within a one-mile radius of the office.[61] Ironically, given the banks support of a large geographic market area, Mr. Fred Potts, then president of PNB, testified that two banks acquired by PNB were not in competition with each other, though the banks were only ten miles apart.[62]

Even if it is true, as it appears to be, that for many banking services each customer is limited to a very local area, the fact that some customers are on the margin of that area, and therefore mobile into an adjacent area, tends to widen the appropriate geographic market area. Much of economic analysis is based upon this premise: that not everyone need make an adjustment to bring about some market equilibrium but rather only those on the margin need do so. And it is the bank customer on the margin, in spite of limited mobility, that tends to widen the geographic market area.

The price element, i.e., the existence of different prices in different areas, may be consistent with distinct geographic market areas where the price differential exceeds transportation costs. The Government has made little use of this, except in *Pabst,* but there no evidence was offered (by either side) that the price differentials are not due to offsetting transport

---

60 *Plaintiff's Proposed Findings of Fact . . .*, pp. 42-44.

61 *United States* v. *PNB, Trial Transcript,* vol. IV, Ex. D-56.

62 *Ibid.*, vol. I, p. 840. The banks constantly faced this dilemma of having argued that their earlier acquisitions were not anticompetitive—because the banks were a few miles apart—then later proposing the argument that the market is actually very broad.

costs, tax differences, or marketing requirements between states.

As mentioned earlier, price data will seldom be adequate in geographic market delineation due to the problems in specifying *the* price and *the* transportation rate. In commercial banking, the problems in using this approach are, perhaps, insurmountable. The work of Hoskins, Shaaf, and Taylor indicates some of the problems in the interregional comparison of bank "prices" due to the difficulties of compensating for different loan mixes, dissimilar risk factors due to varied regulatory statutes, monopoly elements, differences in costs per unit of volume due to density differences, etc.[63]

The industry recognition element has some validity since any effort at geographic market delineation is partly an attempt at predicting the response of businessmen to various demand and supply shifts. Thus it might appear logical to question these individuals about their reaction to possible events inside and outside the hypothetical geographic market area. But there are two obstacles in using this element to delineate a geographic market area. They are not apparent in *Pabst* since the Government basically asserted the element there. But in *United States* v. *Schlitz,* where this element was stressed,[64] the obstacles are apparent.

First, in the context of an adversary proceeding, this element is used predictably, i.e., those business witnesses whose companies' interests are consistent with a finding of a narrow geographic market area tend to testify that the industry recognizes a narrow market—and vice versa for those

---

[63] William Lee Hoskins, "Public Policy Towards Bank Mergers" (Ph.D. diss., UCLA, 1969), pp. 109-11; A. H. Shaaf, "Regional Differences in Mortgage Financing Costs," 21 *Journal of Finance* 85 (March 1966); Charles T. Taylor, "Average Interest Charges, the Loan Mix, and Measures of Competition: The Sixth Federal Reserve District Experience," 23 *Journal of Finance* 793 (December 1968).

[64] *Op. cit., Trial Brief of Plaintiff,* November, 1965, pp. 24–25.

industry spokesmen whose firms might benefit from a finding of a broader geographic market area.[65]

Second, the term "market," as mentioned earlier, is one with a different meaning in economics than in common parlance. While some businessmen use the term in its more formal sense, there is no doubt that questioning businessmen about a geographic market area frequently yields little insight because the term "market" becomes synonymous with "selling territory" or the like. In business parlance, a market is often an area with many customers.[66]

Moreover, the division of a firm's selling territories, done to enable the management of the marketing effort, frequently becomes synonymous with a "market," though the sales territory represents a business decision based on factors generally independent of those that delineate a geographic market area. For example, the Miller Brewing Company has its sales organization established on a state-by-state basis—not because each state is a distinct market in an economic sense but rather to delineate responsibility and evaluate marketing performance.[67] Robert Uihlein explained why Schlitz had divided up the United States into areas:

> The only reason we had area directors was to give individual attention to specific wholesalers. And obviously no man could give attention to all of our wholesalers . . . So it was simply a matter of convenience that we divided up responsibility . . . in various areas.[68]

---

[65] Cf. the testimony of Norman R. Klug, President of Miller Brewing Co. (a disgruntled suitor of Burgermeister) and Jess Nicks, President of General Brewing Co. with John Flanigan, Vice-President of Anheuser-Busch and Robert A. Uihlein, Jr., President of Joseph Schlitz, *Trial Transcript,* Serial No. 14, pp. 197–98; No. 15, p. 456; No. 16, pp. 592–95; No. 21, pp. 1334–35 respectively.

[66] For example, Jess Nicks of General Brewing Co. argued that California was a market, the basic reason being "the mass of population there." William W. Wessinger of Blitz-Weinhard considered California to be a separate market because it had a greater population than any Western state: "That makes it a market." Nicks, *ibid.;* Wessinger, No. 14, p. 337.

[67] Klug, *op. cit.,* No. 14, p. 198.

[68] Uihlein, *op. cit.*

The industry recognition element is particularly susceptible to misuse, either because it can be easily distorted through self-serving testimony or because businessmen, regardless of the parameters of an economic geographic market area, will frequently be "in a convention in Chicago talking of what Coors is doing in the California market." [69] They will talk this way because it is convenient to refer to some specific marketing area, independent of whether that location is a geographic market area and because it is seldom befitting for a businessman to refer to an area that specifically is to represent the configurations of a geographic market area.

The Government's use of the turnover element has a certain intuitive appeal but does not command any clear showing of relevance from economic analysis. The turnover element rests on the premise that market share stability is a sign of moribund rivalry. But the element itself offers no guidance for selecting what area about which to consider turnover. Moreover, economists are presently uncertain, or at least not in agreement, as to whether turnover among firms in concentrated industries is in fact a sign or indicator of business rivalry.[70]

IV. The Measurement of Market Areas for Antitrust Purposes

The basic economic theory of market areas, while logically correct, provides limited guidance to practitioners engaged in geographic market delineation. Partly as a consequence of this limitation, current legal theories of geographic market delineation have, at least in certain well-known instances, logical deficiencies. In what follows, we propose and illustrate an operational procedure for geographic market delineation that (1) is consistent with existing economic the-

---

[69] Wessinger, *op. cit.*, p. 338.

[70] Cf. U.S. Senate, Subcommittee on Antitrust and Monopoly, 89th Cong., 1st Sess., *Hearings on Economic Concentration*, statement of Leonard Weiss, March, 1965, pp. 728-43, and *ibid.*, statement of John Blair, 88th Congress, 2nd Sess., July, 1964, p. 207.

ory, (2) avoids the LIFO and LOFI errors observed in past legal decisions, and (3) can be readily implemented in a variety of circumstances.

Estimating a Market Area

The size and shape of a market area are determined by elements, such as legal restrictions and transportation cost, that may affect demand and supply. These elements typically "collapse" or manifest themselves in their impact upon the relative delivered prices of products; however, as noted earlier, there are both conceptual and operational problems in translating price data into the estimation of market areas. On the other hand, all of the demand and supply elements that affect price also affect quantity—or shipments—and these figures can be used in estimating market areas. Specifically, the only data required to estimate market areas—at least in most cases—are shipments data in physical terms (e.g., barrels), but the data for this one variable must be organized in a certain manner. Specifically, shipments must be classified by two categories simultaneously: destination (e.g., Nebraska) and origin (e.g., Kansas City).[71] Given such data, estimation of market size in terms of area and volume requires a minimum of four steps, as follows:

1. Begin with the location of the larger of the merging firms (or its largest plant). Find the minimum area required to account for at least 75 per cent of the appropriate "line of commerce" shipments of that firm (or plant). Designate this area as the hypothetical market area. If the merging firms are separate geographically,[72] this step is to be followed for each firm.

---

[71] Note that our point of departure is the plant (or shipping center), not the firm. Patterns of ownership are of minor concern.

[72] "Separation" is a matter of judgment. Automobile firms in different parts of the same city are not separated geographically while grocery stores might very well be.

Otherwise simply determine the hypothetical market area for the larger firm.[73]

2. Of the total sales of this product within the hypothetical area, are 75 per cent or more shipped from plants located within this area? If so, the LIFO test is met and step 3 can be completed. If not, the hypothetical market area must be redrawn. In redrawing the hypothetical area,[74] determine the minimum area necessary to account for 75 per cent of the shipments of this product from all plants within the area (or in the absence of other plants, the largest firm shipping into the area). Continue doing this until the LIFO test is met. If it never is met, the market is (at least) national in scope.
3. If the LIFO test is met, determine if at least 75 per cent of the shipments by the firms within the hypothetical market area are to customers within the area. Of course, if there is only one plant (that of one of the merging firms) in the hypothetical area, the LOFI test is met through step 1. But if there is more than one plant, this last step is necessary to meet the LOFI criterion.
4. If both tests have been met, then calculate total consumption (from all shipping points) within the hypothetical market area to get market size in terms of volume.

The 75 per cent figure is obviously somewhat arbitrary. It represents a conservative estimate of the percentage of

[73] Note that the hypothetical market area can be square miles, city blocks, or number of states. Furthermore, the components of the hypothetical market area need not be contiguous. Thus, for a product X, the states of Florida, New York, and California might constitute a hypothetical market area.

[74] Failure to satisfy the LIFO test may mean that the original choice of producing center or base location was inappropriate. Thus, the location of the acquiring or acquired firm may be an unsuitable starting place. In most circumstances, such a situation will be revealed from elementary knowledge of the industry in question.

shipments which encompass the primary demand and supply forces and may understate the true scope of the relevant market. Some might argue that the figure should be, say, 90 per cent, on the grounds that "overlooking" 25 per cent of the shipments is overlooking too much. The 75 per cent benchmark reflects our view that this satisfactorily encompasses the primary demand-supply forces at reasonable costs of estimation. Those objecting to this benchmark can readily substitute a higher (or lower) one into the estimating procedure.

It is of course possible that two distinct geographic market areas might be found following this estimation procedure. If so, this shows a geographic market extension merger. It is also possible, for geographically distinct firms, that the procedure will result in two areas that overlap. If the overlap is substantial, i.e. it accounts for at least 25 per cent of the shipments of either area taken by itself, then the entire area, the overlapping and nonoverlapping segments, may be assumed to constitute a geographic market area.

We are aware of data problems in using this procedure. Plant shipments data will probably not be as difficult to secure as the various area consumption statistics. But in some cases data limitations will require that the hypothetical area be altered slightly to conform to more readily available data. For many markets, particularly retail ones, sampling techniques will be required to estimate shipments; fortunately, sampling is already established in Section 7 cases.[75]

The proposed estimating procedure is less useful as the product market is less clearly defined. For example, applying this procedure to commercial banking is unworkable since to speak of the shipments or sales of "commercial banking" (as opposed to "trust services") is meaningless. This is both a weakness and strength of the estimating procedure. Its

---

[75] Where the appropriate product market is a set of heterogeneous goods, or where there is product differentiation, or where there are important physical differences among units within the product market, adding together physical units will be difficult if not impossible. In such cases, measuring output in sales instead of physical units might be necessary.

strength is its requirement of parties to Section 7 suits to delineate more accurately the relevant product market. As indicated earlier, this estimating procedure hinges upon a clearly delineated product market.[76]

A difficulty in the proposed procedure is that it may involve securing data from firms not immediately party to the merger. These firms will presumably be unwilling to provide their shipments data since such information would be useful to rivals. The court would have to be convinced of the necessity of these data in geographic market delineation and such data should probably remain *in camera* where the supplying firms feel a public record would be harmful.

Whether this estimating procedure will be less costly than present methods is unclear. There is no doubt that certain data not now collected must be gathered, but the converse is also true.[77] The savings, if any, will accrue in having a clear procedure to follow, one that will eliminate the not insignificant legal resources now expended on developing various theories that might strategically support one's desired "market."[78]

The Case of Beer: An Illustration

The previous section mentioned two Section 7 cases involving the Joseph Schlitz and Pabst Brewing Companies. In the former case, the California district court ruled that an eight-Western-state area was a distinct geographic market; in the latter case, the Supreme Court designated the state of

---

[76] In some circumstances, defining the relevant line of commerce and delineating the geographic market area may be interdependent. In such cases the approach adopted by Lozowick, Steiner, and Miller, *op. cit.*, is perhaps unavoidable despite its inherent complexity and substantial cost.

[77] Historically, data collection in merger cases has often comprised data on wholesale prices, prevailing transportation rates, and numerous other variables. Our procedure requires data, other than that readily available from public sources, on shipments only.

[78] Our suggested procedure, since it relies exclusively on historical data, may not adequately indicate future expansions or contractions in a given geographic market area where prices do change substantially from historical levels. However, we believe that our procedure will comprise a reasonably accurate estimate, given only small (future) changes in demand and costs (supply).

Wisconsin a distinguishable market area. In both instances the courts appeared to err in calculating the relevant market area.

In *Pabst*, estimation of the wholesale market area centered at Milwaukee would have required shipments data classified by destination, for all breweries located in Milwaukee. Such data are unavailable, but the case in question did generate data on the shipments of Blatz Pilsner Beer to the contiguous states, including the District of Columbia. As a first approximation, Blatz, with its single plant in Milwaukee, may be taken as a "representative" producer. The share of Blatz shipments to various states for 1949–61 is contained in Tables 1 and 2. Two noteworthy facts are revealed by these tables: (1) the state of Wisconsin has typically absorbed less than one-half the shipments of Milwaukee producers and cannot, by any stretch of the imagination, be considered a distinct geographic market; (2) the market for beer centered at Milwaukee comprises at least 4 or 5 states, not all contiguous.[79]

TABLE 1

SHARE (PER CENT) OF PRODUCTION (NO. OF BARRELS) OF BLATZ PILSNER BEER SOLD IN SELECTED AREAS DURING 1949–61

Year	*Wisconsin*	*Wisconsin, Illinois, Michigan*
1949	31.8%	53.8%
1950	34.8	57.5
1951	34.0	57.4
1952	39.1	61.9
1953	43.4	66.7
1954	46.2	71.8
1955	47.6	73.4
1956	41.5	71.2
1957	31.3	66.7
1958	23.4	63.2
1959	19.5	56.9
1960	17.4	54.7
1961	17.0	56.2

79 For example, the states of Florida and California absorbed a significant portion of Blatz sales during the 1950s; however, the bulk of sales were in central midwestern states.

TABLE 2

ESTIMATES OF MINIMUM NUMBER OF STATES REQUIRED TO ACCOUNT FOR (AT LEAST) 75% OF BLATZ SHIPMENTS FROM MILWAUKEE

Year	*Number of States*	*Per Cent of Blatz Shipments*
1949	8	77.1%
1950	8	77.4
1951	8	75.7
1952	7	76.3
1953	6	76.9
1954	4	75.8
1955	4	77.2
1956	5	77.9
1957	5	77.8
1958	5	78.9
1959	5	75.9
1960	5	75.7
1961	5	79.5

Thus, these data suggest a hypothetical market area for the period, 1957–61,[80] consisting of the states Illinois, Indiana, Ohio, Michigan, and Wisconsin.

Were data available, our next step would comprise the LIFO test. Given the importance of Milwaukee as a producing center, it is likely that the LIFO test would be passed. On the other hand, "exports" from Milwaukee to states other than the five cited above are presumably quite substantial. Thus, it is likely that complete data would suggest an expansion of the hypothetical market area.

Suppose the LOFI test were not passed; we would then expand the market area and subsequently perform *both* the LIFO and LOFI tests once more.[81] Assuming both tests were passed on the second round, we would calculate total consumption within the hypothetical market area from public sources

---

80 These five years constitute a representative collection in that both "boom" and "recession" years are represented. More important, they are the most recent data available.

81 The LIFO test would require repetition because expansion of the areal size might bring our "borders" within the range of other producing centers (e.g., St. Louis, Newark, etc.).

(in this case, *Brewer's Almanac*). Having completed all four steps satisfactorily, we could then proceed to compute market shares, concentration ratios, etc.

In the *Schlitz* case, the Courts erred in the opposite direction. Whereas in the *Pabst* case, the market area was significantly underestimated, the eight Western state area appears—*at first sight*—to be too large.

As indicated in Tables 3 and 4, step 1 of our procedure suggests a hypothetical market area of one to three states. Conceivably, further data sufficient to carry out steps 2 and 3 would result in a large number of states as the hypothetical market area. Nonetheless, the point is that absent such data and calculations, the eight-state area is a simplistic estimate.

TABLE 3

ESTIMATES OF MINIMUM NUMBER OF STATES REQUIRED TO ACCOUNT FOR (AT LEAST) 75% OF J.S.B. SHIPMENTS FROM LOS ANGELES

Year	*Number of States*		*Per Cent of J.S.B. Shipments*	
1960	3	(6)*	78.39	(89.65)*
1961	5	(13)	79.42	(91.91)
1962	3	(13)	77.22	(90.33)
1963	1	(3)	78.28	(93.37)

* Numbers in parentheses are the minimum number of states required to account for 90 per cent of (Los Angeles) shipments and the actual per cent accounted for, respectively.

TABLE 4

ESTIMATES OF MINIMUM NUMBER OF STATES REQUIRED TO ACCOUNT FOR (AT LEAST) 75% OF J.S.B. SHIPMENTS FROM CALIFORNIA (LOS ANGELES AND SAN FRANCISCO)

Year	*Number of States*		*Per Cent of J.S.B. Shipments*	
1960	4	(13)*	77.53	(85.63)*
1961	4	(13)	75.71	(88.22)
1962	1	(3)	81.44	(89.67)
1963	1	(4)	78.08	(89.07)

* Numbers in parentheses are the minimum number of states required to account for 90 per cent of (Los Angeles) shipments and the actual per cent accounted for, respectively.

An authoritative estimate of the relevant market area in the *Pabst* and *Schlitz* cases would have required shipments data by origin and destination (e.g., from Milwaukee to Ohio, but not to Akron, Ohio) for almost all producers. To the extent that such data were unavailable, recourse to "representative firm" arguments would have to be made.

For example, if Blatz could be considered a typical brewery, then estimates of market area based on the Blatz experience alone would suffice. In fact, at the time of the Pabst-Blatz merger, Pabst Brewing was representative of premium beer producers while Blatz was a typical "popular" beer. Even with fragmentary data for a few local breweries in two or three states, one could construct an average hypothetical market area.

This average would comprise a weighted average of the hypothetical market areas for premium, popular, and local beers with the weights consisting of market shares for these types of brewers on a nationwide basis.

Assuming ale and beer to be mere categories in the general market for malt beverages, one could estimate market areas only if access were had to shipments data for more representative producers. Fortunately, the less representative the acquiring and acquired firms, the less likely is the merger to produce anticompetitive effects.

V. Conclusion

Predicting anticompetitive effects from a merger sans a relevant market context is a job for a mystic, not an economist. Until 1966 it seemed clear that determining the appropriate geographic market was necessary in Section 7 suits and was to be an exercise in economics, not mysticism. Thus far, however, the economics has not been top drawer.

Without gainsaying the weaknesses in the Government theories, perhaps the more serious threat to economically sound geographic market delineation is the Court's carte blanche acceptance of "any old geographic market" as articulated in the *Pabst* decision. In spite of an earlier statement to the contrary,[82] the Court wrote:

> the District Court thought that in order to show a violation of Section 7 it was essential for the Government to show a "relevant geographic market" . . . [but the] . . . language of this section requires merely that the Government prove the merger has a substantial anticompetitive effect somewhere in the United States . . . This phrase does not call for the delineation of a "section of the country" by metes and bounds as a surveyor would lay off a plot of ground.[83]

This seemed to indicate that all the Government need do is select some territory in which significant sales of the product in question were consummated. Fortunately for the reputation of Section 7, the Government has not chosen to exploit this decision by henceforth asserting market areas *ad libitum*.

One reason for the Court's gift to the Government might be the apparent lack of clear, noncontroversial estimating procedures to determine market boundaries. The procedures outlined above, however, should prove useful in meeting this void. These procedures, to repeat, have the advantage of being generally consistent with economic analysis, reasonably applicable by antitrust practitioners, designed independently of any need to support a particular case, and analytically far superior to the eclectic methods now being used.

---

82 *Brown Shoe Co.* v. *United States,* 370 U.S. 294, 320, 336–37 (1962).

83 *United States* v. *Pabst,* p. 548.

[5]

ROBERT D. WILLIG
Department of Justice

Merger Analysis, Industrial Organization Theory, and Merger Guidelines

THE LEADERSHIP of the Antitrust Division of the U.S. Department of Justice has, over the past two years, emphasized that the department's 1984 merger guidelines are a sound prescription for horizontal merger enforcement, that as a matter of policy they are being applied in enforcement decisionmaking, and that there may be a need for "clarification and fine-tuning" of the guidelines.[1] This paper examines some facets of the antitrust analysis of horizontal mergers in the light shed by industrial organization (IO) theory, in order to stimulate discussion of some possible directions for fine-tuning and clarification of the guidelines. I focus on the possible anticompetitive effects of horizontal mergers and the role of potential entry in merger analysis. However, to set the context for these subjects, it will be helpful first to sketch the nature of the merger guidelines.

Except where specifically noted, the views expressed in this paper do not necessarily reflect those of the Department of Justice. Robert D. Willig is on leave from Princeton University. He gratefully acknowledges stimulating conversations with and helpful comments from Jonathan Baker, Paul Denis, Jim Langenfeld, Janusz Ordover, Steve Salop, Marius Schwartz, Dave Simpson, and Greg Werden. They should not be held accountable for the outcome.

1. See Rill (1990b); and U.S. Department of Justice (1984), hereafter cited as Guidelines.

The 1984 Merger Guidelines

Under section 7 of the Clayton Act, a merger is prohibited if its effect "may be substantially to lessen competition, or to tend to create a monopoly." The purpose of the merger guidelines is, for the sake of the predictability and accuracy of the enforcement program, to indicate the circumstances in which the Department of Justice is likely to challenge mergers (and acquisitions) under section 7.[2] The 1984 guidelines, and the 1982 guidelines from which they evolved, are dramatic departures from the previous guidelines published in 1968. The 1968 guidelines relied almost exclusively on measures of concentration and provided little precise guidance on how to define the relevant market, the universe over which concentration would be measured. In contrast, the 1982 and 1984 guidelines articulate a conceptually rich framework for merger analysis "that is largely consistent with the perspectives of theoretical economics. Indeed, the noteworthy intellectual feat of the guidelines' authors is the creation of a forensically useful framework that embodies much of the best available economic learning."[3] These guidelines aim squarely at predicting with economic tools whether a merger will create or enhance market power, or facilitate its exercise, while avoiding unnecessary interference with mergers that are competitively beneficial or neutral.[4]

The analytic process defined by the 1984 guidelines for horizontal mergers can be described as a series of discrete steps:[5]

—Delineation of the relevant product and geographic market;

—Identification of firms included as participants in the relevant market;

2. Essentially the same standards are also applied to challenges of mergers and acquisitions under section 1 of the Sherman Act.

3. Ordover and Willig (1983).

4. According to the 1984 guidelines, section 1.0 "This ability of one or more firms profitably to maintain prices above competitive levels for a significant period of time is termed 'market power.' Sellers with market power also may eliminate rivalry on variables other than price." In addition, market power may also refer to analogous monopsony effects.

5. The sketch that follows is very incomplete for the sake of brevity. See Werden (1983) or Salop and others (1987) for a more complete interpretive treatment, or the guidelines themselves.

—Calculation and interpretation of market shares and concentration;
—Assessing ease of entry;
—Consideration of other factors; and
—Assessing efficiencies.

Each step has its own complexities, subtleties, and relationships to industrial organization theory. A basic understanding of many of the steps is necessary to appreciate the economic rationality of the guidelines' analytic framework and the issues discussed later regarding fine-tuning and clarification. Delineation of the relevant market is the most novel and central portion of the framework.

The relevant market is delineated by means of an analysis of what set of products (at associated locations) has sufficiently inelastic demand as a group that a hypothetical profit-maximizing monopoly supplier of the set would impose at least a "small but significant and nontransitory increase in price" (henceforth abbreviated to SSNIP).[6] A SSNIP is typically, but not rigidly, taken to be a 5 percent increase in price. Conceptually, this analysis begins separately with each of the products of the merging firms and asks whether a hypothetical monopolist over this product would profitably raise its price by 5 percent or more. This question is addressed only in terms of the reaction of demand to the hypothesized price increase, with no attention paid to possible efficiencies created by the merger or to reactions by potential entrants. Such possibly important effects are fully considered in other steps of the guidelines' analysis, while this step of delineating relevant markets focuses exclusively on demand-side effects.

If the hypothetical monopolist would profitably raise its price by 5 percent or more, then this starting-point product alone constitutes a relevant product market. If not, then the product that is the closest substitute to the first product is considered along with it, and the 5 percent test is applied to the two together. It is likely that this group has less elastic demand than the first product considered alone, since diversion of demand from the first to the second now remains within the set.

This conceptual process proceeds until the smallest group of products is found that has the property that a hypothetical profit-maximizing

6. Guidelines, section 2.1. See Boyer (1979) for a valuable precursor.

monopolist would impose at least a 5 percent increase in price. This group is taken to be the relevant product market with respect to the starting point, one of the products of one of the merging firms.

An analogous process is carried out (simultaneously, in principle) to delineate the geographic scope of the relevant markets. The guidelines mandate consideration of the relevant markets for each of the products (and locations) of the merging firms. The merger is viewed as horizontal if both of the merging parties are included as participants in any one of these relevant markets, and the merger is not horizontal if there is no such overlap.[7]

It is important to note that this process of delineating relevant markets calibrates the market power that is of concern in a horizontal merger. If the merger created a complete monopoly in an overlap relevant market, the analysis predicts that demand would permit the imposition of at least a small but significant and nontransitory price rise for the products and locations in this relevant market. Of course, a host of pertinent questions remains for subsequent steps of the analysis. Prominent among them are the extent to which the merger would structurally or behaviorally create a monopoly in the relevant market, and whether de novo entry would react to or deter the enlargement or exercise of the market power that is of concern. Before turning to these topics, it is necessary to explain a novel feature of the guidelines' step of identifying the firms to be included as participants in the relevant market.

All firms that currently produce and sell any of the products (at any of the locations) that constitute the relevant market are considered participants in it. In addition, "If a firm has existing productive and distributive facilities that could easily and economically be used to produce and sell the relevant product within one year in response to a [SSNIP], the Department will include that firm in the market."[8] Even though such a firm, termed a production substituter, is not currently supplying products in the relevant market, it is nevertheless considered a partic-

7. As a matter of policy, if rigid adherence to the 5 percent figure masks a competitive interaction between merging firms, then a somewhat larger price rise will be employed for the process of market delineation in order to investigate the horizontal nature of the merger. See Rill (1990a). Corresponding adjustments in other steps of the guidelines' analytic process may be appropriate.

8. Guidelines, section 2.21.

ipant in it. I shall return to a discussion of this feature of the guidelines in the subsequent part of this paper that focuses on entry.

Once the analytic process has delineated relevant markets, identified the participants in them, and found one or more overlap markets, the next step specified by the guidelines is to calculate and interpret market shares and concentration in the overlap relevant markets. When data permit, shares are determined on the basis of capacity where relatively homogeneous products are involved, and on the basis of sales where the relevant products are relatively differentiated. For production substituters, and other participants with capacity that is utilized elsewhere, the determination of shares is based on only sales likely to be made or capacity likely to be used in the relevant market in response to a SSNIP.

Concentration is measured by means of the Herfindahl-Hirschman Index (HHI), calculated by summing the squares of the market shares (in percentage terms) of all the market participants.[9] The postmerger HHI is calculated by assigning to the merged firm the sum of the premerger shares of the merging parties, and assigning to the other participants their premerger shares.[10] The difference between the postmerger and premerger values of the HHI, termed the change in concentration (or the delta), is algebraically given by twice the product of the shares of the two merging firms.

According to the general standards of the guidelines, a horizontal merger will almost never be challenged if the postmerger HHI lies in the ''unconcentrated'' range below 1,000.[11] In the ''moderately con-

9. This is a well-known index with many desirable arithmetic properties. It increases if share is transferred from a smaller to a larger firm. For n equal-sized firms its value is $1/n$, so that 1/HHI can be interpreted as the ''numbers equivalent.'' If shares are given by fractions, the HHI is 1.0 for monopoly, and it approaches 0 for a large number of firms each having a small share. When shares are measured in percentages, as they are in the 1982 and 1984 guidelines, the HHI runs from 0 to 10,000.

10. While these assignments may be predictive when shares are calculated according to capacity, they are unlikely to be accurately predictive when shares are based on sales. For example, a merger that creates market power is likely to lead to a decrease in the total share of sales held by the merging firms. See Ordover and Willig (1983); and Farrell and Shapiro (1990a) on this point. Nevertheless, the postmerger HHI can be viewed as an indicator with analytic value apart from its ability to predict concentration after the merger's effects eventuate. See Werden (1990).

11. Guidelines, section 3.11. Here it is pointed out that despite the general standards, ''market share and concentration data provide only the starting point for analyzing the

centrated'' range, between 1,000 and 1,800, there is a virtual safe harbor for mergers that change the HHI by less than 100, and otherwise, the enforcement decision will weigh a host of other factors along with the level of and change in concentration. In the ''highly concentrated'' range, where the postmerger HHI is above 1,800, the safe harbor applies only to mergers with a delta of less than 50, and otherwise, ''Additional concentration resulting from mergers is a matter of significant competitive concern.''[12]

It is key to note that these general standards embody the idea that a horizontal merger of a given size, as measured by the shares of the parties or by the HHI delta, is of greater concern the greater the market concentration. For example, a merger between two firms each with an 8 percent market share (and hence a delta of 128) would lie in the safe harbor if the market were unconcentrated, would trigger an assessment of other factors if the market were moderately concentrated, and would raise ''significant competitive concern'' if the market were highly concentrated. In addition, for a given level of market concentration above the unconcentrated range, a horizontal merger is of greater concern the greater the change in concentration it is measured to produce.

Heuristic Theoretical Representation

Fundamental rationales for the steps of the guidelines' process that have been discussed above can be illustrated by means of a heuristic representation based on IO theory. I term this treatment heuristic because it is deliberately oversimplified and underspecified in order to focus on the connections among market delineation, concentration, and the welfare impact of a merger. This treatment assumes that there are no efficiencies directly or indirectly created by the merger, no dynamic effects, and that there is no possibility of entry into the market.[13]

To the first order in static partial equilibrium, where dW is change

competitive impact of a merger. Before determining whether to challenge a merger, the Department will consider all other relevant factors that pertain to its competitive impact.''

12. Guidelines, section 3.11.

13. See note 19 for additional assumptions that render this model merely heuristic. For somewhat analogous treatments, see Jacquemin and Slade (1989); and Ordover, Sykes, and Willig (1982).

in consumer plus producer surplus, dQ is change in market output, P is market price, and c is the marginal cost of the market product,

$$dW = dQ\,(P-c). \tag{1}$$

Taking ϵ to be the constant elasticity of demand for the market output, $\epsilon = -(dQ/dP)\,(P/Q)$, and R to be the value (PQ) of market output, (1) can be rewritten as

$$-dW/R = (dP/P)\,\epsilon\,(P-c)\,/P. \tag{2}$$

This shows that the welfare impact of a price rise resulting from a merger depends on the elasticity of market demand and on the Lerner index, $(P-c)\,/P$, applicable to the market experiencing the price rise.

Specification of an oligopoly model is necessary to see how concentration can be related to the welfare impact and to provide a context for the representation of market delineation. Many simple theories of oligopoly have had their equilibria characterized in the following convenient fashion:[14]

$$(P-c)\,/P = H\beta/\epsilon, \tag{3}$$

where H is the HHI and β is a parameter that represents the mode of conduct among the firms in the market.[15] For example, price-taking behavior corresponds to $\beta = 0$, Cournot behavior is represented by $\beta = 1$, and pure cartel behavior corresponds to $\beta = 1/H$.

Market delineation can now be represented as the choice of a universe over which to measure concentration such that the monopoly price, satisfying $(P-c)\,/P = 1/\epsilon$, is 5 percent greater than the current price, satisfying $(P^0-c)\,/P^0 = H^0\beta^0/\epsilon$. This calibration yields the following expression for the elasticity of demand of the products in the relevant market:[16]

14. For example, see Cowling and Waterson (1976); Dansby and Willig (1979); and Bresnahan (1989); as well as Jacquemin and Slade (1989) and Ordover, Sykes, and Willig (1982).

15. Equation (3) is typically built up from the relationship between a firm's price-cost margin and its market share, s_i:

$$(P_i - c_i)/P_i = s_i\beta_i/\epsilon. \tag{3'}$$

16. While ϵ is assumed to be constant with respect to price, it is not invariant to the scope and composition of the relevant market that is delineated here.

$$(4) \qquad \epsilon = (1.05 - H^0\beta^0)/0.05.$$

Applying (3) to the market both premerger and postmerger yields these expressions for the percentage change in price caused by the merger:

$$(5) \qquad dP/P = d(H\beta/\epsilon - H\beta)$$

and substituting (5) and (3) into (2), applying the mean value theorem, and employing (4) yields as the conclusion:

$$(6) \qquad -\Delta W/R^* = 0.05(H^*\beta^*)(H'\beta' - H^0\beta^0) / (1.05 - H^0\beta^0 - .05H^*\beta^*),$$

where $H^*\beta^*$ lies between $H^0\beta^0$ and $H'\beta'$, and R^* lies between R^0 and R'.

This result provides a validation of the guidelines' approach to merger analysis. First, note that while equation (2) required knowledge of the market elasticity of demand in order to assess the welfare impact of the merger, this factor does not appear in equation (6) due to the market delineation step that served to calibrate the market power at stake. Instead, the only factors in (6) relate to modes of firm conduct and to concentration, where the universe over which the concentration is measured is set by the market delineation that accounted for the influence of demand.[17] Second, if the values of β were set to a standardized

17. The remarks in note 10 apply to H′. Note too that in some contexts, it may be important to recognize that the process of market delineation did not yield a set of products and locations over which a hypothetical monopolist would profitably raise price by only 5 percent. For example, starting with one of the products of one of the merging firms, it might be the case that the hypothetical monopolist would profitably raise the price of that product by a greater percentage, t, and that the other merging firm also produces that product. Then the relevant market could not include less than that product. In such cases, the following modification of equation (6) applies, where the value t replaces the 5 percent figure:

$$(6') \qquad -\Delta W/R^* = t(H^*\beta^*)(H'\beta' - H^0\beta^0)/(1 + t - H^0\beta^0 - tH^*\beta^*).$$

It is straightforward to see that this expression is increasing in t. Thus for given values of concentration and for given modes of firm conduct, the larger the percent by which a hypothetical monopolist would profitably raise price over the relevant market, the larger the welfare loss caused by the merger. This is consistent with the statement in section 3.412 of the 1984 guidelines that "the larger the 'gap' at the edge of the product and geographic markets, the more likely the Department is to challenge the merger."

positive constant level, the influence on welfare impact of the measures of concentration would qualitatively correspond to the ways that concentration enters into the guidelines. Welfare impact is more pronounced the larger the delta, and the impact of a given sized delta is more pronounced the larger the level of concentration. For sufficiently low levels of concentration, the welfare impact of a merger is low even if the delta is big enough to raise concerns at higher levels of concentration. Obversely, at sufficiently high levels of concentration, even relatively small levels of delta can yield sizable welfare impacts.

Equation (6) also shows the importance of the mode of behavior of the firms in the market, and the significance of a change in that mode resulting from a merger.[18] For constant β, the greater its value, signifying a less competitive mode of conduct, the greater the welfare impact of a given merger. And the welfare impact of a merger would be greater than that indicated by concentration alone in equation (6) if the merger led to a greater value of β, and hence to a less competitive mode of conduct.[19]

18. Dansby and Willig (1979) and Ordover, Sykes, and Willig (1982) find that such considerations may well be quantitatively more significant than changes in concentration apart from impacts on the mode of firm conduct. See Stigler (1964) for a model of oligopoly in which the likelihood of collusion is related to the HHI.

19. It is significant to note that all of the above qualitative conclusions would hold if the objective were taken to be consumer surplus instead of the sum of consumer and producer surplus. In this case, equation (6) would apply without the $H^*\beta^*$ term in the numerator. At this juncture, take note of some of the particular oversimplifications and underspecifications that lead me to term as "heuristic" the model that has just been exercised. First, the formal treatment of welfare presupposes that output is homogeneous, while that surely is not generally the case, especially when the model attempts to represent the process of market delineation. Second, taken literally, the model assumes that all firms have the same levels of constant marginal cost, thus leaving unexplained why different firms might possess different market shares. If firms are thought to have diverse levels of marginal costs, then the welfare measure omits effects arising from transfers of output among firms. Third, the oligopoly representation leaves exogenous the determination of the mode of firms' behavior, while one of the important facets of merger analysis may be the attempt to predict impacts on this very important influence on industry performance. Fourth, the model does not consider the information that may be derived from the fact that the merger is desired by at least one and perhaps both of the parties. And finally, as already noted, the model deliberately abstracts away from complications arising from possibilities of dynamic impacts, entry, and merger efficiencies.

Assessing Efficiencies

Efficiencies that might be caused by a horizontal merger enter into the guidelines' analytic process in two ways. First, directly, the department will consider "clear and convincing evidence" that a merger "may be reasonably necessary to achieve significant net efficiencies."[20] While this precept sounds desirable, serious issues arise in determining what standards should be applied to the ideas of "reasonably necessary" and "significant net efficiencies." Although I believe that economic analysis can contribute much to resolving such issues, they are well outside the scope of this paper.[21]

Second, efficiencies enter intrinsically, though indirectly, into the guidelines' analytic process. "Because the antitrust laws and, thus, the standards of the Guidelines, are designed to proscribe only mergers that present a significant danger to competition, . . . in the majority of cases, the Guidelines will allow firms to achieve available efficiencies through mergers without interference from the Department."[22]

More analytically, the guidelines might be viewed as implicitly incorporating the *inference* of likely significant efficiencies where there is no finding that the merger would significantly increase market power. The profitability of a voluntarily proposed horizontal merger can only stem from some combination of efficiencies, competitively neutral effects, and increased market power. Where the last of these has been found by an investigation to be unlikely or insubstantial, the posterior expected value of the efficiencies is much raised from its prior expected value, even in the absence of direct evidence on efficiencies. Since efficiencies add to social welfare as well as to profit, while increased market power subtracts from social welfare as it adds to profit, the expected social welfare impact of a profitable merger can be readily swung to positive by a finding that the expected addition to profits does not stem from a significant increase in market power. From this consideration, the guidelines' structure of safe harbors with respect to concentration and entry can be analytically derived.

20. Guidelines, section 3.5.
21. See Williamson (1983) for a stimulating discussion of some of the issues involved.
22. Guidelines, section 3.5.

Consideration of Other Factors and Competitive Effects in the 1984 Guidelines

The rich analytical framework established in the 1984 guidelines leaves considerable room for influences beyond market delineation and concentration, even apart from efficiencies and entry. The likely future competitive significance of a firm in the market is to be evaluated directly, in the event it is not accurately reflected by the firm's current share. Many ''other factors'' are specifically suggested for consideration, especially when the department's decision about whether to challenge a merger is otherwise close. These factors include the degree of heterogeneity of the relevant product; the degree of difference between the products and locations in the relevant market and the next-best substitutes; similarities and differences in the products and locations of the merging firms; information about specific transactions and characteristics of the buyer market; the ability of small or fringe sellers to increase sales; and indications of conduct of firms in the market. All of these other factors are cited as relevant to the extent that they relate to the ease and profitability of collusion.[23]

Indeed, although there is some general language in the guidelines concerning how a concentrating merger might lessen competition, most of the discussion of anticompetitive effects is cast in terms of whether the merger at issue would raise the likelihood of tacit or explicit collusion among the market's suppliers. Until recently, ''tacit collusion'' might have been interpreted as any oligopolistic behavior that deviated in its outcome from perfect competition, although some texts surely held to finer distinctions. Today, however, with the research literature squarely committed to the conceptual framework of game theory, tacit collusion is associated with a particular class of equilibria in supergames, while other forms of oligopolistic behavior have their own and distinct representations.[24] Mergers might, for example, be analyzed in the context of a Cournot or a Bertrand oligopoly, an address or a

23. Guidelines, section 3.4.

24. See Friedman (1977); Porter (1983); Green and Porter (1984); and Abreu, Pearce, and Stacchetti (1986) for highlights in the evolution of the association between tacit collusion and supergame equilibria.

symmetric model of monopolistic competition, a dominant firm model (which is separately evoked in the guidelines under the "leading firm proviso"), or a "carrot and stick" equilibrium of a repeated game with or without complete information.[25]

Fine-Tuning and Clarifying Competitive Effects

From this perspective, ignoring the general language of the 1984 guidelines and focusing on collusion as the only competitive effect of concern leads to a confining and confusing framework for merger analysis. When analysts or merger proponents are led by the language of the guidelines to focus their attention on collusion in the specific meaning that the term has taken on today, they are likely to overlook possible other competitive impacts of a merger that might be of equal or greater concern in the applicable circumstances. Moreover, some of the guidelines' "other factors" are not relevant to the analysis of competitive effects apart from collusion, and, obversely, some extant or additional "other factors" acquire new and particular importance in the analysis of particular competitive effects apart from collusion. Thus I believe it is a worthwhile challenge to attempt to glean from IO theory an elaboration of horizontal mergers' competitive effects that might be of concern and to link them to relevant patterns of fact and "other factors."

It may be useful as a matter of terminology to divide theories of possible anticompetitive effects of mergers into two categories: unilateral effects and coordinated effects. Unilateral effects are changes in the actions of the merging firms that would be profitable for them as a result of the merger if the nonparties did not alter their actions or if the nonparties reacted unilaterally themselves. Coordinated effects are changes in the actions of the merging firms that would be profitable for them as a result of the merger only if the changes are accompanied by alterations in the actions of the nonparties that are motivated in part by fears of reprisals. The leading example of coordinated effects is the elevation of prices charged by the merging firms, along with those charged by the nonparties,

25. See Shapiro (1989) or Tirole (1988) for surveys of theories of oligopoly, and Eaton and Lipsey (1989) for a survey of work on monopolistic competition and other market forms with product differentiation.

where the merger enables tacit collusion to become stable. Here, the price increases are profitable because deviation by a firm would likely trigger retaliatory price decreases. A unilateral effect would arise, in contrast, when a merger between sellers of close substitutes impels them to raise prices profitably whether or not rivals in fact follow. In essence, unilateral effects are those that arise when all market participants undertake unilateral actions, whereas coordinated effects arise from the anticipation of coordinated actions and reactions.[26]

It is the class of coordinated competitive effects on which most of the explicit language of the 1984 guidelines focuses, and these effects remain as important concerns in merger analysis. The guidelines' treatment of such effects and the associated "other factors" is largely consistent with current economic thought on the subject.[27] Since it is the class of unilateral competitive effects that is neglected in the language of the 1984 guidelines, it is here that I next place my attention. Although many variants could usefully be analyzed, two stand out as most fundamental. The next section discusses unilateral effects in the context of Cournot oligopoly models of a homogeneous product industry, and the subsequent section focuses on Bertrand oligopoly models of industries with differentiated products. Then the paper turns to a discussion of the treatment of entry in merger analysis.

Cournot Models of Homogeneous Product Industries

For a century and a half, much of the economics profession's intuition about the connection between market power and concentration has been shaped by Cournot models of oligopoly in homogeneous product industries.[28] Here, as in equation (3) above, equilibrium margins between prices and marginal costs are a decreasing function of the number of

26. Unilateral effects can be represented in a static model, in the repeated stage-game equilibrium of a supergame, or in a supergame where information problems make it impossible for equilibrium strategies to condition current actions on past ones. Coordinated effects can be represented in Nash equilibria of supergames when equilibrium strategies call for actions to depend on the histories of action profiles.

27. See Scherer (1980) for a classic exposition; and Jacquemin and Slade (1989, section 2) and Tirole (1988) for recent surveys.

28. See Shapiro (1989) and Tirole (1988) for background surveys.

symmetric firms in the industry and an increasing function of each firm's market share. It is straightforward to show that in a Cournot model with symmetric firms, linear demand, and constant returns to scale, the deadweight loss associated with the industry equilibrium, as a fraction of industry sales, is one-half the HHI squared divided by the elasticity of market demand. This evocative result suggests that in the absence of potential competition and efficiency effects, horizontal mergers raise deadweight loss to an extent that increases with the level of concentration and with the change in concentration.

This conventional wisdom was challenged by the demonstration by Salant, Switzer, and Reynolds that in such a model, horizontal mergers without cost savings are unprofitable so long as they are just a bit short of creating a full monopoly.[29] The possible implication was thought to be that socially inefficient mergers are unprofitable, so that voluntary mergers short of monopoly would necessarily be socially efficient.

Subsequent research stimulated by this challenge suggests otherwise and points to different important lessons. One is the recognition that applicable models must explicitly analyze mergers in terms of the assets they combine. With this approach, Perry and Porter showed that anticompetitive mergers can be profitable, because the rising marginal cost curves resulting from fixed-asset positions dampen postmerger expansion by the nonparties (that is, by the firms not involved in the merger). It is this expansion by the nonparties having constant marginal costs that renders mergers unprofitable in the Salant, Switzer, and Reynolds treatment.[30]

Most recently, and most elegantly, Farrell and Shapiro showed that in general, absent potential competition, synergies, and learning, asset-based mergers elevate prices in a Cournot setting.[31] They emphasized that such mergers may nonetheless raise welfare inasmuch as they might lead to reallocation of industry output from high- to low-marginal-cost producers. They asserted that the greater the HHI among nonparties, the more opportunity there is for this effect to occur, since the nonparties with relatively large shares have relatively low marginal costs.[32] How-

29. Salant, Switzer, and Reynolds (1983).
30. Perry and Porter (1985); and Salant, Switzer, and Reynolds (1983).
31. Farrell and Shapiro (1990a, 1990b).
32. See Werden (1990) for a contrary interpretation.

ever, examples indicate that no observable condition has yet been identified that reveals whether the bigger nonparties are likely to be the ones to accomplish the greater postmerger output expansion; that is, whether output reallocation is likely to be a beneficial side-effect of an otherwise inefficient merger.

I now proceed to introduce a somewhat novel framework that proves powerful for the analysis of the effects of a horizontal merger in a Cournot context. The framework constructs the aggregate best-response function of the nonparties. This is the total output the nonparties would offer, X, as a function $N(Y)$ of the total output of the parties, Y. Similarly, the aggregate best-response function of the parties, before the merger, is $B(X)$. The best-response function of the merged firm is denoted $A(X)$.[33] The premerger Cournot equilibrium is characterized by X, Y such that $B(X) = Y$ and $N(Y) = X$. The postmerger equilibrium is characterized by X' and Y' such that $A(X') = Y'$ and $N(Y') = X'$. These characterizations are well defined since the second-order conditions and the standard stability conditions imply that the best-response functions are all decreasing.[34]

It generally holds, in the absence of cost savings from the merger, that $B(X) > A(X)$; that is, the merger impels the parties to suppress output, for any given output of the nonparties.[35] If it were the case that

33. The best response functions are built up in the following fashion: Let firms 1 and 2 be the parties to the merger, firms 3, . . . , $n=m+2$ be the m nonparties, q_i be the output of firm i, $C_i(q_i)$ be the cost function of firm i, $X=q_3+ \ldots +q_n$, $Y=q_1+q_2$, and $P(X+Y)$ be the industry inverse demand function. The best response of firm i maximizes $q_iP(X+Y)-C_i(q_i)$ with respect to q_i, holding fixed other firms' output levels. The corresponding first-order condition is $q_iP'(\Sigma q_j)+P(\Sigma q_j)-C'_i(q_i)=0$. Taking $q_1+q_2=Y$ as parametric, there are m such equations for the nonparties, permitting their solution for q_3, ... ,q_n as functions of Y. The sum of these m functions yields $X=N(Y)$. Similarly, there are two such equations for the parties, taking $q_3+ \ldots +q_n = X$ as parametric, permitting their solutions for q_1 and q_2 as functions of X. The sum of these two functions yields $Y=B(X)$.

After the merger, $N(Y)$ is still applicable, but the situation for the parties is different. Now the merged firm chooses q_1 and q_2 to maximize $(q_1+q_2)P(X+Y)-C_1(q_1)-C_2(q_2)$, taking X as parametric, where q_1 and q_2 are the amounts to be produced with the parties' premerger technologies, on the assumption of no efficiencies from the merger. The choices of q_1 and q_2, as functions of X, are added to yield $Y=A(X)$.

34. See Dixit (1982) for an elegant and detailed development of the relationships among second-order conditions, stability conditions, and the slopes of best-response functions. See Shapiro (1989) for a survey treatment.

35. This can be shown by an adaptation of the proof in Farrell and Shapiro (1990a, 1990b) that, without synergies and learning, mergers in Cournot settings raise price.

Figure 1. Merger Suppresses Total Output

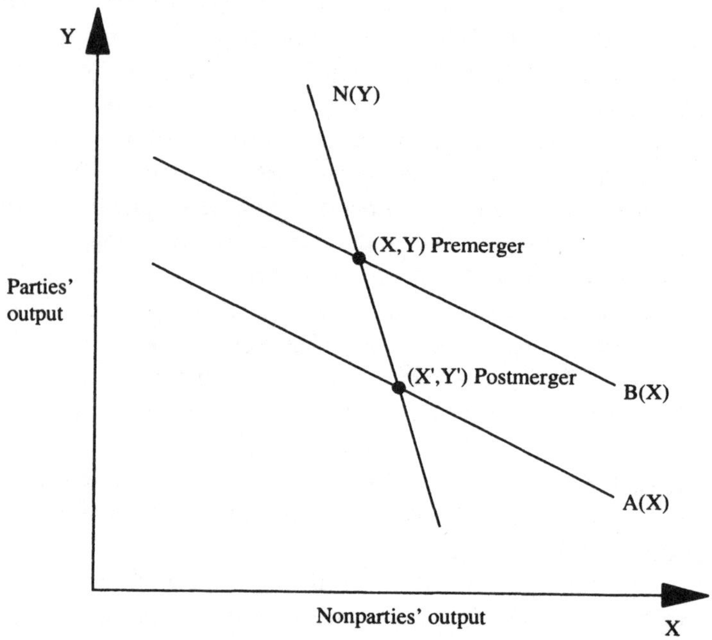

$dN(Y)/dY = -1$, the nonparties would react to this suppression of output with an equal-sized total expansion of output, thereby leaving the market price unchanged by the merger, and rendering the merger unprofitable. Outside of special cases, however, $dN(Y)/dY > -1$, and as depicted in figure 1, the postmerger equilibrium as compared to the premerger equilibrium has smaller production by the parties, greater total production by the nonparties, and smaller total output. In the model of costs and capacity utilized by Perry and Porter; Farrell and Shapiro; and Werden, it can be seen that the larger the capacities of the parties, the greater the difference between $A(X)$ and $B(X)$, and hence the larger the rise in market price caused by the merger.[36]

More novel is the result that less concentration among the nonparties corresponds to $dN(Y)/dY$ being closer to -1 in value. In particular, with m symmetric nonparties having marginal costs that are nonde-

36. In this model, market demand is linear, and a firm's cost of producing q is $cq + q^2/k$, where k is its capital stock, or its capacity level.

creasing convex functions of output, raising m while adjusting the level of their marginal cost curves to keep the premerger equilibrium unchanged has the effect of driving $dN(Y)/dY$ monotonically toward -1.[37] Thus for a given shift due to the merger in the parties' best-response curve, the impact on industry output will be less, the more diffusely spread the total output of the nonparties. With the nonparties replacing the output suppressed by the parties, the merger cannot be profitable in the absence of efficiencies, and if it were profitable, it would not harm consumers. Obversely, the more highly concentrated the nonparties, the less likely they are to make up for the output reduction of the parties.[38]

Another significant finding in this framework pertains to the relationship between the shape of a firm's marginal cost function and the slope of its best-response function. Generally, the greater the slope of its marginal cost curve, holding fixed the relevant level of marginal cost, the greater the slope of its best-response function. Thus the flatter the marginal cost curves of the nonparties, the more elastic their output response to the merger will be, and the less the merger will raise price and profitability increase market power for the parties.[39]

37. Continuing the notation of note 33, let $q_i = q$ and $C_i(q_i) = cq_i + f(q_i)$ for $i = 3, \ldots, m+2 = n$, where $f''(\cdot) \geq 0$ and $f'''(\cdot) \geq 0$. The first-order condition for each nonparty is $qP'(X+Y) + P(X+Y) - c - f'(q) = 0$, where $X = mq$. Adding these yields this characterization of $X = N(Y)$: $XP'(X+Y) + mP(X+Y) - mc - mf'(X/m) = 0$. We investigate the impact of m on $dN(Y)/dY$, while varying c with m in order to keep X constant. In this fashion we can uncover the effect of concentration among the nonparties, without altering their total share and the share of the parties as well. The path $c(m)$ along which X is constant has slope $dc/dm = -(\partial X/\partial m^2)/(\partial X/\partial c) = [(P - f' - c)/m] + f''X/m^2 > 0$. Further differentiation of the characterization of $N(Y)$ yields $dX/dY = -[mP'(X+Y) + XP''(X+Y)]/[mP'(X+Y) + XP''(X+Y) + P'(X+Y) - f''(X/m)]$.

Clearly, along the $c(m)$ path that leaves X constant, dX/dY approaches -1 as m grows large. Moreover, differentiation of dX/dY with respect to m, along the $c(m)$ path, shows that this derivative is assured to be negative if $P' + XP''/m \leq 0$. It suffices for this that inverse demand be concave or that the nonparties' residual marginal revenue be decreasing in their output with $m \geq 2$.

In the model specified in note 36, if the capital of each nonparty is inversely proportional to m, then as m rises, DX/DY declines monotonically to a limit greater than -1.

38. Thus, even where nonparty concentration indicates that output rearrangement among them might bring efficiencies, that concentration can signify that a merger is, on net, more likely to diminish social welfare. Werden (1990) reaches the same conclusion.

39. Let $C_i(q_i) = cq_i + \alpha f(q_i)$, where $f'(\cdot) > 0$ and $f''(\cdot) > 0$. The first-order condition characterizing the best response function of firm i is $q_iP'(q_i + Z) + P(q_i + Z) - c - \alpha f'(q_i) = 0$, where Z is the total output of all other firms in the market. Here we investigate the impact

The following lessons for merger analysis are suggested by these results. In a Cournot homogeneous-product setting, a merger between firms with significant market shares raises the concern that they will find it profitable to suppress their output. This incentive arises because their combined postmerger base of capacity and output makes the consequent rise in price applied to the bigger base outweigh the lost markup on the suppressed sales. There may be offsetting efficiency gains from expansion by nonparties with large shares, but these are difficult to predict. If the nonparties have unconcentrated shares of sufficient total magnitude, or if nonparties having significant total share can individually expand with little cost penalty, then consumers are likely to be protected by the incentives of the nonparties to expand. In such an instance, the parties are unlikely to find their merger profitable unless it creates synergies or other forms of genuine cost savings, and such efficiencies might be inferred from the voluntary character of the combination. In these circumstances, the merger is likely to be socially beneficial.

Little doubt should remain that Cournot models can provide a productive setting for derivation of rich results concerning unilateral competitive effects of horizontal mergers. A remaining question, however, is the applicability of these models to the analysis of real mergers.[40] At their foundational level, these models are based on a particular view of business behavior—that firms unilaterally decide on their levels of output to be sold and that the level of price is that which clears the market of the total output produced.[41] This view of business behavior

of varying α, which parameterizes the slope of the firm's marginal cost curve, along the path $c(\alpha)$ that leaves $c+\alpha f'(q_i)$ unchanged, and hence $q_i(Z)$ unchanged. The slope of the best-response function is $dq/dZ = -(P' + q_iP'')/[2P' + q_iP'' - \alpha f''(q_i)]$. The derivative of this slope is positive with respect to α, along $c(\alpha)$, provided that $q_iP'' + P' < 0$, which follows from a declining market marginal revenue curve and $q^i \leq Z$.

40. See the debate in this volume among Franklin Fisher and his discussants and commentators.

41. An important advance by Kreps and Scheinkman showed that the Cournot model could apply to a different scenario where symmetric firms first unilaterally commit to their levels of capacity, and, subsequently, compete with each other by setting prices. However, recent work by Deneckere and Kovenock (1989) shows that simultaneous capacity investment decisions followed by a second-stage pricing game do not necessarily lead to Cournot outcomes when the firms have significantly different levels of variable cost. In addition, Herk (1990) explores the variety of results that can be obtained from such games as the

may very well be a sufficiently apt description of unilateral conduct in markets for commodity products where production capacity and production runs play important roles. However, there is little reason to believe that Cournot models are sufficiently descriptive when firms have direct control over the pricing of their proprietary differentiated products and when production levels can be readily adjusted in response to demand. For such circumstances, the Bertrand models discussed in the next section are far more appropriate.

Differentiated Product Bertrand Models

Differentiated product Bertrand models describe firms' unilateral incentives to set prices for their proprietary products. Here it is clear that in the absence of potential competition and efficiencies, horizontal mergers between sellers of substitutes create incentives for price elevation by the parties, and that rival nonparties have incentives to raise their prices in response. This was shown in a rather general setting by Davidson and Deneckere.[42]

The articulation is that, premerger, firms set price to balance the added revenue on inframarginal sales against the lost markup on diverted sales. Postmerger, this balance is upset to the extent that a share of the diverted sales would go to a product of the merger partner, so that the lost markup is offset by added net revenue from added sales of that product. Thus, to the first order, the incentive to raise the price of good 1 following a merger with the seller of good 2 is greater the larger the product of the markup on 2 and the derivative of the demand for 2 with respect to the price of 1. This cross-price derivative is meaningfully scaled in relation to the absolute value of the (own-price) derivative of the demand for 1 with respect to the price of 1, to indicate the share of the marginal sales of 1 that would divert to 2. Of course, the obverse holds for the incentive to raise the price of good 2 following the merger.[43]

demand-rationing mechanism is varied. Two-stage capacity games might be further modified to incorporate the anticipated possibility of subsequent mergers.

42. Davidson and Deneckere (1985).

43. These effects can most readily be seen in the context of a linear model of two substitute products. Let the demand for goods 1 and 2 be $Q_1 = a_1 - b_1P_1 + gP_2$ and

Consequently, in principle, a direct way to ascertain whether a merger between sellers of differentiated products raises concern is to estimate the ratios of cross-price and own-price derivatives of demand for the relevant products, in conjunction with the pertinent price-cost margins. The larger in absolute value these ratios, the more the premerger competitive restraints on the pricing of the parties' products arise from the products of the merger partner, and so the more likely (absent other important considerations) the merger is to diminish competition and drive up prices.

There may well be circumstances where data and time permit econometric estimation of the requisite demand system in order to inform enforcement decisionmaking about mergers. There may also be circumstances where business records or other sources of information permit sound inferences to be drawn in a more qualitative fashion about the key concepts of demand.

On the face of it, this perspective appears to remove consideration of market shares from merger analysis since there are no obvious sys-

---

$Q_2 = a_2 - b_2P_2 + gP_1$. Facing constant marginal costs of c_1 and c_2, independent sellers of the two goods would maximize their separate profits in the Bertrand fashion by charging prices that satisfy these first-order conditions:

$$2b_1P_{1o} - gP_{2o} = a_1 + b_1c_1$$
$$-gP_{1o} + 2b_2P_{2o} = a_2 + b_2c_2.$$

After a merger of these sellers, they would set P_1' and P_2' to maximize the total profits derived from these products. These prices would satisfy:

$$2b_1P_1' - 2gP_2' = a_1 + b_1c_1 - gc_2$$
$$-2gP_1' + 2b_2P_2' = a_2 + b_2c_2 - gc_1.$$

While these two systems could be easily solved and their solutions compared, it is more revealing to rearrange them to see that

$$(P_1' - P_{1o}) = g(P_{2o} - c_2)/2b_1 + g(P_2' - P_{2o})/b_1$$
$$(P_2' - P_{2o}) = g(P_{1o} - c_1)/2b_2 + g(P_1' - P_{1o})/b_2.$$

The first of these says that the merger will elevate the price of good 1 according to two effects. One focuses on the initial price-cost margin of good 2, multiplied by the absolute value of the ratio of the cross-price and own-price derivatives of demand for goods 2 and 1. The second effect adds further price elevation to good 1, depending on the elevation in the price of good 2 and the same ratio of demand derivatives. Analogous effects apply to the pricing of good 2.

It should be noted that in a larger demand system, encompassing additional substitute products sold by non-parties, there would be further impetus to elevation of the prices of 1 and 2 arising from unilateral elevations of the nonparties' prices.

tematic relationships among market shares and cross-price derivatives of demand. However, there are rigorously characterized scenarios in which market shares can be accurate indicators of the competitive effect of a merger between producers of differentiated products. In those circumstances, the bigger the market share of 2, the more attractive a product it is, and so the more appealing it is as an alternative to those who buy 1. Thus the bigger the share of 2, the more of the marginal buyers of 1 who would divert to 2 in reaction to a rise in the price of 1. Further, the more attractive 2 is, the lower (in absolute value) its own price elasticity of demand is likely to be, and hence the greater its price-cost margin is likely to be. On both scores, then, the bigger 2's share, the more the merger will drive up the price of 1, and obversely. Moreover, the bigger the shares of other goods in the market, the smaller (in absolute value) their own price elasticities of demand, and thus the greater their price-cost margins. Hence, the greater the welfare loss will be from decreases in their outputs caused by the increases in their prices that are unilaterally profitable responses to the price increases on the merging parties' products.

There are several formal ways to model scenarios of this kind. The value in doing so for present purposes is to carefully expose the substantive content of the underlying assumptions. We shall see that the assumptions are unlikely to be valid in many areas of application where specific information can be developed about product characteristics and about consumer preferences for them. For such applications, merger analysis that focuses exclusively on market shares is likely to go awry. Nonetheless, the models suggest that merger analysis in terms of concentration can be valid in the absence of specific information concerning the detailed structure of products' demand and that market concentration can be a valid benchmark for adjustment in response to incomplete information about demand.

Formally, let U_i be the random utility derived by a particular representative consumer from one unit of good i. The consumer will choose i from the set S if i yields the greatest utility of all options in S.[44] The structure of these random preferences is said to satisfy Luce's Choice Axiom if the ratio of the probabilities that i and j respectively are chosen

44. See Perloff and Salop (1985) for the first model of oligopoly based on such foundations for demand.

from the set of alternatives S is invariant to the membership of S.[45] This implies, but is stronger than, the condition that U_i is uncorrelated with U_j. Luce showed that it is necessary and sufficient that there exist values V_i such that the probability that i is chosen from the set S is equal to $V_i/\sum_S V_j$. Then, s_i, the market share of i out of the universe N, is $V_i/\sum_N V_j$. Consequently, with a large population, the probability that 2 is second best for a consumer choosing 1 is

$$\frac{V_2}{\sum_N V_j - V_1} = \left(\frac{V_2}{\sum_N V_j}\right)\left(\frac{\sum_N V_j}{\sum_N V_j - V_1}\right) = \frac{S_2}{1 - S_i}.$$

Thus for preferences having this strong independence property, the greater the shares of 1 and 2 among the products in the market, the greater the expected number of buyers of 1 who find 2 their favorite alternative to 1.

A convenient demand system built up from such a random utility foundation is the logit.[46] Here, the demand for product i at prices p_j is given by

$$\alpha_i e^{-p_i} / \sum \alpha_j e^{-p_j}$$

This system has the properties that the own-price derivative of demand for product i is $-s_i(1-s_i)$, and the derivative of the demand for j with respect to the price of i is $s_i s_j$.

Then, this demand system has the very features highlighted above.

Products with relatively large shares have relatively small positive own-price elasticities of demand.

For a product j with a relatively large share there is a relatively large absolute value $(s_j/1 - s_i)$ of the ratio of the derivative of its demand with respect to p_i to the derivative of the demand for i with respect to p_i. Consequently, for a market where the structure of demand was well represented by the logit model, or by preferences that satisfy Luce's Choice Axiom, analysis of horizontal mergers would be accurately based on market shares, together with entry and efficiencies and other

45. See Luce (1959).

46. See Anderson and de Palma (1990); and Besanko, Perry, and Spady (1991) for applications of logit demand systems to oligopolies with differentiated products. See McFadden (1973) for the fundamental econometrics of such systems.

pertinent factors. Relatively high shares of the merging parties and relatively high concentration among the nonparties would signify, other things equal, greater reason for concern that the merger would raise the parties' prices and cause significant welfare losses.

It is crucial to recognize that this conclusion rests sensitively on the substance of the assumptions underlying the demand systems. Consider the assumption that a consumer's random preferences for products 1 and 2 are stochastically independent. If products 1 and 2 are close in their endowments of particular salient characteristics, then for those consumers whose U_1 is large, U_2 will be large also, and conversely, so that the random utilities will be positively correlated across consumers. Obversely, if the products are unalike in their salient characteristics, the random utilities will be negatively correlated. Either way, the assumption of stochastic independence would be wrong.

Consider, next, the assumption of Luce's Choice Axiom. Suppose, for example, that product 3 is closer to product 1 than to product 2 in salient characteristics, and that product 4 is closer to product 2 than to product 1. Then the ratio of the probabilities that 1 and 2 will be chosen will be smaller with respect to the set {1, 2, 3} than to the set {1, 2, 4}, thereby contradicting Luce's Axiom.

Finally, consider the possibility that instead of the logit model, a nested logit were the better representation of demand.[47] Then, cross elasticities of demand would depend not only on market shares, as in the logit representation, but also on whether the two products were found to be on the same branch of the tree. Similarly, the relationships between own-price elasticities and market shares would be different for different branches of the tree.

From each of these perspectives, rejection of the strong assumptions on the structure of preferences and demand in a particular market would imply rejection of the foundation for the primary reliance on shares of that market in merger analysis. From each of these perspectives, the reason for the rejection is information that indicates that the products in the market are differentiated by characteristics salient to consumers and that relevant products vary in their similarities to one another in regard to these characteristics. Thus the inferences from market shares

47. See Anderson and de Palma (1990) for developments of oligopoly models in markets with logit and nested logit demand systems.

in this setting are valid only if the products are neither markedly close nor distant from one another in the space of salient characteristics. Otherwise, the products' shares either understate or overstate the expected competitive effects from a merger between their sellers.

It is significant in some settings to recognize that products in a relevant market may have a clustered or local structure to their demand interactions without the salient characteristics being evident to an outside observer. For such instances, the framework of random preferences presented above may be of direct value. For example, where consumers invite in sellers to make bids, the stochastic correlations of the matchups can be investigated. If independence were found, reliance on market shares would be supported, and positive (negative) correlation between the matchups involving merging parties would indicate that the shares understate (overstate) likely competitive effects.

I believe that this is the first rigorous identification of circumstances in which it is appropriate to rely on market shares in the analysis of mergers in differentiated product markets. This finding provides a basis for the use of shares when the associated assumptions fit, and perhaps when there is no better information available on the structure of demands. The analysis here also points to the strong need to develop information beyond shares in markets with differentiated products, particularly the relative proximity of the products of the merging firms in the space of salient characteristics. And finally, the analysis shows that reliance on shares is the benchmark that logically corresponds to the case of stochastic independence of the appeals that different relevant products have across the population of the market's consumers. Hence, information about positive or negative correlation of these degrees of appeal should be considered as grounds for deviation from the benchmark provided by market shares.

Before leaving this subject, an important caution should be emphasized. The above discussion proceeded on the implicit assumption that the pattern of demand relationships and products' characteristics are not subject to endogenous change. Although this may be an accurate assumption in many contexts, in others firms may be readily and quickly able to reposition their products in response to market incentives. As such, there would be little reason for special concern about the effects of a merger between two firms just because their products happened to be close substitutes at the current point in time. If they were to merge and raise their prices, they would be likely to find their rivals repositioning their products in response—in a fashion that would at once protect consumers and render unprofitable a price rise and perhaps an anticompetitive merger itself.

Clarifying Entry Considerations

What a businessperson would call entry appears in the guidelines in two different forms. As already discussed, a firm is termed a *production substituter* if it could enter into supply of a relevant product in response to a SSNIP within one year, without the need to commit significant investment in new facilities. A firm is called an entrant instead of a production substituter if its reponse would take longer than a year, or if its new supply of the relevant product would require significant commitment to new investment. The guidelines hold that production substituters should be considered participants in the relevant market; they should be assigned market shares based on an assessment of what their sales of or capacity for producing the relevant products would be in reaction to a SSNIP; and their market shares should be included in calculations of the market's concentration both before and after the merger.

To see why this is an accurate way to analyze unilateral competitive effects, consider the following two-stage oligopoly game. In the first stage, symmetric firms A, B, and C simultanteously choose the capacities of the stamping machines in which they will be irreversibly investing. In the second stage, the firms play a pricing game over the sale of the services of the stamping machines (with the institution of efficient rationing). By the results of Kreps-Scheinkman, the equilibrium of the two-stage game has each firm fully utilizing its capacity, which is equal to the level of quantity that would have been the solution to a one-stage Cournot game.[48] The demand for the machines' services is derived from the demand for mailboxes and hubcaps, which can only be produced by the addition of elastically supplied inputs to the stamping machines. Firms A and B wind up producing mailboxes, and firm C produces hubcaps.

48. Kreps and Scheinkman (1983).

An analyst coming upon a merger between A and B might ponder how to treat firm C, since he or she would be focusing on the market for mailboxes, delineated in terms of demand. However, the model makes it clear that the merger fundamentally is between two of the three sellers of services of stamping machines. This correct perspective is equivalent to the perspective suggested by the guidelines: define the relevant product market to be mailboxes and consider firm C a full participant since it is a production substituter from hubcaps to mailboxes.

In this respect, the guidelines' approach defines an insightful analytic path. Here, if one knew that the fundamental competition at stake centered on stamping machine services, one couldn't do better than follow the equivalent procedure suggested by the guidelines. However, if one did not know that to be true, following the guidelines' process would either reveal the equivalent approach, or, on different facts, lead to a different conclusion.

Entrants who must commit to significant new investments are treated differently from production substituters in the guidelines. They are not counted as participants in the market for calculation of concentration either before or after the merger. In order for a firm to be considered a potential entrant under the guidelines, it must be the case that it would be likely to enter in response to a SSNIP that persisted over the course of two years. However, IO theory today rarely considers price a state variable in dynamic settings where investment commitments are under analysis. While contemporaneous prices may influence the anticipated profitability of entry as a result of such factors as incumbents' menu costs, incumbents' reputations in the eyes of buyers, inferences about information that is private to the incumbents, and opportunities for medium- and long-term contracts between buyers and entrants, predictions of postentry prices, which may be unrelated to preentry prices, must also be seen as playing a role. Of course, this role is more important the more significant the sunk costs needed to effect efficient entry.

Rather than focus primarily on price, current IO theory would evaluate entry commitments in response to the competitive effect of concern. This competitive effect could be taken to be a diminution of competition that would cause a SSNIP in the absence of entry. Alternatively, the competitive effect could be the particular one, or several, that emerge as concerns from stages of guidelines' analysis that could precede entry analysis.

Evaluating entry commitments as possibly responding to the competitive effect of concern places the focus on the change in the anticipated profitability of entry caused by the structural change inherent in the merger, rather than on the effects of hypothetical price rises. Then, viewed from the perspective of a typical dynamic IO model of unilateral competitive effects, likely, timely, and sufficient entry would deter anticompetitive mergers, not anticompetitive price rises after a merger. Thus, if potential entry met these criteria of effectiveness, voluntary mergers could be inferred to arise from forces distinct from any increase in market power. One possible inference would be that the competitive environment would not in fact be softened by the merger, and an alternative inference would be that any softening of the competitive environment would be offset by efficiency gains created by the merger. Either way, the conclusion would be that the merger was harmless.

The different treatments of production substitutability and entry could then be encapsulated as follows: Production substituters are in the market pre- and postmerger and should be taken into account as part of the competitive environment in which the merger is occurring. Indeed, should it be the case that there are practically unlimited sources of such potential entry within one year, and without the need for commitment to significant irreversible investment, then inclusion in the market of this group of production substituters would necessarily drive concentration measures into the safe-harbor range.[49] In contrast, entrants who might be induced by the merger to sink significant costs in order to participate in the market may or may not be predicted to bring sufficient new competition to replace the competition otherwise lost as a result of the merger.[50] Here, the likelihood, timeliness, and sufficiency of the induced entry are the critical elements of the analysis.

49. In such circumstances, this method of analysis would reach the same conclusion about the impact of a horizontal merger as would the theory of contestable markets. See Baumol, Panzar, and Willig (1982).

50. From this point of view, there is nothing wrong in the following seeming paradox: findings of the need for entrants to sink significant costs can mean that potential entry is strong enough to allay concerns about a merger, whereas findings of no need to sink costs by a limited group of firms can mean that the resulting supply-side substitution is not strong

Figure 2. Merger without Entry

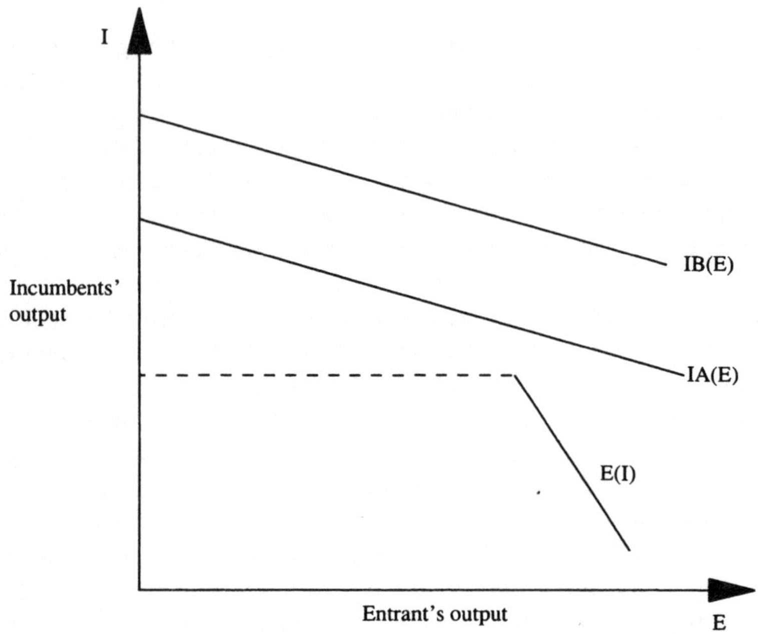

The following example illustrates important facets of the analysis of entry that require significant commitment. Suppose that the interactions among old and new incumbents in the relevant market can be described by a Cournot model. As shown in figures 2 and 3, if entry were to occur with output E, the best responses of the incumbents would total $IB(E)$ before the merger, and the smaller level of output $IA(E)$ after the merger. Entrants' total best response to incumbents' total output of I is given by $E(I)$. Before the merger, market output is $IB(0)$, since the potential entrants are not then participating in the market. If entry were not induced by the merger, postmerger industry output would be $IA(0)$, and price would signficantly rise.

Figure 2 illustrates a case in which entry would not be induced by

enough to alleviate the concerns.

Were the limited group of potential entrants production substituters, their influence on competition would already be reflected in the market price, while if they were instead entrants facing the need to sink costs, their influence on competition would not be present unless induced to commit to the market by the merger.

Figure 3. Merger Induces Entry

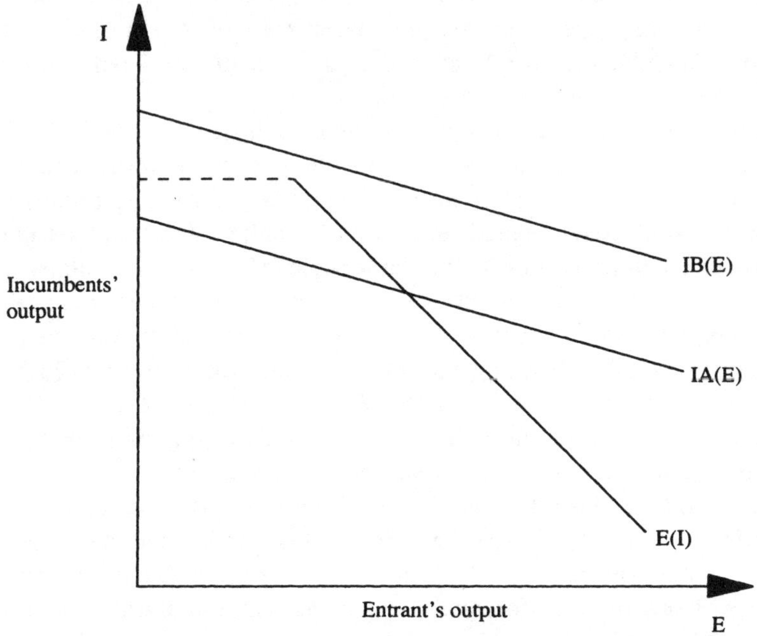

the merger. This can be seen from the lack of an intersection between *IA*(*E*) and the positive region of *E*(*I*). Here, *E*(*I*) cuts discontinuously to 0 where the output of incumbents is too large to leave sufficient room for entrants to sell enough to cover their fixed and sunk costs of set-up.[51] Consequently, the merger would be anticompetitive, and the indicated conclusion would be to challenge it.

In contrast, figure 3 illustrates a case in which merger would induce entry, and the postmerger equilibrium is given by the intersection between *E*(*I*) and *IA*(*E*). Here, as pictured, total industry output has not fallen from the premerger level of *IB*(0), although a portion of this output has been shifted from the incumbents to the entrants. Thus the merger is unlikely to be profitable, unless it brings about efficiencies. The conclusion of this analysis would be that the merger would be

51. More carefully phrased, at this level of incumbent output the residual demand curve available to an entrant lies everywhere below the entrant's average total cost curve. See the survey by Gilbert (1989) for more detail on such constructs and for further references on the subject.

unlikely to raise price and suppress output, as a result of likely entry sufficient to replace the feared diminution of competition. In fact, the analyst would suspect that the merger, in view of its being voluntary, would likely be socially beneficial as a result of efficiencies inferred from the lack of anticompetitive effect.

The difference between figures 2 and 3 lies only in the location of the discontinuous cut to 0 in $E(I)$. In figure 3, the entrants can cover their total costs at a higher level of incumbents' output, because the fixed and sunk costs needed for entry are smaller. This contrast places the focus on entrants' minimum viable scale (MVS)—the smallest scale of output at which an entrant would expect to cover its complete entry and operating costs at current levels of price.[52] As the figures illustrate, the smaller the MVS is for entrants, the more likely there is to be an intersection between $IA(E)$ and the positive portion of $E(I)$, signifying that an otherwise anticompetitive merger would trigger entry that might be sufficient to replace the feared loss in competition.

It should be clear that the facets of the analysis of entry requiring significant commitment that have been illustrated in the above setting apply in other settings as well. Consider, for example, a merger between sellers of substitute differentiated products with unilateral competitive effects of concern. Here, absent efficiencies and entry possibilities, the parties will find it profitable to raise their prices as a result of the merger, and the nonparties are likely to raise their prices as well. The issue then becomes whether this softened competitive environment will be sufficiently attractive to induce entry commitments that would have been unprofitable without the merger. The added inducement to entry is that postmerger incumbents' prices will be higher for any given set of offerings by entrants than they would have been without the merger, thereby presenting entrants with more demand for their substitute products. This enriching of the opportunities available to entrants is more likely to swing to positive their anticipated profits the smaller their MVS and the smaller the required amount of sunk cost that entry places at risk.

In general, when entry does require a commitment of significant sunk costs, the smaller the MVS, and the smaller the necessary sunk costs associated with that scale of entry, the more likely entry is to either

52. See Salop (1986) for the original explanation of this concept.

cure a loss of competition or to give comfort that the merger must not be anticompetitive even in the absence of actual entry. Without attempting a complete list, it is clear that the less important scale economies are, the more flexible production is; and the less important commitment to advertising expenditures is and the more fungible production facilities are, the smaller the MVS and the accompanying sunk costs are likely to be.

These considerations do not obviate analysis of other possible impediments to entry. The longer it would take for entry to be effectively accomplished, regardless of its ultimate profitability, the longer the time would be that the parties to an anticompetitive merger could profit before experiencing the negative impact of the entrants' arrival in the market; the longer consumers would be vulnerable to elevated prices; and the less likely potential entry would deter an anticompetitive merger. For potential entrants to be able to respond to a merger's diminishing of competition, they must have the necessary inputs and technology available to them on terms that make their average costs comparable to prevailing market prices, and they must not face daunting legal impediments.

Thus, in any setting, gauging the power of potential competition to replace competition lost as a result of merger requires a multifaceted assessment of various factors. There can be no doubt of the value of a coherent framework drawn from IO theory to suggest the relevant factors, organize them, and determine their relative importance. Ideally, the consideration of potential competition and competitive effects would be closely linked in a common scenario, so that the analysis could focus on the key question of whether timely entry would be likely to replace the loss of competition that is of concern.

Conclusion

It is easy to assert that further research would be productive in generating more understanding of the competitive effects of horizontal mergers and which observable factors should play roles in their assessment. Perhaps the least explored, and one of the more important, areas for such research is the possible impact of horizontal mergers on competition for innovation. While there is a copious literature on connections between concentration and research and development, little of it has taken the asset-based approach that is now understood to be necessary for the meaningful theoretical study of mergers.[53] Yet it is a commonplace in today's economy that innovation is an important battleground for competition, and it seems evident that market power and efficiencies based on asset holdings play significant roles in shaping its contours and vigor. It would not be surprising to find that merger enforcement policy articulated in a discussion of its impacts on prices and static deadweight loss does in fact work to preserve competition in innovation at the same time. Whether or not this is the case and what additional analytic steps might be warranted from this perspective are questions that press for further research.

It is even easier to assert that more empirical work would be of great benefit to bolster an understanding of the mapping between observables and industry performance and to test theories of how to assess the impacts of mergers.[54] Nevertheless, even while calling for more pertinent research, I am pleased to assert that a great deal is already known that is of real benefit to the task of assessing the effects of horizontal mergers.

The 1984 guidelines reflect much of that knowledge and are well connected to IO theory. Fine-tuning and clarification can deepen and enrich those connections and strengthen the guidelines as a forensically useful framework for merger analysis.

53. See Ordover and Willig (1985) for a modest start down this path.

54. See Bresnahan (1989) and Schmalensee (1989) for surveys of the empirical literature dealing with industry market power and structure and performance. See Kessides (1986) and Hurdle and others (1989) for excellent recent empirical studies of the causes and effects of potential competition. There are very few empirical studies of the effects of mergers. See Barton and Sherman (1984); Werden, Joskow, and Johnson (1991); and Schumann, Rogers, and Reitzes (1990).

References

Abreu, Dilip, David Pearce, and Ennio Stacchetti. 1986. "Optimal Cartel Equilibria with Imperfect Monitoring." *Journal of Economic Theory* 39 (June):251–69.

Anderson, Simon P., and Andre de Palma. 1990. "The Logit as a Model of Product Differentiation: Further Results and Extensions." Discussion Paper 913. Northwestern University.

Barton, David M., and Roger Sherman. 1984. "The Price and Profit Effects of Horizontal Mergers: A Case Study." *Journal of Industrial Economics* 33 (December):165–77.

Baumol, William J., John C. Panzar, and Robert T. Willig. 1982. *Contestable Markets and the Theory of Industry Structure*. Harcourt Brace Jovanovich.

Besanko, D., M. K. Perry, and R. H. Spady. 1991. "The Logit Model of Monopolistic Competition." *Journal of Industrial Economics*, forthcoming.

Boyer, Kenneth D. 1979. "Industry Boundaries." In *Economic Analysis and Antitrust Law*, edited by Terry Calvane and John Siegfried. Little, Brown and Co.

Bresnahan, Timothy F. 1989. "Empirical Studies of Industries with Market Power." In *Handbook of Industrial Organization*, edited by Richard Schmalensee and Robert D. Willig. 2 vols. Amsterdam and New York: North-Holland.

Cowling, Keith, and Michael Waterson. 1976. "Price-Cost Margins and Market Structure." *Economica* 43 (August):267–74.

Dansby, Robert E., and Robert D. Willig. 1979. "Industry Performance Gradient Indices." *American Economic Review* 69 (June):249–60.

Deneckere, Raymond, and Carl Davidson. 1985. "Incentives to Form Coalitions with Bertrand Competition." *Rand Journal of Economics* 16 (Winter):473–86.

Deneckere, Raymond J., and Dan Kovenock. 1989. "Capacity-Constrained Price Competition When Unit Costs Differ." CMSEMS Discussion Paper 861. Northwestern University.

Eaton, B. Curtis, and Richard G. Lipsey. 1989. "Product Differentiation." In *Handbook of Industrial Organization*, edited by Richard Schmalensee and Robert D. Willig. 2 vols. Amsterdam and New York: North-Holland.

Farrell, Joseph, and Carl Shapiro. 1990a. "Horizontal Mergers: An Equilibrium Analysis." *American Economic Review* 80 (March):107–26.

———. 1990b. "Asset Ownership and Market Structure in Oligopoly." *Rand Journal of Economics* 21 (Summer):275–92.

Friedman, James W. 1977. *Oligopoly and the Theory of Games*. Amsterdam: North-Holland.

Gilbert, Richard. 1989. "Mobility Barriers and the Value of Incumbency." In *Handbook of Industrial Organization*, edited by Richard Schmalensee and Robert D. Willig. 2 vols. Amsterdam and New York: North-Holland.

Green, Edward J., and Robert H. Porter. 1984. "Non-Cooperative Collusion under Imperfect Price Information." *Econometrica* 52 (January):87–100.

Herk, Leonard F. 1990. "Consumer Self-Selection and the Cournot Solution in a Duopoly Model of Capacity and Price Competition." Mimeo, Johns Hopkins University.

Hurdle, Gloria J., and others. 1989. "Concentration, Potential Entry, and Performance in the Airline Industry." *Journal of Industrial Economics* 38 (December):119–39.

Jacquemin, Alexis, and Margaret E. Slade. 1989. "Cartels, Collusion, and Horizontal Merger." In *Handbook of Industrial Organization*, edited by Richard Schmalensee and Robert D. Willig. Amsterdam and New York: North-Holland.

Kessides, Ioannis N. 1986. "Advertising, Sunk Costs, and Barriers to Entry." *Review of Economics and Statistics* 68 (February):84–95.

Kreps, David M., and Jose A. Scheinkman. 1983. "Cournot Precommitment and Bertrand Competition Yield Cournot Outcomes." *Bell Journal of Economics* 14 (Autumn):326–37.

Luce, R. Duncan. 1959. *Individual Choice Behavior: Theoretical Analysis*. John Wiley and Sons.

McFadden, Daniel. 1973. "Conditional Logit Analysis of Qualitative Choice Behavior." In *Frontiers in Econometrics*, edited by Paul Zarembka. Academic Press.

Ordover, Janusz A., A. Sykes, and Robert D. Willig. 1982. "Herfindahl Concentration, Rivalry and Mergers." *Harvard Law Review* 95 (June):1857.

———. 1985. "Antitrust for High-Technology Industries: Assessing Research Joint Ventures and Mergers." *Journal of Law and Economics* (May):311–33.

Perloff, Jeffrey, and Steven C. Salop. 1985. "Equilibrium with Product Differentiation." *Review of Economic Studies* 52 (January):107–20.

Perry, Martin K., and Robert H. Porter. 1985. "Oligopoly and the Incentive for Horizontal Merger." *American Economic Review* 75 (March):219–27.

Porter, Robert H. 1983. "Optimal Cartel Trigger Price Strategies." *Journal of Economic Theory* 29 (April):313–38.

Rill, James F. 1990a. "Merger Enforcement at the Department of Justice." Paper presented before the American Bar Association (March).

———. 1990b. "Antitrust Enforcement at the Department of Justice." New England Antitrust Conference (November).

Salant, Steven, Sheldon Switzer, and Robert J. Reynolds. 1983. "Losses from Horizontal Merger: The Effects of an Exogenous Change in Industry Structure on Cournot-Nash Equilibrium." *Quarterly Journal of Economics* 48 (May):185–99.

———. 1986. "Measuring Ease of Entry." *Antitrust Bulletin* 31 (Summer):551–70.

Salop, Steven C., and others. 1987. "Symposium on Horizontal Mergers and Antitrust." *Journal of Economic Perspectives* 1 (Fall):3–54.

Scherer, F. M. 1980. *Industrial Market Structure and Economic Performance*, 2d ed. Houghton Mifflin.

Schmalensee, Richard. 1989. "Inter-Industry Studies of Structure and Performance." In *Handbook of Industrial Organization*, edited by Richard Schmalensee and Robert D. Willig. 2 vols. Amsterdam and New York: North-Holland.

Schumann, L., R. Rogers, and J. Reitzes. 1990. "Case Studies of the Price Effects of Horizontal Mergers." Paper presented at the meeting of the Southern Economic Association.

Shapiro, Carl. 1989. "Theories of Oligopoly Behavior." In *Handbook of Industrial Organization*, edited by Richard Schmalensee and Robert D. Willig. 2 vols. Amsterdam and New York: North-Holland.

Stigler, George J. 1964. "The Theory of Oligopoly." *Journal of Political Economy* 72 (February):44–61.

Tirole, Jean. 1988. *The Theory of Industrial Organization*. MIT Press.

U.S. Department of Justice. 1984. Merger Guidelines. Reprinted in Commerce Clearinghouse. 1984. *Trade Regulation Reports*. ¶13, 103.

Werden, Gregory J. 1983. "Market Delineation and the Justice Department's Merger Guidelines." *Duke Law Journal* 3 (June):514–79.

———. 1990. "Antitrust Policy toward Horizontal Mergers. A Comment on Farrell and Shapiro." Economic Analysis Group Discussion Paper 90–4 (May 15, 1990). *American Economic Review*, forthcoming.

Werden, Gregory J., Andrew S. Joskow, and Richard L. Johnson. 1991. "The Effects of Mergers on Price and Output: Two Case Studies from the Airline Industry." *Managerial and Decision Economics*, forthcoming.

Williamson, Oliver E. 1983. "Vertical Merger Guidelines: Interpreting the 1982 Reforms." *California Law Review* 71 (March):604–00.

[6]

FOCUSING MARKET DEFINITION:

HOW MUCH SUBSTITUTION IS NECESSARY?

Barry C. Harris and Joseph J. Simons

ABSTRACT

Significant advances have occurred in antitrust analysis over the last five to ten years, but the central inquiry in most merger cases remains one of market definition. This paper attempts to provide a focus for market delineation analysis under both the Department of Justice Merger Guidelines and the case law. The Merger Guidelines define a market as a group of producers for whom a "small but significant and nontransitory" price increase would be profitable. Unfortunately, guidance is not provided for determining the profitability of such price increases. The case law on market definition has a comparable shortcoming. This article attempts to fill the void. Specifically, a formula is presented that can be used to determine the percentage loss in sales necessary to make a given price increase unprofitably, which we term the Critical Loss. Solving for the Critical Loss requires knowledge only of the market price and average variable cost. Having identified the Critical Loss, the analysis can then be focused on the issue of whether

Research in Law and Economics, Volume 12, pages 207–226.

ISBN: 1-55938-008-X

that level of sales is likely to be lost in the face of a price increase, and thus, whether a cartel would be profitable. Examples are presented that show how the Critical Loss concept is used in practice. The significance of the Critical Loss for analyses of entry, fringe expansion and oligopoly coordination is also discussed.

Over the last five to ten years, antitrust merger analysis has undergone significant changes. These changes, which have occurred both at the enforcement agencies and in the courts, have been particularly evident since the publication of the Department of Justice 1982 Merger Guidelines and their revision in 1984 ("Merger Guidelines"). The Guidelines adopted what some commentators consider to be a novel approach to market delineation, defining a market as a group of producers for whom a "small but significant and nontransitory" price increase would be profitable.[1] Although this concept is the principal focus of the analysis described in the Merger Guidelines, the issue of how to determine when such price increases would be profitable is not addressed. The Guidelines have been harshly criticized for this omission, with some critics contending that such an omission makes the Guidelines unworkable in practice.

This omission has a counterpart in the case law. The Supreme Court has enunciated the standard of "reasonable interchangeability" such that two products are in the same market only if they are reasonably interchangeable.[2] Most products are employed in a variety of uses, and often there are substitute products available for only some of those uses. The Court has never told us, however, whether products must be interchangeable in 10 percent of their sales, 50 percent of their sales or 75 percent of their sales to be considered in the same market. The Court has instead turned to seemingly arbitrary and ad hoc line drawing to resolve this issue.

This article suggests a practical approach that narrows the focus of market definition analysis and is applicable to market delineation under both the Merger Guidelines and the reasonable interchangeability standard. Specifically, a formula is presented that enables the analyst to determine the percentage loss in sales necessary to make a given price increase unprofitable, which we have called the Critical Loss. Solution of the formula requires that the analyst know only the contribution margin facing firms in a provisional market. The contribution margin in turn depends only on the market price and average variable cost, data typically employed by companies in the normal course of business. Having used the formula to determine Critical Loss, the analysis can then focus on ascertaining whether the level of sales is likely to be lost in the face of a given price increase.

Without first focusing on the Critical Loss calculation, the Guidelines analysis would still contain much of the arbitrariness that characterizes the reasonable interchangeability standard. Applying the calculation of the Critical Loss to actual market conditions permits a melding of the Guidelines' approach and that of reasonable interchangeability. A finding that sales in excess of the Critical Loss would be lost demonstrates that the provisional market is not an appropriate antitrust market under the Guidelines and arguably that there are reasonably interchangeable substitutes.

The remainder of this article is organized into four sections. Section I describes the market definition analysis contained in the Merger Guidelines and discusses some of the criticisms of that approach. Section II describes our suggested approach, including the formula for determining the loss in sales necessary to make a price increase unprofitable. Section III discusses some of the implications of the proposed formula for merger analysis generally. Conclusions are presented in Section IV.

I. MARKET DEFINITION UNDER THE MERGER GUIDELINES

The unifying theme of the Merger Guidelines is that mergers should not be permitted to create or enhance market power or facilitate its exercise.[3] It is for this purpose that the Guidelines' theory of market definition is directed. The Guidelines define a market for purposes of analyzing mergers as:

> a product or group of products and a geographic area in which it is sold such that a hypothetical, profit-maximizing firm, not subject to price regulation, that was the only present and future seller of those products in that area would impose a 'small but significant and nontransitory' increase in price above prevailing or likely future levels.[4]

In essence, the Guidelines attempt to define a group of products and a geographic area for which the sellers of those goods (assuming they could coordinate their actions) could profitably raise price above prevailing levels.

The Guidelines state that this definition process will be performed in two steps. First, the Department determines the relevant product market with respect to each of the products of the merging firms. This is done as follows:

> Specifically, the Department will begin with each product (narrowly defined) produced or sold by each merging firm and ask what would happen if a hypothetical monopolist of that product imposed a 'small but significant and nontransitory' increase in price. If the price increase would cause so many buyers to shift to other products that a hypothetical monopolist would not find it profitable to impose such an increase in price, then the Department will add to the product group the product that is the best substitute for the merging firm's product and ask the same question again. This process will continue until a group of products is identified for which

> a hypothetical monopolist could profitably impose a 'small but significant and nontransitory' increase in price.[5]

Next, the Department determines the geographic market for each of the products of these merging firms. This step is almost identical to the one used to identify the product market, except that the effects of the hypothetical price increase are only explored with respect to substitution to producers from other geographic areas.[6]

The Guidelines' method of market definition clearly hinges on a determination of whether hypothesized "small but significant and nontransitory" price increases would be profitable. Many commentators have argued that there is no practical way to make such a determination, and, thus, the Guidelines are nonoperational. For example, Stigler and Sherwin have stated:

> This [Guidelines] market definition has one, wholly decisive defect: it is completely nonoperational. No method of investigation of data is presented and no data, even those produced by coercive process, are specified that will allow the market to be determined empirically.[7]

Other commentators, Harris and Jorde, have argued:

> [T]his construct is simply impracticable. It would require an enormous number of calculations of cross-price elasticities between any given provisional product or geographic market definition and all possible additions to it. There will virtually never be adequate data to make such calculations, and we doubt that the Department has the resources to make the calculations if the data were available.[8]
>
> [T]his highly theoretical, hypothetical approach to market definition is useless when carried into a courtroom. . . . Thus, we fully expect that if the Department does use the Guidelines' approach to market definition in litigation, it will continue to confront profound evidentiary and proof problems stemming from the speculative nature of the hypothetical inquiry.[9]

Some courts have expressed similar skepticism. One court, in choosing not to rely on the Merger Guidelines, concluded that, "a decision based on these Guidelines remains as inexact as the data gathered to make the assessment . . . [T]hese Guidelines are more useful for setting prosecutorial policy than delineating judicial standards."[10]

The Guidelines have been criticized for numerous other reasons that are unrelated to the ability of the enforcement agencies, courts and practitioners to apply them.[11] These other issues are not addressed here. This paper discusses a method of analysis that overcomes perceived difficulties in applying the Guidelines' "highly theoretical, hypothetical approach." In the next section, the data necessary to perform market definition analysis under the Guidelines are discussed and a practical approach is suggested that can be typically be implemented using available data.

II. A SUGGESTED APPROACH

As discussed above, the essence of market definition under the Merger Guidelines is whether "small but significant and nontransitory" price increases would be profitable. The parameters that determine the profitability of such price increases are the demand and cost conditions facing the firm or firms in the provisional market.[12] Specifically, it is necessary to determine the amount of sales that will be lost as a result of the price increase and the effect that this loss in sales, in conjunction with the price increase, will have on the firms' profits. It is then possible to compare the firms' profits before and after the price increase to determine whether increasing price would increase profitability.

The task of performing such an analysis is most easily done in two distinct steps. First, by examining the relationship of marginal or variable cost to price, it is possible to determine, for any given price increase, the percentage loss in sales necessary to make the specified price increase unprofitable. For ease of exposition, this loss of business is termed the Critical Loss. Next, the amount of business that would actually be lost must be determined. This step can be undertaken in several ways, including using substantially the same methods now employed by the courts in determining reasonable interchangeability. Each of these two steps is discussed in turn. The process is then applied to the facts of a recently litigated case, *FTC v. Occidental Petroleum Corporation*.

A. The Critical Loss

This section presents the derivation of a simple formula for determining the Critical Loss. The derivation of the formula is motivated by asking what producers could gain or lose from a price increase.

Typically, a price increase will cause a firm to lose some sales and the revenues associated with those sales. At the same time, the firm experiences increased revenues from the sales that it retains, because these sales are now made at a higher price. The firm also faces decreased costs from the sales it loses because it no longer must bear the incremental costs associated with these sales. To determine whether any given price increase will be profitable, it is necessary to determine whether the additional revenue gained from the price increase and the decreased costs caused by a reduction in sales would be sufficient to outweigh the loss in revenue from the reduction in sales. If the former gains are greater than the latter losses, then the price increase is profitable.

From this simple relationship it is possible to identify the critical percentage reduction in sales that would make a particular price increase unprofitable. In Figure 1, MC represents the marginal cost curve and D the demand curve facing the hypothetical monopolist producing the product being analyzed.[13] It is assumed that the hypothetical monopolist is formed from the consolidation of numerous firms, which were previously in competitive equilibrium. Consequently, the hypothetical monopolist is assumed to inherit a situation where price is initially equal to marginal cost.[14] The initial price and quantity are designated by P_0 and Q_0, respectively. The marginal cost at Q_0 is designated MC_0. The profit earned in this initial situation is denoted Profit_0, and is equal to the firms' revenues (P_0Q_0) minus the total costs incurred in producing Q_0. Total costs are comprised of variable costs and fixed costs. The variable cost term is equal to Q_0 times average variable cost ($Q_0{*}AVC_0$) or equivalently $\sum_{i=1}^{Q_0} MC_i$, which is the sum of all points along the marginal cost curve from one to Q_0. Thus:

$$\begin{aligned}\text{Profit}_0 &= P_0Q_0 - Q_0{*}AVC_0 - \text{Fixed Costs}\\ &= P_0Q_0 - \sum_{i=1}^{Q_0} MC_i - \text{Fixed Costs} \qquad (1)\end{aligned}$$

Figure 2 shows the situation after the imposition of the price increase hypothesized by the Guidelines. The new and increased price is designated by P_1 and the

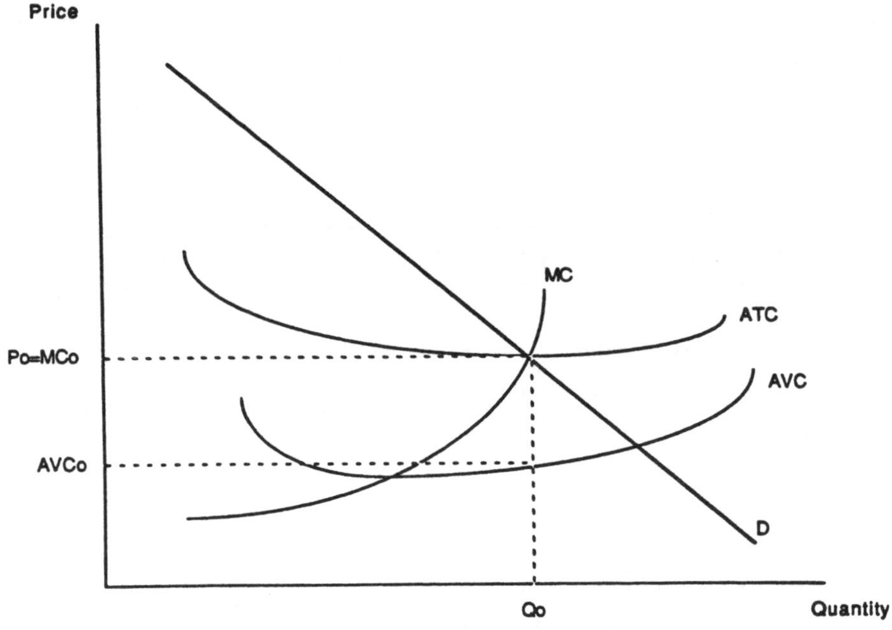

Figure 1.

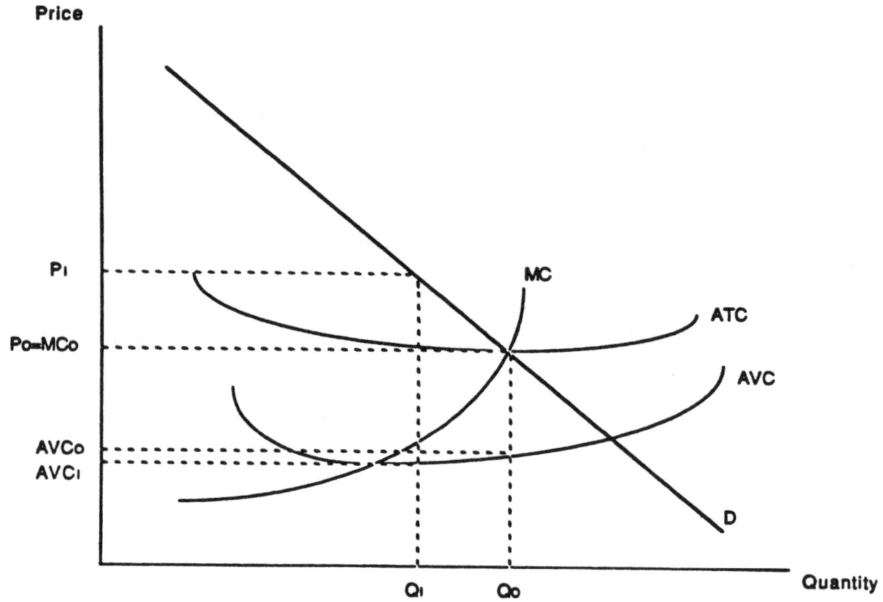

Figure 2.

associated quantity and marginal cost are labeled Q_1 and MC_1, respectively. The resulting profit, labeled Profit_1, is equal to $P_1Q_1 - Q_1{*}AVC_1 -$ Fixed Costs $= P_1Q_1 - \sum_{i=1}^{Q_1} MC_i -$ Fixed Costs, where AVC_1 is the average variable cost of producing Q_1 and $\sum_{i=1}^{Q_1} MC_i$ is the sum of the points along the marginal cost curve from one to Q_1.

The Critical Loss in sales that would make a given price increase unprofitable is the level that makes firms indifferent between market prices P_0 and P_1. Put slightly differently, the Critical Loss is the level that implies that Profit_0 equals Profit_1.

From above, the equality of Profit_0 and Profit_1 implies that:

$$P_0Q_0 - \sum_{i=1}^{Q_0} MC_i - \text{Fixed Costs} = P_1Q_1 - \sum_{i=1}^{Q_1} MC_i - \text{Fixed Costs} \quad (2)$$

By definition:

$$P_1 = P_0(1 + Y) \text{ and} \quad (3)$$

$$Q_1 = Q_0(1 - X) \quad (4)$$

where Y denotes the hypothesized proportionate price increase which is defined as $Y = (P_1 - P_0)/P_0$ (i.e., for a 5 percent price increase, $Y = .05$) and X equals the proportionate reduction in Q that would occur in response to such a price increase (e.g., if a 10 percent loss in sales would occur as a result of the price increase then $X = 0.10$).[15] Q_1 represents the number of customers that are retained in the face of the price increase and is merely Q_0 minus the number of customers lost due to the price increase. Substituting Eqs. (3) and (4) into (2) yields:

$$P_0Q_0 - \sum_{i=1}^{Q_0} MC_i - \text{Fixed Costs} = P_0(1 + Y)\,Q_0(1 - X) - \sum_{i=1}^{Q_1} MC_i - \text{Fixed Costs} \qquad (5)$$

which, after collecting terms, yields:

$$X = \frac{Y}{1 + Y} + \frac{\sum_{i=1}^{Q_0} MC_i - \sum_{i=1}^{Q_1} MC_i}{P_0Q_0(1 + Y)} \qquad (6)$$

Using this equation, as written, to calculate X might require significant amounts of marginal cost data, and would thus be of little practical use. The summation of the two marginal cost terms yields the total variable cost of producing Q_0 and Q_1 respectively. The difference between these two terms is also equal to the difference between the variable costs of producing Q_0 and Q_1, since the same fixed costs are incurred whether Q_0 or Q_1 is produced.[16] Thus, we can rewrite Eq. (6) in terms of average variable cost. By definition:

$$\sum_{i=1}^{Q_0} MC_i = AVC_0 * Q_0 \text{ and} \qquad (7)$$

$$\sum_{i=1}^{Q_1} MC_i = AVC_1 * Q_1 = AVC_1 * Q_0(1 - X) \qquad (8)$$

Substituting Eqs. (7) and (8) into Eq. (6) yields:

$$X = \frac{Y}{1 + Y} + \frac{AVC_0Q_0 - AVC_1Q_0(1 - X)}{P_0Q_0(1 + Y)} \qquad (9)$$

which, after collecting terms, yields:

$$X = (YP_0 + AVC_0 - AVC_1)/(P_0 + YP_0 - AVC_1) \qquad (10)$$

With one exception, the values of the variables in Eq. (10) are usually identifiable from existing business data; Y is identified from the percentage price increase hypothesized and P_0 is merely the currently prevailing market price. There may be difficulty, however, with respect to AVC_1. Most companies maintain data in the normal course of business that allow the calculation of AVC at the current level of production (i.e., AVC_0). These data may not be appropriate for calculation of AVC at the lower quantity associated with the higher price (i.e., AVC_1). When a good estimate of AVC_1 is not available, the Critical Loss can be estimated by assuming that $AVC_0 = AVC_1$.[17] Recalculating Eq. (10) under this assumption yields:

$$X = YP_0/(P_0 + YP_0 - AVC_0) \qquad (11)$$

Dividing the right side of Eq. (11) by P_0/P_0 yields

$$X = Y \div (P_0/P_0 + Y - AVC_0/P_0)$$
$$= Y \div [Y + (P_0 - AVC_0)/P_0] \quad (12)$$

Defining $(P_0 - AVC_0)/P_0$ as the contribution margin (denoted as CM), Eq. (12) can be rewritten as: $X = Y/(Y + CM)$, which when stated in percentage terms, becomes

$$X = [Y/(Y + CM)]*100 \quad (13)$$

The only variable needed to solve for the Critical Loss is the contribution margin, which only depends upon the current price and the current average variable cost.

An example may help to illustrate the use of this formula. Suppose that Alcoa were purchasing the aluminum manufacturing assets of Kaiser, that the only product that the companies have in common is aluminum ingot, that each company has only one plant, and that these plants are adjacent to each other. Also assume that the price of one bar of aluminum ingot is $100 and that the average variable cost for each company is $50 at current levels of output.

Under this example, a Guidelines analysis would first test to see if the plants of the merging firms constitute a market. If the hypothesized ''small but significant and nontransitory'' price increase is defined to be 5 percent, then $Y = 0.05$. Using Eq. (13):

$$X = [Y/(Y + CM)]*100$$
$$= 0.05/(0.05 + 0.5)*100$$
$$= 9.1$$

Thus, the Critical Loss equals 9.1 percent. That is, if the combined firm of Alcoa and Kaiser would lose 9.1 percent or more of its current sales as a result of the price increase, then the two firms alone would not constitute a market and more firms or products would have to be included. If the combined Alcoa and Kaiser would lose less than 9.1 percent of sales as a result of the price increase, then the two firms would constitute a relevant market under the Guidelines. Having calculated the Critical Loss for this merger, it is then necessary to determine whether that number of customers would actually be lost. The following section contains a discussion of methods used to make this determination.

This example illustrates that the determination of the Critical Loss depends on the costs and prices facing producers in the provisional market. Table 1 provides calculations of the Critical Loss associated with hypothesized price increases ranging from 5 to 25 percent and contribution margins ranging from 0 to 100 percent. For example, Table 1 shows that for a hypothesized price increase of five percent, the Critical Loss ranges considerably, including values from 5.3 percent for firms with a 90 percent contribution margin to 33.3 percent for firms with a 10 percent contribution margin. This relationship reflects the greater reduction in profit caused by the loss of higher margin sales. Table 1 also

Table 1. **Critical Loss in Sales Associated with Different Price Increases and Different Contribution Margins**

Percentage Contribution Margin	*Percentage Price Increase*				
	5	*10*	*15*	*20*	*25*
0	100.0	100.0	100.0	100.0	100.0
10	33.3	50.0	60.0	66.7	71.4
20	25.0	33.3	42.9	50.0	55.6
30	14.3	25.0	33.3	40.0	45.5
40	11.1	20.0	27.3	33.3	38.5
50	9.1	16.7	23.1	28.6	33.3
60	7.7	14.3	20.0	25.0	29.4
70	6.7	12.5	17.6	22.2	26.3
80	5.9	11.1	15.8	20.0	23.8
90	5.3	10.0	14.3	18.2	21.8
100	4.8	9.1	13.0	16.7	20.0

Source: Eq. (13)

illustrates that the Critical Loss is sensitive to the hypothesized percentage price increase chosen. For example, the Critical Loss for a group of firms with contribution margins of 50 percent is 9.1 percent for a 5 percent price increase. By contrast, the Critical Loss for the same group of firms jumps to 16.7 percent for a 10 percent price increase and to 38.5 percent for a 25 percent price increase.

This sensitivity to the size of the hypothesized price increase is inherent in the Merger Guidelines' market definition test. As Werden has noted, a small increase in price may not be profitable while a larger increase may be profitable.[18] As an example, consider the same hypothetical group of firms with contribution margins of 50 percent. If customers representing 25 percent of the group's sales are the only customers that can switch to alternative products and would do so for slight price increases, then a five percent increase will be unprofitable because the Critical Loss is 9.1 percent and the firms will actually lose 25 percent of sales. If the firms were to raise price by 25 percent, however, the Critical Loss would increase to 38.5 percent. The firm, however, would still only lose 25 percent of sales, making the price increase profitable. Thus, Table 1 provides some insight into the importance of the choice of the benchmark price increase.[19]

Although Eq. (13) is appropriate for calculating the Critical Loss under most circumstances, there are two important instances where adjustments are necessary. One of these occurs when the reduction in the supply of the product at issue allows an increase in the production of other products. For example, a reduction in jet fuel production at an oil refinery previously operating at capacity may allow some increase in the production of other refinery products. When this occurs, the profit reduction due to lost sales is decreased by the amount earned on the increased sale of other products.[20] For a given profit margin, alternative uses of production facilities attenuate the effects of lost sales and thus increase the Critical Loss associated with an hypothesized price increase.

The existence of joint products is a second circumstance requiring an adjustment in the Critical Loss calculation. Joint products occur when two or more products necessarily result from a production process. For example, the production of chlorine necessarily results in the production of approximately equal quantities of caustic soda as well. A decision to reduce the production of one product necessarily implies a reduction in the level of production of the other. The profits lost as a result of a supply reduction is equal to the revenues previously earned on the lost sales by all of the joint products less the cost of the joint production.[21] This implies that the level of the Critical Loss associated with a chlorine product market depends in part on the results of a market analysis for caustic soda.[22] To see this, first consider the situation where caustic soda is known to be sold in a world market and the provisional chlorine geographic market is the United States. A world market for caustic soda implies that a reduction in the U.S. supply of caustic soda will have little effect on the price of caustic soda. That is, the lost profits on the reduced sales of caustic soda are not compensated by a concomitant increase in the price of caustic soda. This implies that a five percent price increase in chlorine will not be profitable unless it compensates for the profits lost when sales of both chlorine and caustic soda are reduced. As a result, the Critical Loss will be relatively small when caustic soda is sold in a world market. By contrast, if caustic soda is sold in a United States market, the reduction in U.S. chlorine production will raise both the price of chlorine and the price of caustic soda. Consequently, the Critical Loss will be higher than when caustic soda is sold in a world market.

B. The Estimated Loss

To estimate the lost sales that would actually occur for a specified group of producers in the face of a hypothesized price increase, it is necessary to know the likely reactions of (1) producers of other products, (2) other producers of the same product, and (3) customers of the same product. These reactions can be summarized in a concept known as the residual demand elasticity.[23] Residual demand refers to the demand facing the firms that constitute a provisional market. The residual demand elasticity refers to the extent to which the sales of those firms will decline as their prices rise. Consequently, there is a critical residual demand elasticity that corresponds to each Critical Loss. These critical elasticities are calculated by dividing the appropriate Critical Loss shown in Table 1 by the assumed increase in price. Values of critical elasticities are reported in Table 2.[24]

Although an econometric technique for estimating the residual demand elastic-

Table 2. Critical Residual Demand Elasticities Associated with Different Price Increases and Different Contribution Margins

Percentage Contribution Margin	*Percentage Price Increase*				
	5	*10*	*15*	*20*	*25*
0	20.0	10.0	6.7	5.0	4.0
10	6.7	5.0	4.0	3.3	2.9
20	5.0	3.3	2.9	2.5	2.2
30	2.9	2.5	2.2	2.0	1.8
40	2.2	2.0	1.8	1.7	1.5
50	1.8	1.7	1.5	1.4	1.3
60	1.5	1.4	1.3	1.2	1.2
70	1.3	1.2	1.2	1.1	1.1
80	1.2	1.1	1.1	1.0	1.0
90	1.1	1.0	1.0	0.9	0.9
100	1.0	0.9	0.9	0.8	0.8

Source: Table 1

ity has been developed recently,[25] it is often impossible to use because data limitations exist. However, the reactions summarized by the residual demand elasticity can be analyzed through other means and, indeed, are typically so examined in litigation and during investigations by the federal enforcement agencies.

Much of the market definition analysis applied in the litigated cases utilizes one or more approaches in an attempt to quantify these reactions. Many of these approaches can be adopted easily for use in determining whether a sales loss in excess of the Critical Loss is likely. For example, by estimating the cost of switching from one product to another, it may be possible to predict the likelihood and extent of switching that would occur if prices actually did rise.[26] If past conditions are indicative of current conditions, examples of switching under previous price changes can be examined. Courts have also considered the uses of a consumer product and have reached conclusions concerning the extent to which other products can fulfill those uses at comparable price/quality levels.[27] The most direct approach, of course, is to consider testimony of people actually confronted with these decisions.[28]

The implementation of each of these approaches, however, has a common flaw. Each lacks a benchmark for determining how much interchangeability is sufficient to put two products or geographic areas in the same market. Courts have often been confronted with instances where some substitution among products or geographic areas is present for some consumers, but not for others. In such cases, courts have often resorted to ad hoc and arbitrary line drawing.[29]

The use of the Critical Loss calculation can provide a benchmark for the reasonable interchangeability standard.

C. *FTV v. Occidental Petroleum Corporation:* An Illustration

A recent acquisition that was challenged by the Federal Trade Commission provides a good opportunity to demonstrate the applicability of the Critical Loss calculation. In *FTC v. Occidental Petroleum Corp.*, the FTC sought to enjoin Occidental from obtaining the polyvinyl chloride resin ("PVC") assets of Tenneco Polymers.[30] The FTC alleged several product markets, including markets for suspension homopolymer PVC resin and dispersion PVC resin. The parties agreed that these products constituted relevant product markets and, consequently, the analyses focused on identifying the relevant geographic markets.

Industry documents were in general agreement concerning the price and variable cost of both suspension homopolymer PVC resin and dispersion PVC resin. The price of suspension homopolymer PVC resin was approximately 25 cents per pound, with a variable cost of approximately 18 cents per pound. The price of dispersion PVC resin was approximately 49 cents per pound, with a variable cost of approximately 27 cents per pound. These prices and costs produce contribution margins of 28 percent for suspension homopolymer PVC resin and 44 percent for dispersion PVC resin. Applying these values to (13) produces Critical Loss estimates of 15 percent for suspension homopolymer PVC resin and 10 percent for dispersion PVC resin when the hypothesized price increase is defined to be 5 percent. These Critical Loss estimates are equivalent to approximately 875 million pounds of suspension homopolymer PVC resin and 45 million pounds of dispersion PVC resin in 1985.

The analysis to determine whether such volumes of foreign-produced PVC resin could profitably be sold in the United States first considered whether PVC resin users would substitute foreign PVC resin. Testimony by customers and business documents produced by Occidental and Tenneco indicated that a sufficient number of customers of both resin types were willing to purchase foreign-produced PVC resin in the event of a price increase by U.S. producers. The analysis next considered the ability of foreign PVC resin producers to supply additional PVC resin to the United States. Foreign producers already supplying the United States were able to supply the additional product from two sources. First, significant excess capacity was present abroad and could be used to produce additional resin. Second, exports to destinations other than the United States could be diverted. The amount of PVC resin from these two sources was shown to be well in excess of the Critical Loss estimates for both suspension homopolymer PVC resin and dispersion PVC resin. The district court's decision and the Critical Loss calculation each indicated that the United States was an inappropriately small geographic market for both types of PVC resin.[31]

This example illustrates that many of the methods currently used in litigation can be utilized to determine if the loss of sales from a price increase will be sufficient to make a price increase unprofitable. For a provisional market, testimony or analysis can focus on relatively homogeneous groups of users of the product to ascertain each group's ability to substitute other producers. Some groups of users may be able to use alternative products and others may be able to use foreign sources. Still others may be unable to do either. If groups of users representing more sales than the Critical Loss are identified as being likely to substitute suppliers outside the provisional market, then the provisional market must be expanded.

III. OTHER IMPLICATIONS FOR MERGER ANALYSIS

As shown above, the relationship between average variable cost and price is significant for market definition. This relationship is also important for analysis of entry, fringe expansion and some of the market characteristics that affect the ability of firms to collude. Its significance for entry and fringe expansion is related to its use in market definition analysis and serves to determine how much entry or fringe expansion is necessary to prevent the exercise of market power. The relationship of average variable cost to price also provides insight into the incentives of a group of firms to establish and maintain a collusive agreement.

A. Entry and Fringe Expansion

The Merger Guidelines recognize that market definition and the associated measurement of concentration are only the starting points of merger analysis and that qualitative factors such as entry and fringe expansion can be of overriding importance. The Guidelines specifically state: "If entry into a market is so easy that existing competitors could not succeed in raising price for any significant period of time, the Department is unlikely to challenge mergers in that market."[32] The Guidelines' analysis of entry differs only in degree from its market definition analysis. Market definition deals with substitution to other products or other producers within one year, while entry involves substitution to new suppliers over two years. The Guidelines consider fringe expansion as a subgroup of entry. As a result, the Guidelines' approach to the analysis of entry and fringe expansion is subject to the same criticisms raised in the analysis of market definition. Consequently, the approach to applying the Guidelines' market definition test suggested in Section II above is also applicable here.

The Critical Loss identifies how much entry or fringe expansion would have to occur in order to frustrate attempts to exercise market power. Some of the methods currently employed in litigated cases and discussed in Section II(B)(2) above can then be used to determine if sufficient entry or expansion is likely to occur.[33] When only some firms are able to enter or provide fringe expansion, the calculation of the Critical Loss is a necessary step in the analysis. If the ability of the entrants and fringe group to expand production is less than the Critical Loss, the non-fringe suppliers will find it profitable to allow entry and fringe expansion and to raise prices to remaining customers.

B. Oligopoly Coordination

The importance of the magnitude of the contribution margin and the related Critical Loss calculation extend beyond issues of market definition to issues of oligopoly coordination. The coordination problem facing every oligopoly is related to the tension between individual incentives and group incentives. On the one hand, each firm's profits can be increased if the group of firms is able to reduce the supply they offer jointly. This reduction in supply will cause prices to rise and ultimately profits to increase. On the other hand, each firm in the group has an incentive to cheat on the group agreement. The firm that cheats on the agreement can increase its profits by lowering its price below that of the group and, as a result, increase its share. Significant cheating will undermine the group agreement to restrict supply and will cause prices to fall toward the competitive level.

The incentive for a firm to cheat is significantly influenced by the size of its contribution margin. The extent of this incentive is influenced by the level of sales that a particular firm can afford to lose before a price increase will prove to be unprofitable. While the form of the calculation is identical to the calculation of Critical Loss used to identify markets, a single firm must also consider any sales that would be lost to other members of the provisional market. That is, each firm must consider the likelihood that other firms in the provisional market will price below the agreed upon level and obtain sales at the expense of firms that adhere to the agreed upon price.

If a firm expects to lose more sales than the Critical Loss associated with its contribution margin, then it will cheat on the price agreement. That is, it will not choose to raise its price by the agreed upon amount. Similarly, a firm will initiate lower price if it expects its offer of lower prices to result in a sufficiently higher level of sales. This implies that, all else being equal, the larger the contribution margin, the greater the incentive of individual firms to cheat on a group agreement. This is true if a firm is an aggressive cheater that wishes to increase its share at the expense of other firms or if it is defensively cheating to avoid loss of shares to other firms.

Three market characteristics that can further affect the ability of an oligopoly to coordinate its behavior are the percentage of total sales accounted for by individual transactions, the similarity of firms' cost structures and the similarity of the demand facing different suppliers. First, consider the well-known concept that large, infrequent transactions can have a significant restraining influence on the ability of sellers to exercise market power.[34] How large and infrequent the sales must be is largely determined by the Critical Loss facing each firm. To see this, consider a market in which each of the sellers has a cost structure such that a 5 percent price increase results in a Critical Loss of 15 percent. If this product is sold through long-term (e.g., one year) agreements and individual buyers account for a high percentage of a firm's sales, then the 15 percent Critical Loss can occur through the loss of only one or two accounts. The lost profits associated with the loss of a small number of accounts makes each firm vulnerable to the effects of cheating, which in turn increases each firm's incentive to cheat. Thus, when per-unit contribution margins are high and the resulting Critical Loss is low, sales need not be as infrequent and in such large quantities to induce cheating as when margins are low and the Critical Loss is high.

Cheating is not the only reason why a group-imposed price increase will cause some firms to lose more sales than are lost by other firms. Firms, while in the same market, may face different demands for their products. For example, product characteristics or the location of plants may cause demand to differ among firms in the market.[35] When demands differ among firms, a given price increase may cause some firms to lose sales greater than their Critical Losses, while other firms may lose sales less than their Critical Losses.[36] Unless individual firms that lose more sales than their Critical Loss are compensated by those firms that do not, the coordination necessary to raise prices will not occur. Such compensation, however, is difficult to bring about under many conditions and may be nearly impossible to achieve without direct discussions among competitors. The magnitude of the destabilizing influence of dissimilar demands facing firms in a market is significantly influenced by differences in both their contribution margins and their resulting Critical Losses.

A similar difficulty faces a group of firms with dissimilar cost structures. Dissimilar cost structures cause each firm to face a different Critical Loss. Thus, a given price increase that causes each supplier to lose the same amount of sales may increase the profits of some suppliers, while decreasing the profits of others. Just as with variation in the demands faced by individual firms, the greater the variation in the cost structures of firms, the more difficult the coordination problem facing the group of firms.

IV. CONCLUSIONS

Despite the significant changes that have occurred in antitrust over the last five to ten years, the central inquiry in most cases is still one of market definition. This paper attempts to provide a focus for market delineation that uses data produced in the normal course of business and that removes an aspect of arbitrariness from market definition analysis under the standards of both the Department of Justice Merger Guidelines and the case law. The formula presented in this article can readily be used to determine the magnitude of a loss of sales that is necessary to make a price increase unprofitable under the Guidelines' market definition test. Similarly, the formula can be used to determine how much interchangeability is reasonable under the standards of case law. The same Critical Loss formula, when applied to individual firms, also provides insight into the difficulties of oligopoly coordination facing firms in a particular market.

ACKNOWLEDGMENTS

Barry C. Harris and Joseph J. Simons are employed at Economists Incorporated and Wachtell, Lipton, Roson, Katz respectively. Formerly both were with the Federal Trade Commission. The views expressed in this paper do not necessarily reflect those of the Federal Trade Commission or any individual Commissioner. The authors would like to thank Jonathan Baker, James Hurdle, Katherine Leupold, Philip Nelson, John Preston, Steven Salop and Robert Skitol for helpful comments.

NOTES

1. 1984 Department of Justice Merger Guidelines § 2.0, reprinted in 2 Trade Reg. Rep. (CCH) ¶ 4491 *et seq.* (1984). The logic of this approach is that such a group of producers, if they are able to coordinate their behavior, have the joint ability and incentive to lessen compensation and raise prices. By contrast, a proper subset of these producers would not have this ability.

2. See, *e.g.*, *United States v. DuPont & Co.*, 351 U.S. 377, 394–95 (1956); *Brown Shoe Co. v. United States*, 370 U.S. 294, 325 (1962); *United States v. Continental Can Co.*, 378 U.S. 441, 449 (1964).

3. Merger Guidelines § 1.

4. *Id.* at § 2.

5. *Id.* at § 2.11. Each group of products for which this iteration is performed is referred to as a "provisional" product market with the exception of the group of products in the last iteration, which is known as the "relevant" product market.

6. *Id.* at § 2.31.

7. G. Stigler and R. Sherwin, "The Extent of the Market," *J. Law and Econ.*, 28, 555, 582 (1985).

8. R. Harris and T. Jorde, "Market Definition in the Merger Guidelines: Implications for Antitrust Enforcement," 71 *Cal. L. Rev. 464*, 481 (1983); See also T. Dunfee, L. Stern and F. Sturdivant, "Bounding Markets in Merger Cases: Identifying Relevant Competitors." 78 *NW U. L. Rev.* 733, 754 (1983).

9. *Id.* at 491.

10. *Monfort of Colorado, Inc. v. Cargill, Inc.*, 761 F. 2d 570, 579 (10th Cir. 1985), *rev'd*, ______ U.S. ______, 107, S. Ct. 484 (Dec. 9, 1986). See also *United States v. Virginia National Bank-Shares, Inc.*, 1982–2 Trade Cas. (CCH ¶ 64,871 (W.D. Va. 1982).

11. See e.g., E. Fox, "The 1982 Merger Guidelines: When Economists Are Kings," 71 *Cal. L. Rev.* 281 (1983) and articles cited therein.

12. The Guidelines ask whether a group of firms taken together would find a price increase profitable. Different firms, however, may have different cost functions or may face different demand elasticities. As a consequence, a price increase that produced profits for the group may nonetheless reduce the profits of some firms in the market. The relevant issue for market definition is whether firms as a group could profitably raise price. The effects of different cost and demand features on

individual firms are factors in determining the likelihood of successful collusion within a market. See Section IIIB below.

13. For purposes of simplification, it is assumed that all firms producing the product have the same cost curve. The relationship between price and marginal costs thus will be the same for every firm, which means that the profitability of a price increase will be the same for each firm.

14. These results do not depend on the market initially being in a competitive equilibrium or any other particular state. The results are generated from a comparison between any initial state and the state that results from a marketwide price increase. Producers in a provisional market typically are not maximizing their joint profits before the imposition of a price increase.

15. The ratio X/Y is the elasticity of demand facing the group of firms in the provisional market.

16. The difference between the two marginal cost summations is equal to $\sum_{i=Q_0}^{Q_1} MC_i$, which represents the additional cost of producing $Q_0 - Q_1$ units.

17. AVC_0 will often provide a good estimate of AVC_1. Many production processes have relatively flat average variable cost curves. Even when this is not the case, AVC_0 may approximate AVC_1. In long-run competitive equilibrium Q_0 is to the right of the minimum point of the AVC curve. A reduction in Q will first lower and then raise the AVC. This change in direction of AVC attenuates any tendency of AVC_0 and AVC_1 to differ. Assuming that AVC_1 equals AVC_0 will cause X to be underestimated by (13) if AVC_1 actually is less than AVC_0. Similarly, X will be overestimated if AVC_1 actually is greater than AVC_0.

18. G. Werden, "Market Delineations and the Justice Department's Merger Guidelines," 1983 *Duke L.J.* 514, 543–545 (1983).

19. Table 1 also shows that there may be situations where a small price increase would be profitable, but a larger one would not. This result occurs when relatively few sales would be lost at a slightly higher price, but a relatively large amount of sales would be lost as prices increase further.

20. George A. Hay and Robert J. Reynolds, "Competition and Antitrust in the Petroleum Industry: An Application of the Merger Guidelines," in *Antitrust and Regulations: Essays in memory of John J. McGowan*, Franklin M. Fisher, ed., 1985.

21. Direct storage or disposal of large amounts of chlorine may be difficult. If chlorine could not be stored in any form, an increase in its price might require a reduction in the amount produced. When storage, disposal or other use of a joint product is economically feasible, it is possible to reduce the supply of one product without reducing overall production. This likely is the case for chlorine because its principal downstream product, EDC, is easily stored or shipped worldwide. Consequently, it would be possible to restrict the supply of chlorine in the United States without also reducing the supply of caustic soda.

22. This point was made by Robert Willig during discussions with one of the authors.

23. See Landes & Posner, "Market Power in Antitrust Cases," 94 *Harv. L. Rev.* 937 (1981).

24. Table 2 demonstrates that, without making strong assumptions about the relationship between price and cost, there is no unique critical elasticity.

25. J. Baker and T. Bresnahan, "The Gains from Merger or Collusion in Product-Differentiated Industries," 33 *Journal of Industrial Economics*, 427 (1985), pp. 427–444. D. Scheffman and P. Spiller, "Geographic Market Definition Under the DOJ Merger Guidelines," 30 *J. Law & Econ.* 123 (1987).

26. *E.g., FTC v. Occidental Petroleum Corp.*, 1986–1 Trade Cases (CCH) ¶ 67, 071 at 62, 512 (D.D.C. 1986) *vacated as moot*, C.A. No. 86–0900 (Oct. 20, 1986); *United States v. Calmar*, 1985–1 Trade Cases (CCH) ¶ 66,588 at 65, 927–28.

27. *United States v. DuPont & Co.*, 351 v.s. 377, 396–404 (1956).

28. There are, of course, numerous other methods, but a detailed accounting is outside the scope of this paper. For a listing of suggested inquiries, see Salop & Simons, "A Practical Guide to Merger Analysis," 29 *Antitrust Bulletin* 663 (1984).

29. The National Association of Attorneys General has issued merger guidelines dictating that a substitute product must be interchangeable for 75 percent of sales in order to be included in the

market. Table 1 indicates that this 75 percent figure is not appropriate for at least two reasons. First, the appropriate figure can vary greatly depending on the costs of the firms involved and the magnitude of the expected price increase. Second, if one number were chosen to apply in all cases, Table 1 suggests it would be significantly lower than 75 percent.

30. 1986–1 Trade Cas. (CCH) ¶ 67,071 (D.D.C. 1986), *vacated as moot*, C.A. No. 86–0900 (October 28, 1986). Both authors were retained by the Occidental Petroleum Corporation in defense of this action.

31. This conclusion depends on the assumption that it is not possible to price discriminate among users of PVC. If price discrimination were possible, those users of PVC that could not economically use foreign alternatives would be offered a higher price. In such a situation, the United States, would be a relevant geographic market.

32. Merger Guidelines § 3.3.

33. It should be noted that merely to conclude that entry or fringe expansion is physically easy is not sufficient. The Guidelines' test is whether entry or expansion *would* occur in response to a "small but significant and nontransitory" price increase. Entry may be physically easy, but not profitable. For example, in depressed industries, prices are often too low to justify new investment. Although all of the factors of production necessary to enter the market can be readily obtained, a new entrant may not be able to recover its investment at existing prices or at the hypothesized higher price. In such a case, entry would not be profitable and thus, would not be expected to occur. A more complete discussion of factors affecting the likelihood of entry is contained in Steven C. Salop, "Measuring Ease of Entry" 31 *Antitrust Bulletin* 551 (1986).

34. For example, see Section 3.42 of the Department of Justice Merger Guidelines.

35. Merger Guidelines §§ 3.411 and 3.413.

36. The group of firms is assumed to lose sales less than it Critical Loss. Otherwise, the group would not constitute a market.

REFERENCES

Articles

Baker, J., and T. Bresnahan, (1985) "The Gains From Merger or Collusion in Product-Differentiated Industries," *The Journal of Industrial Economics*, Vol. 33, pp. 427–444.

Dunfee, T., L. Stern, and F. Sturdivant (1983) "Bounding Markets in Merger Cases: Identifying Relevant Competitors," *Northwest University Law Review*, Vol. 78, pp. 733–773.

Fox, E. (1983) "The 1982 Merger Guidelines: When Economists Are Kings," *California Law Review*, Vol. 71, pp. 281–302.

Harris, R., and T. Jorde. (1983) "Market Definition in the Merger Guidelines: Implications for Antitrust Enforcement," *California Law Review*, Vol. 71, pp. 464–496.

Hay, George A., and Robert J. Reynolds (1985) "Competition and Antitrust in the Petroleum Industry: An Application of the Merger Guidelines," pp. 15–48 in Franklin M. Fisher, ed., *Antitrust and Regulation: Essays in Memory of John J. McGowan*, Cambridge, Massachusetts, The MIT Press.

Landes, William M., and Richard A. Posner, (1981) "Market Power in Antitrust Cases," *Harvard Law Review*, Vol. 94, pp. 937–996.

Salop, Steven C., (1986) "Measuring Ease of Entry," *Antitrust Bulletin*, Vol. 31, pp. 551–570.

Salop, Steven C., and Joseph J. Simons, (1984) "A Practical Guide to Merger Analysis," *Antitrust Bulletin*, Vol. 29, pp. 663–703.

Scheffman, D., and P. Spiller (1987). "Geographic Market Definition Under the DOJ Merger Guidelines," *Journal of Law and Economics*, Vol. 30, pp. 123–147.

Stigler, G., and R. Sherwin. (1985) "The Extent of the Market," *Journal of Law and Economics*, Vol. 28, pp. 555–586.

Werden, G. (1983) "Market Delineations and the Justice Department's Merger Guidelines," *Duke Law Journal*, pp. 514–579.

Regulations

United States Department of Justice Merger Guidelines, Washington, D.C.: U.S. Department of Justice, June 14, 1982. Reprinted in 2 Trade Regulation Reporter ¶¶ 4501–4505. (Commerce Clearing House).

United States Department of Justice Merger Guidelines, Washington, D.C.: U.S. Department of Justice, June 14, 1984. Reprinted in 2 Trade Regulation Reporter ¶¶ 4491–4495 (Commerce Clearing House).

Cases

Brown Shoe Co. v. United States, 370 U.S. 294 (1962).

FTC v. Occidental Petroleum Corp., 1986–1 Trade vs. (CCH) ¶ 67,071 (D.D.C. 1986), *vacated as moot*, C.A. No. 86–0900 (Oct. 28, 1986).

Monfort of Colorado, Inc. v. Cargill, Inc., 761 F. 2d 570 (10th Cir. 1985), rev'd, ______ U.S. ______ 107 St. Ct. 484 (1986).

United States v. Calmar, 1985-1 Trade Cas. (CCH ¶ 66,588 (D.N.J. 1985).

United States v. Continental Can Co., 378 U.S. 441 (1964).

United States v. DuPont & Co., 351 U.S. 337 (1956).

United States v. Virginia National Bank-Shares, Inc. 1982-2 Trade Cas. (CCH) ¶ 64,871 (W.D. Va. 1982).

[7]

International Journal of Industrial Organization 6 (1988) 283–300. North-Holland

ESTIMATING THE RESIDUAL DEMAND CURVE FACING A SINGLE FIRM*

Jonathan B. BAKER

Dartmouth College, Hanover, NH 03755, USA

Timothy F. BRESNAHAN

Stanford University, Stanford, CA 97035-6072, USA

Final version received November 1987

This paper presents an econometric technique for estimating the single firm residual demand curve that does not require the estimation of demand cross-elasticities. The technique is particularly suited for the estimation of firm market power in product differentiated industries, where cross-elasticities are notoriously difficult to measure. One estimated parameter is directly related to a firm's markup of price over marginal cost when product differentiation is extensive, when an industry consists of a dominant firm and a price-taking fringe, when a Consistent Conjectures Equilibrium is the correct oligopoly solution concept, when firms are Stackelberg leaders relative to their environment, or when firms are perfect competitors. The estimates can indicate power over price in other circumstances. An instrumental variables technique is employed, using firm-individuated factor prices to identify firm-specific residual demand. Yet even when instruments are unavailable, the technique produces elasticity estimates biased in the conservative direction of disproving market power. This methodology is applied to estimate the market power of three firms in an industry characterized by product differentiation: brewing. Over our 1962–82 sample period, Pabst and Coors had similar national market shares and each had high shares in several states. Yet Pabst was virtually a price-taker while Coors possessed substantial market power. Anheuser-Busch had market power in the early part of the sample, but little after 1975 when Miller Brewing changed the competitive nature of the industry.

1. Introduction

In industries with differentiated products, the extent of market power is hard to measure quantitatively. Any empirical method for measuring market power must take into account the theoretical insight that firms could interact in a variety of ways, each leading to different industry performance.[1] With

*We would like to thank the Sloan Foundation and the Stanford Workshop on the Economics of Factor Markets for support and the National Science Foundation for financial assistance under Grant no. SES-8111491.

[1]See Landes and Posner (1981) and Ordover, Sykes and Willig (1982) for recent theoretical treatments. Econometric studies quantifying the impact of firm conduct on market power include Rosse (1970), Iwata (1974), Gollop and Roberts (1979), Appelbaum (1979, 1982), Sumner (1981), and Bresnahan (1980, 1981b).

product differentiation, an additional problem for measuring market power arises: substitutability in demand. A firm producing a unique product may have substantial market power, as when no other firm produces a close substitute. But when another firm produces a nearly identical product, the first firm's 'monopoly' may be inconsequential. In an industry with many products, market power inferences therefore seem to require estimates of a great number of own- and cross-elasticities of demand, a project that is often stymied by data limitations. Several authors have attacked this problem by employing observable indicators of substitution closeness, like 'quality' or 'location',[2] to reduce the number of parameters that must be estimated. However, the data required for that approach cannot be observed in many industries.

In this paper we develop a new econometric approach to the problem of market power estimation, based on specification and estimation of the residual demand function facing a single firm. By residual demand function we mean the relationship between one firm's price and quantity, taking into account the supply response of all other firms. The residual demand curve of a firm in a perfectly competitive industry is flat, that of a monopolist is the same as the industry demand curve, and that of a firm in a product-differentiated industry lies between these extremes. The point of estimating a single firm residual demand curve rather than a structural demand system involving all firms in an industry is to economize on data. Even when the available data would not allow estimation of all of the elasticities with any precision, it is still possible to estimate the degree of market power through the appropriate summary statistic, the elasticity of the residual demand curve.[3] This approach should be particularly fruitful when the degree of product differentiation is uncertain or when the boundaries of the relevant market are unclear. In these same circumstances, accounting profits will be a poor indicator of market power; product differentiated firms may be earning socially valuable rents on superior product design, not monopoly profits.

The model presented in section 2 below specifies a general demand and supply system for all products; the 'supply curves' need not be those of perfect competitors, nor need the different products be perfect substitutes. Solving out the prices and quantities of all other firms' products the residual demand function for the firm of interest. By this procedure, any model of the demand and supply for all firms in an industry implies an equation for each firm's residual demand, and thus a demand elasticity for that firm. Under perfect competition with homogeneous products, one firm's contraction of output will be offset exactly by another's expansion, so that the residual

[2]See Bresnahan (1987), Cowling and Cubbin (1979) and Joskow (1983) for three such approaches to the automobile industry.

[3]See Lerner (1934) for this definition of market power. Landes and Posner (1981) provide a recent treatment.

demand curve is infinitely elastic. In the more general model, either product differentiation or oligopoly behavior[4] can lead to a residual demand curve with a negative slope. While the slope of the residual demand curve is a sensible definition of market power under product differentiation, the relationship between the residual demand elasticity and the firm's markup of price over marginal cost is unclear in some oligopoly theories; this issue is taken up in section 3.

Section 4 specifies and estimates the slopes of the residual demand curves for three U.S. brewing firms, Anheuser-Busch, Coors, and Pabst. The brewing industry has substantial product differentiation, but no satisfactory estimates of structural demand elasticities and cross-elasticities exist to support traditional methods of assessing market power.[5] Antitrust enforcers and some economists who study the industry have suspected that brewers have substantial market power, but no study has yet claimed to quantify the degree of that market power.[6] However, several recent proposed mergers in the industry have been prevented on antitrust grounds.

This paper provides a methodology to detect single-firm power by econometric means. In a competitive world, movements in market price will be completely explained by the supply curve of other firms. If Firm 1, a competitor, should autonomously decide to change its output, Q_1, that will have no effect on price. Thus all changes in Q_1 which originate within Firm 1 will have no predictive power for price; its residual demand curve is flat. We show below how this observation leads to an econometric test for whether a firm has market power and just give the intuition here. The econometric method predicts Firm 1's price P_1 on the basis of Q_1 and of variables that shift other firm's costs. If, empirically, the variables shifting other firms' costs, rather than the firm's own quantity, explain prices, we conclude that the firm has no market power. In this analysis, Q_1 is treated as endogenous, and instrumented for with variables that shift Firm 1's costs alone. In an application, these instruments will be an important part of the procedure. In our brewing application, the natural experiment is created by regional variations in wage rates and by firm capacity, as brewing plant alterations are infrequent and plant capacity is a lumpy investment.

We find that for the period 1962–82, Anheuser-Busch had some market power, Coors had substantial market power, and Pabst faced a flat residual demand curve. These estimates sharply distinguish the market power held by

[4]See Ordover, Sykes and Willig (1982) and section 3.

[5]Elzinga (1982) presents a detailed review of brewing industry history. The demand for beer has been discussed by Greer (1971, 1981), Hogarty and Elzinga (1972), and Kelton and Kelton (1982). Product differentiation issues are discussed in Greer (1981).

[6]Brewing industry market power is evaluated in Elzinga (1982), Horowitz and Horowitz (1965), and Greer (1981). These studies dispute the importance of market power in the industry. Ornstein (1981) describes several beer industry anti-merger enforcement actions brought by the Justice Department during our sample period.

Pabst and Coors even though the two firms had similar nationwide market shares. These empirical findings and other institutional details are used to form a unified picture of the brewing industry in the discussion below.

2. Derivation of residual demand

In this section, the notion 'residual demand curve facing a particular firm' is derived. This notion is familiar in the case of a dominant firm with a price-taking fringe. We first show how the same notion can be derived in an arbitrary context. Throughout this derivation demand curves are arbitrary, so that product differentiation may or may not be present. Similarly, the supply of substitutes can vary, as the conduct of other firms may vary from perfect competitors with flat marginal cost curves to part of a cartel with the firm of interest.

The (inverse) demand function for Firm 1, the firm of interest, is

$$P_1 = P^1(Q_1, Q, Y; \alpha^1). \tag{1}$$

Here P_1 and Q_1 are price and quantity for Firm 1's (single)[7] product, Q is a vector of quantities for other firms' products, Y are exogenous variables entering the demand system, and α^1 are parameters. Q_i is a typical element of Q. Q includes all possible substitutes for the product including production by firms in different 'industries'. No a priori market delineation has been performed. In the special case where all firms' products are identical, eq. (1) would be written

$$P_1 = P^1\left(Q_1 + \sum_i Q_i, Y; \alpha^1\right) \tag{1'}$$

In this case, the parameters α^1 are the own-price demand elasticity, the income elasticity, etc., for the 'market' as a whole. If, as in (1′), there is no product differentiation, both market definition analyses and econometric estimation of α^1 are straightforward. In the more general (and usual) case, (1), both of these can form formidable undertakings. Then α^1 includes cross-price as well as own-price demand elasticities.

[7]The methods described in this article can also be used to estimate the market power of an aggregate of firms. Estimating the market power of a group of firms is of particular interest because a hypothetical cartel price increase of five percent forms part of the algorithm for an antitrust market under the U.S. Department of Justice Merger Guidelines (1984, section 2.0). In this way, our methods have been applied to a market definition problem by Scheffman and Spiller (1987). The present paper is extended to estimate the gains from merger in product differentiated industries in Baker and Bresnahan (1985).

The model also includes (inverse) demand equations for Q, the vector of quantities of all other relevant products.

$$P_i = P^i(Q, Q_1, Y; \alpha^i) \quad \text{for all} \quad i \neq 1. \tag{2}$$

Eq. (2) continues the notational convention of treating Q_1 asymmetrically. The parameters α^i include many also found in α^i the parameters of the demand curve for Firm 1. For example, if (1′) holds, then the α^i are constrained so that Q and Q_1 enter $P^i(\cdot)$ only through their sum. The vector of prices P_i, for $i \neq 1$, is denoted P.

The third element of the model is the supply behavior of all the firms $i \neq 1$. Their supply relations are written in the form 'marginal cost equals perceived marginal revenue' (PMR)

$$MC^i(Q_i, W, W^i; \beta^i) = PMR^i(Q, Q_1, Y; \alpha^i, \theta^i) \quad \text{for all} \quad i \neq 1, \tag{3}$$

where $PMR^i(\cdot)$ is $P^i(\cdot) + Q_i \cdot \sum_j ((\partial P^i/\partial Q_j)(\partial Q_j/\partial Q_i))$.

Marginal cost depends on quantity and on a vector of industry-wide factor prices, W. It further depends on firm-specific factor prices, W^i, none of which are in the industry-wide vector W. Firm i may face different prices for some inputs because of its location, or W^i may be reinterpreted as the shadow rental value of some untraded asset of firm i. Costs also depend on parameters β^i. On the marginal revenue side, PMR's first four determinants are the variables in the structural demand curves (2). Following Bresnahan (1981a) and Ordover et al. (1982), we also let PMR depend on conduct variables denoted θ^i; the vector θ^i indexes the oligopoly solution concept for all firms and thus determines the 'conjectures' $\partial Q_j/\partial Q_i$.

Just as the investigator does not know the cross-price elasticity of demand, so too are the conduct parameters θ^i unknown. The approach taken by the sources cited in footnotes 1 and 2 is to, at this stage, specify functional forms for (1), (2), and (3), and to complete the model by adding another equation like those in (3) for Firm 1. Then the parameters α^i, β^i, and θ^i are estimated econometrically on industry data. Our approach will be to first manipulate the model so that we only estimate a single equation – Firm 1's residual demand curve. This approach will not separately estimate any of the individual cost, demand, or behavioral parameters β^i, α^i and θ^i. Instead, we estimate only their joint impact on market power through the slope of the residual demand curve.

The first step in deriving the single-firm residual demand function is to solve the eqs. (2) and (3) simultaneously for the vectors Q and P. The notation β^I is the union of all cost parameters β^i, and α^I represents all demand parameters α^i, for all $i \neq 1$. W^I is the union of the W^i, and θ^I the union of the θ^i, for all $i \neq 1$. This emphasizes that W^I and θ^I are the firm-specific costs and conduct variables for all the firms *except* the one under study. In this notation, the solution to (2) and (3) for Q is

$$Q = E^I(Q_1, Y, W, W^I; \alpha^I, \beta^I, \theta^I), \tag{4}$$

where $E^I(\cdot)$ means that this is the equilibrium quantity in all of the markets $i \neq 1$. $E^I(\cdot)$ is a vector of functions of the form $Q_i = E^i(\cdot)$. Each element of E^I is a partial-reduced form; the only endogenous variable on the right is Q_1. The elasticity of Q_i with respect to Q_1 in this partial-reduced form is denoted ε_{i1}

$$\varepsilon_{i1} = \frac{\partial \ln E^i}{\partial \ln Q_1}.$$

The residual demand curve facing Firm 1 is derived by substituting E^I into (1)

$$P_1 = P^1(Q_1, E^I(Q_1, Y, W, W^I; \alpha^I, \beta^I, \theta^I), Y; \alpha^1). \tag{5}$$

Substituting out the redundancies, and employing the notation α for the union of α^I with α^1 we have

$$P_1 = R(Q_1, Y, W, W^I; \alpha, \beta^I, \theta^I), \tag{6}$$

where the notation $R(\cdot)$ means (inverse) residual demand. The observable arguments of the residual demand curve are threefold: own quantity, structural demand variables, and other firms' cost variables. The parameters of the residual demand curve are functions of the underlying structural parameters α and β^I, and the behavioral parameters θ^I. A residual demand curve has the costs of all other firms included, so that factor prices paid by those firms are properly incorporated in $R(\cdot)$. Except in the case of perfect competition, however, the costs of other firms do not completely determine P_1, so that $R(\cdot)$ varies with Q_1.

Differentiating (5) in the logarithm shows that its elasticity with respect to Q_1 depends on all of the elasticities of $P_1(\cdot)$, the (inverse) demand function in eq. (1), as well as on the elasticities of other firms' reactions, ε_{i1}

$$\eta_1^R \equiv \frac{\partial \ln R}{\partial \ln Q_1} = \eta_{11} + \sum_{i \neq 1} \eta_{1i} \varepsilon_{1i}. \tag{7}$$

In eq. (7), η_1^R is the parameter we will estimate, and η_{1j} is $\partial \ln P^1(\cdot)/\partial \ln Q_j$.[8] The underlying parameters α, β^I, and θ^I cannot in general be recovered by estimating (6). Only the degree of market power, given by η_1^R, can be estimated, not its source. Because the (inverse) residual demand curve for Firm 1, eq. (6), contains only one quantity (Q_1), $1/\eta_1^R$ is the elasticity of residual demand and η_1^R is the (inverse) elasticity or flexibility of residual demand.

The model is closed by specifying the supply relation for Firm 1.

$$P_1 - MC^1(Q_1, W, W^1; \beta^1) = M^1(Q, Q_1, Y; \alpha^1, \theta^1), \tag{8}$$

where $M^1(\cdot) = MR^1(\cdot) - P_1$. Eq. (8) can be thought of as a transformation of the familiar equilibrium condition equating marginal revenue with marginal cost. To write the model entirely in (P_1, Q_1) space, we substitute out the Q on the right of (8). Again, we use E^I and suppress redundancies

$$P_1 - MC^1(Q_1, W, W^1; \beta^1) = MK^1(Q_1, Y, W, W^I; \alpha, \beta^I, \theta), \tag{9}$$

where $MK(\cdot)$ is the residual markup, and θ is the union of θ^I and θ^1. The intersection of supply relation (9) and residual demand curve (6) determines P_1 and Q_1.

In oligopoly theory, specifying the model this way would be a peculiar but correct way to determine equilibrium values. Our purpose in doing so is to demonstrate that the residual demand curve (6) is econometrically identified, because we estimate (6) at the level of the firm. Eq. (6) can be econometrically estimated when a firm-specific cost variable W^1 exists because W^1 is the exogenous variable in eq. (9) excluded from eq. (6).

3. The residual demand elasticity and the markup

Unless the firm is a price taker, its residual demand curve will not be flat. Thus a nonzero η_1^R implies $P_1 > MC_1$. It is important to clarify, however, that there is not always an exact relationship between η_1^R and the markup.

First, consider a firm which is a Stackelberg leader relative to its environment. For such a firm

$$-\eta_1^R = \frac{P_1 - MC_1}{P_1}, \tag{10}$$

and it *is* proper to infer the markup from the residual demand curve. The point is more general than the simple Stackelberg model. For example, in the

[8] Thus η_{ij} is a demand 'flexibility'. See Frisch (1959).

case of a dominant firm with a fringe of smaller producers, Firm 1 is in fact a leader relative to its whole environment. It knows that the fringe's supply curve affects the elasticity of demand it faces, and acts accordingly. Thus, the markup it chooses will be directly related to the residual demand curve it faces.

More generally, firms in a Consistent Conjectures Equilibrium (Bresnahan 1981a) will have markups given by (10). For such firms, there is no distinction between the residual demand curve and the demand curve the firm acts as if it is facing. Such a firm will chose its output to equate

$$\frac{P_1 - MC_1}{P_1} = -\left(\eta_{11} + \sum_{i \neq 1} \eta_{1i}\hat{\varepsilon}_{i1}\right), \tag{11}$$

where $\hat{\varepsilon}_{i1}$ are Firm 1's 'conjectural variations' in elasticity form. In a Consistent Conjectures Equilibrium $\hat{\varepsilon}_{i1} = \varepsilon_{i1}$ for all i, so the right-hand side of eq. (11) equals $-\eta_1^R$ in eq. (7). Thus, a direct relationship between the residual demand elasticity and markup, eq. (10), holds for this case.

Product differentiation provides another cirumstance in which $-\eta_1^R$, is likely to be near the markup. When the bulk of a firm's market power arises because its products are distinct from others', then the distinction between actual and conjectured marginal revenue is less important. Questions of oligopoly strategic variables are known to disappear as the products become very poor substitutes.[9] There will not be an exact relationship between $-\eta_1^R$ and the markup except in the limit in which strategic variables do not affect the equilibrium, but a large $-\eta_1^R$ will generally indicate substantial market power for firms selling differentiated products.

A final noncooperative example in which our method will reveal the markup of price over marginal cost is perfect competition in an unconcentrated industry. Then our method correctly estimates the flat residual demand curve.

4. Empirical estimates of demand elasticities facing three brewing industry firms

In this section we estimate on yearly data the slopes of the residual demand curves facing three brewing firms: Anheuser-Busch, Pabst, and Coors. These three firms played different market roles over our 1962–1982 sample period. Both Anheuser-Busch (A-B) and Pabst benefited from the late 1950s demand shift from 'popular' to 'premium' beers such as their Budweiser and Pabst Blue Ribbon brands. A-B was the largest brewer over the entire sample period; its market share rose from under ten percent to over 30

[9] See Sonnenschein (1968) for a demonstration.

percent of nationwide unit sales, overwhelmingly through internal growth. Pabst's national market share, on the other hand, remained in the 7.5 percent to 11.5 percent range throughout the last decade. Its regional market share was substantially higher in the upper midwest,[10] but there is considerable dispute about how much market power this implied.[11]

The third firm, Coors, was slightly smaller than Pabst on a nationwide basis, but had the largest market share in each of ten western states; over the last decade Coors averaged a 40 percent market share in the mountain states and nearly 30 percent in the Pacific states.[12] Many industry observers believe that Coors' products (or their images) are distinct in product space, as well. Coors chose a different balance between scale economies and transportation costs than other brewers by using only a single brewery, the largest in the industry, in Golden, Colorado. By contrast, A-B had ten plants, many much smaller. Throughout our sample period the size of the largest plants in the industry increased steadily, and small firms exited in large numbers, suggesting the exploitation of scale economies.[13]

We estimate eq. (6) in double log form for each of three firms j so that the coefficients are elasticities. Let $\langle , \rangle$ denote the inner product operation, let δ_j and γ_j be vectors of parameters, and let lowercase stand for the natural logs of variables. Recall that the vector of W's represents cost side variables and the vector of Y's represents demand side variables. We then estimate eq. (6″) for each firm:

$$\rho_j = \eta_j^R q_j + <\delta_j, (w, w^I)> + <\gamma_j, y> + \varepsilon_{dj}. \qquad (6'')$$

Eq. (6″) will be different for each of the three firms, since the parameters vary across firms.

We specify the industry-wide cost variables w to include prices and industry average plant size.[14] The effects of factor prices other than capital are summarized by short-run average variable cost, calculated by dividing all non-capital costs by quantity. If short-run marginal cost is rising, short run average variable cost will be endogenous in our system of demand and supply equations. We therefore instrument for it using exogenous factor prices: the brewing industry wage rate, an agricultural materials price index,

[10] *Beer Marketer's Insights* reports that Pabst maintained a one-quarter share of dollar sales in the East North Central states (Illinois, Indiana, Michigan, Ohio, and Wisconsin) through the 1970s. Market share figures exclude imports, which were below three percent throughout the upper Midwest.

[11] The Justice Department has often attempted to prevent Pabst from merging. In contrast, Elzinga (1982, p. 226–228) argues that Pabst has little regional market power in the upper midwest.

[12] These market share statistics, based on dollar sales, are reported in *Beer Marketer's Insights.*

[13] Brewing industry scale economies are carefully investigated in Scherer (1975).

[14] All data series are defined in the appendix.

a packaging materials price index, and a price index for advertising services brought by brewers. Industry-wide capital costs enter through a cost of capital measure. Individual cost variables for other firms in the industry, w^I, are summarized as industry excess capacity (nameplate capacity minus production) excluding the firm at hand.

Demand side variables include real per capita national income, advertising expenditure, time, and several demographic measures. The reported estimates omit advertising and the demographic measures as they failed to attain significance or affect the coefficient of any other variable.[15]

Miller's nationwide marketing introduction of light beer in 1975 changed the nature of product differentiation in the brewing industry, and may also have altered the nature of the strategic interaction among firms.[16] We deal with this innovation by including a dummy variable for the period from 1975 onward, both by itself and interacted with each firm's quantity. The expected effect of this new product is unclear. A-B, the largest firm, introduced its own light beer shortly after Miller. The impact of a rival's successful innovation on A-B is clearly negative, although it could take the form of a shift of the residual demand curve toward the origin rather than as a flattening of the demand curve. In theory, the market power of A-B could remain unchanged despite the negative shock to firm demand. The structural interpretation of the light beer dummy variable in each firm's demand equation is also unclear. It could represent a change in the structural demand curve because consumers had more choices, or a change in the conditions of competition because of added product differentiation, or simply stand for the increase in advertising and marketing efforts after 1975.

We use two different definitions of firm price: beer revenue divided by gallons sold[17] and the price of the firm's flagship brand (Budweiser, Coors,

[15]Tests of these exclusion restrictions described in Baker and Bresnahan (1984) show little effect of advertising or demographics on demand for three firms studied. In the unrestricted specification, advertising is treated as endogenous. We are not surprised by the small effect, since a mid-1970s bulge in brewer advertising is collinear with the marketing introduction of light beer, which we treat with a dummy variable in our estimated equations. Advertising remains in our specification as an (endogenous) cost.

[16]Miller acquired the rights to Meister Brau Lite beer in 1972, which had been unsuccessfully marketed as a diet beer for women by a small Chicago brewery. Miller's innovation was in the nationwide marketing of light beer. Light beers, now made by many firms, are lower in alcohol and calories than premium beers. In estimating demand curves from time series data, we implicitly assume that no unobserved changes in product quality or reputation occur. The one exception to this is the obvious change in the relative attractiveness of different brands after the invention of light beer, which we treat by introducing a dummy variable in the residual demand curve of each firm. At the same time, Miller 'repositioned' the Miller High Life brand closer to A-B's Budweiser brand and heavily advertised it. Industry advertising/sales ratios increased dramatically during the mid-1970s. As a result of the collinearity between advertising and the dummy, we are uncertain of its interpretation.

[17]Data on each firm's beer revenue were obtained with the help of Professor George Foster of the Stanford Graduate School of Business. We are unable to construct this price series for Miller or Schlitz, so we do not study them.

Table 1
Correlations among prices.[a]

	$P_{A\text{-}B}$	P_{Coors}[b]	P_{Pabst}	P_{Bud}	$P_{Coors\ Br}$[c]	P_{BlueR}
$P_{A\text{-}B}$	1.0	0.82	0.93	0.96	0.84	0.91
P_{Coors}[b]		1.0	0.65	0.80	0.94	0.58
P_{Pabst}			1.0	0.95	0.65	0.99
P_{Bud}				1.0	0.86	0.93
$P_{Coors\ Br}$[c]					1.0	0.60
P_{BlueR}						1.0

[a]Log of real prices.
[b]Coors, the firm.
[c]Coors, the brand.

or Pabst Blue Ribbon) in northern California.[18] The use of average revenue as a measure of firm-wide price may make the brewing industry appear more competitive than it truly is because of a bias introduced by the changing brand composition of total sales. This bias is empirically not important; use of the flagship brand price and quantity in place of average revenue does not alter the elasticity estimates reported below. This is not surprising: table 1 shows that the flagship brand produces correlation coefficients of 0.96, 0.94, and 0.99 with average revenue for the three brewers, much higher correlations than shown between the prices of different brewers. Because of this high correlation, the results of this section are little different from the flagship-brand results [reported in Baker and Bresnahan (1984).]

Own quantity is endogenous in (6) because of the presence of a simultaneous relation (9) connecting price and quantity.[19] We instrument for it with different exogenous variables for each firm. All of the instruments we employ can be viewed as proxies for firm-individuated factor prices, W^1, which are the natural instruments for identifying residual demand. For each firm we use its capacity as one instrument for quantity. The nature of brewing industry investment suggests that capacity is exogenous in the short run, since capacity is altered infrequently and in large increments. Although A-B has between one-quarter and one-third of nationwide sales in our sample, it typically adds capacity in increments of 20 percent of its annual production. Capacity is typically added in anticipation of growth, so that each firm has long periods of capacity constraint followed by long periods of substantial excess capacity. As a result, firm short-run marginal cost varies according to location in the investment cycle: marginal cost is lowest immediately following capacity expansion and highest immediately before the next plant

[18]Source: *Beverage Industry News of Northern California*, various issues. When we use a single product price, we also use that product's quantity as the output measure in our regressions.

[19]As an econometric matter, however, it is not important on our data to treat own Q as endogenous.

Table 2
Glossary.

Price and quantity	
qj	Log per capita barrels of beer sold by firm *j*
pj	Log real average revenue of firm *j*
qaltj	Log per capita barrels of beer sold for firm *j*'s flagship product
paltj	Log real price of firm *j*'s flagship product in northern California
Cost variables	
sravc	Log real short-run average variable cost for industry
APS	Average industry plant size
pk	Log real user cost of capital for industry
EKTIj	Per capita excess capacity in the rest of industry
Demand variables	
pcdi	Log per capita real disposable income
POP<45	Percentage of over-18 population under 45 years old
FBEER	Percentage of women reporting they drink beer
Instruments	
Kj	Per capita capacity of firm *j*
APSj	Average plant size for firm *j* (A-B and Pabst only)
cw	Log real manufacturing wage rate in Colorado (Coors only)
pl	Log real brewing industry wage rate
pm	Log real brewing industry materials price index
pa	Log real brewing industry advertising price index
Other variables	
LITE	Dummy variable for 1975 and later
MC	Industry marginal cost [see eq. (12)]
TIME	Years
LITExqa−b	Interaction between LITE and A-B quantity

comes on line. Under this investment process, both excess capacity and capacity will be correlated with firm marginal cost. Excess capacity is an unattractive instrument for quantity, however, as it is endogenous even in the short run.

We also employ a second instrument for quantity. For Anheuser-Busch and Pabst, both multiplant firms, we use average capacity of all firm plants because this variable is related to the exploitation of plant-level scale economies over time, and thus to cost. For Coors, which has a single brewery in Colorado, we use the level of manufacturing wages in that state as a second instrument. Since the nationwide brewing industry wage is included as an industry-wide cost variable, the independent movement of Colorado wages shifts costs for Coors alone.

A glossary of variable names used in our regression appears in table 2. As table 2 indicates, we deflated monetary values and put quantity variables in per capita terms to conserve degrees of freedom. The appendix reports the origins of the data.

We estimate eq. (6″) jointly for Coors, Pabst, and A-B by three-stage least squares.[20] The joint estimation takes advantage of information available from the correlation of errors in the three equations, and allows us to conserve degrees of freedom by imposing the cross-equation restriction in eq. (12)

$$\delta_{1j} sravc + \delta_{2j} APS + \delta_{3j} pk + \delta_{4j} EKTI$$

$$= \delta_j(sravc + \beta_{APS} APS + \beta_{KAP} pk + \beta_{EKTI} EKTI) \equiv \delta_j(MC). \qquad (12)$$

The restriction in (12) has the interpretation of assuming that all of the firms in the industry other than Firm 1 use different inputs in the same proportions.[21]

Results for our preferred specification appear in table 3. This specification was reached by deleting all demand variables with coefficients estimated to be smaller than their standard errors in absolute value. As a result, no demographic variables appear. The Lite beer dummy variable, alone and interacted with output, appears only for A-B. Time is not dropped from the equations for Pabst and Coors only.[22] We have not deleted cost-side variables, even if they are statistically insignificant.[23] The estimates in table 3 incorporate the restriction of eq. (12).

The coefficient on log quantity directly estimates η_1^R. As the industry has been characterized by substantial product differentiation throughout our sample period, these estimates are interpreted under the assumption that they correspond to estimates of firm markup of price over marginal cost. Thus, Coors had very substantial market power over our sample period; its inverse demand elasticity of -0.74 corresponds to a 74 percent markup over marginal cost. This coefficient is estimated with a very small standard error. At the other extreme Pabst faced an insignificantly downward-sloping

[20] Similar results were obtained for each firm's elasticity using single equation estimation employing two-stage least squares with little noticeable efficiency loss.

[21] Tests of this restriction do not reject it, although they have little power because δ_j is imprecisely estimated when (12) is not imposed. Demand elasticity results are robust to the imposition of this restriction.

[22] Time most likely serves as a proxy for demographic variables omitted from these equations.

[23] Industry-wide cost variables enter both the residual demand curve and the supply relation (9). Omitting them would tend to make the structural supply and demand equations more (positively) correlated, which would tend to bias point estimates of the residual demand elasticity in the direction of finding market power. Omitting industry-wide demand shift variables is less troublesome, because this specification error would tend to bias the results in the conservative direction of not finding market power. These issues are considered more fully in Baker and Bresnahan (1984).

Table 3
Results.

Variable	Coefficient estimate	Standard error
A-B equation (*pa−b*)		
Constant	2.113	0.505
qa−b	−0.312	0.064
PCDI	0.040	0.157
MC	0.278	0.019
LITE	0.591	0.068
LITExqa−b	0.282	0.040
Pabst equation (*ppb*)		
Constant	3.979	0.362
qpb	−0.058	0.031
PCDI	−0.041	0.132
MC	0.107	0.089
TIME	−0.017	0.004
Coors equation (*pcs*)		
Constant	−1.638	0.805
qcs	−0.745	0.054
PCDI	0.440	0.306
MC	0.266	0.226
TIME	0.032	0.010
Common parameters		
APS	−0.194	0.291
PK	0.042	0.115
EKTI	−0.033	0.022
Summary statistics		
Equation	Durbin-Watson	Sample size
pa−b	2.13	21
pab	1.95	21
pcs	1.70	21

demand curve. This firm had very little market power, only raising price six percent above marginal cost by our point estimate, with a 95 percent confidence interval varying between one percent and 11 percent. Industry leader Anheuser-Busch had considerable market power (with an estimated markup of 31 percent) before the introduction of Lite beer by a rival. This point estimate is reduced to just three percent when Lite beer was introduced.

The general pattern of these inferences is robust to the log-log functional form. In results not shown, we used a linear functional form and calculated the elasticities at the sample means. This had no qualitative impact on the pattern of market power, and the two sets of elasticities, linear and log-log, are not statistically significantly different (under the conservative assumption of independence). As a quantititative matter, the linear model suggested somewhat less market power for A-B in the early period and for Coors overall, though still substantial market power for these firms. We prefer the log-log estimates because the linear specification involves substantial serial correlation in the errors.

The interpretation of these estimates as revealing the firms' markups in an exact, quantitative way may be too strong. Nonetheless, the results clearly show that Coors is a very valuable monopoly, that A-B once was a valuable monopoly, and that A-B post-1975 and Pabst are less valuable monopolies. These results are consistent with the price premium received by Coors through much of the sample period.

These estimates lead to several inferences about the nature of competition in the brewing industry over our sample period. First, product differentiation is important. Coors' and A-B's downward-sloping demand curve probably originate in products distinct in image and geography. Second, regional market share is a poor indicator of market power since Pabst has so little market power.[24] Third, the increased concentration and product differentiation in the industry since 1975 appears to reflect competition, not anti-competitive acts. A-B's residual demand curve reflects a significant loss of market power following the introduction of Lite beer, even though the new product apparently raised the demand for all beer. Fourth, it is unlikely that brewers price in a tacitly collusive way. If they did, we would expect to observe that each firm's residual demand curve has significant slope, and that prices are highly correlated across firms. Pabst belies both conditions. It has negligible market power and its price is not highly correlated with other brewers.[25]

In general, the coefficients other than the residual demand elasticity have no clear interpretation since other coefficients may reflect both direct effects on the firm's demand and indirect effects through the adjustments of other firms. For example, the positive coefficient on PCDI in the Coors equation does not imply positive income elasticity for that brand; instead, it implies that the net effect of an income increase, including the effects through other brands' demands, is to shift sales to Coors. [See eq. (5).] Nonetheless, it is probably not misleading to label Coors as a normal good in (residual) demand, and Pabst as inferior. That is, the coefficients probably mean that Coors is more income elastic than other brands, Pabst less. In this interpretation, our results are consistent with the view of Keithan (1978)

[24] Therefore our estimate lends support to Elzinga's argument that Pabst's market share in the upper midwest overstated that brewer's market power.

[25] However, we cannot reject the unlikely possibility that all firms except Pabst collude to raise price to the level charged by Pabst, the high-cost producer.

that shifts in demand toward a brand or group of brands (like premium or light brands) are what create market power in this industry.

If no firm-individuated factor prices are observed, the residual demand curve (6) will not be identified, and no instruments will be available to estimate its elasticity consistently. Eq. (6) can be estimated, for example by ordinary least squares, but the resulting parameter estimates will be subject to simultaneous equations bias.[26] In that event, the likely bias is in the direction of disproving the presence of market power. Hence, estimating the residual (inverse) demand curve without correcting for the endogeneity of own-quantity will provide a conservative estimate of the residual demand elasticity.

5. Conclusion

The beer industry, characterized by product differentiation, provided a suitable situation to test our technique for estimating firm market power. Our technique, applied to three of the firms in the industry, allows us to describe both the main features of industry structure and the behavior of individual firms. The results appear quite robust to changes in specification. We are able to differentiate the market power of the three firms with a great deal of confidence despite the fact that all have high market shares, both nationally and regionally. Coors had substantial market power over our sample period, A-B lost most of its market power in the middle of the period, and Pabst is a price-taker. Individual firm market power appears to arise because products are distinct in demand, not because of cooperative behavior by firms. Otherwise, Pabst would surely have market power.

Appendix

This appendix describes the source for the variables employed in our study. Variable names are listed in table 2 of the text.

Price and quantity

Nationwide production figures are available from trade publications and firm revenue from beer production is reported in the annual reports of publicly traded brewers. Per capita adjustments were made using the U.S. population over age 18. Prices were transformed into real terms by dividing by the GNP deflator. Flagship brand prices are reported in issues of the *Beverage Industry News of Northern California.*

[26] This bias is shown in our data, but is small. When we treat quantity as exogenous, the residual demand elasticities are estimated as Coors −0.738, Pabst −0.053, and A-B −0.312.

Factor prices (cost variables)

Time series on four factors of production were assumed to apply industry-wide: labor, materials, variable capital, and advertising. The price of labor is the average hourly wage of brewing production workers collected by the Bureau of Labor Statistics, reprinted annually in *Brewers Almanac*. The price of variable capital is the user-cost measure developed by Fraumeni and Jorgensen (1982) for food and beverage industries, and updated by us through the end of the sample period.

Two variants of the materials price series were used. The first uses data on the prices and quantities of a list of specific inputs: malt, corn, rice, hops, cans, bottles, and power. The second divides cost of materials for brewers, as reported in *Brewers Almanac*, by quantity of beer manufactured in barrels. The quantitites consumed of all specific inputs are found in *Brewers Almanac*, except power. *MBA Bluebook* reports expenditures on power. The price series for the specific inputs are from *Producer Prices and Prices Indexes*. In real terms, the two materials price series are correlated at 0.99. The advertising price series is computed as an index of media prices; brewing industry weights are from *Leading National Advertisers*.

Demand variables

Population and income variables are taken from Census and other Commerce Department Sources.

Instruments

Brewer capacity, by plant, is reported in *Beer Marketer's Insights*. This is the basis of both K and APS. The Colorado manufacturing wage rate series is from the *Statistical Abstract of the United States*.

Other variables

Advertising variables, used to compute table 5, include each firm's expenditures on advertising, as reported in *Brewers Almanac*. These variables are normalized either by sales, or by the industry price of advertising as described above and a population index.

References

Appelbaum, E., 1979, Testing price-taking behavior, Journal of Econometrics, July, 313–331.
Appelbaum, E., 1982, The estimation of the degree of oligopoly power, Journal of Econometrics 19, 287–299.

Baker, J. and T. Bresnahan, 1984, Estimating the elasticity of demand facing a single firm: Evidence on three brewing firms, Research paper no. 54 (Stanford Workshop on Factor Markets, Department of Economics, Stanford University, Stanford, CA).
Baker, J. and T. Bresnahan, 1985, The gains from merger or collusion in product-differentiated industries, Journal of Industrial Economics 33, 427–444.
Bresnahan, T., 1981a, Duopoly models with consistent conjectures, American Economic Review 71, 934–945.
Bresnahan, T., 1981b, Departures from marginal-cost pricing in the American automobile industry: Estimates for 1977–78, Journal of Econometrics 11, 201–227.
Bresnahan, T., 1987, Competition and collusion in the American automobile industry, The 1955 price war, Journal of Industrial Economics, June, 457–482.
Cowling, K. and J. Cubbin, 1981, Hedonic price indexes for cars in the U.K., Economic Journal, Sept.
Elzinga, Kenneth G., 1982, The beer industry, in: Walter Adams, ed., The structure of American industry, 6th ed. (Macmillan, New York).
Fraumeni, B. and D. Jorgenson, 1980, The role of capital in U.S. economic growth, 1948–1976, in: G. von Furstenberg, ed., Capital, efficiency, and growth (Ballinger, Cambridge).
Frisch, R., 1959, A complete scheme for computing all direct and cross demand elasticities in a model with many sectors, Econometrica 27, 177–196.
Gollop and Roberts, 1979, Firm interdependence in oligopolistic markets, Journal of Econometrics, July, 313–331.
Greer, Douglas F., 1971, Product differentiation and concentration in the brewing industry, Journal of Industrial Economics 19, July, 201–219.
Greer, Douglas F., 1981, The causes of concentration in the brewing industry, Quarterly Review of Economics and Business, Winter, 87–106.
Hogarty, Thomas F. and K.G. Elzinga, 1972, The demand for beer, Review of Economics and Statistics 54, May, 195–198.
Horowitz, Ira and A. Horowitz, 1965, Firms in a declining market: The brewing case, Journal of Industrial Economics, March, 129–153.
Iwata, G., 1974, Measurement of conjectural variations in oligopoly, Econometrica, Sept., 947.
Joskow, A., 1983, A welfare analysis of industry product variety, Mimeo. (Yale University, New Haven, CT).
Keithan, C., 1978, Staff report on the brewing industry (Staff Report on the Brewing Industry, Federal Trade Commission, Washington, DC).
Kelton, Christina M.L. and W.D. Kelton, 1982, Advertising and intra-industry brand shift in the U.S. brewing industry, Journal of Industrial Economics 30, March, 293–303.
Landes, W. and R. Posner, 1981, Market power in antitrust cases, Harvard Law Review 94, 937–996.
Lerner, A., 1934, The concept of monopoly and the measurement of monopoly power, Review of Economic Studies 1, 157–175.
Ordover, J., A. Sykes and R. Willig, 1982, Herfindahl concentration, rivalry, and mergers, Harvard Law Review 95, 1857–1874.
Ornstein, S., 1981, Antitrust policy and market forces as determinants of industry structure: Case histories in beer and distilled spirits, The Antitrust Bulletin, Summer, 281–313.
Rosse, J., 1970, Estimating cost function parameters without using cost data: Illustrated methodology, Econometrica, March, 150.
Scheffman, D. and P. Spiller, 1987, Geographic market definition under the DOJ guidelines, Journal of Law and Economics 30, April, 123–147.
Scherer, F. et al., 1975, The economics of multi-plant operation (Harvard University Press, Cambridge, MA).
Sonnenschein, H., 1968, The dual of duopoly is complementary monopoly, Journal of Political Economy 76, March/April, 316–318.
Sumner, D., 1981, Measurement of monopoly behavior: An application to the cigarette industry, Journal of Political Economy 89, Oct., 1010–1019.
U.S. Department of Justice, 1984, Merger guidelines (Washington, DC).

[8]

JLEO, V10 N2 407

The Effects of Mergers in Differentiated Products Industries: Logit Demand and Merger Policy

Gregory J. Werden
U.S. Department of Justice

Luke M. Froeb
Vanderbilt University

Using the logit model, and assuming Nash equilibrium in prices and constant marginal cost, it is straightforward to estimate critical demand parameters and simulate mergers. In this way, the logit model can be used to predict the price and welfare effects of mergers. We explore the effects of mergers in this model both analytically and through simulations of hypothetical mergers of U.S. long distance carriers. We find that only mergers involving AT&T would be likely to lessen welfare significantly. Simulations such as these provide a firmer foundation for antitrust policy than traditional structural indicators. The logit model is not always appropriate, but the basic methodology can be adapted to other demand systems.

1. Introduction

The price and welfare effects of mergers in Cournot models with homogeneous products have been the subject of several analyses in recent years (for example, Farrell and Shapiro, 1990; McAfee and Williams, 1992; Werden, 1991). However, Bertrand models with differentiated products may be of greater relevance to antitrust policy. Few industries have a truly homogeneous product and only one price, and despite the insights of Kreps and Scheinkman (1983), there remain doubts about the quantity-setting assumption. In addition, the assumption of a noncooperative competitive interaction is more likely to be reasonable with differentiated products than with homogeneous products.[1]

The most notable studies on Bertrand mergers are those by Levy and Reitzes (1992) and Deneckere and Davidson (1985). Levy and Reitzes consid-

The views expressed herein are not purported to represent those of the U.S. Department of Justice. We thank George Parsons and for helpful discussions and Timothy Tardiff especially for his invaluable assistance on the simulations of long-distance carrier mergers. We also thank the editorial board and two referees for their comments and suggestions.

1. We believe that the competitive interaction is likely to be noncooperative in most differentiated product industries, in part because product differentiation tends to make it more difficult to reach collusive agreements (unless it is straightforward to allocate customers or the like). We recognize, however, that some sort of collusion is widely thought to have occurred in some differentiated products industries, notably breakfast cereals and cigarettes.

er a model of localized, spatial competition, with each firm competing directly with only the adjoining firms around a circle. Deneckere and Davidson consider a model of generalized competition with linear demand. Neither study provides useful guidance for merger policy by indicating how the price and welfare effects of mergers relate to market shares, demand elasticities, and other factors that can be assessed in an antitrust case.[2] This is partially due to the fact that both consider only the symmetric case, even though differentiated products industries are often highly asymmetric. Moreover, Levy and Reitzes consider strictly localized competition in a single dimension, which certainly is not typical.

We examine the price and welfare effects of Bertrand mergers in the context of a more appealing model of generalized competition—the logit model. Although the logit model has substantial limitations, it is of significant interest for several reasons. First, the logit model is simple enough to permit the derivation of analytic results, which significantly extend the work of Levy and Reitzes and Deneckere and Davidson. Second, the logit model has direct policy relevance, since the 1992 Horizontal Merger Guidelines use it as the base case for the analysis of mergers in differentiated products industries. The logit model is a base case in the sense that the merging firms are neither especially close in product space nor especially far apart.[3] Finally, the logit model is very practical for use in antitrust cases with limited data and severe time pressure.[4] The only inputs required for simulating mergers in our version of the logit model are market shares and prices, which can be easily observed, and two demand elasticity parameters, which can be fairly easily estimated using well established methods, or guessed at in a pinch.

Among the implications of this model are: The prices of all products in the industry increase as a result of a merger, but the magnitudes of the price increases are very different for different products. If the merging firms are of different size, their merger has asymmetric effects on their prices; the price of the smaller-share product is increased much more than that of the larger-share product. In addition, the merged firm typically increases the weighted average of its two prices much more than any nonmerging firm increases its price. Larger nonmerging firms increase price more than smaller ones, so increased concentration among the nonmerging firms increases the price effect of a merger, but the effect is typically fairly weak. Finally, mergers may enhance welfare even though they increase price, and increased concentration among the nonmerging firms may reduce the welfare loss from a merger, or even reverse it.

2. Deneckere and Davidson do offer a fairly general proof that prices increase as a result of Bertrand mergers in differentiated products industries. In another recent study, McElroy (1993) shows that it is possible for some prices to fall as a result of a Bertrand merger.

3. See U.S. Department of Justice and Federal Trade Commission (1922: § 2.21) and compare with Willig (1991: 299–304).

4. The law requires that the government be given just 30 days advance notice of mergers, and it may be infeasible to undo a merger after it is consummated.

To illustrate the application of the model, we analyze the price and welfare effects of mergers among existing U.S. long-distance carriers. We make two alternative assumptions concerning the effects of mergers on costs. One assumption is that mergers have no effect on costs, and this is probably the most reasonable assumption. Under this assumption, mergers involving AT&T have significant adverse welfare effects, and mergers not involving AT&T have much smaller welfare effects. The alternative cost assumption is that a merged firm has a marginal cost equal to the lesser of the two marginal costs of the merging firms. Under this assumption, all mergers of pairs of long-distance carriers enhance total welfare, except that of AT&T with MCI.

Section 2 presents our version of the logit model; Section 3 considers the effects of mergers in logit oligopoly on price and welfare; and Section 4 briefly examines the comparative static effects of changing the two demand elasticity parameters. Section 5 illustrates the application of the logit model to hypothetical mergers among U.S. long-distance carriers. Section 6 considers the limitations of the logit model and discusses alternatives. Section 7 offers a few observations on the Merger Guidelines' specific enforcement standards for differentiated products industries. Finally, Section 8 offers some concluding remarks.

2. Logit Oligopoly

A logit demand system generally is motivated by a random utility model in which consumers make a discrete choice among a set, C, of n alternatives, selecting the alternative yielding the greatest utility (see Ben-Akiva and Lerman, 1985: 55–57, 100–104; McFadden, 1974: 106–10). We consider a version of the model that specifies the indirect utility of consumer i associated with the choice of product j as

$$U_{ij} = \alpha_j - \beta p_j + e_{ij}. \tag{1}$$

The price coefficient, β, is assumed to be constant for all consumers and products,[5] and all generally perceived quality differences among products are summarized by the α_j's. The disturbance term, e_{ij}, represents an individual-specific component of utility that is uncorrelated with price, p_j. If the e_{ij}'s are independently and identically distributed according to the extreme value distribution, the choice probabilities have the familiar logistic form (see Ben-Akiva and Lerman, 1985: 104–6; McFadden, 1974: 110–12):

$$\pi_j = \exp\,(\alpha j - \beta p_j) \,/ \sum_{k \in C} \exp(\alpha_k - \beta p_k). \tag{2}$$

5. This formulation is appropriate only if price is appropriately normalized. For example, if different-size packages of detergent are alternative choices, price must be per unit of volume or weight, rather than per package.

For our purposes, it is more convenient to express the model in traditional antitrust terms. We define product n to reflect the choice of "none of the above" (i.e., to be the outside good) and we assume $p_n \equiv 0$ to make the utility of the outside good a constant. The vector of the remaining prices is denoted $\mathbf{p}$, and the share-weighted average premerger price for the inside goods is denoted $\bar{p}$. We term as "shares," denoted $\mathbf{s}$, the vector of choice probabilities for the "inside goods" (i.e., those other than the outside good), conditional on the choice being an inside good.

The (positive) own-price and cross-price elasticities of demand for particular inside goods, ε_j and ε_{jk}, are

$$\varepsilon_j = \beta p_j(1 - \pi_j) = [\beta\bar{p}(1 - s_j) + \varepsilon s_j]p_j/\bar{p} \tag{3}$$

$$\varepsilon_{jk} = \beta p_k \pi_k = s_k(\beta\bar{p} - \varepsilon)p_k/\bar{p}. \tag{4}$$

There is also an implied (positive) "aggregate elasticity of demand for the inside goods," specifically

$$\varepsilon \equiv -[\partial\pi_I(\lambda\mathbf{p})/\partial\lambda][\bar{p}/\pi_I(\mathbf{p})] = \beta\bar{p}\pi_n, \tag{5}$$

where $\pi_I(\mathbf{p}) \equiv 1 - \pi_n(\mathbf{p})$ is the sum of the choice probabilities for the inside goods, λ is a scalar, and the derivative is evaluated at $\lambda = 1$.

The primitives of our version of the model, which completely characterize an industry, are shares, $\mathbf{s}$, and prices, $\mathbf{p}$, both of which can be observed, and the parameters ε and β, both of which can be estimated. Roughly speaking, β is the cross elasticity of demand parameter, controlling the substitutabilities among the inside goods; and ε is the aggregate elasticity of demand parameter, controlling the substitutability between the inside goods and the outside good.

There are several reasons for making ε rather than π_n a primitive of the model. First, economists are accustomed to dealing with demand elasticities, so the underpinnings of a merger simulation will be better understood if an assumption is made with respect to ε rather than π_n. Second, discrete choice models are not designed to estimate the implied aggregate demand elasticity. It is, therefore, preferable to estimate that elasticity using aggregate data and the corresponding econometric tools. We link the aggregate demand estimation with the discrete choice estimation by choosing the value for π_n that is consistent with the aggregate estimate of ε. In our model, π_n is not really a probability at all, but rather a scaling factor used to achieve this consistency.[6]

6. The conventional approach has been to let π_n be the actual probability of choosing none of the above and to place the remaining products in a nest to make the inside goods better substitutes for each other than the outside good is for them. This approach links in an undesirable way the aggregate elasticity of demand with the cross elasticities of demand within the nest. A change in the nesting parameter that makes products in the nest better substitutes for each other necessarily makes outside goods less good substitutes for the products in the nest.

Differences among the α_j's are all that matter, and they are unaffected by the arbitrary choice of one of them. Thus, we set α_n equal to an arbitrary constant, and calculate the α_j's for the inside goods in two steps. First, **s** is converted into a vector of π_j's:

$$\pi_n = \varepsilon/\beta\bar{p}, \qquad \varepsilon \in (0, \beta\bar{p}) \tag{6}$$

$$\pi_j = s_j(1 - \pi_n), \qquad j = 1, 2, \ldots, n - 1. \tag{7}$$

The logs of the ratios of π_j to π_n,

$$\ln(\pi_j/\pi_n) = \alpha_j - \alpha_n - \beta p_j, \tag{8}$$

are then solved for the α_j's, given α_n and **p**.

To complete the model, we assume: each product is initially sold by a single firm; each firm has constant marginal cost, c_j; and there are no fixed costs. We also assume that the equilibrium is Nash in prices both pre- and postmerger. We also assume for the present that economies of scale and scope cannot be realized through merger. Finally, we assume that product characteristics other than price are fixed, so that a merger cannot result in any strategic effects other than those involving price. In particular, mergers cannot lead to entry, or to product repositioning by established firms.

Given these assumptions, each of the first-order conditions for profit maximization [Equation (14) below] can be solved uniquely for the implied value of c_j.[7] With all the demand and cost parameters, it is straightforward to calculate the effects of a merger on prices and shares by solving the post-merger first-order conditions for profit maximization.[8] Anderson and de Palma (1992) and Anderson, de Palma, and Thisse (1992: 264–66) have proved the existence and uniqueness of the equilibrium.

In logit models, the welfare effect of a change in any argument of the utility function is calculated as the compensating variation necessary to restore consumers to the original level of utility. As Small and Rosen (1981) have shown, the change in consumer welfare brought about by changing prices from $\mathbf{p}^0$ to $\mathbf{p}^1$ is given by[9]

7. For certain parameter values, negative marginal cost is implied by Equation (14) if a firm's share is sufficiently great. Negative marginal costs would cause mergers to have unrealistic welfare effects, so we assume throughout that all shares are small enough that all marginal costs are positive. With all product prices equal to unity, as we generally assume, avoiding negative marginal costs requires $\text{argmax}\{s_j\} < (\beta - 1)/(\beta - \varepsilon)$, and there can be a negative marginal cost only if demand is inelastic.

8. As Berry (1994) notes, this must be done numerically. We do this calculation and all calculations using Mathematica. We would be happy to provide the Mathematica code upon request.

9. Raising one or more prices reduces this measure of change in consumer welfare as long as both the terms in square brackets in Equation (9) are positive. To assure that they are, we choose a large value for α_n.

$$\left[\ln \sum_j \exp(\alpha_j - \beta p_j^1) - \ln \sum_j \exp(\alpha_j - \beta p_j^0) \right] \beta^{-1}. \tag{9}$$

Setting α_n arbitrarily does not affect this measure,[10] but it does preclude the calculation of the total consumer welfare pre- or postmerger. For comparison purposes, we express the change in consumer welfare and the change in total welfare (change in consumer welfare plus the increase in industry profits) as a percentage of premerger total revenue for inside goods.

The analysis of the nested-logit model is quite similar. With a single nest, for example, the choice set, C, is divided into two subsets. One subset, N, consists of the goods in the nest, which are especially good substitutes for each other. The other subset, O, consists of the remaining goods in C. Letting $\delta \in (0, 1)$ be the parameter that controls the strength of the nest, and defining

$$D = \sum_{k \in O} \exp(\alpha_k - \beta p_k) + \left[\sum_{k \in N} \exp((\alpha_k - \beta p_k)/\delta) \right]^{\delta}, \tag{10}$$

the choice probabilities are

$$\pi_j = \exp(\alpha_j - \beta p_j)/\delta \left[\sum_{k \in N} \exp((\alpha_k - \beta p_k)/\delta) \right]^{\delta - 1} D^{-1}, \qquad j \in N \tag{11}$$

$$\pi_j = \exp(\alpha_j - \beta p_j) D^{-1}, \qquad j \in O\,. \tag{12}$$

It is simple to verify that setting $\delta = 1$ reduces this to Equation (2). Thus, the effect of the nest is weaker the closer the nest parameter is to unity. As shown by Morey (1992), the change in consumer welfare brought about by changing prices from $\mathbf{p}^0$ to $\mathbf{p}^1$ is given by

$$[\ln D(\mathbf{p}^1) - \ln D(\mathbf{p}^0)]\beta^{-1}. \tag{13}$$

3. The Effects of Mergers on Price and Welfare in Logit Oligopoly

The first-order conditions for profit maximization premerger for the simple logit simplify to

$$p_j - c_j = 1/\beta(1 - \pi_j) = \bar{p}[\beta\bar{p}(1 - s_j) + \varepsilon s_j]^{-1}. \tag{14}$$

Equation (14) implies: Larger firms have higher price–marginal cost margins; increasing β and thus the substitutability among the inside goods decreases all

10. This is easily shown. Increasing any α_j by $\Delta\alpha_j$, while holding the choice probabilities constant, increases all the others by the same amount. By totally differentiating Equation (9), it can be verified that increasing all of the α_j by the same amount leaves the value of Equation (9) unchanged.

margins; and increasing ε, and thus substitutability between the inside goods and the outside goods, also decreases all margins.

It is straightforward to show that the derivatives of the merged firm's profit function with respect to the prices of its two products, evaluated at premerger shares and prices, are both positive. Since Anderson, de Palma, and Thisse (1992: 270–72) have shown that the profit function is quasi-concave, it follows that the merged firm increases both prices as a result of the merger.

The first-order conditions for profit maximization postmerger simplify to

$$p_1 - c_1 = p_2 - c_2 = 1/\beta(1 - \pi_m) = \bar{p}[\beta\bar{p}(1 - s_m) + \varepsilon s_m]^{-1}, \tag{15}$$

with the subscript m used to denote the merged firm. Since the price–marginal cost margin is the same for both products, it follows that the merged firm increases the price of the product with the smaller share by a greater *absolute* than it increases price for the product with the larger share.[11] The intuition behind this result is straightforward. The effect of the merger on the price of the smaller-share product is the greater one because the merger causes a larger portion of its loss in sales from a price increase to be recaptured by the other product involved in the merger [as indicated by the cross elasticities of demand in Equation (4)] and because the premerger markup is smaller for the smaller-share product [as indicated by the first-order condition in Equation (14)].

Analyzing first-order conditions does not suffice to demonstrate how different the price increases are for the two products. That is illustrated in Table 1, which gives the percentage price increases for the products of the merged firm for various mergers for which the combined share of the merging firms is 40 percent.

At premerger shares and prices, the slope of the best-response function for the price of product k with respect to a change in the price of product j is

$$\pi_j\pi_k/(1 - \pi_k) = s_j s_k(\beta\bar{p} - \varepsilon)^2/\beta\bar{p}[\beta\bar{p}(1 - s_k) + \varepsilon s_k]. \tag{16}$$

This slope is clearly positive and greater for larger-share products. This slope is always less than one, and if the two merging firms (firm j's) have equal shares, this slope is less than one-half. For nonmerging firms smaller than both merging firms, this slope is less than one-sixth. Consequently, all of the nonmerging firms increase price as a result of a merger, but larger firms increase price more than smaller ones, and nonmerging firms increase price less than, often much less than, the merged firm increases the weighted average of its two prices. Further, greater concentration among the nonmerging firms causes a merger to result in a greater increase in the industry average price.

11. If the product with the smaller premerger share has the higher price, its price may increase *proportionately* less than that of the product with the larger premerger share.

Table 1. Price Increases for the Products of the Merged Firm Resulting from Mergers with a Combined Share for the Merging Firms of 40 Percent

Shares of the Merging Firms	Percentage Price Increase for the Smaller-Share Product	Percentage Price Increase for the Larger-Share Product	Share-Weighted Average Percentage Price Increase
1, 39	9.09	0.18	0.33
5, 35	7.88	0.93	1.57
10, 30	6.47	1.90	2.86
15, 25	5.19	2.92	3.71
20, 20	4.01	4.01	4.01

Note: For all mergers it is assumed that all premerger prices equal unity. $\beta = 5$, $\varepsilon = 1$, and there are two nonmerging firms with equal shares.

Even though all prices rise, the share-weighted industry average price may fall if higher priced products experience proportionately greater output reductions. Such would be the case if the merging firms had higher than average premerger prices. On the other hand, because all prices increase, it follows from Equation (9) that consumer welfare decreases as a result of a merger. Each firm's profits also increase as a result of a merger.

A merger leads to a reallocation of output from the merging firms to the nonmerging firms, because the nonmerging firms raise price less than the merged firm raises the weighted average of its two prices. If the nonmerging firms, on average, were larger than the merging firms, their costs would be lower or perceived quality higher, and this shift in relative outputs would enhance welfare. A merger would cause a net increase in welfare if the output reallocation were relatively large because of relatively high cross elasticities of demand (specifically $\beta\bar{p}$), and if there were relatively little substitution to the outside good because of a relatively low aggregate elasticity of demand.[12]

If the shares of the merged firm's products differ premerger, there is a shift in output from the product with the smaller premerger share to the product with the larger premerger share because the merged firm raises the price of the former product more than the price of the latter. Thus, the average cost of the merged firm is less than that of the merging firms or the perceived quality higher. A merger would cause a net increase in welfare if the output reallocation were relatively large because of relatively high cross elasticities of demand and a substantial inequality of the merging firms' shares, and if there were relatively little substitution to the outside good because of a relatively low industry elasticity of demand. Indeed, it is possible for mergers to en-

12. As an example, the merger of two firms with shares of 10 percent enhances welfare if $\beta\bar{p} = 7$, $\varepsilon = 1$, and there is one nonmerging firm.

hance welfare even though they involve firms with a combined share in excess of 50 percent.[13]

While either of the foregoing effects may cause a merger to produce a net increase in welfare, that is far more likely with the former effect. In particular, the former effect causes mergers to produce a net increase in welfare over a significantly larger range of the demand parameters. Both of the effects arise in Cournot models as well.[14] In the Cournot context, the only possible source of an efficiency gain from a merger is the exploitation of cost differences among firms. That is not the case with differentiated products because there are perceived quality differences, which also affect welfare.

In the logit context, larger firms generally are inferred to have both lower marginal costs and higher α_j's than their smaller counterparts, but that is not the case if larger firms have significantly higher prices. It is easy to see from Equation (14) that, with sufficiently high prices, larger firms would have higher costs despite higher markups. It might seem that the welfare effects of mergers must depend a great deal on premerger prices and inferred marginal costs and α_j's. That is not the case, however, because the effects of a merger on our measures of change in consumer welfare and change in total welfare are independent of premerger relative prices.[15] Holding s, β, ε, and $\bar{p}$ constant, while changing individual prices, forces offsetting changes in the c_j's and the α_j's that maintain the premerger price–marginal cost margins and differences among the $(\alpha_j - \beta p_j)$'s. With the α_j's changing in this way, the postmerger first-order conditions are satisfied by the same markups and shares for any set of relative premerger prices, and premerger prices do not affect the welfare change calculations.

The effects of merger efficiencies in the form of cost reductions are easily incorporated into the analysis of a merger. If a merger would be expected to reduce one merging firm's marginal cost, then the simulations of the postmerger equilibrium can incorporate that assumption. One possibility we consider below is that the merged firm's marginal cost is equal to the lesser of the marginal costs of the two merging firms. Estimates of fixed cost savings are even more easily incorporated into the welfare calculations. Finally, it is possible in some instances to incorporate effects of mergers on perceived product quality, for example, if the estimated logit demand system has a linear function of product characteristics instead of just α_j constants. Any predict-

13. As an example, the merger of firms with shares of 45 and 10 percent enhances welfare if $\beta\bar{p} = 15$, $\varepsilon = .5$, and there is one nonmerging firm.

14. See Farrell and Shapiro (1990) and Werden (1991). The literature on Cournot models has not focused on shift of production from the merging firms to nonmerging firms as we do. The importance of these effects may be greater in a differentiated products model than in a homogeneous product Cournot model, because firm asymmetries may be greater. Cournot mergers also tend not to be privately profitable, but that is not the case for Bertrand mergers (see Deneckere and Davidson, 1985).

15. This statement no longer holds if mergers are assumed to reduce the marginal cost of the higher-cost merging firms to a level dependent on the marginal cost of the lower-cost merging firm.

able effects of a merger on product characteristics could then easily be taken into account.

4. Comparative Statics Involving the Demand Elasticity Parameters

To facilitate the discussion in this section and the next, it is useful to introduce some additional notation to refer to the price and welfare effects resulting from a merger:

$\Delta p_j \equiv$ the percentage price increase for firm j

$\Delta p_{\text{Ind}} \equiv$ the share-weighted average percentage price increase for the industry

$\Delta CW \equiv$ change in consumer welfare as a percentage of premerger revenue

$\Delta W \equiv$ change in total welfare as a percentage of premerger revenue.

The comparative static effect of changing the demand elasticity parameters is of interest for the conventional reasons and also because it indicates the importance of uncertainty about the values of these parameters. If the estimates are very sensitive to small changes in parameter values, precise estimates of parameter values are important, and if the reverse is true, rough estimates or guesses are satisfactory. Unfortunately, it is not possible to derive analytically general comparative static results relating to the magnitudes of the effects of changing parameter values.[16] Nevertheless, it appears from numerous simulations that the effect of changing the demand elasticity parameters is very much the same on Δp_m, Δp_{Ind}, and ΔCW, and is quite consistent from one merger to the next.

For various parameter values, Table 2 gives the effect on Δp_{Ind} of the merger of two firms with shares of 20 percent, assuming two nonmerging firms with equal shares. The figures in the table are relative to those for a base case of $\beta\bar{p} = 5$ and $\varepsilon = 1$.[17] The relative effects of the merger on ΔCW are almost exactly the same, and the effects on Δp_m are approximately the same. Moreover, for a large number of other mergers we have examined, the relative effects are approximately the same as those presented in Table 2.

There are three notable features of Table 2. First, the effects of mergers are more sensitive to changes in ε than to changes in $\beta\bar{p}$. Second, if either $\beta\bar{p}$ or ε is high, the effect of changing the other is rather modest. Thus, if either of the parameters is known to be high, uncertainty about the other is of limited importance. Third, Δp_m, Δp_{Ind}, and ΔCW are not monotonic in $\beta\bar{p}$; all three peak between $\beta\bar{p} = 4.3$ and $\beta\bar{p} = 4.6$. The reason for this is straightforward. If $\beta\bar{p}$ is very large, the inside goods are such good substitutes for each other that a merger matters little, and if $\beta\bar{p}$ is very small, the inside goods are such poor substitutes for each other that a merger matters very little. Consequently, the effect of a merger must be greatest at some intermediate value of $\beta\bar{p}$.

16. It can be shown analytically that multiplying both β and ε by the same positive constant has the effect of multiplying the price and welfare effects of mergers by the reciprocal of that constant.

17. These parameter values are not arbitrarily chosen. The empirically based value of $\beta\bar{p}$ used in the next section is roughly 4.8, and unitary demand elasticity is in the range of many empirical estimates.

Table 2. Relative Effects of Mergers on Δp_{Ind} with Various Values of β and ε

β \ ε	0.5	1	2	4
2.5	2.00	1.31	0.38	—
5.0	1.24	1.00	0.65	0.19
7.5	0.89	0.76	0.58	0.32
10.0	0.70	0.62	0.50	0.33

ΔW is not considered in Table 2 because the effect of changing parameter values is quite different on ΔW than on Δp_m, Δp_{Ind}, and ΔCW, and because the effect of changing parameter values is not consistent from one merger to the next. Within the range of parameter values considered, ΔW is not monotonic in either $\beta\bar{p}$ or ε. For the merger considered in Table 2, if $\beta\bar{p} = 5$, the maximum welfare loss occurs at $\varepsilon \approx 1.97$. If $\varepsilon = 1.97$, the maximum welfare loss occurs at $\beta\bar{p} \approx 3.22$. If both parameters are allowed to vary (and all marginal costs must be positive), the maximum welfare loss occurs at $\beta\bar{p} \approx 1.25$, $\varepsilon \approx 0.43$. ΔW is not monotonic in ε because the profit increase from mergers rises much more rapidly as ε is decreased than ΔCW decreases.

5. Calculated Price and Welfare Effects of Mergers among U.S. Long-Distance Carriers

To illustrate both the process of simulating mergers with a logit model and the sort of predictions that flow from the logit model, we consider hypothetical mergers among existing U.S. long-distance carriers. There are three major long-distance carriers in the United States—AT&T, MCI, and Sprint—all serving throughout the nation. In 1991, they accounted for 87 percent of the long distance revenues. The remaining 13 percent of revenue was divided among roughly 500 minor carriers, most of which operate in only a small fraction of the U.S., and no one of which accounted for as much as 1 percent of industry revenues. For the purposes of estimating the effects of hypothetical mergers, we assume that choice set faced by any particular subscriber consists of the three major carriers and three of the many minor carriers, assumed to have equal shares.

For market shares, we use actual 1991 nationwide shares of minutes of usage.[18] For prices, we use actual July 1991 average revenue per minute.[19] We take ε to be 0.7, which is in the range of widely cited, published estimates

18. The raw data are from Federal Communications Commission, *Statistics of Communications Common Carriers*, 1991/1992 ed., which reports revenues. The revenue shares are: AT&T, 62.2 percent; MCI, 15.0 percent; Sprint, 9.7 percent; all others, 13.1 percent. We convert these into minutes shares using the average price data. The minutes shares we use are: AT&T, 61.4 percent; MCI, 15.5 percent; Sprint, 9.8 percent; each of the three minor carriers, 4.4 percent.

19. The price data were supplied by Michael Ward and are for five south central states. The average revenues in cents per minute are: AT&T, 16.6; MCI, 15.9; Sprint, 16.2. We have no price data for the minor carriers and assume that their average price was the same as Sprint's.

Table 3. Calculated Price and Welfare Effects of Possible Mergers Assuming that Mergers Do Not Affect Marginal Costs

Merger	$\Delta p_{AT\&T}$	Δp_{MCI}	Δp_{Sprint}	Δp_{Minor}	Δp_{Ind}	ΔCW	ΔW
AT&T–MCI	4.87	25.70	0.49	0.21	5.06	−5.63	−2.296
AT&T–Sprint	2.90	0.48	24.42	0.12	2.82	−3.40	−1.243
AT&T–Minor	1.22	0.20	0.12	23.82, 0.05	1.18	−1.45	−0.488
MCI–Sprint	0.58	2.10	3.35	0.03	1.01	−0.98	−0.046
MCI–Minor	0.25	0.89	0.03	3.28, 0.02	0.44	−0.43	−0.011
Sprint–Minor	0.16	0.04	0.85	1.96, 0.01	0.27	−0.27	−0.0003
Minor–Minor	0.07	0.02	0.01	0.84, 0.00	0.12	−0.12	0.003

Note: For mergers involving a minor firm, the Δp_{Minor} column lists first the price increase for the merging minor firm(s), then that for the nonmerging minor firms(s).

of the elasticity of demand for long-distance service (see Taylor, 1980: 170; and Taylor, 1993). We use an estimate of β derived from a proprietary study of intra-LATA (Local Access Transport Area) carrier choice based on a survey of choices in hypothetical situations, so β could be estimated without instrumental variables. What matters for the welfare effects of mergers is $\beta\bar{p}$, and a β of 29 with the prices we use gives roughly the same value of $\beta\bar{p}$ as in the proprietary study.[20]

Table 3 presents the calculated price and welfare effects for all possible mergers among the carriers, assuming that costs are unaffected by mergers. A striking feature of these results is the substantial asymmetry of the price increases between the two merging firms and between the merging and nonmerging firms. For the mergers involving firms of very different size—those involving AT&T and those between MCI or Sprint and a minor firm—the smaller merging firm increases price at least several times as much as the larger merging firm. For all of the mergers, the nonmerging firms increase price by a fraction of the amount that the larger merging firm increases price.

The merger of two minor firms actually enhances total welfare slightly, and the remaining mergers not involving AT&T lessen welfare very little; even the MCI–Sprint merger reduces welfare by less than 0.05 percent of premerger revenues. Mergers not involving AT&T have such small effects on welfare because AT&T's very large share implies that it has a combination of cost and perceived quality advantages over its rivals,[21] so the substitution to AT&T induced by mergers of its rivals has a welfare-enhancing effect. Mergers involving AT&T are far less likely to be welfare enhancing. As noted above, shifts in production between two merging firms are less likely to cause mergers to enhance welfare than are shifts in production from the merging firms to the nonmerging firms.

20. Additional parameter values within the confidence interval of $\beta\bar{p}$ are considered in Froeb, Werden, and Tardiff (1993).

21. As explained above, it does not matter for the welfare calculations whether the advantage is in cost or perceived quality.

Table 4. Calculated Price and Welfare Effects of Possible Mergers with Non-AT&T Carriers in a Nest, Assuming that Mergers Do Not Affect Marginal Costs

Merger	$\Delta p_{AT\&T}$	Δp_{MCI}	Δp_{Sprint}	Δp_{Minor}	Δp_{Ind}	ΔCW	ΔW
AT&T–MCI	3.71	17.34	0.84	0.36	3.89	−4.22	−1.546
AT&T–Sprint	2.20	0.85	16.69	0.21	2.19	−2.59	−0.762
AT&T–Minor	0.92	0.35	0.20	16.48, 0.09	0.91	−1.10	−0.274
MCI–Sprint	0.77	2.84	4.49	0.13	1.33	−1.30	0.012
MCI–Minor	0.32	1.14	0.12	4.19, 0.05	0.56	−0.55	0.024
Sprint–Minor	0.20	0.13	1.03	2.39, 0.03	0.34	−0.34	0.030
Minor–Minor	0.09	0.06	0.03	0.98, 0.01	0.15	−0.15	0.018

Note. For mergers involving a minor firm, the Δp_{Minor} column lists first the price increase for the merging minor firm(s), then that for the nonmerging minor firms(s).

It has been suggested that consumers perceive non-AT&T carriers as especially close substitutes for each other. Thus, the proper specification of demand may be a nested-logit model, with the non-AT&T carriers in a nest. We do not know what value of the nest parameter would be appropriate, and arbitrarily choose 0.7 so we can illustrate the effects of adding a nest. As Table 4 shows, all mergers not involving AT&T enhance welfare. Adding the nest makes the non-AT&T firms closer substitutes and thus introduces greater competition. This causes mergers not involving AT&T to have greater price effects. Introducing a nest also affects the inferred marginal costs and α's, and these effects cause the mergers not involving AT&T to be welfare enhancing. With lower nest parameter values, the welfare gain from these mergers is even greater.

Finally, we consider the possibility that the cost advantages of large firms can be extended through merger. Table 5 presents the calculated price and welfare effects of the mergers under that assumption, using the simple logit model. All the mergers except AT&T–MCI enhance welfare although the

Table 5. Calculated Price and Welfare Effects of Possible Mergers Assuming the Cost Advantages of Large Firms Can be Extended Through Merger

Merger	$\Delta p_{AT\&T}$	Δp_{MCI}	Δp_{Sprint}	Δp_{Minor}	Δp_{Ind}	ΔCW	ΔW
AT&T–MCI	5.95	10.96	0.44	0.19	4.92	−5.06	−0.587
AT&T–Sprint	3.77	0.41	6.33	0.10	2.75	−2.91	0.130
AT&T–Minor	1.64	0.16	0.10	4.14, 0.04	1.15	−1.21	0.162
MCI–Sprint	0.33	2.35	0.14	0.02	0.59	−0.56	0.306
MCI–Minor	0.10	1.04	0.01	−1.14, 0.01	0.18	−0.20	0.195
Sprint–Minor	0.12	0.03	0.89	0.89, 0.01	0.20	−0.20	0.047
Minor–Minor	0.07	0.02	0.01	0.84, 0.004	0.12	−0.13	0.003

Note For mergers involving a minor firm, the Δp_{Minor} column lists first the price increase for the merging minor firm(s), then that for the nonmerging minor firms(s).

welfare gains are all small. The welfare effects of the mergers are much more favorable in this case not only because of the direct effect of the cost savings from the mergers of different-sized firms. Also important is the indirect effect the cost reduction has on the price increases resulting from the mergers. The smaller-share merging firm generally raises price a great deal under the assumption that marginal costs are unaffected by merger. Under the assumption that the marginal cost of the smaller-share merging firm is reduced to that of the larger-share merging firm, the reduction in the marginal cost of the smaller-share merging firm causes its price to be increased far less. If MCI were to merge with a minor firm, the marginal cost reduction for the product of the minor firm would be sufficiently great that the merged firm would reduce the price for the minor firm's product.

6. Limitations of the Logit Model and Alternative Models

The logit model is based on the restrictive assumption known as Independence of Irrelevant Alternatives (IIA) (see Ben-Akiva and Lerman, 1985: 108–11). This assumption implies that when the price of one product is increased, consumers switch to others in proportion to the relative shares of those products. Actual preferences, however, may yield very different substitution patterns because certain goods may be viewed as closer substitutes than others. For example, in response to a price increase for BMWs, the IIA assumption implies that much of the substitution will be to top-selling models like Ford Taurus and Honda Accord and very little to models sold by Acura, Cadillac, Lincoln, and Mercedes Benz, which have much smaller shares. We suspect that the IIA assumption does not hold in this situation.

The logit model is easily generalized by the incorporation of nests, as we did above. In the car example, there could be a nest for luxury cars and a nest within that nest for foreign or German luxury cars. This certainly makes the logit model more general, but it is still restrictive in two senses. The IIA assumption still applies within a nest and between nests. In addition, a single nest parameter controls how close the goods in a nest are as substitutes for each other and how close they all are as substitutes for goods outside the nest. This means, for example, that making goods in a nest better substitutes for each other requires making them worse substitutes for all other goods. Finally, Brownstone and Small (1989) find that a common estimation technique used for the nested logit is both unstable and inefficient, and yields biased standard errors.

Whether the logit model—simple or nested—fits a particular data set can be examined through an explicit test of the IIA assumption. The leading test was derived by Hausman and McFadden (1984). Its application and the application of alternative tests are discussed by Ben-Akiva and Lerman (1985: 183–94). The IIA assumption has been rejected as a null hypothesis by some empirical studies, but it has been accepted by others (for example, Ben-Akiva and Lerman). When the IIA assumption is not rejected by the data, the logit model can be considered to be a reasonable approximation.

We believe that it is always useful and appropriate to supplement the traditional, structural analysis of mergers in differentiated products industries with simulations. As we discuss presently, logit is not the only possible model and another model may be preferable. We would not hesitate, however, to use the logit model whenever a lack of time or money effectively foreclosed other options. Unlike other modeling approaches, the logit model with our parameterization requires very little information—just readily observable prices and shares, and two demand elasticity parameters, which can be guessed at in a pinch. Even when the logit model is not strictly applicable and the specific predictions of logit simulations cannot be considered reliable, logit simulations provide much needed perspective. They indicate asymmetries in, and order of magnitude of, the price effects of mergers, and they provide a basis for trading off possible cost savings against price increases.

One alternative to using the logit model is to assume that all of the relevant elasticities are invariant to the price and quantity changes resulting from a merger. With this strong assumption, the effects of a merger are easily calculated from postmerger first-order conditions and elasticities. One notable example of this approach is Baker and Bresnahan (1985). They calculate the price effects of several beer mergers using estimated residual demand elasticities. Their approach assumes that elasticities are constant and that the merged firm acts as a Stackelberg leader. Although this approach has the advantage of requiring the estimation of very few elasticity parameters, it still requires some individual-firm cost shifters as instruments. This may be a significant drawback since good instruments are hard to find and weak instruments yield estimates with very large standard errors (see Froeb and Werden, 1991: 44–46).

Most significantly, the assumption of price-invariant elasticities is not tested, and it is unlikely to hold. Most often, increasing the price for a product increases the elasticity of its demand. There is a strong tendency for this to occur, because the price increase induces a quantity decrease, and both of these effects tend to increase the demand elasticity. If the elasticity of demand does increase as price is increased, assuming the contrary leads to an overestimate of the price increases from mergers. Froeb and Werden (1992) explore this phenomenon, and illustrate its significance. As a further illustration, consider the merger of AT&T with MCI, assuming logit demand. The percentage price increases calculated using the Baker-Bresnahan approach are 48.6 for AT&T and 101.8 for MCI.[22] These estimates exceed the actual figures in Table 3 by a factor of 10 in the case of AT&T and a factor of 4 in the case of MCI.[23] Virtually all of the error arises from the assumption of constant elasticity of demand; the assumption of Stackelberg equilibrium turns out to be unimportant.

Hausman, Leonard, and Zona (1994) also calculate the price effects of sev-

22. The calculations involve dividing both sides of Equation (14) by p_j, evaluating the right-hand side at premerger prices, then solving for p_j.

23. The margins of error are smaller for the other mergers and quite small when the price increases predicted by the logit simulations are very small.

eral beer mergers. They assume a multilevel, almost ideal demand system (AIDS), and estimate a host of elasticities, using a panel of scanner data from supermarkets for various cities. To identify the parameters of the demand system, they assume that costs are the same across cities and that demand is independent across cities. This allows them to use prices in one city as an instrument for price in each other city, thus avoiding problems associated with using cost shifters as instruments, and making it possible to use high-frequency scanner data, which may be superior to alternatives. However, the assumption of demand independence across cities is likely to be violated for products, including beer, that have significant seasonal effects or have special promotions at the same time in many cities. In addition, they assume that elasticities are constant in estimating the effects of a merger.

A very different approach has been taken by Berry (1994) and Berry, Levinsohn, and Pakes (1993). They also use panel data, but their data are for various models of products like automobiles, and consumers are assumed to base their choices on observable product characteristics (or on unobservable attributes correlated with observable characteristics). Rather than assuming that elasticities are invariant to changes in prices and quantities, this approach exploits the fact that they do vary. A given product's equilibrium price is affected by variation in the characteristics of competing products, provided that the first product's equilibrium demand elasticity changes. Thus, the model is identified by using characteristics of competing products as instruments.

This approach assumes that characteristics of competing products are independent of demand shocks. This assumption is difficult to test, and it is likely to be violated if firms compete on the basis of model characteristics. This approach is similar to ours in that it uses first-order equilibrium conditions to estimate marginal costs. This line of research was only recently begun and has not yet been applied to mergers, but such an application would be a logical step.

Another solution to the identification problem, and the one used to generate the estimate of the cross elasticity parameter used in the simulations of long-distance carrier mergers, is to use hypothetical choice data rather than actual choice data. Hypothetical choice data are generated by asking consumers what choices they would make at specified prices. Specifying exogenous price variation obviates the need for any instruments. It also eliminates the need to extrapolate outside the range of observations, which is typically required with data on actual choices and can lead to significant error in estimation (see Froeb and Werden, 1991: 39; Froeb and Werden, 1992: 243–46). Furthermore, a consumer survey can be designed so that the right-hand-side variables are orthogonal. When that is the case, White (1980) has shown that a specific functional form, such as the logit, can be motivated as a first-order approximation to the unknown true function.

7. The Structural Standards of the Merger Guidelines

The 1992 Merger Guidelines state the specific enforcement standards used by the two federal antitrust enforcement agencies—the U.S. Department of Justice and the Federal Trade Commission. The general enforcement standards are based on two concentration measures[24]—the *increase in the HHI*, defined as twice the product of the shares of the merging firms, and the *postmerger HHI*, defined as the Herfindahl-Hirschman Index (HHI) for the relevant market plus the increase in the HHI. Mergers fall in a safe harbor if the postmerger HHI for the relevant market is at most 1,000 or the increase in the HHI is at most 50. If the postmerger HHI exceeds 1,800, the 1992 Guidelines (§ 1.51) "presume that mergers producing an increase in the HHI of more than 100 points are likely to create or enhance market power," but they provide that this presumption may be overcome by any of a number of other factors they discuss in later sections, including one on product differentiation.

Section 2.21 of the 1992 Guidelines articulates a special enforcement standard for mergers in differentiated products industries. Under that standard, a merger is presumed to harm consumers significantly if the combined share of the merging firms is at least 35 percent. By negative implication, one may infer that a merger will be presumed not to harm consumers significantly if the combined share of the merging firms is below 35 percent. Typically, a combined share for the merging firms of 35 percent translates into a change in the HHI of 400–500 points, which is far in excess of the 100–point threshold of the general standard.[25]

The foregoing analysis suggests several observations about these standards.[26] First, a standard based on the combined share of the merging firms is problematic because the price and welfare effects of mergers vary greatly for a given combined market share. This is illustrated in Table 1, in which all the mergers have the same combined share for the merging firms. A far better measure for use as a structural standard would have been the product of the shares of the merging firms or, equivalently, the change in the HHI.

The overall level of concentration, holding the shares of the merging firms constant, is a relevant factor since the nonmerging firms increase price more the greater the concentration among them. On the other hand, this effect is rather small, and greater concentration among the merging firms gives rise to a welfare gain from the reallocation or production. The net effect of an increase in concentration among the nonmerging firms, holding the shares of

24. These concentration measures are not meant to be predictions about the actual shares and concentration that will prevail postmerger (see Werden, 1991: 1002–3).

25. The section on mergers in differentiated products industries was just added in the 1992 edition of the Guidelines. At the same time, a 35 percent test was added (in § 2.22) for mergers in homogeneous goods industries, when the effect of concern does not involve coordination (i.e., when the effect is that in a Cournot model). There is no similar test when the effect of concern does involve coordination (i.e., when it stems from explicit collusion or some sort of repeated game equilibrium). Thus, the 1992 Guidelines must reflect a conscious decision to reduce the range of mergers subject to challenge on the basis of effects termed "unilateral," that is, effects not arising from coordination. This is curious because noncooperative models such as Cournot and Bertrand offer a far firmer basis for merger policy than does any notion of collusion (see Hay and Werden, 1993).

26. There is a much more extensive discussion on this subject in Werden and Froeb (1993).

the merging firms constant, is likely to be to mitigate the adverse welfare effects of a merger, and it can even reverse them.

Most importantly, if the logit model, which motivates the Guidelines' discussion of mergers in differentiated products industries, is appropriate, then it is far better to simulate the effects of a merger using that model than to rely on simple structural indicators. Simulations are more accurate generally; they identify asymmetric price effects; they identify possible welfare gains from production reallocation; and they provide a means of trading-off possible merger efficiencies. The last point is particularly significant because trading off price effects and possible efficiencies is a hopeless task if price effects are simply proxied for by market shares.

8. Conclusions

Economists have long been critical of the practice in antitrust law of predicting the competitive effects of mergers on the basis of shares of a delineated relevant market.[27] Early critics of this practice were advocates of monopolistic competition theories, and the argument that market shares are inadequate predictors is strongest in differentiated products industries. As Edward Chamberlin (1950: 86–87) put it:

> "Industry" or "commodity" boundaries are a snare and a delusion—in the highest degree arbitrarily drawn, and, wherever drawn, establishing at once wholly false implications both as to competition of substitutes within their limits, which supposedly stops at their borders, and as to the possibility of ruling on the presence or absence of oligopolistic forces by the simple device of counting the number of producers included.[28]

These criticisms are well taken, and they can be addressed by replacing the traditional structural approach with simulations of the effects of mergers within the context of a specified oligopoly model. We consider the logit model, but other models can also be used. Our version of the logit model is specifically designed to capture one of the important factors to which Chamberlin refers—competition from products outside the designated group. More generally, simulations capture the other factor to which Chamberlin refers—the oligopolistic interaction within the designated group. Taking cost differences and consumer preferences into account, simulations predict the complex, asymmetric price effects of mergers in differentiated products industries. Simulations also indicate effects on welfare of production reallocation induced by mergers, and they make it straightforward to incorporate reductions in fixed or marginal costs in an explicit welfare analysis.

Simulating the effects of mergers unfortunately requires undertaking some-

27. This practice in merger cases can be traced to the Supreme Court's 1948 *Columbia Steel* decision. Economists began expressing opposition to the practice in 1934 (see Werden, 1992: 125–29).

28. Much the same argument was made recently by Fisher (1987: 27), and Hausman, Leonard, and Zona (1992) make a related argument based on the Lerner index.

thing like market delineation, because it is necessary to impose some structure, such as delineating a set of inside goods. The simulations are affected by the delineation of this set because the inside substitutabilities are different from those between the inside and outside goods. On the other hand, narrowing the set of inside goods increases the aggregate elasticity of demand for the inside goods (and possibly the estimated cross elasticity parameter as well), so the simulations may not be very sensitive to the market delineation.

The logit model used here is a reasonable approximation to the structure of demand in some differentiated products industries. Our version of the logit model is also very practical. The two demand elasticity parameters can be easily estimated, or guessed at in a pinch, and premerger prices and market shares are the only other information required for simulations. Thus, we offer a simple, low-cost way in which to get some idea of the effects of mergers in differentiated products industries. The logit model can always be used to obtain a "quick and dirty" estimate, and it is possible to test whether the model is a good approximation to the actual demand system.

There are many situations in which the logit model is not appropriate. A nested logit model may be used in such cases, as may a probit model. In either case, estimation and simulation are more difficult, but still possible. Berry (1994) and Berry, Levinsohn, and Pakes (1993) employ far more complicated models, and such models may also be used to simulate the effects of mergers. These models may prove preferable to the logit model, but their advantages and disadvantages remain to be explored.

References

Anderson, Simon P., and André de Palma. 1992. "Multiproduct Firms: A Nested Logit Approach," 40 *Journal of Industrial Economics* 261–76.

———, ———, and Jacques-François Thisse. 1992. *Discrete Choice Theory of Product Differentiation*. Cambridge, Mass.: MIT Press.

Baker, Jonathan B., and Timothy F. Bresnahan. 1985. "The Gains from Merger or Collusion in Product-Differentiated Industries," 33 *Journal of Industrial Economics* 427–44.

Ben-Akiva, Moshe, and Steven R. Lerman. 1985. *Discrete Choice Analysis*. Cambridge, Mass.: MIT Press.

Berry, Steven T. 1994. "Estimating Discrete Choice Models of Product Differentiation," 25 *RAND Journal of Economics* 242–62.

———, James Levinsohn, and Ariel Pakes. 1993. "Automobile Prices in Market Equilibrium," National Bureau for Economic Research Working Paper 4264 (January 1993).

Brownstone, David, and Kenneth A. Small. 1989. "Efficient Estimation of Nested Logit Models," 7 *Journal of Business and Economic Statistics* 67–74.

Chamberlin, Edward H. 1950. "Product Heterogeneity and Public Policy," 40 *American Economic Review (Papers & Proceedings)* 85–92.

Deneckere, Raymond, and Carl Davidson. 1985. "Incentives to Form Coalitions with Bertrand Competition," 16 *RAND Journal of Economics* 473–86.

Farrell, Joseph, and Carl Shapiro. 1990. "Horizontal Mergers: An Equilibrium Analysis," 80 *American Economic Review* 107–26.

Fisher, Franklin F. 1987. "Horizontal Mergers: Triage and Treatment," 1 *Journal of Economic Perspectives* 23–40.

Froeb, Luke M., and Gregory J. Werden. 1991. "Residual Demand Estimation for Market Delineation: Complications and Limitations," 6 *Review of Industrial Organization* 33–48.

426 The Journal of Law, Economics, & Organization, V10 N2

———, and ———. 1992. "The Reverse *Cellophane* Fallacy in Market Delineation," 7 *Review of Industrial Organization* 241–47.
———, ———, and Timothy J. Tardiff. 1993. "The Demsetz Postulate and the Effects of Mergers in Differentiated Product Industries," Economic Analysis Group Discussion Paper 93-5 (August 24, 1993).
Hausman, Jerry A., Gregory Leonard, and J. Douglas Zona. 1992. "A Proposed Method for Analyzing Competition Among Differentiated Products," 60 *Antitrust Law Journal* 889–900.
———, ———, and ———. 1994. "Competitive Analysis with Differentiated Products," 34 *Annales d'Economique et Statistique* 159–80.
———, and Daniel McFadden. 1984. "Specification Tests for the Multinomial Logit Model," 52 *Econometrica* 1219–40.
Hay, George A., and Gregory J. Werden. 1993. "Horizontal Mergers: Law, Policy, and Economics," 83 *American Economic Review (Papers and Proceedings)* 173–77.
Kreps, David M., and Jose A. Scheinkman. 1983. "Cournot Precommitment and Bertrand Competition Yield Cournot Outcomes," 14 *Bell Journal of Economics* 326–37.
Levy, David T., and James D. Reitzes. 1992. "Anticompetitive Effects of Mergers in Markets with Localized Competition," 8 *Journal of Law, Economics, & Organization* 427–40.
McAfee, R. Preston, and Michael A. Williams. 1992. "Horizontal Mergers and Public Policy," 40 *Journal of Industrial Economics* 181–87.
McElroy, F. W. 1993. "The Effects of Mergers in Markets for Differentiated Products," 8 *Review of Industrial Organization* 69–81.
McFadden, Daniel. 1974. "Conditional Logit Analysis of Qualitative Choice Behavior," in P. Zarembka, ed., *Frontiers in Econometrics*. New York: Academic Press.
Morey, Edward R. 1992. "Derivation of the Nested-Logit Model of Consumer Choice: A Synthesis," unpublished paper, University of Colorado.
Small, Kenneth A., and Harvey S. Rosen. 1981. "Applied Welfare Economics with Discrete Choice Models," 49 *Econometrica* 105–30.
Taylor, Lester D. 1980. *Telecommunications Demand*. Cambridge, Mass.: Ballinger.
———. 1993. "Pricing of Telecommunications Services: Comment on Gabel and Kennet," 8 *Review of Industrial Organization* 15–19.
U.S. Department of Justice and Federal Trade Commission. 1992. Horizontal Merger Guidelines, April 2, 1992, reprinted in 4 Trade Reg. Rep. (CCH) ¶ 13,104.
Werden, Gregory J. 1991. "Horizontal Mergers: Comment," 81 *American Economic Review* 1002–6.
———. 1992. "The History of Antitrust Market Delineation," 76 *Marquette Law Review* 123–215.
———, and Luke M. Froeb. 1993. "The Effects of Mergers in Differentiated Products Industries: Logit Demand and Structural Merger Policy," Economic Analysis Group Discussion Paper 93-4 (August 23, 1993).
White, Halbert. 1980. "Using Least Squares to Approximate Unknown Regression Functions," 21 *International Economic Review* 149–70.
Willig, Robert D. 1991. "Merger Analysis, Industrial Organization Theory, and Merger Guidelines," *Brookings Papers on Economic Activity, Microeconomics (1991)*, pp. 281–332.

Part III
Collusion

[9]

A THEORY OF OLIGOPOLY

GEORGE J. STIGLER[1]
University of Chicago

No one has the right, and few the ability, to lure economists into reading another article on oligopoly theory without some advance indication of its alleged contribution. The present paper accepts the hypothesis that oligopolists wish to collude to maximize joint profits. It seeks to reconcile this wish with facts, such as that collusion is impossible for many firms and collusion is much more effective in some circumstances than in others. The reconciliation is found in the problem of policing a collusive agreement, which proves to be a problem in the theory of information. A considerable number of implications of the theory are discussed, and a modest amount of empirical evidence is presented.

I. THE TASK OF COLLUSION

A satisfactory theory of oligopoly cannot begin with assumptions concerning the way in which each firm views its interdependence with its rivals. If we adhere to the traditional theory of profit-maximizing enterprises, then behavior is no longer something to be assumed but rather something to be deduced. The firms in an industry will behave in such a way, given the demand-and-supply functions (including those of rivals), that their profits will be maximized.

The combined profits of the entire set of firms in an industry are maximized when they act together as a monopolist. At least in the traditional formulation of the oligopoly problem, in which there are no major uncertainties as to the profit-maximizing output and price at any time, this familiar conclusion seems inescapable. Moreover, the result holds for any number of firms.

Our modification of this theory consists simply in presenting a systematic account of the factors governing the feasibility of collusion, which like most things in this world is not free. Before we do so, it is desirable to look somewhat critically at the concept of homogeneity of products, and what it implies for profit-maximizing. We shall show that collusion normally involves much more than "the" price.

Homogeneity is commonly defined in terms of identity of products or of (what is presumed to be equivalent) pairs of products between which the elasticity of substitution is infinite. On either definition it is the behavior of buyers that is decisive. Yet it should be obvious that products may be identical to any or every buyer while buyers may be quite different from the viewpoint of sellers.

This fact that every transaction involves two parties is something that economists do not easily forget. One would therefore expect a definition of homogeneity also to be two-sided: if the products are what sellers offer, and the purchase commitments are what the buyers offer, full homogeneity clearly involves infinite elasticities of substitution between both products and purchase

[1] I am indebted to Claire Friedland for the statistical work and to Harry Johnson for helpful criticisms.

commitments. In other words, two products are homogeneous to a buyer if he is indifferent between all combinations of x of one and (say) $20 - x$ of the other, at a common price. Two purchase commitments are homogeneous to a seller if he is indifferent between all combinations of y of one and (say) $20 - y$ of the other, at a common price. Full homogeneity is then defined as homogeneity both in products (sellers) and purchase commitments (buyers).

The heterogeneity of purchase commitments (buyers), however, is surely often at least as large as that of products within an industry, and sometimes vastly larger. There is the same sort of personal differentia of buyers as of sellers—ease in making sales, promptness of payment, penchant for returning goods, likelihood of buying again (or buying other products). In addition there are two differences among buyers which are pervasive and well recognized in economics:

1. The size of purchase, with large differences in costs of providing lots of different size.
2. The urgency of purchase, with possibly sufficient differences in elasticity of demand to invite price discrimination.

It is one thing to assert that no important market has homogeneous transactions, and quite another to measure the extent of the heterogeneity. In a regime of perfect knowledge, it would be possible to measure heterogeneity by the variance of prices in transactions; in a regime of imperfect knowledge, there will be dispersion of prices even with transaction homogeneity.[2]

The relevance of heterogeneity to collusion is this: It is part of the task of maximizing industry profits to employ a price structure that takes account of the larger differences in the costs of various classes of transactions. Even with a single, physically homogeneous product the profits will be reduced if differences among buyers are ignored. A simple illustration of this fact is given in the Appendix; disregard of differences among buyers proves to be equivalent to imposing an excise tax upon them, but one which is not collected by the monopolist. A price structure of some complexity will usually be the goal of collusive oligopolists.

II. THE METHODS OF COLLUSION

Collusion of firms can take many forms, of which the most comprehensive is outright merger. Often merger will be inappropriate, however, because of diseconomies of scale,[3] and at certain times and places it may be forbidden by law. Only less comprehensive is the cartel with a joint sales agency, which again has economic limitations—it is ill suited to custom work and creates serious administrative costs in achieving quality standards, cost reductions, product innovations, etc. In deference to American antitrust policy, we shall assume that the collusion takes the form of joint determination of outputs and prices by ostensibly independent firms, but we shall not take account of the effects of the legal prohibitions until later. Oligopoly existed before 1890, and has existed in countries that have never had an antitrust policy.

The colluding firms must agree upon the price structure appropriate to the transaction classes which they are prepared to recognize. A complete profit-maximizing price structure may have

[2] Unless one defines heterogeneity of transactions to include also differences in luck in finding low price sellers; see my "Economics of Information," *Journal of Political Economy*, June, 1961.

[3] If the firms are multiproduct, with different product structures, the diseconomies of merger are not strictly those of scale (in any output) but of firm size measured either absolutely or in terms of variety of products.

almost infinitely numerous price classes: the firms will have to decide upon the number of price classes in the light of the costs and returns from tailoring prices to the diversity of transactions. We have already indicated by hypothetical example (see Appendix) that there are net profits to be obtained by catering to differences in transactions. The level of collusive prices will also depend upon the conditions of entry into the industry as well as upon the elasticities of demand.

Let us assume that the collusion has been effected, and a price structure agreed upon. It is a well-established proposition that if any member of the agreement can secretly violate it, he will gain larger profits than by conforming to it.[4] It is, moreover, surely one of the axioms of human behavior that all agreements whose violation would be profitable to the violator must be enforced. The literature of collusive agreements, ranging from the pools of the 1880's to the electrical conspiracies of recent times, is replete with instances of the collapse of conspiracies because of "secret" price-cutting. This literature is biased: conspiracies that are successful in avoiding an amount of price-cutting which leads to collapse of the agreement are less likely to be reported or detected. But no conspiracy can neglect the problem of enforcement.

Enforcement consists basically of detecting significant deviations from the agreed-upon prices. Once detected, the deviations will tend to disappear because they are no longer secret and will be matched by fellow conspirators if they are not withdrawn. If the enforcement is weak, however—if price-cutting is detected only slowly and incompletely—the conspiracy must recognize its weakness: it must set prices not much above the competitive level so the inducements to price-cutting are small, or it must restrict the conspiracy to areas in which enforcement can be made efficient.

Fixing market shares is probably the most efficient of all methods of combating secret price reductions. No one can profit from price-cutting if he is moving along the industry demand curve,[5] once a maximum profit price has been chosen. With inspection of output and an appropriate formula for redistribution of gains and losses from departures from quotas, the incentive to secret price-cutting is eliminated. Unless inspection of output is costly or ineffective (as with services), this is the ideal method of enforcement, and is widely used by legal cartels. Unfortunately for oligopolists, it is usually an easy form of collusion to detect, for it may require side payments among firms and it leaves indelible traces in the output records.

Almost as efficient a method of eliminating secret price-cutting is to assign each buyer to a single seller. If this can be done for all buyers, short-run price-cutting no longer has any purpose. Long-run price-cutting will still be a serious possibility if the buyers are in competition: lower prices to one's own customers can then lead to an expansion of their share of their market, so the price-cutter's long-run demand curve will be more elastic than that of the industry. Long-run price-cutting is likely to be important, however, only where sellers are providing a major cost component to the buyer.

There are real difficulties of other sorts

[4] If price is above marginal cost, marginal revenue will be only slightly less than price (and hence above marginal cost) for price cuts by this one seller.

[5] More precisely, he is moving along a demand curve which is a fixed share of the industry demand, and hence has the same elasticity as the industry curve at every price.

to the sellers in the assignment of buyers. In general the fortunes of the various sellers will differ greatly over time: one seller's customers may grow threefold, while another seller's customers shrink by half. If the customers have uncorrelated fluctuations in demand, the various sellers will experience large changes in relative outputs in the short run.[6] Where the turnover of buyers is large, the method is simply impracticable.

Nevertheless, the conditions appropriate to the assignment of customers will exist in certain industries, and in particular the geographical division of the market has often been employed. Since an allocation of buyers is an obvious and easily detectible violation of the Sherman Act, we may again infer that an efficient method of enforcing a price agreement is excluded by the antitrust laws. We therefore turn to other techniques of enforcement, but we shall find that the analysis returns to allocation of buyers.

In general the policing of a price agreement involves an audit of the transactions prices. In the absence or violation of antitrust laws, actual inspection of the accounting records of sellers has been employed by some colluding groups, but even this inspection gives only limited assurance that the price agreement is adhered to.[7] Ultimately there is no substitute for obtaining the transaction prices from the buyers.

An oligopolist will not consider making secret price cuts to buyers whose purchases fall below a certain size relative to his aggregate sales. The ease with which price-cutting is detected by rivals is decisive in this case. If p is the probability that some rival will hear of one such price reduction, $1 - (1 - p)^n$ is the probability that a rival will learn of at least one reduction if it is given to n customers. Even if p is as small as 0.01, when n equals 100 the probability of detection is .634, and when n equals 1000 it is .99996. No one has yet invented a way to advertise price reductions which brings them to the attention of numerous customers but not to that of any rival.[8]

It follows that oligopolistic collusion will often be effective against small buyers even when it is ineffective against large buyers. When the oligopolists sell to numerous small retailers, for example, they will adhere to the agreed-upon price, even though they are cutting prices to larger chain stores and industrial buyers. This is a first empirical implication of our theory. Let us henceforth exclude small buyers from consideration.

The detection of secret price-cutting will of course be as difficult as interested people can make it. The price-cutter will certainly protest his innocence, or, if this would tax credulity beyond its taxable capacity, blame a disobedient subordinate. The price cut will often take the indirect form of modifying some nonprice dimension of the transaction. The customer may, and often will, divulge price reductions, in order to have them matched by others, but he will learn from experience if each disclosure is followed by the withdrawal of the lower price offer. Indeed the buyer will frequently

[6] When the relative outputs of the firms change, the minimum cost condition of equal marginal costs for all sellers is likely to be violated. Hence industry profits are not maximized.

[7] The literature and cases on "open-price associations" contain numerous references to the collection of prices from sellers (see Federal Trade Commission, *Open-Price Trade Associations* [Washington, 1929], and cases cited).

[8] This argument applies to size of buyer relative to the individual seller. One can also explain the absence of higgling in small transactions because of the costs of bargaining, but this latter argument turns on the absolute size of the typical transaction, not its size relative to the seller.

fabricate wholly fictitious price offers to test the rivals. Policing the collusion sounds very much like the subtle and complex problem presented in a good detective story.

There is a difference: In our case the man who murders the collusive price will receive the bequest of patronage. The basic method of detection of a price-cutter must be the fact that he is getting business he would otherwise not obtain. No promises of lower prices that fail to shift some business can be really effective—either the promised price is still too high or it is simply not believed.

Our definition of perfect collusion, indeed, must be that no buyer changes sellers voluntarily. There is no competitive price-cutting if there are no shifts of buyers among sellers.

To this rule that price-cutting must be inferred from shifts of buyers there is one partial exception, but that an important one. There is one type of buyer who usually reveals the price he pays, and does not accept secret benefices: the government. The system of sealed bids, publicly opened with full identification of each bidder's price and specifications, is the ideal instrument for the detection of price-cutting. There exists no alternative method of secretly cutting prices (bribery of purchasing agents aside). Our second empirical prediction, then, is that collusion will always be more effective against buyers who report correctly and fully the prices tendered to them.[9]

It follows from the test of the absence of price competition by buyer loyalty—and this is our third major empirical prediction—that collusion is severely limited (under present assumptions excluding market-sharing) when the significant buyers constantly change identity. There exist important markets in which the (substantial) buyers do change identity continuously, namely, in the construction industries. The building of a plant or an office building, for example, is an essentially non-repetitive event, and rivals cannot determine whether the successful bidder has been a price-cutter unless there is open bidding to specification.

The normal market, however, contains both stability and change. There may be a small rate of entry of new buyers. There will be some shifting of customers even in a regime of effective collusion, for a variety of minor reasons we can lump together as "random factors." There will often be some sharing of buyers by several sellers—a device commending itself to buyers to increase the difficulty of policing price agreements. We move then to the world of circumstantial evidence, or, as it is sometimes called, of probability.

III. THE CONDITIONS FOR DETECTING SECRET PRICE REDUCTIONS

We shall investigate the problem of detecting secret price-cutting with a simplified model, in which all buyers and all sellers are initially of equal size. The number of buyers per seller—recalling that we exclude from consideration all buyers who take less than (say) 0.33 per cent of a seller's output—will range from 300 down to perhaps 10 or 20 (since we wish to avoid the horrors of full bilateral oligopoly). A few of these buyers are new, but over moderate periods of time most are "old," although some of these old customers will shift among suppliers. A potential secret price-cutter has then three groups of customers who would increase their patronage if given secret price cuts: the old customers of rivals;

[9] The problem implicitly raised by these remarks is why all sales to the government are not at collusive prices. Part of the answer is that the government is usually not a sufficiently large buyer of a commodity to remunerate the costs of collusion.

the old customers who would normally leave him; and new customers.

Most old buyers will deal regularly with one or a few sellers, in the absence of secret price-cutting. There may be no secret price-cutting because a collusive price is adhered to, or because only an essentially competitive price can be obtained. We shall show that the loyalty of customers is a crucial variable in determining which price is approached. We need to know the probability that an old customer will buy again from his regular supplier at the collusive price, in the absence of secret price-cutting.

The buyer will set the economies of repetitive purchase (which include smaller transaction costs and less product-testing) against the increased probability of secret price-cutting that comes from shifting among suppliers. From the viewpoint of any one buyer, this gain will be larger the larger the number of sellers and the smaller the number of buyers, as we shall show below. The costs of shifting among suppliers will be smaller the more homogeneous the goods and the larger the purchases of the buyer (again an inverse function of his size). Let us label this probability of repeat purchases p. We shall indicate later how this probability could be determined in a more general approach.

The second component of sales of a firm will be its sales to new buyers and to the floating old customers of rivals. Here we assume that each seller is equally likely to make a sale, in the absence of price competition.

Let us proceed to the analysis. There are n_0 "old" buyers and n_n new customers, with $n_n = \lambda n_0$ and n_s sellers. A firm may look to three kinds of evidence on secret price-cutting, and therefore by symmetry to three potential areas to practice secret price-cutting.

1. *The behavior of its own old customers.*—It has, on average, n_0/n_s such customers, and expects to sell to $m_1 = pn_0/n_s$ of them in a given round of transactions, in the absence of price cutting. The variance of this number of customers is

$$\sigma_1^2 = \frac{(1-p)pn_0}{n_s}.$$

The probability of the firm losing more old customers than

$$\frac{(1-p)n_0}{n_s} + k\sigma_1$$

is given by the probability of values greater than k. The expected number of these old customers who will shift to any one rival is, say,

$$m_2 = \frac{1}{n_s - 1}\left[\frac{(1-p)n_0}{n_s} + k\sigma_1\right],$$

with a variance

$$\sigma_2^2 = \frac{n_s - 2}{(n_s - 1)^2}\left[\frac{(1-p)n_0}{n_s} + k\sigma_1\right].$$

The probability that any rival will obtain more than $m_2 + r\sigma_2$ of these customers is determined by r. We could now choose those combinations of k and r that fix a level of probability for the loss of a given number of old customers to any one rival beyond which secret price-cutting by this rival will be inferred. This is heavy arithmetic, however, so we proceed along a less elegant route.

Let us assume that the firm's critical value for the loss of old customers, beyond which it infers secret price-cutting, is

$$\begin{aligned}\frac{(1-p)n_0}{n_s} + \sigma_1 &= \frac{(1-p)n_0}{n_s}\left[1 + \sqrt{\left(\frac{p}{1-p}\frac{n_s}{n_0}\right)}\right]\\ &= \frac{(1-p)n_0}{n_s}(1+\theta),\end{aligned}$$

that is, one standard deviation above the mean. Any one rival will on average attract

$$m_2 = \frac{1}{n_s - 1}\left[\frac{(1-p)n_0}{n_s} + \sigma_1\right]$$

of these customers, with a variance of

$$\sigma_2^2 = \frac{n_s - 2}{(n_s - 1)^2}\left[\frac{(1-p)n_0}{n_s} + \sigma_1\right].$$

Let the rival be suspected of price-cutting if he obtains more than $(m_2 + \sigma_2)$ customers, that is, if the probability of any larger number is less than about 30 per cent. The joint probability of losing one standard deviation more than the average number of old customers and a rival obtaining one standard deviation more than his average share is about 10 per cent. The average sales of a rival are n_0/n_s, ignoring new customers. The maximum number of buyers any seller can obtain from one rival without exciting suspicion, minus the number he will on average get without price-cutting ($[1 - p]n_0/n_s\ [n_s - 1]$), expressed as a ratio to his average sales, is

$$\frac{[\theta(1-p)n_0/(n_s - 1)n_s + \sigma_2]}{n_0/n_s}.$$

This criterion is tabulated in Table 1.

TABLE 1

PERCENTAGE GAINS IN SALES FROM UNDETECTED PRICE-CUTTING BY A FIRM

Criterion I: $\frac{1}{(n_s - 1)}\left[\theta(1-p) + \sqrt{\frac{n_s(n_s - 2)(1-p)(1+\theta)}{n_0}}\right]$ $\quad \theta = \sqrt{\frac{p}{1-p}\frac{n_s}{n_0}}$

Probability of Repeat Sales (p)	No. of Buyers (n_0)	No. of Sellers					
		2	3	4	5	10	20
p=0.95	20	6.9	11.3	11.3	11.4	11.8	12.7
	30	5.6	8.9	8.8	8.8	9.0	9.6
	40	4.9	7.5	7.4	7.4	7.5	7.9
	50	4.4	6.6	6.5	6.4	6.5	6.8
	100	3.1	4.4	4.3	4.3	4.2	4.4
	200	2.2	3.0	2.9	2.8	2.8	2.8
	400	1.5	2.1	2.0	1.9	1.8	1.8
p=0.90	20	9.5	14.8	14.7	14.6	14.8	15.7
	30	7.8	11.7	11.5	11.4	11.4	12.0
	40	6.7	10.0	9.7	9.6	9.5	9.9
	50	6.0	8.8	8.6	8.4	8.3	8.6
	100	4.2	6.0	5.8	5.6	5.4	5.5
	200	3.0	4.1	3.9	3.8	3.6	3.6
	400	2.1	2.8	2.7	2.6	2.4	2.4
p=0.80	20	12.6	19.3	18.9	18.7	18.6	19.4
	30	10.3	15.4	15.0	14.7	14.5	15.0
	40	8.9	13.1	12.7	12.5	12.2	12.5
	50	8.0	11.6	11.2	11.0	10.6	10.8
	100	5.7	8.0	7.7	7.4	7.1	7.1
	200	4.0	5.5	5.3	5.1	4.8	4.7
	400	2.8	3.8	3.6	3.5	3.2	3.2
p=0.70	20	14.5	22.3	21.8	21.5	21.2	21.9
	30	11.8	17.8	17.3	17.0	16.6	16.9
	40	10.2	15.2	14.8	14.5	14.0	14.2
	50	9.2	13.5	13.1	12.8	12.3	12.4
	100	6.5	9.3	9.0	8.7	8.2	8.2
	200	4.6	6.5	6.2	6.0	5.6	5.5
	400	3.2	4.5	4.3	4.2	3.8	3.7

The entries in Table 1 are measures of the maximum additional sales obtainable by secret price-cutting (expressed as a percentage of average sales) from any one rival beyond which that rival will infer that the price-cutting is taking place. Since the profitability of secret price-cutting depends upon the amount of business one can obtain (as well as upon the excess of price over marginal cost), we may also view these numbers as the measures of the incentive to engage in secret price-cutting. Three features of the tabulation are noteworthy:

a) The gain in sales from any one rival by secret price-cutting is not very sensitive to the number of rivals, given the number of customers and the probability of repeat sales. The aggregate gain in sales of a firm from price-cutting—its total incentive to secret price-cutting—is the sum of the gains from each rival, and therefore increases roughly in proportion to the number of rivals.

b) The incentive to secret price-cutting falls as the number of customers per seller increases—and falls roughly in inverse proportion to the square root of the number of buyers.

c) The incentive to secret price-cutting rises as the probability of repeat purchases falls, but at a decreasing rate.

We have said that the gain to old buyers from shifting their patronage among sellers will be that it encourages secret price-cutting by making it more difficult to detect. Table 1 indicates that there are diminishing returns to increased shifting: The entries increase at a decreasing rate as p falls. In a fuller model we could introduce the costs of shifting among suppliers and determine p to maximize expected buyer gains. The larger the purchases of a buyer, when buyers are of unequal size, however, the greater is the prospect that his shifts will induce price-cutting.

In addition it is clear that, when the number of sellers exceeds two, it is possible for two or more firms to pool information and thus to detect less extreme cases of price-cutting. For example, at the given probability levels, the number of old customers that any one rival should be able to take from a firm was shown to be at most

$$(1-p)\frac{n_0(1+\theta)}{n_s-1},$$

with variance

$$\frac{(n_s-2)(1-p)(1+\theta)}{(n_s-1)^2}n_0.$$

At the same probability level, the average number of old customers that one rival should be able to take from T firms is at most

$$\frac{T(1-p)n_0}{n_s-T}\left(1+\frac{\theta}{\sqrt{T}}\right),$$

with the variance

$$\frac{(n_s-T-1)}{(n_s-T)^2}(1-p)\left(1+\frac{\theta}{\sqrt{T}}\right)n_0T.$$

Each of these is smaller than the corresponding expression for one seller when expressed as a fraction of the customers lost by each of the firms pooling information.

There are of course limits to such pooling of information: not only does it become expensive as the number of firms increases, but also it produces less reliable information, since one of the members of the pool may himself be secretly cutting prices. Some numbers illustrative of the effect of pooling will be given at a later point.

2. *The attraction of old customers of other firms is a second source of evidence of price-cutting.*—If a given rival has not cut prices, he will on average lose $(1-p)$ (n_0/n_s) customers, with a variance of σ_1^2. The number of customers he will retain with secret price-cutting cannot exceed

a level at which the rivals suspect the price-cutting. Any one rival will have little basis for judging whether he is getting a fair share of this firm's old customers, but they can pool their information and then in the aggregate they will expect the firm to lose at least $(1 - p)(n_0/n_s) - 2\sigma_1$ customers, at the 5 per cent probability level. Hence the secret price-cutter can retain at most $2\sigma_1$ of his old customers (beyond his average number), which as a fraction of his average sales (ignoring new customers) is

TABLE 2

OLD CUSTOMERS THAT A SECRET PRICE-CUTTER CAN RETAIN, AS A PERCENTAGE OF AVERAGE SALES

Criterion II: $2\sqrt{\frac{p(1-p)}{2}\frac{n_s}{n_0}}$

PROBABILITY THAT OLD CUSTOMER WILL REMAIN LOYAL (p)	NO. OF OLD CUSTOMERS PER SELLER (n_0/n_s)			
	10	20	50	100
0.95	13.8	9.7	6.2	4.4
.90	19.0	13.4	8.5	6.0
.85	22.6	16.0	10.1	7.1
.80	25.3	17.9	11.3	8.0
.75	27.4	19.4	12.2	8.7
.70	29.0	20.5	13.0	9.2
.65	30.2	21.3	13.5	9.5
.60	31.0	21.9	13.9	9.8
.55	31.5	22.2	14.1	10.0
0.50	31.6	22.4	14.1	10.0

$$\frac{2\sigma_1}{n_0/n_s} = 2\sqrt{\frac{(1-p)pn_s}{n_0}}.$$

This is tabulated as Table 2.

If the entries in Table 2 are compared with those in Table 1,[10] it is found that a price-cutter is easier to detect by his gains at the expense of any one rival than by his unusual proportion of repeat sales. This second criterion will therefore seldom be useful.

3. *The behavior of new customers is a third source of information on price-cutting.*—There are n_n new customers per period,[11] equal to λn_0. A firm expects, in the absence of price-cutting, to sell to

$$m_3 = \frac{1}{n_s}\lambda n_0$$

of these customers, with a variance of

$$\sigma_3^2 = \left(1 - \frac{1}{n_s}\right)\frac{\lambda n_0}{n_s}.$$

If the rivals pool information (without pooling, this area could not be policed effectively), this firm cannot obtain more than $m_3 + 2\sigma_3$ customers without being deemed a price-cutter, using again a 5 per cent probability criterion. As a percentage of the firm's total sales, the maximum sales above the expected number in the absence of price cutting are then

$$\frac{2\sigma_3}{n_0(1+\lambda)/n_s} = \frac{2}{1+\lambda}\sqrt{\frac{(n_s - 1)\lambda}{n_0}}.$$

We tabulate this criterion as Table 3.

Two aspects of the incentive to cut prices (or equivalently the difficulty of detecting price cuts) to new customers are apparent: the incentive increases rapidly with the number of sellers[12] and the

[10] For example, take $p = .95$. The entry for 10 customers per seller is 13.8 in Table 2—this is the maximum percentage of average sales that can be obtained by price reductions to old customers. The corresponding entries in Table 1 are 6.9 (2 sellers, 20 buyers), 8.9 (3 and 30), 7.4 (4 and 40), 6.4 (5 and 50), 4.2 (10 and 100), etc. Multiplying each entry in Table 1 by $(n_s - 1)$, we get the maximum gain in sales (without detection) by attracting customers of rivals, and beyond 2 sellers the gains are larger by this latter route. Since Table 1 is based upon a 10 per cent probability level, strict comparability requires that we use 1.6 σ, instead of 2 σ, in Table 2, which would reduce the entries by one-fifth.

[11] Unlike old customers, whose behavior is better studied in a round of transactions, the new customers are a flow whose magnitude depends much more crucially on the time period considered. The annual flow of new customers is here taken (relative to the number of old customers) as the unit.

[12] And slowly with the number of sellers if customers per seller are held constant.

incentive increases with the rate of entry of new customers. As usual the incentive falls as the absolute number of customers per seller rises. If the rate of entry of new buyers is 10 per cent or more, price-cutting to new customers allows larger sales increases without detection that can be obtained by attracting customers of rivals (compare Tables 1 and 3).

Of the considerable number of directions in which this model could be enlarged, two will be presented briefly.

The first is inequality in the size of firms. In effect this complication has already been introduced by the equivalent device of pooling information. If we tabulate the effects of pooling of information by K firms, the results are equivalent to having a firm K times as large as the other firms. The number of old customers this large firm can lose to any one small rival (all of whom are equal in size) is given, in Table 4, as a percentage of the average number of old customers of the small firm; the column labeled $K = 1$ is of course the case analyzed in Table 1.

The effects of pooling on the detection of price-cutting are best analyzed by

TABLE 3

MAXIMUM ADDITIONAL NEW CUSTOMERS (AS A PERCENTAGE OF AVERAGE SALES) OBTAINABLE BY SECRET PRICE-CUTTING

Criterion III: $\frac{2}{1+\lambda}\sqrt{\frac{\lambda(n_s-1)}{n_0}}$

RATE OF APPEARANCE OF NEW BUYERS (λ)	NO. OF OLD BUYERS (n_0)	NO. OF SELLERS					
		2	3	4	5	10	20
1/100	20	4.4	6.3	7.7	8.9	13.3	19.3
	30	3.6	5.1	6.3	7.2	10.8	15.8
	40	3.1	4.4	5.4	6.3	9.4	13.6
	50	2.8	4.0	4.8	5.6	8.4	12.2
	100	2.0	2.8	3.4	4.0	5.9	8.6
	200	1.4	2.0	2.4	2.8	4.2	6.1
	400	1.0	1.4	1.7	2.0	3.0	4.3
1/10	20	12.9	18.2	22.3	25.7	38.6	56.0
	30	10.5	14.8	18.2	21.0	31.5	45.8
	40	9.1	12.9	15.8	18.2	27.3	39.6
	50	8.1	11.5	14.1	16.3	24.4	35.4
	100	5.8	8.1	10.0	11.5	17.2	25.1
	200	4.1	5.8	7.0	8.1	12.2	17.7
	400	2.9	4.1	5.0	5.8	8.6	12.5
1/5	20	16.7	23.6	28.9	33.3	50.0	72.6
	30	13.6	19.2	23.6	27.2	40.8	59.3
	40	11.8	16.7	20.4	23.6	35.4	51.4
	50	10.5	14.9	18.3	21.1	31.6	46.0
	100	7.4	10.5	12.9	14.9	22.4	32.5
	200	5.3	7.4	9.1	10.5	15.8	23.0
	400	3.7	5.3	6.4	7.4	11.2	16.2
1/4	20	17.9	25.3	31.0	35.8	53.7	78.0
	30	14.6	20.7	25.3	29.2	43.8	63.7
	40	12.6	17.9	21.9	25.3	38.0	55.1
	50	11.3	16.0	19.6	22.6	33.9	49.3
	100	8.0	11.3	13.9	16.0	24.0	34.9
	200	5.7	8.0	9.8	11.3	17.0	24.7
	400	4.0	5.7	6.9	8.0	12.0	17.4

comparing Table 4 with Table 1. If there are 100 customers and 10 firms (and $p = 0.9$), a single firm can increase sales by 5.4 per cent by poaching on one rival, or about 50 per cent against all rivals (Table 1). If 9 firms combine, the maximum amount the single firm can gain by secret price-cutting is 28.9 per cent (Table 4). With 20 firms and 200 customers, a single firm can gain 3.6 per cent from each rival, or about 30 per cent from 9 rivals; if these rivals merge, the corresponding figure falls to 14.0 per cent. The pooling of information therefore reduces substantially the scope for secret price-cutting.

This table exaggerates the effect of inequality of firm size because it fails to take account of the fact that the number of customers varies with firm size, on our argument that only customers above a certain size relative to the seller are a

TABLE 4

PERCENTAGE GAINS IN SALES FROM UNDETECTED PRICE-CUTTING BY A SMALL FIRM

Criterion IV:

$$\frac{1}{n_s - K}\left[\theta(1-p)\sqrt{K} + \sqrt{\frac{n_s K(1-p)(n_s - K - 1)(1+\theta/\sqrt{K})}{n_0}}\right]$$

$$\theta = \sqrt{\frac{p}{1-p}\frac{n_s}{n_0}}$$

Probability of Repeat Sales (p)	No. of Firms ($n_s - K + 1$)	Buyers per Small Seller (n_0/n_s)	Size of Large Firm (K)			
			1	2	5	9
$p=0.9$	2	10	9.5	13.4	21.2	28.5
		30	5.5	7.7	12.2	16.4
		50	4.2	6.0	9.5	12.7
	3	10	11.7	15.8	23.9	31.4
		30	6.3	8.7	13.3	17.6
		50	4.8	6.6	10.2	13.5
	4	10	9.7	13.1	19.7	25.7
		30	5.2	7.1	10.9	14.4
		50	4.0	5.4	8.3	11.0
	10	10	5.4	7.2	10.7	14.0
		30	2.9	3.9	5.9	7.7
		50	2.2	2.9	4.5	5.9
$p=0.8$	2	10	12.6	17.9	28.3	37.9
		30	7.3	10.3	16.3	21.9
		50	5.7	8.0	12.6	17.0
	3	10	15.4	21.0	32.1	42.3
		30	8.4	11.6	18.0	23.9
		50	6.4	8.9	13.8	18.4
	4	10	12.7	17.3	26.3	34.7
		30	6.9	9.5	14.7	19.5
		50	5.3	7.3	11.3	15.0
	10	10	7.1	9.5	14.4	18.9
		30	3.8	5.2	8.0	10.6
		50	2.9	4.0	6.1	8.1

feasible group for secret price-cutting. The small firm can find it attractive to cut prices to buyers which are not large enough to be potential customers by price-cutting for the large seller.

The temporal pattern of buyers' behavior provides another kind of information: What is possibly due to random fluctuation in the short run cannot with equal probability be due to chance if repeated. Thus the maximum expected loss of old customers to a rival in one round of transactions is (at the 1σ level)

$$\frac{n_0}{(n_s-1)n_s}(1-p)(1+\theta),$$

but for T consecutive periods the maximum expected loss is (over T periods)

$$\frac{T}{n_s-1}(1-p)\frac{n_0}{n_s}[1+\theta\sqrt{T}],$$

with a variance of

$$\sigma_5^2=\frac{(n_s-2)}{(n_s-1)^2}T(1-p)\frac{n_0}{n_s}[1+\theta\sqrt{T}].$$

This source of information is of minor efficacy in detecting price-cutting unless the rounds of successive transactions are numerous—that is, unless buyers purchase (enter contracts) frequently.

Our approach has certain implications for the measurement of concentration, if we wish concentration to measure likelihood of effective collusion. In the case of new customers, for example, let the probability of attracting a customer be proportional to the firm's share of industry output (s). Then the variance of the firm's share of sales to new customers will be $n_n s(1-s)$, and the aggregate for the industry will be

$$C=n_n\sum_1^r s(1-s)$$

for r firms. This expression equals $n_n(1-H)$, where

$$H=\Sigma s^2$$

is the Herfindahl index of concentration. The same index holds, as an approximation, for potential price-cutting to attract old customers.[13]

The foregoing analysis can be extended to non-price variables, subject to two modifications. The first modification is that there be a definite joint profit-maximizing policy upon which the rivals can agree. Here we may expect to encounter a spectrum of possibilities, ranging from a clearly defined optimum policy (say, on favorable legislation) to a nebulous set of alternatives (say, directions of research).[14] Collusion is less feasible, the less clear the basis on which it should proceed. The second modification is that

[13] A similar argument leads to a measure of concentration appropriate to potential price-cutting for old customers. Firm i will lose

$$(1-p)n_0 s_i$$

old customers, and firm j will gain

$$(1-p)n_0\frac{s_i s_j}{1-s_i}$$

of them, with a variance

$$(1-p)n_0\frac{s_i s_j}{1-s_i}\left(1-\frac{s_j}{1-s_i}\right).$$

If we sum over all i ($\neq j$), we obtain the variance of firm j's sales to old customers of rivals

$$(1-p)n_0 s_j(1+H-2s_j),$$

to an approximation, and summing over all j, we have the concentration measure,

$$(1-p)n_0(1-H).$$

The agreement of this measure with that for new customers is superficial: that for new customers implicitly assumes pooling of information and that for old customers does not.

[14] Of course, price itself usually falls somewhere in this range rather than at the pole. The traditional assumption of stationary conditions conceals this fact.

the competitive moves of any one firm will differ widely among non-price variables in their detectability by rivals. Some forms of non-price competition will be easier to detect than price-cutting because they leave visible traces (advertising, product quality, servicing, etc.) but some variants will be elusive (reciprocity in purchasing, patent licensing arrangements). The common belief that non-price competition is more common than price competition is therefore not wholly in keeping with the present theory. Those forms that are suitable areas for collusion will have less competition; those which are not suitable will have more competition.

TABLE 5

RESIDUALS FROM REGRESSION OF ADVERTISING RATES ON CIRCULATION*

No. of Evening Papers	*n*	Mean Residual (Logarithm)	Standard Deviation of Mean
One	23	0.0211	0.0210
With morning paper	10	− .0174	.0324
Without morning paper	13	.0507	.0233
Two	30	−0.0213	0.0135

* The regression equation is

$$\log R = 5.194 - \underset{(.620)}{1.688} \log c + \underset{(.063)}{.139} (\log c)^2 ,$$

where R is the 5 M milline rate and c is circulation.

Source: American Association of Advertising Agencies, *Market and Newspaper Statistics*, Vol. VIIIa (1939).

IV. SOME FRAGMENTS OF EVIDENCE

Before we seek empirical evidence on our theory, it is useful to report two investigations of the influence of numbers of sellers on price. These investigations have an intrinsic interest because, so far as I know, no systematic analysis of the effect of numbers has hitherto been made.

The first investigation was of newspaper advertising rates, as a function of the number of evening newspapers in a city. Advertising rates on a milline basis are closely (and negatively) related to circulation, so a regression of rates on circulation was made for fifty-three cities in 1939. The residuals (in logarithmic form) from this regression equation are tabulated in Table 5. It will be observed that rates are 5 per cent above the average in one-newspaper towns and 5 per cent below the average in two-newspaper towns, and the towns with one evening paper but also an independent morning paper fall nearly midway between these points. Unfortunately there were too few cities with more than two evening newspapers to yield results for larger numbers of firms.

The second investigation is of spot commercial rates on AM radio stations in the four states of Ohio, Indiana, Michigan, and Illinois. The basic equation introduces, along with number of rivals, a series of other factors (power of station, population of the county in which the station is located, etc.). Unfortunately the number of stations is rather closely correlated with population (r^2 = .796 in the logarithms). The general result, shown in Table 6, is similar to that for newspapers: the elasticity of price with respect to number of rivals is quite small (−.07). Here the range of stations in a county was from 1 to 13.

Both studies suggest that the level of prices is not very responsive to the actual number of rivals. This is in keeping with the expectations based upon our model, for that model argues that the number of buyers, the proportion of new buyers, and the relative sizes of firms are as important as the number of rivals.

To turn to the present theory, the only test covering numerous industries so far devised has been one based upon profitability. This necessarily rests upon company data, and it has led to the exclusion of a large number of industries for which the companies do not operate in a well-defined industry. For example, the larger steel and chemical firms operate in a series of markets in which their position ranges from monopolistic to competitive. We have required of each industry that the earnings of a substantial fraction of the companies in the industry (measured by output) be determined by the profitability of that industry's products, that is, that we have a fair share of the industry and the industry's product is the dominant product of the firms.

Three measures of profitability are given in Table 7: (1) the rate of return on all capital (including debt), (2) the rate of return on net worth (stockholders' equity); (3) the ratio of market value to book value of the common stock.

In addition, two measures of concentration are presented: (1) the conventional measure, the share of output produced by the four leading firms; and (2) the Herfindahl index, H.

The various rank correlations are given in Table 8. The various concentration measures, on the one hand, and the various measures of profitability, on the other hand, are tolerably well correlated.[15] All show the expected positive relationship. In general the data suggest that there is no relationship between profitability and concentration if H is less than 0.250 or the share of the four largest firms is less than about 80 per cent. These data, like those on advertising rates, confirm our theory only in the sense that they support theories which assert that competition increases with number of firms.

Our last evidence is a study of the prices paid by buyers of steel products in 1939, measured relative to the quoted prices (Table 9). The figure of 8.3 for hot-

TABLE 6

REGRESSION OF AM SPOT COMMERCIAL RATES (26 TIMES) AND STATION CHARACTERISTICS, 1961

(n = 345)

Independent Variables*	Regression Coefficient	Standard Error
1. Logarithm of population of county, 1960	.238	0.026
2. Logarithm of kilowatt power of station	.206	.015
3. Dummy variables of period of broadcasting:		
a) Sunrise to sunset	−.114	.025
b) More than (*a*), less than 18 hours	−.086	.027
c) 18–21 hours	−.053	.028
4. Logarithm of number of stations in county	−.074	0.046
	R^2= .743	

* Dependent variable: logarithm of average rate, May 1, 1961 (dollars).

Source: "Spot Radio Rates and Data," *Standard Rate and Data Service, Inc.*, Vol. XLIII, No. 5 (May 1961).

[15] The concentration measures have a rank correlation of .903. The profitability measures have the following rank correlations:

	Return on All Assets	Ratio of Market to Book Value
Return on net worth	.866	.872
Ratio of market to book value	.733	....

TABLE 7

PROFITABILITY AND CONCENTRATION DATA

INDUSTRY*	CONCENTRATION (1954)		AVERAGE RATE OF RETURN (1953–57)		RATIO OF MARKET VALUE TO BOOK VALUE (1953–57)
	Share of Top 4	H†	All Assets	Net Worth	
Sulfur mining (4)	98	0.407	19.03	23.85	3.02
Automobiles (3)	98	.369	11.71	20.26	2.30
Flat glass (3)	90	.296	11.79	16.17	2.22
Gypsum products (2)	90	.280	12.16	20.26	1.83
Primary aluminum (4)	98	.277	6.87	13.46	2.48
Metal cans (4)	80	.260	7.27	13.90	1.60
Chewing gum (2)	86	.254	13.50	17.06	2.46
Hard-surface floor coverings (3)	87	.233	6.56	7.59	0.98
Cigarettes (5)	83	.213	7.23	11.18	1.29
Industrial gases (3)	84	.202	8.25	11.53	1.33
Corn wet milling (3)	75	.201	9.17	11.55	1.48
Typewriters (3)	83	.198	3.55	5.39	0.84
Domestic laundry equipment (2)	68	.174	9.97	17.76	1.66
Rubber tires (9)	79	.171	7.86	14.02	1.70
Rayon fiber (4)	76	.169	5.64	6.62	0.84
Carbon black (2)	73	.152	8.29	9.97	1.40
Distilled liquors (6)	64	0.118	6.94	7.55	0.77

* The number of firms is given in parentheses after the industry title. Only those industries are included for which a substantial share (35 per cent or more) of the industry's sales is accounted for by the firms in the sample, and these firms derive their chief revenues (50 per cent or more) from the industry in question.

† H is Herfindahl index.

TABLE 8

RANK CORRELATIONS OF MEASURES OF PROFITABILITY AND MEASURES OF CONCENTRATION

MEASURE OF CONCENTRATION	MEASURE OF PROFITABILITY		
	Rate of Return on All Assets	Rate of Return on Net Worth	Ratio of Market Value to Book Value
Share of output produced by four largest firms	.322	.507	.642
Herfindahl index (H)	.524	.692	.730

TABLE 9

PRICES OF STEEL PRODUCTS, 1939, AND INDUSTRY STRUCTURE, 1938

PRODUCT CLASS	PRICES, 2D QUARTER, 1939 (PER CENT)		HERFINDAHL INDEX	OUTPUT IN 1939 RELATIVE TO 1937
	Average Discount from List Price	Standard Deviation		
Hot-rolled sheets	8.3	7.3	0.0902	1.14
Merchant bars	1.2	4.5	.1517	0.84
Hot-rolled strip	8.5	8.3	.1069	0.56
Plates	2.6	4.8	.1740	0.85
Structural shapes	3.2	4.3	.3280	0.92
Cold-rolled strip	8.8	9.8	.0549	0.88
Cold-rolled sheets	5.8	5.0	.0963	1.14
Cold-finished bars	0.9	3.4	0.0964	0.83

Source: Prices: "Labor Department Examines Consumers' Prices of Steel Products," *Iron Age*, April 25, 1946; industry structure: 1938 capacity data from *Directory of Iron and Steel Works of the United States and Canada;* output: *Annual Statistical Report, American Iron and Steel Institute* (New York, 1938, 1942).

rolled sheets, for example, represents an average of 8.3 per cent reduction from quoted prices, *paid by buyers*, with a standard deviation of 7.3 per cent of quoted prices. The rate of price-cutting is almost perfectly correlated with the standard deviation of transaction prices, as we should expect: the less perfect the market knowledge, the more extensive the price-cutting.

In general, the more concentrated the industry structure (measured by the Herfindahl index), the larger were the price reductions. Although there were no extreme departures from this relationship, structural shapes and hot-rolled strip had prices somewhat lower than the average relationship, and cold finished bars prices somewhat higher than expected, and the deviations are not accounted for by the level of demand (measured by 1939 sales relative to 1937 sales). The number of buyers could not be taken into account, but the BLS study states:

> The extent of price concessions shown by this study is probably understated because certain very large consumers in the automobile and container industries were excluded from the survey. This omission was at the request of the OPA which contemplated obtaining this information in connection with other studies. Since a small percentage of steel consumers, including these companies, accounts for a large percentage of steel purchased, prices paid by a relatively few large consumers have an important influence upon the entire steel price structure. Very large steel consumers get greater reductions from published prices than smaller consumers, often the result of competitive bidding by the mills for the large volume of steel involved. One very large steel consumer, a firm that purchased over 2 pct of the total consumption of hot and cold-rolled sheets in 1940, refused to give purchase prices. This firm wished to protect its suppliers, fearing that "certain transactions might be revealed which would break confidence" with the steel mills. However, this company did furnish per-cent changes of prices paid for several steel products which showed that for some products prices advanced markedly, and in one case, nearly 50 pct. The great price advances for this company indicate that it was receiving much larger concessions than smaller buyers.[16]

These various bits of evidence are fairly favorable to the theory, but they do not constitute strong support. More powerful tests will be feasible when the electrical equipment triple-damage suits are tried.[17] The great merit of our theory, in fact, is that it has numerous testable hypotheses, unlike the immortal theories that have been traditional in this area.

[16] See "Labor Department Examines Consumers' Prices of Steel Products," *op. cit.*, p. 133.

[17] For example, it will be possible to test the prediction that prices will be higher and less dispersed in sales on public bids than in privately negotiated sales, and the prediction that price-cutting increases as the number of buyers diminishes.

APPENDIX

The importance of product heterogeneity for profit-maximizing behavior cannot well be established by an a priori argument. Nevertheless, the following simple exposition of the implications for profitability of disregarding heterogeneity may have some heuristic value. The analysis, it will be observed, is formally equivalent to that of the effects of an excise tax on a monopolist.

Assume that a monopolist makes men's suits, and that he makes only one size of suit. This is absurd behavior, but the picture of the sadistic monopolist who disregards consumer desires has often made fugitive appearances in the literature so the problem has some interest of its own. The demand curve of a consumer for suits that fit, $f(p)$, would now be reduced because he would have to incur some alteration cost a in order to wear the suit. His effective demand would therefore decline to $f(p + a)$. Assume further that the marginal cost of suits is constant (m), and that it would be the same if the monopolist were to make suits of various sizes.

The effect on profits of a uniform product—uniform is an especially appropriate word here—can be shown graphically (Fig. 1). The decrease in quantity sold, with a linear demand curve, is

$$MB = \tfrac{1}{2} a f'(p) \; .$$

The decrease in the price received by the monopolist is

$$DN = \frac{MB}{f'(p)} - a = -\frac{a}{2},$$

so if π is profit per unit, and q is output, the relative decline in total profit is approximately

$$\frac{\Delta\pi}{\pi} + \frac{\Delta q}{q},$$

or

$$\frac{MB}{OB} + \frac{ND}{AD}.$$

Since

$$OB = \frac{f(m)}{2}$$

$$AD = -\frac{p}{\eta},$$

where η is the elasticity of demand, the relative decline of profits with a uniform product is

$$\frac{af'(p)}{f(m)} + \frac{a\eta}{2p} = \frac{a\eta}{2p} + \frac{a\eta}{2p}$$

$$= \frac{a\eta}{p}.$$

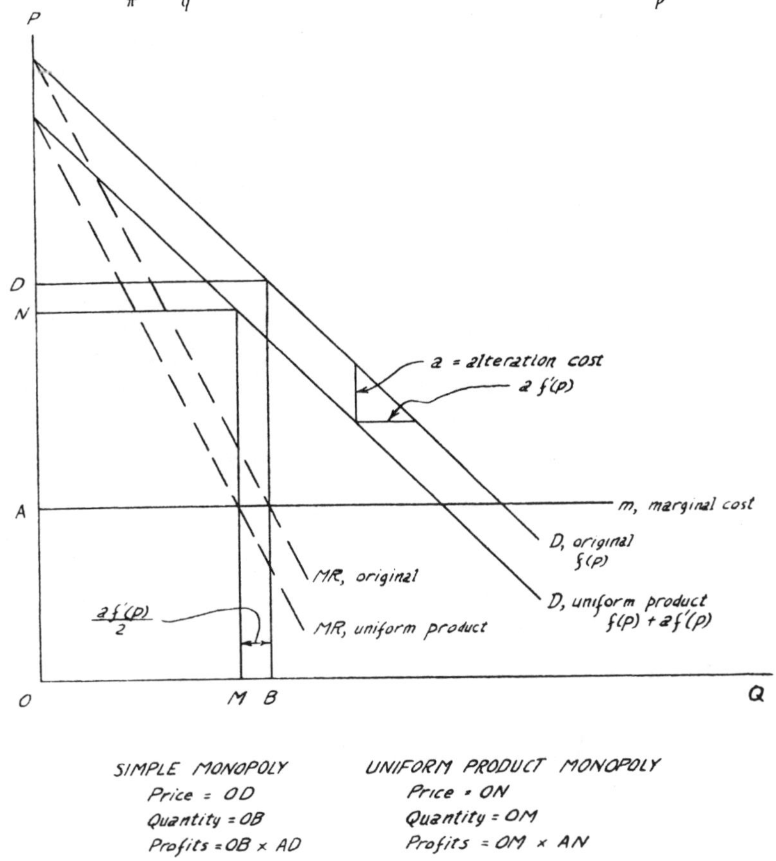

FIG. 1

The loss from imposed uniformity is therefore proportional to the ratio of alteration costs to price.

Our example is sufficiently unrealistic to make any quantitative estimate uninteresting. In general one would expect an upper limit to the ratio a/p, because it becomes cheaper to resort to other goods (custom tailoring in our example), or to abandon the attempt to find appropriate goods. The loss of profits of the monopolist will be proportional to the average value of a/p, and this will be smaller, the smaller the variation in buyers' circumstances.

Still, monopolists are lucky if their long-run demand curves have an elasticity only as large as -5, and then even a ratio of a to p of 1/40 will reduce their profits by 12 per cent. The general conclusion I wish to draw is that a monopolist who does not cater to the diversities of his buyers' desires will suffer a substantial decline in his profits.

[10]

AN EMPIRICAL SURVEY OF PRICE FIXING CONSPIRACIES*

GEORGE A. HAY and DANIEL KELLEY
U.S. Department of Justice

THIS paper reports on a study of recent Antitrust Division horizontal price fixing cases. The objective of the study was to determine if there has been a specific set of characteristics associated with the product or product markets that have been the subjects of price fixing. If such a pattern exists, it might provide empirical insight into some aspects of oligopoly behavior. From a policy point of view, any pattern that is found could be used in a positive enforcement program designed to investigate the "most likely" areas of price fixing. Section I reviews the academic literature which has dealt with the problem of horizontal conspiracy;[1] Section II describes the sample and the methodology used in the study; and Section III summarizes the results.

I

For present purposes collusion will be defined as formal or explicit agreement among competitors. Collusion is normally viewed as a means for firms without significant individual market power to earn greater than competitive profits. The structural characteristics which are hypothesized to affect the

* This paper reflects our own view and does not necessarily represent the position of the Antitrust Division. We are grateful for helpful comments from several colleagues. Joseph Mashi provided invaluable assistance in gathering the data sources.

1 Recent contributions in this area include: George J. Stigler, A Theory of Oligopoly, in The Organization of Industry 39 (1968); Peter Asch, Collusive Oligopoly: An Antitrust Quandary, John M. Kuhlman, Nature and Significance of Price Fixing Rings, & Walter B. Erickson, Economics of Price Fixing, all in 2 Antitrust Law & Econ. Rev. 53-122 (1969). Joseph C. Gallo, Oligopoly and Price-Fixing: Some Analytical Models, 4 Antitrust Law & Econ. Rev. 101 (1970); Roger D. Blair, The Sherman Act and the Incentive to Collude, 17 Antitrust Bull. 433 (1972); Richard A. Posner, Oligopoly and the Antitrust Laws: A Suggested Approach, 21 Stan. L. Rev. 1562 (1969); James M. Clabault & John F. Burton, Jr., Sherman Act Indictments 1955-65, (1966); Roger Sherman, Oligopoly, An Empirical Approach (1972). For a textbook treatment see Frederick M. Scherer, Industrial Market Structure and Economic Performance chs. 6, 7, & 19 (1970). Richard A. Posner, A Statistical Study of Antitrust Enforcement, 13 J. Law & Econ. 365 (1970), provided both a point of departure and a sense of direction to this paper.

incentive to engage in collusive behavior can be enumerated under two categories: (1) those conditions which lower the difficulty of achieving effective collusion by making coordination easier; and (2) those conditions which raise the cost of non-collusive conduct by increasing the potential instability of non-collusive behavior. The factors most often cited in the first category are fewness of numbers, concentration, product homogeneity, industry social structure, inelasticity of demand, and sealed bidding. Lumpiness and infrequency of orders and a high ratio of fixed to marginal costs are factors which fall into the second category.

Effective coordination through collusion requires the ability for the firms involved not only to reach but also to enforce an agreement. Enforcement involves the detection and possibly the disciplining of cheaters. The policing of cheating is important because successful collusion, by raising price above the competitive level, creates incentives for individual conspirators to slightly lower their prices and thus greatly increase their sales. Each of the characteristics above must be evaluated in the light of its effect upon coordination and enforcement.

1. *Factors Which Facilitate Coordination*

a. Fewness of Numbers

Fewness of numbers should be an important factor in the ability of firms to collude successfully. In the process of agreeing upon a price to be set, divergent ideas are a handicap. The conspirators can have divergent views about the optimal price because their cost structures vary or because their views about demand conditions may differ; the smaller the number of competitors the less likely it is that these differences will appear.

In his theory of collusion, Stigler[2] emphasizes the importance of the cheating factor. By analyzing the conditions under which secret price reductions will be detected he reaches the conclusion that, holding variables such as the number and size distribution of the buyers constant, the likelihood of competitors detecting each other's price reductions decreases with the number of firms involved. If these reductions can be easily detected either they will cease or the conspiracy will collapse. The implication is that the smaller the number of firms selling in the market in question, the higher the probability that a conspiracy will be successful, and thus the greater the incentive to enter into such a conspiracy.

b. Concentration

It is frequently argued that firms in highly concentrated industries often do not need to collude explicitly, but can rely on tacit collusion or "conscious

[2] George J. Stigler, *supra* note 1.

parallelism" to achieve a near-monopoly price. Alternatively it is possible that the high degree of interdependence which characterizes oligopolistic markets naturally leads to collusive activity. If the latter is true, high degrees of concentration lead to a greater likelihood that this interdependence will be recognized and that actual collusion will follow.

c. Product Homogeneity

Product homogeneity is among the characteristics frequently cited as facilitating collusive behavior; however the term can be used in at least three senses. One way to define homogeneity is linked to the elasticity of substitution between competitors' products. If the products (or product lines) of two competitors are perfect substitutes for each other, then the "product" is homogeneous. Sometimes, however, homogeneity is used to describe a situation in which the product itself is not complicated. An example will illustrate the difference. Purchasers of steel castings can probably acquire a casting of given specifications from any casting manufacturer. In the sense of the first definition above castings are a homogeneous product. However casting manufacturers produce a wide variety of types and grades of castings, using a wide variety of alloys and "extras," with no single type of casting accounting for a large percentage of total output. From this point of view the product is heterogeneous. To say that in the latter case the product has not been defined narrowly enough overlooks the nature of the problem at hand, which is the ability of competitors to reach a mutually satisfactory agreement.

If a product is homogeneous under both definitions a single price can be negotiated by the conspirators. However, if a product is heterogeneous under either definition an array of prices must be negotiated. This is an inherently more difficult task unless some sort of formula or customer allocation scheme can be arranged.

Still another type is homogeneity over time. If product characteristics remain stable through time then agreement is inherently easier to reach and maintain. Therefore, industries with high rates of technological change should not be expected to be found engaging in collusion with the same frequency as industries without rapid change.

In sum, inter-firm, intra-firm and over-time product differences, by increasing the number of issues to be negotiated, make collusion more difficult.

d. Demand Inelasticity

The more inelastic is industry demand, the greater are the potential rewards to the price fixers. Concomitantly the smaller will be the sacrifice in terms of capacity utilization.

e. Sealed Bidding

The Federal Government's procurement practices are said to facilitate coordination among firms who bid on Government contracts. The results of sealed bid competitions are announced publicly, thus providing conspirators with an excellent means of monitoring the incidence of cheating. If it is a certainty that a firm that cheats will be detected by co-conspirators the incentive to do so will obviously be reduced.

f. Industry Social Structure

This characteristic, although it falls within the realm of sociology rather than economics, cannot be ignored. In the formative stages of a conspiracy, unless it is organized under the aegis of an organization such as the NRA, someone must take the lead in making the contacts and organizing the meetings. Given the illegality of such arrangements some competitors must be coaxed into joining, and a dominant individual will often overcome the inertia and take the lead. Such a person can often exert enough pressure to overcome characteristics which might otherwise prevent a conspiracy from forming. Such an individual may also be necessary to the maintenance of a scheme by acting as a chairman and policeman of meetings. Conversely, a maverick in the industry, by virtue of his desire for independence may prevent conspiracy in an industry otherwise very ripe for it.

2. *Factors Which Increase the Risk of Non-Collusive Coordination*

Intended for discussion in the section are those attributes of a market which are often said to lead to excessive or "cut-throat" competition. When such behavior occurs it is argued that collusion will be used in an attempt to maintain discipline in the industy. A paradox exists in that the factors which lead to "excessive" competition in the first place, frequently are those that increase the likelihood of cheating on any collusive agreement that evolves. The preliminary conclusion is that where these factors are present collusion is likely to be attempted but is not likely to be of lasting duration. The only reason that collusion is attempted in these circumstances is that the payoff, if even for limited duration, can be high.

a. Lumpiness and Infrequency of Orders

Stigler points out that secret price cuts will not be made to ". . . buyers whose purchases fall below a certain size relative to his aggregate sales."[3] It follows that if a few buyers purchase large quantities in relation to a firm's aggregate sales there will be great temptation for the firm to grant

[3] *Id.* at 43.

price reductions to such buyers either to keep them as customers or win their business from another competitor. In the absence of collusion prices will be driven down towards the competitive level. Of course, even if collusion is attempted it will not be successful unless cheating is policed. Nevertheless collusion may be the only potential mechanism for raising industry profits. A corollary, applicable to the conditions listed in Section I above, is that ". . . collusion will often be effective against small buyers even where it is ineffective against large buyers."[4]

b. High Fixed Costs

Price wars are a phenomenon often associated with high fixed costs industries. When demand falls (during a recession for example) unutilized capacity develops. It is tempting in these circumstances for a firm to reduce its price, expand output and sales and thus generate revenue to offset the burden of its high fixed costs. If all firms do this a downward price spiral may be the result. It is not surprising therefore for the firms to attempt to prevent or stop such a spiral by an agreement. Even if an agreement is reached, it may be a fragile one, subject to disintegration during the next downturn.

3. *Methods of Collusion*

Collusion is not a uniform concept. Different industry structures can, *a priori,* be expected to lead to different types of collusive conduct. Where, for example, numbers of competitors are large or where the product differs among transactions (for example, construction) regularly scheduled formal meetings with or without the aid of a trade association can be expected. Conversely, with small numbers and/or a simple product, communication can be effective under less formal, but nevertheless quite illegal, circumstances. Where purchases are repetitive a single list price (or a price list) may be agreed upon —with or without the added attribute of customer allocation; but for non-repetitive purchases, job or territorial allocation, where feasible, may be used in conjunction with a complementary bidding system.

II

This section deals with the sample and the methodology used in the present study. Public information about Antitrust Division price fixing cases comes from two sources: (1) the court record when cases proceed to trial, and (2) the indictments, complaints and press releases which accompany a case filing. Information from the first source is limited due to the fact that most cases are settled by *nolo contendere* pleas and therefore no substantive

[4] *Id.* at 44.

court record is generated.[5] Indictments, complaints and press releases contain some useful information; however most of these documents are written in a standard form detailing little more than the technical nature of the violation, the names of the defendants and the nature of the product. Press releases sometimes give an indication of the volume of commerce involved in the alleged violation but provide little information beyond that found in the indictments or complaints.

For the present study the fact memoranda and other supportive documents prepared by Antitrust Division staff which investigated the violation were also examined.[6] These memoranda have some limitations but in general provide a rich source of detail.[7] Because they are written by the legal staff in preparation for trial, fact memoranda describe in full the conduct of individual conspirators. Less attention is paid to structural matters but some relevant information is available as a by-product. Very little attention is paid to performance since, of course, it is largely irrelevant to proving illegality in the type of case investigated.

All Section 1 criminal cases which were filed *and* won in trial or settled by *nolo contendere* pleas from January 1963, to December 1972, were examined.[8] Cases involving vertical agreements (between producers and distributors for example) were excluded, as were agreements which were not covert. Thus the recent cases involving alleged price fixing for the services of various professional groups were excluded.

[5] A plea of *nolo contendere* or "no contest" entered in a criminal case is equivalent to a plea of guilty for purposes of sentencing but is not an admission of guilt by the defendant. A trial is not necessary when a *nolo contendere* plea is accepted by the court. The courts occasionally accept *nolo contendere* pleas over the objection of the Department of Justice.

[6] A fact memorandum is a summary of the evidence which has been gathered up to the point at which a decision to file a case must be made. In a criminal case the fact memorandum is ordinarily written after all Grand Jury testimony has been heard but before an indictment is presented to the jurors. The fact memoranda were found in Department of Justice files. These files are exempt from the Freedom of Information Act and therefore are not available to the public. We have attempted to provide as much information as possible consistent with the legal constraints.

[7] To cite one example, many indictments will allege that co-conspirators were involved; however they are usually not named and their relation to the conspiracy is unknown. The fact memorandum will indicate their names and their exact relationship to the indicted firms.

[8] The Minnesota bank cases, Trade Reg. Rep. Case Nos. 1734-1736 (Transfer Binder for U.S. Antitrust Case Summaries 1961-1970), and the Los Angeles pipe cases, Trade Reg. Rep. Case Nos. 1785-1789 (Transfer Binder for U.S. Antitrust Case Summaries 1961-1970) were excluded because no data were available. United States v. Bethlehem Steel Co., Trade Reg. Rep. Case No. 1871 (Transfer Binder for U.S. Antitrust Case Summaries 1961-1970) was not included because of the ambiguous result; of a total of 18 counts charged against 11 defendants, 5 *nolo contendere* pleas were accepted; the remaining counts were dismissed.

Each case in the sample was abstracted for product market, geographical market, names of the conspirators and, to the extent possible, their size distribution. Then any useful information about the particular product and market characteristics was noted. Finally, the conspiracy was described and the method of detection, if that information was available, was listed. The information about the conspiracy recorded included the origins of the conspiracy (if known), the method of operation, and any available knowledge of its success.

III

Some of the results of the study are summarized in the appendix.[9] The cases there are listed by CCH Trade Regulation Reports ("Blue Book") number, the name of the product and (in parentheses following the product name) the Standard Industrial Classification number (SIC).[10] The next column indicates whether the geographical scope of the conspiracy was local, regional or national.

The information in the next three columns is designed to describe the number and size distribution of the firms in the industry. The traditional four-firm concentration ratio is computed from sales data found in the fact memoranda.[11] In most cases the data are taken from the last year in which the conspiracy was fully operative. Information which could be used to gauge temporal changes in the market shares was not available. Exact concentration ratios could not be computed in every case. In some instances market share data were presented for all of the firms which were factors in the market being investigated; in other instances data were presented only for the conspirators. In the latter situation, if there was reason to believe that the conspirators supplied a substantial portion of the market, the relative share of the top four is listed in the table with a "less than" sign. Such numbers represent the upper limit of the actual concentration ratio but provide an approximation. When the latter technique could not be used because data for too many firms were lacking or when no market share data appeared in the fact memorandum, market concentration is not reported.

[9] *Infra* at 29. Regulations pertaining to Grand Jury evidence precludes disclosure of some of the information which was gathered.

[10] Summaries of cases listed in order by "Blue Book" number can be found in Trade Reg. Rep. (Transfer Binder for U.S. Antitrust Case Summaries, 1961-1970) and Trade Reg. Rep. ¶¶ 45,070-45,072 at 53,201-53,514. Note that the four-digit Census industry number is also reported. The products in the sample would in most cases be assigned five, six, or seven digit numbers by the Census Bureau. The Standard Industrial Classification (SIC) numbers were assigned by the authors.

[11] The resultant concentration ratios are unique in one sense—they are based on a product concept narrower than the common four-digit "industry" level. The possible importance of this level of detail will be discussed *infra*.

The figure reported next is the number of conspirators (followed in parentheses by the combined market share of all of the conspirators). The number of conspirators is not the same as the number of indicted firms; if there were co-conspirator firms they are included, or if two or more indicted firms were actually controlled by one set of interests, only one of the entities is counted. A firm may be listed as a co-conspirator but not indicted if the evidence against it was of lower quality than the evidence against the indicted firms or if the firm did not actually participate in all of the meetings but had knowledge of the collusive activity. The number of competitors in the market column gives the number of firms who were known to be factors in the market.

The "Trade Association" column simply indicates whether a trade association existed, and if so, if it was in some way involved in the conspiracy.

The column entitled "Nature of the Buyers" is intended as a rough indicator of the type of market in which the conspirators sold their products or services. If the buyers were a very heterogeneous group, or if their identity simply was not known, the entry is blank. An important feature of this column is that if the fact memorandum indicated that significant amounts of sales were made to Government agencies this is reported.

"Nature of the Offense" is a description of the conduct in which the conspiring firms engaged. Such conduct could range from simple price fixing to agreements on various terms of sale to bid-rigging on a job by job basis.

The determinants of collusive behavior listed in Section I can be evaluated in the light of both the information presented in the appendix and other information available from the case abstracts which were prepared. The sample of cases consists of conspiracies which were both discovered and successfully prosecuted; as such they are not necessarily a random sample of all existing conspiracies. This fact may tend to bias the results; however the cases in the sample were discovered in a variety of ways such as customer complaints, observation of performance by Government agencies, and industry informants (see Table 1). The variety of methods of detection tends to argue for the proposition that most conspiracies are subject to possible detection although it is probably reasonable to assume that concentrated industries are more likely than unconcentrated ones to escape detection.

a. Fewness of Numbers

If the four cases in which the number of conspirators is fifty or more are excluded, the average number of firms involved in the conspiracy is 7.25. Table 2 below provides a more useful summary of the number of conspiring firms per conspiracy. In 79 per cent of the conspiracies ten or fewer firms were involved. The number of firms is a variable which was very much on

TABLE 1
METHOD OF DETECTION IN 49 CASES[a]

Method	Number of Cases
Grand Jury investigation in another case	12
Complaint by a competitor	10
Complaint by a customer	7
Complaint by Local, State or Federal Agency	6
Complaint by current or former employees	3
Complaint by Trade Association Official	2
Investigation of conduct or performance initiated by Antitrust Division	2
Newspaper account	2
Referred to Antitrust Division by the Federal Trade Commission	2
Complaint by anonymous informant	1
Merger investigation	1
Private suit	1
Total	49

[a] This information was not available for the remainder of the cases in the sample.

the minds of the potential conspirators; in one of the cases studied the product which was to be subject to agreement was deliberately defined narrowly in order to keep the number of participants small.

The results also show that in many cases larger groups do conspire. It has often been assumed that a formal trade association is the basic mechanism which allows (or is used for) large group collusion. Table 2 also shows the distribution of trade association involvement by number of conspirators. In seven out of eight cases with more than fifteen firms in the conspiracy, a formal industry trade association was involved. The table also shows that trade associations were often used with small numbers, but were not necessarily used even with groups of between ten and fifteen where an association was involved in only four out of twelve cases. What the table fails to reveal is that many conspiracies were in fact highly organized with chairmen, rules of order, agendas and regularly scheduled meetings, but without the cover of a formally organized industry trade association.

A comparison of the number of conspirators column with the number of firms in the market column shows that it is not necessary for a conspiracy to include all of the firms in the market to exist, or indeed, to be successful. It is interesting to speculate on the role of the non-conspirators. In some cases they may occupy product or territorial submarkets not recognized by the staff which wrote the fact memorandum. In general, they seem to be the smallest competitors. It is difficult to believe that these non-conspirators were unaware of the conspiracy. It might be assumed that they were willing silent accomplices living under the price umbrella provided by the conspirators.

TABLE 2

NUMBER OF CONSPIRATORS AND TRADE ASSOCIATION INVOLVEMENT

Number of Conspirators	2	3	4	5	6	7	8	9	10	11-15	16-20	21-25	> 25	Total
Number of Cases	1	7	8	4	10	4	3	5	7	5	2	—	6	62
Trade Association Involvement	—	—	1	—	4	1	—	1	3	1	1	—	6	18

Concentration Ratios

Concentration (Percentage)	0-25	26-50	51-75	76-100	Total
Number of Cases	3	9	17	21	50

b. *Concentration*

Information which could be used to compute concentration ratios was more likely to be available for relatively concentrated industries. Therefore a table listing only the concentration ratios shown in the appendix would be biased towards high values. In those situations in which data were not available, if the total number of firms in the market was known, a "minimum concentration ratio" was estimated by dividing the number of firms into 100 and multiplying by 4. "Minimum concentration ratios" could also be calculated from the market share information reported in the number of conspirators column. In thirty-eight of fifty cases for which estimates could be made the concentration ratio was greater than 50 per cent (see Table 2). This suggests that concentration is an important determinant of the ability of firms to collude. An examination of those cases in which minimum concentration ratios could not be calculated (because it was not felt that they would be appropriate or because the total number of firms in the market was not known) indicates that the conclusions would not be changed even if they could be included.[12]

Clabault and Burton[13] analyzed structure-conduct relationships in industries indicted under the Sherman Act between 1955 and 1965. Their conclusion was that conspiracies were most likely to develop in relatively unconcentrated markets. Clabault and Burton used Census concentration data at the four-digit level, while the concentration ratios reported herein, are oriented to the specific products that were the subject of conspiracy.

When the 1967 Census four-firm concentration ratios for the four-digit SIC industries in which the products in our survey are classified were examined, and compared to the product concentration ratios as reported in the appendix, the Census ratios for the products of the thirteen *national* conspiracies were lower than the product concentration ratios by an average of 39 percentage points (see Table 3). Thus, although the Clabault and Burton sample differs from that used here, it is reasonable to infer that their use of four-digit Census concentration figures resulted in a serious underestimate of the "true" level of concentration in the product markets in which price fixing conspiracies were found.[14]

The implications of this result are significant. Despite the writings of

[12] Calculations for the share of the largest firm divided by the share of the largest four were made. These show that there were many situations in which asymmetric oligopoly was present. However, this tendency was not dominant and no special significance can be attached to it.

[13] *Supra* note 1.

[14] It may, of course, be true that all product markets as defined here are generally much more concentrated than the Census categories and the sample simply reflects this. We know of no reason why this should be true *a priori* however.

TABLE 3
CONCENTRATION RATIOS IN NATIONAL CASES

Blue Book Number	SIC Number	Census Ratios	Fact Memo Ratios
1743	3312	48%	85%
1744	3494	14%	67%[a]
1748	2515	26%	61%
1749	2542	24%	60%
1751	3323	20%	32%[a]
1754	3452	18%	97%
1778	2339	16%	69%
1796	3312	48%	59%
1802	3623	38%	77%
1883	3999	10%	77%
1890	3545	20%	56%
1921	3261	62%	76%
1965	3432	28%	64%
Average		28.6%	67.7%

[a] Estimated from partial market share data.

Stigler and Posner, it has frequently been assumed that conspiracy would be largely restricted to relatively unconcentrated industries, since high concentration would permit extensive non-collusive coordination through what has been termed "conscious parallelism." This assumption has been based primarily on the gross benefits of collusion which are almost surely higher for unconcentrated industries for whom non-collusive coordination is only a remote possibility.

The results of the present study however, suggest that the low cost of planning and enforcing a conspiracy and the smaller likelihood of being caught in concentrated markets, are equally if not more significant factors in stimulating conspiracy.[15] This is not to suggest that some non-collusive coordination does not take place: but it now appears possible that some of the non-competitive price levels alleged to exist in concentrated industries may be the result not of "conscious parallelism" but of formal conspiracy.

c. Homogeneity

A column to show the subjectively estimated degree of inter-firm homogeneity is not presented because virtually all of the entries would read "high" product homogeneity. In terms of the simplicity of the product there appears to be some variety, although most of the products seem to be relatively simple. Some complicated products or services can be allocated on a job-by-job

[15] It should be kept in mind that most of the conspiracies were found in concentrated markets even though *a priori* these are the conspiracies which are most likely to escape detection. Thus if there is a bias, it should result in the underreporting of conspiracies in markets with high concentration.

basis and therefore do not present a great obstacle to coordination. Moreover, even where differentiated or complicated products are involved competitors appear to have isolated some factors which they can usefully agree upon. An agreement to delay end of season discounts in the swimming suit case (No. 1778 in the appendix) is an example.

d. Inelasticity of Demand

Little or no evidence from fact memorandum sources is available.[16]

e. Sealed Bidding

Sealed bidding, where the results are announced, was a factor in some cases. However, it is interesting to note that situations were found in which bids to Government agencies were specifically excluded from the agreements. Motivation for this behavior apparently derived from the belief that collusive activity is more likely to be detected and prosecuted if it is directed against the Federal Government. There were other situations in which market segments were not included in agreements in order to reduce potential friction and this may account for deliberate exclusion of Government bids. In any event, a look at the nature of the offense column shows that bid-rigging was a popular form of conduct.

f. Social Structure

The social structure variable cannot be quantified or briefly described in a table. Suffice it to say that the fact memoranda demonstrated that a dominant individual can force a group of firms to overcome natural barriers to coordination such as large numbers or low concentration ratios. This may explain much of the large group collusion which occurred.

Where the firms are all located in a single area, collusion seems to develop quite naturally and Adam Smith's oft quoted maxim is confirmed: "People of the same trade seldom meet together, even for merriment and diversion, but the conversation ends in a conspiracy against the public, or in some contrivance to raise prices."

g. Lumpiness and Infrequency of Orders

Evidence relating to situations in which individual sales occur infrequently and/or account for a large share of total output can be derived from the

[16] However, the Houthakker and Taylor estimates of short-run demand elasticity for four industries which overlapped our sample were all less than 1 (in absolute value), thus partially confirming the proposition that conspiracy is more likely when demand is inelastic. See H. S. Houthakker & Lester D. Taylor, Consumer Demand in the United States: Analyses and Projections (1970).

"nature of the offense" and "nature of the buyers" columns. If bid-rigging and/or allocation of jobs were involved then it can be assumed that orders were relatively large compared to total sales; this could also be assumed to be true if the buyers market or segments thereof tended toward oligopsony. Bid-rigging was a factor in fifteen cases. Several of those were related to construction, an activity that is inherently "lumpy."

h. High-Fixed and Low Marginal Costs

Any information about the ratio of fixed to marginal costs must be inferred from prior knowledge of the industries in the sample. Industries with such characteristics can be identified, but no strong pattern appears to emerge.

i. Duration

Theoretically, those industries with structural characteristics most conducive toward conspiratorial conduct should display the most success as measured by the duration of the conspiracy. Success was plotted against both the number of firms and concentration in order to provide a rough test of this proposition. Since most of the cases had ten or fewer conspirators the dispersion of observations was not great enough to allow any significant pattern to emerge. The most that can be said is that numbers as large as ten will, in certain circumstances, still allow collusion to continue for long periods of time. The concentration-years observations show a clearer pattern; the preponderance of conspiracies lasting ten or more years were in markets with high degrees of concentration. In those industries where attempts were made to organize large numbers of firms, the conspiracies were generally discovered very quickly. Details of some of the large-group organizational meetings were often printed in local newspapers.

Details concerning the beginning of the conspiracies were often available although there were many situations in which the agreements had been in existence for so long that no one could remember the origins. Several conspiracies had their roots in the NRA. Some meetings which began then continued for decades. One conspiracy began with discussions incident to the meetings of a Webb-Pomerene export association. Many, by far the largest number, were organized in response to price wars or general lack of discipline in the market.

Conclusions

A brief summary of our empirical results would be that conspiracy among competitors may arise in any number of situations but it is most likely to occur and endure when numbers are small, concentration is high and the product is homogeneous. We suspect these results will conflict with at least some previously held opinions on the expected locus of conspiracy, and conversely on the ability of oligopolists to regularly attain monopoly profits through tacit collusion.

This is not to suggest that tacit collusion does not occur or that where it occurs it cannot be attacked under existing antitrust laws,[17] or that a program of deconcentration such as suggested by Senator Hart's proposed Industrial Reorganization Act is either unnecessary or unjustified. It does suggest however that some of the non-competitive pricing attributed to concentrated industries is reachable even under a fairly conservative interpretation of current laws. To discover this kind of conduct would require investigations in those industries for which product markets display the characteristics that appear to be associated theoretically and empirically with collusion. Prime candidates would obviously be industries with a past history of conspiracy. To go much further would require concentration data at something like the seven-digit SIC level for regional or local markets. If such data cannot or will not be made available, however, the relative advantages of this approach to concentrated industries is sharply diminished.

A second implication of our findings has to do with relief. Very little previous work has been done in the area of structure-conduct relationships of the type investigated here. Perhaps as a result of this, scant attention has been paid to structural remedies in Sherman Act Section 1 cases.

The traditional remedies of fines and criminal convictions are generally considered to be inadequate as currently applied.[18] Legislative proposals have been made to increase fines in criminal antitrust cases. A supplementary (or alternative) approach would be to apply the court's powers to reorganize offending industries.

Justification for the reorganization approach is provided by two sorts of evidence: (1) The bulk of the violations prosecuted by the Antitrust Division appear to be in concentrated markets. Concentration and fewness of numbers can be said to facilitate (if not, in some instances *cause*) collusion. The most effective (if not the only effective) means to alter behavior, therefore, may be to alter the structure.[19] (2) Industries which are found to be colluding in

[17] See Richard A. Posner (1969), *supra* note 1.

[18] See Roger D. Blair, *supra* note 1.

[19] Obviously, this is likely to be an attractive remedy only where the firms involved operate two or more plants. Presumably it would not have to be the case that both plants currently serve the narrow geographic or product market in which the conspiracy occurred for dissolution to be effective however. Creating separately-owned entities can be beneficial in two ways even though the "new" firm is not currently in the same geographic or product market. First, because of its experience in serving its own market, the

one local market are often to be found colluding in other local markets. The number of dairy, bread, concrete and linen supply cases in the sample attest to this fact. If anything, this is stronger evidence of the structure-conduct link. Corollary evidence is that industries colluding at one point in time often can be found to be colluding at later points in time, in spite of Antitrust action in the interim.

In several cases the Antitrust Division has sought the dissolution of industry trade associations. The current study demonstrated that trade associations are often used as a coordinating device, especially when more than a given number of firms are involved. The logic of altering the structure of some industries by requiring the dissolution of their trade associations might be extended to breaking up industries with small numbers of competitors when other structural conditions permit.

The demonstration effect of moving for dissolution or divestiture in a price fixing case should not be overlooked. The electrical conspiracy cases seem to have done more for the enforcement of Section 1 than all of the cases prosecuted previous to them. As a start, applying dissolution to habitual offenders may provide the publicity needed to raise further the perceived cost of violating the antitrust laws and thus force compliance by firms in industries prone to conspiracy.

---

new firm probably faces lower barriers to entry for establishing a new plant in the relevant market. Second, even without actually building a new plant, the new company may influence the behavior of firms in the relevant market by its status as a potential entrant.

APPENDIX
Recent Horizontal Price Fixing Cases

Blue Book No.	Product (SIC No.)	Territorial Scope	Concentration Four-Firm (Percentage)	Number of Firms Conspirators (Percentage Sales)	Number of Firms Market
1743	Wrought Steel Wheels (3312)	National	85	5 (100)	5
1744	Rolled Steel Pipe Flanges & Rings (3494)	National		6	6
1748	Bed Springs (2515)	National	< 61	10	20
1749	Metal Library Shelving (2542)	National	60	7 (78)	9
1751	Steel Castings (> 30,000 lbs.) (3323)	National		10 (80)	
1754	Self-Locking Nuts (3452)	National	97	4 (97)	6
1756	Liquified Petroleum Gas Delivery (5984)	Regional		5 (100)	5
1763	Refuse Collection (4953)	Local		86	102
1773	Linoleum Installation (1752)	Local		12	
1778	Women's Swimsuits (2339)	National	< 69	9	
1779	Fabricated Structural Steel (3312)	Regional	91	6 (99)	
1796	Carbon Steel Sheets (3312)	National	59	10	
1800	Commercial Baking Flour (2041)	Regional	50	9 (65)	
1801	Fertilizer (2871)	Regional	< 100	4	

APPENDIX (Continued)

Blue Book No.	Trade Association Involved	Not Involved	Nature of the Buyers	Nature of the Offense
1743	—	—	Railroads and Transit Authorities	List price fixing; identical bids to NYC Transit Authority
1744	x	—		List price fixing
1748	—	—		List price fixing
1749	—	—	Schools, Universities, Federal, State and Local Governments	Complementary bidding; allocation of jobs
1751	—	x		List price fixing
1754	—	—	Aerospace Industry and the Federal Government	List price fixing and identical bidding
1756	—	—	Homeowners and Small Businesses	List price fixing
1763	x	—	Households and Businesses of all types	Customer allocation, coercion of non-members
1773	—	—	Contractors for Commercial and Government Building Projects	Complementary biddings; allocation of jobs
1778	—	—	Retailed by Small Shops and Department Stores	Agreement on end of season sale dates
1779	—	—	Contractors for Large Building Projects	Complementary bidding; allocation of jobs
1796	—	—	Major users are Automobile, Appliance, Container and Construction Industries	List price fixing and agreement on extras
1800	x	—	Commercial Baking Establishments	List price fixing
1801	—	—	Commercial Farmers	Terms of discounts and allowances were agreed upon

APPENDIX (Continued)

Blue Book No.	Product (SIC No.)	Territorial Scope	Concentration Four-Firm (Percentage)	Number of Firms: Conspirators (Percentage Sales)	Number of Firms: Market
1802	Stainless Steel Welding Electrodes (3623)	National	77	7 (87)	8
1818	Steel Products (Wholesale) (5091)	Regional	66	5 (72)	
1842	Acoustical Ceiling Materials (1799)	Local		10 (90)	
1845	Hydraulic Hose (3069)	National		6 (90)	
1847	Non-Premium Beer (5095)	Local		10	10
1849	Gasoline (2911)	Regional	> 49	12	
1860	Liquid Asphalt (2911)	Regional	56	20 (95)	
1880	Milk (2026)	Local		11*	13
1883	Book Matches (Resale) (3999)	National	77	10	10
1885	Concrete Pipe (3272)	Regional	100	4	4
1887	Cement Installations (1794)	Local		125	
1888	Concrete Pressure Pipe (3272)	Regional	100	2	2
1890	Drill Jig Bushings (3545)	National	56	9 (82)	13
1907	Linen Supplies (7213)	Local	49	31 (90)	

* Four firms were acquitted by a jury, the others pleaded *nolo contendere*.

APPENDIX (Continued)

Blue Book No.	Trade Association Involved	Trade Association Not Involved	Nature of the Buyers	Nature of the Offense
1802	—	x	Military, Railroad, Trucking and Chemical Industries use electrodes for Equipment Repair	List price fixing and identical bidding to the Government
1818	—	—		List price fixing
1842	—	—	Contractors subcontract with Ceiling Installation Firms	Complementary bidding, allocation of jobs
1845	—	—	Hose Assembly Manufacturers	List price fixing
1847	x	—	Military Installations	Elimination of discounts
1849	—	—	Affiliated and Independent Retail Dealers	List price fixing, market exclusion of independents
1860	—	—	The State of Missouri	Complementary bidding, allocation of jobs (in part territorial)
1880	x	—	Grocery Stores and Institutions	List price fixing
1883	x	—	Retail Stores and Commercial Institutions	List price fixing
1885	—	—	Highway and Sewer Construction Contractors	Allocation of jobs; complementary bidding
1887	x	—	Housing Contractors	Minimum price fixing and customer allocation
1888	—	—	Highway and Sewer Construction Contractors	Allocation of jobs; complementary bidding
1890	—	—	Machinists (large aircraft manufacturers are the single largest buyers)	List price fixing, identical bidding to Government
1907	x	—	Hotels and Restaurants	Customer allocation

APPENDIX (Continued)

Blue Book No.	Product (SIC No.)	Territorial Scope	Concentration Four-Firm (Percentage)	Number of Firms Conspirators (Percentage Sales)	Market
1909	School Construction (1511)	Local			
1921	Plumbing Fixtures (Majors)** (3261)	National	76	7 (98)	> 15
1925	Dairy Products (2026)	Regional			45
1928	Fuel Oil (5983)	Local		26	
1930	Class Rings (3911)	Regional	< 100	3 (90)	5
1951	Gasoline* (5541)	Local		200	
1954	Tickets (2751)	Regional	< 78	9 (< 91)	> 10
1957	Plumbing (Contracting) (1711)	Regional	< 63	14 (90)	
1962	Tickets (2751)	Regional	> 95	3 (95)	
1963	Bread (Wholesale) (2051)	Regional		50	
1965	Plumbing Brass Fittings (3432)	National	64	6	30
1970	Baked Goods (Wholesale) (2051)	Regional	46	7	> 8
1994	Auto Repair (7531)	Local		16	

** Violations were alleged in both vitreous china and enameled cast iron, a parallel indictment named the smaller (shortline) vitreous china firms. The figures reported are for vitreous china.

* Four separate conspiracies in the Northern California region were identified and prosecuted.

APPENDIX (Continued)

Blue Book No.	Trade Association Involved	Trade Association Not Involved	Nature of the Buyers	Nature of the Offense
1909	—	—	School Districts	Complementary bidding
1921	x	—	Building Contractors	List price fixing
1925	x	—	Grocery Stores; Home Delivery Routes	List price fixing
1928	x	—	Homes, Apartment Buildings, etc.	List price fixing
1930	—	—	Students	Bid rigging
1951	x	—	Motor Vehicle Owners	Price fixing
1954	—	x	Amusement Parks, Transportation Companies, etc.	Customer allocation
1957	—	—	Building Contractors	Complementary bidding; allocation of jobs
1962	—	—	Amusement Parks, Transportation Companies, etc.	Customer allocation
1963	x	—	Grocery Stores, Restaurants, Schools and Hospitals	Customer allocation, price fixing
1965	x	—	Building Contractors, Plumbing Contractors	List price fixing
1970	—	—	Grocery Stores, Restaurants, Schools and Hospitals	List price fixing, elimination of discounts
1994	x	—	Motor Vehicle Owners	Price fixing, reciprocal non-entry agreement with towing companies

APPENDIX (Continued)

Blue Book No.	Product (SIC No.)	Territorial Scope	Concentration Four-Firm (Percentage)	Number of Firms: Conspirators (Percentage Sales)	Number of Firms: Market
1997	Bread (Wholesale) (2051)	Local		6	> 12
2001	Linen Supply (7213)	Local	89	6 (100)	6
2009	Athletic Equipment (5952)	Local		6 (100)	6
2025	Linen Supplies (Industrial) (7213)	Regional		3	
2030	Linen Supplies (7213)	Local		4	
2032	Maple Floors (1752)	Local		4	
2034	Dairy Products (2026)	Regional	> 95	3 (95)	13
2035	Ready-Mix Concrete (3273)	Regional		8	17
2036	Industrial Chemicals (5029)	Local	< 93	5	
2090	Vending Machines (7394)	Local	93	6 (100)	6
2104	Snack Foods (2099)	Regional	95	4 (95)	
2124	Ready-Mix Concrete (3273)	Local		10	
2136	Ready-Mix Concrete (3273)	Local	86	9 (100)	9
2145	Rendering (2094)	Local	< 69	13	16

APPENDIX (Continued)

Blue Book No.	Trade Association Involved	Trade Association Not Involved	Nature of the Buyers	Nature of the Offense
1997	—	—	Grocery Stores, Restaurants, Schools and Hospitals	List price fixing; elimination of discounts
2001	—	—	Hotels and Restaurants	Allocation of customers
2009	—	—	School Districts	Bid rigging; customer allocation
2025	—	—	Gasoline Stations, Automobile Dealerships, etc.	Customer allocation
2030	x	—	Commercial Establishments	Price fixing; allocation of customers
2032	—	—	Contractors	Allocation of jobs
2034	—	—	Grocery Stores and Institutions	List price fixing and bid rigging to institutions
2035	—	—	Contractors	List price fixing
2036	—	—		List price fixing
2090	x	—	Restaurants, Hotels, etc.	Price fixing; customer allocation; coercion and threats
2104	—	—	Grocery Stores and Schools	List price fixing; identical bidding to schools
2124	x	—	Contractors	List price fixing; customer allocation
2136	—	x	Contractors	List price fixing
2145	—	—	Stores, Packing Plants, Restaurants	Price fixing in supply market; allocation of accounts

APPENDIX (Continued)

Blue Book No.	Product (SIC No.)	Territorial Scope	Concentration Four-Firm (Percentage)	Number of Firms: Conspirators (Percentage Sales)	Number of Firms: Market
2156	Autobody Repair (7531)	Local			
2177	Rendering (2094)	Local	100	3 (100)	3
2182	Bread (Wholesale) (2051)	Local		3	6
2189	Dairy Products (2026)	Local		4	7
2192	Retail Shoes (5661)	Local		3	
2211	Overhead Garage Doors (2431)	Regional		6	8
2243	Plumbing Supplies and Services (5074)	Local		8	
2246	Automobile Glass Replacement Parts (7539)	Local	75	8	11
2277	Baking (Wholesale) (2051)	Local	96	4 (96)	5
2278	Wholesale Meat (5047)	Local		6	6

APPENDIX (Continued)

Blue Book No.	Trade Association Involved	Trade Association Not Involved	Nature of the Buyers	Nature of the Offense
2156	x	—	Insurance Companies and Motor Vehicle Owners	Price fixing; elimination of discounts
2177	—	—	Retail Meat Stores	Price fixing in supply market
2182	—	—	Grocery Stores	Price fixing; agreement on terms of sales
2189	—	—	Grocery Stores, Institutions	Price fixing; bid rigging and territorial allocation
2192	—	—	Households	List price fixing
2211	x	—	Contractors, Households	List price fixing
2243	—	x	Contractors	Allocation of jobs; complementary bidding
2246	—	—	Motor Vehicle Owners	Reduction of discounts
2277	—	—	Grocery Stores and Restaurants	List price fixing
2278	—	—	Hotels, Restaurants, Schools and other Public Institutions	List price fixing

[11]

Rand Journal of Economics
Vol. 17, No. 3, Autumn 1986

Most-favored-customer pricing and tacit collusion

Thomas E. Cooper*

This article examines the role of the most-favored-customer pricing policy as a practice facilitating coordination in a dynamic model of price-setting duopoly. This policy is a promise by a firm that if it later lowers price, it will rebate to current customers the difference between the price they pay now and the lower future price. By reducing each firm's incentive to reduce price, the policy enables both firms to offer higher prices and to enjoy higher profits. Consequently, at least one firm offers the policy in equilibrium. We illustrate these general results in an example.

1. Introduction

■ A major question of oligopoly theory is whether firms can collude to achieve the monopoly outcome. Overt formal coordination, such as actual agreements to fix prices, has been the primary object of antitrust law. A more subtle form of coordination that resembles the monopoly outcome is tacit collusion, in which firms choose higher prices because of mutual recognition of their interdependence.[1] But it is usually difficult for firms to collude tacitly, since they may not be able to agree on mutually acceptable prices or they may find price cuts too profitable to resist. If either of these obstacles is present, prices are held down by firms' rivalrous efforts to achieve higher profits.

The possibility of tacit collusion would deserve more attention if there were facilitating practices, actions that firms could take to reduce their agreement or enforcement problems. Some authors have noted that the most-favored-customer pricing policy may be a facilitating practice.[2] The most-favored-customer policy is a guarantee to current customers that becomes

* University of Florida.

This article is based on Chapter 2 of my dissertation, which was partly supported by an NSF Graduate Fellowship. I am grateful to David Brownstone, Leonard Cheng, Avinash Dixit, Philip Dybvig, Andrew Postlewaite, Richard Romano, Hugo Sonnenschein, Joseph Stiglitz, and Robert Willig for helpful comments and discussion. Comments from the Editorial Board and an anonymous referee have greatly improved this article. Of course, I am responsible for any errors that may remain.

[1] This concept has also been known as conscious parallelism, as in Posner (1976). Clearly, this idea has its roots in Chamberlin's (1962) discussion of oligopoly behavior.

[2] Several good discussions of facilitating practices include reference to the most-favored-customer policy. The term most-favored-customer pricing comes from Hay's (1982) article, in which he presents several examples of facilitating practices and discusses their import for antitrust policy. Throughout this article, this term is used interchangeably with price protection policy, another term offered by Hay.

Salop (1986) offers an interesting discussion of how facilitating practices can credibly generate improved tacit coordination. He considers several commonly employed practices, like most-favored-customer pricing, most-favored-nation pricing, meeting-competition clauses, and meet-or-release clauses. Chapter 1 of Cooper (1984) consists of a formal characterization of facilitating practices and application of this definition to a variety of proposed facilitating

effective only if the firm offers a lower price during some specified future period. In that event the firm will pay past customers the difference between the price they paid and the lowest price offered during the prescribed period. If firms institute this policy and offer a collusive price in one period, the rebate provision penalizes later attempts to shade the price. Previous discussions of the most-favored-customer policy have focused on its ability to support a collusive price once that price is reached. Little effort has been directed to determining whether firms would ever willingly adopt this practice and raise prices initially.[3] In the absence of formal coordination firms may be unwilling to offer price protection because the reduction in pricing flexibility could put them at a competitive disadvantage. And even if all firms offer the most-favored-customer policy, each can still undercut the collusive price in the first period, before the policy takes effect. Most-favored-customer pricing cannot generate a more profitable outcome in a noncooperative equilibrium unless it resolves these difficulties. The purpose of this article is to show how the most-favored-customer policy solves these problems and, hence, facilitates tacit collusion.

To demonstrate the effects of the most-favored-customer policy, we consider a perfect information model of price-setting duopoly with differentiated products. If a firm offers the price protection policy, then charging a price slightly above the single-period Nash equilibrium price commits the firm to maintaining that price into the future. The firm would not lower price later, because the rebates required by the policy outweigh the gains from the reduction. Since this commitment induces the other firm to raise its price, both firms can earn greater profits if one offers the policy. Therefore, a firm has an incentive to adopt the most-favored-customer policy unilaterally. In equilibrium at least one firm offers price protection and both earn greater profits as a result. The practice facilitates tacit collusion by generating increased industry profits without formal coordination.

The remainder of this article shows how the price protection plan works. In the next section we present the duopoly model and describe the game played by the firms. Section 3 contains the discussion of the role of most-favored-customer pricing as a facilitating practice. After graphically demonstrating that committing to a high price can be profitable, we present some formal results about the effects of the policy in equilibrium. Section 4 presents an example to demonstrate the quantitative significance of the policy. In Section 5 we present a case in which price protection was used, and in Section 6 we consider factors that may make offering price protection not so attractive. Finally, we conclude with a brief summary.

2. The model

■ In this model there are two firms, designated A and B. There is no possibility of entry or exit. The duopolists produce differentiated, nondurable goods in an effort to serve a single market. The demand and cost conditions that they face remain unchanged over time. In each period firms set prices p^A and p^B and make sales of $Q^i(p^A, p^B)$ at a cost $C^i(Q^i)$ for $i = A, B$.[4] As a result, firm i earns profit $\Pi^i(p^A, p^B) = p^iQ^i - C^i(Q^i)$.

We shall refer to the single-period equilibrium of this price-setting game as the Bertrand equilibrium. The subscript n indicates solutions to this simple Nash game, so p_n^A and p_n^B are the Bertrand prices and Π_n^i is firm i's Bertrand profit. Let us assume that there is a unique

practices. There are even references to facilitating practices in the standard industrial organization literature as embodied in Scherer's (1980) text. In addition to a general discussion of the topic in Chapters 5 through 7, he discusses the effects of the most-favored-customer policy explicitly on pp. 163–164.

[3] There are two exceptions. Hay (1982) contends that firms would adopt the policy as a show of good faith. Salop (1986) discusses benefits from offering the policy unilaterally. His discussion is based on an earlier version of this article.

[4] Unless otherwise noted, any function with designation i is for $i = A$ and for $i = B$. Also, the superscripts i and j are used in a single expression if it applies to the cases $i = A, j = B$ and $i = B, j = A$. Notice that arguments of a function such as Q are suppressed when they are obvious.

Bertrand equilibrium and that both prices and outputs are positive in the equilibrium.[5] In addition, we assume the following conditions are satisfied whenever both quantities are positive:

Assumption 1. $Q^i(p^A, p^B)$ is twice continuously differentiable, decreases in p^i (own price), and increases in p^j (rival's price).

Assumption 2. $C^i(Q^i)$ is twice continuously differentiable with $C^{i\prime}(Q^i) \geqq 0$ and $C^{i\prime\prime}(Q^i) \geqq 0$.[6]

Assumption 3. $\Pi^A_{12} > 0$ and $\Pi^B_{21} > 0$.

Assumption 4. $\Pi^A_{11} + \Pi^A_{12} < 0$ and $\Pi^B_{22} + \Pi^B_{21} < 0$.

These assumptions are fairly standard, but they do impose two restrictions on the interdependence of the firms. First, since the goods are substitutes, firms are actually competing to serve a single market. Second, Assumption 3 states that a price increase by one firm makes a price increase more attractive to the other. As a result, the firms' single-period reaction curves slope upward in price space. This condition provides an opportunity for tacit coordination, because a firm's best response to a cooperative gesture (a price increase) is also a seemingly cooperative price increase.[7]

When the duopolists make a decision, they know the cost functions, the demand functions, and all actions taken in previous periods. In this article, they must take three actions. At time zero, before the market opens, they announce their choices of the policy variable M^i, which is defined by

$$M^i = \begin{cases} 1 & \text{if firm } i \text{ offers a most-favored-customer policy} \\ 0 & \text{otherwise.} \end{cases}$$

The most-favored-customer policy requires rebates to past customers if prices are subsequently reduced; therefore, the choice of M^i affects the profit function in the second period. Incorporating this variable into the profit function changes firm i's second-period profits from Π^{i2} to

$$\hat{\Pi}^{i2} = \begin{cases} \Pi^{i2} & \text{for} \quad p^i_2 \geqq p^i_1 \\ \Pi^{i2} - M^i(p^i_1 - p^i_2)Q^i_1 & \text{for} \quad p^i_2 \leqq p^i_1, \end{cases}$$

where the time period is indicated by the second superscript for profit and by subscripts for all other variables. Clearly, a firm's choice of M^i is merely a choice of second-period profit function. The two remaining actions of the firms are announcements of prices. At the beginning of the first period, each firm sets p^i_1. Similarly, each selects a price p^i_2 as the second period begins.

Each firm selects a closed-loop strategy that indicates what actions to take. The strategy consists of a choice for the policy variable M^i, a rule for setting p^i_1 as a function of $M = (M^A, M^B)$, and a rule for setting p^i_2 as a function of M and $p_1 = (p^A_1, p^B_1)$. We restrict the firm to choose a subgame-perfect strategy.[8] A strategy is subgame perfect if it calls for optimal actions in every possible subgame, or known set of circumstances, that the players may face (Selten, 1975). Since such strategies require rational behavior both on and off the

[5] Friedman (1977) presents sufficient conditions for this result and proves that they yield the unique Nash equilibrium desired. Assumptions 1, 2, and 4 are special cases of some of his sufficient conditions.

[6] As is customary, $C^{i\prime} = \partial C^i/\partial Q^i$ and $C^{i\prime\prime} = \partial^2 C^i/\partial Q^{i2}$. In addition, $\Pi^i_1 = \partial\Pi^i/\partial p^A$, and Π^i_{jk} is the cross partial derivative with respect to the jth and kth arguments.

[7] Bulow, Geanakoplos, and Klemperer (1985) would call these goods strategic complements because more aggressive action begets a more aggressive response.

[8] I am grateful to Andy Postlewaite for suggesting this restriction.

equilibrium path, a firm cannot support an equilibrium by making threats that it would not want to execute.

The problem for each firm is to select a strategy that maximizes the undiscounted sum of its profits in the two periods, given the strategy of the other firm.[9] A subgame-perfect Nash equilibrium is a pair of strategies that simultaneously solve the two firms' problems. We assume that an equilibrium exists. To simplify the exposition let us also assume that a firm's choice of p_1^i is a pure strategy for any value of M in equilibrium.[10] Since the example in Section 4 satisfies this condition, one may consider it reasonable.[11] The latter assumption is useful because it collapses the game to a simple one with M^i as the only choice. Once each firm selects M^i, firms know both first-period prices from the assumption, and they know p_2 since it is a unique function of M and p_1 in this model. The firm's choices of M^i completely determine their payoffs. To see the effects of the most-favored-customer policy, one only needs to consider the levels of prices and profits associated with each possible value of M in this simple noncooperative game.

It is appropriate to examine a noncooperative solution because we are considering tacit collusion, which occurs without binding contracts.[12] Unconstrained by a meaningful cooperative agreement, a firm will select the strategy that is best from its individual point of view. Only in a noncooperative equilibrium will each firm be satisfied with its chosen strategy. Since each strategy contains rules for setting prices, there is ample opportunity for duopoly interaction in this Nash equilibrium. A strategy simply dictates how a firm's actions depend on the previous actions of its rival. Therefore, each firm must select a strategy that anticipates the manner in which its rival will react. Firms are fully aware of their interdependence when they make decisions.

The duopolists have an opportunity to punish departures from a cooperative plan, and they also recognize this fact. Nevertheless, without price protection the firms earn the Bertrand profit in each period, as they would if they could not respond to actions taken. This result occurs because strategies must be subgame perfect and the horizon is finite. Any punishments proposed by a subgame-perfect strategy must be rational. Only a threat to move to a noncooperative equilibrium satifies this condition. A threat of this type may support a seemingly cooperative plan over an infinite horizon, but in this model it carries no weight if the horizon is finite.[13] By backward induction one can see that the only solution without price protection is to offer the Bertrand prices in each period (Luce and Raiffa, 1957). Firms could earn the Bertrand profit in a single-period model which offers no chance to cooperate; therefore, we let the Bertrand solution serve as a benchmark of competitive behavior. Since this model has two periods, we consider twice the Bertrand profit to be the competitive level of a firm's total profit. We shall say that the most-favored-customer policy facilitates tacit collusion if it enables both firms to earn more than their competitive profit.

3. The most-favored-customer policy as a facilitating practice

■ One can see the potential for the most-favored-customer policy to facilitate tacit collusion by recognizing two facts. The first is that in a one-period price-setting duopoly, a firm can

[9] The qualitative results of the model would not be affected if discounting were added.

[10] Allowing mixed strategies would not alter the nature of the results. All statements made about p_1^i would just apply to any of the possible values. If there are multiple solutions for p_1, any one of them could be viewed as a signalling equilibrium. If both firms believe one solution for p_1 is "correct," it would be an equilibrium.

[11] The spatial model of product differentiation found in Salop (1979) also meets this assumption, as is discussed in Chapter 2 of Cooper (1984).

[12] Hugo Sonnenschein first pointed out to me the apparent anomaly in referring to the outcome of a noncooperative game as tacit collusion. Tacit collusion is not cooperative behavior in this model. This approach seems consistent with the use of the term by Stigler (1964) and Spence (1978). Since they imply that expected reactions support tacit collusion, they appear to speak of firms that pursue their own best interests.

[13] Friedman (1977) discusses the balanced temptation equilibrium, in which the threat of moving to a noncooperative equilibrium does support a more profitable outcome.

increase its profit by establishing a binding legal minimum on its own price. Both firms will earn greater profits once the other firm reacts to the minimum by raising its price. The second key fact is that the most-favored-customer policy effectively enables a firm to set a minimum price.

Figure 1 illustrates the value of setting a minimum price. In this diagram $p^{A*}(p^B)$ and $p^{B*}(p^A)$ are the single-period best reply functions of the firms. The intersection of these functions is the Bertrand equilibrium. At the Bertrand prices (p_n^A, p_n^B), the isoprofit curve for firm A is tangent to the horizontal line $p^B = p_n^B$. Since $p^{B*}(p^A)$ is increasing, a portion of it lies above firm A's Bertrand isoprofit curve at values of p^A above p_n^A. Establishing a minimum price above p_n^A enables firm A to move the industry to these more profitable points.[14] Firm B would respond to the minimum by charging its best-response price; therefore, varying the minimum would move the industry along $p^{B*}(p^A)$. To make the most of this opportunity, firm A should set the minimum at $p^{A'}$, thereby achieving the profit that a von Stackelberg leader would earn. Since profits increase as prices move above an isoprofit curve, the minimum price enables both firms to earn greater profit. It is possible for both firms to benefit because the leadership results in reduced competition in this model.[15]

One can see that the most-favored-customer policy effectively enables a firm to commit itself to a minimum price in the future by considering Figure 2. Assume that firm A has

FIGURE 1

EFFECT OF SETTING MINIMUM FOR p^A ABOVE p_n^A

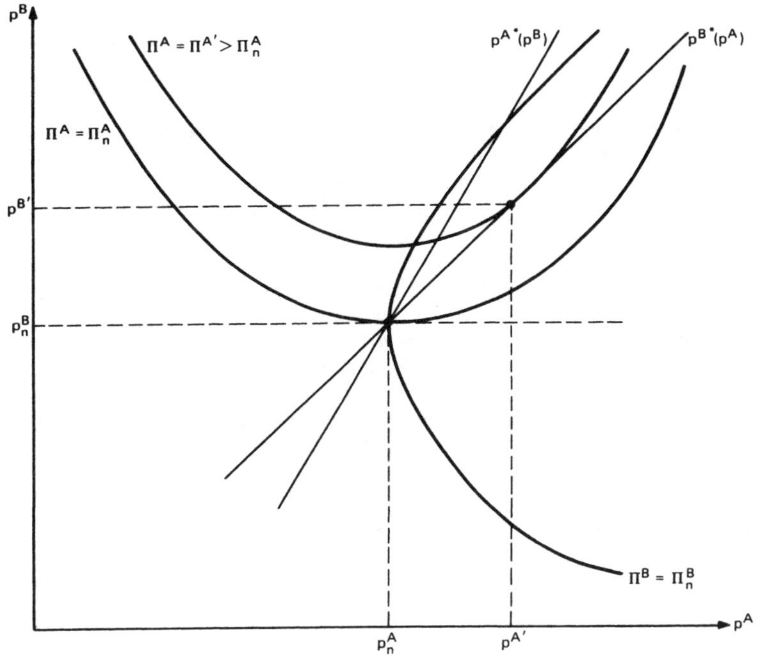

[14] It is obvious that a maximum would be desirable if reaction curves slope downward. Only if they are horizontal at the Bertrand prices is this type of incentive absent.

[15] A similar result involving voluntary export restrictions as a facilitating practice is discussed in Krishna (1985).

FIGURE 2

EFFECT OF THE MOST-FAVORED-CUSTOMER POLICY ON SECOND-PERIOD REACTION FUNCTION OF FIRM A

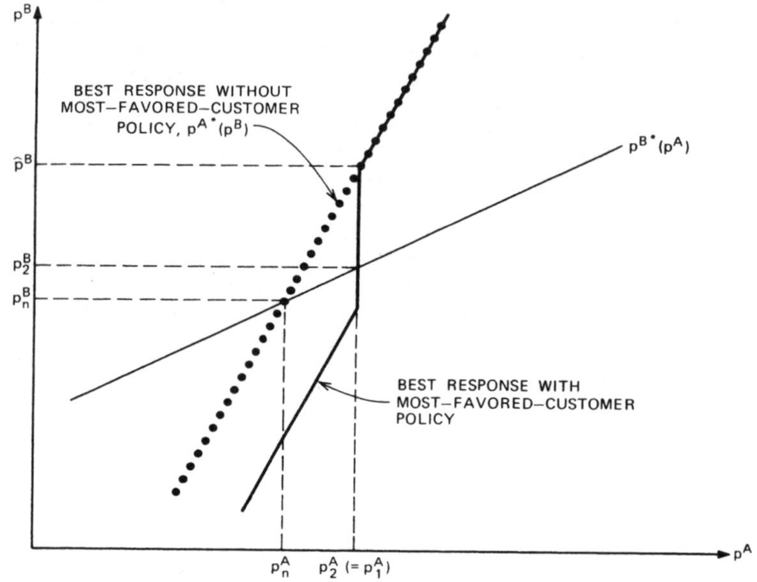

offered the policy in the first period and set its initial price at p_1^A, which exceeds p_n^A. Without price protection firm A would continue to charge p_1^A in the second period only if it expected firm B to charge the price marked $\hat{p}^B$ in the figure. After offering the most-favored-customer policy, firm A finds that keeping price at p_1^A is its best second-period response to a range of values of p^B, all less than or equal to $\hat{p}^B$. This occurs because, when contemplating a price reduction, the firm must consider rebates to previous customers. For small price cuts the loss from rebates exceeds the gains from increased sales. Since the policy induces firm A to forgo some price reductions that would otherwise be profitable, it creates a flat section on firm A's second-period reaction curve. Provided firm B selects a price close enough to $\hat{p}^B$, firm A will not wish to lower its price.[16] In Figure 2 this commitment is effective, since the new Nash equilibrium prices are $p_2^A = p_1^A$ and $p_2^B = p^{B*}(p_1^A)$. The most-favored-customer policy has created a situation in which firm B can charge $p^{B*}(p_1^A)$ because it knows that firm A will not cut price below p_1^A. Thus, the outcome is the same as if firm A had set a legal minimum for p_2^A at the value of p_1^A.

Because of the most-favored-customer policy, firm A's choice of first-period price affects both firms' prices in the second period. The intertemporal price dependence created by the policy is the key to achieving higher prices. To demonstrate this fact, we assume that only firm A offers the policy. In that case the firms do not simply set the Bertrand prices in each

[16] The length of this flat section is an increasing function of this firm's first-period sales. For zero first-period sales, there is no flat section.

The firm selects a value of p_2^A that is less than p_1^A if the reaction curves do not intersect in the flat section, but firms A's second-period price still exceeds p_n^A if $Q_1^A > 0$ and $p_1^A > p_n^A$. It is easier to see the commitment arising from the policy if the firm does not lower price at all. For this reason we restrict our discussion to the case depicted in Figure 2.

period. Firm A could improve on that strategy by raising p_1^A slightly above the Bertrand price. Switching strategies in this manner induces both firms to set prices above the Bertrand prices in the second period. The most-favored-customer policy prevents firm A from setting p_2^A below p_1^A, and that commitment enables firm B to increase p_2^B. Since the change in strategies increases the price of a substitute, firm A receives some benefit from the switch. The cost to firm A from raising its own prices is zero to first order because the original prices were single-period profit-maximizing prices. Thus, we find that adopting the policy gives firm A both the incentive and the ability to raise prices in the industry.

The intertemporal price dependence also enables firm B to increase p_1^B. If firm A lowered p_1^A in response to a higher p_1^B, that reaction would reduce both prices in the second period. The resulting loss in future profit outweighs the immediate gain; therefore, firm B can raise p_1^B without fearing that p_1^A will be lower than expected. Although we have seen how the policy affects prices, we have not yet considered its effects on profits. The following lemma shows that both firms earn greater profits if only one adopts the policy.[17]

Lemma. If only one firm offers the most-favored-customer policy, both firms' prices exceed the Bertrand prices in each period, $\Pi^{A1} + \hat{\Pi}^{A2} > 2\Pi_n^A$, and $\Pi^{B1} + \hat{\Pi}^{B2} > 2\Pi_n^B$.

Proof. We only consider the case with $M = (1, 0)$. Prices cannot be below the Bertrand prices because the policy limits only price reductions. From the preceding discussion it is obvious that prices exceed the Bertrand prices in both periods.

Note that firm A does not lower its price over time. If it did so, then it would earn $\Sigma\Pi^A = p_2^A Q_1^A - C^A(Q_1^A) + p_2^A Q_2^A - C^A(Q_2^A)$. This expression decreases in p_1^A. Because of the envelope theorem, raising p_1^A has no effect through p_2^A, but it lowers p_2^B.[18] Consequently, firm A wants to lower p_1^A out of the range that calls for a future price cut. Thus, we find that in equilibrium $p_1^A = p_2^A$ and $p_1^B = p_2^B = p^{B*}(p_1^A)$.

We find $\Sigma\Pi^A > 2\Pi_n^A$ by considering a suboptimal strategy for firm A. Since $p_1^B > p_n^B$, firm A could earn more than $2\Pi_n^A$ by offering the prices that generate the Bertrand level of sales each period.[19] The optimal strategy must yield at least this profit, so $\Sigma\Pi^A > 2\Pi_n^A$. Since p_1^A and p_2^A exceed p_n^A, one finds that firm B earns more by a straightforward application of the envelope theorem. *Q.E.D.*

Considering the effects of the policy, we find the increase in profits quite reasonable. Offering price protection enables a firm to act as a von Stackelberg leader in the second period. The firm's choice of price in the first period effectively determines both firms' prices for the second period. It is hardly surprising that the firm, as a von Stackelberg price leader, gains by exercising its control over prices. Since the leader raises the price of its product, the seller of the substitute good must also benefit. Thus, if one firm offers the policy, the noncooperative prices generate increased profits for both.

The firm without the policy contributes virtually nothing to the effort to raise prices. This firm always selects its myopic profit-maximizing responses to the leader's actions. Since the firm with the policy bears the burden of raising industry prices, each firm may want the other to be the only one to adopt the policy. Such a situation may make it difficult to reach equilibrium, but this problem does not affect the characteristics of the Nash equilibrium.[20] Far more important is the fact that both firms earn greater profits if one offers the policy.

---

[17] For this lemma we need the implicit assumption that rebate payments are the only cost associated with the policy. We discuss the importance of this assumption in Section 5.

[18] The Appendix contains a general specification of second-period prices and their dependence on first-period prices.

[19] If there were no such price, raising p_1^A indefinitely would yield profit greater than $2\Pi_n^A$ immediately.

[20] If there are two equilibria in which a single firm offers the policy, the situation parallels the Battle-of-the-Sexes game. Since there is no dominant strategy equilibrium, each firm prefers to wait for the other to offer the policy. It would be difficult to select which equilibrium to play because the firms prefer different selections.

This ensures that at least one firm will use the policy in equilibrium. The following theorem contains this result.

Theorem. There is an equilibrium in which at least one firm offers a most-favored-customer policy. At equilibrium both firms earn higher profits and set higher prices than in the Bertrand game (with no most-favored-customer policies).

Proof. Since the game reduces to selecting M^i, we must show that $M = (1, 1)$, $M = (1, 0)$, or $M = (0, 1)$ is an equilibrium. From the lemma we know that both firms find $M = (0, 0)$ less profitable than $M = (1, 0)$ and $M = (0, 1)$. Hence, there is an equilibrium in which someone offers the policy because cycling of choices is impossible.

From the lemma we see that the rest of the results hold if only one firm adopts the policy. Since $M = (1, 1)$ only if that is more profitable than $M = (1, 0)$ and $M = (0, 1)$, then equilibrium profits exceed Bertrand profits. Moreover, if $M = (1, 1)$, a firm has an incentive to raise price from the Bertrand prices, exactly as if $M = (1, 0)$. Hence, prices exceed the Bertrand prices. *Q.E.D.*

These results indicate that the most-favored-customer policy does facilitate tacit collusion. The firms select their best actions independently, but each considers how the other will respond to its choice before making a decision. In the absence of the policy neither firm's actions depend on previous choices, so the recognition of their interdependence has no effect. If at least one firm offers the policy, however, both firms know that first-period prices affect second-period prices. The intertemporal price dependence created by the policy leads to higher noncooperative prices in the first period. Then the rebate provision of the policy enables the firms to keep prices high in the second period as well. Since the higher prices yield increased profits, it is in the best interest of at least one firm to adopt price protection.

4. Example

■ Although we have seen that there are always benefits from offering the policy, it is important to know how large the gains are. An example provides an indication of the magnitude of the effects. Suppose that we have the following demand function, provided both demands are positive:

$$Q^i = \begin{cases} 22 - 9\sqrt{p^i} + p^j & \text{if} \quad p^i \leqq 16 \\ 4 - \frac{9}{8}p^i + p^j & \text{if} \quad p^i \geqq 16 \end{cases}$$

for $i = A, B$ and for $j = B, A$.[21] Total industry demand declines if either firm raises its price. In addition, total demand decreases to zero as both prices increase proportionally. To simplify matters further, let us assume that production is costless. As a result, firms simply try to maximize revenues.

Table 1 sets out the equilibrium values. Each firm's equilibrium strategy calls for it to set the same price in both periods; therefore, we present the values of price, quantity, profit, and total surplus for a single period, t.[22] We omit the case with $M = (0, 1)$, since it is symmetric to the case with $M = (1, 0)$, but we add the perfect cartel's solution for comparison.

Although it is not the equilibrium, let us first consider the case in which $M = (1, 0)$.

---

[21] This function satisfies all of our assumptions except that of twice continuous differentiability, which fails at $p = 16$. The results of the example do not depend on the change in the second derivative at this point. Therefore, we use this demand function to simplify the analysis. It is merely a special case of $Q^i = r - s\sqrt{p^i} + tp^j$ in the relevant region, but we have replaced r, s, and t with numbers to produce an interpretable solution.

[22] We use profit plus consumer surplus to measure welfare, as discussed in Willig (1973). When prices are equal, we calculate consumer surplus as the sum of the areas under the demand curves while assuming both prices change equally.

TABLE 1 Equilibrium Values of *p*, *Q*, and Π in Period *t*

Variable	$M = (0, 0)$	$M = (1, 0)$	$M = (1, 1)$	Perfect Cartel
p_t^A	3.594	3.758	6.351	7.563
p_t^B	3.594	3.640	6.351	7.563
Q_t^A	8.532	8.193	5.670	4.813
Q_t^B	8.532	8.587	5.670	4.813
Π^{At}	30.664	30.789	36.010	36.395
Π^{Bt}	30.664	31.257	36.010	36.395
TS_t	196.032	194.993	168.302	156.408

Both firms gain from having firm *A* adopt the policy, but firm *B* gains more than firm *A*. This occurs because firm *A* must bear the burden of raising prices by assuming the position of the high-priced firm. With no cooperation from firm *B*, both prices rise by less than 5%, industry sales fall by less than 2%, welfare falls by less than .6%, and firm *A*'s per period profit rises by .145, or only .5%. If there were any costs to adopting the policy, firm *A* may prefer $M = (0, 0)$ to $M = (1, 0)$. In that event there could be an equilibrium without the policy.

In the equilibrium of this example, however, both firms offer the price protection policy.[23] With both firms' contributing to the effort to raise profits, prices are 77% higher, quantities are 33% lower, profits are 17% higher, and welfare falls 14% from the Bertrand case.[24] It is interesting to note how effective tacit collusion can be. In this example the price protection policy enables the firms to achieve 93% of the increase in profits they would have obtained if they colluded perfectly.

5. A case involving the use of the most-favored-customer policy

■ The two manufacturers of turbine generators, General Electric and Westinghouse, both used the most-favored-customer policy for some time.[25] From the early 1960s to the mid-1970s, each firm offered a price protection policy that was effective for the six months following a sale. Several factors combined to make the policy profitable in this industry. First, the costs of adopting and administering the policy were low. The major cost of adopting price protection is informing potential buyers and rival sellers. Only if everyone concerned knows about the policy can it profitably constrain pricing. General Electric and Westinghouse publicly announced the new policy to inform most buyers. In addition, the manufacturers could use the trade associations of buyers, who were public utilities, to inform others at a low cost. Administering the policy was inexpensive because few purchases were made during any six-month period. The manufacturers assured buyers that all promised rebates were paid by allowing them to check the records for any relevant price cuts. Consequently, the manufacturers did not face great costs of adopting and implementing the policy.

The major obstacle to using the policy profitably lay in the fact that most generators were custom-built. Unless a firm happened to sell two identical generators in a six-month period, the most-favored-customer policy would not constrain pricing. The firms overcame this problem by publishing price books that contained relative prices for all components

[23] The firms offer prices that simultaneously solve $(\partial \Pi^i/\partial p^i) + Q^i = 0$ for $i = A, B$. If either shades the expected price, the other has an incentive to reduce its price in the second period.

[24] Although welfare falls in this example, this need not be the case. There is an example in which the policy leads to greater welfare in Chapter 2 of Cooper (1984).

[25] The description of this case is based on information in Hay (1982), Sultan (1974), and the Department of Justice's memorandum concerning the proposed modification of the final judgment in *United States* v. *General Electric Co.*, *Federal Register*, 42 (March 30, 1977), pp. 17,005–17,010.

and the information needed to determine the price of any generator. Since each firm announced that it would change prices only by adjusting the multiplier used to convert relative prices into actual prices, reductions in the price of one generator would trigger the rebate provision for all sales in the previous six months. As a result, the publication of the price book made the most-favored-customer policy constraining despite product heterogeneity.

The structure of the turbine-generator industry made the policy particularly profitable. The benefits from price protection were fairly large because this was a duopoly where each firm received a large share of the gains from coordination. Moreover, the threat of entry did not limit these gains. The time to construct a new production facility exceeded the six-month duration of the policy; therefore, using the most-favored-customer policy would not encourage entry. Considering all these facts, one should not be surprised to learn that price protection was profitable in this industry. The firms found inexpensive ways to constrain their pricing with the policy, and they only shared the rewards from coordination with each other. These firms finally agreed to end the practice as part of a settlement to avoid antitrust prosecution.[26]

6. Factors reducing the profitability of the most-favored-customer policy

■ Except for the turbine generator industry, there are very few cases in which firms have adopted the most-favored-customer policy despite its apparent ability to facilitate coordination. Therefore, the disadvantages of offering the policy may often outweigh the benefits. In this section we look at some factors that reduce the profitability of the policy.

A firm may have to incur some costs to reap the benefits of the price protection policy. The practice is only effective if information flows to many agents. The firm that wants to use the policy must ensure that the necessary information transfers occur. At the outset, a firm must announce its adoption of the policy to customers and competitors alike. Once they know about the policy, rivals will react to it only if they believe that rebates will accompany price cuts. To provide such assurances, a firm must keep detailed records of past customers and find a method of announcing price changes to them.

Although there are costs involved in transmitting information about price protection policies and price cuts, they may be small in some industries. For example, a firm could use trade association meetings or trade publications as a public forum for making announcements. In industries such as many producer good industries, where customers maintain a continuing relationship with suppliers, it is virtually costless to inform customers. On the other hand, the cost of providing the requisite information may exceed the benefits if there are many customers with whom it is difficult to communicate.

Structural conditions in an industry may also reduce or eliminate the benefits from the most-favored-customer policy. We have seen that the return to being the only firm to offer the policy may be quite small. With significant costs of offering price protection, there could be an equilibrium in which no one offers the policy. As a rule, factors that make tacit collusion difficult also make this facilitating practice less valuable.

Let us consider some structural features that tend to reduce the benefits from the policy. First, most-favored-customer pricing becomes less profitable as the number of firms increases. The policy lets a firm restrict its ability to compete, but other firms still compete among themselves. As more firms remain in competition, the policy has less effect on their prices; therefore, a firm receives a smaller gain from this strategy. Second, price protection is less valuable if entry barriers are low. The policy leads to greater profits by helping firms set

---

[26] *United States* v. *General Electric Co.*, "Plaintiff's Memorandum in Support of a Proposed Modification to the Final Judgment Entered on October 1, 1962 against Each Defendant." In *Federal Register*, 42 (March 30, 1977), pp. 17,005–17,010.

higher prices. Not only do the increased profits invite entry, but the policy also interferes with lowering price in response to entry. Without high entry barriers firms may have to limit increases in prices and profits to discourage entry. Third, the policy is less attractive in a rapidly changing environment. After a firm commits itself to a high price, a change in costs or demand could make that price inordinately high. Since the policy reduces pricing flexibility, the firm could not make the desired adjustment. Moreover, any adjustment must be accompanied by rebates. Thus, the gains from the policy could completely vanish. Any of these factors could prevent firms from offering the policy, especially if information costs are significant.

In addition to these considerations, there are some industries in which the most-favored-customer policy does not provide useful constraints. Firms in some industries change product design frequently. A firm could easily hide a price reduction behind a design change. As a result, the policy would hardly affect a firm's ability to adjust price. Firms could use a price book to mitigate this problem, but even that solution would fail in the face of design changes involving components not included in the book. Finally, firms may not use the policy because setting a minimum is of no value. This situation occurs if single-period reaction curves slope downward.

7. Summary

■ If a firm offers a price protection policy, lowering price later imposes a penalty in the form of rebate payments to past customers. By penalizing price cuts, the policy may help support a more cooperative outcome; however, firms must still agree to adopt the policy and to raise prices. In this article, we have shown that the price protection policy enables firms to accomplish these objectives without formal coordination. In our model a firm gains limited control over its rival's future price by offering the policy. As the firm exercises this control, both firms raise their prices and thus earn greater profits. Therefore, at least one firm offers the policy in a noncooperative equilibrium. Since the policy enables both firms to earn more in a noncooperative setting, we say that it facilitates tacit collusion. A variety of structural features affect the value of this facilitating practice. It is most likely to be profitable in stable, concentrated industries with high entry barriers.

Appendix

■ For the presentation of the reaction functions for second-period price, I shall define $p^{AD}(p^B)$ by $(\partial \Pi^A/\partial p^A)(p^{AD}, p^B) + M^A Q_1^A = 0$ and define $p^{BD}(p^A)$ similarly. If a firm chooses to reduce its price in the second period, p^{iD} is the appropriate response to p^j. In writing the reaction functions, I shall take two simplifying steps. One is to write the functions generally for firms i and j, so that symmetric situations are presented only once. The relations are true for $i = A, B$ and $j = B, A$. Second, I shall simply write the second-period responses as functions of second-period prices if they are simultaneously solved to yield unique functions of first-period prices. The functional dependence on earlier prices is then implicit. Then the optimal response, $p_2 = (p_2^A, p_2^B)$, is[27]

$$p_2^i = p_n^i, \quad p_2^j = p_n^j \quad \text{if} \quad p_1^i \leq p_n^i \quad \text{and} \quad p_1^j \leq p_n^j; \tag{A1}$$

$$p_2^i = p_1^i \quad \text{and} \quad p_2^j = p^{j*}(p_1^i) \quad \text{if} \quad p_1^i \geq p_n^i, \quad p^{iD}(p^{j*}(p_1^i)) \geq p_1^i, \quad \text{and} \quad p^{j*}(p_1^i) \geq p_1^j; \tag{A2}$$

$$p_2^i = p^{iD}(p_2^j) \quad \text{and} \quad p_2^j = p^{j*}(p_2^i) \quad \text{if} \quad p^{iD}(p^{j*}(p_1^i)) \leq p_1^i \quad \text{and} \quad p^{j*}(p^{iD}(p_1^j)) \geq p_1^j; \tag{A3}$$

$$p_2^i = p^{iD}(p_1^j) \quad \text{and} \quad p_2^j = p_1^j \quad \text{if} \quad p^{iD}(p_1^j) \leq p_1^i, \quad p^{j*}(p^{iD}(p_1^j)) \leq p_1^j, \quad \text{and} \quad p^{jD}(p^{iD}(p_1^j)) \geq p_1^j; \tag{A4}$$

$$p_2^i = p^{iD}(p_2^j) \quad \text{and} \quad p_2^j = p^{jD}(p_2^i) \quad \text{if} \quad p^{iD}(p^{jD}(p_1^i)) \leq p_1^i \quad \text{and} \quad p^{jD}(p^{iD}(p_1^j)) \leq p_1^j; \tag{A5}$$

$$p_2^i = p_1^i \quad \text{and} \quad p_2^j = p_1^j, \quad \text{if} \quad p^{i*}(p_1^j) \leq p_1^i, \quad p^{j*}(p_1^i) \leq p_1^j, \quad p^{iD}(p_1^j) \geq p_1^i, \quad \text{and} \quad p^{jD}(p_1^i) \geq p_1^j. \tag{A6}$$

[27] The proof that these are the unique optimal responses is available from the author upon request.

References

BULOW, J.I., GEANAKOPLOS, J.D., AND KLEMPERER, P.D. "Multimarket Oligopoly: Strategic Substitutes and Complements." *Journal of Political Economy,* Vol. 93 (1985), pp. 488–511.

CHAMBERLIN, E.H. *The Theory of Monopolistic Competition,* 8th ed. Cambridge: Harvard University Press, 1962.

COOPER, T.E. "Facilitating Practices and Most-Favored-Customer Pricing." Ph.D. Dissertation, Princeton University, 1984.

FRIEDMAN, J.W. *Oligopoly and the Theory of Games.* Amsterdam: North-Holland, 1977.

HAY, G.A. "Oligopoly, Shared Monopoly, and Antitrust Law." *Cornell Law Review,* Vol. 67 (1982), pp. 439–481.

KRISHNA, K. "Trade Restrictions as Facilitating Practices." NBER Working Paper No. 1546, January 1985.

LUCE, R.D. AND RAIFFA, H. *Games and Decisions.* New York: John Wiley, 1957.

POSNER, R.A. *Antitrust Law.* Chicago: University of Chicago Press, 1976.

SALOP, S.C. "Monopolistic Competition with Outside Goods." *Bell Journal of Economics,* Vol. 10 (1979), pp. 141–156.

———. "Practices That (Credibly) Facilitate Oligopoly Coordination" in J.E. Stiglitz and G.F. Mathewson, eds., *New Developments in the Analysis of Market Structure,* Cambridge: MIT Press, 1986.

SCHERER, F.M. *Industrial Market Structure and Economic Performance,* 2nd ed. Chicago: Rand-McNally, 1980.

SELTEN, R. "Reexamination of the Perfectness Concept for Equilibrium Points in Extensive Games." *International Journal of Game Theory,* Vol. 4 (1975), pp. 25–55.

SPENCE, A.M. "Tacit Coordination and Imperfect Information." *Canadian Journal of Economics,* Vol. 11 (1978), pp. 490–505.

STIGLER, G.J. "A Theory of Oligopoly." *Journal of Political Economy,* Vol. 72 (1964), pp. 44–61.

SULTAN, R.G.M. *Pricing in the Electrical Oligopoly,* 2 vols. Cambridge: Harvard University Press, 1974.

WILLIG, R.D. "Welfare Analysis of Policies Affecting Prices and Products." Center for Research in Economic Growth Memorandum No. 153, Stanford University, 1973.

Part IV
Vertical Restraints

[12]

WHY SHOULD MANUFACTURERS WANT FAIR TRADE?

*LESTER G. TELSER**
University of Chicago

I. Introduction

A LONG-STANDING puzzle to economists is that some manufacturers prefer that their products are sold at not less than "fair trade" retail prices.[1] Before the courts upset the legal status of resale price maintenance, some of these manufacturers spent millions to prevent distributors from selling their products below the list price. The manufacturers' interests seem to be best served when distributors resell their products under such competitive conditions as may exist at the level of distribution and at the lowest prices resulting from that competition. If manufacturers set a floor to the resale price then they also set a ceiling to their sales and thus apparently support a policy that runs counter to their own self-interest. Let the manufacturers fix a price at the factory gate at which all distributors may buy the product. Would not the manufacturers' sales and profits be greater the lower is the price at which distributors resell their products to consumers? If so, then what explains the strong desire of some manufacturers to prevent distributors from

* Professor A. Director first proposed that I study the court record of United States v. General Elec. Co., 272 U.S. 476 (1926) and has given me valuable assistance throughout the study. I am also grateful to Professors R. Kessel, J. McGee, D. Meiselman, and G. Stigler.

[1] One of the first economists to recognize that manufacturers' endorsement of resale price maintenance is puzzling is T. H. Silcock, Some Problems of Price Maintenance 48 Econ. J. 42–51 (1938). He gives three reasons for their endorsement of this policy: by fixing a minimum retail price they reduce the consumers' incentive to shop around which would expose them to the temptation of possibly buying some other product; the manufacturer may obtain more services from retailers which would increase sales of his product; the manufacturer may obtain a wider distribution of his product. His analysis is quite perceptive though incomplete. Even earlier Professor Taussig noted the paradox. See Price Maintenance, 4 Am. Econ. Rev. 170–84 (Supp. 1916). One of his explanations of resale price maintenance assumes some degree of "irrational" consumer behavior. If consumers associate price and quality then he argues that reductions in the retail price may reduce sales because consumers believe the product quality is deteriorated. Of course the coercion of manufacturers into setting resale prices by a retail cartel is a different and easily comprehensible phenomenon: see B. S. Yamey, The Economics of Resale Price Maintenance (1954). This is also the main explanation of the Federal Trade Commission in its 1945 Report on Resale Price Maintenance.

reselling their product at prices below the level set by the manufacturers? The purpose of this paper is to examine some arguments appropriate to different market structures that explain why some manufacturers may impose resale price maintenance on distributors.[2]

We retain all of the essential elements of the puzzle if for simplicity we suppose that manufacturers sell their product to retailers who resell it to final consumers thus ignoring the other stages of distribution. Of course, the manufacturers need concern themselves with imposing resale price maintenance on the firms engaged in distribution only if they do not themselves deal directly with the consumers of their products. For instance, a firm may own retail outlets and its salaried employees may sell its product to final users: by choosing this course it can avoid any legal obstacles in the way of resale price maintenance. However, the cost disadvantages of such an arrangement may outweigh the advantages it thinks to gain by exercising direct control over the retail price. Therefore, the need for resale price maintenance arises only if there is separate ownership of the producing and distributing firms.[3]

Any manufacturer who can sell as much of the product to retailers as he pleases without affecting its price at the manufacturing level is manifestly foolish if he attempts to force resale price maintenance on retailers. What is more to the point, a manufacturer in a competitive industry could not control the price at the manufacturing level by changing his rate of output and surely could not affect the price at the retail level by so doing. Hence a necessary condition to a manufacturer's use of resale price maintenance is that he must possess some degree of monopoly control over the price of the product because his product is differentiated in economically relevant respects from competing products.

Some British data are consistent with the hypothesis that only manufacturers enjoying some degree of monopoly power use resale price maintenance. Assuming the degree of concentration of production crudely measures manufacturers' monopoly power, the data of Table 1 indicate that the prevalence of resale price maintenance by consumer commodities is associated with manufacturing monopoly. For example, of the commodities for

[2] Manufacturers have sold a number of products under resale price maintenance agreements. Examples are Victor and Edison Talking Machines, Ford and Packard Motor Cars, Welch's Grape Juice, Kellogg's Corn Flakes, B.V.D.'s, Ingersoll and Hamilton Watches, Beechnut Products, Bissell carpet sweepers, and Waterman pens. W. S. Bowman, Jr., Prerequisites and Effects of Resale Price Maintenance, 22 U. Chi. Law Rev. 825, 833–35 (1955). Another long list of products appears in Report of the Federal Trade Commission on Resale Price Maintenance 498 (1945).

[3] Even though a manufacturer may strongly desire resale price maintenance, the cost of enforcement may be too great to make this a profitable policy. For example, retailers offer trade-in allowances on some products. Manufacturers who maintain the retail prices of such products need also to cope with the difficult problem of regulating trade-in allowances,

which the three leading producers together account for between 50 and 60 per cent of industry's employment, nine are sold with and two are sold without the aid of resale price maintenance. Unfortunately, there are apparently no similar data for the United States.

Although monopoly control by manufacturers is a sine qua non to their espousal of resale price maintenance, matters stand on a different footing with regard to the presence or absence of monopoly power of retailers.

TABLE 1

PRICE MAINTENANCE OF CONSUMER GOODS IN GREAT BRITAIN, 1938

Degree of Concentration of Production* (Per Cent)	No. of Commodities Price Maintained†	
	Insignificant or Non-existent	Significant (Half or More of the Commodity Was Price Maintained)
0–10	24	0
10–20	14	3
20–30	3	7
30–40	0	7
40–50	1	5
50–60	2	9
60–70	1	7
70–80	0	4
80–90	3‡	3§
90–100	0	0
Total	48	45

Source: James B. Jeffreys, The Distribution of Consumer Goods: A Factual Study of Methods and Costs in the United Kingdom in 1938, Table 7, pp. 46–48 (1950).

* The degree of concentration of production is the ratio of the employment in the three largest units to the total number employed in the production of the commodity.

† The list of commodities includes almost all consumer goods. Some of the commodities are price maintained at the instigation of the PATA—the British retail druggists' association.

‡ The three commodities are sugar, wallpaper, and linoleum.

§ The three commodities are salt, petrol (gasoline), and vacuum cleaners.

Under some circumstances manufacturers may employ resale price maintenance even if there is perfect competition among retailers. I describe these circumstances in the sections on the special service argument and the cartel argument. Most explanations of resale price maintenance turn on attempts by retailers to form associations that would enable them to eliminate price competition among themselves and bend manufacturers to their will. Such explanations are compatible with the existence of perfect competition among the manufacturers and they require that retailers, though powerless singly, collectively have monopoly power. The following arguments apply when retailers individually are either monopolists or are in perfect competition.

II. The Service Argument[4]

Suppose sales at the retail level depend both on retail prices and on the services the retailers provide jointly with the product. Specifically, assume that the quantity sold at the retail level varies inversely with retail prices and directly with the amount of services the retailers provide jointly with the product.

A diagram is helpful. D_0 is the demand schedule for the product at the retail level when retailers offer S_0 of services. If they offer more services, $S_1 > S_0$, the demand shifts to the right to D_1 (see Fig. 1). For a given quantity OQ, $P_1 - P_0$ equals the price per unit of the product that consumers are willing to pay for an increment in services, $S_1 - S_0$, that is provided jointly with the product.

We must understand these retailers' services to be specific to the commodity and unrelated to the retailers' methods of generally doing business. If, on the contrary, the retailers' general business methods are at issue such as whether they provide their customers with a pleasant atmosphere, delivery, credit and the like then there is no need for the protection of resale price maintenance on the particular commodity to be sold jointly with these services.

To convince ourselves of the latter point let us assume it to be false. That is, suppose that retailers of a certain type may only be induced to handle the product if the manufacturer sets a minimum retail price. This implies that in the absence of resale price maintenance consumers prefer to purchase the product from those retailers who provide less services and sell goods at lower prices. It is only by preventing such retailers from selling the goods in question at a lower price that the manufacturer is able to have his product sold by the retailers who provide more services. Therefore, if resale price maintenance is necessary to get the product sold in, say, fancy shops then consumers really

[4] Bowman analyzes the service argument in terms of two kinds of markets, service and non-service. His argument, it seems to me, does not fully recognize the point that the services are special to the product and are not related to the kinds of services connected with the distributors' methods of business. See W. S. Bowman, Jr., Resale Price Maintenance, 22 U. Chi. Law Rev. 825, 840–43 (1955). Yamey does recognize the point that the services are special to the product. He produces essentially the same argument as mine and offers it in explanation of book publishers' support of resale price maintenance for their product. See Yamey, Economics of Resale Price Maintenance, 62–68 (1954).

". . . where the sale depends upon demonstration or service on the part of the distributor, especially when the distributor has substitute items in stock, the injury to the manufacturer is probable. Good examples of this are plumbing equipment and automobiles, for in these cases an important role is played by the distributor in leading the customer to a final decision. Scarcely inferior to the articles mentioned in this respect are kodaks, certain toilet articles, medicines—at least at certain stages in their distribution—and mechanical contrivances such as radios, victrolas, and talking machines. In all these instances the likelihood of a sale depends in no small measure upon the distributor himself." E. R. A. Seligman and R. A. Love, Price Cutting and Price Maintenance, 193 (1932). This quotation shows that some aspects of the special service argument have long been recognized.

prefer to buy the good at low prices in plain stores. Moreover, under these circumstances, since resale price maintenance must increase the average retail price, it tends to reduce total retail sales of the product. Therefore, no wise manufacturer would adopt a policy of retail price maintenance merely to get competing stores of different kinds to sell his product.

Clearly, retailers of all kinds in competition with each other sell many products not price maintained jointly with whatever services they provide. They will not deprive their customers of these services on any sale regardless of whether or not the product in question is protected by a resale price main-

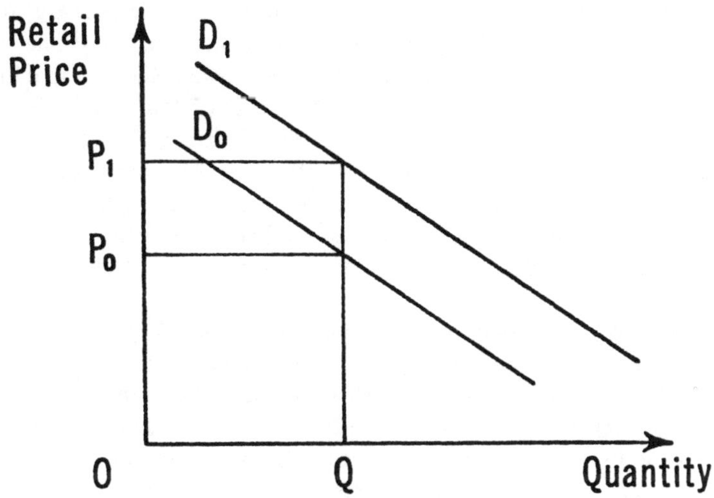

FIG. 1

tenance agreement with the manufacturer. In the absence of resale price maintenance we can expect many kinds of retailers offering all kinds of different services to sell the product at prices that differ by the cost of providing these services. The fact that many retailers offer different kinds and combinations of services is a reflection of the diversity of consumers' tastes. Inter-store price differentials that equal the difference in the costs of providing services of different kinds and amounts is a reflection of the competition among the retailers. Resale price maintenance is intended to alter these normal price differentials that we may expect for a product that is sold by many different kinds of retailers.[5]

[5] The argument in the text assumes perfect competition in retailing. However, if individual retailers are monopolists the argument needs modification. By protecting the minimum mark-up the manufacturer offers retailers more inducement to handle the product. This results in wider retail distribution, which may increase retail sales; simultaneously the average retail price is somewhat higher and that tends to decrease retail sales. A wise manu-

However, a product that is protected by a resale price maintenance agreement is one for which the minimum gross mark-up—the difference between the retail and the manufacture price—is fixed. Because of this, the manufacturer hopes to induce retailers to single out his product for *special* pre-sale treatment. A cogent example of a special service is pre-sale demonstration of the product by retailers. Thus the amount of these special retailers' services that are provided jointly with the physical product is expected by the manufacturer to vary directly with the retailers' remuneration from the sales of that product.

If at some mark-up all the retailers provide the *same* amount of special services jointly with the product then the manufacturer, seemingly, need not maintain a minimum retail price. By choosing appropriately the price at which he is willing to sell his product to the retailers he can maximize his profits and avoid concerning himself with the level of the retail price, leaving that to be freely determined by the competition among the retailers. Therefore, assume for the moment that the manufacturer does not set a floor to the retail price. He sells his product to retailers at a low enough price to induce them all to provide the same amount of special services. But, under these circumstances, do all retailers have incentives to carry out the manufacturer's wishes?

Since the services provided are, by hypothesis, special, some retailers have good reason not to provide these special services and offer to sell the product at lower prices. They reduce their prices because they avoid the additional cost of the special services. If some retailers do provide these services and ask for a corespondingly higher price whereas others do not provide the services and offer to sell the product to consumers at a lower price then an unstable situation emerges. Sales are diverted from the retailers who do provide the special services at the higher price to the retailers who do not provide the special services and offer to sell the product at the lower price. The mechanism is simple. A customer, because of the special services provided by one retailer, is persuaded to buy the product. But he purchases the product from another paying the latter a lower price. In this way the retailers who do not provide the special services get a free ride at the expense of those who have convinced consumers to buy the product.

As a result few or none of the retailers offer the special services the manufacturer thinks necessary to sell his product. If the manufacturer is correct in his belief that point-of-purchase services increase the demand for his product then because less than the optimal amount of services are provided his sales decrease. He can prevent the diversion of sales from one kind of retailer to another if he removes the incentive to diversion. He accomplishes this by

facturer weighs the net effect of these opposing forces and adopts resale price maintenance only if greater net revenue results. In the rest of the paper, the argument is valid irrespective of the state of retailing competition.

establishing a minimum retail price that guarantees a minimum gross mark-up. Therefore retailers are forced to compete by providing special services with the product and not by reducing the retail price.[6]

Although effective resale price maintenance thus prevents diversion, it may permit retailers, who are able to sell the product without providing the special services at the maintained price, to obtain extraordinary profits. They can do so if the manufacturer is mistaken in his belief that he needs special services to sell his product. None will be offered by retailers all of whom can get profits equal to the cost of these special services provided the manufacturer fixes a minimum retail price. For example, if in the course of time consumers become so won over to a product or so familiar with it that costly special persuasion by retailers becomes an unnecessary inducement to purchase it, the manufacturer will discover that he need not maintain the retail price and will rationally abandon his fair trade policy.

The argument explaining the rationale for resale price maintenance is incomplete because it fails to consider the manufacturer's alternatives to the policy that could apparently obtain the same effects. Perhaps the most promising is this. Let the manufacturer arrange with retailers to have the special services sold separately to potential customers. In this way a customer may buy the product without buying the special services or vice versa. For example, imagine that retailers would charge customers a fee for demonstrating the product to them. In this way the problem of free riding by other retailers is eliminated and the special services are indeed provided those customers who wish to pay for them. Although this scheme seems to do away with the difficulties manufacturers face by adopting resale price maintenance it has formidable complications of its own.

The main complication is the necessity of devising a method of charging customers for the special services they obtain. If all the customers want the same amount of special services then a single price equal to the marginal cost of these services is sufficient. Indeed under this assumption all retailers would offer the same amount of special services and the manufacturer would find resale price maintenance unnecessary.

For some commodities, however, consumers surely differ in their desire for special services and it may be very costly to use a system of marginal cost pricing whereby each customer pays a price equal to the marginal cost of the services he obtains. One reason for this may be that the extent of the market

[6] Suppose an undifferentiated product made under competitive manufacturing conditions is of such a nature that the provision of special retailing services is thought to facilitate sales. Were a single manufacturer to adopt resale price maintenance to obtain the provision of the optimal amount of special services then his scheme would succumb to the same kind of forces as are described in the text. The manufacturers not adopting retail price maintenance may benefit from the special services he induces and obtain a free ride at his expense. Only if the group collectively adopts resale price maintenance may they ensure the provision of the optimal amount of special services.

for the product is too limited to make feasible the specialization needed for a system of marginal cost pricing. Suppose, for example, that one-third of the customers want no special services, one-third want special services that cost $6 and one-third want special services that cost $12. Assume that these special services are sold separately and that the price of the product is $100. If marginal cost pricing of the services is too cumbersome or unattainable and all customers pay a flat fee for special services regardless of the amount they obtain then those who want none purchase none and those who want an amount that costs $12 pay $12. But no single price equal to the average cost of the services suffices to induce those who wish to purchase $6 worth to buy any. Or if the consumer alternatives are no special services or $6-worth then some part of the demand for services remains unsatisfied because those desiring $12-worth obtain half as much. Thus because customers differ in the amount of special services they desire and because marginal cost pricing of these services is impractical, the manufacturer finds that consumers purchase less than the optimal amount even though the services are available separately from the product.

There is another alternative. The special service argument shows that the need for resale price maintenance arises when not all the retailers provide the same amount of special services and all may buy the product from the manufacturer at the same price. Hence those who do not provide the services get a profit equal to the cost of these special services they do not provide only if they pay the manufacturer the same price for the product as those retailers who do provide the special services. This suggests that the manufacturer should not charge all retailers the same price for the product to induce them to promote sales by guaranteeing a minimum gross mark-up. That is to say, he could charge retailers different prices according as they do or do not provide the special services. Let those who agree to provide special services jointly with the product pay a lower price at the factory gate than those who do not provide the special services. If he establishes the proper price differentials for his product then he can, apparently, obtain the same result as by imposing resale price maintenance on the retailers.

In addition, the manufacturer needs to prevent those retailers who are ostensibly willing to push his product thereby incurring greater costs, from reselling his product to other retailers who, because they are unwilling to push the product, may obtain it from the manufacturer but only at a higher price. That is, the manufacturer needs to prevent trans-shipments of his product from the retailers who pay him the lower price to those who pay him the higher price. If he cannot prevent trans-shipments among retailers then he also cannot prevent diversion of consumers' purchases among retailers. Because some retailers bootleg his product to others who resell it without special services at lower retail prices, the same mechanism of free riding at the expense of retailers who do provide special services and charge higher prices comes into play. Therefore, the manufacturer either needs to prevent sales among retailers, if he sells his product to them at different prices, or, if all the retailers pay him the same price, he needs to prevent price cutting to induce them to offer special services jointly with his product.

Since there may be a fatal objection to selling the product at different prices to different retailers, the manufacturer may hope to accomplish the same thing by paying retailers directly an amount equal to the cost of the special services they provide. He would need to check the performance of the retailers to be sure that they actually provide these requisite services. Resale price maintenance may better serve the manufacturer's interest because the retailers are compensated for providing special services only to the extent of their sales. Balanced against this advantage of price maintenance is the cost of its enforcement. It seems likely, however, that it is easier to police violations of minimum prices than to survey retailers to see that they do indeed provide the special services and do not simply fritter away the direct payments. But the most compelling point is that direct payment by the manufacturer to retailers who provide special services is equivalent to selling the services separately to the consumers and both are feasbile only if marginal cost pricing of the special services is economic.

The manufacturer has still another alternative to resale price maintenance. He may refuse to sell his product to any retailer who does not provide the requisite special services. A manufacturer could not logically adopt this policy uness he arranges somehow to remunerate those retailers he approves for providing the special services.[7] Therefore, if he does carefully select retailers who will distribute his product then he must also devise a system of paying them that does not suffer from the same objections one makes to direct payment to retailers.[8]

The special service argument has several implications. These have to do

[7] Retailers not approved by the manufacturer might buy the product from those who are approved. The cost of policing a refusal to sell policy includes the cost of detecting and preventing such sales among retailers.

[8] Two other points are worth mentioning. The special service argument does not imply that the rise of discount houses was a reaction to widespread use of resale price maintenance. A discount house offers its customers a less costly bundle of services and therefore lower prices. However, these services are typically unrelated to particular commodities and are not special according to the usage in this paper. They offer no free credit or charge accounts, have a less elegant decor, fewer sales people per customer, and the like. Their success is to be attributed to consumers' demand for this type of retailing rather than to their alleged erosion of price maintenance. This conclusion is buttressed by the fact that discount houses carry many goods that are not price maintained. Manufacturers who sell their products both under their own label and to retailers who resell them under their own private labels have no incentive to adopt resale price maintenance. This is manifestly the case if the manufacturers are in competitive industries. Even if the manufacturer is a monopolist, sales of the same product under different labels is symptomatic of price discrimination and this technique leads to a more efficient separation of markets than would be obtained by the use of resale price maintenance (see p. 104 infra).

primarily with the nature of the product. Only branded products that are unfamiliar to the mass of consumers are price maintenance candidates on this argument.[9] To gain wide acceptance for their products, manufacturers often direct national advertising at the final consumers. However, if they choose to maintain minimum retail prices then they believe that such advertising by itself is insufficiently effective to persuade consumers of the merits of their products and that the retailers' personal sales efforts are a valuable adjunct. Thus resale price maintenance substitutes to some extent for impersonal national advertising. Since part of the sales expense of nationally advertised products not price maintained is borne by the manufacturers, we anticipate on that account that the gross mark-up of such goods is less than that of price-maintained commodities.

Pursuing this line somewhat further, recall that prior to the 1920's national advertising was limited to the newspapers and magazines. First radio and then televison gave rise to the great technological change in advertsing. Hence prior to the 1920's manufacturers had fewer alternatives to the use of the retailers' services. We might on this account expect a weakening desire by manufacturers for the special services of the retailers purchased by means of resale price maintenance. However, it is hard to establish that there was a secular withdrawal from resale price maintenance by manufacturers, and even if it could be demonstrated it would be subject to alternative explanations. For example, during this period the courts continued to place obstacles in the way of price maintenance.

New branded products are obviously unfamiliar to the mass of consumers and are, thereby, candidates for resale price maintenance. If the manufacturer wishes the special services of retailers, he may set a floor to the retail price of this new product. After a new product has gained wide consumer acceptance, its producer no longer needs to maintain a minimum retail price. We may expect to observe the resale price maintenance agreements of new products to persist for as long as it takes the product to become familiar to consumers. Electrical appliances are a case in point. Manufacturers introducing new appliances often impose resale price maintenance on the distributors to induce them to offer special services.

Old branded products purchased infrequently by relatively few households may also be logical candidates for resale price maintenance agreements. Such products are in a sense new to the mass of consumers and may never gain wide acceptance. Because they are unfamiliar, the manufacturer of such products may find retailers' point-of-purchase special services particularly

[9] "Where, for instance, a manufacturer of well-known items brings out an entirely new product he may try, rather than resort to the expensive expedient of far-reaching advertising, to follow a policy of price maintenance, utilizing for this purpose his long established name in conjunction with a liberal margin granted to the retailer in order to secure his close cooperation." Seligman and Love, Price Cutting and Price Maintenance, 209 (1932).

valuable. For example, bows and arrows are very old products bought infrequently by relatively few people. Potential buyers are probably susceptible to the persuasive efforts of those retailers who sell this product, and if the manufacturers of bows and arrows have some degree of monopoly power, I would not be surprised to learn that there is a minimum retail price schedule for this product. In fact, manufacturers of sporting goods often use resale price maintenance.

Drug manufacturers making differentiated products over which they have some degree of monopoly power may strongly favor resale price maintenance because consumers of such articles rely heavily on the druggists' advice. Resale price maintenance is an effective way for a manufacturer to remunerate druggists for these special services and insure that they will be forthcoming. It also happens that retail druggists' associations are not averse to price maintenance even for those commodities made by manufacturers who would gladly have them sold at competitive retail prices.

The special service argument explains why one manufacturer may want to establish minimum retail prices but it cannot explain why a group of competing manufacturers would favor this policy. The next section gives a rationale for a group of manufacturers who adopt resale price maintenance.

III. The Cartel Argument

The cartel argument analyzes the particular problems facing a combination of manufacturers that make a substantial proportion of its sales via competing distributors to households. This is in contrast to a cartel of manufacturers making an intermediate good, that is, one which is ultimately purchased primarily by other manufacturing firms.

A cartel like a monopoly needs to choose a rate of output or, equivalently, a price that maximizes profits. But unlike a monopoly a cartel faces special difficulties. Because their members have conflicting interests, cartels are fragile organizations. Each member of a cartel wants the other members to abide by the terms of the cartel agreement but has powerful incentives to violate these terms in the pursuit of its self-interest. What rules must the members of a cartel establish to ensure compliance and render the cartel a sturdy instrument that will extract monopoly profits for the benefit of its membership?

Obviously the cartel members must agree on the price at which they are willing to sell the product to distributors. But if any member of the combination offers distributors the product at a price somewhat lower than that agreed-upon, he may increase his sales and reduce the profits of the other cartel members. If the cartel rules impose penalties on price-cutters that compensate the non-price-cutters for their loss of profits, these penalties must impose costs on the price-cutters greater than their increased profits. That is, the cartel needs rules that nip in the bud attempts to spoil the market for all. One such rule is resale price maintenance. Thus no retailers, for example, may sell the product to consumers at a price lower than that agreed upon. How does resale price maintenance preserve the cartel's monopoly profits?

Let a member of the cartel try to increase sales by giving retailers secret price concessions. Since the retailers are unable openly to reduce the price at which they can sell the product to final consumers, they manifestly are deprived of the most powerful instrument to increase sales to customers. Therefore, a manufacturer who would induce retailers to increase their purchases from him by offering them lower prices loses profits to no avail. Nonetheless, a secret concession may give an advantage to a manufacturer. If retailers sell a number of brands of the product—brands of the cartel members—they may be induced to single out the brand of some manufacturer for special treatment if they are bribed to do so because of getting a secret price concession from that manufacturer.

One way of preventing this is for the members of the cartel to agree that distributors may handle only a single brand. Thus each distributor becomes an exclusive dealer in one brand and cannot favor one manufacturer at the expense of another.[10]

A dealer who is given a secret price cut by a manufacturer may in turn attempt to increase sales to final consumers by granting them special terms of sale that have the effect of price concessions. For example, customers may be offered favorable credit terms, free delivery service, less than the prevailing price on a tied article, and the like. Insofar as possible the members of the cartel must agree on terms of sale that outlaw any device that has the effect of allowing retailers to cut prices.

A resourceful member of the cartel may try to increase his sales in still another way. He may try to win away the retailers handling the product made by other members of the cartel to his own brand. Secret price concessions to retailers might accomplish such changes in allegiance. The rules of the cartel must guard against this eventuality. They must stipulate that a retailer handling the brand of one cartel member may not drop it in order to replace it by the brand of another cartel member. Such a rule prevents the members of the combination from competing for distributors.

[10] B. S. Yamey interprets "exclusive dealing" coupled with resale price maintenance quite differently. He sees the former as a valuable concession from the retailer to the manufacturer and the latter as the reverse. Thus the two together are a kind of quid pro quo arrangement whereby distributors and manufacturers form a vertical cartel. B. S. Yamey, The Economics of Resale Price Maintenance, 34–35 (1954). He does, however, recognize that "Resale price maintenance may be an indispensable, or at least a valuable, adjunct to formal or tacit agreement among a group of manufacturers," at 18. It seems to me that Yamey misses the the essential point, namely that exclusive dealing and resale price maintenance are both needed to make effective the collusion among the manufacturers. See also pp. 19–22.

Bowman also analyzes the quid pro quo argument. W. S. Bowman, Jr., Prerequisites and Effects of Resale Price Maintenance, 22 U. Chi. Law Rev. 825, 838–39, 844–48 (1955). His description of the marketing of spark plugs and enameled iron ware indicates that the cartel argument may apply there.

The viability of a cartel requires other terms of agreement. Clearly the members must agree on the same retail price schedule. Moreover, they must agree on the same mark-up. All the other terms of sale between distributors and members of the combination must be the same so that no distributor has a pecuniary incentive for preferring one manufacturer over another. For a cartel to provide for every partciular eventuality threatening its existence is impractical if not impossible. For example, a manufacturer may attempt to induce new retailers, who have never before handled his product, to choose his brand and secretly offer them lower prices in compensation. If the cartel has a rule that imposes penalties on any of its members who exceed agreed upon market shares then these penalties serve as catchalls designd to guard against this tactic—secret price concessions to new distributors by those members of the cartel who wish to exceed their sales quotas—as well as other competitive tactics a manufacturer might employ in conjunction with cooperating retailers that would have the effect of spoiling the common interest of the cartel.

That a combination of manufacturers may practice price maintenance (impose the same minimum prices on each other) is easily understandable and indeed is a common cartel feature.[11] It is the use of *resale* price maintenance by a cartel that presents interesting problems. Typically price maintenance agreements cover so-called industrial products. Such industrial products are purchased by other firms who utilize them in their manufacturing processes to make other goods. Obviously in those cases resale price maintenance would serve to combine manufacturers at another stage of production into a cartel.[12] Although such vertical cartels undoubtedly exist, they must be less common than the kind described above, legal difficulties aside, because the number of conspirators necessary for the combination is typically too great to allow viability.

[11] There are numerous cartels of manufacturers embodying price maintenance agreements. Some examples are the following: sanitary pottery, a combination of 23 corporations producing 82 per cent of the output of this product, United States v. Trenton Potteries Co., 273 U.S. 392 (1927); hardboard producers, United States v. Masonite Corp., 316 U.S. 265 (1942); producers of certain kinds of electrical fuses, United States v. Line Material Co., 333 U.S. 287 (1948); makers of gypsum wallboard, United States v. United States Gypsum Co., 333 U.S. 364 (1948); and wrinkle finish varnish, enamel, and paint, a combination of virtually all the producers of this product, United States v. New Wrinkle, 342 U.S. 371 (1952).

[12] Perhaps the most interesting example is ethyl compound, a chemical product added to gasoline to increase the octane rating. The patent on ethyl was jointly owned by DuPont and Esso who licensed refiners to make ethyl gasoline. Ethyl gasoline was to be sold at a fixed price differential above the average net sales prices of the licensee's best non-premium grade of commercial gasoline. The licensed refiners produced 88 per cent of all the gasoline and 70 per cent of all the ethyl gasoline. Ethical (non-price cutting) jobbers were licensed to handle ethyl gasoline and 11,000 of the 12,000 gasoline jobbers were so licensed. Thus the owners of the patented ethyl compound formed most of the gasoline refiners into a cartel. Moreover, jobbers and retailers as a common practice anteceding ethyl compound handled one brand of gasoline exclusively. Ethyl Gasoline Corp. v. United States, 309 U.S. 436 (1940).

When we see all the contingencies a cartel must guard against we are struck by the implicit rigidities in the face of changing economic conditions that compliance with the rules of the cartel require. New price schedules appropriate to new conditions must be arrived at in concert as the result of committee deliberation. Though monopolies may respond sluggishly to a changing environment for the same reasons as do cartels, the reaction speed of a cartel which turns on the deliberations among the sovereign members must be even slower. Even so the cartel reward is a monopoly profit diminished to the extent that deliberations to change prices lag behind events, but if the cartel survives we must conclude that the game is worth the candle.

The cartel argument is admirably illustrated by the resale price maintenance of light bulbs.[13] The story of light bulbs is the subject of the next section.

IV. Light Bulbs and Resale Price Maintenance

The resale price maintenance of light bulbs was a major issue in a famous anti-trust case in 1926—the United States v. General Electric, Westinghouse, and others.[14] It is remarkable that the system the defendants devised for distributing light bulbs fits the cartel argument of the preceding section in every respect.

In 1906 the General Electric Company acquired exclusive United States rights to a number of patents governing the production of tungsten filament incandescent lamps. It "introduced its tungsten filament lamps into the United States late in 1907, under exclusive patent rights for the United States purchased in 1906 for $100,000 from the German Welsbach Company."[15] It acquired two other important patent applications and inventions governing the production of this type of light bulb in 1909. In 1911 GE introduced ductile tungsten filament incandescent lamps to the American market.[16]

[13] Many of the features of the light bulb combination are foreshadowed in the cartel among producers of enameled iron ware formed around 1909. There were 16 members in that cartel producing 85 per cent of the total output. Standard Sanitary Mfg. Co. owned the key patent and licensed the others under it. Minimum prices were established by a committee of 6, including the patent owner (whose market share was 50 per cent), who initiated price changes subject to the approval of a majority of the other 5 committee members. Ninety per cent of all the jobbers in the trade were licensed by the manufacturer and resale price maintenance imposed on them. Such jobbers were prohibited from dealing with unlicensed manufacturers, except with express written permission of the licensor. To aid in compliance, licensees paid royalties rebatable in part on condition of adherence to the license terms. Exclusive dealing by jobbers is not mentioned in the Supreme Court's opinion. Standard Sanitary Mfg. Co. v. United States, 226 U.S. 20 (1912).

[14] United States v. General Elec. Co., 272 U.S. 476 (1926). Although this case has become a classic textbook example, see for instance, C. Wilcox, Public Policies toward Business, 157–58, 412 (1955), no one seems to have offered the interpretation of the case which follows.

[15] A. A. Bright, Jr., The Electric Lamp Industry, 190, 192 (1949).

[16] *Id.* at 192–98.

In 1912 the Westinghouse Electric Company entered into a new license agreement with General Electric. The agreement contained these important provisions regarding royalties:

> The royalty payable on tungsten filament lamps sold and shipped for use in domestic territory during the period of three years from the first day of January, 1912 shall be 2% of the Licensee's net sales of said lamps.
>
> If, in the year beginning with the expiration of said period, or in any subsequent year, the Licensee's net sales of tungsten filament lamps, for use in domestic territory, amount to 15% (changed to 17.25% in 1919) or less of the aggregate net sales of such tungsten filament lamps by the Licensor and the Licensee for use in said territory in the said period, the royalty payable on tungsten filament lamps shall be 2% of the Licensee's net sales of said lamps; but if the Licensee's net sales exceed 15% of the said aggregate net sales, the royalty shall be 2% of the Licensee's net sales up to and including said 15% and shall be 10% of the excess of said net sales over said 15%.[17]

Similar license agreements were entered into between General Electric and other United States producers of light bulbs.[18] In 1923 General Electric and its licensed manufacturers accounted for 86% of total sales of light bulbs in the United States.[19] Based on this evidence it is plausible to regard General Electric and its licensed manufacturers as forming a cartel. Yet there seems available a simpler hypothesis. May we not regard General Electric as a monopolist by virtue of its ownership of key patents which it permits others to use in return for the payment of royalties? Cartel implies greater weakness and appears wrongly applied in this context.

Certainly with regard to the Westinghouse Electric Company there is little doubt that General Electric had a formidable rival. In its own right Westinghouse owned valuable and important patents and had an active research laboratory.[20]

Because of this General Electric could not feel secure in its position of acknowledged power as of 1912 and it needed to come to terms with a danger-

[17] Record, p. 118, United States v. General Elec. Co., 272 U.S. 476 (1926).

[18] The so-called "B" licenses granted manufacturers other than Westinghouse differed in some important respects from the Westinghouse license. Although "B" licensees could establish their own prices and terms of sale, they could not use the Mazda trademark (used on General Electric and Westinghouse products), they paid GE a higher royalty rate (3 per cent) than did Westinghouse (2 per cent shortly reduced to 1 per cent), their production quotas were small and they could make only few types of incandescent lamps, Bright, op. cit. supra n. 15 at 238, 240–43. Although the agreement between GE and Westinghouse benefitted the small licensed manufacturers, their ability to compete was curtailed by the terms of the "B" licenses. The cartel argument of section III applies to the GE-Westinghouse agreement.

[19] Record, p. 6, United States v. General Elec. Co., 272, 476 (1926).

[20] Bright, op. cit. supra n. 15 at 180, 188–89. GE and Westinghouse entered a cross licensing agreement in 1896, see p. 137.

ous rival whose market share was then 13 per cent.[21] The license agreement served to protect General Electric from increased output by its licensees but the structure of distribution that it established can only be understood if interpreted as a system to protect the licensees from abuses by General Electric. Surely by charging higher royalties on Westinghouse's sales in excess of 15% of the total, General Electric could have deterred Westinghouse sufficiently from increasing its sales. Therefore, the entire system of distribution is a confession of weakness on the part of General Electric.[22]

All the members of the light bulb cartel adopted the same system of distributing that product to the public.[23] Because of the shaky legal status of straightforward resale price maintenance and in particular because of the terms of the Consent Decree of 1911, the defendants in the 1926 court action resorted to a legal stratagem to acccomplish the effects of resale price maintenance.[24] Distributors received light bulbs on consignment. Legal title to the bulbs remained in the hands of the manufacturers who were thus free to fix any retail price they liked—presumably, one that would maximize their monopoly profits. The manufacturers presented the jobbers and retailers with price lists and permitted sales at not less than the list prices.[25] Therefore, General Electric had no incentive to give secret price concessions to the jobbers and the retailers because these distributors could not lower resale prices in order to increase sales. Therefore distributors would not purchase more bulbs from General Electric even at secretly reduced prices.

[21] In 1919, seven years after the license agreement, General Electric actually reduced the royalty payments from Westinghouse by having the penalty rate come into effect when the sales of Westinghouse exceeded 17.25 per cent of the combined sales instead of 15 per cent. See Record, p. 118, United States v. General Elec. Co., 272 U.S. 476 (1926). For the 1911 market share of Westinghouse, see Bright, op. cit. supra n. 15 at 151.

[22] In 1919 the Westinghouse royalty rate was actually reduced to 1 per cent. Bright, op. cit. supra n. 15 at 236 n. 2.

[23] Record, p. 109, United States v. General Elec. Co., 272 U.S. 476 (1926). The terms of the license agreement between Westinghouse and General Electric required that both adopt the same method of distribution. Moreover, Westinghouse could not pay its agents greater commissions than General Electric.

[24] On March 3, 1911 the Department of Justice brought equity proceedings under the Sherman Anti-Trust Act against General Electric, Westinghouse and 32 other companies. The defendants accepted a consent decree that prohibited the continuance of resale price maintenance as it was carried out prior to 1911. The decree stated that any such licensor is hereby enjoined and prohibited from requiring or imposing upon the licensee the fixing of resale price to be observed by the licensee's vendee; and the purchasers of such lamps from either the licensor or from the licensee or from the vendees of either the licensor or the licensee, whether at wholesale or retail, shall not be in any manner restricted as to the price at which such lamps shall be sold to the public or to any dealer or consumer. Record, p. 860, United States v. General Elec. Co., 272 U.S. 476 (1926).

[25] From the General Sales Rules of March 1, 1912, Number 14, "The prices given in the schedule are minimum prices. Sales may be made at higher prices." Record, p. 153, United States v. General Elec. Co., 272 U.S. 476 (1926).

No agent shall be appointed to act for more than one Manufacturer, to whom these rules apply [that is, members of the cartel], or to sell or distribute more than one brand of lamp for any such Manufacturer.[26]

Thus the distributors were made exclusive agents of the manufacturer. Here we encounter an important condition of the cartel argument.

A concern acting as Agent for a Manufacturer may not be given a Form B Appointment [Form B Appointments applied to jobbers] by another Manufacturer, even if eligible thereto, unless specific approval is obtained in advance of any solicitation whatever by the Manufacturer proposing the Form B Appointment.[27]

Thus the cartel members eliminated competition for distributors. A third condition of the cartel argument is encountered. However, any jobber or retailer who previously handled the merchandise of an unlicensed manufacturer could be enticed by the licensed producers. Such distributors received a discount based on two-thirds of their net sales of the unlicensed bulbs during the period when these were handled.[28]

In effect, General Electric set the pace for the total quantity sold. By increasing its sales it permitted the other licensed manufacturers to increase their sales in proportion without paying a greater royalty rate.

A number of provisions in the agreements between manufacturers and their agents prevented the latter from offering their customers special terms that would have the effect of reducing the retail price. For example, agents could not give their customers free samples. Retailers had to account for every bulb in stock including those claimed to be damaged or missing.[29] Light bulbs were a common enough product so that consumers did not need special services from retailers to be convinced of the merits of or to be taught the finer points of light bulbs. All a retailer needed to enter the retail bulb business was a rack to store the bulbs and a contract from a jobber. Hence the manufacturers had little incentive to give secret reductions to their agents to pay for their providing special services jointly with the bulbs.

Only one kind of distributor could deal in several light bulb brands—the central station power company offering its customers a "free" renewal service. This fact does not contradict the cartel argument. The power company gave customers free light bulbs and charged higher electricity rates to cover the cost of these free bulbs.[30] Since these rates did not depend on the brand of the

[26] Record, p. 543.

[27] Record, p. 542. Similar provisions applied to retailers.

[28] Record, p. 249.

[29] Record, p. 159.

[30] "Prior to September, 1902, the [electricity] rates to small customers approximated, on the average, 20 cents a kilowatt hour, or, something, perhaps, in excess of that figure. The price included the supply of incandescent lamps for which the cost was in the neighborhood of 1 cent a kilowatt hour." T. C. Martin, Forty Years of Edison Service: 1882–1922, 137

bulbs given customers, the power stations could not reduce the price of bulbs to its customers.

Transactions among jobbers and retailers could not be made unless the agents involved received special permission to do so from the manufacturer.[31] Consumers could purchase light bulbs but only to the extent of their requirements.[32] The manufacturers gave quantity discounts to jobbers and retailers. In addition some consumers purchased bulbs under contract directly from the manufacturer and others dealt with retailers.[33] Could there be price discrimination between these two kinds of customers—the former being typically large industrial purchasers of light bulbs and the latter households?

Clearly if anyone purchases bulbs outright, that buyer could legally resell them at any price of his choosing. The agency technique for accomplishing resale price maintenance would fail if some purchasers did in fact resell bulbs at less than the list price. Even more important, without such restriction on sales to direct purchasers, any resale price maintenance scheme adopted by a group of manufacturers would fail. Without such limitations manufacturers could give secret price cuts to direct purchasers and, if these buyers resold the bulbs at lower prices than the jobbers and retailers, they could divert sales from the agent distributors. It was therefore necessary to limit their purchases

---

(1922). This statement applies to New York City but it is reasonable to believe similar arrangements held elsewhere. Speaking of July, 1911, Mr. Martin goes on to say, "This schedule for the first time provided an allowance to those customers who relieved the [New York Edison] Company of the supply of incandescent lamps, who, if they guaranteed 1500 kilowatt hours of monthly consumption, were allowed to purchase their lamps independently of the service rate, to offset which they were allowed a discount of 1 cent a kilowatt hour" (p. 141). To the best of my knowledge, in those cities in which there is a lamp renewal service those purchasers of electricity who use this service pay a certain sum each month with their electricity bill.

[31] A jobber could obtain special authority to deal with another who handled the same brand. Such arrangements could be made for limited periods of time. The primary agent received as compensation "the difference between the net amount due the Manufacturer from the sale of lamps to the Secondary Agent and the net amount which would have been due the Manufacturer had the lamps been sold directly by the Primary Agent." Record, p. 551, United States v. General Elec. Co., 272 U.S. 476 (1926). Arrangements among other kinds of distributors had similar conditions.

[32] "Lamps may be sold to any consumer within domestic territory, to the extent of the consumer's requirements for immediate delivery, at the discounts fixed in the schedule for Purchasers Without Contract, which discounts are subject to change without notice. Electrical contractors requiring incandescent lamps to complete installation work will be regarded as consumers of such lamps." Sales under contract may be made only to the extent of the consumer's requirements. Record, pp. 272–73, United States v. General Elec. Co., 272 U.S. 476 (1926).

[33] General Electric's total sales of light bulbs had this composition: 22 per cent was made up of sales to purchasers under contract who dealt directly with GE employees, 37 per cent to purchasers under contract who dealt with agents, and 41 per cent to customers not under contract who dealt with agents. The corresponding figures for Westinghouse are 36 per cent, 30 per cent, and 34 per cent.

to the extent of their requirements and to offer them exactly the same terms as agents buying equal amounts. These stipulations in the rules governing sales to direct purchasers do not, therefore, necessarily indicate the existence of price discrimination.

Although the same quantity discount schedule applied to the agents as to the direct purchasers,[34] the possibility of price discrimination is not thereby excluded. Direct purchasers may have bought larger amounts than the agents and a discount schedule based on quantities is consistent with price discrimination.

Resale price maintenance coupled with restrictions on sales among distributors and other customers is circumstantial evidence of price discrimination. The former prevents leakages of sales among distributors and the latter prevents those distributors getting the product at the lower price from selling not to final consumers but to other distributors who would have to pay the manufacturer a higher price for the merchandise. Either kind of leakage spoils that segment of the market in which the manufacturer sells his product at the higher price. There is not enough relevant evidence in the court record of the case to decide the issue of price discrimination one way or another.[35] However, all the evidence in the case is consistent with the implications of the cartel argument.

V. Conclusion

Because resale price maintenance suppresses price competition among retailers, we may readily understand why as a group they often support it. This is commonly thought the chief explanation of the existence of minimum retail prices—that retailers press price maintenance on reluctant manufacturers. However, this explanation fails in those cases in which the impetus clearly comes from one or more manufacturers. There are two arguments to rationalize manufacturers' support of the policy. First, a single manufacturer producing a differentiated product over which he possesses some degree of monopoly power may find it advantageous to establish minimum retail prices in order to induce those retailers who handle his product to offer special services jointly with it thereby increasing total sales. Second, a group of manufacturers may couple resale price maintenance with a kind of exclusive dealing as part of their broad scheme to create a producers' cartel.

In the first or special service argument the manufacturer's advocacy of re-

[34] The record shows the discount schedule for purchasers under contract on p. 286. Basic rates of compensation for Agents are on pp. 288–89. These indicate that the discounts for a given amount of net sales were about the same for both kinds of transactions.

[35] One student of the case does believe in the price discrimination theory. See W. S. Bowman, Jr., Resale Price Maintenance—a Monopoly Problem, 25 J. Bus. 153–54 (1955), and also by the same author, Prerequisites and Effects of Resale Price Maintenance, 22 U. Chi. Law Rev. 825, 839–40 (1955).

sale price maintenance depends on the nature of the product. This argument applies to products which are unfamiliar to the mass of consumers either because the product is new (or embodies new features) or because it is purchased infrequently by a relatively small proportion of households. To test the significance of this explanation we need a list of consumer goods classified according to the presence or absence of price maintenance schemes such that the price maintained goods are further classified according as manufacturers (as distinct from retailers) initiated the pricing policy. If the special service argument is valid then a high proportion of the commodities price maintained at the initiative of manufacturers who possess monopoly power should require special point of purchase sales efforts whereas products sold by monopolistic manufacturers at unrestricted resale prices are not offered jointly with special services.

Of those price maintained commodities not offered jointly with special services such that the initiative stems from the manufacturer, the cartel argument should apply. We may expect that producers of these commodities sell them via distributors on the same terms. Moreover, the distributors of these goods handle only a single brand for which the manufacturer fixes a minimum price.

[13]

VERTICAL RESTRAINTS AS CONTRACT ENFORCEMENT MECHANISMS*

BENJAMIN KLEIN *and* *KEVIN M. MURPHY*
University of California, Los Angeles — *University of Chicago*

It is now generally recognized that there are many cases of vertical restraints that do not fit the standard "consumer free riding on special services" theory.[1] For example, the widespread use of resale price maintenance in the marketing of brand name clothing cannot be explained as inducing retailers to supply services such as dressing rooms. It is unlikely that consumers must be prevented from trying on clothing free of charge at a full-service retailer before purchasing the clothing at a discount from retailers who do not supply dressing rooms. A number of authors recently have attempted to correct this deficiency in the standard theory by expanding the type of services that vertical restraints may induce retailers to supply and the corresponding retailer free-riding problems.[2]

The standard economic analysis of how vertical restraints operate to induce desired retailer behavior has remained essentially unchanged, however. The standard analysis assumes that when it is not feasible for a manufacturer to write explicit, court-enforceable contracts with retailers for the supply of particular services, the only alternative mechanism manufacturers can use to induce the supply of desired services is to increase the direct return retailers receive from consumers when those

* We are grateful to the Sloan Foundation grant to the University of California, Los Angeles, for the study of contractual relationships for research support and to Armen Alchian, Harold Demsetz, Roy Kenney, Frank Mathewson, Tim Opler, Stanley Ornstein, John Wiley, and referees of this *Journal* for useful comments.

[1] The classic statement of the theory is in Lester G. Telser, Why Should Manufacturers Want Fair Trade? 3 J. Law & Econ. 86 (1960). Similar reasoning can be found in earlier articles by T. H. Silcock, Some Problems of Price Maintenance, 48 Econ. J. 42 (1938); and F. W. Taussig, Price Maintenance, 6 Am. Econ. Rev. 170 (Suppl. 1916). Since Continental T.V., Inc. v. GTE Sylvania, Inc., 97 S. Ct. 2549 (1977), such reasoning has been frequently accepted by the courts as a procompetitive rationale for nonprice vertical arrangements.

[2] For example, Howard P. Marvel & Stephen McCafferty, Resale Price Maintenance and Quality Certification, 15 Rand J. Econ. 346 (1984), consider the supply by retailers of product "certification services."

[*Journal of Law & Economics*, vol. XXXI (October 1988)]
 0022-2186/88/3102-0004$01.50

services are supplied. Resale price maintenance increases this direct return by increasing the retail margin, creating an incentive for individual retailers to engage in nonprice competition and to supply the desired services. Exclusive territories increase the direct return by eliminating nearby retailers, lessening the possibility that some of the gain from the supply of desired services will accrue to other retailers.

This standard economic analysis of vertical restraints is fundamentally flawed. Vertical restraints, by themselves, do not create a direct incentive for retailers to supply desired services. Consider the standard case of a retailer free riding on other retailers' product demonstrations. Even if the manufacturer fixes the retail price and does not permit price competition, retailers still have an incentive to free ride by supplying nonprice services that are not desired by the manufacturer but are of value to consumers. For example, free-riding retailers of personal computers could encourage consumers to obtain a product demonstration from a full-service retailer before purchasing the product from them with, say, lower priced tied accessories. No matter how large a margin is created by resale price maintenance, there appears to be no incentive for competitive free-riding retailers to supply the desired demonstration services. The standard economic analysis of vertical restraints makes sense within this context only under the unrealistic assumption that the sole avenue of nonprice competition available to retailers is the supply of the particular services desired by the manufacturer.[3]

Further, even if nonprice competition is unidimensional, retailers may merely take the additional money created by the vertical restraint and continue to free ride. This is obvious in cases where consumers cannot, before purchase, detect retailer services that influence product quality, such as rotation of a product with a limited shelf life. Competitive retailers have an incentive to "free ride" on the reputation of the manufacturer by reducing such services, thereby supplying a lower quality product than consumers anticipate and than the manufacturer desires. Such free riding entails an extra short-run profit to the retailer, and, no matter how large a margin is created by the vertical restraint, retailers will have no incentive to incur the added costs of supplying the desired services.

Our analysis presents an alternative theory of how vertical restraints

[3] This erroneous assumption is made both in the original Telser analysis, *supra* note 1, and in the work that has been done since to extend the free-riding analysis. See, for example, G. F. Mathewson & R. A. Winter, An Economic Theory of Vertical Restraints, 15 Rand J. Econ. 27 (1984); Victor P. Goldberg, The Free Rider Problem, Imperfect Pricing, and the Economics of Retailing Services, 79 Nw. U. L. Rev. 736 (1984); Martin K. Perry & Robert H. Groff, Resale Price Maintenance and Forward Integration into a Monopolistically Competitive Industry, 100 Q. J. Econ. 1293 (1985).

operate to induce desired dealer services. Manufacturers are assumed to induce desired dealer services through a private enforcement mechanism by which active manufacturer monitoring and the threat of manufacturer termination assures dealer performance. Within this framework, the manufacturer uses vertical restraints to decrease the short-run gain to nonperforming dealers (by limiting their ability to expand output) and to increase the long-run gain to performing dealers (by creating a quasi–rent stream).

This analysis explains the use of exclusive territories and resale price maintenance in the *Coors* case,[4] where desired dealer services are unobserved by consumers and, hence, where the standard "consumer free riding on special services" theory is clearly inapplicable. It is then extended to the more general case of product promotion, where dealer services, such as shelf space or product demonstrations, are observed by consumers, but where the manufacturer's desire for targeted marketing to marginal consumers implies a greater level of these services than would be supplied by unrestrained dealers. Manufacturers employ vertical restraints, not to avoid consumer free riding, but to optimally compensate dealers on a per unit of sales basis for an increased supply of product promotion services and to prevent price competition that would eliminate the desired targeted marketing scheme. This analysis is shown to be consistent with the use of exclusive dealing arrangements, with the use of resale price maintenance in the marketing of brand name clothing such as Levi Strauss jeans, and with the facts of *Monsanto*.[5] More generally, our theory of vertical restraints is shown to be applicable to any situation where it is not economical for the manufacturer to write an explicit contract with its dealers regarding some aspect of desired dealer performance.

I. Private Enforcement of Dealer Performance

We take as the starting point of our analysis the same assumption implicitly taken by the special services free-riding analysis, namely, that it is not economically feasible for a manufacturer to write an explicit, enforceable contract with a dealer for the supply of desired dealer services. We assume that the manufacturer can observe dealer performance, but that an explicit contract regarding this performance cannot be made because dealer performance may be prohibitively costly to measure and to

[4] Adolph Coors Co. v. FTC, 497 F.2d 1178 (10th Cir. 1974), cert. denied, 419 U.S. 1105 (1975).

[5] Monsanto Co. v. Spray-Rite Service Corp., 104 S. Ct. 1464 (1984).

specify in a way that contractual breach and the extent of damages can be proven to the satisfaction of the court. Rather than relying on a third-party enforcer, some elements of dealer performance are privately enforced solely by the threat of termination of the transactional relationship.[6]

If a manufacturer chooses to rely on such a private contract enforcement mechanism to assure that dealers supply desired services, then an expected future quasi–rent stream must exist. The potential loss of this future quasi–rent stream takes the place of a potential court-imposed sanction in assuring dealer performance. If the expected present discounted value of the future quasi–rent stream earned by an honest dealer exceeds the expected value of the gain to a dealer who shirks on the supply of desired services, then the capital loss that can be imposed on a dealer by manufacturer termination will be sufficient to assure dealer performance.

If a dealer's short-run per-unit time gain from shirking on the supply of services is π_ℓ, then the minimum perpetual dealer quasi–rent stream that will assure dealer performance, π_h, is given by

$$\pi_h = [1 - e^{-rt}]\, \pi_\ell, \tag{1}$$

where r is the interest rate and t is the time to detection and termination by the manufacturer of a shirking dealer, determined by manufacturer expenditures on monitoring of dealer performance.

It is important to note that the existence of a performance-assuring quasi–rent stream need not represent more than a normal rate of return to dealers. If dealers have made investments that are manufacturer specific, termination will be costly even if they are earning no premium. If these manufacturer-specific investments are of sufficient magnitude, the threat of loss of the quasi–rent stream on the investments will assure dealer performance without the creation of a premium stream.[7] Nevertheless, many dealers, such as department stores selling a particular clothing manufacturer's merchandise, make insufficient manufacturer-specific in-

[6] Since contract law places legal constraints on the ability of manufacturers to unilaterally terminate dealers without cause, notice, or compensation, pure private enforcement in this sense does not exist. Even within these legal constraints, however, a continuum exists between degrees of private and court enforcement. Under some contractual arrangements, manufacturers may retain substantial termination discretion with significantly less court intervention into the enforcement process than would be required under alternative contractual arrangements.

[7] Significant manufacturer-specific reliance investments may make it more difficult to legally unilaterally terminate dealers without compensation. Avoidance of such legal constraints may explain why all manufacturers do not demand initial lump sum payments from dealers equal to the present discounted value of any anticipated premium stream.

vestments to insure dealer performance solely through the threat of losing the return on these specific investments; a premium stream must be generated in order for a private enforcement mechanism to work.

Further, for the private enforcement mechanism to work, the manufacturer must be able to commit to terminating dealers who shirk on the supply of services and to commit to providing dealers who do not shirk with the required future quasi–rent stream. The manufacturer will terminate shirking dealers either because the manufacturer learns something about the dealers who shirk (that they possess high discount rates or relatively high costs of supplying the desired level of services) or because failure to terminate would lead dealers to learn that the manufacturer has a high cost of terminating them. In either case the manufacturer can commit to terminate because it would be costly for the manufacturer not to terminate shirking dealers.

Similarly, the manufacturer's ability to commit to payment of a future quasi–rent stream and the dealers' belief that a quasi–rent stream will be forthcoming depend upon the cost to the manufacturer of violating such a commitment. Since the manufacturer knows that violation of such a commitment would lead to dealer shirking, violation requires that the manufacturer adopt an alternative marketing arrangement, such as handling distribution with its own employees.[8] Hence, as long as the manufacturer's cost of distribution inherent in the next best alternative exceeds the dealer's cost of distribution inclusive of the quasi rent, the manufacturer's commitment to provide the dealer quasi–rent stream can be credible.[9]

The present discounted value of the cost advantage associated with independent dealer distribution is also what limits minimization of monitoring costs. Since manufacturer monitoring is a costly process, while the

[8] The only example we know of mass dealer terminations and vertical integration is the Ralston Purina termination in 1971 of all 642 Jack-in-the-Box franchises with thirty-day notification. This is not a likely example of reverse cheating, however, since it occurred only after Ralston Purina settled a class action suit that forced it to alter substantially its franchise arrangement.

[9] This should be contrasted with the case of consumer enforcement of high quality supply. See Benjamin Klein & Keith B. Leffler, The Role of Market Forces in Assuring Contractual Performance, 89 J. Pol. Econ. 615 (1981). In that case, consumers cannot make credible commitments regarding future premium payments to manufacturers because costs cannot be imposed on reneging consumers who do not pay a higher price in the future. Since consumers cannot make credible commitments regarding future premium payments, the mechanism suggested by Shapiro, whereby a zero profit equilibrium is reached with a sufficiently low (below cost) price in the initial period equal to the present discounted value of the premium stream, is not realistic. See Carl Shapiro, Premiums for High Quality Products as Returns to Reputations, 98 Q. J. Econ. 659 (1983). Instead, Klein & Leffler reach a zero profit equilibrium by the use of firm-specific initial investments that provide a future service flow and, hence, a future demand that will be lost if the firm shirks.

quasi–rent stream is an income transfer that entails no real resource cost, the efficient level of manufacturer monitoring may appear to be extremely low with the associated quasi–rent stream extremely high. However, there is a limit to the economizing process where the manufacturer can decrease expenditures on monitoring (thereby increasing the time to detection of shirking dealers) while simultaneously increasing the promised quasi–rent stream (and the cost to the dealer from termination). The limit is the ability of the manufacturer to commit to providing an increased quasi–rent stream. The manufacturer cannot credibly commit to provide a quasi–rent stream greater than the cost to him of violating the commitment or the cost advantage associated with independent dealer distribution compared to employee distribution.

The maximum quasi rent that the manufacturer can commit to provide the dealer as a premium for future performance is also determined, in part, by reverse cheating problems. Consider the extreme case where the manufacturer is assumed to give dealers all the quasi rents associated with the sale of the product by lowering the wholesale price to the manufacturer's marginal cost and creating exclusive territories for each dealer. In return, the dealer could pay the manufacturer an initial lump sum equal to the discounted value of all the rents associated with the present and future sale of the product.[10] In such a situation, however, the manufacturer would not have the proper incentive to maintain the quality of the product. Unless the dealer can write a costlessly enforceable contract with the manufacturer for the supply of the manufacturer's product and for the level of manufacturer monitoring, the manufacturer will certainly shirk on product quality and monitoring effort. A fully symmetrical reverse-cheating problem is created unless the manufacturer also has something to lose from his nonperformance. In order to assure performance on both sides of the transaction, an appropriate distribution of rents between the transacting parties must exist.

II. Vertical Restraints as Enforcement Devices

The necessity of a quasi–rent stream to assure dealer performance and the use of vertical restraints to both increase the quasi–rent stream earned by dealers and decrease the dealer's short-run gain from shirking can be seen most clearly by considering an idealized exclusive territory arrange-

[10] This is the solution adopted by manufacturers in the Rey and Tirole model when dealers are risk neutral. Rey and Tirole use dealer-risk aversion to explain why such an arrangement is inefficient and ignore the significant manufacturer incentive problems present. See Patrick Rey & Jean Tirole, The Logic of Vertical Retraints, 76 Am. Econ. Rev. 921 (1986).

ment where the manufacturer attempts to solve the dealer free-riding problem by fully assigning customers to particular dealers and imposing maximum resale price maintenance at the "competitive" dealer level to solve the "successive monopoly" problem created by the exclusive territory arrangement.

This solution is illustrated in Figure 1. Figure 1*a* depicts the demand for the manufacturer's product, $D(P,S)$, which is assumed to be negatively related to market price, P, and positively related to the per-unit level of services provided by dealers, S.[11] Figure 1*b* depicts a representative dealer's costs of marketing the manufacturer's product to consumers with the manufacturer's desired level of dealer services. The minimum average cost of dealer distribution is given by C_0 with the efficient dealer size given by q_0.

If contractual enforcement were costless, the manufacturer could assure that dealers supply the desired level of services by simply specifying contractually the desired level of dealer services and allowing competition to occur among dealers. Competition would drive the retail-wholesale price gap down to the representative dealer's minimum average cost of marketing the product with the desired services, C_0, and a potential court-imposed sanction would guarantee performance by dealers.

This competitive, costless enforcement equilibrium is represented in Figure 1*a*. For expositional simplicity we assume that the manufacturer has a constant marginal cost of production, which we denote MC_M. The manufacturer then adds the constant marginal cost of selling his product through competitive dealers, C_0, to the constant marginal cost of production to obtain the total marginal cost of producing and selling his product, MC_T, where MC_T equals $C_0 + MC_M$. The manufacturer's output, Q_0, is determined where the marginal revenue schedule, MR, intersects total marginal cost, MC_T. This implies a profit-maximizing wholesale price, P_{W_0}, of $P_{R_0} - C_0$. In Figure 1*b* this profit-maximizing wholesale price, P_{W_0}, is added to the dealer's costs to represent marketing conditions facing

[11] Although we assume that the manufacturer faces a negatively sloped demand curve for its product, we do not focus on the "monopoly" distortion implied by less than perfectly elastic demand curves. This should be contrasted with recently published works by Rey and Tirole, *id.*, and Perry and Groff, *supra* note 3, which consider vertical restraints, not as devices to prevent dealer free riding, but as devices that the manufacturer uses to extract monopoly rents. The rents earned by manufacturers in our model may represent a return on the manufacturer's investment in product reputation, particular location, or any other firm-specific product characteristic that creates a negatively sloped demand within an imperfectly competitive environment. It is important to recognize that such firm-specific assets serve the socially useful function of encouraging product innovation. It is not socially desirable, as Rey and Tirole and Perry and Groff maintain, to eliminate this return by driving the manufacturer's price to his marginal production cost.

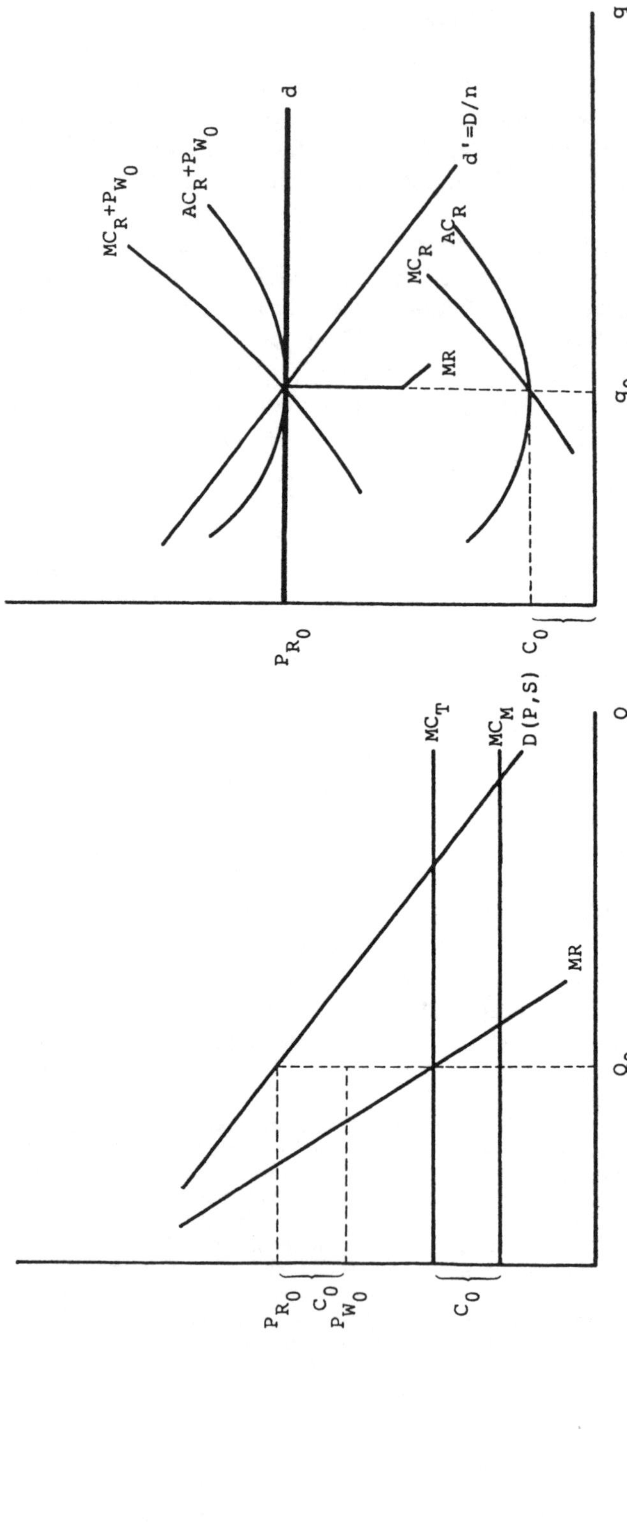

FIGURE 1*a*.—Manufacturer

FIGURE 1*b*.—Dealer

FIGURE 1.—Dealer exclusive territories and maximum resale price maintenance

dealers. Each dealer faces a perfectly elastic demand curve, *d*, at the equilibrium price, $P_{R_0} = P_{W_0} + C_0$. Competition between dealers insures that distribution is provided at minimum cost to the manufacturer and consumers, and the contractual arrangement insures the supply of the desired dealer services.

When the manufacturer cannot contractually specify the supply of desired services, and services are subject to free riding, each dealer can increase its short-run profit by shirking on the supply of services. Exclusive territories may appear to provide a solution to this problem. An idealized exclusive territory arrangement is illustrated in Figure 1*b*, where each dealer's demand curve, d', is assumed to be the market demand of the dealer's assigned customers or D/n if each of n dealers is given an equal share of the market. The manufacturer, by choosing the optimal number of exclusive dealers, $n_0 = Q_0/q_0$, and by setting a maximum resale price equal to P_{R_0}, may appear to guarantee that distribution is accomplished at minimum cost and that dealers earn no monopoly profits. Customer assignment implies that no dealer can free ride on other dealers, and maximum resale price maintenance at the competitive distribution level implies that no dealer can take advantage of market power to increase price. Therefore, in spite of the fact that the supply of dealer services cannot be contractually specified, manufacturers appear to have the best of both worlds—competitive margins for dealer distribution services and monopolistic dealer-customer assignment to prevent interdealer free riding.[12]

While an exclusive territory-"competitive" maximum price arrangement solves interdealer free-riding problems, it does not solve all free-riding problems between the dealer and the manufacturer. For example, consider the case where consumers cannot detect prepurchase dealer services that influence product quality, such as rotation of a product with limited shelf life. In such a case, dealers have the ability and incentive to shirk on the supply of services. Even with complete customer assignment, if maximum resale price maintenance squeezes the dealer's margin

[12] To avoid legal restrictions on the use of maximum resale price maintenance, manufacturers may modify the exclusive territory arrangement by permitting interterritory sales, but only at a specified, minimum list price. By creating a threat of sales from dealers in other territories, the manufacturer sets an effective maximum price that dealers can charge customers in their own territory without explicitly fixing such a maximum price. This may explain the marketing arrangement challenged in Eastern Scientific Co. v. Wild Heerberg Instruments, Inc., 572 F.2nd 883 (1st Cir.), cert. denied, 439 U.S. 833 (1978) and upheld as less restrictive than a legal, pure exclusive territory arrangement. The fact that the manufacturer set a minimum price on interterritory sales is consistent with the existence of a premium on intraterritory sales that the manufacturer did not want competed away.

to the point where the dealer earns no quasi rents, a dealer can achieve a larger return by shirking on the supply of services. Although future consumer demand and, hence, dealer sales will be reduced, this results in the loss of manufacturer profits, not dealer profits. The threat of lost future sales will not prevent the dealer from reducing services since the costs from the reduction in sales will be borne by the manufacturer. In addition, when dealers earn no quasi rents the threat of manufacturer termination will not be a costly sanction to the dealer and will not prevent the dealer from shirking.

One way for a manufacturer to create a margin sufficient to guarantee dealer performance is to employ exclusive territories with maximum resale price maintenance but to let the dealers earn some of the "monopoly" rents associated with assigned customers. An exclusive territory thereby creates a valuable asset for the dealer that would be lost upon termination. The manufacturer can be thought of as imposing a maximum price at the same profit-maximizing level, P_{R_0}, so as to keep the output at the same level, Q_0.[13] The number of dealers can also be kept at the same level, n_0, so that each dealer's share of the total market will be at the same optimum (minimum-cost) point on the dealer distribution cost function, q_0. As Figure 2 illustrates, however, the manufacturer must now lower the wholesale price from P_{W_0} to some point, say P_{W_1}, where the rents earned by the dealer are sufficient to assure the supply of the desired level of dealer services. The manufacturer must share with dealers some of the rents earned on the sale of the product.[14]

In addition, an exclusive territory arrangement lowers the dealer's gain from shirking by reducing a shirking dealer's ability to expand sales and, hence, short-run profits. This lowers the required premium and, when dealers have made specific investments, the exclusive territory arrange-

[13] This is approximately correct. More precisely, since any premium payment is a marginal cost to the producer, the profit-maximizing price will increase. The premium stream, however, is generally not very large. For example, if the desired services (and, hence, short-run gain) represent 20 percent of the value of a good, and shirking dealers cannot expand sales but can shirk for one year before being terminated, then, with an interest rate of 5 percent, the quasi rent need be only 1 percent of sales (which may be covered in part by the dealer's return on manufacturer specific investments). If a shirking dealer can expand sales, the short-run gain and, hence, the required premium may be substantially larger.

[14] In general, lowering the wholesale price is superior to generating the required premium stream with a fixed per-unit time payment to dealers. If the per-unit time payment was set at a level sufficient for the expected level of output for the average-sized dealer, those dealers with larger than expected output would find it profitable to shirk on the supply of dealer services. Because the sizes of dealers are likely to vary substantially in ways that cannot be predicted by the manufacturer ex ante, a proportional premium generated by lowering the wholesale price is preferred.

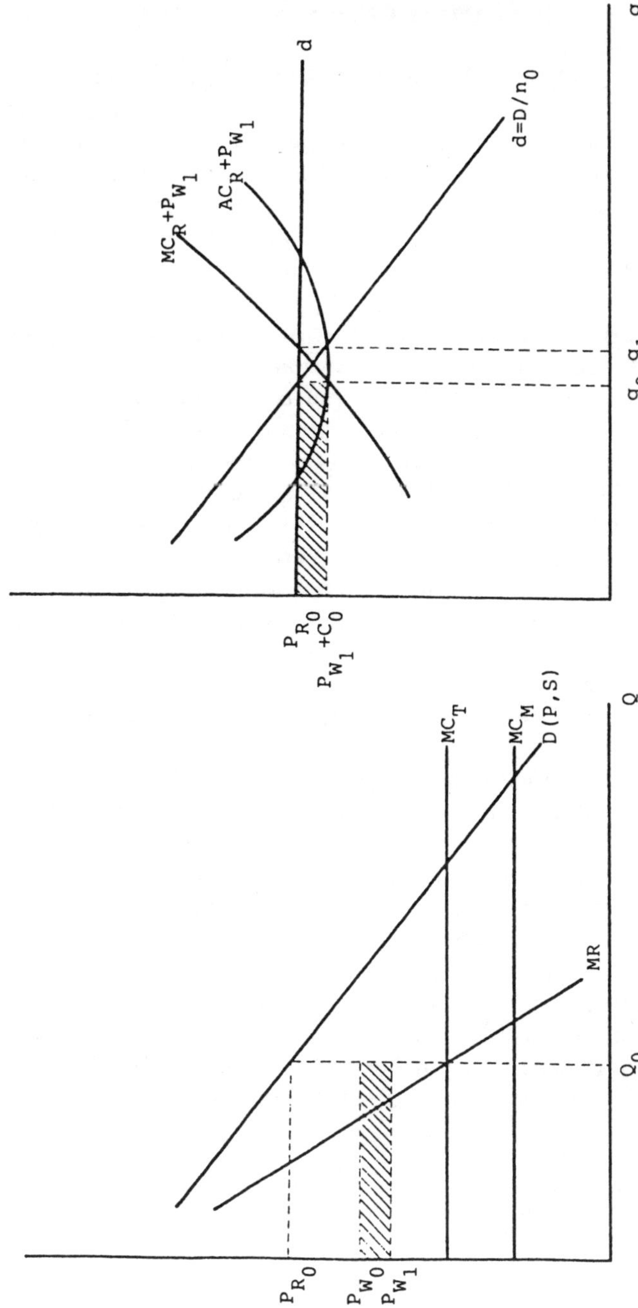

FIGURE 2a.—Manufacturer

FIGURE 2b.—Dealer

FIGURE 2.—The generation of a dealer premium

ment in itself may be sufficient to prevent dealer shirking. If the lower short-run shirking return is less than the quasi rents on the dealer's manufacturer specific investments, then manufacturer monitoring and the threat of termination, together with exclusive territories, will be sufficient to prevent dealer shirking without lowering the wholesale price.

Similarly, if minimum resale price maintenance is to be effective in assuring dealer performance, it must create a situation where dealer quasi rents exceed the short-run shirking potential. Consider Figure 2 once again. As opposed to our analysis of exclusive territories, where each dealer was assumed to face a market sharing demand curve, d', we can now assume that each dealer faces a perfectly elastic demand curve, d. As in our analysis of exclusive territories, the imposition of resale price maintenance at P_{R_0} will have two effects. First, resale price maintenance limits the ability of shirking dealers to expand output. For example, without resale price maintenance, potentially large expansions in sales may occur via telephone mail-order marketing. Resale price maintenance thereby lowers the potential short-run shirking gain and the required dealer quasi–rent stream.[15] If quasi rents on manufacturer-specific investments are greater than this new low shirking potential, then the imposition of resale price maintenance, together with manufacturer monitoring, will be sufficient to assure dealer performance without lowering the wholesale price.

Second, resale price maintenance may be used to create a dealer premium stream. When the short-run dealer shirking potential exceeds the quasi rents from manufacturer-specific investments, then the manufacturer must lower the wholesale price from P_{W_0} to P_{W_1} to generate a dealer premium. Without minimum resale price maintenance, the dealer price would fall by the same amount as the wholesale price decrease, and no premium would exist. If, however, the manufacturer enforces minimum resale price maintenance at P_{R_0} and fixes the number of dealers at n_0, then a premium stream will be generated. Although individual dealers would desire to expand their output beyond q_0 to q_1, the minimum price constraint prevents dealers from expanding output through price cutting.[16]

[15] This may explain why restrictions on price advertising are commonly employed in vertical restraint marketing arrangements. See Thomas R. Overstreet, Jr., Resale Price Maintenance: Economic Theories and Empirical Evidence (Bureau of Economics staff report to the Federal Trade Commission 1983), at 84–101.

[16] A maximum output arrangement would appear to be a logically equivalent alternative to such a minimum price arrangement. Fixing prices is generally superior to fixing output, however, when demand differs across dealers or differs for a particular dealer over time. If changes in dealer demand are due to changes in the number of customers, that is, every customer has the same demand for the product but there is variability over time and across

III. Manufacturer Monitoring of Nonprice Competition

The resale price maintenance equilibrium illustrated in Figure 2 implicitly assumes that, although a positive price-marginal cost gap exists, dealers cannot expand output through nonprice competition such as tie-in sales, discounts on other items, or giveaways. Such dealer nonprice competition would eliminate some of the dealer quasi-rent stream and reduce the effectiveness of resale price maintenance in assuring dealer performance. The standard free-riding analysis of resale price maintenance ignores the problem of unauthorized nonprice competition by erroneously assuming that the desired special services represent the only avenue for nonprice competition. Our model, on the other hand, recognizes that many types of nonprice competition are available.

Clearly, if resale price maintenance is to be effective, the manufacturer must monitor the most obvious forms of nonprice competition that are the closest substitutes for price reductions. Nevertheless, even if the manufacturer can effectively monitor these forms of nonprice competition, some avenues will remain. In order for our equilibrium to be viable, nonprice competition along these other margins must not eliminate the dealer premium.

To evaluate this possibility, consider Figure 2 again, where each dealer is assumed to have a price-marginal cost gap equal to the amount of the per-unit premium, $P_{R_0} - (P_{W_1} + C_0)$. Further, assume that dealers can make per-unit expenditures on nonprice competition that lower the effective price to the consumer by α dollars per dollar spent on nonprice competition, where α is greater than zero and less than one.[17] Under the assumption of perfect competition among dealers, expenditures on nonprice attributes would occur up to the point where the dealer's marginal cost of output equals the price net of expenditures on the nonprice attributes. No matter how inefficient nonprice competition, that is, no matter how small is α, dealers will engage in such competition until all marginal profit is eliminated. Resale price maintenance would not be effective in creating a dealer premium stream.

The result that unlimited nonprice competition eliminates all marginal profit depends upon the assumption of perfect competition. In other con-

---

dealers in the number of customers each dealer has, then it will be easier for a manufacturer to fix the correct premium stream with minimum resale price maintenance than attempting to estimate the corresponding maximum-output level for each dealer at every point in time. On the other hand, see our discussion of automobile marketing arrangements in Section VII *infra*.

[17] If α equals one, then consumers value the added service just as much as a reduction in price, and hence the minimum price restraint is completely ineffective.

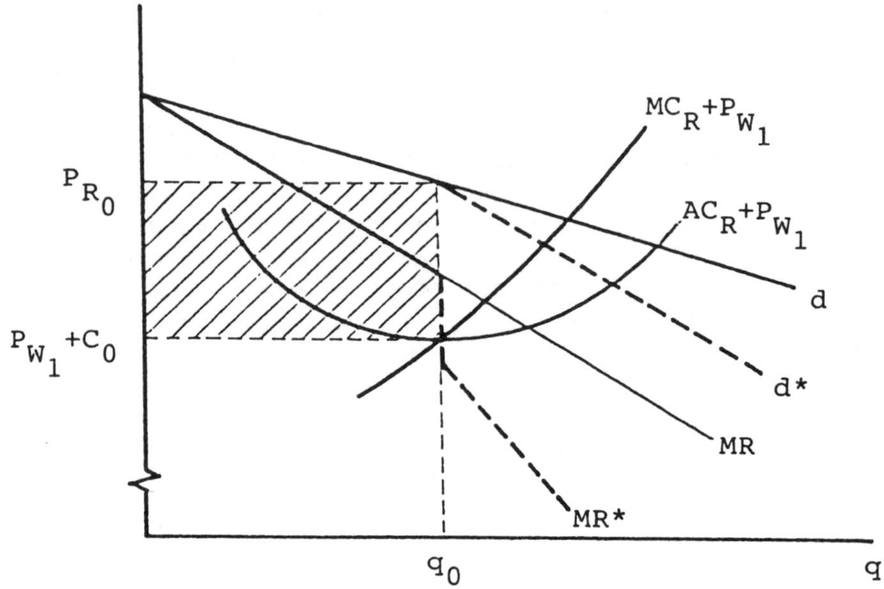

FIGURE 3.—Dealer equilibrium with nonprice competition

texts this assumption, although unrealistic, is generally useful since it simplifies the analysis and produces results that are close to those likely to be actually observed. For analyzing nonprice competition, however, the perfect competition model produces results that are qualitatively different from what could be expected under even slightly imperfect competition. In particular, if we assume that sales cannot be increased by an arbitrarily large amount with an arbitrarily small decrease in the effective price to consumers, then dealers will not have the incentive to engage in a broad range of nonprice competition.[18]

To illustrate, Figure 3 represents an individual dealer's demand curve, *d,* as less than perfectly elastic. Further, the dealer's ability to expand output by nonprice means is represented by the more inelastic demand curve, *d**. This demand curve can be thought of as representing the quantity the dealer can sell by varying expenditures on nonprice competition. The inefficiency of nonprice competition ($\alpha < 1$) implies that dealer in-

[18] This is the primary difference between our model of nonprice competition and that presented in George Stigler, Price and Nonprice Competition, 76 J. Pol. Econ. 149 (1968), where an assumption of perfect competition at the dealer level implies that nonprice competition, no matter how inefficient, eliminates all marginal profit.

creases in expenditures on nonprice competition result in a larger reduction in the net price received by the dealer, $P_R - z$, than in the effective price paid by the consumer, $P_R - \alpha z$. Therefore, expenditures on nonprice competition result in smaller increases in sales than under price competition. Since it takes $1/\alpha$ dollars to lower the effective price to consumers by one dollar, the slope of the dealer's effective demand curve for output greater than q_0 is $1/\alpha$ times the original slope.[19]

The dealer's effective demand curve has a kink at the minimum dealer price. This kink implies a discontinuity in the dealer's marginal revenue schedule. If the dealer's marginal cost curve (equal to average cost at this equilibrium) passes through this discontinuity, that is, if marginal cost exceeds marginal revenue at any output beyond the kink, then increases in sales through nonprice competition are not profitable. As α goes to zero, that is, as nonprice competition becomes less effective, the size of this gap in the marginal revenue schedule increases, and nonprice competition is less likely to occur.

Since the dealer will attempt to expand output whenever the dealer's price-cost margin, $[P_R - (MC_R + P_W)]/P_R$, is greater than one over the individual dealer's effective demand elasticity, a necessary condition for the dealer not to engage in nonprice competition is that

$$\pi_h/q_0 P_{R_0} < -1/(\alpha E_d), \tag{2}$$

where αE_d is the elasticity of the dealer's effective demand curve and π_h/q_0 is the per-unit premium.

Equation (2) indicates that the likelihood that nonprice competition will occur is positively related to the elasticity of dealer demand, the size of the premium as a fraction of price, and the effectiveness of the nonprice competition. Nonprice competition is unlikely to occur, even for relatively effective nonprice competition channels and relatively large individual dealer-demand elasticities, as long as the premium is a small fraction of the product price. For example, if the premium stream is 5 percent of the dealer price, even if the dealer demand elasticity is 25, any nonprice competition that is 80 percent or less as effective as price competition, that is, $\alpha \leq .80$, will not be engaged in by dealers. The manufacturer need not monitor such forms of nonprice competition since expenditures on them will not be made and the premium stream will not be reduced.

[19] The manufacturer may eliminate the kink for the nonprice expenditures it desires the dealer to make by paying $(1 - \alpha)$ percent of those particular expenditures. Cooperative advertising programs are a common example of this phenomenon.

IV. Price and Nonprice Restraints: The *Coors* Case

Our framework unifies the efficiency theory of price and nonprice vertical restraints.[20] Both minimum resale price maintenance and nonprice restraints, such as exclusive territories, assure dealer performance of elements of the contractual understanding that are not enforceable in court. And both price and nonprice restraints accomplish this purpose in essentially the same way. Both forms of vertical restraints raise the quasi–rent stream earned by the dealer relative to the dealer's short-run shirking potential.

Our analysis of nonprice competition also indicates that both minimum resale price maintenance and exclusive territories increase dealer quasi rents and reduce the short-run shirking potential by reducing dealer demand elasticity. Resale price maintenance decreases the elasticity of a dealer's effective demand curve because of the relative inefficiency of nonprice competition; exclusive territories decrease the elasticity of demand facing each dealer by creating individual dealer market power.

Whether a manufacturer chooses resale price maintenance, exclusive territories, or some other distribution arrangement to generate the required quasi–rent stream and to reduce the short-run gain from shirking will depend upon the particular case. Exclusive territories generally have some advantages over resale price maintenance in terms of a lower dealer shirking potential. The shirking potential is reduced by eliminating the interdealer free-rider problem. However, while it is often economical to assign wholesale distributors to a relatively small number of retail accounts fixed at particular locations, customer assignment is not feasible for retail distribution.

These economic forces are illustrated in the *Coors* case, where an exclusive territory (and maximum resale price maintenance) arrangement was employed at the wholesale level, and a resale price maintenance arrangement was employed at the retail level.[21] The marketing problem

[20] It is important to recognize that there is also a collusive theory of vertical restraints with widely different implications for price and nonprice restraints. While the simultaneous imposition by all firms in an industry of vertical resale price maintenance is equivalent in form to a horizontal price fix, the simultaneous imposition of vertical exclusive territories is not equivalent in form to a horizontal market-sharing agreement. Therefore, industrywide price restraints may serve as an enforcement device for a cartel arrangement and represent more of a potential antitrust problem than nonprice restraints.

[21] *Supra* note 4. In addition to Coors' use of exclusive territories at the wholesale level and minimum resale price maintenance at the retail level, the Federal Trade Commission claimed that Coors had unfair termination provisions with its wholesalers (termination with cause on five days' notice and without cause on thirty days' notice). This clause is consistent with our theory that termination should be a sanction. See Andrew McLaughlin, An Economic Analysis of Resale Price Maintenance (unpublished Ph.D. dissertation, Univ. Calif. at Los Angeles 1979) for further discussion and analysis of the Coors litigation.

solved by the use of these vertical restraints is related to the unique production process employed by Coors. Coors developed a sterile-fill or aseptic brewing process as an alternative to pasteurization. The aseptic brewing process controls the amount of live bacteria in the bottled beer by enclosing the product in a sterile, refrigerated system after the malt extract is boiled with the hops. This process, while creating a high quality beer, also creates a product that deteriorates fairly rapidly at room temperature. Coors is essentially an unpasteurized draft beer sold in bottles and cans and, like draft beer that is shipped in chilled barrels and marketed under refrigerated conditions, Coors must be kept refrigerated to maintain its quality. Coors beer was shipped by refrigerated trucks and insulated rail cars to distributors who were required to have refrigerated warehouses. Dealers were also encouraged to refrigerate, and a strict policy of product rotation and limited inventories was followed, with distributors required to visit every account once a week.[22]

It is clear that these refrigeration and product rotation services do not fit the standard "consumer free-riding" paradigm. It is not possible for consumers to receive a "complete" product by first obtaining the refrigeration services separately and free of charge from a dealer who refrigerates the beer and, then, purchasing the beer at a discount price from a dealer who does not refrigerate. A dealer free-riding problem exists, however, because consumers cannot detect quality deterioration before purchase, and consumers who receive a low quality product do not blame the particular dealer for the poor quality. If consumers even partially attribute the poor quality to the product generally, that is, to the manufacturer, then a dealer who shirks on supplying these services imposes an external cost on the manufacturer and on the other dealers of the product.[23]

Coors solved this free-riding problem at the wholesale level by creating a perfect exclusive territory arrangement with each dealer account as-

[22] If dealer refrigeration space was not available, dealers were required to have a strict product rotation policy and to maintain even more limited inventories with distributors recommended to service such accounts twice weekly. See Beer Quality and Refrigerated Marketing, statement by Jeffrey H. Coors to the Annual Distributors' Meeting of March 1, 1977, at 8.

[23] It may be rational for consumers to "blame" the manufacturer and to decrease demand for the product generally when they receive a poor quality product from a particular dealer because consumers know that product quality is determined by inputs that are supplied at both the manufacturer and dealer levels. Hence, rational consumers assign some probability that poor quality products are due to manufacturer production problems or manufacturer failure to properly monitor dealers. Benjamin Klein, Transaction Cost Determinants of "Unfair" Contractual Arrangements, 70 Am. Econ. Rev. 356 (Papers and Proceedings 1980), discusses this problem in a franchising context, denoting it as the "superhighway" or low probability of repeat sale problem.

signed to a particular wholesale distributor.[24] Coors denied distributors the right to ship beer into other distributors' territories and terminated distributors who did so. In addition to increasing the probability of repeat sale and preventing interdealer free riding, the evidence indicates that the exclusive territories represented valuable assets. Although Coors imposed maximum resale price maintenance on its distributors, a premium stream appears to have been created. When Coors opened new areas of distribution, significant excess demand existed for the initial grant of the exclusive territory, and the exclusive franchises sold for significant values when ownership rights were transferred.

On the retail level, Coors faced the same problem that it faced on the wholesale level. Because a consumer shops at different stores and cannot detect the quality of Coors beer before purchase, retailers have an incentive to shirk on the supply of refrigeration and rotation services. On the retail level, however, it is completely impractical for Coors to assign customers to individual dealers or to give retailers exclusive geographic territories. For these territories to possess the market power necessary to generate the correct premium stream and to internalize the interdealer free-rider problem, the territories would have to be uneconomically large. Therefore, on the retail level, Coors employed minimum resale price maintenance rather than an exclusive territory arrangement and monitored retailers' provision of refrigeration and product rotation services.

V. Manufacturer Purchase of Dealer Promotional Services

The problem solved by the Coors marketing arrangement is caused by the fact that consumers cannot detect dealer services before purchase. This gives dealers the incentive to shirk on the supply of these services. Nevertheless, even when consumers are fully aware of the extent of dealer services before they make a purchase, less than the desired quantity of dealer services may be supplied when there is a high manufacturer price-marginal cost margin and it is in the manufacturer's interest to have significant expenditures made by dealers on promotional services that increase sales. This is the case for wholesale distribution of all "premium" brands of beer, whether pasteurized or not, and other highly

[24] After the Federal Trade Commission decision, Coors adopted contracts with their wholesale distributors that included area of prime responsibility provisions. These provisions, since the Sylvania case, *supra* note 1, have been upheld as legal and important elements for protecting the quality of the product. See Maykuth v. Adolph Coors Co., 690 F.2d 689 (9th Cir. 1982), Mendelovitz v. Adolph Coors Co., 693 F.2d 570 (5th Cir. 1982), and Del Rio Distributing, Inc. v. Adolph Coors Co., 589 F.2d 176 (5th Cir.), cert. denied, 444 U.S. 840 (1979).

advertised products.[25] At the retail level, consider, for example, a department store's marketing of a brand name perfume, where the manufacturer's margin is extremely high and where the manufacturer desires the store to supply services such as shelf space and salespeople providing product demonstrations. Dealers determining the level of these services will not take account of the effect of the services on increased manufacturer sales and profits.

If the desired promotional services increase the value of the product on all units to all consumers by the same amount and the value of the services is greater than the cost of the services, then competing dealers will have the correct incentive to supply services despite the fact that dealers do not take account of manufacturer profitability. Since a dealer can increase the price of the product by the value of the services he supplies, services will be provided to the point where the marginal value of services to consumers is equal to the marginal cost to dealers of providing services. The competitive process will lead to the supply of the optimum quantity of services from both the consumers' and manufacturer's point of view.[26]

When consumers differ in the value they place on promotional services, however, competing dealers will not supply the services because they will not be able to increase the price on the particular units sold to the particular consumers that value the services. Moreover, the manufacturer may desire dealers to provide promotional services even though the total cost of the services exceeds the amount consumers are willing to pay for the services.[27] For example, assume that the wholesale price of an ounce of perfume is $45, that the competitive retail price is $50, and that there are inframarginal consumers who are purchasing the product and receiving consumer surplus. Further assume that there is a potential marginal consumer who values the product at only $40. Absent the promotional ser-

[25] The increased importance of advertising and distributor promotional efforts has led beer producers, as well as soft drink bottlers, to establish exclusive territory wholesale marketing arrangements for their products.

[26] Goldberg, *supra* note 3, argues that competitive dealers will supply less than the desired level of services, such as shelf space, by drawing an inappropriate analogy between consumers as fish and dealers as fishermen and assuming the existence of an "overfishing" externality. As opposed to their being caught like nonrational fish, however, it is useful to consider consumers as having property rights in themselves and making voluntary utility maximizing decisions in choosing the desired level of services. Moreover, if supplying promotional services such as shelf space is analogous to putting a fishing line into a lake, then dealer "overfishing" is likely to lead to too much shelf space rather than too little.

[27] The following analysis is similar to that provided in William S. Comanor, Vertical Price-Fixing, Vertical Market Restrictions, and the New Antitrust Policy, 98 Harv. L. Rev. 983 (1985). As we shall see, however, Comanor draws incorrect and misleading policy implications.

vices, such as a product demonstration, this marginal consumer will not purchase the product. If a product demonstration that has a total cost of, say, $30 increases the value of the product to the marginal consumer by only $10 and is not valued at all by the inframarginal consumers, the demonstration would not be voluntarily supplied by dealers. The added $50 sale to the marginal consumer will not cover the $30 promotional expenditure. As long as the manufacturer's marginal cost of producing the perfume is less than $15, however, it will pay the manufacturer to have the product demonstration provided because the manufacturer's profit on the additional unit is greater than the $30 cost of the demonstration. In effect, the manufacturer desires to price discriminate in favor of the demonstration-sensitive marginal consumer by having $30 spent to cut the effective price of the product to that consumer by $10.[28]

If the manufacturer were vertically integrated into retailing, this targeted promotion could be accomplished by the direct provision of the desired promotional services free of charge to consumers. Provision of promotional services is more profitable for a vertically integrated manufacturer than increasing sales by decreasing the price of the product because there are different types of consumers. The manufacturer cannot determine ex ante which consumers should receive selective price cuts, and, even if he could, the manufacturer cannot prevent arbitrage between consumers. Therefore, if the manufacturer lowers the price of his product, he must decrease the price for all consumers. However, if the manufacturer supplies promotional services that are of particular value to marginal consumers, this action provides a focused price decrease merely for these consumers.

Marginal consumers who are deciding whether to purchase the manufacturer's product can be thought of as consuming a relatively large fraction of promotional services such as product demonstrations. And, because consumption of product demonstrations entails a time cost, inframarginal consumers who are already purchasing the product are unlikely to consume the promotional services. Alternatively, instead of assuming that marginal consumers have increased consumption rates of the

[28] Subsidization of product promotion as targeted marketing may take many forms. For example, sales effort may be required to convince a consumer contemplating the purchase of a "stripped" standard model that he ought to buy a deluxe model with extra features; or sales effort may be required to convince a consumer to purchase "extra" units of a product. Our analysis of promotional services merely requires a larger effect of the services on any of these margins compared to its effect on units already sold. For simplicity of exposition we refer to particular types of consumers and assume that without the promotional services the marginal consumer will not purchase from the manufacturer at all.

promotional services, the manufacturer can be thought of as supplying promotional services that are public-type goods, such as advertising, displays, or shelf space, which marginal consumers are more sensitive to than are inframarginal consumers. The empirical relevance of the increased sensitivity of marginal customers to promotional services is evidenced by the fact that manufacturers and dealers often provide such services at a zero price. In fact, the underpricing of services to obtain additional sales is almost a definition of promotional services—if the services were priced at cost, they would be considered as part of the product.[29]

In the absence of vertical integration, the manufacturer must adopt a marketing arrangement that assures the supply by dealers of a greater level of promotional services than those dealers would voluntarily supply. The manufacturer accomplishes this by creating an implicit contractual understanding with the dealer whereby the dealer agrees to provide the desired level of promotional services in exchange for a payment from the manufacturer. The contract is implicit because measurement problems prevent the manufacturer and dealer from contracting on the services directly. The payment may be made by the manufacturer with the use of vertical restraints such as an exclusive territory or resale price maintenance arrangement, which creates a dealer price-cost margin sufficient to cover the costs of providing the desired increased level of promotional services. This implies that the manufacturer payment for promotional services is made on the basis of dealer output, which is a good measure of services supplied (if the dealer is selling at the correct price).[30] If insufficient manufacturer-specific dealer investments exist, the manufacturer also must use the vertical restraints marketing arrangement to provide dealers with a premium above the cost of the desired services. In any event, the manufacturer must always monitor dealer performance and terminate dealers who violate the implicit contractual understanding regarding the supply of promotional services.

[29] The underpricing of promotional services cannot be explained by the minimization of transaction costs. In many cases it would be economically feasible for the manufacturer or dealer to charge the customer directly for services such as demonstrations. The charge would not be too small relative to the cost of collection because the services are not cheap to provide, and dealers often do charge for other less expensive items such as shopping bags.

[30] Some dealer services, such as linear feet of shelf space, may appear to be easily measurable, and, therefore, a direct manufacturer contract with the dealer for the supply of these services in return for a per-unit time payment may appear to be possible. The *value* of the services in terms of added manufacturer sales may be difficult to measure, however, and, since value is likely to be closely related to actual dealer sales, an implicit payment based on dealer output frequently is preferred.

VI. The Prevention of Dealer Overcompensation for Promotional Services

There are two general ways in which the dealer can violate the implicit contractual understanding with the manufacturer regarding the supply of promotional services—by supplying fewer services than implicitly contracted for or by increasing the compensation received for the implicitly contracted quantity of services. Consider the first potential violation. Since the payment from the manufacturer for promotional services is in a per-unit output form, dealers will have an incentive to reduce the level of services below the desired level whenever there are diminishing returns to services. The dealer is paid for a desired average level of services per unit sold, but the marginal unit of service desired by the manufacturer produces less than the average increase in sales. As in our perfume example above, the dealer will not have the appropriate incentive to make the $30 expenditure on promotional services necessary to sell the last unit of the product. The dealer is compensated by the manufacturer to make this expenditure, but the compensation is paid on all the dealer's previous sales. When a profit-maximizing dealer reduces services to a level below that desired by the manufacturer, the dealer is overcompensated for the services actually supplied.

The prevention of dealer overcompensation can also explain manufacturer use of exclusive dealing as a complementary marketing device that is used with resale price maintenance and exclusive territory arrangements.[31] For example, consider a marketing arrangement where a manufacturer grants an exclusive territory or area of prime responsibility to dealers in order to create the correct quasi–rent stream that will assure dealer supply of promotional services. Recognizing the distortion of marginal dealer incentives to supply services given the average compensation scheme implied by this arrangement, the manufacturer must monitor dealer performance and terminate dealers who do not supply the desired level of services, that is, dealers who do not fully develop and take advantage of their assigned areas. The manufacturer, however, has only an imperfect measure of what the sales in each territory should be. Therefore, the manufacturer will also monitor the level of promotional services directly, such as the number of salespeople hired by the dealer. These measures will also be imperfect, however, and, because of the manufacturer's "average sales" compensation scheme, dealers will have the incentive to use their promotional efforts to switch marginal consumers to

[31] Overstreet, *supra* note 15, at 84–101, documents the fact that exclusive dealing is frequently employed in conjunction with exclusive territories or resale price maintenance.

other relatively unknown (unadvertised) brands that sell for a lower retail price, but which possess higher dealer margins.

Although competition among manufacturers, including manufacturers of relatively unknown products, for dealer sales effort is desirable, the ability of dealers to obtain double compensation for the same sales effort is undesirable. Dealers are reneging on the implicit contractual understanding with the manufacturer if they first accept payment for desired dealer services with an exclusive territory–maximum resale price or minimum resale price maintenance arrangement, both accompanied by a reduction in the wholesale price, and then do not supply the services but, instead, switch marginal consumers to an alternative product. Exclusive dealing prevents such switching and thereby lowers the required quasi–rent stream necessary to assure dealer performance.

Our explanation for exclusive dealing is distinct from the explanation given by Howard Marvel.[32] Marvel emphasizes the use of exclusive dealing to prevent dealer "free riding" on tangible and intangible manufacturer investments, such as advertising or dealer training, which get the consumer in the dealer's door to begin with. Marvel distinguishes this theory from the conventional textbook view of exclusive dealing, where the practice does not protect manufacturer investments but, rather, is said to encourage dealer sales efforts. Although the Marvel analysis correctly explains the motivation for exclusive dealing in many cases, many of the examples of exclusive dealing more closely fit this conventional textbook view that Marvel rejects.

For example, consider the *Standard Fashion*[33] dress pattern case that Marvel discusses in great detail. Marvel recognizes that manufacturer investments in advertising or dealer training were relatively unimportant in this case and instead emphasizes the manufacturer's investment in pattern designs as the economic rationale for exclusive dealing. He is correct in recognizing that successful patterns could be easily copied by rival manufacturers, but he is incorrect in claiming that exclusive dealing prevents such copying. Exclusive dealing would not prevent established full-line firms from copying the pattern and adding it to their line. Collusion among the established firms would be necessary to prevent such copying. Further, exclusive dealing would not prevent new limited-line firms from copying the pattern unless exclusive dealing also created a barrier to entry.

Instead, consistent with our theory, it appears much more likely that

[32] Howard P. Marvel, Exclusive Dealing, 25 J. Law & Econ. 1 (1982).

[33] Standard Fashion Co. v. Magrane-Houston Co., 258 U.S. 346 (1922).

exclusive dealing encouraged the supply of dealer promotional services for a product with a low marginal cost relative to price. Dealer services were extremely important in the marketing of dress patterns, with the manufacturer-dealer contractual arrangement explicitly specifying that dealers provide a pattern department at a suitable, generally first-floor location, a "lady attendant" to assist customers, and a minimum inventory level.[34] Most important, in addition to the exclusive-dealing requirement, dealers were also subject to resale price maintenance. This suggests that exclusive dealing, by preventing switching, did not prevent free riding on a manufacturer investment but, rather, prevented free riding on the manufacturer's payment scheme for dealer services.

The second general way dealers can violate the implicit contractual understanding with the manufacturer is, not by reducing the level of services they supply to promote the manufacturer's product, but by taking actions that increase the compensation they receive for a given level of services. Since service compensation is made in per-unit output terms, a dealer who keeps the level of services constant but lowers product price and thereby expands his sales will increase his service compensation. The dealer will be overpaid for the level of services provided, and other (non-price-cutting) dealers will be underpaid for the service they provide. Therefore, we can expect the other dealers to cut back their supply of services or perhaps (given fixed costs of handling distribution of a product) to drop the manufacturer's product completely.[35]

The individual dealer who engages in price competition to attract the manufacturer's inframarginal consumers could claim that these consumers do not demand the promotional services. Therefore, even though the dealer's per-unit service level is reduced by the price competition, they could claim that consumers are not harmed. Such dealers are merely arbitraging the manufacturer's targeted promotional services marketing scheme and taking advantage of the manufacturer's decrease in the wholesale price that is necessary to create an appropriate average dealer margin. It makes little economic sense to claim that "competition" merely offers consumers a choice of alternative price and service levels because such unlimited price competition gives inframarginal consumers the ability to pay a price below cost. Although such inframarginal con-

[34] Marvel, *supra* note 32, at 13.

[35] As the Seventh Circuit notes in Valley Liquor, Inc. v. Renfield Importers, Ltd., 678 F.2d 742 (1982), at 744, "If a supplier wants his distributors to emphasize non-price rather than price competition, . . . he will be hostile to price cutters because they will make it harder for his other distributors to recoup the expenditures that he wants them to make on presale services to consumers and on other forms of nonprice competition."

sumers do not demand services and, therefore, are not "free riding" in the standard sense of first shopping at a full-service dealer to receive services before buying the product at a no-service discount dealer, they are "free riding" on full-service retailers in the sense that they are taking advantage of the manufacturer's quasi rent–generating marketing arrangement and lower wholesale price on all units as a mechanism to subsidize the supply of promotional services to the marginal consumers. Such free riding is just as harmful to full-service retailers as the standard type of free riding and, if permitted, could not survive in long-run equilibrium.

This analysis is applicable to a great number of vertical-restraints marketing arrangements. For example, consider the use of resale price maintenance by brand name clothing manufacturers marketing their products through department and specialty stores.[36] The key features of these cases are that the manufacturers have substantial margins and that retail sales effort and shelf space are key determinants of aggregate demand, but that these services are not generally subject to consumer free riding.

An alternative explanation for manufacturer control of dealer distribution is the prevention of consumer free riding on "certification services."[37] According to this alternative explanation, consumer free riding occurs when consumers observe that an authorized brand name department store carries a product and then purchase the product at an unauthorized discount store. The certification services hypothesis implies that we would expect resale price maintenance for new, relatively unknown products where the potential free riding is greatest. Instead, we observe resale price maintenance being used as a marketing technique for many very well known apparel manufacturers who do not appear to require certification services, while relatively unknown, nonbrand name products infrequently employ the price-maintenance marketing technique.

[36] For example, resale price maintenance has been used for the sale of London Fog raincoats, Florsheim shoes, Levi Strauss jeans, Jonathan Logan and Palm Beach sportswear, and Gant shirts. See Overstreet for a list of products subject to Federal Trade Commission resale price maintenance litigation over the 1965–82 period. Overstreet, *supra* note 15, at 84–101. A list of products covered by resale price maintenance during an earlier period can be found in Ward S. Bowman, Jr., The Prerequisites and Effects of Resale Price Maintenance, 22 U. Chi. L. Rev. 825, 833–35 (1955).

[37] See Howard P. Marvel & Stephen McCafferty, Resale Price Maintenance and Quality Certification, 15 Rand J. Econ. 346 (1984); Sharon Oster, The FTC v. Levi Strauss: An Analysis of the Economic Issues, in Impact Evaluations of Federal Trade Commission Vertical Restraints Cases 47 (R. N. Lafferty, R. H. Lande, & J. Kirkwood eds., FTC Bureau of Competition and Bureau of Economics 1984); and Timothy Greening, Analysis of the Impact of the Florsheim Shoe Case, in Impact Evaluations of Federal Trade Commission Vertical Restraints Cases 91 (R. N. Lafferty, R. H. Lande, & J. Kirkwood eds., FTC Bureau of Competition and Bureau of Economics 1984).

Oster attempts to explain this discrepancy by arguing that the Levi Strauss resale price maintenance policy may have been profitable initially when the brand was little known, but that Levi Strauss continued to use the policy when it was no longer profitable. This "mistake" explanation for the existence of resale price maintenance, that is, that the Federal Trade Commission was doing Levi Strauss a favor by bringing action against them,[38] seems extremely implausible. First of all, it suggests that such "mistakes" were coincidentally also being made in the marketing of a great number of other brand name apparel products. Second, contrary to Oster's claim, Levi's were well known long before Levi Strauss adopted resale price maintenance. It was only after Levi Strauss left the Army and Navy stores and moved upscale into major department stores that it adopted resale price maintenance. Resale price maintenance was necessary to enforce the supply of the new higher level of desired dealer promotional services.

The analysis also appears to explain the arrangement adopted by Monsanto in marketing agricultural herbicides to distributors who, in turn, resold the herbicides to retail dealers.[39] Although the Supreme Court correctly recognized that "[t]he manufacturer often will want to ensure that its distributors earn sufficient profit to pay for programs such as hiring and training additional salesmen or demonstrating the technical features of the product, and will want to see that 'free riders' do not interfere,"[40] the standard form of consumer free riding does not appear to have been practiced by Spray-Rite. Monsanto claimed that "Spray-Rite's distributorship had been terminated because of its failure to hire trained salesmen and promote sales to dealers adequately."[41] While Spray-Rite did fail to promote the product, however, it does not appear to have sold to individuals who first obtained the promotional services from another distributor. Instead, Spray-Rite primarily sold at a discount to knowledgeable, large volume customers who did not require the promotional services. While these customers did not obtain services from other distributors, they did take advantage of how Monsanto paid for the supply of such services—by setting a margin at the distribution level "to ensure that its distributors earned sufficient profit to pay for" the services. Spray-Rite and its customers were free riding on this implicit contractual arrangement.[42]

[38] See FTC v. Levi Strauss & Co., D-9081 (July 12, 1978) and subsequent state actions.

[39] *Supra* note 5.

[40] *Id.* at 1470.

[41] *Id.* at 1467.

[42] To avoid this free riding, many manufacturers often handle such large established customers themselves.

When the manufacturer's margin is large and, hence, one is likely to observe the use of vertical restraints as part of an arrangement to insure the supply of promotional services, it is also likely that such arrangements will be efficiency enhancing because the increase in sales to the marginal consumers implies a large increase in producer surplus.[43] Moreover, there may be a substantial increase in consumer surplus to the now inframarginal—previously marginal—consumers who learned about the product and now are receiving substantial benefits.

Against these gains one must trade off any loss in consumer welfare from a potential increase in the price charged previously inframarginal consumers. It is unclear, however, that vertical restraints cause prices to rise for these inframarginal consumers. If promotional expenditures are not marginal costs, the price change will depend solely upon the change in the elasticity of demand at the price charged absent the vertical restraint. Promotional services shift out the demand curve and, therefore, make it more inelastic, increasing the price. Since marginal consumers value the promotional services more than inframarginal consumers, however, the demand curve also becomes flatter and more elastic, decreasing the price.

More importantly, promotional services, especially those dealing with a product's image, are likely to create some value for inframarginal consumers. Further, as the court recognized in *Sylvania,* declaring vertical restraints illegal is not likely to eliminate the promotional services but merely may result in "a shift to less efficient methods of obtaining the same promotional effects."[44] This, in fact, may explain the increase in direct manufacturer advertising of brand name clothing since repeal of the Miller-Tydings and McGuire acts in 1975.[45]

[43] Comanor, *supra* note 27, correctly states that the efficiency criterion is the change in the sum of consumer plus producer surplus but then ignores producer surplus throughout his analysis and concentrates solely on the possibility that consumer surplus may decline. Although he creates a hypothetical example where inframarginal consumers experience a loss of consumer surplus, he fails to trade off this loss with the increase in producer surplus. It certaintly does not follow from his analysis, as he asserts, that vertical restraints on "established" products should be either per se illegal or that manufacturers should have the burden to demonstrate that the restraints have benefitted consumers generally. Such a broad policy conclusion based on an incomplete result derived from a hypothetical example merely reveals Comanor's bias against promotional services. His identical analysis could be applied to a vertically integrated firm supplying such services directly without any vertical restraints.

[44] *Supra* note 1, at 2560 n.25.

[45] Peter B. Pashigian, Demand Uncertainty and Sales: A Study of Fashion and Markdown Pricing (Working Paper No. 49, Univ. of Chicago, Center for the Study of the Economy and the State, 1987) documents that apparel manufacturers in the last decade have assumed more of the promotion function previously carried out by retailers, but he has mistakenly attributed this change to "the reduced cost of contacting customers through the television and print media and the increased cost of using sales people to inform consumers." *Id.* at 13. It is unlikely that any large shift has occurred in these factors over the last ten years.

Independent of legal constraints, the vertical integration solution, where the manufacturer provides desired services directly rather than relying on the dealer to provide the services, is frequently adopted when the manufacturer's margin is very large and the quantity of desired dealer services is also very large and not easily measurable. For example, perfume and cosmetics manufacturers often rent space in a department store and use their own employees to provide product demonstrations.[46] Even when manufacturers do not adopt a vertical integration solution, they often directly supply some of the services by providing racks, displays, and other forms of advertising.[47] In general, the manufacturer will provide services directly when the desired services are a large fraction of the value of the product and a shirking dealer can easily expand output. Under such conditions the premium stream required to prevent dealer shirking may be greater than the manufacturer's possible cost disadvantage of providing the service directly.

VII. Manufacturer Control of the Number and Type of Dealers

A form of promotional services that may be desired by a manufacturer is an increased number of retail outlets, where the use of retail outlets is analogous to other attention-getting promotional devices such as shelf space. Increased outlets, with individual dealers operating at outputs less than their minimum average cost, may be optimal from the manufacturer's perspective when marginal consumers are differentially sensitive to the number of outlets. As with other promotional services, a greater number of retail outlets than would exist in an uncontrolled environment can be supported only by restricting price competition.[48]

An interesting example is automobile marketing, where the manufacturer's margin is large and dealer marginal costs are rising slowly. The marginal cost to a dealer of selling an additional automobile is essentially equal to the manufacturer's wholesale (invoice) price plus dealer inventory and preparation cost. This marginal cost remains essentially flat over a wide range of dealer selling rates. Hence, letting dealers order and

[46] See, for example, FTC v. Germaine Montiel Cosmetiques Corporation, C-3098 (November 19, 1982). This solution is also frequently adopted within a department store for fur retailing, which often entails a significant amount of services.

[47] Esprit and Ralph Lauren are among the brand name clothing manufacturers that build entire "boutiques" in department stores.

[48] This is the "outlets hypothesis" for resale price maintenance presented by Gould & Preston, See J. R. Gould & L. E. Preston, Resale Price Maintenance and Retail Outlets, 32 Economica 302 (1965). A similar argument is also presented in B. S. Yamey, The Economics of Resale Price Maintenance (1954), 49–52. These authors do not explain why dealers cannot get consumers to pay for the manufacturer-desired number of outlets.

receive as many automobiles as they wish, and compete freely on the basis of price, would lead to a small number of very large dealers. But automobile manufacturers do not want the average size of a dealer determined at the point where a dealer's marginal cost finally rises sufficiently to cover the dealer's fixed cost of operation.

Automobile manufacturers cannot use resale price maintenance or exclusive territories to get the larger desired number of dealers in their distribution network. Since the sale of automobiles involves substantial price bargaining and corresponding price differences across customers, and because partial payment is often made in terms of an automobile trade-in, resale price maintenance is not feasible. In addition, given the large value of an individual purchase, consumers are willing to travel significant distances to shop. Therefore, exclusive territories would have to be extremely large to generate the required premium.

Instead of vertical price or territorial restraints, automobile manufacturers rely on a quantity allocation arrangement to maintain "small dealer" quasi rents. Dealers generally cannot obtain unlimited quantities of all models but are allocated automobiles on a formula based on past dealer sales and zone-level sales and on current market conditions. Allocations vary with market demand in order to provide dealers with a normal rate of return on their fixed cost capital investments at a sales rate where price is above the dealer's marginal cost. The allocations change dealer pricing incentives by increasing the dealer's "effective" marginal cost of selling an auto.[49]

In addition to controlling the number of dealers, manufacturers may also want to control the type of dealers who market their products. Manufacturer control of the outlets where consumers may purchase their product is a key element in the marketing of many goods where the manufacturer is concerned about the product's image.[50] Given such concern, the mere existence of the product at a discount dealer destroys some of the product's image.[51] Within this marketing context, resale price mainte-

[49] This arrangement should be distinguished from the complementary attempt by manufacturers to assure that dealers receive a minimum number of automobiles to maintain reasonable inventory levels, thereby preventing "book dealers" from free riding on inventories of full-service dealers. For a description of such standard free-riding problems, see, for example, United States v. General Motors Corp., 384 U.S. 127 (1966).

[50] A Lenox china marketing vice president testified that "we would lose our identity as being a prestige product if every conceivable type of retail outlet were to carry our . . . line." See Victor P. Goldberg, Enforcing Resale Price Maintenance: The FTC Investigation of Lenox, 18 Am. Bus. L. J. 225, 246 (1980).

[51] See, for example, Jacob Jacoby & David Mazursky, Linking Brand and Retailer Images: Do the Potential Risks Outweigh the Potential Benefits? 60 J. Retailing 105 (1984). Jacoby and Mazursky also note that a discount outlet may use a high-end product, even if selling at a nondiscount price, to enhance its own reputation for high quality merchandise.

nance prevents image deterioration by creating a premium stream and, therefore, a potential sanction that prevents the product from being transshipped from an authorized dealer to the discounter.

More generally, such a mechanism is necessary if the manufacturer is to control distribution of its product for whatever reason it desires. For example, if the manufacturer wishes to avoid the standard form of consumer free riding on dealer product demonstrations, and if manufacturer-specific dealer investments do not exist, the manufacturer will not be able to avoid this free riding without a premium stream generated by a vertical restraint. Without such a potential sanction the manufacturer will not be able to prevent transshipping of its product from authorized dealers to, for example, unauthorized free riding telemarketers. This is because once an authorized dealer takes title to a product, the dealer generally can legally sell it to whomever he pleases. A vertical restraint that creates a premium stream gives the manufacturer the ability to control dealer distribution by being able to effectively terminate dealers who transship their product to unauthorized dealers.

VIII. Conclusion

Our framework contrasts with the standard economic paradigm of an optimal, incomplete contractual arrangement, which involves the setting of explicit contract terms so that the direct returns of alternative actions make the incentives of the transacting parties correct. This standard contract does not describe real world contract arrangements. Consider, for example, the employment of a worker. First of all, it is generally recognized that it is uneconomic to create a complete contingent contract to govern the employment relationship. A complete contingent contract entails large transaction costs, rigidities, and hold-up potentials associated with initial contractual negotiation and renegotiation in the face of changing market conditions. In addition, many elements of performance, such as the energy and enthusiasm the worker devotes to a particular task, are essentially unmeasurable (although not unobservable) and must remain unspecified and unenforceable in court.

Once we have an incomplete contract, the question becomes one of how the employer will motivate employees to perform along the contractually unspecified elements of performance. The employer generally will not adopt a contractual arrangement that motivates employees by changing the direct return from performance. For example, if the employer attempts to induce desired behavior along the unspecified dimensions of employee performance by giving each employee a share of the firm's profit, the optimum share would have to equal 100 percent—with offsetting initial lump sum payments by each employee to the employer. This arrangement would create great distortions, including an incentive for the employer to sabotage production (or pay off an individual worker not to perform). In addition, the employer certainly would not want to perform in a manner that results in an unanticipated profit expansion (for example, by introducing a product innovation). It is obvious that one sees incredible contracts like this only in the hypothetical worlds of theoretical economics.

In the real world, an employee is hired or a manufacturer-dealer distribution agreement is made under incomplete contracts, where both the employee and the dealer derive at least part of their motivation to perform well by the threat of termination. Employers police their employees, as manufacturers police their dealers, by observing their behavior and by reserving the option of terminating underperformers. Employers or manufacturers do not attempt to induce worker or dealer performance solely by changing the direct returns from alternative behaviors. Once it is recognized that it is efficient for transactors to adopt a premium-termination enforcement mechanism, the contractual arrangement must be designed to optimally distribute quasi rents between the transacting parties. Vertical restraints, by shifting some rents from the manufacturer to the dealers, have this effect and thereby help to assure dealer performance of unspecified but essential elements of the contractual understanding.

This framework has great explanatory power. In addition to explaining how vertical restraints can induce dealers to supply special services that consumers can obtain free of charge from other dealers, a mechanism for which is lacking in the standard free riding on special services theory, the framework explains dealer supply of services that cannot be detected by consumers before they make a purchase (the *Coors* case) and dealer supply of the desired level of promotional services when there is no consumer free riding (the marketing of branded clothing or the *Monsanto* case). More generally, this framework is applicable to any service that a manufacturer wishes a dealer to perform that is not in the dealer's own short-run self-interest and where an explicit contract cannot be written and enforced.

This analysis may help the public and the courts to understand the important economic role of vertical restraints. Most economists recognize that vertical restraints are usually voluntarily adopted by transacting parties as a way to efficiently distribute products that require point-of-sale services, and that much private litigation surrounding their use actually involves contract disputes rather than antitrust problems. As a logical matter, vertical restraints employed by transactors with no market power cannot be anticompetitive. Nevertheless, it has been difficult to persuade noneconomists that this view, especially with regard to resale price maintenance, is valid. This conclusion remains unpersuasive because an empirically relevant procompetitive explanation for vertical restraints has been missing. In particular, many of the instances of the practice do not correspond with the classic consumer free riding paradigm upon which the standard economic analysis is built. Our theory, which empirically rests not upon consumer free riding but upon a more general desire of the manufacturer that dealers adequately promote its product, corresponds much more closely with reality.

Bibliography

Bowman, Ward S., Jr. "The Prerequisites and Effects of Resale Price Maintenance." *University of Chicago Law Review* 22 (1955): 825–73.

Comanor, William S. "Vertical Price-Fixing, Vertical Market Restrictions, and the New Antitrust Policy." *Harvard Law Review* 3 (1985): 983–1002.

Goldberg, Victor P. "Enforcing Resale Price Maintenance: The FTC Investigation of Lenox." *American Business Law Journal* 18 (1980): 225–58.

Goldberg, Victor P. "The Free Rider Problem, Imperfect Pricing, and the Economics of Retailing Services." *Northwestern University Law Review* 79 (1984): 736–57.

Gould, J. R., and Preston, L. E. "Resale Price Maintenance and Retail Outlets." *Economica* 32 (1965): 302–12.

Greening, Timothy. "Analysis of the Impact of the Florsheim Shoe Case." In *Impact Evaluations of Federal Trade Commission Vertical Restraints Cases,* edited by R. N. Lafferty, R. H. Lande, and J. Kirkwood, p. 91. Washington, D.C.: Federal Trade Commission, Bureau of Competition and Bureau of Economics, 1984.

Jacoby, Jacob, and Mazursky, David. "Linking Brand and Retailer Images: Do the Potential Risks Outweigh the Potential Benefits?" *Journal of Retailing* 60 (1984): 105–22.

Klein, Benjamin. "Transaction Cost Determinants of 'Unfair' Contractual Arrangements." *American Economic Review: Papers and Proceedings* 70 (1980): 356–62.

Klein, Benjamin, and Leffler, Keith B. "The Role of Market Forces in Assuring Contractual Performance." *Journal of Political Economy* 89 (1981): 615–41.

McLaughlin, Andrew. *An Economic Analysis of Resale Price Maintenance.* Unpublished Ph.D. dissertation, University of California, Los Angeles, 1979.

Marvel, Howard P. "Exclusive Dealing." *Journal of Law & Economics* 25 (1982): 1–26.

Marvel, Howard P., and McCafferty, Stephen. "Resale Price Maintenance and Quality Certification." *Rand Journal of Economics* 15 (1984): 346–59.

Mathewson, G. F., and Winter, R. A. "An Economic Theory of Vertical Restraints." *Rand Journal of Economics* 15 (1984): 27–38.

Oster, Sharon. "The FTC v. Levi Strauss: An Analysis of the Economic Issues."

In *Impact Evaluations of Federal Trade Commission Vertical Restraints Cases,* edited by R. N. Lafferty, R. H. Lande, and J. Kirkwood, p. 47. Washington, D.C.: Federal Trade Commission, Bureau of Competition and Bureau of Economics, 1984.

Overstreet, Thomas R., Jr. *Resale Price Maintenance: Economic Theories and Empirical Evidence*. Bureau of Economics staff report to the Federal Trade Commission. Washington, D.C.: 1983.

Pashigian, Peter B. "Demand Uncertainty and Sales: A Study of Fashion and Markdown Pricing." Working Paper No. 49. Chicago: University of Chicago, Center for the Study of the Economy and the State, 1987.

Perry, Martin K., and Groff, Robert H. "Resale Price Maintenance and Foreward Integration into a Monopolistically Competitive Industry." *Quarterly Journal of Economics* 100 (1985): 1293–1312.

Rey, Patrick, and Tirole, Jean. "The Logic of Vertical Restraints." *American Economics Review* 76 (1986): 921–39.

Shapiro, Carl. "Premiums for High Quality Products as Returns to Reputations." *Quarterly Journal of Economics* 98 (1983): 659–80.

Silcock, T. H. "Some Problems of Price Maintenance." *Economic Journal* 48 (1938): 42–51.

Stigler, George. "Price and Nonprice Competition." *Journal of Political Economy* 76 (1968): 149–54.

Taussig, F. W. "Price Maintenance." *American Economic Review,* Suppl. 6 (1916): 170–84.

Telser, Lester G. "Why Should Manufacturers Want Fair Trade?" *Journal of Law and Economics* 3 (1960): 86–105.

Yamey, B. S. *The Economics of Resale Price Maintenance*. London: Pitman, 1954.

Part V
Predatory Pricing

[14]

PREDATORY PRICE CUTTING: THE STANDARD OIL (N.J.) CASE

JOHN S. McGEE
University of Chicago

He [Rockefeller] applied underselling for destroying his rivals' markets with the same deliberation and persistency that characterized all his efforts, and in the long run he always won.—IDA TARBELL.

I. INTRODUCTION

THE purpose of this paper is to determine whether the pre-dissolution Standard Oil Company actually used predatory price cutting to achieve or maintain its monopoly. This issue is of much more than antiquarian or theoretic interest. Settling it is of direct importance to present anti-trust policy. At the very least, finding the facts should aid in defining certain hazy notions that now figure in discussions of monopoly and its control.

The *Standard Oil* case of 1911[1] is a landmark in the development of anti-trust law. But it is more than a famous law case: it created a legend. The firm whose history it relates became the archetype of predatory monopoly.

It is sometimes said that *Standard Oil* was influential because it revealed deadly and reprehensible techniques by which Monopoly on a heroic scale could be achieved and, probably more important, perpetuated. Historians tell us that the facts revealed in *Standard Oil* were in good part responsible for the emphasis that the antitrust laws came to place upon unfair and monopolizing business practices.

Perhaps the most famous of all of the monopolizing techniques that Standard is supposed to have used is local price cutting. Given the bad repute in which monopoly has long been officially held in this country, and the prominence of predatory pricing in *Standard Oil,* it is not surprising that the practice received special attention in the law. Monopoly was not new in 1911, but a predatory giant may have seemed novel. The vision of a giant firm that used a brutally scientific, and completely effective, technique for acquiring and maintaining monopoly must have aroused uncommon concern. Standard was invincible. Anything economists could say about the transience of monopoly must have seemed hopelessly unrealistic in view of the vigor and success with which Standard was said to have prevented entry.

In any case, by 1914, in the Clayton Act, predatory price discrimination was included among a select group of business practices the character or effect of which called for explicit statutory prohibition. The Robinson-Patman

[1] Standard Oil Co. of New Jersey v. United States, 221 U.S. 1 (1911).

amendment of 1936 lengthened the list, but certainly did not weaken the hostility toward local price cutting. Indeed, its legislative history and subsequent interpretation reveal a continuing dread of the device.

Predatory discrimination thus occupies a special and almost unquestioned place in law and economics. This has led to a certain amount of difficulty, especially in connection with the Robinson-Patman Act. Some critics claim that this statute unnecessarily restricts rivalry, thereby softening competition. Yet even the critics apparently fear that if we permit the helpful kind of discrimination we will encourage the lethal kind. Most are obliged to rely on the tenuous standard of intent to distinguish one kind from the other.

This fearful ambivalence, in which the spectre of *Standard Oil* figures prominently, may be responsible for the continuing, and somewhat fruitless, arguments about the proper role of a "good faith" defense under Section 2(B) of the Robinson-Patman Act. It may also account for the popular view that disciplinary price cutting makes cartelization easier and its benefits more lasting. It surely has influenced thinking about small firms that face large rivals.

For these reasons, a re-examination of *Standard Oil* may be worthwhile.

II. Predatory Price Cutting: Some Hypotheses

According to most accounts, the Standard Oil Co. of New Jersey established an oil refining monopoly in the United States, in large part through the systematic use of predatory price discrimination. Standard struck down its competitors, in one market at a time, until it enjoyed a monopoly position everywhere. Similarly, it preserved its monopoly by cutting prices selectively wherever competitors dared enter. Price discrimination, so the story goes, was both the technique by which it obtained its dominance and the device with which it maintained it.

The main trouble with this "history" is that it is logically deficient, and I can find little or no evidence to support it.[2]

A brief examination of the logic of predatory price discrimination is helpful in interpreting the facts. In the beginning, oil refining in the United States apparently was competitive. Necessary capital was relatively slight, because of the modest quality demands imposed by consumer preferences and the primitive technological character of the refining process itself. The number of re-

[2] I am profoundly indebted to Aaron Director, of the University of Chicago Law School, who in 1953 suggested that this study be undertaken. Professor Director, without investigating the facts, developed a logical framework by which he predicted that Standard Oil had not gotten or maintained its monopoly position by using predatory price cutting. In truth, he predicted, on purely logical grounds, that they never systematically used the technique at all. I was astounded by these hypotheses, and doubtful of their validity, but was also impressed by the logic which produced them. As a consequence, I resolved to investigate the matter, admittedly against my better judgment; for, like everyone else, I knew full well what Standard had really done.

finers was evidently large, since the Standard interests bought out more than a hundred of them. Standard Oil was not born with monopoly power: as late as 1870 it had only 10 per cent of the refining business.

The usual argument that local price cutting is a monopolizing technique *begins* by assuming that the predator has important monopoly power, which is his "war chest" for supporting the unprofitable raids and forays. Evidently the technique could not be used until the Standard interests achieved the necessary monopoly power. Similarly, advantages from monopsonistic bargaining[3] would not be available until the buyer attained considerable stature.

A simpler technique did exist, and Standard used it. Unless there are legal restraints, anyone can monopolize an industry through mergers and acquisitions, paying for the acquisitions by permitting participation of the former owners in the expected monopoly gains. Since profits are thus expanded, all of the participants can be better off even after paying an innovator's share to the enterpriser who got the idea in the first place.

Under either competition or monopoly, the value of a firm is the present worth of its future income stream. Competitive firms can be purchased for competitive asset values or, at worst, for only a little more. Even in the case of important recalcitrants, anything up to the present value of the future monopoly profits from the property will be a worthwhile exchange to the buyer, and a bountiful windfall to the seller.

It is conceivable that Standard did not merge to the full size it wanted, but did achieve whatever size was necessary to use predatory techniques to grow the rest of the way. How would it go about using them? Assume that Standard had an absolute monopoly in some important markets, and was earning substantial profits there. Assume that in another market there are several competitors, all of whom Standard wants to get out of the way. Standard cuts the price below cost. Everyone suffers losses. Standard would, of course, suffer losses even though it has other profitable markets: it could have been earning at least competitive returns and is not. The war could go on until average variable costs are not covered and are not expected to be covered; and the competitors drop out. In the meanwhile, the predator would have been pouring money in to crush them. If, instead of fighting, the would-be monopolist bought out his competitors directly, he could afford to pay them up to the discounted value of the expected monopoly profits to be gotten as a result of their extinction. Anything above the competitive value of their firms should be enough to buy them. In the purchase case, monopoly profits could begin at once; in the predatory case, large losses would first have to be incurred. Losses would have to be set off against the prospective monopoly profits, discounted appropriately. Even supposing that the competitors would not sell for

[3] Example: railroad rebates. Although this subject lies outside the present inquiry, I am convinced that the significance of railroad rebates has also been misunderstood.

competitive value, it is difficult to see why the predator would be unwilling to take the amount that he would otherwise spend in price wars and pay it as a bonus.

Since the revenues to be gotten during the predatory price war will always be less than those that could be gotten immediately through purchase, and will not be higher after the war is concluded, present worth will be higher in the purchase case. For a predatory campaign to make sense the direct costs of the price war must be less than for purchase. It is necessary to determine whether that is possible.

Assume that the monopolizer's costs are equal to those of his competitors. The market has enough independent sellers to be competitive. Otherwise the problem of monopolizing it ceases to concern us. This implies that the monopolist does not now sell enough in the market to control it. If he seeks to depress the price below the competitive level he must be prepared to sell increasing quantities, since the mechanism of forcing a lower price compels him to lure customers away from his rivals, making them meet his price or go without customers. To lure customers away from somebody, he must be prepared to serve them himself. The monopolizer thus finds himself in the position of selling more—and therefore losing more—than his competitors. Standard's market share was often 75 per cent or more. In the 75 per cent case the monopolizer would sell three times as much as all competitors taken together, and, on the assumption of equal unit costs, would lose roughly three times as much as all of them taken together.[4]

Losses incurred in this way are losses judged even by the standard of competitive returns. Since the alternative of outright purchase of rivals would have produced immediate monopoly returns, the loss in view of the alternatives can be very great indeed.[5] Furthermore, at some stage of the game the competitors may simply shut down operations temporarily, letting the monopolist take all the business (and all the losses), then simply resume operations when he raises prices again. At prices above average variable costs, but below total unit costs, the "war" might go on for years.

Purchase has an additional marked advantage over the predatory technique. It is rare for an industrial plant to wear out all at once. If price does not cover average variable costs, the operation is suspended. This will often leave the plant wholly intact. In the longer run, it may simply be the failure of some key unit, the replacement of which is uneconomic at the present price level, that precipitates shut-down. In either case, physical capacity remains,

[4] Any assumption that the monopolizer's size gives him sufficient cost advantages rapidly takes us away from a predatory price cutting example and into the realm of so-called natural monopolies.

[5] It must not be supposed that, just because he enjoys profits elsewhere, anyone will be so stupid as to assume that it is costless to use them for anything but the best alternatives.

and will be brought back into play by some opportunist once the monopolizer raises prices to enjoy the fruits of the battle he has spent so much in winning.

All in all, then, purchase would not be more expensive than war without quarter, and should be both cheaper and more permanent. It may at first be thought that predatory pricing more than makes up for its expense by depressing the purchase price of the properties to be absorbed. In effect, this requires that large losses reduce asset values less than smaller losses. This is not at all likely. Furthermore, assuming that the properties in question are economic,[6] it is unlikely that their long-run market value will be much reduced by an artificially low price that clearly will not be permanent. The owners can shut down temporarily, allowing the monopolist to carry all of the very unprofitable business, or simply wait for him to see the error of his ways and purchase. Even if there is widespread bankruptcy, wise men will see the value to the monopolist of bringing the facilities under his control, and find it profitable to purchase them at some price below what the monopolist can be expected to pay if he must. Since the monopolist is presumably interested in profits, and has a notion of the effect of discount factors upon future income, he cannot afford to wait forever. Properties that a would-be monopolist needs to control can be an attractive investment.

Predation would thus be profitable only when the process produces purchase prices that are so far below competitive asset figures that they more than offset the large losses necessary to produce them. One empirical test, for those who suspect the logic, would be to examine prices paid for properties in cases where predatory pricing is alleged to have been practiced.

Some of the most strategic factors to be monopolized may be the skilled managerial and technical personnel of competitors. Reproducing them can be a much more formidable and longer job than the construction of physical facilities. But short of murder, the cost of which can also be expected to be high if undertaken in any quantity, the only feasible way of preventing their embarrassing and costly reappearance is to hire, retire, or share with them. None of these things can be accomplished well or permanently if these people are too much badgered in the process.[7]

There are two other crucial issues that must be examined, the first dealing with the extent to which monopolization is profitable; the second, with the

[6] If they are not, they need not concern us, since their extinction might be expected or welcomed under competition.

[7] "[A]s Mr. Rockefeller and Mr. Archbold testified, most of the concerns which were brought together continued to be operated and managed by the former owners." Brief for the U.S., Vol. 1, at 19.

Further, "There are only a few cases in which the Standard interests, during this period [1872–80], acquired stock in concerns without taking the former owners in as stockholders of the Standard, or bringing them into the combination by leaving them a minority interest in the original concern." Id., at 32.

necessary conditions for its success. Monopolization as such will be carried only so far as is necessary to maximize profits, since it inevitably involves certain expenses of planning, purchase, and rationalization. In the case of a vertically integrated industry the would-be monopolist will choose to monopolize the level that will produce the largest net profit. This requires choosing that one which is both cheapest to control and over which control is likely to endure. If a monopoly can be achieved at the refining level, for example, there is little sense trying to achieve one at the crude oil producing level, or marketing. Standard Oil of New Jersey achieved a refinery monopoly; anything more would have been redundant.[8]

This should not be taken to mean that the monopolist will not care what happens to the other levels; for he has every interest in seeing to it that the other levels are not monopolized by someone else. In marketing, for example, he would prefer that the product be distributed as cheaply as possible, since he can then extract full monopoly revenues from the level in his control. This point is important in interpreting the facts of the *Standard Oil* case.

Obstacles to entry are necessary conditions for success. Entry is the nemesis of monopoly. It is foolish to monopolize an area or market into which entry is quick and easy. Moreover, monopolization that produces a firm of greater than optimum size is in for trouble if entry can occur even over a longer period. In general, monopolization will not pay if there is no special qualification for entry, or no relatively long gestation period for the facilities that must be committed for successful entry.

Finally, it is necessary to examine certain data that are often taken to be symptomatic of predatory price cutting, when in fact they may be nothing of the sort. Assume that a monopolist sells in two markets, separated effectively by transport costs or other impediments to free interchange, and that he has a complete monopoly in both. Elasticity of demand is assumed to be the same in both markets, and monopoly prices are identical. Assume that, for some unknown reason, entry occurs in one market but not in the other. Supplies are increased in the first and price falls; price in the second remains unchanged. There are now two different prices in the two markets, reflecting the existence of alternative supplies in the first. The theory of the dominant firm, maximizing by taking into account the outputs of his lesser rivals at various prices, appears to fit the case. An objective fact-finder discovers that the monopolist is discriminating in price between the two markets. A bad theorist then concludes that he is preying on somebody. In truth, the principle established is only that greater supplies bring lower prices.

[8] This abstracts from any cost reductions that integration may make possible. These have nothing to do with the problem at hand.

See Bork, Vertical Integration and the Sherman Act, 22 U. of Chi. L. Rev. 157 (1954). Standard began producing crude oil in 1889, and by 1898 produced 33 per cent of the total. By 1906, its share declined to 11.11 per cent. Transcript of Record Vol., 19, at 626 (Def. Exh. 266).

Compare this example with another. Assume that we have two separate markets, and that each is in short-run competitive equilibrium with firms earning super-normal returns. Assume that, for some reason, entry takes place in one market but not in the other. Supply increases and price falls in one but not in the other. From this evidence of price changes in both the monopoly and competition examples, the inference is simply that greater supplies lower prices. We should not infer from the price data that either case has anything to do with predatory price-cutting.

To sum up: (1) Predatory price cutting does not explain how a seller acquires the monopoly power that he must have before he could practice it. (2) Whereas it is *conceivable* that someone might embark on a predatory program, I cannot see that it would pay him to do so, since outright purchase is both cheaper and more reliable. (3) Because monopolization by any technique always involves some expense, a firm *qua* monopolizer will carry it to the one securest level in an integrated industry, not to all. (4) Actual variations in prices among markets may be accounted for in terms of variations in demand elasticities, but do not imply or establish that anybody is preying on anybody else.

III. Testing the Hypotheses

The voluminous Record in the Standard Oil of N.J. dissolution suit furnishes a test of these propositions.[9]

The Record shows that Standard established a refining monopoly.[10] Collusion among 100 to 200 different sellers was unstable. Standard achieved its monopoly position through merger and acquisition.[11] Although the Govern-

[9] The Transcript of Record consists of over 11,000 printed pages of exhibits and testimony; Appellants' briefs and oral argument covers more than 900 pages; Appellee's briefs and arguments almost 1300 pages. The full record is thus more than 13,500 pages long. Unless otherwise noted, volume references are to the Transcript of Record.

[10] In 1879, Standard and those concerns "in harmony" with it, apparently refined from 90 to 95 per cent of the U.S. output. See Vol. 6, at 3303. It is not clear just what these data mean. Mr. Archbold testified that in 1870 Standard did about 10 per cent of the refining business in the United States; and that for 1888 Standard's share was probably 75 per cent. Id., at 3246–68. I think that much work remains to be done to determine how Standard's market position really changed over time. See e.g., Vol. 2, at 783–784.

In any case, Standard's position in crude oil production was relatively small; it did very little retailing and did not perform all of its own wholesaling; several major railroads and the pipeline systems of Pure, Tidewater, Texas Co., Gulf, and others competed in the transportation of crude oil. Its strongest position was evidently in refining.

[11] "Q. Had you difficulty before you entered into relations with the Standard Oil Company to make money out of the business? A. The competition was always very sharp, and there was always some one that was willing to sell goods for less than they cost, and that made the market price for everything; we got up an association, and took in all the refiners until some of them went back on us, and that would break up the association; we tried that two or three times." Vol. 6, at 3303.

See also Mr. Rockefeller's interesting testimony on the difficulty of effecting stable conspiracies. Vol. 16, especially at 3074–75.

ment alleged that Standard employed other techniques as well, it concluded that:

Unquestionably the principal means used by the defendants to monopolize and restrain trade and commerce in petroleum has been the combination of previously independent concerns. . . .[12]

. . . Standard acquired 123 refineries (many of which also did a marketing business), 11 lubricating oil works, 24 pipeline concerns, and 64 exclusively marketing concerns; a total number of 223.

Neither did these acquisitions all occur at an early date. about half of them, in number, occurred since 1879, and many important ones between 1890 and 1902. . . .[13]

Of the refineries it acquired, Standard dismantled at least 75, and ultimately produced a greatly increased volume in only 20 separate installations.[14]

1. PRICE CUTTING AGAINST COMPETING REFINERS

Standard's monopoly was in refining. Is there any evidence that predatory price cutting helped to achieve it?[15] To discover whether local price cutting played any part in the many refinery acquisitions made by the Standard interests, I checked the whole Record for testimony about every refinery known to have been bought.[16] Furthermore, I have tried to check every alleged case of local price cutting involving competitive refiners that Standard did *not* buy. I can find few specific references to refiners in connection with allegations that Standard cut prices to drive out competitors. The following are the principal examples, including cases in which the marketing subsidiaries or branches of Standard's integrated competitors were involved. They are certainly the most significant ones.

a) "SUSPECT" CASES INVOLVING ACQUISITIONS

The Cleveland Acquisitions.—During 1871–72 the Rockefeller interests purchased at least 17 Cleveland refineries.[17] I can find no real evidence that predatory price cutting or any other type of coercion figured in the acquisitions. According to Mr. Rockefeller, the consolidation of the Cleveland refineries was a blessing to all concerned, and arose

In a most natural way. . . . We were; [*sic*] neighbors, acquaintances, friends, having had our prosperity there together in the business in the good days; and beginning

[12] Brief for the United States, Vol. 1, at 169.

[13] Reply Brief for the United States, at 62.See Appendix C, Sheets 1–11. [14] Id., at 63–64.

[15] The first problem is to discover which companies were really refiners. Oddly enough, many of the firms mentioned in the record have "Refining Company" as part of their names, but were apparently not refiners at all. One example is Mr. Castle's Columbia Refining Co., wholly a marketing concern. Possibly the owners concluded that customers are better disposed towards marketers who make the products they sell.

[16] Brief for the United States, Vol. 1, Appendices C & D; Vol. 19, at 662–63; Vol. 17, at 3290.

[17] Reply Brief for the United States, Appendix C, Sheet 1.

generally to recognize the changes that were coming, and the lessening of the chance of good returns from the refining business on account of the overproduction of refined oil, or the overproduction of the refinery construction.[18]

On the other hand, Mr. Lewis Emery, Jr., a long-time crude oil producer and refiner from Bradford, Pennsylvania, offered the following hearsay on the subject: "I talked with quite a number of them afterwards, and they said they thought the case was hopeless and they had arranged with the combination."[19]

Predatory price cutting had nothing to do with the acquisitions, according even to Mr. Emery's version. There is some question about Mr. Emery's testimony in any case: Emery was testifying, in 1908, about events that occurred 36 years earlier. Furthermore, he had evidently not been in Cleveland at this time and had no first-hand knowledge of the affair.[20]

There are very good reasons to suppose that no kind of coercion figured in the Cleveland purchases. The stock records and a great deal of testimony confirm that Standard's usual practice during this time was to employ the managers and owners of the firms they absorbed, and often to make them shareholders as well. Victimized ex-rivals might be expected to make poor employees and dissident or unwilling shareholders.

Mr. Emery's Own Experience.—Lewis Emery entered the industry as a crude oil producer in 1865. By 1870 he became interested in the Octave Oil Company and Refinery. In 1875, Emery closed down the Octave, and in 1876 sold it to the Standard interests for $45,000.[21] Emery claimed that the railroad pool agreement of 1874 had squeezed him out along with other small Western Pennsylvania refiners. Predatory price cutting clearly had nothing to do with it.[22]

[18] Vol. 16, at 3065.

[19] Vol. 6, at 2625. According to Emery, the refiners were pushed into consolidation because of the rail rate "preferences" given to Standard in the South Improvement Company program and the succeeding pool agreement of 1874. The South Improvement program apparently never became effective; and the contract of 1874, which Emery said sealed the doom of Pennsylvania independent refiners, simply *equalized* rail freight from Cleveland and Western Pennsylvania refineries. Id., at 2724, 2732. See testimony of Archbold, id., at 3244–45.

[20] Though it does not really prove anything, it is interesting that Emery was first of all a crude producer and like any raw materials supplier had little affection for the monopsony that faced him. He was also a successful politician during a period in which anti-trust had great popular appeal. Id., at 2642.

[21] Id., at 2610, 2640. It was small, and must have been relatively high cost, since Standard dismantled it forthwith.

[22] See Note 19, supra. Apparently even the railroad rebates, which Emery claimed built Standard, were also available to the small refiner:

"[I]n the very early history of the Octave Oil Company, when we were shut down, we went to the railroads and they said they would give us 25 cents rebate. . . . [p]er barrel on oil." Id., at 2772–73.

See also the testimony of Archbold, id., at 3244–45; and Josiah Lombard, an independent: "They gave . . . all shippers over that road a rebate of ten per cent, which we got with others." Vol. 1, at 265. See also note 37, infra.

Whatever his reasons for selling the Octave, Mr. Emery was apparently not discouraged. For, in 1879, Emery and two partners formed Logan, Emery & Weaver, and started a new refinery at Philadelphia.[23] By 1880 the refinery was completed.[24] Nevertheless, he testified, his firm soon had trouble getting empty railroad cars.[25] Seven years later, Logan, Emery & Weaver sold out to Standard.[26] According to Emery, the original cost of the refinery, lands and wharves was $350,000. Standard bought the refinery for $275,000 and promptly dismantled it, though Emery claimed that the plant was "[f]irst class in every sense."[27] He did admit that refinery depreciation was commonly 10 to 15 per cent per annum.[28] Emery said he sold because he could not get crude oil. The problem was, according to Emery, that Standard and the crude oil producers had agreed to reduce crude output after the excessive production of 1887.[29]

Mr. Emery had also been interested in the Equitable Company, which built a crude oil pipeline in 1878, and sold it to the Tidewater interests for $178,000 in 1879. In 1889 Mr. Emery bought a small Bradford refinery for $5,000, commencing business with 250-barrel stills.[30] By 1908, output was 1,500 barrels per day. The Emery Manufacturing Company at Bradford, Pennsylvania thus had a much-enlarged refinery worth $250,000 to $400,000 and gathering lines worth $200,000. Sales had expanded from about $20,000 per year to between $480,000 and $600,000 per year. Standard's "predatory" tactics, if there were any, had apparently neither discouraged nor ruined Mr. Emery's own business.[31]

[23] Mr. Emery was by this time a member of the Pennsylvania Legislature and remained in office for 10 years thereafter. Vol. 6, at 2642.

[24] Interestingly enough, Mr. Emery had borrowed $25,000 from—of all people—the Standard Oil Company. Id., at 2643.

[25] Id. General rail car shortages were not infrequent during this period. Some oldtimers indicated that certain rail centers attracted refiners because they typically provided plenty of empty freight cars.

[26] Id., at 2645.

[27] Id., at 2646. Emery asked $750,000 for the refinery, but accepted $275,000. Id., at 2768. Emery thought the plant was worth the money, "[b]ecause we had a large export trade, what independent refineries there were, and a very good opportunity to make a margin on our oils if we could get them there at the same price the Standard Oil Company did." Id.
It is not clear whether Standard bought only the refinery for $275,000 or refinery, wharves, and real estate.

[28] Id., at 2738.

[29] Id., at 2646. It seems strange that Standard, a large net purchaser of crude oil, would acquiesce in any scheme to increase the price of its principal raw material. In any case, abortive crude oil producers' cartels attempted, from time to time, to monopolize and shut in wells. See testimony of Rockefeller on the 1872–74 shut down. Vol. 16 at 3073 et seq.; also testimony of Tarbell, Vol. 3, at 1430.

[30] With a probable daily output of 90 to 150 barrels.

[31] Vol. 6, at 2769–70.

Furthermore, Emery became president of the United States Pipeline Company, which, in 1891, constructed a crude oil pipeline. The United States Pipeline Company later sold out to the Pure Oil Company.[32] When Emery sold the company, he took about $100,000 in Pure Oil Company stock, and retained a $15,000 interest in U.S. Pipeline. By 1893, Standard had bought a four-tenths interest in the United States Pipeline, but Emery and his colleagues frustrated their efforts to vote the stock.[33] In 1908, Emery's Philadelphia refinery had a capacity of 2,000 barrels per day, and his other oil interests were extensive. Emery clearly had a successful career, an important part of which consisted of selling companies to Standard and others. However rough the competitive storm may have been, Emery certainly weathered it well.

Emery's sole allegation of local price cutting concerns his Philadelphia marketing business, which he ultimately leased to Pure Oil Co. He admits he did not know who really started the Philadelphia price war.[34]

Holdship & Irwin.—In 1878 this Allegheny, Pennsylvania firm, with an output of 1,000 barrels of products per day, leased their refinery to Standard for 5 years.[35] Under the lease, the partners continued to run the refinery for Standard on a salary basis till 1883, when the lease expired and Holdship & Irwin resumed operation on their own account.[36] In 1886, they sold the refinery to Standard, with the understanding that they would not go back into the oil refining business. Mr. Irwin's testimony does not indicate that Standard used coercion of any kind.[37]

The Empire Oil Works, and the Globe Refining Co.—In 1875 or 1876, Mr. David P. Reighard started the Empire Oil works in Pittsburgh. When Holdship & Irwin sold in 1886, Reighard also sold out to Standard.[38] Reighard stayed out of the oil business till 1887, when he built the Globe Refining Company at Pittsburgh.[39] He ran the Globe for 18 to 20 months, then sold out to Standard again. At the same time, Mr. Reighard sold a large Phila-

[32] Emery summed up Pure Oil's business by saying that "Their money has been principally made in the production of crude oil." Id., at 2718. According to Emery, Pure Oil's sales rose at least 15 per cent to 20 per cent between 1900 and 1908; dividends were 8 per cent per annum.

[33] Id., at 2659–60.

[34] Id., at 2668–69. Emery did admit that he had cut Standard's prices, at 2785 ff.

[35] Id., at 3013—Testimony of Lewis Irwin.

[36] Id., at 3014.

[37] Id. Irwin's testimony is also interesting on other grounds. (1) He claims that Standard accomplished considerable economies of scale. Id., at 3022. (2) In the period 1872–74, when both the railroad and oil industries were overbuilt and "demoralized," everyone in the oil business was getting rail freight rebates ("drawbacks"). In Irwin's words, "There were drawbacks and drawbacks within drawbacks. . . . Everybody got drawbacks in those days." Id., at 3026–27.

[38] The Empire and Holdship & Irwin were co-owners of a pipeline system. Id., at 3131.

[39] It had 12 crude stills, each of 600 barrels capacity, and some pipelines. Id., at 3134.

delphia refinery, which he was in the process of building.[40] The sale was no occasion for sadness, for as Mr. Reighard put it:

> Well, the reason I sold out was I found that the bonus that I asked those people (the Standard Oil) was as much as I could actually make on the profits for 15 or 20 years to come. [41]

Reighard sold for $1,224,800 in trust certificates and $50,000 cash.[42] Each of the last two refineries that Reighard sold to Standard had cost between $200,000 and $250,000. Thus it was that Mr. Reighard managed to build and sell three refineries to Standard, all on excellent terms.

Woodland Oil Company (Mr. C. J. Castle).—Mr. Castle was an important government witness on predatory price cutting and other unfair competition. He had been an oil refiner, and was still a marketer of petroleum products when he testified. At this point we will deal only with Mr. Castle's early role as a refiner who sold out to the Rockefeller group.

In 1883, Mr. Castle and a partner started the Woodland Oil Company, a small Cleveland refinery.[43] They began with $8,000 to $10,000 capital. By 1886, book capital was $14,000, and Woodland sold to the Rockefeller interests for the same amount. Castle implied that one reason he sold was inability to get crude oil from the Standard Oil pipeline. But he did not allege that predatory price cutting played any part in the sale, and did not feel aggrieved at the price Standard paid for his property.[44] Indeed, after selling the refinery, he went to work for Standard and remained in their employ for about 14 years.

Castle told several other stories about Standard's predatory price cutting during the period in which he worked for them.[44a] Nevertheless, I think it is significant that when he left Standard in 1900 he was clearly unafraid: he immediately started a rival oil marketing firm.

The Rocky Mountain Oil Company.—Mr. E. M. Wilhoit's brief but pointed version of this affair clearly implies intent and ability to crush out competition. Wilhoit was employed by Standard at the time this incident took place, and claimed to know something about it. In his words,

[40] Id., at 3136.

[41] Id., at 3135.

[42] "Well, they didn't want us to take any certificates at all. . . . I forced them, or went after them several times till I got them to give me some certificates." Ibid. The value given for the trust certificates was par value. Market value was higher. Vol. 17, at 3332. The Government gives the "competitive value" of the two Reighard properties as $823,000. Reply Brief for the United States, Appendix C, Sheet 8.

[43] Capacity: 200 barrels per day. Vol. 6, at 3060. By 1908, capacity of Standard's Whiting, Indiana refinery was 25,000–30,000 barrels per day.

[44] Id., at 3029.

[44a] The relevant anecdotes are analyzed in the Marketing section of this paper.

Before the Refinery got in operation, the Standard Oil made our fight on the Rocky Mountain Company and the Union Pacific went into the hands of a receiver and the Refinery was afterwards dismantled—went broke of course.[45]

On the surface, this incident is the nearest thing to predatory price cutting that I found in the Record. But there are reasons to suppose that there was something more here than meets the eye.

First, it is interesting that no complaint from the Rocky Mountain interests appears in the Record. Second, Continental—the Standard Company in the area—had entered into an agreement with the Florence Oil and Refinery Company and the United Oil Company, both located at Florence, Colorado.[46] Under the agreement, the two refiners sold their whole output of refined products to Continental. Prices were presumably attractive to the refiners, though, in view of the almost complete marketing monopoly of Standard in the area, quantities taken must have been limited.[47]

The United commenced refining oil about 1887 or 1888.[48] Sometime after Florence and United entered into the exclusive arrangement with Continental, shareholders of United and Florence started the Rocky Mountain Company at Pueblo, Colorado. A price war with Continental ensued. About 1894, after some two years of conflict, Rocky Mountain sold its crude oil properties to Western Oil Company, a producing subsidiary of United and Rocky Mountain. It is not clear what happened to the refinery itself, except that Rocky Mountain no longer ran it.[49]

What does this episode mean? Although the facts are not as ample as we would like, there is one hypothesis that is both logical and wholly consistent with what facts we do have: Standard had marketing facilities in the area, but no local supplies. Standard's refined products had to be brought in from Whiting, Indiana. The United-Florence interests had crude oil and refinery capacity. There may have been other competing refiners in the market as well.

Standard agreed to take certain quantities of refined products from United-Florence, at specified prices, in return for which the refiners agreed not to sell to anyone else. A restricted refinery output could be better for all concerned. But to get it, Standard would have to share monopoly gains with the refiners.

[45] Vol. 3, at 1216. The Government's position runs less to intent and causes, and more to a history of events. For, in Volume 2 of Brief for the United States, at 157, the Government says: "parties connected with the United Company undertook to establish another refinery known as the Rocky Mountain . . . a violent price-cutting competition started in between the Standard's marketing company, the Continental, and this company . . . the Rocky Mountain Company failed and went out of business."

[46] Standard later came to own 17 per cent of the stock of the United. Ibid. This may raise certain questions of minority shareholders' interests.

[47] The government claimed that a little over 1 per cent of the market was supplied by independents and "the marketing of oil in this territory is extremely profitable." Ibid.

[48] Vol. 1, at 155.

[49] Id., at 181.

In that way duplication of marketing facilities and refining capacity could be avoided.

In this case, as in other such sales arrangements, there must have been a temptation for the producers to sneak out a little more output on the side, in violation of the agreement, and thereby make supernormal returns on a larger output. That would be the best of all possible worlds: the monopoly price could be gotten from Standard on a limited quantity; in addition, a larger amount could be disposed of, on the side, at higher than competitive prices. Since United and Florence had an agreement with Standard for limited quantities, one way to chisel or to work their way into a larger share of the cartel profits would be to start a new firm. This they did in the form of the Rocky Mountain Company. Mr. Wesley H. Tilford, Treasurer of the Standard Oil Company of New Jersey, explained the purpose of Rocky Mountain in these words:

> They were not satisfied with the interest in the United and they built another refinery to take part of their own business.[50]

Mr. Henry M. Tilford, President of Continental since 1893, confirmed and elaborated Wesley Tilford's recollection of the incident:

> Early in 1891 or 1892 Mr. Daniel Eells came to our office, and had an interview with W. H. Tilford and myself in which he stated that he and some friends proposed to build a refinery in Colorado, and asked if the Continental Oil Company would take their output. He was told the Continental Oil Company was getting from the Florence Oil and Refining Company and the United Oil Company all the oil they could market in that vicinity. Some little time afterwards he came back to the office and said that the refinery had been built, and asked again if the Continental Oil Company could take the output, and he was advised that they could not, that the situation was the same as it was before. . . . They commenced business and they commenced cutting prices.[51]

What happened after the reabsorption of Rocky Mountain is also consistent with the cartel hypothesis: The refiners *raised* the prices of refined products to Continental. Whatever their object, then, the net result was that United and Florence apparently emerged from the conflict with more favorable contract terms *vis a vis* Standard.[52] Tilford did not regard Rocky Mountain as having failed, but simply as having been reabsorbed by those who started it.[53]

With the passage of time, more refineries were built in the Rockies. By 1907, when Mr. Henry Tilford testified, refineries had been built in Sugar Creek and Evanston, Wyoming; Spring Valley, and Boulder, Colorado. At

[50] Id., at 156.

[51] Vol. 2, at 730–31.

[52] It may be that the cartel had more refiner members than United and Florence, for Tilford said "there were other people in the oil business selling oil to the Continental, and indirectly it affected them, of course." Vol. 1, at 177, and see also 180.

[53] Id., at 181.

least two, those at Spring Valley and Boulder, were independent, and built between 1905 and 1906.[54] This suggests either that memories are short; or that those who were familiar with the episode did not regard the Rocky Mountain incident as a case of predatory price cutting.

The 1895 Purchases.—James W. Lee, Vice President and Director of Pure Oil, testified that in the 1890's a group of Pennsylvania refiners sent emissaries to Standard to moderate the "destructive competition" that plagued them.[55] Standard offered to purchase their pipelines and facilities, for cost plus 12 per cent. Whether for those terms or not, some of the group sold out, including Mr. Ramage.[56] It is interesting that none of those who sold out came forward to testify that they had been abused in any way.

Most did not sell, but banded together and formed the Pure Oil Company in 1895.[57] Pure Oil thus became the largest independent oil company in the United States. It was also a profitable one.[58]

Although Lee did not allege local price cutting, he claimed that Standard had squeezed the independent refiners by bidding up the price of crude oil in 1895.[59] As it turns out, however, since Standard was actually buying 90 per cent of the crude oil in question, such a maneuver would have cost Standard a great deal more than those it was seeking to punish.[60]

The Argand Refining Company.—In spite of having "the regular severe competition of the Standard all the way through,"[61] this refinery was a profitable business. It earned "a little over $35,000" a year, net, with 600 barrel still capacity and $50,000 beginning capital.[62] Dividends were paid regularly at the rate of 2½ per cent per quarter.

Argand included among its stockholders several railroad officials.[63] According to Cram,

[54] Vol. 2, at 731–32.

[55] Vol. 6, at 3169–70. Lee did not refer to local price-cutting as a factor.

[56] Ramage evidently took some Standard stock, for he appears on the Standard stockholder lists. Messrs. Fertig and Burwell also sold.

[57] Consistent with logic, but not with a theory of predation, are Standard's persistent efforts to buy stock control in Pure Oil Company affiliates. Vol. 6, at 3176–79.

[58] Id., at 3191.

[59] Id., at 3192–93.

[60] Id., at 3192–3194. Apart from this elementary fact, quite acceptable and logical alternative explanations were given.

[61] Testimony of Cram, Volume 3, at 1349. Earlier he had said: "Not anything more than ordinary competition in their business, I should judge. . . . Well, I cannot say they cut on us particularly; they were a larger concern than we were and we followed their prices." Vol. 5, at 2422.

[62] Vol. 3, at 1351. At that time, a still would be "run off" about once every two or three days at best. This would have made a 200 barrel per day output, or 73,000 barrels per year without allowance for down time and "turnarounds." Actual output was probably lower. See Vol. 5, at 2419–20.

[63] Vol. 3, at 1349.

> There were no threats as to what they [Standard] would do if we didn't sell out. Our railroad stockholders became convinced that we would lose our railroad business, from which we derived half of our net profit.[64]
>
> The refinery was finally disposed of [to Standard] on a lease basis for $20,000 a year, for a period of ten years. It was afterwards adjusted on a cash basis on which our stockholders, on which the company, got $180,000.[65]

Predatory price cutting obviously had nothing to do with the sale.[66]

Scofield, Shurmer and Teagle.—This firm was one of the last large refiners purchased by Standard before its dissolution. SS&T had a refinery at Cleveland,[67] and sold about 200,000 barrels of refined products a year in Michigan, Illinois, Indiana, Iowa, Nebraska, Kansas and Missouri.[68] SS&T and Standard were old rivals, and had several clashes over the years. In 1876 Standard and SS&T ended one competitive struggle by signing a market-sharing contract. Under its terms Standard guaranteed a minimum profit to SS&T, in exchange for output limitation; and shared additional profits in specified proportions.[69] But in 1880, SS&T broke the contract, and, when Standard sought to enforce it, denounced the instrument as a tool of an unlawful monopoly.[70]

Nevertheless, when SS&T sold out, Walter Teagle joined Standard, as did the old staff. According to Walter C. Teagle, son of the head of SS&T, Standard continued to employ all but three SS&T employees after the acquisition.[71] Standard operated the SS&T facilities under the style of Republic Oil Company till about 1905.[72] Claims that Standard operated SS&T as a "bogus independent" only strengthen the hypothesis that there was no coercion surrounding the sale. For it is impossible to keep a secret when those who must be relied on to keep it can injure their enemies by betraying it.

[64] Id., at 1350. About half of the $200,000 capital stock was held by officials of the B&OSW and the Marietta & Columbus Northern Railroads. These railroads bought about one-fourth or one-fifth of Argand's output.

[65] Id., at 1352. The sale apparently was consummated in 1897. Cram agreed to stay out of the oil business, as did some others. Vol. 5, at 2424.

[66] It is curious that in his much earlier testimony Cram did not mention the possible loss of railroad business as a factor in the sale. Whereas in his later testimony he is not really hostile to Standard, and certainly does not claim local price cutting, Cram seems less happy with the sale. Perhaps he came to regret it. One possibility is that Cram felt aggrieved when the ample "stand-by" salaries Standard paid the managers under the original settlement gave way to a cash settlement to stockholders.

[67] According to Teagle, "We had a refinery at Cleveland, but the refinery at Cleveland was old and out of date, and the capacity of it was limited as compared with the sales end of our business. I don't suppose we refined, during the years immediately previous to our sale, over 35 to 40 per cent of the refined oil products that we sold. Cleveland had ceased to be a refining center." Vol. 3, at 1467.

[68] Id., at 1468. [69] Vol. 16, at 3204. [70] Id., at 3205.

[71] Vol. 3, at 1150. SS&T sold out in 1901. Id., at 1153. After the dissolution Mr. Teagle became president of Standard Oil of New Jersey.

[72] Id., at 1153 ff.

In any case, there is no evidence that predatory price cutting had anything to do with the SS&T acquisition, or with the terms on which Standard purchased it.[73]

Summary.—The record does not indicate that predatory price cutting forced any refiner to sell out. The only doubtful case is that of the Rocky Mountain Company and, in my opinion, this incident is no exception to the rule. Furthermore, there is no evidence that predatory price cutting was used to depress asset value of any of the more than one hundred-twenty competitive refineries that Standard bought.[74] So far as I can make out, Standard's purchase terms were generally very good, and sometimes lavish. Abstracting from purchases, the mortality rate in refining was evidently low after Standard achieved a monopoly position.

b) "SUSPECT" CASES THAT DID NOT RESULT IN MERGER OR PURCHASE

There remains the possibility that Standard used local price cutting to drive rival refiners to the wall without purchasing them. Perhaps Standard, without having to buy them out, simply exterminated them.

The following integrated refining firms at one time or another had local, or general, clashes with Standard. Standard did not buy, or merge with, any of these firms. Testimony about these incidents was often vague, which is not too surprising in view of the very long period covered.[75] There is also a large amount of pure hearsay, and many facts were hotly controverted.

Fehsenfeld (The Red C Interests).—Mr. W. H. Fehsenfeld was president of the Red C Oil Manufacturing Co. of Baltimore.[76] Red C was a marketing company, but Fehsenfeld was also president of Island Petroleum, a refiner.[77]

Fehsenfeld testified that up to about 1897, Red C and Standard competed in the South in the sale of barreled refined products. After 1897, Standard relied increasingly upon the tank wagon method of distribution. Red C continued to emphasize barrel distribution.[78] According to Fehsenfeld, Standard

[73] One independent oil man made the following observation about SS&T: "They had a plant that they maintained and they maintained it until they *succeeded* in selling out to the Standard." Vol. 2, at 987. (Italics supplied.)

There is no real evidence that the "bogus" Republic waged predatory price cutting campaigns, either. See testimony of Crenshaw, for example, on the amicable settlement of one price cutting flurry in 1902: Vol. 3, at 1173–74.

[74] See Mr. Lombard's testimony on the "very fair" prices Standard paid the refiners it bought out. Vol. 1, at 250.

[75] Testimony covered the period 1865 through 1908.

[76] Vol. 5, at 2302.

[77] Id., at 2330. Fehsenfeld was also President of the Columbia Oil Co., and Vice-President of both the Georgia Oil Co. and the Richmond Oil Co. All but Island were marketing companies. Island owned stock in the various marketing companies.

[78] Red C did sell by tank wagons in and around Baltimore, and had various commission agents and jobbers over the country.

systematically offered price inducements to merchants to prevent Red C from making up carload shipments of 60 barrels, and sometimes induced Red C customers to countermand their orders.[79]

At one time or another, Red C faced competition from five different "bogus independents" operated by Standard.[80] According to Fehsenfeld, "[T]hey sold regardless of price, in order to secure our business. . . ."[81] On some occasions, at least, Red C clearly started the price cutting. Indeed, Red C evidently employed price cutting whenever it served their interests. As Fehsenfeld explained:

> I did certainly cut the price in order to get the business. . . . As occasion was necessary; that is to say, *in going into a territory we would have to offer some inducement*. . . . Sometimes I would sell—it would depend entirely upon the quality of the oil—at prices lower than the Standard or sell at prices higher than the Standard.[82]

According to C. T. Collings, Second Vice-President of the Standard Oil Company of Kentucky, Red C had always been a price cutter. Standard, on the other hand, found price cutting an unattractive policy. In Collings' words,

> Red C . . . had a way every once in a while of sending out one or two men, rushing them around over the South Carolina Field, and making up carload orders by cutting our prices from a half to one and a half cent a gallon. . . . we had lost quite a good deal of business in years gone by by this system. . . . As you will see here in every one of those letters where their prices are mentioned, they are from half a cent to a cent and a half below our price. . . . We didn't go down to their very low prices, except, I believe, in one case, and that was at Union, South Carolina. . . . We do not initiate the cut. We rely on our having been the pioneers in establishing the business, serving the trade with good oil in the most-up-to-date manner, and that if a competitor comes in there to get our business he must necessarily cut the price or offer some inducement in order to wean the trade away from us. Therefore, it is not necessary for us to cut prices.[83]

Although he said that thirty years of competing with Standard were hard, Fehsenfeld acknowledged that the Red C interests had grown steadily and prosperous since their modest beginning in 1878.[84] Before 1903, Standard twice tried to purchase the Red C group but failed.[85]

[79] Id., at 2303.

[80] Id., at 2311.

[81] Id., at 2319.

[82] Id., at 2341. (Italics supplied).

[83] Vol. 12, at 895–96. See also Vol. 13, at 1536–37. There is a great deal of corroborating testimony. See, for example, Vol. 13, at 1306 et seq., 1322 et seq., 1362 et seq., 1364–65, 1440. The Record is liberally sprinkled with evidence, and anecdotes of competition between Red C and Standard. For example, see Vol. 5, at 2303, 2307, 2310, 2313, 2316, 2406–9, 2476; Vol. 10, at 1747–58, 1760–1775; Vol. 12, p. 913; Vol. 13, at 1110–13, 1139–44, 1158 et seq., 1167, 1239, 1250, 1305–07; Vol. 15, at 2443–44; Vol. 20 at 100–101, 146–48, 152–3, 156–68, 212 et seq. In fact, much of Volumes 13 and 20 concerns this rivalry.

[84] Vol. 5, at 2333. Island was organized in 1901, when Red C integrated "backwards" into refining. Id., at 2337. Island owned the controlling interest in the Richmond Oil Co.

[85] Id., at 2329.

Cornplanter Refining Company.—Founded about 1888, Cornplanter was an old rival of Standard. Although there was a good deal of hearsay about Standard "attacking" Cornplanter over the years, it is clear that from time to time Standard and Cornplanter entered into agreements to avoid competition.[86] Mr. Todd, Cornplanter's Manager, testified that Standard had threatened Cornplanter with extinction, but that it never materialized.[87] Cornplanter was a Warren, Pennsylvania refiner, but, among other places, also sold in the St. Paul area.[88] The Manager of Standard's Whiting refinery told Todd that Cornplanter was selling too much kerosene in the St. Paul territory, and that if they did not agree to reduce output and regulate sales, Standard would run them out of business. Mr. Todd understood well the economics of local price cutting, for, as he testified:

> Well, I says, "Mr. Moffett, I am very glad you put it that way, because if it is up to you the only way you can get it [the business] is to cut the market, and if you cut the market I will cut you for 200 miles around, and I will make you sell the stuff," and I says, "I don't want a bigger picnic than that; sell it if you want to," and I bid him good day and left.[89]

The Standard threat never materialized.

Todd also testified that about 1898 a Standard Oil executive told him Standard's policy was to put all independents out of business.[90] Standard then launched a price-cutting war against Cornplanter in New York. Todd said Standard started it, but acknowledged that Cornplanter had started a price-cutting campaign around Boston.[91] The "war" was costly to both sides, and they entered into a market-sharing agreement for the Boston territory. Prices rose "from $6\frac{1}{2}$ to 10 cents in a very few days, and they remained there for a long time."[92] The agreement, first for three years and later renewed for five, remained in effect until about 1906. At that time, Cornplanter sold its Boston distribution facilities to the Gulf Refining Company, an aggressive independent concern.

Todd testified to other conflicts,[93] and still other agreements,[94] with Standard. In spite of their difficulties with Standard, Cornplanter's capital had

[86] See, e.g., Vol. 6, at 3209 et seq.

[87] Id., at 3212.

[88] Id., at 3213.

[89] Id., at 3214, and also at 3227.

[90] Id., at 3215–16.

[91] Id., at 3216. Cornplanter's gallonage trebled in Boston. Id., at 3231.

[92] Id., at 3217. Cornplanter had acquired the Boston facilities when it bought out the New England Oil Company about 1897. Id., at 3228, 3230.

[93] Id., at 3220–21. See also testimony of Hopkins, Vol. 3, at 1030 about cutting Standard's prices.

[94] Vol. 6, at 3207–8, 3220, 3223–28.

grown, in the twenty years of its existence, from $10,000 to $450,000. Todd admitted that they were still alive and, indeed, very healthy.[95]

Crew-Levick.—Crew-Levick had several refineries.[96] George J. Wolff, Baltimore manager, testified that a Standard "bogus" concern had waged war on them. Wolff admitted that he sometimes cut Standard's prices in Baltimore,[97] and acknowledged that Standard, whatever its motives, hadn't been able to kill Crew-Levick:

Q. You don't think you need any guardian for carrying on business against the Standard Oil Company, do you?
A. No, by gosh! I don't.[98]

Crew-Levick had apparently done well in Baltimore, for as Wolff testified:

Q. From 1904 until recently you had a pretty steady increase, haven't you?
A. Yes, sir. The day I took charge I only sold 400 gallons, and that was all my own.
Q. And that would be about 2,000 gallons a week?
A. Yes.
Q. And now you sell about 20,00 gallons a week?
A. Yes, Sir.[99]

Some Other Refining Companies.—Defendant's Exhibit 277[100] indicates that in 1908 there were 123 independent refineries in the United States. Some were undoubtedly very small; some were not. The list includes firms which are major companies today and which were substantial even then. Pure Oil, Tidewater, Gulf, The Texas Company, Sun Oil Company, and Union Oil are perhaps the outstanding examples. By 1908, the Texas Company had a refinery of 12,000 barrels per day capacity; Gulf had two: one of 10,800, another of 41,600 barrels per day.[101] Pure, Tidewater, Gulf, and Texas each had large crude oil pipeline systems.

Standard owned about 31 per cent of Tidewater's common stock, and had various agreements with that firm.[102] It also owned a substantial interest in the Pure Oil pipeline affiliate, but never achieved control.

There always had been some competing refiners.[103] At least 10 independent

[95] Id., at 3221. Cornplanter had numerous other oil interests as well. Id., at 3232 et seq. They marketed under several names, including Tiona Oil.
There are many references to the competition of Cornplanter and Standard. See, e.g., Vol. 20, at 45, 61–62, 114; Vol. 6, at 3213–18; Vol. 15, at 2383–87; Pet. Exh. 635.

[96] See Vol. 20, at 105–106. Interestingly enough, they were operated under different names: Crew-Levick, The Glade Oil Works, The Muir Works, The Seaboard Oil Works.

[97] See, e.g., Vol. 20, at 118 et seq., 122, 126, 131. See also Vol. 16, at 2612 et seq.

[98] Vol. 20, at 126. [99] Id., at 109. [100] Vol. 19, at 662–63.

[101] A 40,000 barrel per day refinery is of quite respectable size even today, and very large for its time. Testimony of Emery, Vol. 6 at 2704, 2710–12.

[102] See e.g., Archbold's testimony, Vol. 17, at 3321.

[103] Vol. 1, at 243–44; Vol. 3, at 1467; Vol. 5, at 2542; Vol. 6, at 2626, 2642, 2705, 3015, 3131, 3132; Vol. 16, at 3139; Vol. 17, at 3446; Vol. 20, at 31.

refineries which were built before 1890 were in continuous operation through 1908,[104] By 1895, there were 38 competing refineries.[105] By 1906, the figure had grown to 123.[106]

The Pure Oil Company, formed in 1895, is only one example of the growth and prosperity of independent refiners.[107]

Refining: Summary.—I can not find a single instance in which Standard used predatory price cutting to force a rival refiner to sell out, to reduce asset values for purchase, or to drive a competitor out of business. I do not believe that Standard even tried to do it; if it tried, it did not work.

Standard bought many firms, and paid well to get them. Its purchases continued pretty much up till dissolution, and were apparently necessary to preserve the monopoly position it had built. In addition to purchasing many competitors, Standard entered into market-sharing and price-fixing agreements with still others.[108]

From the beginning of Standard's power, and throughout the period of its greatest strength, new firms sprang up and prospered; old firms survived and grew.

2. PRICE CUTTING INVOLVING JOBBERS AND RETAILERS

It is significant that far and away the largest amount of testimony about price cutting concerns the jobbing and retail levels. Most of the firms alleged to have been involved in price cutting by Standard were non-integrated marketers; the bulk of them were retail merchants and peddlers. Marketing affiliates of competing refiners have already been discussed.

Oil marketing, though different from what we know today, was changing. Before about 1890, refiners sold most of their products in barrels to jobbers, who then distributed the product locally.[109] About that time Standard began "tank wagon" delivery to grocers and other retailers. Under that system, Standard set up bulk stations to which it shipped barrels or tank cars of products, and from which it sent out tank-wagons to serve retailers directly. A tank wagon was just what the name implies: a horse-drawn wagon with a

[104] Vol. 5, at 2542; Vol. 6, at 2651, 2705, 2840, 3015, 3061, 3207; Vol. 20, at 106–107.

[105] Vol. 6, at 2690–2712.

[106] Vol. 2, at 651; Vol. 5, at 2543–45; Vol. 6, at 2691, 2700, 2704, 2710, 2711–12; Vol. 8, at 1002 (Pet. Exh. 396); Vol. 17, at 3290; Vol. 19, at 627 (Def. Exh. 269), 662; Brief For Appellants, Vol. 1, Appendix III, at 266.

For the more rapid growth of competition in the export trade, see Vol. 8, at 904 (Pet. Exh. 377). Competitors' greatest growth was in products other than kerosene. Brief for Appellants, Vol. 2, at 102–03.

[107] Pure's crude oil receipts more than doubled between 1900 and 1906. Vol. 3, at 1443, 1451. Another interesting example is the New York Lubricating Co. Vol. 2, at 532–33, 766–67, 773.

[108] For some of the agreements, see Vol. 1, at 175–76, 214–23; Vol. 2, at 734, 738, 946, 950; Vol. 3, at 1130; Vol. 17, at 3321; Vol. 12, at 955.

[109] Testimony of Archbold, Vol. 17, at 3467–68.

wooden or iron tank mounted on it. Each tank wagon served 30 to 50 specified retail customers. Tank wagon drivers poured or pumped gasoline and kerosene into store-keepers' tanks, taking cash on delivery. Standard ultimately sold most of its products through the tank wagon channel.[110] Collings, of the Standard Oil of Kentucky, testified that as much as 90 per cent of his sales were made in that way.[111] The remainder continued to go to jobbers and peddlers.

Peddlers usually called at a tank station and filled their own wagons. To reflect the savings on delivery, and their larger average purchase, peddlers usually paid ½ to 1 cent per gallon less than the tank wagon price.[112] Retail peddling wagons made 150 or more selling stops per day.

Jobbers were thus being displaced by an integrated marketing apparatus pioneered by Standard and imitated quickly by its competitors. Peddlers too, faced sweeping changes. Gas and electricity had begun to challenge the household kerosene market on which peddlers depended. The rise of the automobile was just beginning. These forces would ultimately make kerosene, then the principal product, a fourth-rate fuel.

At the same time these changes were taking place, refiners were groping for more efficient ways to market their products. Even as it was developing tank wagon delivery, Standard also experimented with its own peddling operations. It tried to keep its ownership of them secret. These constituted most of the "bogus independents" about which we have heard so often. Almost all the rest were jobbing concerns, generally small ones. They were never of great importance quantitatively.[113] And, for whatever it is worth, Standard was not the only company with "bogus" peddlers and jobbers.[114]

Standard gave several reasons for not advertising its connection with these

[110] The proportion varied among the different territories. Barrel, jobber, and commission-agent distribution were more important in very small communities, and in certain mountainous areas. As late as 1904, for example, Standard was still extending tank wagon service to small New York communities. In all areas, tank wagon delivery was coming to be the dominant method.

[111] Vol. 12, at 896.

[112] Standard's competitors also granted these terms.

[113] More than half of the "bogus" concerns were strictly retail peddling outfits. Most were very small; they averaged, perhaps, two or three peddling wagons. In addition, most did not last very long. "They were an experiment in selling oil directly to the consumer, which largely on account of the necessity of giving credit, proved a failure." Brief for Appellants, Vol. 2, at 192. See also Vol. 13, at 1523–25. Most were gradually withdrawn as the equipment wore out. Those few that continued became "Can Departments" of the various Standard companies.

Furthermore, there is some question about just how secret these firms were supposed to be, and grave doubts about how secret they in fact were. Finally, the government, and witnesses for it, erroneously accused Standard of owning and operating firms that it did not really have anything to do with. For example, see Vol. 5, at 2412, Vol. 12, at 779–80, 790–91; Vol. 13, at 1218–20, 1279–83, 1307, 1533–35.

[114] There are many examples, including the firms operated by Mr. Castle, National Refining Co., Red C, Crew-Levick, et al.

firms. First, persistent public attacks on its monopoly and high profits had prejudiced some of the trade against buying Standard products.[115] Second, some of the marketing concerns that it bought had substantial good will and better local market acceptance than Standard could economically create. Third, to break local retailer and peddler cartels and to meet the competition of other peddlers, from time to time Standard found it useful to run in a retail outfit selling at competitive prices. But to do these things without antagonizing its tank wagon customers, secrecy was useful.[116] Fourth, this approach permitted Standard to experiment with new personnel and marketing methods without abandoning the old, and without committing large resources.

As tank wagon distribution largely displaced barrel delivery to jobbers, Standard sought to extend integration further. As Mr. Squires put it:

> [W]e reached a point where it was felt that possibly another step nearer the consumer might be taken and save him money. It was learned that the retailer was making from 50 to 100 percent profit, and it was believed that we could save one-half of this to the consumer. To make this move required a great deal of care and caution, so that the trade which we were supplying might not be antagonized; also for the purpose of developing any impracticable features which in the end might prove it was not the proper course to pursue. Therefore a few towns were selected to make the experiment, and the towns quoted above were used for the purpose. . . .
>
> But a very serious obstacle soon developed itself, namely, the giving of credit. The storekeeper gave credit to his customers, whereas with us they paid cash. This became such a factor as to make it almost impossible to sell the large quantity which was sought through this medium. Various ways were tried to see if it could not be overcome—like the sale of tickets by milkmen—but it did not work. Then credit was given, but our loss by bad debts was in itself sufficient to practically kill the enterprise. In addition to this we discovered that the expense due to wear and tear of the equipment was great. On account of loaning the cans to the consumer, being our property and not theirs, they did not take the proper care of them. More or less were damaged by carelessness and some were lost entirely. Therefore it was decided, after a very careful canvass of the experience of the different towns, to abandon the idea. Gradually from point to point the equipment was withdrawn, with the exception of two, namely, Youngstown and Cleveland, which have always been known by refiners as peddling points, due to the fact that a number of peddlers had been in existence there for years and the consumer had become familiarized with that means of delivery.[117]

Whether these were really Standard's motives, or merely clever rationalizations, is both imponderable and irrelevant. Suffice it to say that such a

[115] It is impossible to know how important this prejudice was, but it is clear that it existed. One possible symptom is the flavor of names adopted by some competitors: Antitrust Oil Co.; Freedom Oil; Uncle Sam Oil Co.; etc.

[116] Collings: "We would much prefer selling to the dealer. That was the business that we were especially engaged in and prepared to take care of." Vol. 12, at 887.

[117] Vol. 13, at 1523–24. Mr. Squire was not exaggerating retail margins, as the Record amply confirms. Whether margins were high because of retailer cartels or high costs does not matter. What does matter is that Standard, like any refiner, had every interest in reducing them. See also, Vol. 2, pp. 757–58; Vol. 3, p. 1109; Vol. 5, pp. 2583, 2602, 2584.

course of action is reasonable in light of the evolution of the industry. This evolution in fact accelerated after the 1911 dissolution when competition increased. It was not a creature of monopoly. After all, where are the kerosene peddlers today? The alternative explanation, that Standard sought to monopolize wholesale and retail distribution, is certainly less logical and is less consistent with the facts that we have.

In retailing, numbers were often very large, and entry was cheap and quick. Standard Oil never had, or apparently sought, a monopoly of retailing. It would have been pointless to try, and probably impossible to achieve. With a refining monopoly, Standard's interest in marketing should logically have been to keep it efficient and highly competitive.[118]

Of all the "levels" in the oil business, retailing would have been the most difficult for Standard to monopolize, and a monopoly there would have been the most transient of all. The reasons are simple. Kerosene retailers were of two sorts: grocers and other retail merchants, who kept tanks or barrels from which they filled customers' oil cans; and peddlers, who operated one or more wagons which went house-to-house on regular routes, much like the milkman of today and the iceman of old.

The skills and resources devoted to refined oil peddling were neither expensive, scarce, nor specific. A wagon, horse, driver, and some cans or a tank made a peddler.[119] A large peddling concern might have two or three wagons. The resources could, and did, move quickly out of oil peddling and back again, lured by the prospects for gain.

Similarly, entry into grocery retailing and general merchandising has never been difficult. Very early in the game, Mr. Rockefeller realized that a private monopoly of crude oil was impossible.[120] He must have realized that a retailing monopoly was even more hopeless. Only governments succeed for very long in monopolizing activities of that kind. Furthermore, Standard evidently

[118] A monopolist in manufacturing would prefer that marketing have zero costs and be competitive. In that way, the maximum monopoly returns could be extracted from manufacturing.

[119] Shea testified that he entered the peddling business in 1892 with $25.00 of his own money, $25.00 borrowed capital, and a borrowed horse. He grew rapidly, and branched off into jobbing as well as retailing. "I would imagine that we are doing about 30 times as much business as we were in 1892 when we first started." Vol. 5, at 2493.

[120] Rockefeller's description of the ill-fated crude producers' agreement of 1872 is classic:

"I could not state how long it was in existence or said to be operative, but the high price for the crude oil resulted, as it had always done before and will always do so long as oil comes out of the ground, in increasing the production, and they got too much oil. We could not find a market for it.

"[O]f course any who were not in this association were undertaking to produce all they possibly could; and as to those who were in the association, many of them men of honor and high standing, the temptation was very great to get a little more oil than they had promised their associates or us would come. It seemed very difficult to prevent the oil coming at that price. . . . There was a limitation beyond which we, as refiners and merchandizers in the oil, could not go. We were their servants in passing on to the consumer

concluded that its interests could usually best be served by letting someone else perform the retailing function.

Thus it was that before the dissolution jobbers and retailers were exposed to evolutionary forces at work in the industry at large. These changes persisted, indeed probably accelerated, after the dissolution.[121] In addition, jobbers and retailers were subject to all the ills and quarrels that characterize petty trade, where size was small and numbers large. It is not surprising, therefore, that most complaints about price cutting involved non-integrated marketers.[122]

It is clearly impossible to review here all of the incidents involving jobbers and retailers. The record is filled with many very similar examples, and commenting on each of them is an unnecessary and uneconomic task.[123] For present purposes, it is enough to review some of the more important and representative cases. The incidents can conveniently be divided into three categories: (*a*) alleged price cutting which involved competing marketers, but which had no particular outcome; (*b*) alleged price cutting accompanied by purchase of competing marketers; (*c*) alleged price cutting accompanied by the disappearance of competing marketers. Alleged incidents of the first class are numerous, but do not support a theory of predatory monopolization. Examples of the second and third class would be more useful for such a theory, but are very scarce.[124]

Only a few representative incidents will be discussed in detail; others will be cited.

a) PRICE CUTTING WITH NO SPECIFIED OUTCOME

The bulk of evidence, and assertion, established only that Standard sold at different prices within the same community or among communities; and that the lower prices often resulted from greater competition.[125]

---

the refined product, and the limitation was there in what we could at that time sell." Vol. 16, at 3074.

[121] In 1911, for the first time, gasoline sales passed kerosene.

[122] Standard claimed that its tank wagons served 37,000 towns in the United States. The number of jobbers and peddlers must also have been large.

[123] To a remarkable degree, the record is freighted with casual hearsay, petty complaints of small traders, and countless unimportant charges and countercharges. This is probably attributable to the nature of the proceedings under which testimony was taken. Witnesses appeared before an Examiner, not a judge, who felt that he had no power to rule on the admissibility of evidence. A large amount of the Government's testimony came from ex-employees of Standard, most of whom had been discharged or resigned under pressure. Several admitted grudges against Standard management. Some of these witnesses were testifying about Standard operations of which they had no direct knowledge. E.g., Vol. 5, at 2347, 2364, 2381; Vol. 15, at 2472.

[124] Because firms often were both jobbers and peddlers, and testimony about them was often scant, it is impossible to segregate the incidents into those involving jobbers or peddlers. Such a distinction would have little value in any case.

[125] See, for example, Vol. 8, at 905–1011 (Petitioner's Exhibit 379–96); Vol. 10, at 1624–1659 (Pet. Exh. 628–635). But compare Vol. 8, at 664; Vol. 10, at 1624; Vol. 21, at 133

Hisgen Brothers.—A typical example of a marketing firm that complained about local price cutting is Hisgen Brothers. The type of evidence presented is also representative of this whole class of incidents.

Hisgen started selling axle grease in 1889.[126] In 1900, they began retailing and wholesaling kerosene, which they purchased from independent refiners. They complained that in 1901, when they started selling kerosene in various small towns along the Hudson River, Standard cut prices to run them out. Prices elsewhere were said to have remained high. Standard's records indicated that their kerosene prices actually rose during the time Hisgen said Standard was cutting in the six towns involved.[127] Six grocers testified that it was Hisgen, not Standard, who started price-cutting.[128] In any case, Hisgen admitted that he sometimes did cut Standard's prices,[129] and was very vague about Standard's cuts against him.[130] Later episodes around Springfield, Massachusetts show that, at least part of the time, Hisgen initiated price cuts against Standard.[131]

Quite apart from the question of who started the price wars, Hisgen apparently did well. During 1904, for example, Hisgen Brothers did 21 per cent of the oil business at Springfield, and increased their share to 30 per cent in 1905.[132] After 1900, they greatly enlarged their territory and business and apparently prospered in the process.[133]

(Pet. Exh. 962). See also, Vol 2, at 937; Vol. 3, at 1046; Vol. 5, at 2484, 2490–91; Vol. 17, at 3620–2, 3628; Vol. 20, at 229–31, 233.

[126] Vol. 4, at 1795. By the second year business trebled, and kept on increasing. By 1900 sales were $80,000 to $100,000. Hisgen twice ran for Governor of Massachusetts on an anti-trust (anti-Standard Oil) platform. Vol. 4, at 1800, 1841, 1848–49, 1852.

[127] Vol. 12, at 713, 813–15. At one time prices did decline, allegedly because of price cutting by Tiona, marketing subsidiary of Cornplanter Refining Co. Id., at 716.

[128] Vol. 12, at 780–82, 812–13, 818–19, 822–24, 826–27, 830–31, 833–35; Vol. 4, at 1894–95, 1963–66.

[129] Vol. 4, at 1813–15, 1856 et seq., 1888–89, 1898, 1977–78. See also id., at 1932–37, 1952, 1964–72; Vol. 12, 729–37, 782–88, 810–17, 822–37.

[130] Vol. 4, at 1861, 1874.

[131] In 1904 Hisgen began selling at 10½¢ per gallon, undercutting Standard by ½¢. Part of the following decline was attributed to a general price reduction over a wide territory; part to further cutting by Hisgen. In 1905, Hisgen stopped cutting, and Standard's prices rose. Vol. 10, at 1636.

[132] Brief for Appellants, Vol. II, p. 177. See also Vol. 12, at 782–85, 809–810; Vol. 10, at 1636.

[133] Vol. 4, at 1836–44.

There are numerous other examples of this class of incidents. See, for example:

H. C. Boardman. In 1904, when Standard fired him, Boardman opened a marketing business in Augusta. Vol. 5, at 2189. Prices fell. Id., at 2169–71. Boardman captured and held one-third of the trade. In his words:

> "If I could get a third of the trade, I was satisfied. I recognized the fact that the Standard had to live, too, and needed the money, and so I thought I would let them live. So I kept it at 11 cents." Id., at 2171.

In 1906 Boardman opened up a tank station in Denmark, South Carolina. While he was

b) PRICE CUTTING AND PURCHASING

There were several allegations that Standard used local price cutting to force independent marketers to sell out. For the most part, the evidence was simply that there was price cutting and someone affected by it sold out to Standard. In a few cases, the testimony was somewhat more pointed. The following are the most important and relevant examples.

G. T. Wofford.—From 1898–1902, Mr. Wofford was chief clerk and assistant to the Manager in the Birmingham headquarters of the Standard Oil Company of Kentucky.[134] He testified that Standard gave rebates to induce countermands or requirements contracts. Collings denied these allegations.[135] About the end of 1902, Wofford and some associates started the Southeastern Oil Company—a marketing firm—in Birmingham. According to Wofford, Kerosene prices fell steadily from 14 cents to 11 cents per gallon. Southeastern lost money, and sold out to Standard about 1904. There are several convincing reasons why this is *not* a case of successful predation: First, Wofford admitted that it was not Standard's price-cutting on kerosene that made the business unprofitable: "We made a reasonable profit on that particular grade of oil, but we lost money on the general business."[136] Second, Standard claimed, and there is some evidence to support it, that Southeastern solicited the sale to Standard.[137] Third, there was even some testimony that Standard did not actually cut prices before Southeastern sold out.[138]

Fourth, the Government claimed that Standard's Birmingham business was profitable during 1903.[139]

---

erecting tanks, Standard cut prices. Id., at 2175. But, cut as they would, Boardman got about 40 per cent of the business. Although he was largely confined to one territory, and therefore should, so we are told, have been particularly vulnerable to "discriminatory sharp-shooting," Boardman prospered. His trade was profitable from the start; by 1908 he had 75 per cent of the Augusta lubricating oil business, and one third of the refined oils trade. Id., at 2171, 2181. Boardman started business with a capital of $3,000, including tanks and a wagon. The first year his sales were $40,000, the second year, $50,000, and the third year $60,000. "I have never had a month yet that I haven't made a nice profit, even from the first month." Id., at 2181.

C. J. Castle. Vol. 6, at 3040, 3044–46, 3055–57, 3067–68, 3088; Vol. 13, at 1483, 1517–18.

St. Louis Oil Co. Vol. 2, at 891, 894, 896, 899, 900. For a similar case, see Vol. 15, pp. 2411–2415, 2425; Vol. 20, pp. 229–33.

E. M. Wilhoit. Vol. 3, at 1037–38 et seq., 1269–70. "In going into a new territory I cut usually the Standard price." Id., at p. 1227.

Cooper Brothers. Vol. 5, at 2358–59, 2392–2400; Vol. 15, at 2434, 2453, 2472–73, 2542–46.

Testimony of Maxon and Kercher. Vol. 5, at 2459–70; Vol. 6, at 2811–13, 2815–33. But see Vol. 12, at 922–23, 969.

[134] Vol. 5, at 2150.

[135] Id., at 2155–56; Vol. 12, at 908.

[136] Vol. 5, at 2156.

[137] Vol. 12, at 848.

[138] Id., at 847–48, 908.

[139] Brief for the United States, Vol. 2, at 486. After the sale, Wofford went on to establish another successful oil marketing firm.

People's Oil Company.—E. N. Wooten, an ex-Standard employee, testified that from 1892 to 1898 Standard cut prices severely at Atlanta to kill off the People's and the Commercial, and that both were forced to sell out to the Standard.[140] Collings denied that Standard started a price war or tried to drive them out.[141] There is both indirect and direct evidence that they were not *forced* out: First, Wooten said the sales were secret, and secrets cannot usually be kept when parties are aggrieved. Second, People's was a *customer* of Standard. Third, the former owner of People's explicitly denied that she was forced out or underpaid.[142] Fourth, Wooten acknowledged that the value of People's and the Commercial had not been higher at any time than when they sold out.[143]

Testimony of Mr. Castle.—Castle testified that while employed by Standard, he forced an independent Port Huron, Michigan dealer—Mr. Campfield—to sell out to Standard sometime after 1889.[144] Correspondence indicated that Castle was supposed to rebate to dealers to keep the Port Huron kerosene price depressed to 6 cents per gallon to combat Campfield.[145] It is not clear who started the price cutting, and I can find no further evidence about the incident. There is no doubt that Castle employed rebates extensively in the Ohio territory;[146] that is why Standard claimed they fired him. Castle also testified that he forced a Cuyahoga Falls peddler named Blackburn to sell out.[147] For one who claimed to have waged war so long and widely, even the results that Castle claimed appear slender, indeed.[148]

[140] Vol. 5, at 2096–2103. Commercial was owned by the Peerless Refining Company of Cleveland. Standard claimed to have fired Wooten because of his alleged "drug habit." Vol. 12, at 906.

[141] Id., at 897–901.

[142] Vol. 18, at 253 (Def. Exh. 92½).

[143] Vol. 5, at 2149. Another example is the purchase of two wholesale marketing organizations started by a Mr. Joseph. According to Cooke, a Government witness,

> "[T]he Standard was anxious to get a location . . . and they realized there was hardly room for two companies (it was not a large town), and they went to Joseph and offered to buy him out; and I must say for the Standard Oil Company, they were very fair and equitable with him because they gave him a darned sight more than the old trap was worth." Id., at 2531.

Joseph agreed to stay out of the oil business, but soon came back, put up another bulk plant, and started cutting prices.

"Q. And the Standard met his cut?

"A. Well, you wouldn't expect them to take bank shots all the time, would you?" Ibid. Joseph sold out again.

[144] Vol. 6, at 3059–60.

[145] Vol. 10, at 1894–95 (Pet. Exh. 836, 837).

[146] Vol. 3, at 1362–3; Vol. 6, at 3030, 3037–38, 3039–45, 3071; Vol. 10, at 1886 (Pet. Exh. 829); Vol. 13, at 1511–15; 1576.

[147] Vol. 6, at 3044. At 3041, he says an unnamed peddler at Columbiana, Ohio also was forced to sell. The Columbiana affair arose out of price-cutting by Freedom Oil, Vol. 13, at 1511–15, as did many incidents in Ohio. Vol. 6, at 3040, 3044.

[148] Mahle, a former Standard stenographer, claimed that Blaustein tried to run Fivel, a peddler, out of Norfolk. Vol. 5, pp. 2211–12, 2360–62. Blaustein denied that, but admitted

c) PRICE CUTTING AND BUSINESS EXTINCTION

There remains the possibility that marketers were exterminated rather than purchased. The evidence is scanty and unconvincing.

Decline of Cleveland Peddlers.—According to Castle, in 1903, when Standard sent peddling wagons into Cleveland, the independent peddlers were doomed.[149] Whereas before that time independent peddlers flourished, their numbers declined drastically:

> [A]t that time peddlers were getting a pretty good rebate and the retail prices hadn't been brought down. They were doing pretty well there for a start. . . . After they brought these wagons on. . . .[I]t made the margin very small, and it had the effect that up to this time there are very few peddlers in the business, at the present time. Out of probably two hundred and fifty at that time, I don't think you could find fifty now.[150]

Squire, of Standard, offered a different and more sensible explanation:

> [I]n 1902 there were 115 peddlers, with no natural-gas meters in use. In 1903 there were 90 peddlers, with 16,194 natural-gas meters in use. In 1904 there were 80 peddlers, with 30,165 natural-gas meters in use. In 1905, there were 78 peddlers, with 46,819 natural-gas meters in use. In 1906 there were 61 peddlers, with 66,743 natural-gas meters in use. In 1907 there were 43 peddlers, with 77,646 natural-gas meters in use. In 1908 there were 40 peddlers, with 83,976 natural-gas meters in use.[151]

Natural gas, of course, was used both for heating and lighting.

The Mahle Testimony.—Mahle gave a great deal of hearsay testimony. For example, he said that three oil dealers in the Baltimore territory had been run out of business by Standard: Tough-Rutherford, McNeil, and the Purse family at Seaford, Delaware. I cannot find any evidence on the first two, but the allegation with respect to Purse is erroneous. The Seaford Company was a Crew-Levick concern, not a Standard "bogus" company,[152] and the Purse family said it was Red C price-cutting that drove them out.

Other Incidents.—H. C. Boardman worked for Standard in Augusta, Georgia from 1886–1904, and testified that during that period Standard cut prices to drive out competitors.[153] Boardman said that one marketer, J. T. Thornhill, "finally abandoned business"; and that other major integrated competitors of

buying Fivel's wagon and supplies. Vol. 15, at 2434–39. Farquaharson said Blaustein ultimately bought Fivel out for $50 more than the "excessive" figure at which he first offered to sell. Vol. 5, at 2211. See also Vol. 2, at 725–27; Vol. 5, 2100–2, 2107, 2279; Vol. 12, at 902–05; Vol. 15, at 2445–7; 2549–52, 2544.

149 Vol. 6, at 3054–56, 3108–19, 3124, 3201, 3206; see also Vol. 3, at 1507–10.

150 Vol. 6, at 3056.

151 Vol. 13, 1532.

152 Vol. 13, at 1218, 1278–79, 1281, 1283, 1307. Cf. Vol. 5, at 2412; Vol. 13, at 1219–20.

153 Vol. 5, at 2163–67.

Standard withdrew from the territory. These allegations were controverted.[154] Even Boardman admitted that Standard cut prices only "as last resort."[155]

Maywood Maxon, once a Standard employee, testified that in 1899 an unnamed independent oil dealer at Paris, Illinois was forced out of business after a year of rebating and price war.[156] Collings denied the whole affair.[157] In another instance, Kercher claimed that a peddler named Wagner left the business.[158]

C. M. Lines testified that he ran a string of bogus peddling wagons for Standard between 1900 and 1903.[159] He said he thought that these concerns lost money.[160] George Lane, who had worked for Lines, said that in Youngstown Lines made a "drive" on another peddler's business, and drove everybody out of business except the man he was after.[161] On the other hand, Vahey, the peddler who was alleged to be the object of Lines' warfare, testified that he did a land office business when the Standard group attacked him.[162] Far from going out of business, he apparently flourished.

Marketing: Summary.—This testimony is voluminous, controverted, and confusing. Many exhibits were ambiguous, and some are of dubious authenticity. Several conclusions stand out, however:

1. If Standard's object was to monopolize marketing—and that would have been irrational to begin with—they failed. For, if we abstract from the decline of kerosene peddling that followed the growth of natural gas in Cleveland, I can find less than 10 small oil dealers whose sale or disappearance appears to have anything to do with local-price cutting. And that is a liberal estimate of the evidence. Some of the firms were nameless; allegations were often vague; most claims were disproved; some, while not controverted, were never really

[154] See e.g., Vol. 12, at 910; Vol. 5, 2163. Boardman himself was a little vague: "I don't know whether they sold out, but the impression was that they sold out to the Standard." Vol. 5, at 2166. Boardman claimed that Tidewater; Crew-Levick; and Blodgett, Moore & Co., all withdrew.

[155] Id., at 2164.

[156] Vol. 3, at 1291, 1293, 1294, 1313. Maxon obviously wanted revenge on Standard; id., at 1294.

[157] Vol. 12, at 890. See also Vol. 5, at 2466–69.

[158] Vol. 6, at 2832–3. But see Vol. 10 at 1846 (Pet. Exh. 798). Kercher was an admitted perjurer. He also had a grudge against Standard, and apparently tried to blackmail them. Vol. 6, at 2949 et seq., 2969 et seq., 2990.

[159] Vol. 6, at 3201 et seq.

[160] Ibid., at 3205.

[161] Vol. 3, at 1356–61.

[162] Vol. 3, pp. 1366–67. Though just a peddler, Vahey was no fool. He claimed that when a Standard employee threatened to put him out of business, he replied that ". . . I was positive it would take him at least two years to put me out of business and maybe he couldn't do it then. . . ." Id., at 1367. For another alleged instance see Nicolai Brothers, Vol. 13, at 1196.

proved. In many cases, probably most of them, the independents clearly initiated price cuts.

The "possible" cases are, therefore, really unexplained cases. Most of them involved peddlers, among whom I would expect failures to be relatively numerous in the absence of predatory practices.

"Fatalities," from all causes, were apparently not very numerous in petroleum retailing and wholesaling, which is surprising in the light of the usual experience in petty trade. There were a fair number of purchases, but fewer than one might have expected.

2. Standard's correspondence and directives to salesmen show that they were intent on getting business that paid, but were not going to give away anything to get it.[163] Salesmen were cautioned to "be as economical in getting this business as possible";[164] were denounced for cutting prices when it was not necessary [165] and for selling too much oil at special prices.[166]

3. It is interesting that most of the ex-Standard employees who testified about Standard's deadly predatory tactics entered the oil business when they left the Standard. They also prospered.

4. Standard apparently had a shrewd and hard marketing organization. It had every interest in distributing as cheaply as possible, and tried to achieve that result.[167]

[163] Standard's salesmen and agents had to fill in "Form 29" requesting permission to cut prices. E.g., Vol. 3, at 1021–22; Vol. 12, at 962. Permission was often withheld. Vol. 10, at 1758–59 (Pet. Exh. 690). See Vol. 12, at 688, 845, 907. Standard's employees by and large appear to have learned what they were told. As one Waters-Pierce man put it:

> "Our goods was [sic] just as good or [a] little better than our competitors and I thought we should get as much for them as possible. [Cutting price] might increase the gallonage, but I figured we would lose money." Vol. 3, at 1170.

Wilmer also testified that Standard expected its salesmen to get the business at remunerative prices, for "[a]nyone could give goods away." Vol. 13, at 1250. Metzell, a competitor's salesman, agreed that "[t]hey are getting all they can." Vol. 5, at 2418. Wilhoit knew that Standard's profitability rested on high prices, not low ones. As he put it,

> "[I]f I could market my goods at such prices as the Standard Oil Company get for them regularly, I would not want but one year's business at their regular prices, if I got twenty-five per cent of the business. One year would be all I want to retire on at their regular price. We don't get their regular price."

Vol. 3, at 1038.

[164] Vol. 10 at 1840 (Pet. Exh. 790).

[165] "I have also corresponded with our agents in the South Carolina field and they fully understand we want to retain our business and would reduce our market ½ cent per gallon rather than see the business go to the other oil companies, but I have impressed upon their minds that we do not want to put this reduction into effect unless it is absolutely necessary." Vol. 10, at 1758–59. (Pet. Exh. 690).

[166] Vol. 12, at 1019.

[167] Collings said that the incidents in Standard of Kentucky territory were in large part caused by excessively high dealer prices that Standard was in the process of breaking down. Vol. 5, at 2462; Vol. 12, at 886–89, 923–927. According to Collings, a peddler working on a 4¢ per gallon margin can do well: As he put it,

> "So that at 4 cents a gallon it will be about, at 150 gallons a day, $6 a day. A man with

IV. Conclusions

Judging from the Record, Standard Oil did not use predatory price discrimination to drive out competing refiners, nor did its pricing practice have that effect. Whereas there may be a very few cases in which retail kerosene peddlers or dealers went out of business after or during price cutting, there is no real proof that Standard's pricing policies were responsible. I am convinced that Standard did not systematically, if ever, use local price cutting in retailing, or anywhere else, to reduce competition. To do so would have been foolish; and, whatever else has been said about them, the old Standard organization was seldom criticized for making less money when it could readily have made more.

In some respects it is too bad that Standard did not employ predatory price cutting to achieve its monopoly position. In doing so it would surely have gotten no greater monopoly power than it achieved in other ways, and during the process consumers could have bought petroleum products for a great deal less money. Standard would thereby not only have given some of its own capital away, but would also have compelled competitors to donate a smaller amount.[168]

It is correct that Standard discriminated in price, but it did so to maximize profits given the elasticities of demand of markets in which it sold. It did not use price discrimination to change those elasticities. Anyone who has relied upon price discrimination to explain Standard's dominance would do well to start looking for something else.[169] The place to start is merger.

It should be quite clear that this is not a verdict of acquittal for the Standard Oil Company; the issue of monopoly remains. What this study says is that Standard did not achieve or maintain a monopoly position through price dis-

---

> one horse and wagon that can make $6 a day is doing very well. . . . [W]e figure that from 2 to 3 cents over the tank-wagon price was a fair price for the peddler. They could make a good living out of that. . . . And where they tried to hold up the customer to a fancy profit above that we used our efforts in one way or another to get them to bring it down, the object being, of course, to increase the consumption of oil. We felt, of course, that if they held the price up to 15 or 20 cents a gallon for oil, people would be more economical in the use of it."

Id., at 890. See also id. at 917–18. Cooke, a Government witness, testified that the effect of Standard's Capital City Wagons was to force peddlers to charge reasonable prices to consumers.

[168] This, of course, ignores certain moral issues. Economics is not a particularly useful tool for dealing with them.

[169] In arguing against the Defendant's motion for adjournment to prepare its case, Government Counsel may have admitted what I have concluded:

> "What is there, then, to prepare for in this case? Simply the question of unfair competition. The Examiner can see from the testimony that has already been taken that that is not a great task; that it won't take any particular time for them to prepare to meet that testimony." Vol. 6, at 3333.

crimination. The issue of whether the monopoly should have been dissolved is quite separate.

I think one further observation can tentatively be made. If the popular interpretation of the *Standard Oil* case is at all responsible for the emphasis that anti-trust policy places on "unfair" and "monopolizing" business practices, that emphasis is misplaced.[170] This limited study suggests that what businessmen do *to* one another is much less significant to monopoly than what they find it useful to do together to serve their common interest.

[170] The Standard Legend may also be responsible for the strained analogy often drawn between business and war. Analogies to chess strike me as being equally weak. Chess is a competitive game which one player wins, while the other loses. Successful quasi-monopoly seeks to avoid the competitive game, since all players lose as soon as they begin playing it.

[15]

7

Injury to Competition: The Law's Basic Theories

THE root trouble with modern antitrust, more damaging even than the confusion over goals, is the unsophisticated, indeed primitive, state of the law's economic doctrines. The seeming complexity of this topic is spurious. The ideas at work are of ancient lineage, few in number, and easily comprehended. To understand them is to understand the otherwise apparently bewildering course of the law and the unity that underlies its surface diversities. To grasp the nature of their error is to perceive the route to reform.

The early period of antitrust laid down two theories of the ways in which competition may be injured that continue to shape and drive the law today:

(1) Competitors may agree to remove the rivalry existing between themselves and thereby injure the competitive process; or

(2) Competitors may inflict injury on their rivals and thereby injure the competitive process.

Each of these theories has an important core of truth, but each has been egregiously overextended so that the law regularly strikes at and destroys normal business practices whose only consequence is enrichment of the community. The mistake is the same in both cases. Each theory contains an obvious dilemma: the agreed elimination of rivalry and the infliction of injury upon rivals are not merely means of injuring the competitive process; they are, even more importantly, means by which productive efficiency is created and by which the forces of competition allocate resources. Because the law has not resolved that dilemma, has not found ways of separating the beneficial eliminations of rivalry and inflictions of injury from the detrimental, it has been forced to ignore the claims of productive efficiency. The law is, therefore, driven by only one economic consideration: fear of injury to allocative efficiency. Considering only one vector in a two-vector situation is bound to give results far off the mark.

If the principles of law made by the courts were consistently applied, not only would competition be outlawed, but a modern (or almost any) economic system would be impossible. This has not happened, of course, but the law is saved from demanding impossible results only by applying its principles erratically and inconsistently. Vigorous and consistent enforcement of present antitrust doctrines would be a national disaster. There is no chance that we will ever see it occur, but that is no reason to be content with the wealth destruction that now takes place within the areas where antitrust's irrationalities are allowed free scope.

Examination of the two basic theories of injury to competition discloses the cause of the law's waywardness.

THE AGREED ELIMINATION OF RIVALRY

The first theory—that competition is injured by the agreed elimination of rivalry—is less than a half-truth. Competition, in the sense of consumer welfare, is in fact injured by such agreed eliminations of rivalry as price-fixing rings, exemplified by the agreements in *Trans-Missouri* [1] and *Addyston Pipe & Steel*,[2] or, very probably, by monopolistic horizontal mergers, as in *Standard Oil*.[3] But it is also true that productive efficiency absolutely requires the agreed elimination of rivalry in many more cases. When men join together in corporations or partnerships, or in any economic unit of more than one person, they either explicitly or tacitly accept the elimination of market rivalry between themselves. Joint effort organized by administrative direction replaces the forces of the marketplace.

Since cooperation and division of labor within such economic units is essential to the tasks of production and distribution, it is impossible to enforce a legal rule that makes the agreed elimination of rivalry unlawful. If the agreed elimination of rivalry were always illegal, the resulting economic system, should one remain, would be unable to support the present population of the United States, much less provide what we have come to regard as a civilized living standard.

It is wrong, therefore, to accept a rule of law that purports to do what it cannot: strike down all agreed eliminations of rivalry. That was Holmes's point in his *Northern Securities* dissent.[4] The correct distinctions for the law are two. Agreed eliminations of rivalry should be illegal when they do not accompany and make more effective the integration of persons or business units in productive economic activity. Thus, price-fixing cartels are properly declared unlawful per se, but partnerships are not. Second, even when economic integration is present, the arrangement may be unlawful if the parties control the market so that restriction of output appears to be the primary effect. These considerations impinge upon current law in several areas: price fixing, market division, and boycotts, among others. Their application requires elaboration which must be deferred to the appropriate chapters.

THE INFLICTION OF INJURY UPON RIVALS

The second theory employed by the law—that competition is harmed by injury inflicted upon rivals, their exclusion from the market or some segment of it—is more complex, and it has also proved more harmful to the integrity and rationality of antitrust. Though we will be dealing with aspects of this theory in various chapters—those, for example, on vertical mergers, conglomerate mergers, exclusive dealing, and price discrimination—a general statement of the argument will be useful at this point.

The law employs a rich, diverse, and confusing vocabulary to describe what it perceives as the problem of market exclusion. We read in the cases not only of "exclusionary practices" but also of "predation," "abuses," "coercion," "foreclosure," "unfair competition," "fencing out," and "barriers to entry." These words all reflect or assume a theory of practices that improperly exclude rivals and hence injure the competitive process.

The problem is to know what exclusion is improper. All business activity excludes. A sale excludes rivals from that piece of business. Any firm that operates excludes rivals from some share of the market. Superior efficiency forecloses. Indeed, exclusion or foreclosure is the mechanism by which competition confers its benefits upon society. The more efficient exclude the less efficient from the control of resources, and they do so only to the degree that their efficiency is superior.

Such exclusion is proper and beneficial. It is the task of antitrust to see that it continues to operate. Antitrust, therefore, must be able to distinguish efficiency exclusion from improper exclusion. The conceptual apparatus now in use is incapable of making that crucial distinction.

The law's theory of exclusionary practices contains two branches. The more modern, and more important, strikes at practices *because* they exclude, without asking whether they exclude through efficiency or improperly. No showing of wrongful intent is required. This will be referred to as the *theory of automatic exclusion.* The older, and nowadays less significant, branch required some indication of wrongful intent as a means of separating normal and efficient behavior from that which inhibits competition improperly. This is the *theory of predation.*

THE THEORY OF AUTOMATIC EXCLUSION

The theory that there exist business practices which are automatically exclusionary, that the exclusion is improper and anticompetitive, and that the law can usefully identify and prohibit them is probably the single most important economic idea in antitrust today. It controls the interpretation of most of the Clayton Act, including the Robinson-Patman Act, and now much of the Sherman Act as well. To cite but a single example: vertical mergers are today all but completely illegal, on the theory that the manufacturer who acquires a retailer also acquires the ability to shut rival manufacturers out of that segment of the market. It is not necessary to a successful government suit to enjoin the merger that the manufacturer display any wrongful or anticompetitive intent in making the acquisition or that the retailer represent a very large share of the market. Vertical mergers are believed inherently exclusionary and are dealt with severely, as are such things as exclusive dealing contracts, requirements contracts, and price differentials. Yet it is clear that the theory of automatically exclusionary practices is utterly without merit.

Inherent in the concept of automatically exclusionary practices are two major fallacies, each of them fatal. The first is the postulation of a category of economic motivation or behavior that does not exist. The second is the simple arithmetical error of counting the same market power twice.

The first fallacy is nowhere more clearly displayed than in Judge Wyzanski's renowned opinion in *United States* v. *United Shoe Machinery Corp.*[5] Judge Wyzanski decided that United had monopolized the shoe machinery market and thus violated Section 2 of the Sherman Act. His determination rested in major part upon the presumed exclusionary effect of United's system of leasing its machines to shoe manufacturers. The leases were thought to make it more difficult for other machinery manufacturers to compete. Yet this exclusionary effect was found not to be predatory, for Judge Wyzanski stated that "United's power does not rest on predatory practices. Probably few monopolies could produce a record so free from any taint of that kind of wrongdoing." But such a finding was unnecessary, Judge Wyzanski thought, because the alternative to predation was not necessarily efficiency. The Sherman Act, therefore, must take account of another possibility.

> When they proposed the legislation, Senators Hoar and Edmunds thought it did little more than bring national authority to bear upon restraints of trade known to the common law, and it could not apply to one "who merely by superior skill and intelligence . . . got the whole business because nobody could do it as well" [21 Cong. Rec. 3146–3152]. They did not discuss the intermediate case where the causes of an enterprise's success were neither common law restraints of trade, nor the skill with which the business was conducted, but rather some practice which without being predatory, abusive, or coercive was in economic effect exclusionary.

The difficulty with this, and hence with all law that rests upon the idea of automatic exclusion, is that the intermediate case described by Judge Wyzanski simply does not exist. It is an idea that has no counterpart in reality, and so law based upon the idea has no relation to reality.

To be clear on this point it is necessary merely to examine the assumptions underlying the notion of the intermediate case. By definition it is a case in which the company has engaged in market behavior with neither the expectation nor the result of making money. The defendant is assumed not to be attempting to do business more efficiently and also not to be attempting to exclude rivals on some basis other than efficiency. But the excluded purposes exhaust the possible motivations for profit-maximizing behavior. There are no other categories of behavior that create revenue for the firm. To postulate an "intermediate case," therefore, is to assume that there is a class of market conduct that is motivated by nothing in particular. Further, it requires us to assume that the conduct, whatever its motivation, does not prove efficient nonetheless.

Judge Wyzanski's concept of the intermediate case asks us to believe that the executives of the United Shoe Machinery Corp. (and every other shoe machinery manufacturer in the history of the industry) spent decades working out and continuously modifying a complex leasing system (and that United, at least, defended that system against repeated antitrust attacks) with no particular purpose in mind. That is flatly impossible. The concept of the "intermediate case," which is the theory of automatically exclusionary practices, thus describes a null set.

Employment of the theory leads the court to deny without investigation the possibility that the questioned practice creates efficiency. Thus Judge Wyzanski:

> In one sense, the leasing system and the miscellaneous activities just referred to (except United's purchases in the secondhand market) were natural and normal, for they were, in Judge Hand's words, "honestly industrial." They are the sort of activities which would be engaged in by other honorable firms. And, to a large extent, the leasing practices conform to longstanding traditions in the shoe machinery business. Yet, they are not practices which can be properly described as the inevitable consequences of ability, natural forces, or law. They represent something more than the use of accessible resources, the process of invention and innovation, and the employment of those techniques of employment, financing, production, and distribution, which a competitive society must foster. They are contracts, arrangements, and policies which, instead of encouraging competition based on pure merit, further the dominance of a particular firm. In this sense, they are unnatural barriers; they unnecessarily exclude actual and potential competition; they restrict a free market.

This passage is not an investigation of the efficiency hypothesis (there is no such investigation anywhere in the opinion) but only an insistence that, for reasons not cited, the leasing system cannot be efficient, that it is "something more"—the intermediate case. And once the system is not efficient, a proposition resting on nothing more than assertion, it becomes an "unnatural barrier" and "unnecessarily" exclusionary. Hence its exclusionary effect is improper, and a market share resting upon improper exclusion is itself improper. The real, the only, issue in the case—was United trying to be efficient or predatory?—was never even discussed.

The theory of automatically exclusionary practices achieves truly spectacular results when it is coupled with the theory of incipiency, as it is in litigation under the Robinson-Patman Act and Sections 3 and 7 of the Clayton Act. The incipiency concept authorizes courts to catch monopolies and restraints of trade in their infancy, before they have matured to Sherman Act size. Thus, the firm employing a practice identified as suspect by the law need not possess a market share anywhere near United's 85 percent in order to run afoul of the law. In these categories of behavior, the possibility of efficiency is eliminated by hypothesis, and any exclusion that seems possible is necessarily improper. Thus, vertical mergers with a mere potential for excluding rivals from less than 1 percent of the market are struck down, as are exclusive dealing contracts. In some Robinson-Patman Act litigation, exclusion itself is inferred from the mere fact of a minor price differential. In all of these cases, as in *United Shoe Machinery,* the real problem is resolutely ignored.

The second major fault in the theory of automatic exclusion is its necessary adoption of the fallacy of double counting. When a court assumes that a firm forecloses its rivals without predatory intent and without creating efficiency, the court also assumes that the firm gets "something more" without noticing it. That can be explained only if the firm pays nothing for the something extra. *United Shoe Machinery* may again be used to illustrate the error.

United was successful in getting most shoe manufacturers to accept its leases, and yet Judge Wyzanski said the effect of the leases was artificially to exclude rival machinery manufacturers, thus preserving United's monopoly position. Such exclusion would of course be detrimental to the shoe manufacturers. They would prefer not to have to deal forever with a monopolist. United could charge for its machines only what they were worth to the shoe manufacturers, and we may call that amount *X*. If *X* was taken by United entirely in rental dollars, it had no power left over to force any disadvantageous terms upon the shoe manufacturer lessees. Yet, by Judge Wyzanski's hypothesis, United must have done just that. We cannot suppose that United lowered its dollar rentals in order to buy the exclusionary lease terms from the lessees, for that would be conscious predation, which is excluded by hypothesis and, for good measure, by explicit finding. Nor can we suppose that United took less in dollars without realizing the fact, for that would mean, first, that its executives over a period of several decades never perceived that they could charge more if they did not impose disadvantageous terms and, second, that no lessee ever pointed out that it would be willing to pay more if some of those terms were relaxed or removed. Such a supposition denies elementary business ability to any of the companies involved. Judge Wyzanski must have assumed that United could capture X in rental dollars and capture it a second time in exclusionary lease terms. Implicit in his reasoning, therefore, is the elementary fallacy of counting the same degree of market power twice. There is no way the theory of automatic exclusion, which ignores the possibilities of efficiency and predation alike, can avoid that additional error.

Double counting is present, for example, in all the vertical merger cases under amended Section 7 of the Clayton Act. Courts assume that a manufacturer can buy a retailer, force the new retail subsidiary to take the manufacturer's products, and thereby foreclose rival manufacturers. For this behavior to work an anticompetitive result, it is necessary to assume that the manufacturer is able to transfer the retailer's market position to itself at the manufacturing level while the retailer retains that same market position at the retail level. Double counting is clearly involved. If a manufacturer with 10 percent of its market buys a retailer with 5 percent of the retail market and forces its products upon the retailer, the theory supposes that the manufacturer winds up with 15 percent of manufacturing, and that the added 5 percent is not based on competitive merit. The theory works only if the retailer continues to enjoy 5 percent of the retail market, and that cannot be, since we started with the assumption that the manufacturer could not have earned that 5 percent on competitive merit. The manufacturer's competitive weakness has been forced upon the retailer along with the products. To assume that improper exclusion flows from such a merger is to assume that the retailer can give its market position to a manufacturer, who does not deserve it, and still retain the market position for its own enjoyment.

A particularly clear double-counting error occurs in the Supreme Court's decision in *United States* v. *Griffith*.[6] The Court found illegal monopolization in a motion picture theater chain's practice of negotiating with each distributor a master agreement for all its theaters. The crucial characteristic of the master agreements, according to Justice Douglas (who wrote the majority opinion), was that "they lumped together towns in which the appellees [defendants] had no competition and towns in which there were competing theatres." Accepting the district court's finding that the chain had no intent to restrain trade or monopolize, Douglas held that even though no threat was made, it was nevertheless likely that the distributor would give the chain exclusive rights in towns where competitive theaters existed, because of the monopoly power of the closed towns.

To exclude the possibility of predation and still to attribute this result to the linking of the towns through the master agreement is to embrace the double-counting fallacy. Again, call the monopoly power of the closed town X. The chain comes to the negotiation armed with X, and only X, for each closed town. It would normally pay the competitive price for films in competitive towns and that same price, minus the dollar value of X, in each closed town. If the distributor charged the chain the competitive price in both open and closed towns but gave it preferential rights worth X in the open towns, the chain would surely notice what was happening. It would be giving up money in the monopoly market for preferential terms that no competitor would be willing to pay for in the competitive market. The only point in that would be to destroy rivals in the competitive market. But that would be predation —excluded by hypothesis. Therefore, the reasoning assumes that the chain gets X in dollars in the closed town and gets X again in preferential terms in the competitive towns—and without noticing it. Aside from the stupidity gratuitously attributed to the chain (the alternative to stupidity is knowledge and therefore predation), the argument assumes that the distributor, unlike the rest of the human race, is willing to pay 2X for a thing worth only X, and to do it without even being asked. The fact that a legal theory with such a premise has gained ascendancy is a tribute both to antitrust as an art form and to the bar's capacity for the willing suspension of disbelief.

Notice that double counting requires the linking of two markets by lease, contract, merger, or ownership of two units. The leases in *United Shoe Machinery* are the equivalent of the master agreement in *Griffith,* of vertical mergers, and of exclusive dealing contracts. Both the use of a conduit for the transfer of power from one market to another and the fallacy of counting the same power twice, once in each market, are essential to the automatic exclusion cases.

The theory of automatic exclusion, then, contains two fatal defects: reliance upon a nonexistent motivation for economic behavior and reliance upon the fallacy of double counting. The theory cannot be accepted upon the terms in which the courts present it.

There remains for examination, however, the possibility that the theory is a "legal fiction" not intended to make sense according to its own terms—just as the old action of ejectment conclusively presumed that the defendant was in possession of the disputed property, no matter that he was standing before the court hotly denying possession. The legal fiction of automatic exclusion might be defended by arguing that it rests upon a judicial intuition that predatory business behavior is extremely common but very difficult to prove so long as wrongful intent is a required element of proof. The law, therefore, may drop the element of specific intent and so arrive at a presumption of automatic exclusion in order to frame a prophylactic rule, believing it more important to block predation than to avoid an occasional injustice and the social disservice of destroying some efficiency. In this view, to demonstrate that the theory of automatic exclusion is fallacious is to miss the point.

The prophylactic justification will not withstand analysis, however. Aside from the fact that it would attribute to the courts a disingenuous willingness to disguise a major, and very debatable, policy judgment, there are two conclusive objections to it: an effective prophylactic rule would require the suppression of all competition; and predation is not more common than efficiency.

The first objection is easily stated. To return to *Griffith,* a court applying a prophylactic rule on the assumption that the chain was demanding preferential rights in order to monopolize the competitive towns could avoid the fallacy of double counting only by assuming that the chain was giving up X, in the form of dollars, in each monopoly town in return for X, in the form of preferential terms, in a corresponding number of competitive towns. But such a transfer of power through the master agreement could easily be duplicated, without the master agreement, by transferring cash from one town to the other. The chain would need only a checking account or a black satchel to get *X* dollars from a closed town to an open town and purchase preferential terms there.

All the transfers of power assumed in the cases can be converted to transfers of equivalent cash, and that poses an insuperable problem. To do any good the prophylactic rule would have to be applied to all uses of money. But money has the same purchasing power whether it comes from a theater monopoly, a competitive haberdashery, a rich aunt, frugal living, or a day at the races. It can all be used, if any can be used, for predation. Since the point of a theory of automatically exclusionary practices (viewed as a prophylactic rule) is to avoid examining intent or otherwise having to distinguish between predation and normal competition, there is no alternative but to prohibit any use of money that could be predatory. This means, to use motion picture exhibition as the example, that courts would have to regulate amounts paid for films, admission prices, interior comfort and décor, and so forth, to ensure absolute equality between theaters in the same town. That is true whether the theaters belong to a chain or are independent. The same reasoning applies to all other types of business. The manufacturer, forbidden to acquire retailers and force its products at a loss to the wholly owned outlets, could accomplish the same result at the same loss by cutting the price to independent retailers. A prophylactic rule would require regulation of both price and quality.

Thus, if we adopt the theory of a prophylactic rule in our anxiety to preserve free competition, we end with the necessity to suppress every vestige of free competition. We cannot, therefore, justify the theory of automatic exclusion as a legal fiction disguising a prophylactic rule.

The second objection—that predation is less frequent than efficiency, so that a prophylactic rule would do more harm than good—is best taken up in the context of the theory of predation.

THE THEORY OF PREDATION

Antitrust law has never clearly defined what it means by predation, but the concept clearly contains an element of wrongful or specific intent, of a deliberate seeking of market power through means that would not be employed in the normal course of competition. We need something a little more definite for purposes of analysis. Predation may be defined, provisionally, as a firm's deliberate aggression against one or more rivals through the employment of business practices that would not be considered profit maximizing except for the expectation either that (1) rivals will be driven from the market, leaving the predator with a market share sufficient to command monopoly profits, or (2) rivals will be chastened sufficiently to abandon competitive behavior the predator finds inconvenient or threatening. Since these results are detrimental to consumer welfare, predation is not to be classed as superior efficiency.

Unsophisticated theories of predation abound, leading to drastic overestimations of its likelihood. The most common "theory" views firms in the market as if they were thugs in a dark alley; evidently a large firm has more muscle and can beat smaller firms to death. Sometimes the figure is changed, as in ominous references to the "law of the jungle" or the sarcasm frequently offered to rebut arguments for market freedom: " 'Everyone for himself,' cried the elephant as he danced among the chickens." Such remarks, though they represent popular "learning" on the subject, do not reflect theory but are only foolishly inapposite metaphors that ignore the constraints the market places upon firm behavior.

An equally foolish theory holds that predation is possible for a multimarket or conglomerate firm because it can lower prices to uneconomic levels in one market and avoid the costs of predation by raising its prices elsewhere. This theory rests upon the often-exploded recoupment fallacy. The predator would already be maximizing profits in all markets and so would have no way of increasing profits elsewhere to finance predation. That statement holds, of course, whether or not the predator has a monopoly position in the other markets.

Any realistic theory of predation recognizes that the predator as well as his victims will incur losses during the fighting, but such a theory supposes it may be a rational calculation for the predator to view the losses as an investment in future monopoly profits (where rivals are to be killed) or in future undisturbed profits (where rivals are to be disciplined). The future flow of profits, appropriately discounted, must then exceed the present size of the losses. So stated, there seems nothing inherently impossible in the theory. The issue is the probability of the occurrence of predation and the means available for detecting it.

A growing body of economic literature contributes to our understanding of the problem. For reasons that will become obvious, however, this literature does not completely solve the problem for modern antitrust.

There was a time not so long ago when everybody knew that the great American trusts had established and maintained monopoly positions by the ruthless extermination of smaller rivals. The prize exhibit was, of course, the known conduct of the Standard Oil Trust, and for that reason a very large crack appeared in what had appeared solid knowledge when John S. McGee published his careful and startling reevaluation of the Standard Oil legend, showing that Standard had not used predatory price cutting in its march to monopoly.[7] McGee's study was done to test Aaron Director's hypothesis, founded entirely upon the logic of price theory, that would-be monopolists would always prefer merger to predation. The study bore out that prediction. After a careful analysis of the entire trial record of the *Standard Oil* litigation, McGee concluded that "Standard Oil did not use predatory price discrimination to drive out competing refiners, nor did its pricing practices have that effect. . . . I am convinced that Standard did not systematically, if ever, use local price cutting in retailing, or anywhere else, to reduce competition. To do so would have been foolish; and, whatever else has been said about them, the old Standard organization was seldom criticized for making less money when it could readily have made more." Standard attained its market share by merger rather than predatory pricing.

Morris Adelman examined the facts underlying the government's successful prosecution of A&P, including the charge that the chain employed predatory price cutting in local markets in order to gain monopolies and the ability to raise prices.[8] He showed theoretically why such behavior would have been foolish and demonstrated empirically that it most certainly never occurred. Yet the Antitrust Division's charges, and judicial acceptance of them,[9] established still another legend of deliberate predation by a large multimarket firm.

Another study of a legend of predatory price cutting is Kenneth Elzinga's review of the history of the Gunpowder Trust.[10] Taking fourteen companies the government had alleged to be victims of such tactics, Elzinga concluded: "the evidence is quite clear six of these . . . suffered no such fate, it is my impression that another . . . was not subjected to this pricing strategy, the evidence does not allow any conclusion as to five of the companies . . . , and possibly two . . . were in fact subjected to the practice, though even here the evidence is hardly conclusive." The Trust "actually relied upon mergers and loose-knit agreements" for the market dominance achieved.

A theoretical analysis of predation by Lester G. Telser starts with the "assumption that the law does not hinder monopoly by merger or predation" and proceeds to evaluate these practices as "alternative means to monopoly return." [11] Telser concludes that, where the merger route is open, "predatory pricing . . . remains a threat and not an actuality among reasonable men, regardless of conditions in the capital market. The carrying out of the threat indicates a mistake either in the valuation of assets, in the cost of predatory pricing, or in the probability of winning." Telser suggests, however, that the threat may be used by either party, the acquiring firm or the firm to be acquired, to affect the price of the merger, which is to say, the share of the monopoly returns to be anticipated from the merger.

These studies, valuable as they are, do not directly address the question of appropriate rules concerning predation today. They leave open at least two major issues. First, the Standard Oil and Gunpowder trusts had merger and cartelization available as alternative routes to monopoly profits, and Telser's analysis begins with the assumption that these paths are available. Modern antitrust law, however, completely closes the merger option and makes cartelization a costly, dangerous, and much less effective method than it once was. We need to estimate, therefore, the likelihood that the closing of alternatives makes predation an attractive form of behavior for would-be monopolists. Second, these studies dealt with only one form of predation, price cutting, and we need to know whether other forms may be more effective.

Predation is a war of attrition, with its outcome determined by the combatants' relative losses and reserves. The war will be a blitzkrieg only if the predator has greatly disproportionate reserves or is able to inflict very disproportionate losses.

The factor of reserves is probably the less important. For our purposes, a firm's reserves may be defined as its liquid assets plus outside capital available to it at a price justified by expectations of future income. It is plausible to assume that the reserves of various firms in one industry will usually be in proportion to their relative degrees of competitive success, hence in proportion to their market shares. The predator, presumably the largest firm, will thus typically have the largest reserves in absolute size, but its reserves are likely not to be much larger in proportion to market share, and this, as we shall see, will usually be the important factor. When reserves are proportionally equal or even close to equality, the large firm will not find predation profitable if it must employ a technique that inflicts proportionally equal losses upon itself and the victim, and it will certainly not employ a technique that inflicts proportionally larger losses upon itself. The likelihood that reserves will be proportionally equal increases when we realize that available outside capital is included.

It is common to hear objections that the victim will not be able to find outside capital because "the capital market is imperfect." George Stigler aptly characterizes this as a "Gabriel-horn phrase": "Not only is imperfections-in-the-capital-market a popular concept, but what is more important, it is a terminal concept. Once this phrase has been written or spoken, the economist has finished with *that* strand of analysis." [12] The general idea of the capital market being more imperfect than other markets is, of course, patently implausible, since, as Stigler notes, "capital (or general credit) is the most fungible, the most divisible, the most mobile of all productive resources."

The difficulty with the concept of imperfections in the capital market is worse than this, however, for it is not evidence of imperfection if a lender refuses to make an unprofitable loan. If resisting predation is a profitable activity, the imperfection theorist would have to explain why capital will not flow to profitable uses, not just because of occasional mistakes in appraisal, but by a systematic refusal to invest in profitable resistance to predation. Nobody has troubled to explain that form of irrationality in capital suppliers, and we are justified in believing that it does not exist.

If the potential victim would find resistance to predation a profitable use for his liquid assets, a lender should find it equally profitable to lend the required capital. In fact, in any case in which the predator must use a technique that inflicts proportionally equal or greater losses upon himself, the victim would merely have to show the predator his new line of credit to dissuade the predator from attacking.

There are costs in raising capital, of course, and a major cost is likely to be the provision of information to potential investors. That cost is likely to loom largest when the amount of capital required is small and the industry is little known. The cost of convincing lenders may then create a sharply rising cost of outside capital and so provide some opportunity for predators. Yet there are also innumerable small investors in our society, and it seems doubtful that any industry is so unknown to any source of funds. And when we speak of industries operating at regional or national levels, we find both widespread information and many corporate and institutional sources of capital. Here the costs of borrowing to resist predation should not be great, and these are the most important markets.

The technique of predation, rather than the question of reserves, is likely to be decisive in the success of the tactic, and the law should focus upon this issue. Stigler states that "all systems of disciplining rivals by imposing losses require that the rival have inferior access to capital." If I understand that proposition, I think it is incorrect. Given equal access to capital, rivals can be killed or disciplined if the predator is able to inflict disproportionately large losses on his victim. This is required not merely so that the predator may be able to outlast the victim in a war, but also so that the predator can win quickly and thus have a reasonable expectation that future gains will outweigh present losses.

TECHNIQUES OF PREDATION

We must, therefore, attempt to classify forms of business behavior according to their capacities to serve as techniques for predation. If that can be done, the law enforcement agencies will be able to concentrate their attention on activities that have a potential for predatory use, and drop their harmful habit of seeing predation in behavior that is actually vigorously competitive.

To illustrate the theory of predation we will discuss three strategies that businesses may employ. The first, price cutting, though conventionally viewed with grave suspicion, does not provide a likely means of predation because it requires the predator to bear losses that are much larger, both absolutely and proportionally, than those inflicted on the intended victim. The second, the disruption of distribution patterns, is a more complex phenomenon. It may be manifested in a variety of ways, from demands for exclusive dealing (which is an extremely unlikely form of predation) to expulsion from cooperative business groups (e.g., boards of trade), a tactic which may enable predators to inflict losses upon victims that are not merely absolutely and proportionally larger than their own but so crushing as to be instantly and completely decisive. The third predatory strategy consists of misuse of courts or other agencies of government. This strategy may well succeed, since the predator will often be able to inflict upon his victim costs that are in absolute terms equal to or larger than his own, and proportionally larger in either case. These techniques are discussed as examples of a general theory; other possible cases will be mentioned under appropriate chapter headings in this book.

Price Cutting. A firm contemplating predatory price warfare will perceive a series of obstacles that make the prospect of such a campaign exceedingly unattractive. The losses during the war will be proportionally higher for the predator than for the victim; merger law will make it all but impossible for the predator to purchase the victim, so the campaign will have to last until the victim's organization and assets are dissolved; ease of entry will be symmetrical with ease of exit; and anticipated monopoly revenues, being deferred, must be discounted at the current interest rate.

Losses during a price war will be proportionally higher for the predator because he faces the necessity of expanding his output at ever higher costs, while the victim not only will not expand output but has the option of reducing it and so decreasing his costs.

The nature of the problem may be illustrated with a hypothetical case. The particular figures used are arbitrary, but their relationship is not. We may assume that a firm with 80 percent of a market wishes to kill a rival with 20 percent in order to achieve the comforts and prerogatives of monopoly status. We shall assume also that these respective shares of the market were determined by the shapes of the firms' marginal cost curves and that each firm is selling where marginal costs equal price.* The situations of predator and victim are shown in Figure 5. (Figure 5 does not show fixed contractual obligations, such as obligations to repay loans, and we may realistically suppose that the predator

* Many persons might suppose that the demand curves of duopolists would slope and that prices would be set above marginal costs. Introducing nonmarginal cost pricing, however, would complicate Figure 5 without changing the nature of the problem.

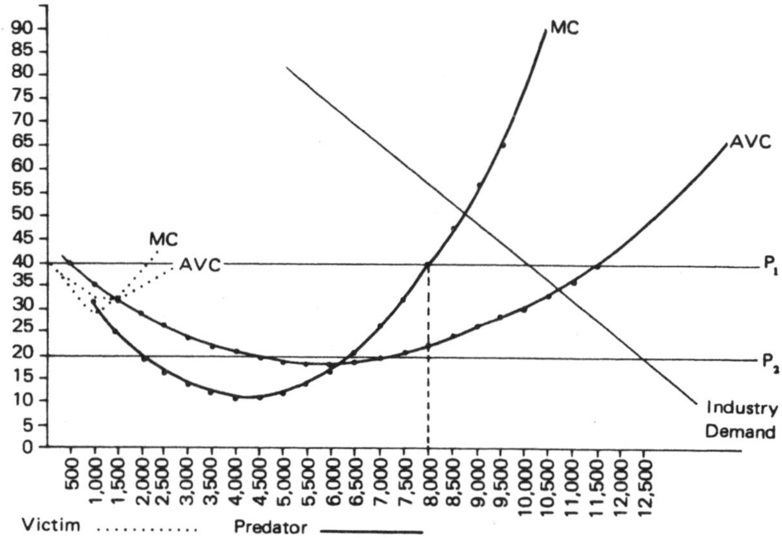

Figure 5. Hypothetical price, output, and cost for predator and victim.

has obligations amounting to $40,000 per week and that the victim's total $10,000.)

The market price is $40 and 10,000 units are being sold per week, of which the large firm sells 8,000 and the small firm 2,000. Let us suppose the predatory large firm opens warfare with a cut in price to $20. This price will cover neither firm's average variable cost,* and neither firm would remain in business if it expected that situation to continue for a long time. Indeed, the predator hopes to convince the victim of the futility of staying in the industry by indicating that $20 will be the price so long as the victim hangs on. But we must analyze the possible adjustments that may be made. These depend largely on the shape of the victim's average variable cost curve and on the feasibility of his closing down altogether until the price cutting ends. I have deliberately given the victim higher marginal and average variable costs than the predator at all relevant ranges of output, in order to

* Average variable cost is total variable cost divided by output. No firm will continue to produce if it does not expect to be able to cover its variable costs. It will continue if it covers variable but not fixed costs, though it will not replace equipment and plant as they wear out. This definition of average variable cost does not include expectations about the future. If it did, the illustration would require additional unnecessary explanation.

heighten the apparent probability of successful predation. If the victim's cost curves were as low as the predator's at any relevant output but rose more sharply (accounting for his lower share of the market), predation would fail even more certainly.

We may begin with the situation that is the worst for the victim, i.e., that he maintains his output at a rate of 2,000 per week. Halving the market price, however, has elicited a total demand of 12,500, which seems a modest enough increase; the predator, if he wishes to keep the price down to $20 for his victim's products, must satisfy this new demand by increasing output from 8,000 to 10,500 units per week. (The precise figures used in the example that follows are taken from a table on which Figure 5 is based. The table is not shown here because Figure 5 shows the relationship, and nothing depends on the exact numbers.)

The price received by the victim is $14.56 below his average variable cost. Given an output of 2,000, he is losing $29,120 in variable costs each week, to which must be added fixed expenses of $10,000, giving a total loss of $39,120. If losses were proportional to the starting market shares, the predator would be losing $116,480 in variable costs. But losses are not proportional, because the predator has had to expand output and because his average variable costs rise with that expansion. Average variable cost at the new output stands at $32.76, still below his victim's, but giving a loss of $12.76 on each of 10,500 units for a loss of $133,980 per week. Adding fixed obligations, he is losing $173,980. These assumptions produce a result so far that is not too bad for the predator, though they are certainly not favorable. If we assume, as is plausible, that the reserves of the two firms are in proportion to their original market shares—that is, in the ratio of 4 to 1—it is apparent that the predator is using up his reserves slightly faster than the victim. The ratio of losses is just over 4.4 to 1. That is not necessarily disastrous, of course. The predator may have reserves proportionally larger. On the other hand, the anticipated blitzkrieg has not materialized.

Yet this is by no means the worst that may happen to the hapless predator. The victim has options he has not begun to use. He may be able to close down operations for the time being, paying only $10,000 in fixed obligations and letting the predator supply the entire demand of 12,500 units at the price of $20. In Figure 5 the predator's average variable cost is $47.52 at that output, bringing his weekly variable costs to $344,000, and total losses to $384,000. The ratio of losses is then 38.4 to 1. A lower rate of increase in average variable cost would reduce the loss, but it would remain considerably higher than the loss necessary where the victim maintains his prewar output. The predator cannot raise the price because the victim would reopen, so he must take his losses as long as the victim retains the capacity to reopen.

But let us imagine a situation not quite so catastrophic for the predator. The victim may wish to avoid certain start-up costs, to keep a nucleus of staff on the job, to retain trade contacts, etc. He may, therefore, cut back to 1,000 units per week, where average variable cost is $33.60; then the loss per unit is $13.60, total loss in variable costs is $13,600 per week, and total losses are $23,600. The predator must now sell 11,500 units at an average variable cost of $39.50; he fails to recover weekly variable costs of $224,250, and absorbs a total loss of $264,250. Thus, while the predator's and the victim's reserves stand roughly in a ratio of 4 to 1, their losses per week stand in a ratio of almost 11.2 to 1. The unsophisticated observer might believe that the predator was winning the battle, since he appears to have "captured" 92 percent of the market, but it is that very fact that is defeating him.

A variety of factors may alter the magnitudes discussed here. Some of these would improve the predator's position somewhat; some would make it much worse. Thus, the predation would fail even more rapidly and disastrously if the victim had lower average variable costs below an output of 2,000, a not unreasonable possibility; or if the industry demand were more elastic, so that the predator had to produce, say, 13,000 units to hold the price down to $20.* However one varies the figures, one essential tendency will always be present: the predator must increase output, both to satisfy the new demand that comes forth at lower prices and to take up the market share relinquished by his victim, so he will sell many more units at a loss than will the victim. Moreover, the predator must move to higher average variable costs, while the victim can move to lower. The predator, therefore, will be taking higher losses, both absolutely and proportionally, than the victim. It looks as if the best method of predation is to convince your rival that you are a likely victim and lure him into a ruthless price-cutting attack.

This analysis is confirmed by the common sense of one Mr. Todd, the manager of a refinery allegedly threatened with price cutting by Mr. Moffett, the manager of the Standard Trust's Whiting refinery. John McGee quotes Todd's testimony:

* The victim might, of course, be driven from the market if he had very high levels of debt that had to be serviced. While this would be unfortunate for the owner, it would not harm competition. If the creditors either took over the business or sold it, the predator would find himself faced with a better-capitalized victim. Driving a company into bankruptcy turns out to be a way of eliminating what some might describe as an imperfection in the capital market.

Well, I says, "Mr. Moffett, I am very glad you put it that way, because if it is up to you the only way you can get it [the business] is to cut the market, and if you cut the market I will cut you for 200 miles around, and I will make you sell the stuff," and I says, "I don't want a bigger picnic than that; sell it if you want to," and I bid him good day and left.[18]

McGee notes, "The Standard threat never materialized."

The costs of predatory price cutting appear prohibitive, but three related considerations make such a tactic even more unattractive and improbable.

First, the modern law of horizontal mergers makes it all but impossible for the predator to bring the war to an end by purchasing his victim. To accomplish the predator's purpose, the merger must create a monopoly, and the law currently forbids mergers forming market shares of 5 percent or less. Even the much less stringent merger law advocated elsewhere in this book would preclude the attainment of the monopoly necessary to make predation profitable. This means that the price war must be protracted until the victim's facilities are entirely driven from the industry, without possibility of return, and there will always be the danger, until the victim's organization and facilities are irretrievably scattered, that an outside purchaser may appear; then the costly war will have been for nothing. Indeed, by depressing the value of the victim's business, the predator makes that business an attractive investment for any purchaser with adequate reserves. The substitution of such a purchaser for the victim will bring the war to an end, since its continuation would be pointless.

Second, as Ward Bowman points out, ease of entry will be symmetrical with ease of exit. The easier it is to drive a firm from the market, the easier it will be for that firm or another to reenter once the predator begins to collect his monopoly profits. Conversely, the more difficult entry is, the more difficult and expensive it will be to drive a rival out. A shoe retailer can be driven out rapidly, but reentry will be equally rapid. Railroading, which involves specialized facilities, is difficult to enter, but the potential victim of predation would be difficult to drive out precisely because railroad facilities are not useful in other industries. The railroad's management would have to be convinced that the long-run prospects, because of the predation, reduced the value of their facilities to little more than they would bring if sold as scrap. This symmetry of entry and exit means that predation by price cutting is a poor investment even if the predator has the reserves to bear the disproportional losses required.

Finally, while costs are immediate, the anticipated monopoly return is in the future, perhaps far in the future, and must be discounted by the rate of interest. This adds to the poor prospects for the firm contemplating predation by price cutting. (It may be added, if a fourth factor is wanted, that demand tends to become more elastic over time, thus further reducing the size of the anticipated future stream of monopoly payments.)

These considerations do not demonstrate that price cutting could never under any circumstances be a successful method of predation. We need more studies such as those by McGee, Adelman, and Elzinga of cases in which such predation is said to have occurred. But the analysis does demonstrate that predation by such techniques is very improbable.

It seems unwise, therefore, to construct rules about a phenomenon that probably does not exist or which, should it exist in very rare cases, the courts would have grave difficulty distinguishing from competitive price behavior. It is almost certain that attempts to apply such rules would do much more harm than good. For this reason, I am unpersuaded by the arguments advanced by Phillip Areeda and Donald Turner,[14] and even less so by F. M. Scherer's response [15] to them.

Areeda and Turner concede that predatory pricing seems highly unlikely and that extreme care must be taken that the rules formulated not deter competitive pricing. Yet they argue that it is well to have rules all the same. The rule they propose is that "a monopolist pricing below marginal cost should be presumed to have engaged in a predatory or exclusionary practice." (Presumably, the rule should apply to any large, established firm, and not merely to monopolists.) Since it is very difficult to ascertain marginal cost, they say, the rule can be applied by using average variable cost, which is shown in conventional business accounts, as a proxy for marginal cost. The suggestion poses a variety of problems.

The most worrisome is that true average variable costs cannot be reconstructed adequately from business records in a firm of any complexity. Areeda and Turner seem to be discussing plant-level costs, which are themselves sufficiently troublesome; but when we move to the level of the firm, particularly a multiplant, multiproduct firm, problems of costs estimation and allocation will ensure that the costs the law uses are only coincidentally related to real economic costs. There is a high probability of mistake, and hence of harassment, by enforcement authorities and private plaintiffs that would harm consumers by inducing noncompetitive price behavior.

We need not examine the theoretical points Scherer disputes with

Areeda and Turner because they lead him to an unworkable proposal, judicial inquiry into such matters as "the relative cost positions of the monopolist and fringe firms, the scale of entry required to secure minimum costs, whether fringe firms are driven out entirely or merely suppressed, whether the monopolist expands its output to replace the output of excluded rivals or restricts supply again when the rivals withdraw, and whether any long-run compensatory expansion by the monopolist entails investment in scale economy-embodying new plant." There could hardly be drawn a list of criteria less fit for judicial employment. Those items on the list that would not be altered by the monopolist's knowledge of the rules are unknowable by either courts or economists. It is a mistake to suppose that all of the questions posed by an abstract geometric representation of demand and cost phenomena can usefully be addressed in a court proceeding.

Roland H. Koller III studied twenty-three cases in which there were "convictions" for predatory price cutting and where the factual record was adequate to determine whether it had in fact occurred.[16] He thinks predatory price cutting was attempted in only seven cases, succeeded to some extent in four, and had harmful effects upon resource allocation in only three (and these three involved predation not to eliminate a rival but to precipitate merger or collusion).

If Koller's findings are accurate (any successful predation by price cutting is surprising and one should be wary of accepting at face value the assertion that even three cases exist), it is apparent at once how harmful the law has been. Twenty-three judge or jury findings of unlawfully low prices and only three cases of apparent harm to consumers. In sixteen cases firms were held liable for low prices when there was not even an attempt at predation. The result can only be to dampen the vigor of price competition. Moreover, in the three cases where Koller found harm to consumers, the mechanism (merger or collusion) is itself prohibited by law. It would appear safer for the law to concentrate on collusion and very large horizontal mergers in order to make predation ineffective than to jeopardize price competition by trying to prohibit predatory price cutting.

The theoretical argument presented here suggests that predatory price cutting is most unlikely to exist and that attempts to outlaw it are likely to harm consumers more than would abandoning the effort. The analysis also indicates that we should look for methods of predation which do not require the predator to expand output and incur disproportionately large costs. There are such techniques, and we turn to a consideration of some major examples.

Disruption of Distribution Patterns. In any business, patterns of distribution develop over time; these may reasonably be thought to be more efficient than alternative patterns of distribution that do not develop. The patterns that do develop and persist we may call the optimal patterns. By disturbing optimal distribution patterns one rival can impose costs upon another, that is, force the other to accept higher costs. This may or may not be a serious cost increase, but if it is (and the matter can only be determined empirically), the imposition of costs may conceivably be a means of predation. The predator will suffer cost increases, too, and that sets limits to the types of cases in which this tactic will be used for predation. There is a further complication, moreover, in that the behavior involved will often be capable of creating efficiencies. Thus, the law cannot properly see predatory behavior in all unilaterally enforced changes in patterns of distribution.

An example of a business practice carrying a very weak possibility of predation and a very strong probability of efficiency is the use of exclusive dealing contracts. Assume an industry with two manufacturers of equal size, ten retailers of equal size, and a pattern of distribution in which each of the manufacturers supplies half of each retailer's requirements. The pattern of distribution may be supposed to be optimal. Suppose that manufacturer *A* then imposes the condition that any retailer who buys from him must buy only from him. Contrary to some formulations of the problem, this does not threaten manufacturer *B* with foreclosure from the retailers. Since there was an equal demand for the products of the two manufacturers, should half of the retailers decide to accept *A*'s condition, the other half will be better off dealing exclusively in *B*'s product and not acceding to *A*. But the distribution pattern has altered, and it is possible that the new pattern is less efficient and hence imposes costs on *B*, though it is far more probable that *A* has merely perceived that exclusive dealing is more efficient and has adopted it for that reason. The law need have little difficulty with this case, however, for the patterns of distribution have changed to the same extent for both *A* and *B*, and each has suffered the same increase in costs, if there is an increase in costs and not a better mode of selling. The law should not interfere. Either *A* is a witless would-be predator and will retract his condition of exclusivity when he realizes his mistake, or, much more likely, he is trying to find a better mode of doing business.

The possibility of predation might arise if *A* started with 90 percent of the market and *B* with 10 percent, each of them selling in those proportions to each retailer. When *A* imposes its exclusive dealing condition, it will perhaps get nine of the retailers and *B* one. Assuming that benefits of the first pattern of distribution are proportional to the sales in each outlet, then *A* loses one retailer making X amount of sales and *B* loses nine whose sales also total X amount. Increased costs would again be equal, but if those costs impose a loss on each firm and their reserves are proportional to their market shares, *A* can bear the loss much better than *B,* and the result could be to drive *B* from the business. These assumptions can be altered in a variety of ways to give different results, but I want merely to note that the possibility of predation, however slim it may be, cannot be entirely excluded on theoretical grounds.

This analysis may be applied to *all* impositions of terms by a seller, which is one way of saying that the analysis alone is of no practical use whatever to antitrust law. Anybody who sells sets terms, and it seems a bit extreme to stop commerce on the ground that some minuscule proportion of it may theoretically involve predation. The search for predation may be narrowed somewhat, for the theory set out can work only if the predator has well over half of the relevant market. Even then it would not work unless the disruption of the distribution pattern imposed significant costs that could not be avoided. That narrowing is not sufficient, however. It would not make sense to deny the right to set terms to all firms with, say, a market share over 80 percent. Aside from the point that such a rule would really be a statement that no such market share should be permitted (a judgment that ought to be debated on other grounds), there is no reason to believe that the terms set, such as exclusive dealing, do not create efficiency far more often than they indicate predation.

The law can usefully attack this form of predation only when there is evidence of specific intent to drive others from the market by means other than superior efficiency and when the predator has overwhelming market size, perhaps 80 or 90 percent. Proof of specific intent to engage in predation may be in the form of statements made by the officers or agents of the company, evidence that the conduct was used threateningly and did not continue when a rival capitulated, or evidence that the conduct was not related to any apparent efficiency. These matters are not so difficult of proof as to render the test overly hard to meet. The real danger for the law is less that predation will be missed than that normal competitive behavior will be wrongly classified as predatory and suppressed.

It would be tempting to dismiss the whole topic on the ground that there is insufficient likelihood that predation of this sort ever occurs, but it seems clear that it can and does in certain classes of cases. It could have occurred in *Griffith,* since purchasing unreasonable clearances over rival theaters does not appear to require the predator to accept losses disproportionately larger than those of his intended victim. We have already canvassed the reasons why *Griffith*'s rationale of automatic exclusion was incorrect, and from this it follows that specific intent must be shown if efficiencies are not frequently to be sacrificed. Moreover, it should be noted that the theory of predation sketched here does not suppose that power flowed from monopoly towns to competitive towns but only that Griffith, being much larger than the independents singly or collectively, had larger reserves than all other theaters in its area and hence could have afforded a war that did not require it to accept disproportionate losses. There was, of course, no evidence cited that this was what happened.

But there is no doubt that predation can succeed when the distribution pattern is so much more efficient than the alternative that those forced out of the pattern cannot compete. The technique of predation is the denial of access to an essential economy of scale. Boards of trade, for example, often control such access, and their members may often easily destroy a troublesome rival by expelling him from membership or, perhaps more commonly, may bring a rival into line with the mere threat of expulsion.

The possible use of this technique may be illustrated by the factual situation underlying *Chicago Board of Trade.*[17] The trial record is inadequate to permit determination of the real purpose of the board regulation fixing prices overnight on grain "to arrive." There is a suggestion in the Supreme Court's opinion, however, of what may have been an unrecognized predatory design. Justice Brandeis noted that defendants averred the purpose of the rule was "to promote the convenience of members by restricting their hours of business and to break up a monopoly in that branch of the grain trade acquired by four or five warehousemen in Chicago." That is an improper use of the word "monopoly," and in any case Justice Brandeis, in arguing that the price-fixing rule affected such a small fraction of total grain sales as to have no adverse effect, indicated that even a real "monopoly" would have had no market power. Yet breaking the grip of four or five traders on this segment of trade may have been the purpose of the rule. Indeed, Brandeis claimed as a benefit of the regulation that "it distributed the business in grain 'to arrive' among a far larger number of Chicago receivers and commission merchants than had been the case there before." If the effect of fixing prices overnight was to take business from the four or five warehousemen and spread it to other grain traders, the most probable explanation would seem to be that the four or five had efficiencies in overnight price making that the others lacked. Perhaps they had night staffs or better connections with the farmers and country merchants and were able to follow the market and make prices more rapidly and accurately. The price-fixing regulation may well have been a move by a political majority within the board to deprive these traders of the benefits of their efficiencies. The tactic would work because it was probably essential for a trader to use the exchange. Thus, the predatory majority could confront the more efficient minority with the alternatives of giving up the benefit of their superior price-making capacities or giving up their membership on the Board of Trade. Loss of membership would be intolerable for such traders. The predators thus had the ability to impose totally unacceptable losses while bearing insignificant losses themselves.

Misuse of Governmental Processes. Misuse of courts and governmental agencies is a particularly effective means of delaying or stifling competition. We are here speaking of legal processes undertaken without regard to the merit of the claim advanced, in order to harm an actual or potential business rival. Litigation can be framed so that the expenses to each party will be about the same, and expenses in complex business litigation can be enormous, not merely in direct legal costs and fees but in diversion of executive effort and disruption of the business organization's activities. Where the object of predatory litigation is to drive an existing rival from a market altogether, the technique will generally be useful only by a larger firm against a smaller, since equal absolute costs will be proportionally greater for the smaller firm. But where delaying the appearance of new competition is the objective, the predator may be any size relative to the victim. The cost of the litigation must be measured against the worth of delay in the appearance of a rival in a lucrative market. The object is not then to inflict unacceptable costs upon the victim but merely to tie him up in proceedings to preserve a market position for a few years more.

The ability of the antitrust laws to deal with predation through this technique is somewhat constricted by countervailing policies. In some part, regulation by administrative agencies is expressly designed to allow firms to suppress the appearance of rivalry. That is not usually true of the court system, but even there the policy of allowing access to the courts, a policy that at times takes on constitutional dimensions, somewhat curtails the ability of antitrust to strike at predation through litigation. There is reason to think, however, that antitrust can and will play a valuable role in punishing predation through this technique. The issues are discussed at greater length in Chapter 18.

* * * *

The argument of this chapter has sweeping implications for antitrust policy. We have examined all of the law's theories about the ways in which business practices or structures may injure competition and found all of them, in varying degrees, to be defective. This is a serious matter, for it means that the law now perceives threats to competition where none exists, and it follows that the law is destroying valuable business arrangements for no reason.

The details of the necessary reforms are worked out in the chapters that follow, but the analysis so far indicates the general nature of those reforms. The law of arrangements that remove rivalry by agreement (e.g., horizontal price fixing, market division, mergers, and the like) must be substantially revised to save those arrangements whose primary effect is an increase in efficiency.

More important are the changes required in the law concerning practices or arrangements thought to be exclusionary (e.g., vertical and conglomerate mergers, exclusive dealing, tying arrangements, price discrimination, and the like). The theories of automatic exclusion and incipiency, upon which the Clayton Act, the Robinson-Patman Act, and the Federal Trade Commission Act are now based, should be abandoned completely. Antitrust should attack no practice or arrangement on the grounds that it is exclusionary or foreclosing unless deliberate predation can be proved. Improper exclusion (exclusion not the result of superior efficiency) is always deliberately intended. There is no "intermediate case" of exclusion resulting from neither efficiency nor predation. The law must become more sophisticated about techniques of predation. Presently, it fears exclusion from such things as price cutting and exclusive dealing, which are very rarely if ever predatory, and tends to pay too little attention to misuse of governmental processes and organized exchanges, where opportunities for predation are plentiful.

These reforms would greatly alter the course of decisions under the antitrust statutes. Just how much will shortly be seen. That alteration would bring the antitrust laws into line with their professed purposes and would represent a clear net gain for consumers as well as for the integrity and intellectual respectability of the law.

Notes

1. *United States* v. *Trans-Missouri Freight Ass'n.*, 166 U.S. 290 (1897), discussed at pp. 22–26, supra.
2. *United States* v. *Addyston Pipe & Steel Co.*, 85 Fed. 271 (6th Cir. 1898), aff'd., 175 U.S. 211 (1899), discussed at pp. 26–30, supra.
3. *Standard Oil Co. of New Jersey* v. *United States*, 221 U.S. 1 (1911), discussed at pp. 33–41, supra.
4. *Northern Securities Co.* v. *United States*, 193 U.S. 197, 400, 410–11 (1904), discussed at pp. 30–32, supra.
5. 110 F. Supp. 295, 345, 341, 344–45 (D. Mass. 1953), aff'd per curiam, 347 U.S. 521 (1954).
6. 334 U.S. 100, 102, 106, 108 (1948).
7. McGee, "Predatory Price Cutting: The Standard Oil (N.J.) Case," 1 *J. of Law and Econ.* 137, 168 (1958).
8. Adelman, *A&P: A Study in Price-Cost Behavior and Public Policy* (Cambridge: Harvard University Press, 1966), pp. 14, 362–79, 390, 394–97, 407–10.
9. *United States* v. *New York Great Atlantic & Pacific Tea Co.*, 67 F. Supp. 626 (E.D. Ill. 1946), aff'd, 173 F.2d 79 (7th Cir. 1949).
10. Elzinga, "Predatory Pricing: The Case of the Gunpowder Trust," 13 *J. Law and Econ.* 223, 236 (1970).
11. Telser, "Cutthroat Competition and the Long Purse," 9 *J. Law and Econ.* 259, 264, 267 (1966).
12. Stigler, "Imperfections in the Capital Market," 75 *J. of Pol. Econ.* 287, 290 (1967).
13. McGee, "Predatory Price Cutting," supra n. 7, at 155.
14. Areeda and Turner, "Predatory Pricing and Related Practices Under Section 2 of the Sherman Act," 88 *Harv. L. Rev.* 697 (1975).
15. Scherer, "Predatory Pricing and the Sherman Act: A Comment," 89 *Harv. L. Rev.* 869, 890 (1976).
16. Koller, "The Myth of Predatory Pricing: An Empirical Study," 4 *Antitrust L. & Econ. Rev.* 105 (Summer 1971).
17. *Chicago Board of Trade* v. *United States*, 246 U.S. 231, 237, 240 (1918).

[16]

JOURNAL OF ECONOMIC THEORY **27**, 280–312 (1982)

Predation, Reputation, and Entry Deterrence*

PAUL MILGROM

J. L. Kellogg Graduate School of Management, Northwestern University, Evanston, Illinois, 60201

AND

JOHN ROBERTS

Graduate School of Business, Stanford University, Stanford, California 94305

Received July 30, 1980; revised July 13, 1981

Economists often argue that predatory practices are irrational, since there exist cheaper or more certain means to gain or maintain a monopoly. Our game-theoretic, equilibrium analysis suggests that if a firm is threatened by several potential entrants, then predation may be rational against early entrants, even if it is costly when viewed in isolation, because it yields a reputation which deters other entrants. Asymmetric information plays a crucial role in our analysis, since it provides the rationale for entrants to base their expectations of the firm's future behavior on its past actions. The analysis also suggests methods to treat general reputational phenomena. *Journal of Economic Literature* Classification Numbers: 611, 022, 026, 612.

1. INTRODUCTION

Allegations of price cutting or similar tactics aimed at driving a rival out of business are frequently heard, both in and out of law courts. Yet a large fraction of the economics profession would argue that such predation is an irrational strategy for attempting to gain or maintain a monopoly position and that it is, therefore, unlikely to be adopted in practice. This position rests on arguments that predation is costly to the predator and is unlikely to

* This work was begun while Roberts was on the faculty at Northwestern and completed while Milgrom was visiting Stanford. We would like to thank Robert Wilson and David Kreps for making their unpublished results available to us and for several helpful conservations, David Besanko and Garth Saloner for their excellent research assistance, the referees for their useful comments, and the Center for Advanced Study in Managerial Economics, the Office of Naval Research (N00014-79-C-0685) and the National Science Foundation (SOC 79-07542, SES 80-01932, and SES 81-08226) for financial support.

succeed in driving out a rival who understands that the price cutting is temporary. Further, it is held that even if the rival is eliminated, any attempt to raise prices so as to reap the benefits of the monopoly position may attract new entrants. Thus, any monopoly gains would be short-lived.[1] (See, e.g., McGee [10, 11] for full expositions of these arguments, as well as some indication of the nature of the opposing views.)

In this paper we present a model in which predation emerges as a rational, profit-maximizing strategy. In this model, predation is practiced not because it is directly profitable to eliminate the particular rival in question, but rather because it may deter future potential entrants. The mechanism by which this deterrent effect comes about is that by practicing predation the firm establishes a reputation as a predator. This reputation then leads potential entrants to anticipate that the incumbent firm will behave similarly if they should enter, and, thus, entry appears less attractive to them.

In this context, it is worth noting that predation will emerge in our model even if, as asserted by those who doubt the rationality and relevance of predatory strategies, predation against a particular rival involves losses that cannot be directly recouped in the given market, even were exit to be induced. Moreover, viability of this predatory strategy does not depend on being able to induce exit. Rather, all that is needed is that the predator usually be able to drive the rival's return from entry below that available elsewhere.

Examples consistent with the sort of analysis we will develop are not hard to find. Government studies in the U.S. and the U.K. in the early part of the century identified many instances of predatory pricing against new entrants in the ocean shipping industry through the use of "fighting ships," and the U.S. Department of Justice [18] has documented more recent episodes in this industry which it views as predatory (see also Yamey [19]). Although it is difficult to determine if any of this price cutting was done with a view to deterring future entrants, one might expect that firms considering entering an industry with a century-long history of aggressive responses to entry would at least entertain the idea that they might meet a similar response. More directly, Brock's discussion [2] of IBM's pricing and product strategies against the "plug compatible" manufacturers (who were marketing peripheral equipment for use with IBM central processing units) suggests that IBM was concerned that failure to respond aggressively would encourage further entry. Finally, the fierce price wars that erupted as Proctor and Gamble introduced its Folger's brand of coffee into local markets in the Eastern U.S. in competition with Maxwell House may well have been central in *P & G*'s

[1] This latter argument seems to suggest the possibility of deterring entry by holding current prices down. For a discussion of some of the problems with this notion of limit pricing, see [13].

decisions not to continue expansion of its distribution area and, in particular, not to enter the New York City market.[2]

Of course, it has long been recognized in the literature on industrial organization that the response that entrants expect from incumbent firms would be a major factor in determining the attractiveness of entry, and much of the traditional literature on entry deterrence effectively hinges on the threat of predation (see, e.g., Dixit [3] or Spence [17]). Most models involving such threats are, however, subject to a telling, fundamental criticism. One should expect that the threat of predation will be effective in preventing entry only if entrants find the threat credible. But in these models, which involve a single entrant, if the entrant were to call the incumbent's bluff by entering despite the threat, the incumbent would not be willing to prey, since sharing the market would typically be more the profitable course. In contrast, the strategy of predation in our model does not involve threats which would not rationally be carried out, since the immediate losses incurred in predation are offset by the gains from a reduced threat of further entry that building a predatory reputation yields.

Thus, in our framework, a multiplicity of potential entrants plays a key role in rationalizing a predatory strategy. If, in fact, the established firm were to face a countable infinity of threats of entry, all of which may be potentially carried out, then it is trivial to identify an equilibrium which involves a credible threat of predation, as we demonstrate in Appendix A. (We also show there that there are numerous other equilibria in this framework.) If, however, there are only a finite number of potential entrants, the issue is more complicated. This point has been made by Selten [16].

Selten considers a model which may be interpreted in terms of a firm which operates in N identical markets (a chain store). Each market has one potential entrant. Sequentially, the entrants must individually decide whether to enter the corresponding markets. If entry does not take place in market n (at stage n), the incumbent enjoys its monopoly position in that market without further threat. This contributes Π^M to its overall payoff. If entry occurs at stage n, the incumbent must decide whether to prey on the entrant (yielding Π^P) or to share the market (yielding Π^C). We assume $\Pi^M > \Pi^C > \Pi^P$: predation is costly. In any event, the next entrant must then make its decision, knowing the history of play up through the preceding stage. Assume that the payoff to any entrant from meeting predation is strictly less than that from staying out, which, in turn, is less than the payoff from entry if no predation occurs.

Selten suggests, and it does seem intuitively appealing, that in early rounds of this game the incumbent would adopt the costly predatory action in order

[2] In Section 4 of their companion paper, Kreps and Wilson present a model which predicts behavior that closely approximates that in the Folgers–Maxwell House competition in several important aspects.

to persuade later entrants that they should best stay out, and that only near the end of the game would it be willing to share a market. Yet Selten also points out that this strategy cannot be consistent with the natural solution concept (that of perfect equilibrium) to employ in such situations.

The argument is the following. Consider the last entrant. It knows that if it enters and meets predation, it would have been better off to stay out. But it also knows that, if faced by actual entry, the established firm is strictly better off if it behaves nonaggressively. Thus, assuming that both firms will always act in their own best interests, entry will occur in the last market to be threatened and will meet a nonaggressive response. Moreover, this will be the result, no matter what has been the history of play to this point.

Now consider the second-last market to be threatened. If entry were to occur there and if the chain store could deter entry in the last market by adopting predatory practices, it might well adopt such measures. However, as just shown, the outcome in the last market is completely determined, independent of the outcome in the second-last market. Thus, if entry occurs, the chain store will share the second-last market peacefully, and, thus, too, entry will occur in this market.

The induction is inexorable and the conclusion clear: in equilibrium, predation will never be practiced. Moreover, even if (for whatever reason) the chain store were observed to have preyed repeatedly against every previous entrant, the logic still will lead the next entrant to anticipate not that past behavior will be repeated but rather that it entry will meet a nonaggressive response. Repeated observations of behavior which, *a priori*, the entrant expected never to see cannot and do not shake its absolute confidence in its predictions of future behavior.

The key factor driving this conclusion is that it is *common knowledge* (see Aumann [1], Milgrom [12]) that accomodation is the best reponse to entry and that entry is the best response to accommodation. This common kwowledge, in turn, arises from the situation represented as a game of complete and perfect information in which all the firms are fully informed about the structure of the tree describing the game being played, about the payoffs accruing to all players, and about the others' past acts. As soon as the complete information assumption on the game is relaxed, so that the common knowledge condition no longer obtains, the logic of the backward induction breaks down. (This point is illustrated in Appendix B.) The possibility of actions taken in the past being a useful guide to future behavior in similar situations now opens up, and with this, reputations[3] can come into

[3] Most generally, a player's reputation in this context would be the beliefs that other players hold about his unknown characteristics and on the basis of which they predict his behavior. These beliefs would depend on their initial beliefs and on their observations of the player's past behavior. In the model we develop here, a simple sufficient statistic for these beliefs will be identified as the firm's reputation.

play. Further, once the lack of complete information gives rise to reputation possibilities, the players' equilibrium behavior will adjust markedly. The resultant equilibrium is then radically different than with complete information, for it has exactly the qualitative properties of Selten's intuitive solution. Practicing predation now gives one a reputation as a predator which is valuable in deterring entry. Thus, if entry occurs at an early stage, it will meet a predatory response, because any other response encourages further entry. Recognizing this, potential entrants at these early stages will enter only if the market is so lucrative that they are willing to face certain predation. Only as the horizon draws near and the number of markets which may still be entered declines will the firm be willing to share a market.

In the following sections we present our analysis of a version of Selten's model of multiple markets with sequential entry possibilities. In contrast to Selten, however, we allow that there is some doubt in the minds of the potential entrants concerning the established firm's options, motivations and behavior. We compute an equilibrium in this context which involves predation even by firms which find such a strategy to be costly in the short run, and we show that this equilibrium is the unique one involving sequential rationality by all players. We also investigate some of the major comparative statics properties of this model. The chief of these relate the value of a reputation—and the costs one will be willing to incur to obtain it—positively to the frequency with which the reputation may be used, as measured by the length of the horizon and the inter-period discount factor. The final sections presents a summary and some suggestions regarding both the implications of this analysis for policy and the possibilities for developing other formal models involving reputations.

2. The Model

As suggested in the previous section, incomplete, asymmetrically distributed information plays a central role in our analysis of predation and, in particular, in undoing the logic leading to Selten's Chain Store Paradox. One obvious way to introduce the requisite informational asymmetry is to allow that the entrants do not know exactly the payoffs accruing to the established firm from an aggressive response to entry and that there is some positive probability that such a response is directly more profitable in any given stage than a response of peaceful coexistence. Kreps and Wilson [7] employ this approach, and we had also explored this avenue in earlier versions of this paper.[4]

[4] While their analysis and ours originated independently, we have since benefitted greatly from having access to their ideas. They have also developed significant extensions of the "one-sided" reputation models studied here. Their paper is highly recommended to the reader.

Here we adopt a different approach in which we assume that the established firm definitely finds predation to be directly less profitable than sharing a given market. However, we also allow that there is some arbitrarily small, but nonvanishing, element of doubt in the minds of the entrants about whether their model of the established firm's options, motivation, and behavior is correct. In particular, our modeling allows that the entrants entertain some possibility that one or another simple behavioral rule guides the actions of the established firm. The nature of these rules is such that past behavior is repeated when similar circumstances arise. While yielding an equilibrium with exactly the same qualitative properties as that identified by Kreps and Wilson and by us in our earlier modeling, the present approach permits somewhat simpler arguments than we had needed before, it yields a strong uniqueness result, and it also appears to have some measure of applicability to a broad range of other problems. We will return to these issues of motivation, interpretation and justification after presenting the formal model.

We consider a game with $N+1$ players. Player 0 is the established firm, while player n, $n = N, \ldots, 1$, is a potential entrant in market n, where N is the first market threatened and 1 is the last. Associated with each player i is a random variable τ_i which is uniformly distributed on $[0, 1]$, independent of the other τ_j. We refer to a realization t_i of τ_i as the "type" of player i, $i = 0, 1, \ldots, N$. As well, we have two strictly increasing, continuous functions, α, and β, where

$$\alpha\colon [0, 1] \to (-\infty, 0)$$

and

$$\beta\colon [0, 1] \to (-\infty, 1).$$

The function α will give the payoffs to firm 0 from preying at a particular stage as a function of its type, while β gives the payoff to an entrant which decides to stay out, again as a function of its type.

The $N+1$ firms will play one of three possible games, each of which involves N repetitions of a particular stage game. (Only the established firm will know which of these actually obtains.) The first possibility is that the game is one where the nth stage is

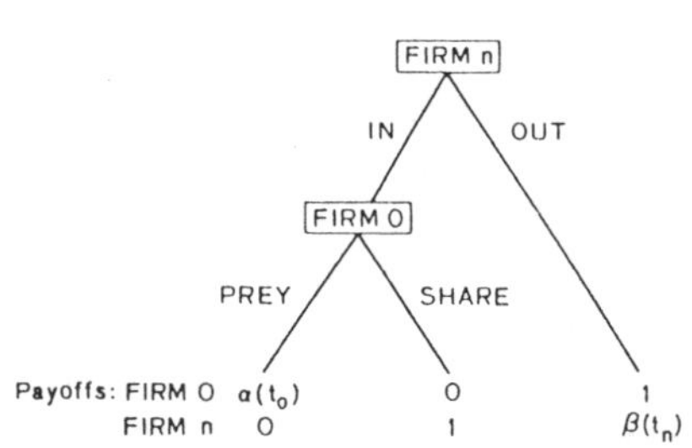

The second possibility is that the game has as its nth stage

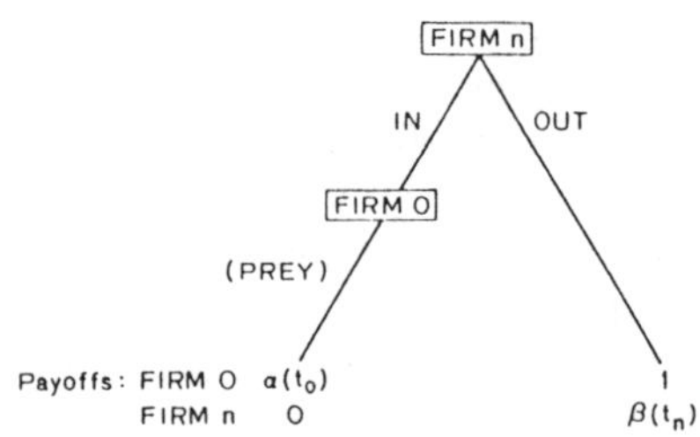

The third possibility is that the nth stage is

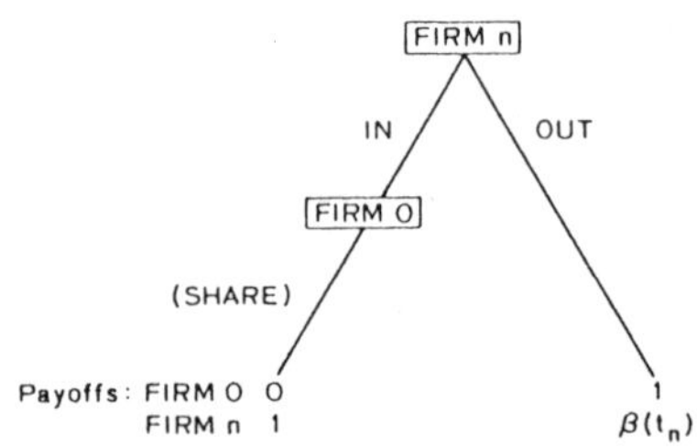

The first pattern is initially assessed a probability of $1/(1+\varepsilon+\delta)$, the second is given probability $\varepsilon/(1+\varepsilon+\delta)>0$, and the third is given probability $\delta/(1+\varepsilon+\delta)\geqslant 0$. We think of ε and δ as being small. Note that the realized value of τ_0 matters only when it is the first of these games that is being played. It is then convenient when referring to the situation where the second game is being played to abuse the notation by saying that $\tau_0=\omega$ ($\omega>1$) in this circumstance. Correspondingly, we will say that $\tau_0=-\omega$ when it is the third game which is being played.

In each case, we have normalized the stage game payoffs so that the profit accruing to the established firm in any market in which it does not experience entry is 1 while its profit when peacefully sharing the market is 0, and so that the profit to the entrant is 0 if it meets predation and 1 if its entry elicits a nonaggressive response. These normalizations in no way effect the results: they solely serve to ease computations. In particular, they do not mean that the entrant "breaks even" when preyed upon, nor do they imply that, for example, the profits of the entrant if it is not preyed upon are equal to the profits of the established firm when there is no entry.

The specifications of the ranges of the α and β functions do have meaning in this context, however. That α is bounded above by 0, which is the profit payoff from preying, means that, other things being equal, any profit maximizing established firm would prefer to share a single market rather than to prey. (We are thus building McGee's arguments into our formal model.) Similarly, the upper bound of 1 on β means that the entrants' outside opportunities are never better than sharing the market if entry will meet a passive response. The condition on α is used in our uniqueness argument, but may not be necessary; the condition on β serves only to simplify the arguments and could definitely be relaxed. Allowing that the realized values of β may be negative recognizes the possibility that entry might occur even if predation were certain. This could, for example, capture the idea that predation would fail against a particular entrant.

Our model is distinguished from Selten's in two major respects, both of which involve aspects of incomplete information. First, we assume that each player has a continuum of possible types, with different payoffs for each type. This assumption serves primarily to generate a pure strategy equilibrium. Taking α and β to be constant functions would eliminate this difference between our model and Selten's but would still generate a predatory equilibrium strategy for the established firm. Hence, the first distinction cannot account for the qualitatively different equilibrium behavior that we will find. The second difference is the positive ε and δ assumed in our model; in Selten's model $\varepsilon = \delta = 0$. We have introduced positive values of ε and δ to capture the ideal that entrants entertain the possibility that a predatory response in one period might be part of a general aggressive pattern, and a cooperative response might be part of a general cooperative pattern. It is important to recognize that, if $\varepsilon = \delta = 0$, there is no compelling reason for an entrant to suspect that any observed behavioral pattern might continue: past behavior, in that case, is utterly irrelevant in forecasting future behavior. It is precisely that irrelevance that leads to and is the heart of Selten's paradox. We shall see later that even as ε and δ approach zero, the potential entrants' strategies do not approach those specified by Selten: As ε, δ approach zero, the probability that predation deters entry can be bounded away from zero. However, the probability that predation actually occurs does converge to zero.

We assume that

$$\alpha(1) > \frac{-\rho(1-\beta^{-1}(0))}{1-\rho(1-\beta^{-1}(0))} \equiv \mathbf{a},$$

where $\rho \in (0, 1)$ is the discount factor used by firm 0. This condition turns out to be necessary for any reputation building to occur. While the basis for this claim must remain somewhat opaque for now, it will be shown that the right-hand side of the inequality represents the critical value of $\alpha(t_0)$ such that a firm of type t_0 is just indifferent about preying when the horizon is infinite and a single act of predation convinces the entrants that predation is certain in every future period. We also assume that $\beta(1) > 0$. Otherwise, there is no possibility of deterring entry, since being preyed upon is always better than the alternative opportunity involved in not entering.

It is worth noting in this context that the assumption that the τ_i are uniform random variables on $[0, 1]$ in fact imposes no restriction on the model. This is because α^{-1} and β^{-1} are the cumulative distributions of the random payoffs.[5] Further, although our assumptions that α and β are increasing functions means that there are no mass points in these distributions, this assumption on α is for convenience only. The strict monotonicity of β does assure some useful continuity in the optimal responses, but this too can be relaxed at the cost of complicating the equilibrium (see [7, Remark A]).

Initially, the structure of the game is common knowledge. This includes the values of δ and ε, the α and β functions, and the distributions of the random variables τ_i which determine the types. As well, it is common knowledge that only player i knows the value of τ_i and that only player 0 knows which of the three repeated stage games is being played. At each point in the game, each firm knows the history of the moves taken to that point by it and the other firms, but firm 0's payoffs in previous rounds are not observable by the other firms. Finally, it is also common knowledge that firm 0's payoff from the whole game is the present value of its profits at each stage, calculated with the discount factor ρ.

This framework corresponds to Harsanyi's treatment of games of incomplete information played by Bayesian players [5]. The distributions α^{-1} and β^{-1} reflect the various firms' beliefs about each other's payoffs, and the ε and δ reflect the doubts that the entrants have about whether their modeling of the established firm via the first repeated game is correct. Since the players are not sure about either the form of the tree describing the game they are playing (i.e., whether τ_0 is $+\omega$, $-\omega$ or in $[0, 1]$) or the payoffs accruing to various strategies (since the realized values of α and β are not public information), the situation is a game of incomplete information. Harsanyi's method for solving such games involves introducing a new game with complete but imperfect information, i.e., one in which the players all know the full game tree and all the payoffs but are not fully informed about the previous moves of the other players. In this game there is an additional player, Nature, which moves first. Nature plays a mixed strategy, selecting the actual types of the various players according to the probability distribution over types that describes the players' prior beliefs about one another. This move by Nature in our framework thus determines which of the three possible games is being played and the actual, realized values of the payoffs to the $N+1$ firms. However, only firm 0 is informed about the

[5] Throughout, for increasing functions $f\colon [0, 1] \to R$, we employ the conventions that if $x < f(0)$, then $f^{-1}(x) = 0$ and if $x > f(1)$, then $f^{-1}(x) = 1$.

outcome of Nature's choice of the game tree and about the value of τ_0, and only firm n is informed about the realized value of τ_n. Thus, the game, while one of complete information, is also one with imperfect information, since a player's information sets typically include several different decision nodes, with the node that actually obtains having been determined by an aspect of Nature's move about which the firm is not informed. Harsanyi's approach is then to identify an equilibrium of this game with complete, imperfect information as the equilibrium of the original game of incomplete information.

In any game, a pure strategy for a player identifies an action to take in each information set. Here, a player's information sets are differentiated in part by its type. For example, given any stage n and any history of play by the firms up to that point, firm 0 still has a continuum of different information sets, one for each possible determination of its type through Nature's move. Thus, if only for this formal reason, a strategy for any firm must be a function of its type and thus must specify what it would do if its type were, say, some value $\bar{t}$, even when its true (realized) type is something different.

This fact often seems to cause difficulties for those who have not previously dealt formally with games of incomplete information. One way to interpret the idea that a strategy must specify behavior for types that don't actually exist is to regard a strategy for a particular player as a conjecture in the minds of the others about its behavior. Then the dependence of the strategy on the player's type simply reflects the other players' making allowances in forming these conjectures that the player's behavior depends on its type, which is unknown to them. In our model, these conjectues by the entrants about firm 1's behavior are first about whether or not they have correctly modeled the established firm as choosing between predation and sharing, and secondly, if it does make such choices rather than reacting mechanistically, about the conditions under which it will prey. With this view, an equilibrium involves each player reacting optimally to its conjectures about the other's behavior, and these conjectures being consistent with the choices actually made.

Our solution of this game employs the concept of sequential equilibrium introduced by Kreps and Wilson [8]. This equilibrium notion requires that, at any decision node, the player take an action that maximizes its expected payoff, given its current beliefs and given that the others will henceforth follow the prescribed equilibrium strategies. These current beliefs (about, e.g., which node in an information set actually obtains) must be consistent with the player's initial beliefs, with any information that it may have available (directly or by inference) and, whenever possible, with the hypothesis that play has evolved to this point under the equilibrium strategies.

To define a sequential equilibrium formally, let H_n denote the history of the moves taken by the various firms from stage N to, but not including, stage n. Let H_n^+ denote the resulting history in stage $n-1$ when predation occurred in stage n, let H_n^- indicate that sharing occurred, and let H_n^0 indicate that there was no entry. Let $\mathscr{H}_n$ denote the possible histories of play up to stage n. Then a strategy for firm 0 consists of N maps

$$s_0^n: \mathscr{H}_n x\{\{-\omega\} \cup [0, 1] \cup \{\omega\}\} \rightarrow \{\text{Prey, Share}\},$$

$n = N, \ldots, 1$, where $s_0^n(\cdot, \omega) \equiv$ Prey and $s_0^n(\cdot, -\omega) \equiv$ Share. A strategy for entrant n is a map $r^n: \mathscr{H}_n x[0, 1] \rightarrow \{\text{Enter, Stay Out}\}$. Then a sequential equilibrium is a strategy for each firm such that:

(1) for each $n = 1, \ldots, N$, each $H \in \mathscr{H}_n$ and each $t_n \in [0, 1]$,

$$\begin{aligned} r^n(H, t_n) &= \text{Enter} \quad \text{if} \quad [1 - p_n(H)] > \beta(t_n), \\ &= \text{Stay Out} \quad \text{otherwise;} \end{aligned}$$

(2) for each $n = 1, \ldots, N$, each $H \in \mathscr{H}_n$ and each $t_0 \in [0, 1]$,

$$\begin{aligned} s_0^n(H, t_0) &= \text{Prey} \quad \text{if} \quad \alpha(\tau_0) + \rho \tilde{V}_{n-1}(t_0, H^+) > \rho \tilde{V}_{n-1}(t_0, H^-), \\ &= \text{Share} \quad \text{otherwise,} \end{aligned}$$

where the value function $\tilde{V}$ is defined recursively, given $\tilde{V}_0 \equiv 0$, by

$$\begin{aligned} \tilde{V}_n(t_0, H) = {} & q_n(H) \max[\rho \tilde{V}_{n-1}(t_0, H^-), \alpha(t_0) + \rho \tilde{V}_{n-1}(t_0, H^+)] \\ & + (1 - q_n(H))[1 + \rho \tilde{V}_{n-1}(t, H^0)]; \end{aligned}$$

and

(3) for all n and all $H \in \mathscr{H}_n$

$$p_n(H) = \text{Prob}\{s_0^n(H, \tau_0) = \text{prey} \mid H\}$$

and

$$q_n(H) = \text{Prob}\{r^n(H, \tau_n) = \text{enter} \mid H\}.$$

In this definition, the p_n and q_n, which are interpreted as perceived probabilities of predation and of entry, respectively, represent the players' conjectures, and condition (3) is the rational expectations consistency requirement.[6]

Sequential equilibria are always Nash. Moreover, Kreps and Wilson have shown [8] that "for 'almost all' games [with finite strategy spaces], the

[6] Note that the conditional expectations in (3) may not be well defined if H is a history of play that occurs with probability zero under the specified strategies. In this case there is some latitude possible in specifying $p_n(H)$ and $q_n(H)$, although not any arbitrary specification will do. See [7 and 13] for further discussion of this point in related contexts.

perfect and sequential equilibria 'nearly' coincide." Although the continuum of choices open here to Nature renders this result formally inapplicable to our model, the sequential equilibrium still clearly captures the basic idea behind perfectness. An advantage of the Kreps–Wilson equilibrium formulation over the perfectness approach is that it greatly eases the problem of computing and verifying that particular strategies constitute an equilibrium, since it allows us to use the methods of dynamic programming to analyze the players' decisions. To apply the methods of dynamic programming, it is necessary to define one or more state variables that summarize some of what the players know about the current position of the game. In the original Kreps–Wilson formulation, the beliefs of each player function as his personal state variable. In our model, the firm's reputation, which will be defined by a statistic that summarizes the history of play, will serve as a state variable.

3. Existence, Uniqueness and Properties of the Equilibrium

To begin analysis of this game, note that at stage 1 (the last market), firm 0 must never prey as long as $t_0 \neq \omega$, since to do so lowers its payoff with no possible compensation. Thus, if it is known that $t_0 \neq \omega$, entry must occur at stage 1. But if firm 0 ever fails to prey, the entrants can all immediately infer that $t_0 \neq \omega$, (since $t_0 = \omega$ automatically yields predation). Selten's argument then applies, since it is common knowledge that firm 0 will not prey at stage 1. Thus, once it has ever failed to prey, firm 0 cannot gain by preying at stage 2, or, for that matter, at any other stage, since to do so simply squanders profits (α is negative) and cannot influence future entry decisions. Thus, if firm 0 ever fails to prey, it is clear that it will never prey again in equilibrium. It is also then clear that entry will occur in every succeeding market, since $\beta(t_n)$ is less than the payoff from unopposed entry for all t_n. Thus, in any sequential equilibrium, failure to prey against a particular entrant implies that the present value of the established firm's future payoffs from this and all succeeding stages is zero.

Now suppose that firm 0 has never failed to prey, but that entry has just occurred in market n. As just seen, failure to prey yields a value of zero to the established firm for the rest of the game. If, however, it adopts an alternative strategy which involves preying at stage n, then, given the strategies of the remaining entrants, it faces some list of possible patterns of future entries, predatory episodes, and unentered markets. In expected present value terms, let E, P, and M represent, respectively, the count of future entries, current and future predatory acts, and unshared markets resulting from the alternative strategy. Then the expected present value of future payoffs from following this strategy of predation is equal to $P\alpha(t_0) + M$, given our normalizations. Since $P \geqslant 1$, this expression is increasing in t_0, the value of τ_0. Thus, if it pays firm 0 to prey at stage n when $\tau_0 = t$ (i.e., $P\alpha(t) + M > 0$), it also pays when $\tau_0 = t' > t$. In fact, then, the maximized value of future payoffs over all possible strategies is also increasing in t_0, since it is the value of the maximum of increasing functions (including the constant function 0).

These points can be effectively illustrated graphically. The axes in Figure 1 are M and P, as defined above. Given the succeeding entrants' strategies, a particular choice of strategy at stage n by firm 0 results in a particular point in (P, M)-space. The convex hull of the resulting points is graphed. Note that $P + M \leqslant n$, and that the origin is always available. Firm 0's preferences over this space are given by the linear indifference curves corresponding to $P\alpha(t_0) + M = C$. Payoffs are increasing as we increase M or decrease P, and the slope of any particular type's indifference curves is $-\alpha(t_0) > 0$. Thus, if $t_0 > t_0'$, then the t_0 indifference curves are flatter than those for t_0'. It then is seen that the optimal P is at least weakly increasing in t_0, and that if a given strategy yields a positive payoff for a particular value of t_0, it yields a positive payoff for all higher values of t_0.

Thus, in searching for an equilibrium, we can limit our attention to pure strategies for firm 0 which call for predation at a particular stage with a given history of play if and only if the value of τ_0 exceeds some critical value, where this value is 1 if the history to that point involves any failure to prey. (Clearly, for $\tau_0 = |\omega|$, there is nothing to specify. The reason we can restrict ourselves to pure strategies is that, with $P\alpha(t_0) + M$ increasing in t_0, at most one single type would ever be indifferent between the two possible actions at any stage.)

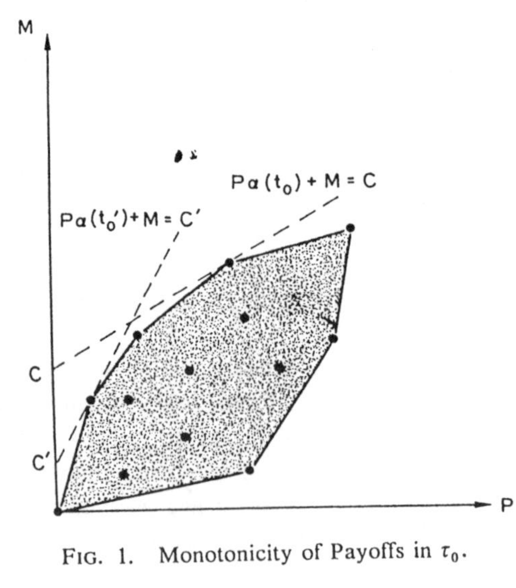

FIG. 1. Monotonicity of Payoffs in τ_0.

Thus, in equilibrium, if firm 0 has preyed whenever entry has occurred, the entrants can infer that either $\tau_0 = \omega$ or the value of τ_0 exceeds the maximum of the critical values governing its past predatory decisions. Let x be this maximum, and call x the *reputation* of firm 0 with the given history of play. We make the special conventions that if the established firm has ever failed to prey, its reputation is $x = -\infty$, and that if no entry has previously occurred, $x = -1$.

We will now characterize an equilibrium for this game in which at stage n:

(1) firm n's decision depends only on the value of τ_n and on firm 0's current reputation x;

(2) firm 0's decision (for the relevant case where $|\tau_0| \neq \omega$) depends similarly only on the value of τ_0 and on x;

(3) firm 0's new reputation on entering stage $n-1$ depends only his reputation entering stage n and the actions taken there.

This equilibrium involves N numbers, $x_N \leqslant x_{N-1} \leqslant \cdots \leqslant x_1$, with the property that, so long as it has never previously failed to prey, firm 0 with $|\tau_0| \neq \omega$ will prey in response to entry in market n if and only if $t_0 > x_n$. Further, we show that $x_1 = 1$, that $x_n < x_{n-1}$ unless $x_{n-1} = 0$ or 1, that $\lim x_n = \max[0, \alpha^{-1}(\boldsymbol{\alpha})]$, and that, if $\alpha(0) > \boldsymbol{\alpha}$, there exists a finite k such that, for all $n > k$, $x_n = 0$. Thus, in this equilibrium, the set of firms which will prey at stage n includes all those which will prey at any later stage when there are fewer markets to protect, and, for large N, any firm for which $\alpha(\tau_0) > \boldsymbol{\alpha}$ will prey in the early rounds, regardless of the immediate cost. We also show how to compute the x_n values, demonstrate that this is the unique sequential equilibrium, and obtain some comparative statics results.

Since the entrants are to be looking only at their own types and firm 0's reputation, and since the revision of the reputation is to depend only on its current value and current actions, the expected present value to firm 0, when entering stage n, of playing optimally in this and all later stage depends only on the value t of τ_0 and on its current reputation x. Let $V_n(t, x)$ denote this value, and recall that, as argued above, V_n is increasing in t as the supremum of increasing functions. We will describe recursively a set of strategies based on these V_n functions, then verify that they do in fact constitute the unique sequential equilibrium.

Step 0. *Initialization.* Let $V_0(t, x) \equiv 0$ for all t and x. This is just an initialization based on a "dummy" stage 0. We also initialize by setting firm 0's reputation entering stage N at -1.

Step 1. *Reputation Revision at Stage n.* Suppose firm 0's reputation entering stage n is $x \neq -\infty$. Then its reputation on entering stage $n-1$ is

Outcome in Market n	Reputation Entering Market $n-1$
No entry	x
Sharing	$-\infty$
Predation	$x \vee x_n$

where "$\vee$" is the max operator and

$$x_n \equiv \inf\{x \in [0, 1] \mid t > x \text{ implies } \alpha(t) + \rho V_{n-1}(t, t) > 0\}.$$

If $x = -\infty$ at stage n, then firm 0's reputation at stage $n-1$ is also $-\infty$, independent of the actions taken at stage n.

Step 2. *Firm* 0'*s Actions at Stage n.* With $\tau_0 = t \in [0, 1]$ and current reputation $x \neq -\infty$, we specify the firm 0 will prey at stage n if and only if

$$\alpha(t) + \rho V_{n-1}(t, x \vee x_n) > 0,$$

i.e., if and only if the current return plus the value of continuing optimally exceeds zero, which, as argued above, is the value of the payoffs resulting from failure to prey (i.e., $V_n(t, -\infty) \equiv 0$). If $x = -\infty$, we specify that the firm will share the market if entry occurs.

This is clearly an optimal strategy for firm 0.

Remark: Suppose now that firm 0 does follow this strategy. What can subsequent entrants correctly infer from seeing firm 0 prey at stage n? If the firm entered stage n with reputation x, then the subsequent entrants need consider only firm types t that exceed x. There are two possible cases.

First, if $x > x_n$, then $x = x \vee x_n$. In this case,

$$\alpha(t) + \rho V_{n-1}(t, x) \geqslant \alpha(x) + \rho V_{n-1}(x, x) > 0$$

so long as $t \geqslant x$, since α and V_{n-1} are increasing in t. The second inequality here follows from the definition of x_n and from $x > x_n$. Thus, if the firm has already demonstrated that it is of type $t > x_n$, it will surely prey at stage n.

Second, if $x \leqslant x_n < 1$, then $x_n = x \vee x_n$. Then the fact that α and V_{n-1} are increasing in t implies that

$$\alpha(x_n) + \rho V_{n-1}(x_n, x_n) \gtreqless \alpha(t) + \rho V_{n-1}(t, x_n)$$

as $x_n \gtreqless t$. Now, if $x_n > 0$, the continuity of V_{n-1} (to be verified shortly) implies that the left-hand side of the inequality is zero. Then the firm will in fact optimally prey if $t > x_n$, will optimally share if $t < x_n$, and is otherwise indifferent. If $x_n = 0$, then the left-hand side is non-negative, t is automatically greater than x_n, and predation is an optimal response, while if $x_n = 1$, then a similar argument shows the optimality of sharing. Thus, we have verified that future entrants could correctly forecast that firm 0 will prey in market n with reputation $x \neq -\infty$ if and only if $\tau_0 > x \vee x_n$. This justifies the evolution of reputations that we specified.

Step 3. *Firm n's Actions at Stage n.* In view of these computations, if $x > x_n$, then entrant n will in equilibrium correctly regard a predatory response as certain. If $x = -\infty$, entry will be correctly anticipated to meet a nonaggressive response. In general, we have

$$
\begin{aligned}
p_n(x) &= \text{the probability in equilibrium that firm 0 will prey at stage } n \text{ with reputation } x, \text{ given that } \tau_0 \geqslant x \\
&= \text{the probability assessed by entrant } n \text{ that, given the reputation } x, \text{ firm 0 will prey at stage } n \\
&= \begin{cases} \dfrac{\varepsilon + [1 - (x \vee x_n)]}{\varepsilon + (1 - x)} & \text{if } x \geqslant 0 \\ 0 & \text{if } x = -\infty \\ \dfrac{[\varepsilon + (1 - x_n)]}{[1 + \varepsilon + \delta]} & \text{if } x = -1. \end{cases}
\end{aligned}
$$

The entrant's best response at n is then to enter if and only if

$$p_n(x) \cdot 0 + (1 - p_n(x)) \cdot 1 \geqslant \beta(t_n),$$

i.e., if and only if

$$t_n \leqslant \beta^{-1}(1 - p_n(x)) \equiv q_n(x).$$

Then $q_n(x)$ is precisely the probability that n enters at stage n when firm 0's reputation is x.

These strategies are clearly optimal responses to firm 0's strategy.

Step 4. *Transition from Stage n to Stage n* + 1. With the initialization for V_0, the preceding steps allow us to calculate V_1 as $V_1(t, x) = 1 - q_1(x)$. To complete the recursive cycle, we now have to specify how to move from stage n to $n + 1$. For $x \neq -\infty$,

$$
\begin{aligned}
V_{n+1}(t, x) = q_{n+1}(x) \max[0, \alpha(t) + \rho V_n(t, x \vee x_n)] \\
+ (1 - q_{n+1}(x))(1 + \rho V_n(t, x)).
\end{aligned}
$$

The first term on the right-hand side is the probability of entry times the maximum of the expected present value of the payoffs either from sharing the market and getting a reputation of $-\infty$ (where we have used the previously established fact that $V_n(t, -\infty) = 0$ or from preying now and then continuing optimally with the new reputation $x \vee x_n$. The second is the probability of no entry times the value of having this market as a monopoly and then continuing optimally with one's reputation unaffected.

Note that it is now clear that V_n is continuous if V_{n-1} is continuous. Thus, since $V_0 \equiv 0$ is continuous, all the V_n are.

It is also clear that V_n is the optimal value function and, thus, that the strategies do constitute a sequential equilibrium. Each firm is maximizing, given its beliefs and its conjectures about the other firms' strategies, the beliefs are consistent, and the conjectures are correct.

Before we turn to characterizing this equilibrium, some further discussion of the determination of the x_n values may be useful. In Fig. 2 we show $[0, 1] \times [0, 1]$ with the diagonal. Think of the horizontal axis as being reputations and the vertical as the type of the established firm. Then we ask: if preying at stage n were to yield a reputation x, which types of firms would be willing to prey? The set of such firms is $\{t \in [0, 1] \mid \alpha(t) + \rho V_{n-1}(t, x) > 0\}$. Thus, the lowest type willing to prey is the inf over this set. Denote this inf as $h_n(x)$, and note that h_n is continuous and monotone decreasing. Then x_n is the unique fixed point of $h_n(x)$, i.e., the point where the graph of h_n crosses the diagonal. To see this, note that if $x \neq x_n$, then the set of firms willing to prey if it yields reputation x would not in fact justify the earning of that reputation.

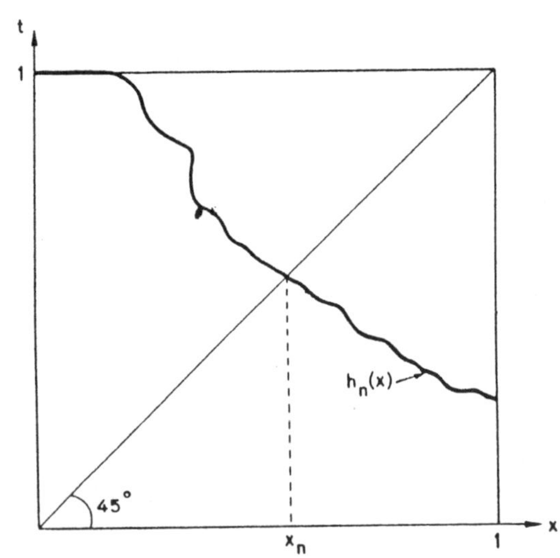

FIG. 2. Determination of x_n.

We now seek to characterize the equilibrium. In so doing, the following function will be useful. Define $g: R^2 \to R$ by

$$g(t, v) = (1 - q_1(1))(t + \rho v) + q_1(1) \max(0, \alpha(t) + \rho v),$$

where $q_1(1)$ is the probability of entry against the "strongest" type of established firm in the last period or, equivalently, the probability of entry in any round against certain predation, i.e., $q_1(1) = \beta^{-1}(0)$. Observe that $V_{m+1}(t, 1) = g(t, V_m(t, 1))$ and for all t, g is increasing in v and

$$|g(t, v_1) - g(t, v_2)| \leqslant \rho\, |v_1 - v_2|,$$

so that $g(t, \cdot)$ is a contraction map. Let $\bar{v}(t)$ be the unique fixed point for each t. Then one can verify that

$$\begin{aligned} \bar{v}(t) &= \frac{1 - q_1(1)}{1 - \rho(1 - q_1(t))} && \text{if} \quad t \leqslant \mathbf{x}, \\ &= \frac{1 - q_1(1)(1 - \alpha(t))}{1 - \rho} && \text{if} \quad t \geqslant \mathbf{x}, \end{aligned}$$

where

$$\mathbf{x} = \alpha^{-1}\left(\frac{-\rho(1 - q_1(1))}{1 - \rho(1 - q_1(1))}\right) = \alpha^{-1}(\boldsymbol{\alpha}).$$

This fixed point will provide a bound on $V_n(t, \cdot)$.

Note, too, that the relationship $\alpha(1) > \boldsymbol{\alpha}$ which was assumed earlier is simply equivalent to $\mathbf{x} < 1$. (At this point, one can straightforwardly verify the claims and interpretations made in connection with this assumption.) Further, since g is an increasing contraction map, we have the following result.

LEMMA. *If $v < \bar{v}(t)$, then $v < g(t, v) < \bar{v}(t)$.*

Proof. Let $v < \bar{v}(t)$. Then

$$g(t, v) < g(t, \bar{v}(t)) = \bar{v}(t).$$

Also,

$$\begin{aligned} \bar{v}(t) - g(t, v) &= g(t, \bar{v}(t)) - g(t, v) \\ &\leqslant \rho(\bar{v}(t) - v) \\ &< \bar{v}(t) - v, \end{aligned}$$

so $v < g(t, v)$. Q.E.D.

Note that $V_0(t, 1) = 0 \leqslant \bar{v}(t)$ (with strict inequality at least for $\mathbf{x} < t$) and that $V_{m+1}(t, 1) = g(t, V_m(t, 1))$. Thus, in particular, we have $V_m(t, 1) \leqslant \bar{v}(t)$ for all m.

PROPOSITION 1. *For any n, $x_{n+1} \leqslant x_n$, with strict inequality if $x_n \neq 0$ or 1. Further $x^* \equiv \lim_{n\to\infty} x_n = \max[0, \mathbf{x}]$.*

The proof of this result is given in Appendix C.

Proposition 1 establishes the key point that any firm (defined in terms of the costs it incurs in preying) which is willing to prey when n markets are still threatened by actual or potential entry will also prey when there are a greater number threatened. It further gives the asymptotic properties of the x_n. If $\mathbf{x} < 0$, so that $x^* = 0$, then the convergence to x^* is necessarily in finite time. Thus, for all n sufficiently large, the established firm will prey for sure unless $\tau_0 = -\omega$. If $\mathbf{x} > 0$, then the convergence is only asymptotic: $x_n > \mathbf{x}$ for all n. Of course, for large enough values of n, the differences between x_n and $\mathbf{x}$, between $V_n(t, x)$ and $\bar{v}(t)$, and between $p_n(x)$ and unity are arbitrarily small.

Note that none of these asymptotic properties depend on the particular values of $\varepsilon > 0$ and $\delta \geqslant 0$.

In terms of Figure 2, the behavior of the h_n functions as n varies gives the evolution of the x_n values. If $\alpha(1)$ is sufficiently negative, no firm would find predation attractive if n is small, and the corresponding h_n functions are identically equal to 1. Eventually, however, acquiring a reputation of 1 (or close to it) by a single act of predation will become attractive for firms with high enough $\alpha(\tau_0)$ values, since such a reputation reduces the threat of entry to (essentially) $\beta^{-1}(0)$. Thus, at least near $x = 1$, $h_n(x)$ lies below x, and x_n becomes strictly less than 1. The correspondence between higher values of n and lower values of x_n then is a matter of h_n (at least near the diagonal) being above h_{n+1}. Finally, all the h_n converge in n to a constant function at $x^* = [0 \vee \mathbf{x}]$, indicating that any type above x^* would be willing to prey to get such a reputation.

The equilibrium evolution of the game thus becomes clear. For large n, if $\mathbf{x} < 0$, then once firm 0 has preyed and thereby revealed that it is not irrevocably committeed to sharing ($\tau_0 \neq -\omega$), entrants correctly regard predation as certain. Thus, the only entrants which will attempt entry for large n after one predatory episode are those whose outside alternatives are so poor, relative to the profits available by entry, that they are willing to face certain predation. The probability of entry is then $\beta^{-1}(0)$, which may be zero. If $\mathbf{x} > 0$, then a second act of predation is not absolutely certain (since $x_{n+1} > x_n > \mathbf{x}$ for all n), but it is close to being so when n is large. Consequently, the probability of entry is close to $\beta^{-1}(0)$. In either case, the established firm sees predation at an early stage as leading to a long string of monopoly returns, possibly interrupted by occasional predatory episodes. If its payoff while preying exceeds $\boldsymbol{\alpha} = \alpha(\mathbf{x}) = [-\rho(1-\beta^{-1}(0))]/[1-\rho(1-\beta^{-1}(0))]$, it prefers this to the continuation value of zero which results from failure to prey. If $t < \mathbf{x}$, sharing is preferred.

Before the first attempt to entry, if $\delta > 0$ it is still possible that the established firm is of the type that never preys. In this case, the probability of predation is strictly less than one, even when $\mathbf{x} < 0$, and so one would expect (with probability strictly greater than $\beta^{-1}(0)$) to see a test of firm 0's fortitude by an entrant with a relatively low value of τ_n and thus low opportunity costs in entering. If this entry meets predation, then the firm's reputation immediately jumps to $x \geqslant x^*$, and the game proceeds as described above.

As the number of markets remaining threatened decreases over time and the horizon approaches, x_n increases. This begins immediately if $\mathbf{x} > 0$, and at some finite date if $\mathbf{x} < 0$. Consequently, the conditional probability that $\tau_0 > x_n$, given the current reputation x, and thus the probability of predation will start to decrease. If at some stage this probability of predation is sufficiently low relative to $\beta(t_n)$, entry will occur. If $t \leqslant x_n$, entry will meet a nonaggressive response. The possibility that $\tau_0 = \omega$ is then eliminated, it thus becomes certain that predation will not occur in market 1, Selten's logic takes over, and unopposed entry occurs in all remaining markets. If $t > x_n$, predation occurs. The established firm's reputation now rises to x_n, the probability of predation at stage $n-1$ now is $p_{n-1}(x_n) > p_{n-1}(x)$, the attractiveness of further entry is reduced from what it would have been if the value of τ_0 were only known to exceed x rather than x_n, and the probability of entry in future rounds correspondingly falls.

We will now demonstrate that this is the unique sequential equilibrium.

We have already observed that, in *any* sequential equilibrium, if the established firm ever fails to prey, then there must be entry and sharing at every later stage. Thus, it suffices to consider only what happens when there has been no sharing. We have also observed that at any stage n with any history of play to that point, firm 0 with $|\tau_0| \neq \omega$ will prey if and only if τ_0 exceeds some critical value. Thus, at any sequential equilibrium all that can be inferred from a given history involving no sharing is that $\tau_0 = \omega$ or $\tau_0 \in (x, 1]$ for some x. As well, we have also observed that we need consider only pure strategies.

We now establish inductively that any sequential equilibrium must agree with the one we have described earlier at all stages $m \leqslant n$. The induction is made on n, and the case $n = 0$ is immediate. Fix any sequential equilibrium and suppose that the result holds for $n = k$. Then the value of entering stage k with $\tau_0 = t$ and reputation x is $V_k(t, x)$. Now consider firm 0 in stage $k+1$, where the history is H and the corresponding reputation is $\bar{x}$. Let $x \geqslant \bar{x}$ denote the reputation that 0 would have at this equilibrium if entry and predation occurred at stage $k+1$. Then firm 0 of type $\tau_0 = t$ would choose to prey or not according as

$$\alpha(t) + \rho V_k(t, x) \gtreqless 0.$$

The reputation x must be consistent with 0's actual strategy at equilibrium, so we must have for $t \geqslant \bar{x}$ that

$$\alpha(t) + \rho V_k(t, x) \gtreqless 0 \qquad \text{as} \quad t \gtrless x.$$

Using the monotonicity of V_k, it is straightforward to check that the unique $x \geqslant \bar{x}$ for which this holds is $x = \bar{x} \vee x_k$. Hence, the conditional probability that entry will meet predation at stage $k+1$ given the history H and reputation $\bar{x}$ is $p_{k+1}(\bar{x})$. The unique best response to this for firm $k+1$ is to enter if and only if $\beta(\tau_{k+1}) < p_{k+1}(\bar{x})$, and this completes the induction. Notice that the fact that strategies depend on history only through reputations has been derived, not assumed. What the induction establishes is that if history affects play only through the reputation for stages $m \leqslant k$, then the same is true at stage $k+1$. Since this is trivially true for $k=0$, it is true for all k.

The comparative statics properties of this equilibrium can be stated rather simply. Those on N have already been established: the values of the x_n are, in fact, independent of N, so that the probabilities of entry and of predation in round $n < N$ do not depend on N. Of course, we have already shown that x_n converges monotonically down to $[0 \vee \mathbf{x}]$. Increases in ρ, the discount factor, tend to lower the x_n's. To see the sense behind this claim, note that against given strategies by the entrants, a higher value of ρ increases (in present value terms) the reward to preying. The costs that the established firm would be willing to incur in preying then increase, lowering the cut-off level of x at which predation occurs. However, such a lower value for x_n will make entry less attractive, lowering $q_n(x)$ and increasing the benefit from predation at stage $n+1$. Thus we have a snowballing effect, with everything working in the same direction. (A formal proof of all the comparative statics results we will claim here is given in Proposition 2.)

Together these two results indicate that the value of a reputation—and the costs one would incur to achieve it—increase with the frequency with which it may profitably be used. Being able to use the reputation either more often at a given rate (increases in N) or with less delay between uses (increases in ρ) increases the incentives for building and maintaining a reputation. We will later suggest some interesting implications that would follow if this intuitively appealing result carries over to other models.

The effects of changing the α or β functions in certain ways can also be identified. Adding any positive function to β (while still maintaining monotonicity and the upper bound of 1) yields a new function whose inverse, as the distribution of the outside opportunities, stochastically dominates the original distribution β^{-1}. This change lowers the probability of entry against any given reputation, given the established firm's strategy. However, the lower values of the q_n tend to increase the value of preying (since they mean that predation is more likely to deter future entry), so again we have the snowballing effect we saw in the case of ρ. Similarly, an increase in α, which shifts α^{-1} in the sense of stochastic dominance, also decreases the x_n. Thus both an increase in the outside profit opportunities of the entrants (which lowers the attractiveness of entry) and a decrease in the costs of preying tend to lower the x_n, thereby increasing the probability of predation with any given reputation and lowering the probability of entry.

Finally, a higher value of ε, the probability put on an automatically aggressive response, also works in the same way to lessen the x_n, and thus to increase the probability of predation with a given reputation and lower the probability of entry.

All these properties are established formally by the following result, which is proven in Appendix D.

PROPOSITION 2. *Suppose* $\rho \geqslant \bar{\rho}$, $\alpha \geqslant \bar{\alpha}$, $\beta \geqslant \bar{\beta}$ *and* $\varepsilon \geqslant \bar{\varepsilon}$. *Then* $x_n \leqslant \bar{x}_n$, *for all n.*

In this modeling, the possibility that $\tau_0 = -\omega$ (with probability δ) was included largely for the sake of symmetry: either form of mechanistic behavior pattern is possible. The sole effect of δ on the equilibrium is that it encourages an early test of firm 0 by some entrant. In particular, the x_n values do not depend on the value of δ. In fact, as long as the probability that $\tau_0 = \omega$ is kept bounded from zero, we could also have allowed that the entrants also entertained all the theories about the established firm's behavior which involve it preying against every entrant until there are exactly k markets left, $k = 1, 2, \ldots$, and then never preying again. The equilibrium would not have been qualitatively changed.

Finally, let us examine the behavior of the equilibrium as $\varepsilon \to 0$ and thus as we approach the original Selten model. Consider the case $N = 2$: the arguments can be extended for any N. By Proposition 2, x_2^ε is increasing as $\varepsilon \to 0$ and so has a limit x_2^0. Then by the definition of x_2^ε, we have $q_1^\varepsilon(x_2^\varepsilon) \to \max(0, 1 + \alpha(x_2^0)/\rho)$. Since α is bounded above by 0, we then have that the limit is strictly less than one. Further, if $x_2^0 \neq 1$, then we have $\lim q_1^\varepsilon(x_2^\varepsilon) = \lim \beta^{-1}[1 - \varepsilon/(\varepsilon + 1 - x_2^\varepsilon)] = 1$, and this contradiction shows that $x_2^0 = 1$. Thus, as $\varepsilon \to 0$, the set of firms which will prey in equilibrium becomes null. However, since $x_2^0 = 1$, predation at stage 2 deters entry with probability equal to $\min[1, -\alpha(1)/\rho] > 0$. Note that this a failure of upper hemicontinuity of the sequential and perfect equilibrium correspondence as we change the information structure: the established firm's equilibrium strategy converges to that identified by Selten, but the entrants' strategies do not.

Another way to express the striking importance of even very small positive values of ε is to consider how the deterrent effect of a strategy of always preying depends on ε. The easiest case to consider is when $\beta(0) > 0$. Suppose entry actually occurs at k dates $m_k, \ldots, m_1$, where m_i occurs after m_{i+1}, and these entries are always met by predation. Then by examining the entrants' strategies we find that for any two successive entry dates m_i and m_{i-1}, $1 - \beta(0) > 1 - \beta(\tau_{m_{i-1}}) > [\varepsilon + 1 - x_{m_{i-1}}]/[\varepsilon + 1 - x_{m_i}]$, where $x_{mk+1} \equiv 0$. This gives a set of k inequalities which when multiplied together lead to $[1 - \beta(0)]^k > [\varepsilon + 1 - x_{m_1}]/[\varepsilon + 1 - x_{m_{k+1}}] > \varepsilon/(1 + \varepsilon)$. Hence, $k < \ln[\varepsilon/(1 + \varepsilon)]/\ln[1 - \beta(0)]$. This provides an upper bound on the number of entries that can arise for *any* realizations of $\tau_1, \ldots, \tau_N$ when entrants follow their equilibrium strategies and firm 0 adheres to an aggressive strategy. Note that the bound is independent of N and grows only logarithmically in ε. Even tiny values of ε can lead to moderate bounds on k. For example, if $\beta(0) = 0.75$, then for $\varepsilon = 10^{-3}$ one obtains $k \leqslant 4$, for $\varepsilon = 10^{-6}$ one obtains $k \leqslant 9$, and for $\varepsilon = 10^{-9}$, $k \leqslant 14$. Thus, tiny elements of uncertainty can produce a significant deterrence of entry.

4. Summary and Conclusions

We have demonstrated that the presence of informational asymmetries can lead a firm operating in several markets to adopt a predatory strategy against entrants, even though such behavior is irrational when viewed in the context of a single market in isolation and even though there are only a finite number of potential entrants. This same point is made in the one-sided uncertainty model in the accompanying paper by Kreps and Wilson [7]. We view this model and our work as complementary, in that they display two different ways in which the recognition of informational asymmetries can "resolve" the Chain-Store Paradox. This resolution comes about because the informational asymmetry gives the entrants reason to forecaset future actions on the basis of past behavior. This in turn gives the establishes firm reason to prey in order to build a reputation which leads future entrants to predict that they too are likely to meet predation.

The particular asymmetry we have introduced involves the entrants being less than certain that they are correct in modeling the established firm as rationally choosing between predation and peaceful coexistence. Specifically, we allow that they entertain the possibility that an episode of predation—which ought never to occur in the complete information set-up—may be part of a general pattern of predatory behavior. The recognition of this possibility then results in the marked change in the equilibrium behavior that we have demonstrated.

There are numerous reasons why this element of uncertainty should exist. On the one hand, the entrants could be not completely sure about the game being played. For example, it might be that the established firm could actually be involved in some bigger game of which the one studied here is only a part and that the firm's equilibrium strategy in this larger game calls for it to prey in these markets. A second possibility is that in the game actually being played, the established firm may be able to precommit itself to an aggressive course of action and may have done so. Other scenarios involve the entrants allowing that the firm is not behaving as a fully rational game theorist.

For example, the fact that firms involve many individuals, each with his or her own preferences and information, suggests that the appropriate model of the firm would be one of group decision making, and there is no compelling reason for choices in such situations to correspond to the maximization of a single utility function. Alternatively, the firm may have well-defined utility function, but it may not calculate fully the equilibrium in the game being played. Instead, it may have some more or less arbitrary conjectures about how the entrants will behave in response to its actions, and its preying is the optimal behavior given these conjectures. In fact, Rosenthal [14] has argued that games of perfect information ought to be analyzed as if the players were decision theorists in this sense, rather than game theorists whose conjectures about others' behavior must be correct. In this context, Rosenthal suggested that his approach could resolve the Chain-Store Paradox, and Macgregor [9] has verified this conjecture. Thus, for example, if the established firm believed that the entrants would simply forecast that past behavior would be repeated, it would be led to prey.

In this regard, Scherer's discussion ([15, pp. 338–339] of predation as a deterrence strategy is of interest. He notes that if entrants perceive different markets as sufficiently similar and if "business managers extrapolate from past events rather than sizing up the probabilities in each new situation", then predation may have a deterrent effect. He goes on to note that very little is known about the extent to which such extrapolation occurs. Our analysis show that even if everyone is fully rational and does "size up the probabilities in each new situation," as long as there is some doubt about whether this is the case, predation can emerge.

The implications of this analysis for antitrust policy are straightforward. In multiple market situations, predation can be a rational strategy which deters entry and thus supports monopoly. Thus, any tendency to discount the likelihood or significance of predation on the basis of its presumed irrationality should be checked when there are multiple markets which might reasonably be regarded by potential entrants as similar. (An interesting paper by Easley *et al.* [4], in which firms can make their markets seem to be intrinsically unprofitable candidates for entry by predation, yields similar conclusions.) Firms serving several geographically distinct markets are only one case where the model and its conclusions might apply. Firms with broad product lines or those in which on-going technological change yields a pattern of new product introduction over time are others. In this context, it is worth noting explicitly that predation will only rarely need to be practiced. The credible threat of predation will deter all but the toughest entrants (those with low values of t_n), and so the occasions when the firm will be called upon to carry out its threat will be infrequent.

Two factors in our model lead to the emergence of reputations: the informational asymmetries and the repeated actions with the possibility of observing past behavior. These conditions will be necessary for reputation building to occur in general, and it would further seem that they are sufficient: in any situation where individuals are unsure about one another's options or motivation and where they deal with each other repeatedly in related circumstances (or where past dealings with other people are observable), we would expect to see reputations develop. A clear example of such a situation is in problems involving the choice of product quality. Other examples in economics arise in credit relationships, in labor negotiations and strikes, in implicit contract models, and in the provision of auditing services, bond ratings, job recommendations and the like. The reader can easily provide more examples. Moreover, applications outside the traditional bounds of economics are at least as numerous. We expect that the methods of this paper can be applied in each of these contexts to yield important insights on the nature of observed behavior. We also would expect that the main comparative statics result of this paper—that the value of a reputation and the extent of reputation building increase with the frequency of the opportunities for its use—will prove generally true. If so, this would provide insight on such issues as the costs of social mobility in terms of reducing the opportunities and incentives for building reputations for honest behavior, quality service, and the like.

The particular way in which we have introduced the informational asymmetry in this paper is to assume that individuals ascribe some positive probability to there being some alternative theory which determines behavior. In some situations, there will be an alternative theory which is particularly natural. In others, however, many perturbations of the "basic" complete information model will exist, and the choice between them may appear arbitrary. This suggests the need for a notion of robustness for these alternative theories. One such notion is that a theory would be robust if its presence led to behavior which did not refute the theory. We plan to explore such ideas in the context of developing reputation models of some of the phenomena discussed above.

Appendix A

In this Appendix we examine an infinite horizon version of Selten's chain-store model. As we demonstrate, one trivially establishes existence of an equilibrium where any attempted entry is met by predation, even with complete information. This equilibrium then resembles that in Section 2 for large N. However, in contrast with the finite horizon, incomplete information model, the set of equilibria in this model is large and contains many intuitively unappealing strategy combinations.

Let Π_0^P, Π_0^C and Π_0^M denote the incumbent's payoffs to predation, coexistence and monopolization in a single market, and let the corresponding payoffs to any entrant be Π_1^P, Π_1^C and Π_1^A. Given a discount factor ρ for the incumbent, and denoting the play at round n by h_n, where $h_n = +1$ denotes predation, $h_n = 0$ denotes no entry and $h_n = -1$ denotes sharing, the incumbent's payoff is

$$\Pi_0^C \sum_0^\infty \rho^n 1_{\{h_n=-1\}} + \Pi_0^P \sum_0^\infty \rho^n 1_{\{h_n=+1\}} + \Pi_0^M \sum_0^\infty \rho^n 1_{\{h_n=0\}},$$

where 1_A is the indicator function for the event (set) A, i.e., $1_{\{h_n=a\}}$ is equal to one for those n such that $h_n = a$ and zero otherwise.

We assume that the game is one of perfect information, so that all players know the structure of the game tree, the payoffs, and the actions taken all previous moves. In contrast to the set-up in the text, number markets forward in time: market n opens before market $n+1$. Assume $\Pi_0^P < \Pi_0^C < \Pi_0^M$ and $\Pi_1^P < \Pi_1^A < \Pi_1^C$.

We now claim that, if $\Pi_0^P + \Pi_0^M \sum_1^\infty \rho^n > \Pi_0^C \sum_0^\infty \rho^n$, then the following strategies constitute a sequential equilibrium:

Firm 0: if $h_1, \ldots, h_{n-1} \geqslant 0$ and entry occurs in market n, then prey.
If $h_k = -1$ for any $k < n$ and entry occurs in market n, then share this market.

Firm n: If $h_1, \ldots, h_{n-1} \geqslant 0$, do not enter.
If $h_k = -1$ for any $k < n$, enter

So long as $\Pi^P + \Pi_0^M \sum_0^\infty \rho^n > \Pi_0^C \sum_0^\infty \rho^n$, not only do these strategies have the mutual best-response property that makes them Nash equilibria, but also this property obtains for the appropriately truncated strategies starting from any node in the game tree, so in fact they yield a sequential equilibrium.

However, as is again easily shown, the strategies of never preying for the established firm and all potential entrants always entering, regardless of the history, also constitute a perfect equilibrium. Moreover, if $\Pi_0^P + \Pi_0^M \sum_1^\infty \rho^n >$

$\Pi_0^C(1 + \sum_1^\infty \rho^n)$, then there are uncountably many pure-strategy perfect equilibria; indeed, there are uncountably many of the following form, parameterized by S.

Firm 0: If conditions (a), (b) and (c) hold at stage n, then prey at n:

(a) $h_k \geqslant 0$ for all $k < n, k \notin S$

(b) $h_k \leqslant 0$ for all $k < n, k \notin S$

(c) $n \notin S$.

Otherwise, do not prey at n.

Firm n: If (a), (b), and (c) hold, stay out. Otherwise, enter.

Among the sets S that make these strategies a perfect equilibrium are: $S = \{k \mid k \geqslant i\}$ for any choice of i, and $S = \{k \mid k$ is divisible by $i\}$, for any sufficiently large integer i. In view of this multiplicity, perfect equilibrium lacks any effective predictive power in this infinite horizon model. Furthermore, predation would never be observed in the pure-strategy equilibria of this model, so it also fails to explain apparent observed behavior.

For these reasons, and because we also believe that the finite horizon model has its own inherent interest, we concentrate on it in the text.

Appendix B

The following example illustrates our claim regarding the role of lack of common knowledge in generating predation.

Specifically, we consider a situation with the established firm, 0, and two entrants, 1 and 2. There are three possible states of the world, a, b, and c, all of which are equally likely. In state a, the game at each stage is such that entry results automatically in predation. In states b and c, the stage game is

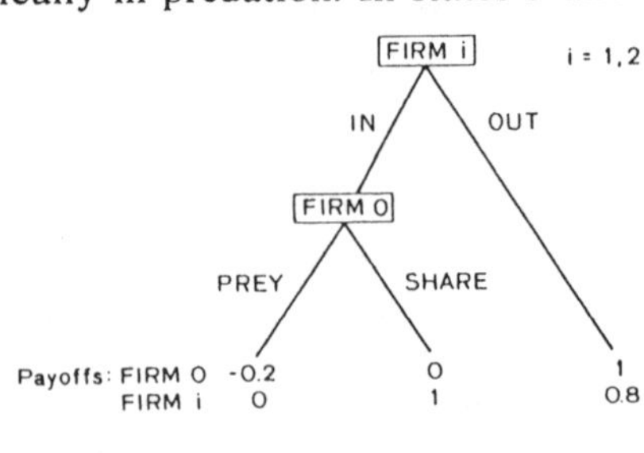

We can think of state a as one where the established firm is a predator.

The firms differ in their information, which can be described by the following partitions:

$$\text{Firm 0: } [\{a\}, \{b, c\}]$$

$$\text{Firm 1: } [\{a, b\}, \{c\}]$$

$$\text{Firm 2: } [\{a\}, \{b\}, \{c\}]$$

Note that firm 2 has perfect information, and that in state c it is common knowledge between the two entrants and also between the established firm and entrant 2 (who is the first to threaten entry) that firm 0 is not a predator. Yet in equilibrium, firm 2 is credibly threatened by predation! To see this, one need only note that the following constitute a set of sequential equilibrium strategies:

Firm 2: Stay out

Firm 1: Enter in event $\{c\}$, or if 2 entered and 0 failed to prey. Otherwise, stay out.

Firm 0: Prey if firm 2 enters. If firm 1 enters, prey in event $\{a\}$, and do not prey in $\{b, c\}$.

What makes this work is that, when the actual state is b or c, firm 0 does not know whether 1 knows that it (0) is not a predator, and everyone knows this. Note that 0 must take the same act in events b and c, since it cannot distinguish them. Thus, it can prey against firm 2 either in both states or in neither. If it shares in both states, it gets an expected return of 0. That this will result when c is the actual state is clear. When b obtains, failure to prey against 2 allows 1 to infer that it will not meet predation, and so entry in the last market again follows. If firm 0 preys in both states, then it absorbs a cost of -0.2 against firm 2. When c is the state, it still experiences entry, so its total payoff is -0.2. In state b, however, the act of predation prevents 1 from inferring whether state a or b obtains. Entry in state a yields 1 a payoff of 0, entry in b yields it 1, and since it views the two as equally likely, it prefers to stay out and receive 0.8. Thus, from 0's point of view, predation yields equal chances of $-0.2 + 1$ and $-0.2 + 0$, for an expected return of 0.3. Since this exceeds the expected return of zero resulting from failure to prey, it preys. Given that 0 will prey no matter what the state, firm 2 is then deterred from entering. This is true even when (in state c) it and firm 0 both know that sharing is directly more profitable for 0, both know that both know this, both know that both know that both know this, *ad infinitum*.

In [6], this type of modeling is used to explain observed behavior in the finitely repeated prisoners' dilemma game.

Appendix C

In this Appendix we establish Proposition 1. The first part of the argument involves a rolling induction on the following list of propositions.

(P0) *$V_n(t, x)$ is continuous in (t, x) and nondecreasing in t.*

(P1) *$V_n(t, x)$ is nondecreasing in x.*

(P2) $x_{n+1} \leqslant x_n$.

(P3) *For all u and all $x \leqslant x_{n+1}$,*

$$1 + \rho V_n(t, x) \geqslant \max[0, \alpha(u) + \rho V_n(t, x_{n+1})].$$

Since we have already established (P0), we turn to proving (P1)–(P3).

Proof of (P1)–(P3). We proceed by a "rolling induction" on n. The initialization for $n = 0$ is straightforward if we define $x_0 \equiv 1$.

Now suppose (P1) to (P3) hold for all $n \leqslant m$, and let us check the case for $n = m + 1$.

(P1): Rearranging the recursion for V_{m+1} yields:

$$\begin{aligned} V_{m+1}(t, x) = {} & \max(0, \alpha(t) + \rho V_m(t, x \vee x_{m+1})) \\ & + (1 - q_{m+1}(x))[(1 + \rho V_m(t, x)) \\ & - \max(0, \alpha(t) + \rho V_m(t, x \vee x_{m+1}))]. \end{aligned}$$

The max term, the $(1 - q_{m+1}(x))$ term, and the bracketed term are all non-negative (by the inductive hypothesis (P3)) and non-decreasing in x (by the inductive hypothesis (P1)). Thus, we have (P1) for $n = m + 1$.

(P2): By the just proven fact that (P1) holds for $n = m + 1$, we have for all x that $V_{m+1}(x, x) \leqslant V_{m+1}(x, 1)$. Together with the observation following the lemma, this gives $V_{m+1}(x, x) \leqslant \bar{v}(x)$. So, using the lemma and the fact that $V_{m+1}(x_{m+1}, x_{m+1}) = g(X_{m+1}, V_m(x_{m+1}, x_{m+1}))$, (which is seen to be just the defining recursion once we note that $q_1(1) = \beta^{-1}(0) = q_{m+1}(x_{m+1})$),

$$\begin{aligned} & \alpha(x_{m+1}) + \rho V_{m+1}(x_{m+1}, x_{m+1}) \\ & \quad = \alpha(x_{m+1}) + \rho g(x_{m+1}, V_m(x_{m+1}, x_{m+1})) \\ & \quad \geqslant \alpha(x_{m+1}) + \rho V_m(x_{m+1}, x_{m+1}). \end{aligned}$$

If $x_{m+1} = 1$, there is nothing to prove. If $x_{m+1} < 1$, then the right-hand side above is at least zero (by definition of x_{m+1} and continuity of V_m). Hence, by the monotonicity and continuity of α and V_{m+1} and by the definition of x_{m+2}, we have $x_{m+2} \leqslant x_{m+1}$. (As we argue in the main text, this inequality will turn out to be strict if $x_{m+1} > [0 \vee \mathbf{x}]$.)

(P3): We now must show that (P3) holds for $n = m + 1$. The case where $0 \geqslant \alpha(t) + \rho V_{m+1}(t, x_{m+2})$ is seen immediately to follow from the nonnegativity of $V_{m+1}(t, x)$. This is turn results from the availability of the strategy of always sharing, which yields a non-negative payoff. Thus we concentrate on the case $0 < \alpha(t) + \rho V_{m+1}(t, x_{m+2})$. Using the recursive expression for V_{m+1}, we then have

$$
\begin{aligned}
1 &+ \rho V_{m+1}(t, x) - \alpha(t) - \rho V_{m+1}(t, x_{m+2}) \\
&= 1 + \rho\{q_{m+1}(x) \max[0, \alpha(t) + \rho V_m(t, x_{m+1})] \\
&\quad + [1 - q_{m+1}(x)][1 + \rho V_m(t, x)]\} \\
&\quad - \alpha(t) - \rho\{q_{m+1}(x_{m+2}) \max[0, \alpha(t) + \rho V_m(t, x_{m+1})] \\
&\quad + [1 - q_{m+1}(x_{m+2})][1 + \rho V_m(t, x_{m+2})]\} \\
&= \rho[q_{m+1}(x_{m+2}) - q_{m+1}(x)]\{1 + \rho V_m(t, x) - \max[0, \alpha(t) + \rho V_m(t, x_{m+1})]\} \\
&\quad + \rho[1 - q_{m+1}(x_{m+2})]\{\rho V_m(t, x) - \rho V_m(t, x_{m+2})\} + 1 - \alpha(t).
\end{aligned}
$$

By the induction hypothesis (P3), the first term in braces is nonnegative. Since $x_{m+2} \geqslant x$ by hypothesis and since q_{m+1} is decreasing in x (as is easily verified), we have $-1 \leqslant q_{m+1}(x_{m+2}) - q_{m+1}(x) \leqslant 0$. Since V_m is increasing in x by the induction hypothesis and since $x \leqslant x_{m+2}$, the second term in braces is non-positive. Thus, replacing $\rho[q_{m+1}(x_{m+2}) - q_{m+1}(x)]$ by -1 and $\rho(1 - q_{m+1}(x_{m+2}))$ by its upper bound, 1, we obtain, for $x \leqslant x_{m+2}$,

$$
\begin{aligned}
1 + \rho V_{m+1}(t, x) &- \alpha(t) - \rho V_{m+1}(t, x_{m+2}) \\
&\geqslant -\{1 + \rho V_m(t, x) - \max[0, \alpha(t) + \rho V_m(t, x_{m+1})]\} \\
&\quad + \{\rho V_m(t, x) - \rho V_m(t, x_{m+2})\} + 1 - \alpha(t) \\
&= \max[0, \alpha(t) + \rho V_m(t, x_{m+1})] - [\alpha(t) + \rho V_m(t, x_{m+2})],
\end{aligned}
$$

which we must show to be non-negative. For this, it is sufficient that

$$V_m(t, x_{m+2}) \leqslant V_m(t, x_{m+1}).$$

But this inequality follows from (P1) and (P2), so we are done.

Thus, in particular, $x_{n+1} \leqslant x_n$. We now establish the remaining claims made in the statement of the Proposition.

Since $\{x_n\}$ is a bounded, nonincreasing sequence, it has a limit $x^* \geqslant 0$. If the firm ever preys (without having failed to do so before), it acquires a reputation $x \geqslant x^*$. For any such x and any n,

$$p_n(x) = \frac{\varepsilon + 1 - (x \vee x_n)}{\varepsilon + 1 - x}$$

$$\geqslant p_n(x^*) = \frac{\varepsilon + 1 - (x^* \vee x_n)}{\varepsilon + (1 - x^*)}.$$

But since $x_n \to x^*$, this last term converges to 1 as $n \to \infty$. Thus, $p_n(\cdot)$ converges uniformly for $x \geqslant x^*$ to 1 as n goes to infinity, and so $q_n(x) = \beta^{-1}(1 - p_n(x))$ converges uniformly to $\beta^{-1}(0) = q_1(1)$. Predation is certain in the limit, and only those willing to be preyed upon will enter.

Then, since

$$V_n(t, x) = q_n(x) \max(0, \alpha(t) + \rho V_{n-1}(t, x \vee x_n)) + (1 - q_n(x))(1 + \rho V_{n-1}(t, x))$$

for $\rho < 1$ we must have (by standard results in discounted dynamic programming)

$$\lim_{n \to \infty} V_n(t, x) = V_\infty(t, x) \qquad \text{for} \quad x \geqslant x^*,$$

where $V_\infty(t, x)$ is the unique solution to

$$\begin{aligned} V_\infty(t, x) &= q_1(1) \max[0, \alpha(t) + \rho V_\infty(t, x)] \\ &\quad + [1 - q_1(1)][1 + \rho V_\infty(t, x)] \\ &\equiv g(t, V_\infty(t, x)). \end{aligned}$$

But, by definition, this solution is the fixed point, $\bar{v}(t)$. Thus, in the limit, predation gives the firm a reputation $x \geqslant x^*$ and a continuation value $\bar{v}(t)$. Then, the limiting condition guaranteeing that the firm will prey is $\alpha(t_0) + \rho\bar{v}(t_0) > 0$, i.e., $t_0 > \mathbf{x}$. Thus, $x^* = \lim x_n = [0 \vee \mathbf{x}]$.

Since we assumed $\mathbf{x} < 1$, we have thus demonstrated that predation which is costly in the short run will still occur for n large enough. Reexamination of the argument establishing (P2) now in fact reveals that $x_n < x_{n-1}$ unless x_{n-1} is 0 or 1, since $\bar{v}(t)$ is strictly greater than $V_n(t, x)$ for all the relevant values of t. Q.E.D.

APPENDIX D

This proof of Proposition 2 involves a rolling induction on n based on the following two statements.

(P4) $\forall n, \quad x_n \leqslant \bar{x}_n$

(P5) $\forall x \leqslant x_n, \quad V_n(x, x) \geqslant \bar{V}_n(x, x) \geqslant 0.$

Proof. Notice that (P5) for $n = k$ implies (P4) for $n = k + 1$. To see this, note that if k were such that $x_{k+1} > \bar{x}_{k+1} \geqslant 0$, then, using the induction hypothesis (P5), the monotonicity of α and V_k, and the fact that $x_{k+1} > 0$, we have

$$\bar{\alpha}(\bar{x}_{k+1}) + \bar{\rho}\bar{V}_k(\bar{x}_{k+1}, \bar{x}_{k+1}) < \alpha(x_{k+1}) + \rho V_k(x_{k+1}, x_{k+1}) \leqslant 0,$$

which contradicts the definition of $\bar{x}_{k+1}$ and the continuity of $\bar{\alpha}$ and $\bar{V}_k$.

To show (P5), note first that both (P4) and (P5) hold trivially for $n = 0$ and that non-negativity was shown in the proof of Proposition 1. Suppose (P5) holds for $n = k$ and (P4) holds for $n = k + 1$. Then, for $x \leqslant x_{k+1}$,

$$V_{k+1}(x, x) = q_{k+1}(x) \cdot 0 + (1 - q_{k+1}(x))(1 + \rho V_k(x, x)),$$
$$\bar{V}_{k+1}(x, x) = \bar{q}_{k+1}(x) \cdot 0 + (1 - \bar{q}_{k+1}(x))(1 + \bar{\rho}\bar{V}_k(x, x)),$$

where the zero payoff in the first expression is because firm 0 will not prey if $x \leqslant x_{k+1}$, and the second follows since $x \leqslant x_{k+1} \leqslant \bar{x}_{k+1}$. For the claimed inequality, it now suffices, given (P5) for $n = k$, to show that $q_{k+1}(x) \leqslant \bar{q}_{k+1}(x)$. But $x_{k+1} \leqslant \bar{x}_{k+1}$ and $\bar{\varepsilon} \leqslant \varepsilon$ implies $\bar{p}_{k+1}(x) < p_{k+1}(x)$, which in turn means that

$$\bar{q}_{k+1}(x) \equiv \bar{\beta}^{-1}(1 - \bar{p}_{k+1}(x)) \geqslant \beta^{-1}(1 - \bar{p}_{k+1}(x))$$
$$\geqslant \beta^{-1}(1 - p_{k+1}(x)) \equiv q_{k+1}(x),$$

and we are done. Q.E.D.

REFERENCES

1. R. AUMANN, Agreeing to disagree, *Ann. Statist.* **4** (1976), 1236–1239.
2. G. BROCK, "The U.S. Computer Industry: A Study of Market Power," Ballinger, Cambridge, Mass., 1975.
3. A. DIXIT, A model of duopoly suggesting a theory of entry barriers, *Bell J. Econ.* **10** (1979), 20–32.
4. D. EASLEY, R. T. MASSON, AND R. J. REYNOLDS, A dynamic analysis of predatory pricing with rational expectations, mimeo, Cornell University, 1981.

5. J. HARSANYI, Games of incomplete information played by Bayesian players (parts I, II, III), *Manage. Sci.* **14** (1967–68), 159–182, 320–334, 486–503.
6. D. KREPS, P. MILGROM, J. ROBERTS, AND R. WILSON, Rational cooperation in the finitely repeated prisoners' dilemma, *J. Econ. Theory* **27** (1982), 245–252.
7. D. KREPS AND R. WILSON, Reputation and imperfect information, *J. Econ. Theory* **27** (1982), 253–279.
8. D. KREPS AND R. WILSON, Sequential equilibrium, *Econometrica*, in press.
9. M. MACGREGOR, A resolution of the chain-store paradox, draft, University of California, Berkeley, 1979.
10. J. MCGEE, Predatory price cutting: the standard Oil (N.J.) case, *J. Law and Econ.* **1** (1958), 137–169.
11. J. MCGEE, Predatory pricing revisited, *J. Law and Econ.* **23** (1980), 289–330.
12. P. MILGROM, An axiomatic characterization of common knowledge, *Econometrica* **49** (1981), 219–222.
13. P. MILGROM AND J. ROBERTS, Limit pricing and entry under incomplete information: an equilibrium analysis, *Econometrica* **50** (1982), 443–459.
14. R. ROSENTHAL, Games of perfect information, predatory pricing and the chain-store paradox, *J. Econ. Theory* **25** (1981), 92–100.
15. F. M. SCHERER, "Industrial Market Structure and Economic Performance," 2nd ed., Rand-McNally, Chicago, 1980.
16. R. SELTEN, The chain-store paradox, *Theory and Decision* **9** (1978), 127–159.
17. M. SPENCE, Entry, capacity investment and oligopolistic pricing, *Bell. J. Econ.* **8** (1979), 534–544.
18. U.S. Department of Justice, "The Regulated Ocean Shiping Industry," Washington, 1977.
19. B. YAMEY, Predatory price cutting: notes and comments, *J. Law and Econ.* **15** (1972), 137–147.

Part VI
Exclusionary Behavior

[17]

THE JOURNAL OF INDUSTRIAL ECONOMICS 0022-1821 $2.00
Volume XXXVI September 1987 No. 1

COST-RAISING STRATEGIES

STEVEN C. SALOP AND DAVID T. SCHEFFMAN*

This paper studies a variety of strategies by which firms could disadvantage rivals by raising their costs. In this paper, we show that strategies designed to raise rivals' costs have a number of advantages over predatory pricing: They are credible, do not necessarily require the victim to exit, and do not necessarily require the existence of classical market power. The paper sets up a general model, proves a number of general results, and then applies the model to specific strategies involving "overbuying" inputs and vertical integration.

I. INTRODUCTION

ECONOMISTS AND courts have long been concerned with conduct that creates or enhances market power by disadvantaging rivals. A variety of cost-raising strategies can be used to disadvantage rivals or drive them out of the market without the need to set low prices. For example, while AT&T was not found liable for predatory pricing, it did not escape liability for denying rivals equal access. In another classic antitrust case, the *Lorain Journal* newspaper conditioned sales of advertising space on advertisers' promises not to purchase additional advertising from a competing radio station.[1] Other possible cost-raising strategies include a variety of exclusive dealing arrangements, inducing input suppliers to discriminate against rivals, lobbying legislatures or regulatory agencies to create regulations that disadvantage rivals, commencing R & D and advertising wars, and adopting incompatible technologies. Because these strategies are predatory, but do not involve classic predatory pricing, they are sometimes referred to as "non-price predation".[2]

In this paper, we show that strategies designed to raise rivals' costs have a number of advantages over predatory pricing. First, cost-raising strategies do not have an inherent problem of credibility. Such strategies may be profitable whether or not the rivals exit, since higher cost rivals have an incentive to cut back output and raise prices immediately, which may make it possible for the predator to reap gains even in the short run.[3] Secondly, unlike predatory pricing, classical, single firm market power (i.e., downward sloping demand

* Professor of Economics at Georgetown University Law Center and Director, Bureau of Economics, Federal Trade Commission, respectively. This paper is a revised version of Salop and Scheffman [1984].

[1] 342 U.S. 143 (1951).

[2] Since these strategies sometimes involve prices (e.g., raising the price of an input), perhaps a better term is "cost-predation".

[3] See Salop and Scheffman [1983].

curve) in the relevant output market is not essential for the success of cost-raising strategies, since even perfect competitors can benefit if rivals have higher costs.[4]

This paper is organized as follows. In sections II and III, we set out the general model for analyzing cost-raising strategies. These sections generalize and extend the results reported in Salop and Scheffman [1983]. The specific model analyzed in section III assumes the predator can fully control a parameter that affects its costs and those of its rivals, for example, where the parameter is a regulatory instrument.[5] In section IV, we define and analyze strategies based on "overbuying" inputs, such as the conduct alleged in *Alcoa*. Finally, section V develops a theory of raising rivals' costs through vertical integration and shows that vertical integration can be anticompetitive, even for technologies in which an input is used in fixed proportions.

II. THE GENERAL MODEL

We begin with a general model of competition between the predator and a competitive (price-taking) fringe, where the predator may be either a price taker or a dominant firm.[6] Let $D(p)$ be market demand, and let the predator's and fringe's cost functions be given, respectively, by the functions $C(x, \alpha)$ and $G(y, \alpha)$, where outputs are given by x and y, and where a cost-raising parameter, α, influences the costs of all firms, perhaps symmetrically.[7] For example, α could be interpreted as a regulatory parameter, the price of an input, or expenditures on advertising or research and development.[8] We adopt the convention that increases in α raise the average and marginal costs of the fringe and the average costs of the predator—i.e., the partial derivatives C_α, G_α, and $G_{y\alpha}$ all are non-negative.[9] We assume that the predator has the power to control the level of α, subject to a general market constraint formalized by the equation $F(\alpha, p, x, y) \geqslant 0$. In subsequent sections, we consider particular forms for this constraint corresponding to specific institutional settings.

The fringe supply curve is denoted $S(p, \alpha)$, which can be derived from the

[4] Inframarginal rents increase with price, and higher cost rivals may shift up the industry supply curve, thereby increasing price.

[5] See Salop, Scheffman, and Schwartz [1984].

[6] See Salinger [1985] for the case of an oligopolistic fringe.

[7] The fringe cost function and resulting supply curve may be treated as long run functions encompassing potential entry by additional price-taking firms. Lack of entry barriers is signalled by constant marginal costs and a perfectly elastic supply curve. Thus, in principle, dynamic elements can be taken into account in the analysis. We treat p and α as scalars, although the results are generalized easily to vector-valued variables.

[8] We will not treat the case where market demand also depends on α (for example, when α represents advertising expenditures), but many of our results are easily generalized to that case.

[9] If increases in α reduce the predator's costs (i.e., if $C_\alpha < 0$), then increases in α would have an independent "efficiency" benefit to the "predator" beyond any exclusionary benefits.

fringe cost function in the usual manner:[10]

$$(1) \qquad S(p,\alpha) = \underset{y}{\operatorname{argmax}}\,[py - G(y,\alpha)]$$

Thus, the predator faces the general profit-maximizing problem:

$$(2) \qquad \max_{\{p,x,\alpha\}} \,[px - C(x,\alpha)],^{11}$$

subject to

$$x + y = D(p)$$

$$y = S(p,\alpha)$$

$$F(\alpha,p,x,y) \geqslant 0$$

Without placing more structure on the market constraint function $F(\alpha, p, x, y)$, the first order conditions for equations (2) do not yield interesting interpretations.

III. DIRECT CONTROL OVER α

In this section we assume that the market constraint has a very simple form: the predator has direct and complete control over α, subject only to the constraint $\alpha \geqslant \bar{\alpha}$. The *ex ante* value $\bar{\alpha}$ may correspond to the predator's choosing α solely on the basis of cost-minimization (that is, $C_\alpha = 0$), an exogenous *status quo*, or an alternative proposed by a rival. Thus, we assume that the predator has a type of market power in an "input market", in the sense that α corresponds to a variable in a relevant input market, such as price.[12] We assume here that the predator's choice of output level has no direct effect on the value of α.[13]

Several institutional settings are suggested by this formal structure. In the *Pennington* case studied by Williamson [1968], it was alleged that a large coal producer induced the labor union to drive up the wage rate. Under this interpretation, $\alpha > \bar{\alpha}$ would correspond to a wage increase.[14] In another

[10] Assuming $y > 0$, fringe supply satisfies the usual first-order condition relating price to marginal cost, $p = G_y(y, \alpha)$. The properties of the supply curve are as follows: $S_p = 1/G_{yy} \geqslant 0$ and $S_\alpha = -G_{y\alpha}/G_{yy} \leqslant 0$. If $G_{yy} > 0$, the fringe supply curve is upward sloping. If $G_{yy} = 0$, then $S_y = \infty$, and the predator has no classical market power in the downstream market, but instead faces a perfectly elastic residual demand curve. Of course, even in that case the predator may benefit from shifts in his residual demand curve.

[11] If the predator does not have classical market power in the output market, price is not a choice variable. Instead, output x is determined by the relationship $p = C_x(x, \alpha)$. See Salop, Scheffman and Schwartz (1984) for a detailed analysis of this case.

[12] In this formulation, regulations can be analyzed as inputs that are forced on the firms, rather than being purchased.

[13] This would not always be the case, for example, if α was the price of an input purchased by both the predator and the fringe in a competitive market. A model of this type is taken up in the following sections.

[14] In this formulation it is assumed that the union rations labor to clear the market at the higher wage.

interpretation, α and $\bar{\alpha}$ can be treated as alternative regulations that could be adopted by an agency the predator is trying to "capture".[15] One also could view α as a level of advertising or research and development expenditures chosen by the predator to which the fringe reacts by raising its own advertising or research levels.[16]

Formally, rewriting the maximization problem in (2), we have

$$(2') \qquad \max_{\{p,\alpha\}} p(D(p) - S(p,\alpha)) - C(D(p,\alpha) - S((p,\alpha),\alpha)),$$

subject to

$$\alpha \geqslant \bar{\alpha}$$

The first order conditions for an interior maximum ($x, y > 0, \alpha > \bar{\alpha}$) are given as follows:

$$(3a) \qquad (p - C_x)/p = 1/\varepsilon^R$$

$$(3b) \qquad (p - C_x) = -C_\alpha/S_\alpha$$

where ε^R is the elasticity of residual demand faced by the predator.[17]

Equation (3a) is the usual Lerner markup equation for a dominant firm. At an interior equilibrium ($\alpha > \bar{\alpha}$), combining (3a) and (3b) yields[18]

$$(4) \qquad S_\alpha/(D_p - S_p) = C_\alpha/x$$

The interpretation of (4) is straightforward. The left-hand side of (4) equals $\partial p/\partial \alpha |_x$, where this derivative represents the change in price arising from the reduction in fringe output resulting from the increase in α, holding the output of the predator fixed. In other words, the left-hand side of (4) is the derivative representing the *vertical* shift in the residual demand curve facing the dominant firm. The right-hand side of (4) is the derivative of *average cost* (AC^D) of the predator with respect to α, holding its output fixed. Therefore, an interior solution must satisfy the condition $\partial p/\partial \alpha = \partial AC^D/\partial \alpha$, where these derivatives are evaluated at the profit-maximizing point (x^*, α^*).

We now state the following *sufficient* condition for a cost-raising strategy to be profitable, that is, for $\alpha^* > \bar{\alpha}$.

[15] Elsewhere, we have presented a model in which we examine the determinants of who controls the regulatory process (Salop, Scheffman and Schwartz [1984]). In that case, the "market power" may simply involve partial control over the regulatory process. For a summary of the literature on the use of regulation as a cost-raising strategy, see McCormick [1984].

[16] The fringe's profit-maximizing reaction function is implicit in the cost derivative G_α. However, under this interpretation, any effects of advertising or R&D on market demand are ignored.

[17] $\varepsilon^R = -(\partial(D-S)/\partial p)(p/(D-S)) = \varepsilon/\sigma + (1-\sigma)\zeta^F/\sigma$, where ε is the price-elasticity of market demand, ζ^F is the price-elasticity of fringe supply, and σ is the market share of the predator.

[18] It can easily be shown that the condition corresponding to (4), if the fringe has constant returns-to-scale technology, is: $[1-(p-C_x)\varepsilon/p]/(C_\alpha/D) = 1/AC^{F'}(\alpha)$, with ε the price elasticity of market demand and $AC^{F'}(\alpha)$ is the derivative of the fringe's average cost with respect to α. The first order conditions for y require $p - C_x \geqslant 0$ and $(p-C_x)y = 0$.

Proposition 1. Let $\bar{x}$ be the profit maximizing output for the predator when $\alpha = \bar{\alpha}$ (that is, $\bar{x}$ is the solution of (3a) for $\alpha = \bar{\alpha}$). $\alpha > \bar{\alpha}$ is profitable if

(5) $$\partial p/\partial\alpha > \partial AC^D/\partial\alpha$$

where the derivatives are evaluated at $(\bar{x}, \bar{\alpha})$.

This sufficient condition requires that the vertical shift in the predator's residual demand curve must exceed the vertical shift in its average cost curve, evaluated at the non-strategic equilibrium ($\alpha = \bar{\alpha}$). This result follows directly from the fact that the predator's profits at $\bar{x}$ equal $(p - AC^D)\bar{x}$, where AC^D is the predator's average costs.[19]

The sufficient condition (5) is more likely to hold: (i) the larger is the vertical shift in the fringe supply curve resulting from an increase in α (S_α large); (ii) the smaller is the impact of an increase in α on the predator's average costs (C_α/x small); and (iii) the less elastic are the market demand curve and the fringe supply curve ($-(D_p - S_p)p/x$ small).

(i). *Effect on price*

Consider now the effect of increasing α on price. If we denote the predator's profit by π^D, $dp/d\alpha$ can be determined by totally differentiating the predator's first order condition for price, $\pi_p^D = 0$. Since the second order conditions require $\pi_{pp}^D < 0$, sign $dp/d\alpha$ = sign $\pi_{p\alpha}^D$, or

(6) $$\text{sign}\, dp/d\alpha = \text{sign}\,[-S_\alpha - C_{x\alpha}(D_p - S_p) - (p - C_x)S_{p\alpha}]$$

The first term on the right hand side of equation (6) is positive. The sign of the second term is ambiguous because of the ambiguity of the sign of $C_{x\alpha}$; that is, the effect of an increase in α on the predator's *marginal* cost is ambiguous.[20] The sign of the third term depends on the sign of $(D_{p\alpha} - S_{p\alpha})$, the effect of an increase in α on the *slope* of the residual demand curve, which is also ambiguous. Thus, it is possible for $dp/d\alpha$ to be negative.[21]

This is a straightforward result, analogous to the well-known ambiguity of the effect of an increase in demand on a monopolist's profit-maximizing price. However, this result alerts us to the fact that if the predator has market power in the output market, both the shift in the fringe supply curve and its slope are critical in determining the effect of an increase in α on price. In summary, we have the following proposition.

[19] The interpretation of (5) is provided in Salop and Scheffman (1983).

[20] We have only assumed that C_α is negative.

[21] An example in which $dp/d\alpha < 0$ is as follows. Suppose market demand is $Q = (1 - p)$, and that initially fringe supply is inelastic at one unit. Suppose further that the predator's costs are zero and that an increase in α changes fringe supply to the function: $y = p^2/100$, $p \leqslant 10$; $y = 1$, for $p > 10$. It is easy to see $S_\alpha \leqslant 0$. The initial equilibrium price is $p^* = 5$, while the equilibrium price after the increase in α is $p^* = 4.7$, so that the price falls with an increase in α. The key to this example is that although $S_\alpha \leqslant 0$, the fringe supply curve becomes much more elastic with an increase in α, making the predator's residual demand curve more elastic.

Proposition 2. Profitable cost-raising strategies may result in a *decrease* in price if the predator has market power in the output market. A sufficient condition for price to increase is $C_{x\alpha} \geqslant 0$ and $S_{p\alpha} \leqslant 0$.[22] If the predator does not have market power in the output market, profitability of cost-predation requires that price increase.

(ii). *Effect on fringe output and profits*

We now examine the effect of an increase in α on fringe output. From the fringe supply function, we have

(7) $$dy/d\alpha = S_p dp/d\alpha + S_\alpha$$

Because, by assumption, $S_\alpha < 0$, then if $dp/d\alpha < 0$, it follows that fringe output necessarily falls ($dy/d\alpha < 0$). However, in some cases it may be profitable for the predator to increase price sufficiently to permit the fringe output even to expand ($dy/d\alpha > 0$), although in such a case the predator must restrict his own output enough so that total output falls in order to effect an increase in price.[23] As with the ambiguous price effect, the result depends on the effect of an increase in α on the elasticity of the predator's residual demand curve. Summarizing, we have the following result.

Proposition 3. An increase in α has an ambiguous effect on fringe output. However, if price falls ($dp/d\alpha < 0$), then fringe output also must fall ($dy/d\alpha < 0$).

Because an increase in α has an ambiguous effect on price and fringe output, it is probably not surprising that the effect of an increase in α on fringe "profits" (inframarginal rents) is also ambiguous.[24] Suppose that fringe supply is upward sloping and that further entry is blocked so that the fringe earns inframarginal rents. Fringe profits are given by $\pi^F = py - G(y, \alpha)$. Differentiating π^F and recalling that $p = G_y$, we have

(8) $$d\pi^F/d\alpha = y(G_{yy} dy/d\alpha + G_{y\alpha} - G_{y\alpha}/y)$$

In the standard case in which fringe output falls ($dy/d\alpha < 0$), fringe profits necessarily fall, unless fringe marginal costs rise sufficiently relative to fringe average costs.[25] Summarizing, we have the following proposition.

[22] This should be clear since the critical issue is how C_x and ε^D change with α (see (3a)), and $-S_{\alpha p} \geqslant 0$ is a sufficient condition for $\partial\varepsilon^D/\partial\alpha \leqslant 0$.

[23] An example in which $dy/d\alpha > 0$ is as follows: Suppose market demand is $Q = (11 - p)$ and the predator's costs are zero. Suppose further that for $\alpha = 0$, fringe supply curve is perfectly elastic at a price of one, but for $\alpha > 0$ the fringe supply curve becomes $y = (p-1)/\alpha$ for $0 < \alpha < 1$, $y = (p-1)$ for $\alpha \geqslant 1$. Then, for $\alpha = 0$, the equilibrium price $p^* = 1$ and output of the fringe is zero. However, if the predator can set α, it will set $\alpha^* = 1$, leading to a new price of $p^* = 5/2$ with fringe output rising to 3/2. Of course the key to this example is that the increase in α makes the fringe supply curve much less elastic.

[24] Thus, characterizing the conduct as necessarily "predatory" in this case would be in error. The conduct could sometimes be characterized as "collusive". Indeed, in the example discussed in footnote 27, fringe profits actually increase with α.

[25] It is easy to see that if fringe marginal costs increase much more than fringe average costs, the fringe's inframarginal rents (the area behind the fringe supply curve) may increase.

Proposition 4. Sufficient conditions for fringe profits to fall are: either (i) $dp/d\alpha < 0$, or (ii) $dy/d\alpha < 0$ and $(G_{y\alpha} - G_\alpha/y) < 0$. A sufficient condition for fringe profits to rise is $dy/d\alpha > 0$ (which itself requires $dp/d\alpha > 0$), and $(G_{y\alpha} - G_\alpha/y) > 0$.

These two conditions are of particular interest because they depend only on price or on the output of the fringe and its technology.

(iii). *Effect on welfare*

In this section, we analyze the welfare effects of these strategies. Let the conventional welfare indicator (the sum of consumer plus producer surplus) be denoted by W. Then, we have[26]

(9) $$dW/d\alpha = [D(p) - S(p, \alpha)]dp/d\alpha - (p - C_x)S_\alpha(p, \alpha) - C_\alpha - G_\alpha + \Omega'(\alpha)$$

where $\Omega(\alpha)$ is a measure of welfare in other markets affected by α.

Without placing more structure on the problem, the properties of $\Omega(\alpha)$ are undefined. If α is a regulatory parameter affecting only the relevant output market, the effects of increased regulation ($\alpha > \bar{\alpha}$) on welfare outside that market are likely to be unimportant, unless there are substantial resources used up (rather than simply transferred) to influence the regulatory authority. If α is the price of an input, then some of the increases in costs arising from an increase in α represent only a transfer to the input owners.[27] Until later sections, where we have sufficient structure to determine the properties of Ω, we will concentrate on partial equilibrium welfare effects. We will denote partial equilibrium welfare by $\hat{W}$, where

(10) $$\hat{W} = W - \Omega$$

From equation (9) it should be clear that the sign of $d\hat{W}/d\alpha$ is ambiguous.[28] For example, if $dp/d\alpha < 0$, it would not be surprising that $d\hat{W}/d\alpha > 0$. Furthermore, even if $dp/d\alpha \geqslant 0$, welfare could rise because the strategy may reduce the output of a higher cost rival, increasing producer surplus more than any decrease in consumer surplus.[29] This result only can occur if the

[26] $W(\bar{p}, \bar{\alpha}) = \int_p^\infty D(p)dp + \bar{p}\bar{x} - C(\bar{x}, \bar{\alpha}) + \bar{p}S(\bar{p}, \bar{\alpha}) - G(S(\bar{p}, \bar{\alpha}), \bar{\alpha}) + \Omega(\alpha)$. We normalize by setting $\Omega(\bar{\alpha}) = 0$.

[27] For example, in the case considered by Williamson [1968], the cost-raising strategy took the form of an increase in the union wage, which resulted in a transfer to union members. However, rent-seeking conduct may transform such transfers into welfare losses.

[28] This follows because if the predator has market power in the output market, fringe and predator marginal costs will not be equalized, leading to a typical second best welfare calculus.

[29] Suppose demand is $Q = (a - bp)$ and the predator's costs are zero. Suppose further that for $\alpha = 0$, fringe supply is $y = [(a - 4b) + bp]$ and for $\alpha = 1$, fringe supply is $y = (a - 6b) + 2bp$. It can easily be shown that the equilibrium price is $p = 2$ for $\alpha = 0$ or $\alpha = 1$, so that consumer surplus is the same in each equilibrium. However, producer surplus is larger in the case of $\alpha = 1$ because a greater proportion of the output is produced by the lower cost predator (which has zero costs). What is driving this example is that the marginal costs of the fringe and the predator are not equalized because of market power exercised in the output market by the predator.

predator has market power that results in $p > MC$. If price equals marginal cost, then the diversion of output to the predator must raise total costs.

Of course, a sufficient increase in price will cause enough reduction in consumer surplus to result in $d\hat{W}/d\alpha < 0$. Substituting (3b) into (9), we have:

$$(11) \qquad d\hat{W}/d\alpha < 0 \text{ if } dp/d\alpha > S_\alpha/(D_p - S_p) - (C_\alpha + G_\alpha)/(D - S)$$

The term $(S_\alpha/(D_p - S_p))$ is the price rise due to an increase in α, assuming the predator holds its output fixed. Therefore, equation (11) holds if the predator does not increase its output when α is increased. Summarizing, we have the following result:

Proposition 5. In general, increasing α has an ambiguous effect on partial equilibrium welfare, even if price rises, when the predator has classical market power. However, if the predator does not increase its output, welfare necessarily is reduced. If price rises, *consumer* welfare is reduced by an increase in α. If the predator is a price taker and price does not fall, total equilibrium welfare must fall.

(iv). *α as an input price*

We now place additional structure on the previous model by specifying the way in which α affects costs. We assume in this section that α is the price of an input A that is used by both the predator and the fringe. Denoting $\bar{\alpha}$ as the competitive price of A, we assume that the predator can raise the input price above the competitive level without increasing its purchases of A.[30] Although the first order conditions for the predator are still given by (3), when α is an input price additional results can be derived because of the properties of C_α and S_α.

By the usual duality properties of cost functions, we have $C_\alpha = A^D$ and $G_\alpha = A^F$, where A^D and A^F are the (cost minimizing) demands for A by the predator and fringe, respectively. On the assumption that fringe supply is given by (1), the fringe's (cost minimizing) demand for A satisfies $\partial A^F/\partial y = G_{y\alpha}$. Therefore, from (4) and (5), a sufficient condition for $\alpha > \bar{\alpha}$ to be profitable is

$$(12) \qquad (-\partial A^F/\partial y)/G_{yy}(D_p - S_p) > A^D/x, \text{ evaluated at } (\bar{x}, \bar{\alpha})$$

As with (5), the left hand side of (12) is $\partial p/\partial \alpha\,|_x$, and the right hand side of (12) is the derivative of average cost of the predator with respect to α for output of the predator kept fixed. Notice that a necessary condition for a cost-raising strategy to be profitable is that A not be an inferior factor for the

[30] Our specification of this model is similar to that of Williamson [1968]. Thus, we are assuming that some actor in the input market, e.g., a union, rations the sales of the input at a higher price. Williamson makes some restrictive assumptions (fixed coefficients, constant-returns-to-scale technology for the predator and the fringe), which, we will see, greatly limit the range of possible equilibrium outcomes.

fringe ($\partial A^F/\partial y \geqslant 0$), since otherwise an increase in α would increase fringe output.

Sufficient condition (12) can be rewritten to facilitate its interpretation. Let $\rho = (\partial A^F/\partial y)(y/A^F)$, the elasticity of fringe demand for input A with respect to fringe output. Then from (12), at $(\bar{x}, \bar{\alpha})$ we have

$$(13) \qquad -S_p/(D_p - S_p) > (A^D/x)/\rho(A^F/y)$$

Since the left hand side of (13) is less than one, (13) requires that $(A^D/x) < \rho(A^F/y)$. Hence, the greater is the fringe's use of input A per unit of output *relative to* the predator's use of that input per unit of output, the more likely that cost-predation will be profitable.[31] The results contained in (12) and (13) are summarized in the following proposition.

Proposition 6. If α is the price of input A, for the predator to raise α profitably, A must not be an inferior factor for the fringe. The profitability of a cost-raising strategy is more likely:

(i) the more elastic is the fringe input-expansion path for A;
(ii) the less elastic is the fringe supply curve;
(iii) the less elastic is the market demand curve; and
(iv) the greater is fringe use of input A per unit of output relative to the predator's.

Welfare effects. In assessing the welfare effects of an increase in the input price, we must recognize that some of the cost increase borne by the predator and the fringe is a transfer to input suppliers. In terms of the notation used above,

$$(14) \qquad \Omega'(\bar{\alpha}) = d[\alpha(A^D + A^F)]/d\alpha$$

i.e., the change in payments to owners of the input, which can be positive. Since $C_\alpha = A^D$ and $G_\alpha = A^F$, the welfare effect summarized in equation (9) can be written:

$$(9a) \qquad dW/d\alpha = [D(p) - S(p,\alpha)]dp/d\alpha - (p - C_x)S_\alpha(p,\alpha) - A^D - A^F + \Omega'(\alpha)$$

Since $dW/d\alpha = d\hat{W}/d\alpha + \Omega'(\bar{\alpha})$ and $\bar{\alpha}(d(A^D + A^F)/d\alpha) < 0$, it is easily seen from (11) that Proposition 5 now holds for *total* welfare W.

IV. OVERBUYING STRATEGIES

In this section we assume that α is the price of an input A that is supplied by a competitive industry according to the supply curve $A(\alpha)$. Now, in order to raise the input price, the predator must purchase additional quantities of the

[31] Since $\rho > 1$ is possible, this input use asymmetry is not necessary for the profitability of cost-predation.

input.[32] As a result, its marginal factor cost of increasing α exceeds C_α (where, as before, $C(x, \alpha)$ is the minimized cost of buying inputs to produce x at input price α).

The equilibrium condition in the input market corresponding to the market constraint $F(\alpha, p, x, y) \geqslant 0$ in (1) now is given by

(15) $$A(\alpha) - A^F(\alpha, p) - A^D = 0$$

where $A^F(\alpha, p)$ is the fringe demand function for input A and A^D is the quantity of A purchased by the predator. We make the standard assumptions that $A' > 0$, $A^F_\alpha < 0$, $A^F_p > 0$. From (15), we can derive the function $A^D(\alpha, p)$ that gives the level of purchases of A required for the predator in order to raise the price of A to α, given p (i.e., the residual supply function for A).

Let $z = (z^1, \ldots, z^m)$ denote the quantities of other inputs, $r = (r^1, \ldots, r^m)$ denote their prices, and let $f(z^D, A^D)$ denote the predator's production function. The predator's cost function, $\tilde{C}(x, \alpha, r, p)$, can be defined as follows:

(16) $$\tilde{C}(x, \alpha, r, p) = \min_{\{z^D\}} [\textstyle\sum r_i z^D + \alpha A^D(\alpha, p)],$$

subject to

$$f(z^D, A^D) = x$$

By the "Envelope Theorem", we have

(17a) $$\tilde{C}_\alpha = A^D + (\alpha - \chi f_A) A^D_\alpha,$$[33] and

(17b) $$\tilde{C}_p = (\alpha - \chi f_A) A^D_p,$$[34]

where $\chi = \tilde{C}_x$, is the predator's marginal cost.

The first order conditions for profit-maximization for the predator can be derived as in (4), yielding

(18a) $$(p - \tilde{C}_x)/p = (1 - \tilde{C}_p/x)/\varepsilon^D,$$ and

(18b) $$(p - \tilde{C}_x) = -\tilde{C}_\alpha/S_\alpha$$

Following equation (5), these equations can be combined to yield

(19) $$S_\alpha/(D_p - S_p) = (\tilde{C}_\alpha/x)/(1 - \tilde{C}_p/x)$$

As before, the left hand side of (19) is the vertical shift in the residual demand curve facing the predator and the right hand side is the vertical shift in its average costs.[35]

[32] This overpurchasing may be carried out by excessive open market purchases of inputs or by excessive purchases of productive capacity to produce inputs, i.e., by excessive vertical integration. We will discuss vertical integration explicitly in the next section.

[33] Notice that if the predator was a perfect competitor in the A-market, then $\tilde{C}_\alpha = A^D$ (the usual duality relationship). If the predator was a simple monopsonist in the A-market, the first order conditions for α would require $\tilde{C}_\alpha = 0$.

[34] $\tilde{C}_p$ is the change in the dominant firm costs arising from a change in p, resulting from the fact that a change in p changes the fringe demand for A and therefore the net supply of A available to the dominant firm.

[35] $\partial AC^D/\partial\alpha = [\tilde{C}_p(\partial p/\partial\alpha)]/x$.

In the model of the preceding section, it was straightforward to determine whether a cost-raising strategy was being pursued; a necessary and sufficient condition was $\alpha > \bar{\alpha}$. In the present model, however, all purchases of A automatically increase α, so that as long as the predator actually uses its purchases of A to produce output, we do not have a simple benchmark.

There are two potential benchmarks we may consider. One useful benchmark is classical (dominant firm) monopoly/monopsony conduct. By this we mean the level of input purchases that would arise if the predator behaved as a dominant firm facing a residual demand curve $R(p, \alpha)$ and a residual supply curve $A^D(\alpha, p)$, but ignored the strategic effects of α on its rivals' input costs and the resulting effects on price.[36] A second benchmark is the cost-minimizing (efficient) level of input purchases.

We take up the simple monopoly/monopsony (MM) benchmark first. In that model, the MM's optimal choice of A would imply $\tilde{C}_\alpha = 0$; that is,

$$A^D(\alpha - \chi f_A)A^D_\alpha = 0 \tag{20}$$

In this case, the MM's marginal revenue product for A equals the marginal factor cost (MFC) of A.[37] In contrast, if a strategically-minded MM also realizes and acts on the knowledge that α affects R and that p affects A^D, the first order conditions for α (17b) require

$$(\alpha - \chi f_A)A^D_\alpha + A^D > 0 \tag{21}$$

Thus, for strategic behavior, the marginal revenue product of A for the predator is below its marginal factor cost.[38] The intuition is straightforward. The predator, recognizing the effect of an increase in α on fringe supply, finds it in its interest to purchase relatively more A than if it were a simple monopsonist. It is in this sense that the predator "over-purchases" the input.[39] The results of this section are summarized in the following proposition.

Proposition 8. A necessary and sufficient condition for increasing α to be profitable is $MFC^D_A - \chi f_A > 0$; that is, the marginal factor cost of A exceeds the predator's marginal revenue product of A.

In principle, MFC^D_A and χf_A could be quantified, in which case an empirical test for overbuying could be carried out.

[36] Formally, this assumes that the dominant firm ignores the effect of α on the predator's residual demand function and the effect of p on A^D.

[37] The marginal revenue product of A is χf_A and the marginal factor cost of A is $\alpha + A^D/A^D_\alpha$.

[38] For a diagrammatic explanation of this result see Salop and Scheffman [1984].

[39] It is not possible to state a general result summarizing the relationship between the strategic and non-strategic equilibria. However, simple examples bear out the intuition about the effects of strategic overbuying. For example, let market demand be $a - bp$. Suppose both the fringe and the predator use one unit of A to produce one unit of output, and that $A^F(\alpha, p) = (p - \alpha)$. Suppose further that A is supplied according to the supply function $A(\alpha) = k\alpha$. Finally, assume that the predator's only cost of production is the cost of A. Then it can be shown that the cost-predation equilibrium has a lower p and higher α than the equilibrium in which the predator acts as a simple monopolist-monopsonist.

Using the simple monopoly/monopsony model as a benchmark has two shortcomings for policy purposes. First, the condition given in Proposition 8 may be difficult to measure in practice. Second, although buying more inputs than would a non-strategic *MM* indicates an *intent* to raise rivals' cost to gain power over price, the strategy may not reduce economic efficiency. This is because a monopsonist under-purchases the input, relative to the efficient level, so that purchasing more than a monopsonist may improve welfare.

These two considerations suggest a second possible benchmark: the input purchase level that would be chosen if the predator were a perfect competitor in both input and output markets. If the predator so overpurchases the input that the value of the input price α exceeds the value of the input's marginal product (pf_A), then it must be true that the purchaser both intended to raise rivals' costs and also bought so much extra input that economic welfare must have declined, even ignoring the additional inefficiencies induced by the increase in competitors' costs. This benchmark clearly is far more permissive than the classical monopoly/monopsony purchase level. However, it can be profitable to raise rivals' costs sufficiently to exceed this benchmark.[40]

This more permissive benchmark is analogous to Areeda and Turner's [1975] marginal cost pricing rule for judging allegations of predatory pricing. Although a price below the short run profit-maximizing level may indicate an intent to drive rivals from the market and may reduce economic welfare even if the entrant is less efficient,[41] Areeda and Turner chose the more permissive static, non-strategic pricing standard. Their arguments in favor of the Areeda-Turner rule can be applied to our competitive benchmark.

Moreover, it is interesting to note that our competitive benchmark also involves a comparison of marginal cost and price. If a perfectly competitive firm purchases inputs beyond the efficient level to a point where the price of the input exceeds its marginal value product, that firm will be in a position where its marginal cost (of increasing its output with an input) exceeds the price it receives for its output. This is easy to show. For a perfect competitor with no monopsony power, the marginal cost of increasing output by expanding use of a particular input equals the price of that input α divided by its marginal product f_A. Formally, if the predator was a perfect competitor, we would have $MC = \alpha/f_A$. It follows that the competitor's marginal cost

[40] Suppose that the fringe requires one unit of A to produce one unit of output. Then, assuming that the fringe has increasing costs in other inputs, a plausible fringe supply function is $S(p, \alpha)$, and fringe demand for A is $A^F(\alpha, p) = (p-\alpha) \geqslant 0$. Suppose that A is supplied inelastically at A^*, but that the predator does not use A in production. Thus, an equilibrium with $\alpha > 0$, $A^D > 0$ proves the result. Assume that the predator has constant average cost of production of c. Finally, assume that industry demand is linear, $D(p) = a-bp$. It is easily shown that the equilibrium in this model is $p^* = (a+bc-A^*)/2b$, $\alpha^* = [a-(b+1)A^*]/2b$, $A^D = (A^*-c)/2$, if $[a-(b+1)A^*] > 0$. If this condition holds $\alpha^* > 0$, then $A^{D*} > 0$, even though the marginal productivity of A for the predator is zero. Thus, the predator purchases A at a price above its marginal revenue product and above the value of the marginal product of A (which in this case are both zero).

[41] See Hay [1981].

exceeds the price of output p if the input price α exceeds the marginal value product pf_A (i.e., if $\alpha > pf_A$, then $MC = \alpha/f_A > p$). Thus, if the predator violates our competitive benchmark, his marginal cost *measured by treating him as a competitor* would exceed price.

V. VERTICAL INTEGRATION

Consider now the case in which the predator is partially vertically integrated; that is, it self-manufactures a portion of its overall input requirements. The model of section IV is easily extended to incorporate this possibility. We will now show that the firm may (over-) purchase inputs on the outside "merchant" market even when it is more efficient to produce the input internally, in order to increase the costs of competitors. This can occur even if the production technology exhibits fixed proportions.

Interpreting $A^D(\alpha, p)$ as *net* purchases of input A by the predator (where $A^D(\alpha, p) < 0$ means that predator is a net seller of A), let A^{*D} be the quantity of input A *produced* by the predator and let $c(A^{*D})$ be its cost of production. Then the predator's cost function is given by

$$(22) \qquad \tilde{C}(x, \alpha, p) = \min_{\{z_i^D, A^{*D}\}} [\textstyle\sum r_i z_i^D + \alpha A^D(\alpha, p) + c(A^{*D})],$$

$$\text{subject to } f(z^D, A^{*D} + A^D(\alpha, p)) = x$$

It is easily seen that the minimization of (22) with respect to A^{*D} requires

$$(23) \qquad c'(A^{*D}) - \chi f_A = 0$$

This condition implies that the predator always *produces* input A efficiently, i.e., at the level at which its marginal cost of production is equal to its marginal revenue product.

The other equilibrium conditions are the same as (17). Therefore, since as shown above, $(\alpha - \chi f_A) > 0$ may be characteristic of an equilibrium, it follows from (23) that $(\alpha - c'(A^{*D})) > 0$ may also obtain.[42] In short, it may be profitable for the predator to purchase the input on the market at a price exceeding its own marginal cost of producing the input internally. This is because purchases of the input raise the costs of the fringe and the reduction in fringe supply may more than compensate for the predator's increased input cost.

Asymmetry in the extent of vertical integration enhances the likelihood

[42] An example in which $(\alpha - c'(A^{*D})) > 0$ can be easily constructed along the lines of the example of footnote 40. Assume now that the predator must also use one unit of A to produce one unit of output and that it can produce A at a constant average cost of c. If we assume the demand curve and technology of the fringe is the same as in footnote 40, the equilibrium in this model is also $p^* = (a + bc - A^*)/2b$, $\alpha^* = [a - (b+1)A^*]/2b$, $A^D = (A - c)/2$, $x^* = [a + bc - A^*]/2$, and $A^{*D} = [a + (2-b)c - A]/2$, where A^{*D} is the amount of A produced by the predator (assuming $(a + (2-b)c - A) > 0$). Since α^* does not depend on c, it is clearly possible to have $(\alpha^* - c) > 0$.

that this strategy will be profitable. This can be illustrated with the following simple example. Suppose the predator and the fringe each have a fixed proportion technology that requires one unit of the input to produce one unit of output. Assume that only the predator is vertically integrated into input production and it produces a fraction β of its input needs internally. In this case, an increase in α by an amount $\Delta\alpha$ increases the predator's average costs by $(1-\beta)\Delta\alpha$. This increase is smaller than the increase in fringe marginal cost of $\Delta\alpha$. Because market prices depend on fringe marginal costs, the asymmetry in vertical integration may be the basis of a profitable exclusionary strategy.

Of course, there is also an indirect effect on the predator's average cost equal to $\Delta\alpha A(\alpha)\varepsilon_A$ arising from the increased purchases required to increase α by $\Delta\alpha$, where ε_A is the price elasticity of supply of A. Nonetheless, the asymmetry between the vertically integrated predator and the unintegrated fringe is more likely to make cost-predation profitable, even if there is no input substitutability.[43] This is summarized in the following result.

Proposition 9. Vertical integration can be anticompetitive, even with a technology that permits no input substitution.

Proposition 9 shows that a fixed coefficient technology is *not* a sufficient condition for the absence of anticompetitive impact of a vertical merger (cf. Bork [1978]).

VI. SUMMARY AND CONCLUSIONS

In this paper, we have developed a general model in which a predator can use cost-raising strategies to increase its profits by disadvantaging its rivals. Our results suggest that cost-raising strategies can be an important anticompetitive instrument even if the "predator" is a price-taker in the output market. Such strategies can include pre-emption in upstream input markets and vertical integration, abuse of the regulatory process, advertising, and product differentiation. In addition, the effects of some cost-raising strategies can sometimes be collusive, in that the fringe's profits sometimes increase.

There is more work needed in this area. First, the models in this paper do not incorporate the possibility of fringe counterstrategies against the predator's conduct. Although we have shown elsewhere (Salop, Scheffman and Schwartz [1984]) that the scope of such counterstrategies is limited, they can provide a constraint on potential cost-raising strategies in some cases. Second, we have focused on the case of a competitive fringe. Some work has been carried out for oligopoly markets (see, e.g., Salinger (1985)), but additional structure could be added to that model and counterstrategies could be studied productively. Third, more detailed analysis of efficiency could allow the welfare results to be made more precise. Finally, models of

[43] The example in the preceding footnote provides proof of this proposition.

optimal antitrust policy in a regime of limited market information for the enforcement authorities could be constructed using the structure set out here.[44]

STEVEN C. SALOP,
Georgetown University Law Centre,
600 New Jersey Avenue, N.W.,
Washington, DC 20001,
USA.

ACCEPTED NOVEMBER 1986

DAVID T. SCHEFFMAN,
Bureau of Economics,
Federal Trade Commission,
Washington, DC 20580,
USA.

REFERENCES

AREEDA, P. and TURNER, D., 1975, 'Predatory Pricing and Related Practices Under Section 2 of the Sherman Act', *Harvard Law Review*, 88.

BORK, ROBERT, 1978, *The Antitrust Paradox* (Basic Books, New York).

EASTERBROOK, F., 1981, 'Predatory Strategies and Counterstrategies', *University of Chicago Law Review*, 48, pp. 263–337.

GILBERT, RICHARD, 1981, 'Patents, Sleeping Patents and Entry Deterrence', in S. SALOP (ed.), *Strategy, Predation and Antitrust Analysis*, pp. 205–270.

HAY, G., 1981, 'A Confused Lawyer's Guide to Predatory Pricing', in S. SALOP (ed.), *Strategy Predation and Antitrust Analysis*, pp. 155–202.

KRATTENMAKER, T. and SALOP, S., 1986, 'Anticompetitive Exclusion: Raising Rivals' Costs to Achieve Power Over Price', *Yale Law Journal*, 96 (November), pp. 209–295.

MALONEY, M. and MCCORMICK, R., 1982, 'A Positive Theory of Environmental Quality Regulation', *Journal of Law and Economics*, 25 (April), pp. 99–124.

MALONEY, M. and TOLLISON, R., 1979, 'Achieving Cartel Profits Through Unionization', *Southern Economic Journal*, 42 (October), pp. 628–634.

MCCORMICK, R., 1984, 'The Strategic Use of Regulation: A Review of the Literature', in ROGOWSKY and YANDLE [1984].

ORDOVER, J. and WILLIG, R., 1981, 'An Economic Definition of Predation: Pricing and Product Innovation', *Yale Law Review*, 91 (November), pp. 8–53.

PLOTT, C., 1981, 'Theories of Industrial Organization as Explanations of Experimental Market Behavior', in S. SALOP (ed.), *Strategy, Predation and the Antitrust Analysis*, pp. 523–578.

ROGOWSKY, R. and YANDLE, B., 1984, *The Political Economy of Regulation: Private Interests in the Regulatory Process* (Federal Trade Commission, Washington, DC).

SALLINGER, M., 1975, 'Vertical Mergers and Market Foreclosure', Columbia Business School, unpublished manuscript.

SALOP, S. C., 1979, 'Strategic Entry Deterrence', *American Economic Review*, 69 (May), pp. 335–338.

[44] For an explicit treatment of the concept of cost-raising strategies in an antitrust context with full market information see Krattenmaker and Salop (1986).

SALOP, S. C., 1981, 'Introduction', in S. C. SALOP (ed.), *Strategy, Predation and Antitrust Analysis* (Federal Trade Commission, Washington, DC), pp. 1–42.

SALOP, S. C. and SCHEFFMAN, D. T., 1983, 'Raising Rivals' Costs', *American Economic Review*, (May), pp. 267–271.

SALOP, S. C. and SCHEFFMAN, D. T., 1984, 'Multi-Market Strategies in a Dominant Firm Industry', (Federal Trade Commission Bureau of Economics Working Paper No. 100, Washington, DC).

SALOP, S. C., SCHEFFMAN, David T. and SCHWARTZ, W., 1984, 'A Bidding Analysis of Special Interest Regulation: Raising Rivals' Cost in Rent-Seeking Society', in ROGOWSKY and YANDLE [1984].

SALOP, S. C. and SHAPIRO, C., 1980, 'A Guide to Test Market Predation', Unpublished Manuscript.

SCHARFSTEIN, D., 1984, 'A Policy to Prevent Rational Test Market Predation', *Rand Journal of Economics*, 2 (Summer), pp. 229–243.

WILLIAMSON, O., 1968, 'Wage Rates as a Barrier to Entry: The Pennington Case', *Quarterly Journal of Economics*, (February), pp. 85–116.

[18]

The Antitrust Bulletin/Spring 1988 95

Understanding "raising rivals' costs"

BY TIMOTHY J. BRENNAN*

Introduction

Raising rivals' costs [RRC] is a phrase rapidly entering the lexicon of the antitrust economist and lawyer. The innovative focus of RRC is on actions taken by firms against their competitors, rather than on the exercise of market power against upstream suppliers or downstream customers. The paradigmatic RRC situation is simple to describe. A dominant firm in an industry exercises some sort of strategy to shift upward the supply curve of its rivals. Assuming no effects on demand, this shifts out the residual demand curve for the dominant firm's product. The

---

* Associate Professor, Graduate School of Arts and Sciences, George Washington University.

AUTHOR'S NOTE: *This research was begun while I was an economist with the Antitrust Division, U.S. Department of Justice. It does not necessarily reflect the views of the department or its officials. Thanks go to Marius Schwartz, Margaret Guerin-Calvert, Robert McGuckin, and Russ Pittman for many helpful suggestions. Special thanks go to Rick Warren-Boulton for sharing his knowledge of the literature in this area, and to Steve Salop and Tom Krattenmaker for many helpful conversations. This article does not necessarily reflect the views of any of those acknowledged, and they bear no responsibility for errors.*

increase in demand leads to increased profits for the dominant firm. Shifting back the rivals' supply curve requires increasing their costs at the margin. Opposing the conventional wisdom that firms injure competitors only by offering higher quality or lower priced products, RRC is offered as a way to revive discredited theories of predation and vertical foreclosure.

A good test for the usefulness of any new antitrust theory is whether it identifies bad practices that are currently legal without adding to the set of good practices that are inappropriately condemned. The purpose of this article is to show that RRC fails both aspects of this test. While RRC can provide insights into various anticompetitive actions firms may undertake, practices properly criticized by RRC necessarily involve horizontal monopolization that can be addressed through conventional antitrust analytical techniques.

On the "costs" side, RRC's focus on harm to competitors through vertical practices invites analysis of the wrong markets, misapplication of anticompetitive conduct "tests," and the revival of antitrust doctrines that condemned welfare-enhancing practices. The vertical aspects of RRC will either be only marginally significant or apply primarily where the exercise of market power in a vertically related market is otherwise constrained, because of regulation or because the government itself possesses the relevant monopoly power. While RRC may stimulate worthwhile investigation of partially vertical integrated industries, prior theoretical work suggests a model helpful for antitrust enforcement is unlikely to be forthcoming.

Concept

The essence of RRC is set out in the 1983 paper *Raising Rivals' Costs* by Salop and Scheffman.[1] RRC is described as a

---

1 Salop & Scheffman, *Raising Rivals' Costs*, 73 AMER. ECON. REV. 267 (1983) [hereinafter cited as *Raising Rivals' Costs*]. A more detailed presentation is in Salop & Scheffman, *Cost Raising Strategies*, 36 J. INDUSTRIAL ECON. 19 (1987). The idea has precursors in Williamson, *Wage Rates as a Barrier to Entry: The* Pennington *Case in Perspective*, 82 Q. J. ECON. 85 (1968), and a number of authors have looked at the compet-

form of nonprice predation carried out by raising rivals' supply cost, rather than the traditional predatory tactic of reducing their output price by flooding the market. Salop and Scheffman argue that with RRC the predator need not absorb the losses incurred in traditional predation, where the overall output market price is lowered for both the predator and the prey. RRC is said also to have the property that the returns from carrying it out are immediate, rather than dependent upon the postpredation response of competitors and future entry deterrence effects. They also find that RRC may be profitable even if the rivals do not actually exist, since the rivals' supply curve is shifted to the left by virtue of the raised costs.[2] "Exclusionary practices," *i.e.*, conduct involving closing off competitors from access to inputs, are looked at as possible RRC tactics.

This theme is developed further in *Competition and Cooperation in the Market for Exclusionary Rights* by Krattenmaker and Salop.[3] There, vertical restraints—specifically contracts with input suppliers that incorporate discrimination against or refusals to deal with the contracting firm's rivals—are examined as potential RRC tactics. They state that where the supplies of the

---

itive effects of exclusive dealing contracts. *See* WARREN-BOULTON, VERTICAL CONTROL OF MARKETS: BUSINESS AND LABOR PRACTICES, 78, 87-88 (1978). The notion that government processes can be used to predate against rivals is analyzed in BORK, THE ANTITRUST PARADOX, 347-64 (1978).

2 Depending upon the strategy selected, the dominant firm will be better off even if the RRC tactic raises its own costs as well, and the rivals themselves may be better off after their costs are raised. If the increase in marginal cost is greater than the increase in average costs, then the price-cost margin increases, potentially increasing profits as well. One can think of an agreement among firms to blow up half of their plants, raising marginal production cost, limiting output and raising price. This, of course, is not the most efficient strategy; resources would have been saved had the extra capacity not been built in the first place.

3 Krattenmaker & Salop, *Competition and Cooperation in the Market for Exclusionary Rights*, 76 AMER. ECON. REV. 109 (1986) [hereinafter cited as *Exclusionary Rights*]. A longer article by Krattenmaker and Salop elaborating the raising rivals' cost theory is *Anticompetitive Exclusion: Raising Rivals' Costs to Achieve Power Over Price*, 96 YALE L. J. 209 (1986) [hereinafter cited as *Anticompetitive Exclusion*].

inputs are not perfectly elastic, the opportunity for rivals to exercise counterstrategies will not alleviate the effects of the RRC tactics. The very expenditure of resources on counterstrategies will raise rivals' cost, thus accomplishing the goal of the strategy. In addition, the benefits of keeping markets competitive are a "public good" that rivals will not fully internalize, making their incentive to fight RRC too low from a social welfare perspective.[4]

Finally, the authors address whether it makes a difference that RRC is considered a vertical tactic, not covered under conventional analyses of horizontal market power. They claim RRC does not require preexisting market power, since market power is created by the accumulation of exclusionary rights contracts. Embedding the accumulation of exclusionary rights in (explicit) vertical rather than (implicit or covert) horizontal contracts may prevent cheating by upstream suppliers, and enables them to capture some of the benefits reaped by the downstream firm which is not subject to the exclusion or discrimination.[5]

---

4 Krattenmaker and Salop concede that the price of exclusionary contracts is likely to rise as input suppliers realize what the value of exclusionary rights are to downstream sellers, but argue that some rights will be purchased nonetheless. They also note that there may be bargaining problems regarding division of the profits from the RRC tactic among the downstream predator and the upstream suppliers of exclusionary input contracts, but those are dismissed as solvable either by competition among input suppliers or through commitments by the downstream predator "to purchase all rights offered at some price or purchase a fixed number of rights from the lowest bidders." *Exclusionary Rights*, *supra* note 3, at 112.

Market-wide commitments are needed to address the "hold-out" problem, in which each seller of exclusionary rights knows the rights will be valuable if everyone else sells their rights and therefore does not sell at a price below that which the predator is willing to pay. The general difficulty in pursuing such a preemptive strategy is pointed out in Lewis, *Preemption, Divestiture, and Forward Contracting in a Market Dominated by a Single Firm*, 73 AMER. ECON. REV. 1092 (1983).

5 Again, it is not the purpose here to criticize some of the specific theoretical claims made in the papers describing RRC. Rather, my goal here is to see whether there are valid theoretical claims implied by RRC that could not be presented and understood effectively using conventional, horizontal market-oriented antitrust analysis.

Critique

The critical issue in assessing RRC is embodied in its name. To raise rivals' costs, by definition one has to raise their input prices.[6] Input prices cannot be raised without either acquiring power over price in the markets for those inputs, or causing preexisting but restrained power in the upstream market to be exercised. If market power is acquired, the dominant firm is monopolizing the input market. This in and of itself ought to be an antitrust violation. Whether it elects to exercise this market power by exclusively dealing with itself is a second-order consideration, with ambiguous welfare effects, *once the upstream monopolization occurs*. On the other hand, if preexisting market power is exercised, one has to explain why that market power had not been exploited and how the actions of the downstream firm change either the ability or the incentive to take advantage of that market position.

If this simple assessment is valid, RRC boils down to either monopolization of an input market, which is already illegal, or an assortment of "special case" theories involving the exercise of upstream market power otherwise constrained by regulation, transaction costs, or government ownership of the relevant assets or property rights.[7] To see this requires a case-by-case examina-

---

6 "Inputs" here includes the varieties of production processes that could be employed to produce the input. Thus, a firm can raise its rivals' costs if it holds market power in the supply of technological processes. An example of this would be tying up the supply of competing patents. The government might also be induced to make production by the rivals more expensive by prohibiting certain kinds of production methods.

7 RRC tactics involving activities outside the property rights system, such as blowing up one's competitors' plants, can be squeezed into this framework, but only awkwardly. One could say that if a firm could take control of the supply of plants, as blowing them up implies, then it has monopolized their supply. However, simply taking the plants is illegal. A tactic less wasteful than blowing up the plants, such as renting them out at a high price, requires a market with well defined "owners." Unfortunately, such a market would imply that the "thieves" behind the acquisition of control of the plants could be identified and punished. Such "thieves" might avoid punishment if they adopted a second-best

tion; thus, we turn to the half-dozen applications of RRC discussed in Salop and Scheffman's 1983 paper.[8]

1. In the *Klors*[9] case, one retailer (Broadway-Hale) allegedly used exclusive dealing contracts to monopolize the supply of manufacturers' products into the relevant geographic market. It would be as if a cartel of manufacturers had been formed for the purpose of charging a high price in that market.[10] This scheme worked only because arbitrage across retail markets could be prevented. If not, the victimized retailer could have obtained goods from retailers in other markets, and there would be no effective monopolization in the relevant San Francisco area.[11]

---

tactic, such as blowing up the plants. Thus, distortions created by the differential costs associated with the enforcement of property rights, depending upon what "thieves" do with the "stolen" property, make otherwise suboptimal tactics optimal.

8 *See Raising Rivals' Costs*, *supra* note 1. Similar analyses can be applied to other cases offered as examples of the applicability of RRC. For some examples, *see*, *e.g.*, Salop, Deregulation, Antitrust, and Exclusionary Conduct (Charles River Associates conference, April 18, 1986); *Anticompetitive Exclusion*, *supra* note 3.

9 Klors, Inc. v. Broadway-Hale Stores, Inc., 359 U.S. 207 (1959).

10 Klors' complaint alleged such collusion among the appliance manufacturers; Broadway-Hale was not the only firm cited.

11 It is possible that there may be a conventional defense of Broadway-Hale's conduct. If Klors offered at discount merchandise for which Broadway-Hale provided valuable point-of-sale information, exclusive dealing arrangements might prevent free-riding by Klors and provide efficient incentives for Broadway-Hale to provide this information. *See* Bork, *supra* note 1, at 331-32.

It should be noted that the number of appliance retailers in the same metropolitan area as Klors and Broadway-Hale, San Francisco, apparently numbered in the hundreds at the time of the case. Many of these stores were within blocks of Klors and Broadway-Hale, carrying products of the alleged boycotters of Klors and of the boycotters' competitors. The lower courts decided against Klors, finding that there was no conceivable harm to consumers as a result of the alleged boycott. 255 F. 2d 214, 223 (1958).

2. In *Pennington*,[12] capital-intensive coal producers induced a labor union to raise wages, injuring labor-intensive competitors. The action in *Pennington* was similar to a unilateral wage increase by the union. Such an increase may cause a redistribution of profits among firms that cannot be captured by the union in the absence of "lump sum" payments. But for transaction costs, though, a union with market power could obtain such payments from the capital-intensive firms. Thus, in cases like *Pennington* there is a competitive problem only if labor's market power is constrained by particular circumstances, *e.g.*, if union agreements to obtain lump-sum payments from employers are not covered under labor's antitrust immunity.[13]

3. Exclusive dealing arrangements, when there are economies of scale in retailing, may raise small firms' distribution costs. If a dominant wholesaler prevents the efficient provision of retail services to its small competitors through exclusive dealing arrangements with the efficient large scale retailers, the dominant firm has effectively monopolized the supply of retailing services in the relevant retail markets. It is as if the efficient retailers had formed a cartel among themselves.

4. Government regulations can raise rivals' costs of conforming to industry standards. Using the government process (or

---

12 United Mine Workers v. Pennington, 381 U.S. 657 (1961). The UMW's RRC conduct in *Pennington* was only alleged; on remand, the lower court found the evidence insufficient to find the UMW liable.

13 Williamson, *supra* note 1 does not address how the UMW was induced to cooperate with the capital-intensive coal producers, or why such cooperation would be necessary for the UMW to maximize profits. Marius Schwartz hypothesizes that the lump-sum transfer from the capital-intensive coal producers to the union might have been a promise to avoid costly negotiations. Avoiding negotiation costs, though, is *prima facie* welfare increasing. In addition, if this is the source of the harm in *Pennington*, would it then follow that capital-intensive employers have an obligation to expend resources fighting unions during wage negotiations solely to keep labor-intensive firms in business? If RRC is intended to include pecuniary externalities of this sort, it offers almost no guidance to help antitrust authorities or courts distinguish welfare-reducing from welfare-increasing practices.

nonprofit standard-setting groups) to impose costs on rivals is the exploitation of monopoly power over the supply of important inputs. The entities holding that power (putatively) have no interest in exploiting it, but effective control over that market may be obtained through a political process.[14]

5. Advertising and R&D activities can reduce the marginal productivity of similar expenditures by rivals. For example, advertising by one firm may cause the advertising of another to be less effective at the margin. Looking at advertising as an input, the firm in that sense becomes less productive, and its costs of operating rise. If a firm's increased advertising or R&D expenditure makes efforts by competitors less productive, it may be because consumers prefer the results of these efforts. If so, such expenditures are part of a welfare-increasing process that should not be subject to interference. An externality associated with these expenditures could provide the firm with effective market power over the price the other firm must pay for a given level of advertising or R&D effectiveness. It is doubtful that this would be considered an antitrust violation; a more conventional externality policy, such as an advertising or R&D tax, would be more appropriate.[15]

6. A dominant firm can integrate backwards to create a "vertical price squeeze." This "backward integration" scenario explicitly involves the monopolization of an upstream market by a downstream firm. The monopoly of the upstream market is the source of the anticompetitive effect and the proper object of antitrust action.

---

14 *See* Stigler, *The Theory of Economic Regulation*, in THE CITIZEN AND THE STATE 114-19 (1975).

15 I am not aware of any actual case where an antitrust claim along these lines has been seriously made. Ironically, where there are such externalities, it may be efficient for the industry to collude on mutual reductions of expenditures of this sort. The benign attitude taken toward R&D joint ventures is in part motivated by these considerations.

Note that if advertising or R&D expenses are not incurred at the margin, this externality will have no effect on rivals' supply curves unless rivals are driven out of business.

These examples indicate that where there is an antitrust problem to which RRC is alleged to apply, there is either a horizontal market being monopolized or preexisting but for some reason unexploited monopoly power being exercised. The "vertical" aspects add little to the competitive analysis not already understood.[16]

Alternatives

Imposing costs through government processes

Looking at uses of RRC by others could illustrate RRC's usefulness, but there unfortunately has been too little time for many applications of RRC to appear in the literature. One, suggested to me as an RRC application by Prof. Salop, is an article on the misuse of antitrust by Baumol and Ordover.[17] There, they discuss the strategic use of governmental processes, particularly antitrust suits, to make it more costly for competitors to enter or employ new production or distribution techniques. More broadly, there is a long-standing argument against economic regulation on the grounds that its strategic abuse by expert incumbents can deter entry and restrain competition. Nothing is gained by renaming this argument "RRC." Moreover, RRC could be used to defend competitors' standing to sue in antitrust cases, as aggrieved rivals whose costs have been raised.[18] This practice, precisely the activity Baumol and Ordover bemoan, is an important illustration of the costs RRC may introduce into antitrust litigation.

16 Vertical restraints may facilitate horizontal collusion at some level, and thus their presence may indicate suspicious activity. This role of vertical arrangements was well known prior to the development of RRC, however. *See* Schwartz & Eisenstadt, Vertical Restraints, Department of Justice Antitrust Division Economic Policy Office Discussion Paper 82-8 (1982).

17 Baumol & Ordover, *Use of Antitrust to Subvert Competition*, 28 J. L. Econ. 247 (1985). *See also* Hovenkamp, Economics and Federal Antitrust Law 158 (1985) for similar arguments.

18 *See Anticompetitive Exclusion*, *supra* note 3, at 292-93.

Partial vertical integration

In another paper, White[19] looked at a combination involving Showtime and The Movie Channel [TMC], two of the three suppliers of movie-oriented pay-cable services (HBO, with many more subscribers than Showtime or TMC combined, is the other). In this transaction, the combined Showtime/TMC would have been run by a joint venture including three of the six major motion picture distributors, Paramount, Warner, and Universal. This deal presented potential horizontal concerns in markets for both pay-cable service and the film exhibition rights.

White went further, however, to offer a vertical RRC theory. The premise for his vertically related concerns was that a vertically integrated firm has a greater incentive to seek upstream collusion than an unintegrated firm. The integrated firm would be able to operate efficiently while its unintegrated downstream rivals would not, because the vertically integrated firm can sell to itself at marginal cost, reaping an efficiency advantage relative to rivals who must pay the monopoly price for the input from the cartel. The upstream monopoly can be exploited more profitably because of the vertical integration, making the gains to monopolization, hence its likelihood, greater.

This suggests an implicit theory of partial vertical integration, *i.e.*, where there exist unintegrated firms downstream of an integrated upstream monopolist.[20] Prior models involving

---

19 White, *Antitrust and Video Markets: The Merger of Showtime and the Movie Channel as a Case Study*, in VIDEO MEDIA COMPETITION: REGULATION, ECONOMICS, AND TECHNOLOGY 338 (Noam ed. 1985).

20 White may be making the more subtle argument that concentration be "taxed." To keep an industry from becoming sufficiently concentrated to pose a significant cartelization risk, keep large firms from achieving potential efficiencies through vertical integration or restraints. Such a policy would be distorting, though, unless the "tax" can be limited to concentration situations where monopoly power can be expected, and where the "tax" would prevent the creation of that market power.

Such a "tax" might prove useful if vertical integration is required to generate profits needed to cover cartelization costs, in that absent vertical integration, collusion would not take place. The benefits from precomplete vertical integration have ambiguous welfare conclusions, but RRC might have something to offer as a theory of the deleterious consequences of partial vertical integration. Partial integration, unlike the complete integration case, has been little explored. Schmalensee[21] models partial vertical integration where the fraction of downstream output held by the upstream monopolist is exogenous. As with most analyses of vertical market relationships, he reached ambiguous welfare calculations.[22]

The more appropriate perspective would look at the percentage of productive assets (or firms) in one market owned by a monopolist in a vertically related market. Perry[23] looks at a downstream monopsonist partially integrated upstream, where the measure of integration is the percentage of a fixed supply upstream factor owned by the downstream monopolist. He finds two incentives for integration. First, the monopolist uses his assets more intensively and profitably than do the unintegrated firms because, as White observed, the latter firms' production decisions are distorted by the noncompetitive price. The second incentive is that the implicit per-unit rents paid to up-

---

serving competition may outweigh any efficiencies lost from preventing the integration. It would be more efficient, however, simply to use conventional merger policy to limit the ability of firms to create concentrated markets, than to impose a tax to reduce their incentive to merge. If a monopoly succeeds in spite of the "tax," welfare losses will be larger since the inability to integrate will raise production costs.

21 Schmalensee, *A Note on the Theory of Vertical Integration*, 81 J. Pol. Econ. 442 (1973).

22 A recent extension of Schmalensee's model to look at the effect of price as the level of vertical integration increases is Quirmbach, *The Path of Price Changes in Vertical Integration*, 94 J. Pol. Econ. 1110 (1986). Quirmbach finds that downstream price rises with the degree of vertical integration by a monopolist, as long as unintegrated competitors survive. However, this situation is not profit-maximizing for this monopolist; it does best once the market is entirely preempted. At that point, downstream price may be lower than before integration. Welfare effects at either the final equilibrium or intermediate points cannot be determined in general.

23 Perry, *Vertical Integration: The Monopsony Case*, 68 Amer. Econ. Rev. 561 (1978).

stream producers for their share of the fixed factor decline as the monopsonist's upstream "share" increases. Moreover, Perry finds upstream output increases as the degree of vertical integration increases in the "normal" case where the marginal expenditure curve facing the monopsonist is rising. Applying his model to the downstream case, we may infer that welfare losses from partial vertical integration would be limited to unusual demand conditions.

These models do not exhaust the potential supply,[24] and RRC may yet inspire useful contributions to partial vertical integration theory. But because current theory gives ambiguous welfare results and indicates that losses are unlikely in usual circumstances, partial vertical integration theory does not yet provide guidance for practical antitrust enforcement policy.

A monopolistic competition approach

A monopolistic competition framework for looking at exclusive practices is offered in a forthcoming paper by Mathewson and Winter.[25] They offer a model with interrelated demand curves for two differentiated products. They find that exclusive dealing proposed by the supplier of the most demanded product can lead to welfare reductions. It forces local retailers to sell ex-

---

24 Salinger (*Vertical Mergers and Market Foreclosure*, QUART. J. ECON., forthcoming) considers two oligopolies, one upstream from the other, in which he assumes that some of the oligopolists are vertically integrated, *i.e.*, participate in both markets. He finds that added vertical integration leaves fewer unintegrated sellers to supply the remaining unintegrated buyers, raising the price of the intermediate good. While this causes "foreclosure" by his definition, he makes no conclusion about either increased downstream prices or welfare.

Katz (*The Welfare Effects of Third-Degree Price Discrimination in Intermediate Goods Markets*, 77 AMER. ECON. REV. 154 (1987)) finds that third-degree price discrimination in intermediate goods markets can raise price to all buyers, unlike the final goods case usually studied. His model suggests that partial vertical integration may reduce welfare if it facilitates such price discrimination.

25 Mathewson & Winter, *Is Exclusive Dealing Anticompetitive?*, 77 AMER. ECON. REV. 1057 (1987).

clusively either the more popular good or the less popular good. The dealers may find it profitable to accept the exclusive dealing arrangement, forcing the less popular good off the market and, in some circumstances, enabling the seller of the more popular good to raise prices. In their model, this may reduce economic welfare from both higher prices and reduction of product variety.[26] This seems to be a potentially productive approach to this question, and deserves more attention as a way to analyze many economic activities, not just vertical restraints.[27]

Costs

So far, the analysis of RRC has focused mainly on whether it embodies any heretofore undeveloped economic theory regarding collusive or anticompetitive practices. Even if it does not, though, its semantic differences can have substantive consequences. Word choice, like any other choice, has potential costs and benefits that should be considered in deciding what terms are optimal. As a theoretical term RRC offers little benefit, in that the harms it identifies can be presented using traditional horizontal market approaches. The other side of the cost/benefit equation asks whether using RRC as an antitrust doctrine would impose costs on the antitrust system or the economy as a whole.

Two related classes of costs can be identified. Most competitive activity, such as charging lower prices, entering new markets, improving product quality, and obtaining discounts from suppliers, makes rivals worse off. In focusing antitrust attention on the effects on competitors rather than on customers, as RRC does, antitrust courts and authorities may become excessively sensitive

---

26 Overall profits may be greater if availability of the more profitable good is tied to a requirement that the less popular good be sold at a markup, and then extracting a lump-sum payment from the downstream suppliers. Such a contract would be equivalent to merger of the two upstream suppliers.

27 Mathewson and Winter's model may apply to *Klors*, although it may be harder to show that there were only two sellers, differentiated from one another, in the relevant retail services market.

to protecting the welfare of competitors rather than the competitive process itself. While RRC eventually may lead to useful theories of partial vertical integration, it may lend academic authority to discredited foreclosure and predation doctrines. Antitrust enforcement will have taken a giant step backward if RRC only manages to bring back the days when efficient vertical integration, exclusive dealing or charging low prices put a firm at legal risk.

A second harm of RRC is that it directs attention toward the market in which the alleged perpetrator operates, rather than on the market in which the anticompetitive concentration of control is being carried out. This can cause the wrong questions to be asked, wrong tests to be carried out, and possibly wrong conclusions to be reached.

This potential harm is best illustrated by a concrete example. Miller and Anheuser-Busch [A-B] breweries were alleged to have engaged in a campaign to raise their competitors, advertising costs. The RRC mechanism was the purchase of exclusionary rights from networks regarding advertising during sports events. Under the terms of the advertising contracts with the networks, no other brewers besides Miller and A-B were allegedly permitted to purchase advertising time from the networks during sports events.[28]

The RRC approach was misleading because it gave the impression that the anticompetitive concern was in the beer industry, with Miller and A-B out to raise the advertising costs of competing brewers. The relevant question, though, was whether Miller and A-B monopolized the supply of network sports advertising time for beer companies, the relevant market given the alleged conduct. Vertical analysis serves only two purposes: market definition—can beer companies substitute other types of advertising for network sports commercials?—and efficiency evaluation—is there an externality justifying contracts where only one beer company may buy network advertising time during a sports event?

---

28 Letter from Assistant Attorney General Douglas Ginsburg to Sen. Howard Metzenbaum, 11/1/85.

This matter offers a noteworthy illustration of the effect of RRC in misdirecting attention: the erroneous application of Easterbrook's output test for monopolization.[29] Easterbrook's test is that it would be wrong to conclude that a practice was monopolistic if it led to an increase in output or share in the relevant market. The intuition behind the test is trivial—monopolists do not typically increase output. If the relevant market were beer, as the RRC vertical construction implies, one might conclude with then Antitrust Division head Douglas Ginsburg that Miller's practice could not have been monopolistic since its market share increased after instituting the exclusive arrangements.[30]

Of course, if Miller and A-B had monopolized the supply of network television advertising, and if such advertising is a relevant market at least as far as beer companies are concerned, the alleged practice may well have been harmful. One might respond that Easterbrook's test must be wrong, but such a response would miss the point. Krattenmaker and Salop[31] claim that the "error" in Easterbrook's test is "obvious" because a firm that dynamites its competitors' factories will expand its market share and probably its output, but it would be silly to infer that blowing up plants is procompetitive. True enough. But to apply Easterbrook's test correctly, one should look at the supply of factories. Dynamiting them would reduce their supply, and the activity was clearly anticompetitive.[32]

While the purpose here is not to defend Easterbrook's test, Krattenmaker and Salop's conclusion that Easterbrook is guilty of "careless drafting"[33] is a product of the error in identifying relevant markets that RRC invites. In the Miller example, Easterbrook's test should have been applied to the monopolized

---

29 Easterbrook, *The Limits to Antitrust*, 63 TEX. L. REV. 1 (1984).

30 *See supra* note 28.

31 *See Anticompetitive Exclusion*, *supra* note 3, at 283, n.231.

32 *See supra* note 7.

33 *Anticompetitive Exclusion*, *supra* note 3, at 283, n.231.

market—network television advertising. The proper question was whether the supply of television advertising in the relevant market to beer companies increased as a result of Miller's practice. If so, one could reasonably infer that there was no output reduction and that the practice was procompetitive. If it was not, one would have to ask whether other efficiency rationales, such as avoiding consumer confusion by advertising differing beers during the same program, outweighed the apparent output reduction. But the problem would be Miller and A-B's monopolization of a relevant upstream advertising market. Whether they would use this market power to increase their shares in beer markets, exclude others from such advertising, or simply sell such television advertising to any beer company willing to pay the monopoly price, adds little to our understanding of the consequences of this monopolization.

Prognosis

The primary purpose of RRC is to direct attention to vertical activities in which one market is made less competitive by making it harder for rivals to compete, lending substance to notions like "foreclosure" and "exclusion" that have become unfashionable in current antitrust parlance. These terms fell out of favor, though, for good reasons. When carelessly applied, especially by private plaintiffs, they tended to make innocent or socially beneficial industrial conduct suspect under the antitrust laws. While not much evidence is in, the record so far suggests that the new language of RRC will not avoid these past problems and may well exacerbate them.

The horizontal framework with which we assess market power and antitrust problems is well suited to the legitimate problems the proponents seek to address. As observed above, the gravamen of RRC is that rivals' costs are raised. This requires power to raise costs, implying power in relevant input markets. If such power had not previously been acquired, then presumably an input market has been monopolized. If such power already had been acquired, then the most one can say is that a preexisting upstream monopolist is limiting the set of downstream firms with which he will deal. The welfare effects of such activity are ambiguous, given the prior input monopoly. The welfare analysis is even more problematic if RRC is stretched to cover any pecuniary input externality.

Since we will rarely have a clear-cut case of monopoly when these purely vertical effects are at issue, we are probably better off looking mainly, if not exclusively, at the horizontal issues. Actions raising rivals' costs obviously outside the property rights system, *e.g.*, a firm blowing up its rivals' factories, are already illegal regardless of antitrust analysis. For actions taken within the property rights system, the relevant input market should be clearly identified, including where pertinent the limitation to a specific set of buyers. In the *Klors* case, for example, the relevant market would be the supply of appliances at the wholesale level into the relevant retailing market served by Klors and Broadway-Hale.

Krattenmaker and Salop[34] argue that horizontal market analysis understates the content of RRC because a vertical relationship reduces the propensity of the cartel members to cheat and enables the capture of benefits when a high price is charged to the competitors of the downstream firm. The first point just restates the proposition that a monopolist is more stable than a cartel. The vertical relationship is a horizontal binding device; but it is the horizontal market power, not the verticality itself, responsible for the competitive effects. With regard to the second point, we may observe that vertical relationships are typically unnecessary. An unintegrated monopolist of "exclusionary rights" would not single out one downstream firm to benefit from the monopolization without charging it for the privilege.

Where the vertical relationship is a necessary component of the competitive problem, there must be market power at one level, constrained or held by an entity not interested in profit maximization, which can be exercised through vertical integration or other vertical practices. In the government's antitrust case

---

34 *See Exclusionary Rights*, *supra* note 3.

against AT&T, for example, AT&T was accused of raising the costs of its rivals in interexchange and customer equipment markets by denying access to its regulated local exchange monopolies.[35] A less obvious case is *Pennington*. If there were profits to be had by the union raising its wages, why did it not do so on its own? Was the case only about the illegality of side payments, lump-sum transfers, or whatever *quid* was given for the *quo* of the high wages?[36]

An encouraging development is that the RRC doctrine may be evolving more toward the traditional horizontal paradigm. One of the contributions of RRC has been the focus of attention on narrowly drawn horizontal markets, such as the local appliance wholesale market in *Klors*[37] or the television network sports advertising of beer in the Miller/A-B matter. The relevant input market monopolizations in these cases did not involve the acquisition of complete control of all appliance manufacturers in the relevant market. What was acquired was, as Krattenmaker and Salop call them, "exclusionary rights."[38] While plaintiffs arguing on RRC-like grounds should be required to demonstrate such monopolization of a relevant input market, it seems that this evolution of RRC to an "exclusionary rights" framework is a step in putting the informative part of RRC into a traditional horizontal framework.

As a new terminology for upstream monopolization, RRC could enable courts to address inefficient business practices that could not be reached under conventional horizontal tests. For this to hold, though, the antitrust laws would have to have the perverse property that the burden of proof for multimarket or

---

35 For a more detailed examination of the problems associated with multimarket strategies to evade regulatory constraints, *see* Brennan, Regulated Firms in Unregulated Markets: Understanding the Divestiture in *U.S. v. AT&T*, EAG Discussion Paper 86-5, Antitrust Division, U. S. Dept. of Justice (1986).

36 *See supra* note 13.

37 *See supra* note 9.

38 *See Exclusionary Rights*, *supra* note 3.

vertical practices was lower than for horizontal practices. Such a systematic adjudicative bias should be corrected, not used to rationalize RRC. If courts may not be able to recognize horizontal monopolization in specific input markets, RRC may offer a means for addressing conduct that would otherwise escape attention. However, if the courts are insufficiently sophisticated to arrive at correct horizontal market definitions, there is little reason to think they will be able to avoid inappropriately applying RRC to protect firms from more efficient competitors.[39]

In summary, RRC explains little that cannot already be understood through careful application of the conventional and proven horizontal market paradigm in antitrust analysis. While RRC may serve as a rhetorical device to enhance awareness of input market monopolization or the use of governmental processes and regulations to injure competitors, experience suggests it is likely to lead to erroneous conclusions. As RRC evolves more toward an "exclusionary rights" framework, it will become more familiar and compatible with the prevailing paradigm and less innovative in appearance. Antitrust understanding would be better served by directing research attention toward substantive analyses of partial vertical integration, antimonopolization policies, and vertical interactions among differentiated competitors.

---

39 A specific way RRC is likely to increase litigation cost is that it will stimulate demand for economic experts, who do not come cheaply, to explain why this new idea does or does not make sense in a particular case.

Equilibrium Vertical Foreclosure

By JANUSZ A. ORDOVER, GARTH SALONER, AND STEVEN C. SALOP*

We formulate a complete, but analytically simple, equilibrium model of vertical mergers to evaluate the logic of standard vertical foreclosure claims and the criticisms made of those claims. The model includes incentives of the integrated firm and unintegrated input suppliers to exclude rivals, the potential counter-strategies of competitors to these foreclosure threats, and the potential hold-out problem. In this fully specified model, vertical foreclosure can emerge in equilibrium. (JEL 610)

The competitive effects of vertical mergers have long been a source of controversy in economics and antitrust. One of the central issues in that debate involves vertical foreclosure; the exclusion that results when unintegrated downstream rivals are foreclosed from the input supplies controlled by the firm that integrates. Analogous effects occur when unintegrated upstream competitors are foreclosed from selling to the downstream division of the integrated firm.[1]

While foreclosure has been accepted in leading court decisions[2] and policy guidelines,[3] critics maintain that the theory itself is logically flawed. They claim that a vertically integrated firm will have no incentive to exclude its rivals, and if it did try to exclude them, rivals could protect themselves by contracting with other unintegrated firms.[4]

This controversy can be seen more clearly by making the vertical foreclosure theory more specific.[5] According to the theory, a single vertical merger can disadvantage downstream rivals as follows.[6] Consider a market in which the supply of inputs is competitive before the merger and there are no production efficiency benefits gained from vertical integration. After the merger, suppose the upstream division of the now-integrated firm refuses to supply inputs to the rivals of its downstream division.

This foreclosure of rivals from these supplies means that remaining suppliers will face less competition. As a result, they may be able to increase their profits by raising their input prices to the unintegrated down-

*Department of Economics, NYU; Department of Economics and Sloan School of Management, MIT; and Georgetown University Law Center, respectively. We have benefited from several useful discussions with Mike Whinston and comments from William Comanor, Louis Kaplow, Julio Rotemberg, Jean Tirole, an anonymous referee, and participants at a conference on Vertical Restraints at Harvard University, September 1987. Financial support from the National Science Foundation (grant IST-8510162), the C.V. Starr Center for Applied Economics at NYU, the Hoover Institution at Stanford University, and the Sloan Foundation is gratefully acknowledged.

[1] The other main strand of the debate concerns how vertical mergers can eliminate inefficiencies due to a double markup of input costs and substitution to other less efficient inputs. Similar models show how vertical mergers can be used to facilitate price discrimination against purchasers with less elastic demands. This literature is reviewed by Martin Perry (1989) and Jean Tirole (1988).

[2] See, for example, *Brown Shoe Co. v. United States*, 370 US 294 (1962) and *United States v. Aluminum Co. of America*, 44 F. Supp. 97, 121-44 (SDNY, 1941), 148 F. 2d 416, 436-38 (2d Cir., 1945).

[3] For example, the Department of Justice's 1984 Vertical Merger Guidelines.

[4] See Robert Bork (1978), pp. 222–45 and pp. 299–309, Richard Posner (1976), pp. 171–84, 196–207, Frank Easterbrook (1984), and Posner and Easterbrook (1981), pp. 869–76.

[5] In what follows, we focus on foreclosure of downstream rivals. The analysis of foreclosure of upstream rivals is analogous.

[6] For a general discussion of potential anticompetitive consequences of vertical mergers see Thomas Krattenmaker and Steven Salop (1986).

stream firms.[7] These higher prices benefit the vertically integrated firm. If rivals' costs of inputs are increased, they will be forced to reduce their production and raise the prices they charge in the downstream market. This reduction in competition allows the downstream division of the integrated firm to increase its market share and its price. Thus the profits of the vertically integrated firm can rise, even if there are no production efficiency benefits flowing from the vertical integration.

The critics of vertical foreclosure raise a number of objections to these assertions. Each of these objections implies that the strategy of vertical integration and foreclosure of supply will not increase the overall profitability of the integrated firm. The objections deny the ability to use power in one market to "leverage" into a position of power in a second market. For example, Robert Bork (1978, p. 231) concludes:

> Vertical merger does not create or increase the firm's power to restrict output. The ability to restrict output depends on the share of the market occupied by the firm. Horizontal mergers increase market share, but vertical mergers do not.

There are six main objections to the foreclosure theory. First, the supply of inputs available to rivals is not necessarily reduced as a result of a vertical merger. This is because the integrated firm also reduces its demand for inputs produced by unintegrated suppliers. For example, if a firm with 10 percent of the output market purchases a supplier that accounts for 10 percent of the input market, it will not reduce the net supply available to rivals. Instead, it merely will necessitate a rearrangement in supply relationships.

[7]Krattenmaker and Salop term this version of the vertical foreclosure theory the "Frankenstein Monster" because the integrated downstream firm creates market power for the remaining upstream firms, giving them the power to raise input prices to its rival.

Second, critics assert that it may not be profitable for the integrated firm to foreclose its downstream rivals. Although the profits of the downstream division rise, the upstream division of the integrated firm loses input sales from its refusal to deal with rival downstream firms. These lost upstream profits may exceed the increased downstream profits. As a result, it does not follow necessarily that it is in the interest of the vertically integrated firm to foreclose downstream rivals.

Third, remaining suppliers may not have the incentive to raise their input prices. The foreclosure theory relies on the incentive of remaining suppliers to increase their input prices after they no longer face competition in the input market from the integrated supplier. But this reduction in competition is more apparent than real. If the remaining suppliers raise their input prices, downstream firms often can begin to produce the input themselves.

Even if such entry is assumed to be impossible, raising prices may still be unprofitable. If the remaining suppliers raise prices, their downstream customers will be placed at a cost disadvantage vis-à-vis the integrated firm and will be forced to reduce their input purchases. Stated more directly, unintegrated firms' input demands are highly elastic. Consequently, suppliers' incentives to increase prices even after the integrated firm forecloses those rivals from its input production are low.

Fourth, the foreclosed rivals have available a number of alternative counterstrategies to battle their exclusion. In particular, they can respond by vertically integrating with the remaining unintegrated input producers. This will enable them to obtain the inputs at the competitive price, thereby eliminating their cost disadvantage. Thus, the first firm to integrate will gain no market power.

Fifth, it is not obvious that the first downstream firm's bid to integrate with an upstream firm will succeed to begin with. The vertical foreclosure theory suffers from a potential holdout problem. Assuming that remaining input producers gain the power to increase their input prices to unintegrated downstream buyers, a holdout supplier would gain an advantage by remaining unintegrated. Unless the downstream firm bids enough to compensate its potential merger partner for this lost opportunity, its bid will fail. Each firm will hold out, in the anticipation that another supplier will merge and give it the ability to profitably raise its input price. If the downstream firm does try to compensate its potential merger partner for this lost opportunity, the profitability of the merger is decreased, possibly to the point that no merger will occur.

Finally, the vertical foreclosure theory suffers from one last potential flaw. Since the firm that is foreclosed is placed at a disadvantage, it ought itself to participate in the bidding for the scarce upstream resource. While this flaw is somewhat different from the earlier criticisms, in that it does not amount to a claim that vertical foreclosure will fail, it does make the theory incomplete.

In this paper, we set out a complete, but analytically tractable equilibrium model to evaluate the logic of the standard vertical foreclosure argument as well as the arguments advanced by its critics. Even though our model is simple, it includes the incentives of the integrated firm and remaining unintegrated input suppliers to exclude rivals, the possible counterstrategies of competitors to these threats of foreclosure, and the potential holdout problem. It also deals explicitly with the bidding for the scarce upstream resource.

We analyze the simplest vertical structure capable of capturing the essential elements of interest. In particular, we consider successive duopoly: two upstream firms initially provide an equal share of a homogeneous input to two downstream producers. These two downstream firms each produce a differentiated product in competition with the other, and initially have equal market shares. In order to focus exclusively on foreclosure rather than efficiency, we have structured the model so that double marginalization does not arise when the firms initially are unintegrated. This is accomplished by assuming Bertrand competition upstream.

We then allow for the possibility that a downstream firm acquires one of the upstream suppliers, leaving the rival with a single independent upstream supplier. However, the net supply available to the rival does not necessarily fall. Of course, if the integrated firm refuses to supply the unintegrated downstream firm, the remaining upstream supplier is endowed with a good deal of market power. We do not assume, however, that the integrated firm will refuse to deal with the remaining downstream rival. Rather, we examine several different scenarios for the way in which the input prices are determined. We also examine the possibility that the remaining downstream rival is able to counter the effect of the first vertical merger by itself merging with the remaining supplier. Finally, we require that the integrating downstream firm outbid its rival for the acquisition of the upstream firm, that is, we require bidding for the right to foreclose.

In this fully specified model, vertical foreclosure does emerge in equilibrium, provided the downstream firms' revenues are increasing in the price of the input. Then, when one of the firms integrates backward, thereby causing an increase in the input prices of the rival, downstream prices and revenues increase. Of course the profits of the unintegrated downstream firm decrease because it must pay the higher input costs. However, the sum of its profits and those of its supplier (which sum equals downstream revenues) increase. Therefore its loss in profits is less than the increase in the profits of its supplier. Accordingly, the unintegrated downstream firm cannot induce the upstream firm to merge and return to the *ex ante* position.

This argument holds for small increases in the upstream price. If the unintegrated upstream firm has an incentive to raise its price excessively, however, the unintegrated downstream firm will lose so much market share to its rival that its revenue will fall. Then the unintegrated firms will have an incentive to merge.

Thus, whereas the conventional critique of foreclosure theory has questioned the ability of the remaining upstream firm(s) to raise price, ironically, in this model a necessary condition is that it not be able to raise its price too much. Its ability to so raise the price will be reduced if it faces competition from other substitutes, or, as seems plausible, if the integrated firm is able to "keep a lid" on that price by announcing a price of its own at which it is prepared to supply the rival downstream firm.

The condition that the downstream firms' revenues be increasing in the price of the input tends to hold in the case of differentiated product price competition. There if a firm increases its price in response to an increase in the price of an input (an action the rival likes), the rival tends to respond in like manner, raising its own price: prices are strategic complements. In the case of Cournot competition with downward sloping best-response functions, in contrast, the firms' actions are strategic substitutes: if a firm reduces its output in response to an increase in the input price (an action the rival likes), the rival responds by increasing its own output, leading to a decrease in the former's revenues. Thus, while the analysis rests on certain features of the market structure, they are not the ones suggested by the conventional critique.

There is an earlier literature on vertical foreclosure which focuses on the case in which either the upstream or downstream tier of the industry is monopolized (or, at least, one firm has a dominant market position). That literature is concerned with the question of whether the dominant firm can increase its profitability by foreclosing some of the firms at the other level.[8] The fundamental difference here is our focus on vertical foreclosure by a firm to increase its market power in the level of the market which it currently shares with another rival.

Our work is related to that of Michael Salinger (1988). He examines whether vertical integration between successive oligopoly leads to higher or lower final goods prices. His model is more general than ours in that he allows for successive oligopoly rather than duopoly, and he allows for differing numbers of upstream and downstream firms. A similar body of work (focusing mainly on the duopoly case) also has been developed in the marketing literature.[9] However, none of this work examines the issues of counterstrategies and bidding which are the focus of our paper.

The paper is organized as follows: We begin by laying out the basic model in Section I. That section also establishes the unintegrated and fully integrated outcomes as benchmarks for our further analysis. In Section II, we analyze the model of vertical integration with differentiated products and establish the rationality of foreclosure in that setting.

In Section III, we study the robustness of our conclusions to changes in model specification. We show that the holdout problem may arise when upstream firms bid for downstream firm rather than vice versa because downstream firms earn positive profits before the merger. We also show that merger incentives depend on the nature of competition among the downstream firms. In particular, when downstream firms compete in quantities there are no foreclosure-creating vertical mergers in equilibrium because it is always profit-increasing for the unintegrated firms to merge in response to the initial

[8] See William Comanor (1967) for an early example of a paper in this line, and Jean Tirole (1988, pp. 193–4) for a survey of the issues. Tirole (1988, ch. 4) also provides an excellent survey of vertical restraints such as "exclusive dealing" (as discussed, for example, in Comanor and H. E. Frech, 1985, Frank Mathewson and Ralph Winter, 1987, and Marius Schwartz, 1987), and "exclusive territories" (as discussed, for example, in Patrick Rey and Joseph Stiglitz, 1986). The paper by Schwartz points to the importance of considering a retailer's rationality in accepting an exclusive dealing arrangement involving a higher wholesale price, while Mathewson and Winter emphasize the importance of considering competition among wholesalers for the right to be selected by the retailer. Those papers underscore the importance of considering a rich set of strategies and counterstrategies of the kind considered in the current paper. In a somewhat different vein, Philippe Aghion and Patrick Bolton (1987) show how a firm with a first-mover advantage can deter entry by entering into an exclusive contract with customers.

[9] Two good examples are Sridhar Moorthy (forthcoming) and Ann Coughlin and Birger Wernerfelt (1988).

vertical merger. Finally, we consider the equilibria that can be implemented with two-part tariffs for inputs in lieu of a vertical merger. We argue that a two-part tariff contract between an input supplier and a buyer that does not specify prices to other buyers will not implement the anticompetitive equilibrium with foreclosure identified in Section II. Section IV concludes.

I. The Industry Structure and Benchmark Outcomes

In this section we lay out the structure of the market setting we examine and illustrate how the standard foreclosure argument can be applied to it. In the following section, we enrich the setting to model merger strategies, price-setting of the upstream good, and merger counterstrategies.

A. *Basic Model*

Two upstream firms, $U1$ and $U2$, provide a homogeneous input to two downstream firms, $D1$ and $D2$. For reasons that will become obvious soon, we assume that the input is produced with a constant returns to scale technology. At this point, we do not make any assumptions regarding the production technology for the outputs of $D1$ and $D2$.

Throughout the paper we assume static competition between the downstream firms and concentrate on the case where the firms produce differentiated products and use prices as their strategic variables. We denote by $Q^i(p_i, p_j)$, $i, j=1,2$, the demand function for the product of firm i.

B. *Vertical Relationships*

There are numerous ways in which vertical relationships can be structured. In order to establish benchmark outcomes, it is useful to analyze two polar cases, (i) where neither downstream firm is vertically integrated (the "stand-alone" case); and (ii) where both are integrated and the internal transfer price is efficiently set at marginal cost. Where neither firm is vertically integrated, the input prices are determined by the nature of upstream competition. In the analysis of the benchmark case, we assume that when the stand-alone case obtains, the input suppliers compete in prices. Thus, Bertrand competition between $U1$ and $U2$ drives the input price to marginal cost.

Between these two extremes lie a variety of alternative pricing mechanisms. Of special interest to us will be those that can obtain when only one of the firms is vertically integrated. Then, the unintegrated firms may use long-term contracts to set nonlinear prices (such as two-part tariffs), for example, while an integrated firm may be able credibly to commit to internal transfer prices different from marginal cost.

C. *Equilibrium in the Downstream Market*

$D1$ and $D2$ engage in Bertrand competition which yields equilibrium prices, p_1^* and p_2^*. These prices are obtained by simultaneously solving the first-order conditions:

$$(1)\quad \pi'_{Di} = (p_i - v'_i)\cdot Q^i_i + Q^i(p_i, p_j) = 0, \qquad i, j=1,2,$$

where $v'_i(Q_i, c_i)$ is Di's marginal cost of producing Q_i units of output when it is paying c_i for the relevant input. Q^i_i is the derivative of demand for the product produced by Di with respect to its own price.

The FOCs in equation (1), also generate the best-response functions, $B_i(p_j; c_i)$. From equation (1), comparative statics yield,

$$(2)\quad \partial B_i/\partial c_i = \left[(\partial v'_i/\partial c_i)\cdot Q^i_i\right]/\pi''_{Di} > 0,$$

as long as the relevant input is normal, as we shall assume from now on. Hence, as the cost of the relevant input to the firm increases, the firm will increase its optimal price, holding rival's price constant.

We assume that the prices of the two final products are strategic complements, in the terminology of Jeremy Bulow et al. (1985), meaning that $\partial B_i/\partial p_j > 0$. This assumption is satisfied if the second cross-partial derivative, Q_{ij}, is not "too negative." It is satisfied, for example, when downstream demands are linear.

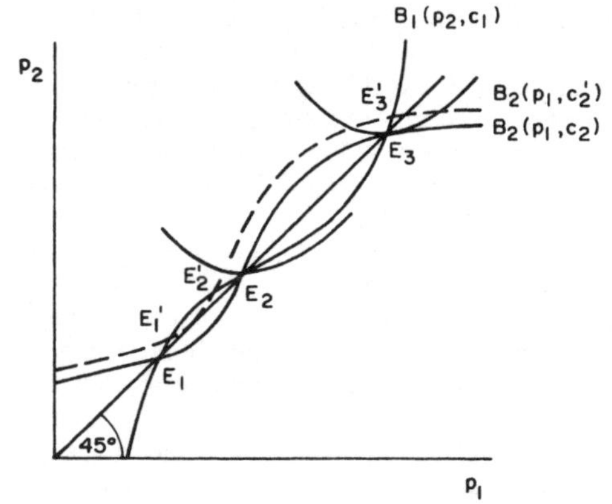

FIGURE 1. STABLE AND UNSTABLE EQUILIBRIA

These minimal restrictions placed on the demand and cost functions in the final goods market raise the possibility that there may be more than one Bertrand-Nash equilibrium in the downstream market. In the case of multiple equilibria, some are "unstable."[10] In Figure 1, E_1, E_2, and E_3 are the intersections of $D1$ and $D2$'s best-response functions. Equilibria E_1 and E_3 are stable, while E_2 is unstable. The dashed curve represents $D2$'s best-response function when its costs are increased slightly to c_2', leading to new equilibria E_1', E_2', and E_3', respectively. As shown, the movement from E_3 to E_3' increases $D1$'s profits, while the movement from E_2 to E_2' decreases them. (The concave curves through E_2 and E_3 represent $D1$'s isoprofit curves through those points: "higher" isoprofit curves represent higher levels of profit.) These results are summarized as:

Remark 1: An increase in the rival's input cost increases (resp., decreases) the equilibrium prices around a stable (resp., unstable) Bertrand-Nash equilibrium.

Furthermore, since

$$\partial \pi_{Di}/\partial c_j = (\partial \pi_{Di}/\partial p_j)\cdot(\partial p_j^*/\partial c_j),$$

then we also have:

Remark 2: An increase in the rival's input cost raises (resp., lowers) the firm's profits around the stable (resp., unstable) Bertrand-Nash equilibrium.

Two other questions regarding the profit effects of cost shifts remain: (i) whether or not an increase in the firm's own input cost may plausibly increase its profits; and (ii) whether or not an industrywide increase in costs increases a firm's profits. Now, an increase in the firm's own costs causes a change in profits given by:

$$(3) \qquad \partial \pi_{Di}/\partial c_i = -x_i + (p_i - v_i')\cdot(Q_j^i)\cdot(\partial p_j^*/\partial c_i),$$

where x_i stands for Di's use of the input. The sign of this expression is ambiguous around a stable equilibrium. The case of interest is where that derivative is negative so that no firm would like to see its costs raised unilaterally. An industrywide cost increase is more likely to raise firms' profits than a unilateral increase because it leads to a greater change in equilibrium prices. In the case of linear demand (worked out in the Appendix), however, both types of cost increase lower firms' profits. Then, $D1$ and $D2$ will not tacitly collude to impose higher costs upon themselves.

D. *The Standard Foreclosure Argument*

With these preliminaries out of the way, we can state the foreclosure argument as follows. $D1$ acquires $U1$, say, and prevents it from selling the input to the unintegrated rival $D2$. $U1$'s withdrawal from the market potentially increases $U2$'s market power over the price of the input. In the market setting posited here, $U2$ becomes a monopolist supplier of the input to $D2$ and sets the price at

[10]See Jesus Seade (1980), Avinash Dixit (1986), or Jean Tirole (1988, pp. 323 ff.) for discussions of stability in oligopoly models. Stability is related to the convergence of dynamic adjustment processes. In this context, one imagines the thought experiment in which firm 1 chooses a price, then firm 2 chooses its static best-response to that price, then firm 1 chooses its best-response to firm 2's best-response, etc. If this process converges to the equilibrium, the equilibrium is said to be stable. Of course, in a static context, there is no practical content to the thought experiment.

level c_2^m which maximizes its profits:

$$(4)\quad \pi_{U2}(c_2) = (c_2 - m)\cdot x_2^*(c_2; c_1 = m),$$

where m is the marginal cost of the input to $U1$. Obviously, $c_2^m > m$, which is the level that obtains under Bertrand competition in the input market.[11]

Focusing on stable equilibria, since $D1$'s profits are increasing in its rival's costs, the strategy of backward vertical integration makes $D1$ better off and lowers rival's profits. In addition, the strategy also increases downstream prices of both products. Because there are no efficiency gains from vertical integration, social welfare falls. Hence, on all accounts, $D1$'s integration with $U1$ is anticompetitive.

The preceding derivation of the anticompetitive consequences of the vertical merger is, however, woefully inadequate. First, why should $U1$ withdraw from the merchant market after the merger? May it not be in the interests of the merged $D1$-$U1$ firm to (partly) constrain $U2$'s market power by standing ready to supply $D2$ at some price? Second, why would $D2$ not be able to employ some counterstrategy that would protect its profit margins, for example by merging with $U2$? Finally, should $D2$ not be allowed to compete with $D1$ for the right to acquire the upstream supplier in the first place? And would such competition not render $D1$'s initial anticompetitive strategy unprofitable?

In the following section we consider a richer model which not only sheds some light on these questions but allows foreclosure through vertical merger to emerge as a fully rational, equilibrium strategy in a well-specified game.

II. A Game-Theoretic Model of Vertical Foreclosure

A. *Description of the Game*

In order to incorporate all the features of interest, we analyze a four-stage game. In the first stage, the "bidding" stage, the downstream firms have an initial opportunity to acquire one of the upstream suppliers. If there is only one merger, following the convention of the previous section, we suppose it to be between $D1$ and $U1$ and denote the merged firm by $F1$.

In the second stage, input prices are determined.[12] As we shall see, how input prices are set is a crucial determinant of the equilibrium of the overall game. It is therefore important to be careful how one models the second stage.

If no vertical merger takes place in stage one, $D1$ and $D2$ pay marginal cost for the input. If there is an acquisition, $D1$ continues to obtain the input at its true marginal cost. However, it is less clear what assumption about the price $D2$ must pay is most reasonable. We consider and contrast three possibilities:

(i) $F1$ and $U2$ simultaneously choose the input prices at which they are prepared to supply $D2$ (a la Bertrand).

(ii) $F1$ can commit to not supplying $D2$ at all. In this case only we consider the possibility that there exists an alternative, albeit inferior, source of the relevant input. The input can be obtained from that source for $\underline{c} > m$. This assumption enables us to parametrize the upstream price. Note, in particular, that if $\underline{c}$ is sufficiently high, $U2$ has monopoly power over $D2$, as in the previous section.

(iii) $F1$ is able to set an upper bound on the price that $D2$ faces by standing ready to supply it at a price c_{12}, which is determined by $F1$. To capture this, we consider the case in which $F1$ announces its linear price to $D2$ *before* $U2$ announces its price.

The major modeling difference is between (ii) and (iii) on one hand and (i) on the other. When (i) pertains, the merged firm is unable to resist the temptation of competing with $U2$ for $D2$'s business. However, a far-sighted $F1$ will realize that entering into competition of this kind will lower $D2$'s input price, which, in turn, will lead to lower

[11]This is true as long as the two downstream products are not perfect substitutes.

[12]Since input prices are determined before the output prices, it is proper to characterize the input suppliers as the upstream firms, as one of the referees reminds us.

downstream prices. The downstream division of $F1$ would, generally, prefer that the upstream division exercises some pricing restraint. Assumption (ii) captures this restraint. However, it may not be in $F1$'s interest to completely withdraw from the upstream market. Indeed, as we shall show, it may not be in the interest of firm 1 to endow $U2$ with "too much" market power over to price of the input. Assumption (iii) provides $F1$ with the ability to constrain $U2$'s market power in the post-merger game.

In sum, as one moves from (i) to (iii), $F1$ has increasing control over the price of the input to $D2$. We show how the equilibrium of the game depends on this assumed degree of control.

In the third stage, if $D1$ acquired $U1$, $D2$ can bid for its supplier, $U2$. This allows us to analyze $D2$'s ability to counter the potentially adverse consequences of the previous merger by becoming vertically integrated itself. Since organization formation is less flexible than choices of prices, one might think that both opportunities for vertical mergers should logically come before the selection of input prices. Our focus, however, is on the desirability of the second merger assuming that the first has taken place. Considerations about the rationality of the second merger depend on the input price that $D2$ believes it will face if it does not merge. Thus considering the setting of input prices in stage 2 is a way of providing the relevant backdrop against which $D2$ makes its merger decision.

In the fourth stage, downstream prices are chosen, given input prices.

B. *Solving for the Equilibrium*

To solve for the equilibrium, we proceed by backward induction.

(i) *Stage Four*. This stage is simply the one-shot game analyzed in Section I.

(ii) *Stage Three*. In this stage, we inquire whether $D2$ should make a bid for $U2$, and whether it can make a bid that is attractive to $U2$. The answer to this question depends on the sum of the profits earned by $U2$ and $D2$, if they were to remain independent, as compared to those they would earn after a merger. If the latter profits are higher than the former, then the $U2$-$D2$ merger generates gains and we would expect such gains to be realized in an efficient bargain and the merger to take place.

If $D2$ and $U2$ merge, there will be full vertical integration in the industry. The profits earned by the merged entities will be $\pi_{Di}(m,m) \equiv \pi_i^O$, $i=1,2$, which are the levels that are realized absent integration and with Bertrand competition in the input market. We refer to these profits as "benchmark" profits. If $D2$ and $U2$ do not merge, $U2$ charges $D2$ an input price c_2 (which is determined in the second stage) and the sum of their profits, which we term "stand-alone profit" and denote by π^S, is

$$(5)\quad \pi^S(c_2) = \pi_{D2}(c_2) + \pi_{U2}(c_2, m).$$

$D2$ and $U2$ will not merge if and only if $\pi_{U2}(m,m) < \pi^S(c_2)$.

We must show that there exists some $c_2 > m$ for which this inequality is satisfied. To this end we differentiate equation (5) with respect to c_2. After using the envelope theorem and Shephard's lemma, we get:

$$(6)\quad \partial\pi^S/\partial c_2 = (c_2 - m)\cdot(dx_2/dc_2) + (\partial\pi_{D2}/\partial p_1)\cdot(\partial p_1{}^*/\partial c_2),$$

where dx/dc denotes the total equilibrium change in $D2$'s demand for the input following its increase in price. Note that, around the stable equilibrium, the first term is negative and the second is positive. Thus, when (6) is evaluated around $c_2 = m$ it leads to:

PROPOSITION 1: *If the initial equilibrium is stable, then a small increase in the price of an input above marginal cost to the unintegrated downstream firm increases the "stand-alone profit,"* π^S, *defined in equation* (5).

The import of Proposition 1 is that, for at least some range of the input price c_2, the stand-alone profit of the two unmerged firms increases above the benchmark level, π_{D2}^0. This means that $D2$ cannot make an attractive enough merger offer to its (monopolistic) upstream supplier, $U2$. Consequently, if

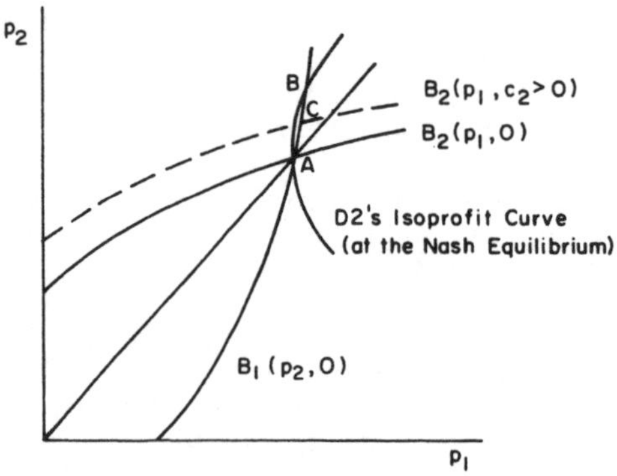

FIGURE 2. BEST-RESPONSE FUNCTIONS WITH PRICE AS THE STRATEGIC VARIABLE

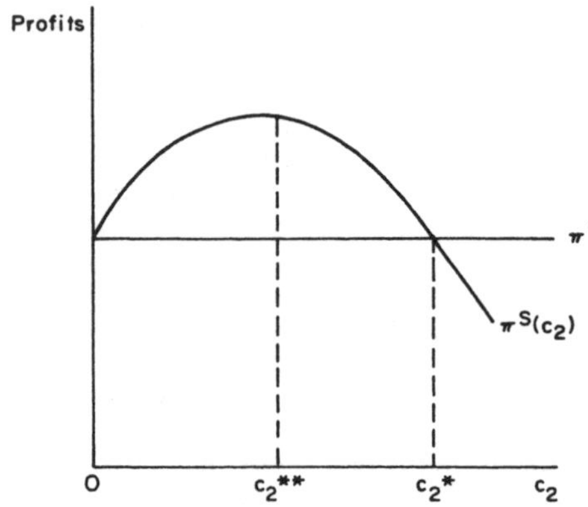

FIGURE 3. THE SUM OF PROFITS OF THE FORECLOSED FIRM AND ITS SUPPLIER

the equilibrium value of c_2 is in that range, $U2$ cannot resort to a merger as an effective counterstrategy.

The reason that such a range exists in the model analyzed here can be seen from Figure 2 which illustrates the benchmark equilibrium. There the locus of points which give $D2$ its benchmark level of profits is superimposed on the best-response curves. Since $D2$ has no costs and $U2$ has no revenues in the benchmark case, that curve also represents the locus of points where the sum of $D2$ and $U2$'s revenues are equal to the benchmark level.

A small increase in c_2 above m causes $D2$'s best-response function to shift up (as represented by the dashed line), and therefore p_1^* and p_2^* to increase, which increases downstream revenues (the new equilibrium, C, lies on a higher iso-revenue curve for $D2$). While $D2$ must pay more for the input, since this additional payment is captured by $U2$, combined profits are equal to $D2$'s revenues which increase.

Eventually a further increase in the input price decreases the "stand-alone" profit. As the markup $(c_2 - m)$ grows, the equilibrium output of $D2$ falls. Ultimately, $D2$'s revenues fall; then the profits earned by $U2$ are insufficient to compensate $D2$ for its lost profits. This occurs in Figure 2 when $D2$'s best-response function intersects $D1$'s best-response function above B. Stand-alone profit cannot fall below the benchmark level, π_{U2}^0, because that level can always be secured via merger. Figure 3 depicts the behavior of the stand-alone profit as a function of c_2.

(iii) *Stage Two*. In this stage input prices are determined. The only substantive case to consider is when $D1$ and $U1$ have merged to form $F1$. We have to consider three alternative pricing scenarios. In the first, $F1$ and $U2$ simultaneously choose the price to be charged to $D2$. Let c_{12} denote the price that $F1$ charges $D2$. Plainly for any c_2, $F1$ has an incentive to undercut, in the usual Bertrand fashion. So, in equilibrium $c_{12} = c_2 = m$.

The second alternative is that $F1$ commits not to sell to $D2$. Consider first the case where $D2$ does not have access to an inferior input substitute. Regardless of whether a $U2$-$D2$ merger subsequently occurs $U2$ earns $\pi_{U2}(c_2, m)$. This is because if a merger occurs, $D2$ must offer a high enough price to compensate $U2$ for what it would earn if it did not merge. Thus $U2$ sets the monopoly price c_2^m. If, however, $D2$ does have access to a substitute inferior product priced at $c < c_2^m$, then $D2$ will set c_{12} just below c.

The third, and most interesting alternative pricing scenario is when $F1$ offers to supply $D2$ at some price c_{12}. $U2$'s best reply to any such $c_{12} > m$ is to undercut it infinitesimally. Given this opportunity to constrain $U2$'s market power by precommiting to c_{12}, $F1$

selects that price that makes the sum of stand-alone profits, π^S, equal to benchmark profits, π_{U2}^0, as calculated in Section I. In Figure 3, this input price is denoted by c_2^*. When input is priced at that level, $D2$ cannot make a merger offer that $U2$ would not refuse.

For the linear-linear case examined in the Appendix, $c_2^* < c_2^m$ so that $F1$ does exercise a competitive constraint over $U2$'s pricing power vis-à-vis $D2$. It is not clear whether this holds for all relevant demand and cost configurations.

To summarize the second stage: If $U2$ and $F1$ move simultaneously, then $c_2 = m$. If $F1$ commits not to supply $D2$ then $c_2^* = c_2^m$ in the case where there is no alternative source of supply and is equal to the lesser of c_2^m and c when there is one. Finally, if $F1$ can set a price to constrain $U2$, then $c_2 = c_2^*$.

(iv) *Stage One*. In this stage the initial acquisition(s) can be made. There are numerous ways in which one could formulate the actions in the acquisition stage. Bidding could be initiated either by the buyers or the sellers of the input. A bidder could bid for only one firm at the time or it could make multiple offers. Alternatively, each firm could be paired with a single target. Here we examine the simplest case where both firms bid for a designated upstream firm, say $U1$. The robustness of the results is taken up in Section III.

To see how this stage plays out, we first compare the payoffs from winning versus losing this initial bidding contest. For consistency, we assume that $D1$ is the winning bidder, in the event that there is a bid. Recall that there will be no bid if both firms correctly expect $D2$ to acquire $U2$ when it has a chance to deploy its counterstrategy in stage 3. Such acquisition will take place if the input is overpriced in stage 2. Then, with both firms vertically integrated profits are again at the "benchmark" level.[13]

So, the only interesting case is when the input is priced at c_2^*, so that $D2$ will be just indifferent between buying and not buying its supplier. How much is $D1$ willing to bid for $U1$? Note that if there is a merger, $D1$, as an owner of $F1$, makes $\pi_{D1}(p_1^*(m, c_2^*), p_2^*(c_2^*, m); m)$ on the downstream account. If $D1$ submits a losing bid, it will earn $\pi_{D1}(p_1^*(c_1^*, m), p_2^*(m, c_1^*); c_1^*)$. Here c_1^* is the input price that $D1$ will have to pay in the event that $D2$ prevails in the bidding game. Obviously, the maximum amount that $D1$ will be willing to bid, W^1, is the difference between these two profit levels. By an earlier assumption, downstream firm's profits decline as its costs increase unilaterally. Hence, $W^1 > 0$. In the symmetric case $W^1 = W^2 = W$. Given the assumed structure of the remainder of the game, $U1$ earns zero if it does not accept the offer so it accepts $D1$'s bid of W.[14]

C. *Equilibrium Summarized*

The unique equilibrium of the game is as follows:

If $F1$ and $U2$ set input prices simultaneously, so that $c_2 = 0$; or if $F1$ can only commit not to supply $D2$ without being able to constrain $U2$ so that $U2$ wants to charge $c_2^m > c_2^*$ and there is no substitute input at $c < c_2^*$, then no vertical merger takes place.

If $F1$ can commit not to supply $D2$ and there is a substitute input at $c < c_2^*$, then both firms bid $W(c)$ for $U1$. The offer is accepted and $D1$ faces the input cost of m while $D2$ pays c.

If there is no substitute product and $F1$ can commit to supply $D2$, both firms bid $W(c_2^*)$. $U1$ accepts the offer and $D1$ faces the input cost of m while $D2$ pays c_2^*.

D. *Welfare in Equilibrium*

It is immediate that a vertical merger between $U1$ and $D1$ raises both downstream prices. Obviously, consumers' welfare falls.

[13]Notice that we do not allow Di to make a bid for a Ui in Stage 3, in the event that the initial merger did not take place.

[14]Note that $D2$ cannot induce $U1$ to remain independent by offering $U1$ a lump-sum payment, L. Plainly, by pitting $D1$ against $D2$, $U1$ can always earn W. Hence L would have to be greater than W. But $D2$ is not willing to pay more than W.

TABLE 1—THE INCENTIVE TO INTEGRATE IN THE LINEAR DEMAND CASE

d	$p_i^*(0,0)$	π_i^O	c_2^*	$p_1(0,c_2^*)$	$p_2(c_2^*,0)$	$\pi_{D1}(0,c_2^*)$	$\frac{\pi_{D1}(0,c_2^*)}{\pi_i^O}$	$\frac{p_1(0,c_2^*)}{p_1^*(0,0)}$
(1)	(2)	(3)	(4)	(5)	(6)	(7)	(8)	(9)
0	0.50	0.25	0.00	0.500	0.500	0.250	1.000	1.000
1	0.33	0.22	0.09	0.345	0.381	0.238	1.073	1.036
2	0.25	0.19	0.13	0.274	0.321	0.225	1.200	1.095
3	0.20	0.16	0.14	0.229	0.278	0.210	1.315	1.147
5	0.14	0.14	0.13	0.175	0.219	0.183	1.492	1.222
10	0.08	0.08	0.09	0.110	0.142	0.133	1.743	1.320
$d \to \infty$	0.00	0.00	0.00	0.000	0.000	0.000	2.250	1.500

The unintegrated downstream firm, $D2$, is made worse off as a result of the merger because only its input cost went up while the rival's cost remained at m. More surprisingly, perhaps, former $D1$ is also worse off: its net payoff is the same as $D2$'s in this symmetric game. Its gross profits are increased by the merger, of course. However, because it paid W to acquire $U1$ its net profits are lower than they would have been had there been no vertical merger: both downstream firms would be better off if the bidding war was never started—if publicly traded, their stock prices fall when the bidding commences! The game has a prisoners' dilemma structure: any firm that believes that the other will not bid for $U1$ can gain by buying up $U1$ at a low price and capturing the rents from the foreclosure of its rival. The fear of being foreclosed drives each firm to attempt to foreclose the other. As a result, all the rents from foreclosure are dissipated through the bidding and all the profits accrue to the upstream firm(s). In a richer model, with asymmetric downstream payoffs, for example, the foreclosing firm also could be made better off in equilibrium.

The clear winners thus are the upstream firms. $U1$ gets $W(c_2^*)$, while $U2$ earns $\pi_{U2}(c_2^*)$. Note that $U1$ is better off than $U2$. This follows from the fact that π_1^* exceeds π^S, due to the inefficient pricing of the input to $D2$. However, $D1$ and $D2$ earn the same *net* profits. Thus, $U1$'s shareholders obtain a better return on their shares than do $U2$'s shareholders. This is an attractive feature of the model because it obviates the possibility of the upstream target holding out hoping that the other firm will be taken over.

The net effect of a merger is a reduction in social welfare. This is because the merger does not remedy any existing market imperfection but, instead, leads to an inefficient pricing of the input to $D2$. The fact that additional profits accrue to the input suppliers does not overcome the losses to consumers.

While our analysis illustrates that vertical foreclosure may be rational, with the degree of generality in the above model, it is not possible to measure the size of the incentives to integrate there. In the Appendix we explicitly calculate the equilibria with and without a vertical merger for the case of linear demand for the case where the integrated firm is able to constrain the price which $U2$ can charge if there is a $U1$-$D1$ merger (scenario (iii)). We assume there that demand for good i is given by $q_i = 1 - bp_i + d(p_j - p_i)$, and that $m = 0$. We have carried out some calculations, setting $b = 1$.

Table 1 reports the results of those calculations for different values of d, which measures the sensitivity of each firm's demand to the difference in the firms' prices.

Notice from columns (2) and (6) that as d grows, competition between the downstream firms becomes so fierce that prices are driven to marginal cost, irrespective of whether there has been a merger or not. Therefore (as one can see from columns (3) and (7)), firm 1's profits vanish in the limit too.

Columns (8) and (9) present the results of most interest. The increase in $D1$'s profitability is given in (8). Clearly if $d = 0$ $D1$'s profitability is the same whether it merges with $U1$ or not. As d increases, however, the merger becomes increasingly profitable. In the limit, as $d \to \infty$, the merged firm's profits are increased by 125 percent.

Because profits become insignificant as d increases, it is possible that even a tiny percentage increase in price can result in a large percentage increase in profitability. In column (9), therefore, we directly examine the effect of a merger on $D1$'s equilibrium market price. While the percentage increases in price are smaller than those in profits, the figures are still sizable.

III. Robustness

In this section, we discuss the robustness of the results of Section II to three changes in the assumptions. First, we examine equilibrium outcomes when downstream firms compete in quantities rather than prices. Second, we discuss changes in the bidding formulation: we discuss what happens if the downstream firms can make offers to either of the upstream firms in stage 1, or if the upstream firms bid for a downstream firm. Finally, we discuss more general vertical contracts, such as two-part tariffs.

A. *Quantity Competition*

We now consider what happens when the downstream firms' actions are strategic substitutes. To do this we assume quantity competition in stage four, that the products are perfect substitutes, and that the unique Cournot equilibrium is stable. Under reasonable assumptions about marginal costs and revenues, Di's best reply to an expansion of output by Dj is to constrict its output.

Using the approach of Section II, we calculate the effect of an increase in c_2 on π^S, the stand-alone profits of $U2$ and $D2$. Differentiation gives:

$$(8)\quad \partial\pi^S/\partial c_2 = (c_2 - m)\, dx_2/dc_2 + (\partial\pi_{U2}/dq_1)\cdot(\partial q_1/\partial c_2).$$

Around $c_2 = m$, the sign of this expression is governed by the sign of the second term. The sign of that term is unambiguously negative because an increase in c_2 induces expansion in $D1$'s output which, in turn, causes p_2 to fall for any given level of q_2. This depresses $D2$'s profits. Hence:

PROPOSITION 2: *When the downstream firms compete in quantities, the only equilibrium of the four-stage game entails no vertical merger.*

The intuition here can be obtained by reference to the taxonomy of strategic actions developed by Drew Fudenberg and Jean Tirole (1984). An increase in $D2$'s costs makes it "soft" (i.e., less aggressive) in its competition with $D1$. Accordingly in the case of strategic complements, apart from the fact that it must bear the higher costs itself, it favors a "fat-cat" posture. That is, if it has a less aggressive position vis-à-vis $D1$, more accommodating pricing results. In the case of strategic substitutes, however, $D2$ wants to maintain a "lean-and-hungry" look. That is, any gain in output and profitability for the $U2$-$D2$ "side of the market" must be gained at the expense of the $U1$-$D1$ side.

Thus the $U2$-$D2$ side of the market is made strictly worse off in aggregate if the price charged by $U2$ rises. Accordingly, $U2$ and $D2$ will always counter a $U1$-$D1$ merger with a merger of their own.

The relevant test of whether a vertical merger for the purposes of foreclosure can be successful, therefore, is whether the sum of the profits of the unintegrated firms will increase or not.

B. *Alternative Bidding Formulations*

As was discussed above, there are many possible alternative formulations of the bidding stages. Here we briefly discuss just two.[15]

First, suppose that the downstream firms can make offers to either upstream firm. If

[15]These cases are discussed in more detail in our working paper, Janusz Ordover, Garth Saloner, and Steven Salop (1988).

we continue to assume that the downstream firms simultaneously make take-it-or-leave-it offers to the upstream firms, then the equilibrium analyzed in Section II remains an equilibrium. If $U2$ believes that $U1$ will accept $D1$'s offer, then there does not exist an offer that $D2$ can profitably make which will be acceptable to $U2$.[16]

Second, suppose that it is the upstream firms that bid for a downstream firm rather than *vice versa*. Thus, consider the case where in stage 1, $U1$ and $U2$ bid for $D1$ and in stage 3, $D2$ can become the target if the first merger occurred.

The main effect from this reformulation of the game is the reallocation of rents and the size of the winning bid in stage 1. The post-merger input and products' prices will be exactly as they would have been had it been the downstream firms bidding for the upstream supplier.[17]

C. *Alternative Vertical Contracts*

We now discuss alternatives to integration as ways of raising downstream prices. Our discussion focuses on the case of differentiated products and price competition, in light of Proposition 2.

To begin with let us note that where it is possible for firms to enter into alternative contractual relationships with their input suppliers, these may appear to be preferable to a merger. The purpose of these alternatives, like that of a fully-fledged vertical merger, is to raise downstream prices by affecting input costs.[18]

The key point of this section is easily illustrated with the help of Figure 3. There, with $c_1 = m$, c_2^{**} maximizes π^S, the sum of $U2$ and $D2$ profits. In order to induce $U2$ to charge that price rather than c_2^*, $D2$ can enter into a two-part tariff contract with its supplier under which the fixed fee transfer compensates $U2$ for not charging c_2^*. (This point is made by Bonanno and Vickers, 1988.) In our setting vertical integration is just the special form of two-part tariff where the price is equal to marginal cost and the fee is the purchase price.

Two observations can now be made. First, even if $U2$-$D2$ counter the $U1$-$D1$ merger with an optimal two-part tariff, the initial merger remains profitable. However, the bid price will be lower because the equilibrium downstream prices will be lower.

Second, it may appear that $U2$-$D2$ could replicate the outcome under a two-part tariff by first merging and then setting the *transfer price* at c_2^{**}. This conclusion is implausible because once these two firms have merged, there is an incentive to cut the transfer price below c_2^{**}. Furthermore, the rival who cannot easily monitor intra-firm pricing will, most likely, proceed on the expectation that transfer prices are set at efficient levels. As a result, the superior equilibrium cannot be replicated with a merger because a firm can-

[16] Of course there are other similar equilibria as well: $U2$ could be designated as the target and either $D1$ or $D2$ could be selected as the winning firms. Notice that providing the downstream firms with all the bargaining power creates an asymmetry in the resulting outcome. Although $U1$ and $U2$ are both viable targets and ought to be expected to compete for the right to be taken over, instead the downstream firms "designate" the winner who then gets the lion's share of the spoils. Formally, since the integrated firms do better than the unintegrated firms, requiring the upstream firms to each do equally well and the downstream firms to each do equally well would have to be accomplished by utilizing mixed strategies (with some resulting inefficiency) or resorting to correlated equilibria.

[17] Another effect of this reformulation is that a hold-out problem (discussed in detail in our working paper) can arise. To see how this might arise, consider the products are almost independent in demand. There the upstream firm that merges gains very little because the profits that accrue to the merged firm are only slightly increased by the increase in the input price to the unmerged rival. The unmerged upstream firm, in contrast, is suddenly endowed with monopoly power over the remaining downstream firm. Thus both upstream firms would prefer to be the firm that does not merge.

[18] This point is similar to that made by Cooper (1986), who points out that in a differentiated products context a firm (and its rival) may be made better off if it can commit to charging a higher price than the noncooperative equilibrium price. In Cooper's model the firm achieves this by offering a "most-favored-customer" contract which, once it has been implemented, gives the firm an incentive not to lower its price in the future.

not credibly commit to internal transfer prices that are inefficient, in our view.[19]

The distinction between two-part tariffs and vertical integration can be brought out again by considering a game in which in the first stage, $D1$ and $D2$ present $U1$ with two-part tariff contracts. For example $D1$ may bid $\{f = W(c_2^*) > 0,\ c_1 = 0,\ c_2 = c_2^*\}$ which potentially replicates the equilibrium outcome under vertical integration. Notice, however, that the vertical contract must specify the price which $U1$ must charge $D2$. Moreover, since $U2$ has an incentive to secretly cheat on this contract and supply $D2$ at a lower price, the restrictive contract will only be feasible if $D1$ can monitor $U1$'s price. However, a contract that specifies $U1$'s merchant market prices is likely to run afoul of the antitrust laws. In contrast, a vertically integrated firm can more credibly commit to its merchant market price and may refuse to sell the input to the rival without risking antitrust litigation.[20]

IV. Conclusions

We have investigated how vertical integration can be used to achieve anticompetitive foreclosure of downstream firms from an essential source of supply. Our main conclusion is that anticompetitive foreclosure arises as an equilibrium phenomenon in a coherent model where sophisticated firms use a wide range of strategies and counterstrategies.

Our analysis indicates that the profitability of foreclosure involves a number of subtleties. However these subtleties are not the ones associated with the standard critique of foreclosure theory discussed in the introduction. Indeed, the central condition for successful foreclosure is simply that the unintegrated upstream firm's gain exceed the downstream firm's loss.

This condition can be satisfied in a model with differentiated products and price-setting because the sum of the profits of the foreclosed firm and its supplier increase (locally) if the foreclosed firm's price rises (and the rival's price adjusts optimally). In a quantity-setting, homogeneous goods model, by contrast, the sum of those profits decrease if the foreclosed firm's output decreases and the rival's adjusts optimally.

Moreover, even in the differentiated products case, the sum of the unintegrated firms' profits is reduced if the unintegrated upstream firm's market power is "too" great. This is because, in that case, the profit-maximizing price that it charges for its input will be so high that the downstream firm will have the incentive and ability to offer a mutually beneficial vertical merger. In this paper we have set out two of the ways in which the unintegrated upstream firm's market power may be limited. One is that the integrated firm may be able to constrain the upstream spot price. The other is that there may be an alternative (and inferior) competitive source of supply.

As another alternative, one could model the upstream industry as an oligopoly rather than a duopoly. In that case, a single vertical merger would not confer complete monopoly power on the remaining upstream firms. While competition among them would naturally constrain the upstream price, reducing the profitability of foreclosure, such competition also would reduce the potential for an effective counterstrategy on the part of the foreclosed downstream firm. The necessary modeling is not entirely straightforward, however. Since the interesting case is one in which the elimination of an upstream firm does have some effect on input prices, this requires specifying an upstream market in which the goods are at least somewhat differentiated (perhaps because of transportation costs). Enriching the model in this way is a possible avenue for future research.

The controversy surrounding the vertical foreclosure argument has traditionally been cast in the context of vertical integration. In

[19]Chaim Fershtman and Kenneth Judd, (1987) for example, analyze a model in which firms distort managers' compensation schedules in order to change their conduct in the product market. As here, there are strong incentives to cheat on these inefficient arrangements, especially in light of the fact that such internal arrangements are not easily monitored for deviations.

[20]It may also be easier to commit to a two-part tariff than an internal transfer price by coupling the two-part tariff with a most favored nation clause as in Salop (1986).

order to address the questions raised in that debate we have, for the most part, kept to that formulation. Yet, as modern contract theory emphasizes, vertical integration is but one particular form of vertical contract. Indeed, as we have shown, there may exist incentives for firms to structure vertical relationships in ways that fall short of full vertical integration if they are so able. This richer formulation raises a number of interesting issues that we have only begun to explore.

APPENDIX

Here we solve the model in the "linear-linear" case. Thus, we assume the following: (i) upstream unit costs are equal to zero, $m = 0$; (ii) downstream marginal cost is equal to c_i, $i = 1,2$; and the demand functions are symmetric, that is, $q_i = 1 - bp_i + d(p_j - p_i)$, $i, j = 1,2$. It is useful to rewrite this as $q_i = 1 - kp_i + dp_j$, where $k = b + d$.

Our main objective is to analyze how the equilibrium prices, input cost, and purchase price vary with the value of d, which determines the degree of substitution between the two products. These comparative statics are reported in the text in Table 1.

Standard calculations yield the following reduced form equations:

$$\text{(A1)} \qquad p_i^* = [(2k + d) + 2k^2c_i + kdc_j]\big/(4k^2 - d^2),$$

$$\text{(A2)} \qquad q_i^* = k[(2k + d) - (2k^2 - d^2)c_i + kdc_j]\big/(4k^2 - d^2),$$

$$\text{(A3)} \qquad \pi_{Di}^* = (q_i^*)^2/k.$$

When input is priced at $c_1 = c_2 = 0$, Di earns

$$\text{(A4)} \qquad \pi_{Di}^0 = k/(2k - d)^2.$$

When $c_1 = 0$, $U2$'s profits are:

$$\text{(A5)} \qquad \pi_{U2}(c_2) = kc_2[(2k + d) - c_2(2k^2 - d^2)]\big/(4k^2 - d^2).$$

Hence, $U2$'s unconstrained profit maximizing price is:

$$\text{(A6)} \qquad c_2^{m} = (2k + d)/2(2k^2 - d^2).$$

The maximum input price that forestalls the $U2$-$D2$ merger, denoted by c_2^*, solves

$$\text{(A7)} \qquad \pi_{U2}(c_2) + \pi_{D2}^*(c_2, c_1 = 0) = \pi_{D2}^0.$$

Thus,

$$\text{(A8)} \qquad c_2^* = (2k + d)d^2/2k^2(2k^2 - d^2) < c_2^{m},$$

since $b, d > 0$.

REFERENCES

Aghion, Philippe and Bolton, Patrick, "Contracts as a Barrier to Entry," *American Economic Review*, June 1987, *77*, 388–401.

Bonanno, Giacomo and Vickers, John, "Vertical Separation," *Journal of Industrial Economics*, March 1988, *36*, 257–66.

Bork, Robert H., *The Antitrust Paradox*, New York: Basic Books, 1978.

Bulow, Jeremy I., Geanakoplos, John D., and Klemperer, Paul D., "Multimarket Oligopoly: Strategic Substitutes and Complements," *Journal of Political Economy*, June 1985, *93*, 488–511.

Comanor, William S., "Vertical Mergers, Market Power, and the Antitrust Laws," *American Economic Review*, May 1967, *57*, 254–65.

______ **and Frech, H. E.,** "The Competitive Effects of Vertical Agreements," *American Economic Review*, June 1985, *75*, 539–46.

Cooper, Thomas E., "Most-Favored-Customer Pricing and Tacit Collusion," *Rand Journal of Economics*, Autumn 1986, *17*, 377–88.

Coughlin, Ann and Wernerfelt, Birger, "Competition and Cooperation in Marketing Channel Choice: Theory and Application," *Marketing Science*, Spring 1988, *4*, 110–29.

Dixit, Avinash, "Vertical Integration in Monopolistically Competitive Industry," *International Journal of Industrial Organization*, September 1983, *1*, 63–78.

Fershtman, Chaim and Judd, Kenneth, "Equilibrium Incentives in Oligopoly," *American Economic Review*, December 1987, *77*, 927–40.

Fudenberg, Drew and Tirole, Jean, "The Fat-Cat Effect, the Puppy-Dog Ploy, and the Lean-and-Hungry-Look," *American Economic Review*, May 1984, *74*, 361–66.

Krattenmaker, Thomas G. and Salop, Steven C. "Anticompetitive Exclusion: Raising Rivals' Costs to Achieve Power Over Price,"

Yale Law Journal, December 1986, *96*, 209–93.

Mathewson, G. Frank and Winter, Ralph, "The Competitive Effects of Vertical Agreements: Comment," *American Economic Review*, December 1987, *77*, 1057–62.

Moorthy, K. Sridhar, "Strategic Decentralization in Channels," *Marketing Science*, forthcoming.

Perry, Martin K., "Vertical Integration: Determinants and Effects," in Richard Schmalensee and Robert Willig, eds., *The Handbook of Industrial Organization*, New York: North-Holland, 1989, 185–255.

Posner, Richard A., *Antitrust Law*, Chicago: University of Chicago Press, 1976.

______ **and Easterbrook, Frank H.,** *Antitrust*, 2nd ed., St. Paul: West Publishing Co., 1981.

Rey, Patrick and Stiglitz, Joseph, "The Role of Exclusive Territories in Producers' Competition," Princeton University, mimeo., September 1986.

______ **and Tirole, Jean,** "The Logic of Vertical Restraints," *American Economic Review*, December 1986, *76*, 921–39.

Salinger, Michael A., "Vertical Mergers and Market Foreclosure," *Quarterly Journal of Economics*, May 1988, *77*, 345–56.

Salop, Steven C., "Practices that (Credibly) Facilitate Oligopoly Coordination," in Joseph Stiglitz and C. Frank Mathewson, eds., *New Developments in the Analysis of Market Structure*, Cambridge: MIT Press, 1986, 265–90.

______ **and Scheffman, David T.,** "Cost-Raising Strategies," *Journal of Industrial Economics*, 1987, *36*, 19–34.

Schwartz, Marius, "The Competitive Effects of Vertical Agreements: Comment," *American Economic Review*, December 1987, *77*, 1063–8.

Seade, Jesus K., "On the Effects of Entry," *Econometrica*, March 1980, *48*, 479–89.

Tirole, Jean, *The Theory of Industrial Organization*, Cambridge: MIT Press, 1988.

[20]

Equilibrium Vertical Foreclosure: Comment

By DAVID REIFFEN*

In the March 1990 issue of this *Review*, Janusz A. Ordover, Garth Saloner, and Steven C. Salop (OSS) claim to show that vertical mergers can increase final product price. While the results are in many ways not very robust (for example, if there are initially three upstream firms rather than two, the results do not hold), their model seems to show that, even with fixed proportions, vertical mergers can have deleterious effects on welfare.

OSS acknowledge on page 133 that this result depends critically on the postintegration pricing game. In effect, OSS show that higher downstream prices will result if the integrated firm can commit not to undercut the rival's price. Absent such commitment ability, vertical integration is ineffective. Perhaps less apparent is that in the framework of OSS, given the ability to commit, vertical integration becomes irrelevant. That is, vertical integration per se is neither necessary nor sufficient to generate higher downstream prices. The key is the ability to make price commitments. Unless some causal nexus between vertical integration and the ability to commit to a pricing strategy is demonstrated, it is difficult to see how the OSS results are related to vertical integration at all.

The OSS model has two upstream firms selling a homogeneous product and two downstream firms selling differentiated products. Since the upstream firms have constant and identical marginal costs, if they compete in price, the resulting Nash (Bertrand) equilibrium is for each to charge upstream marginal cost. The downstream firms have constant and identical marginal cost, but because the products are differentiated, the resulting Bertrand-equilibrium price exceeds marginal cost. OSS then assume that an upstream firm integrates with a downstream firm (D1), and subsequently chooses to charge a price exceeding marginal cost (perhaps an infinite price) to the nonintegrated downstream firm (D2). This permits the nonintegrated upstream firm (U2) to increase price above marginal cost. This in turn increases D2's price (relative to the nonintegrated solution), leading to higher downstream prices and higher profits for the integrated firm. OSS show that for small increases in U2's price above the initial level, the loss to D2 is outweighed by the gain to U2. Therefore, integration by U2 and D2 (which would lead to a return to the initial equilibrium) is not a profitable counterstrategy, and this is OSS's novel insight.

As noted above, while it appears that the higher downstream price results from integration, the key is the ability of the integrated firm to commit to a price in the input market. In the proposed equilibrium, the unintegrated firm (U2) charges D2 a price above marginal cost, and the integrated firm refrains from undercutting this input price. Given that U2's price exceeds marginal cost however, it would be profitable for U1 to charge a price to D2 just below that price, since its downstream profits would remain approximately unchanged, while its upstream profits would increase by D2's purchases times U2's margin. As Oliver Hart and Jean Tirole (1990) independently note, the proposed outcome is not a Nash equilibrium.

OSS's justification for the price-commitment assumption is that "[a] farsighted [integrated firm] will realize that entering into competition of this kind will lower D2's input price" (p. 133). That is, U1 expects U2 to react to a reduction in U1's price by lowering its own price. This justification is unsatisfactory. In a static framework such as that used by OSS, there is no sense in which firms react, since they do not observe the

*Economist, Federal Trade Commission, Washington, DC 20580. I thank Meredith Regan for her assistance with this comment.

other player's action. In this sense, the OSS explanation bears a strong relationship to conjectural variation "explanations" of collusion.[1] For reactions to be relevant, an explicitly dynamic framework is required. It is well known that, in such a framework, collusive outcomes can be supported without any reference to vertical integration.

In a static framework, the OSS analysis is perhaps most appropriately seen as a sequential game, in which the integrated firm sets an input price (thereby committing to that price), and the unintegrated upstream firm chooses its best (price) response. In a sequential game, however, the outcome when neither firm is integrated produces similar results to those of OSS.[2] Consider a game involving just the two downstream firms. If prices are chosen sequentially, it would be profitable for either downstream firm unilaterally to increase price above the Bertrand level, if it could credibly signal its commitment to keep it there. If D1, say, takes D2's reaction into account, the pricing game would be transformed into a Stackelberg leader–follower game. D1 will then choose P_1 to maximize

$$\Pi_1 = (P_1 - C)q_1[P_1 + P_2(P_1)]$$

where $P_2(P_1)$ is D2's best-response function. In the "linear-linear" example detailed in the appendix of the OSS paper, this means that D1 chooses

$$P_1 = \frac{2k + d + dkC}{4k^2 - 2d^2} + \frac{C}{2}$$

and D2 will choose

$$P_2 = \frac{1 + d\left(\dfrac{2k + d + dkC}{4k^2 - 2d^2} + \dfrac{C}{2}\right) + kC}{2k}.$$

[1]Tirole (1989 p. 244) notes that in a static setting any conjecture about another firm's reaction that differs from a conjecture of no reaction is irrational.

[2]More generally, whatever the justification for departing from the static Nash equilibrium concept, a similar rationale would appear to hold in a nonintegrated context.

Just as in the situation OSS describe (i.e., vertical foreclosure), prices and profits will be higher than in the Bertrand equilibrium.[3] One interesting difference between the two methods of increasing price is that, while both increase the profits of both the leader and follower by increasing D2's final product price, in the Stackelberg equilibrium the "follower" (D2) earns higher profits than the "leader" (D1). This occurs in the Stackelberg case because, by increasing its own price, the leader induces the follower to raise its price. This action by the leader would reduce its profits but for the effect on the follower's price. In OSS, the leader (U1/D2) earns higher profits than U2 by integrating and raising D2's costs because it is able to increase D2's price at no cost to itself. That is, in either case, the firm with the lower downstream price earns higher profits; in the Stackelberg case D1 has the higher price, while in OSS D2 has the higher price, and the integrated firm earns higher profits than the combined profits of U2/D2.

The sequential game above presupposes an ability (by the leader) to commit to a price. OSS's model similarly presupposes an ability for the integrated firm to commit to an input price (at which it will sell to D2). Either type of commitment increases the relevant firm's profits relative to the Bertrand equilibrium, and there is no profitable counterstrategy that reverses the increase in the final product price. Although the profitability of making the commitment differs in the two commitment games, the relative profitability is somewhat beside the point. The real question is: when there is no natural sequence to the pricing decision, how do firms make the commitment to a price? In the specific example used by OSS, the commitment required of the integrated firm is rather complex. It cannot simply commit to "foreclose" D2 (refuse to sell to it). Such a commitment would make the unintegrated upstream firm an unconstrained monopolist, and in that case the successive monopoly distortion becomes sufficiently great that the combined profits

[3]See the Appendix for details.

of D2/U2 will increase if those two firms merge. This merger will return the industry to the initial equilibrium.[4] For partial integration (i.e., U2 remaining unintegrated) to be sustainable, the integrated firm must commit to a price below U2's monopoly price, but above marginal cost. It is difficult to imagine how such a commitment could be easier than a commitment by an unintegrated downstream firm to some price above the Bertrand equilibrium price.

As Timothy J. Brennan (1988) notes, while "raising rivals' costs" analyses (a class to which OSS's model seems to fit) are ostensibly vertical, most appear to be ultimately horizontal upon careful consideration. Here again, vertical integration does not raise price, holding all else constant. The mechanism by which credible commitment leads to higher prices is different in the integration and nonintegration cases, but the basic requirement for a credible commitment remains, and the commitment does not appear to become easier by virtue of a vertical relationship.

Appendix

In the "linear-linear" example in the OSS appendix, demand facing downstream-firm i ($i=1,2$) is a linear function of both its own price and its rival's price (i.e., $q_i = 1 - kP_i + dP_j$, where $k > d > 0$). Firms face a constant marginal cost of C_i, so that

$$\Pi_i^{\mathrm{B}} = (P_i - C_i)(1 - kP_i + dP_j).$$

This implies first-order conditions for unintegrated firms of

$$\text{(A1)} \qquad P_1 = \frac{1 + dP_2 + kC_1}{2k}$$

$$\text{(A2)} \qquad P_2 = \frac{1 + dP_1 + kC_2}{2k}.$$

[4]OSS note that another way in which D2 can buy at less than the upstream monopoly price is for there to be an inferior upstream product available to D2 at a price between the Bertrand and monopoly prices.

If $C_1 = C_2 = C$, the resulting downstream Bertrand equilibrium is

$$P_i^{\mathrm{B}} = \frac{2k + d + dkC + 2k^2C}{4k^2 - d^2}$$

(OSS's equation A1).

Suppose instead that D1 can commit to a price and that it knows D2's reaction function [equation (A2)]. Then, D1 acts as a Stackelberg leader and maximizes

$$\Pi_1^{\mathrm{S}} = (P_1 - C)\left[1 - kP_1 + d\left(\frac{1 + dP_1 + kC}{2k}\right)\right].$$

Taking the derivative with respect to P_1 and evaluating at P_1^{B} yields

$$\text{(A3)} \qquad (1 - kP_1) + \frac{d(1 + dP1 + kC)}{2k} + (P_1 - C)\left(\frac{d^2}{2k} - k\right).$$

Evaluated at P_1^{B} this equals

$$2kd^2\left(\frac{2k + d + dkC + 2k^2C}{4k^2 - d^2} - C\right)$$

$$= \frac{2kd^2}{2k - d}[1 + (d - k)C]$$

which is positive since $1/(k-d) > C$. Consequently, firm 1 can increase its profits by increasing price above P_1^{B}. This is an application of Thomas Cooper's (1986) result that starting at a differentiated-product Bertrand equilibrium, unilateral price increases are always profitable. OSS (p. 139) note that their results are also an application of Cooper's principle.

Finally, setting equation (A3) equal to zero, the optimal price for the Stackelberg leader is

$$P_1^{\mathrm{S}} = \frac{2k + d + dkC}{4k^2 - 2d^2} + \frac{C}{2}$$

which is greater than $P_1(0, C_2^*)$ from the OSS model.

REFERENCES

Brennan, Timothy J., "Understanding 'Raising Rivals' Costs'," *Antitrust Bulletin*, Spring 1988, *33*, 95–113.

Cooper, Thomas E., "Most-Favored-Nation Pricing and Tacit Collusion," *Rand Journal of Economics*, Autumn, 1986, *17*, 377–88.

Hart, Oliver and Tirole, Jean, "Vertical Integration and Market Foreclosure," *Brookings Papers on Economic Activity*, Summer 1990, (Special Issue), 205–76.

Ordover, Janusz A., Saloner, Garth, and Salop, Steven C., "Equilibrium Vertical Foreclosure," *American Economic Review*, March 1990, *80*, 127–42.

Tirole, Jean, *The Theory of Industrial Organization*, Cambridge, MA: MIT Press, 1988.

[21]

Contracts as a Barrier to Entry

By PHILIPPE AGHION AND PATRICK BOLTON*

It is shown that an incumbent seller who faces a threat of entry into his or her market will sign long-term contracts that prevent the entry of some lower-cost producers even though they do not preclude entry completely. Moreover, when a seller possesses superior information about the likelihood of entry, it is shown that the length of the contract may act as a signal of the true probability of entry.

Most of the literature on entry prevention deals with the case of two duopolists (the established firm and the potential entrant) who compete with each other to share a market, where one of the duopolists (the incumbent) has a first-move advantage.[1] This basic paradigm has been studied under various assumptions: about the strategy space of the players; the information structure of the game; and the time horizon. Recently, the model has been enlarged to allow for several entrants, several incumbents, several markets, and third parties.[2]

We propose here to extend the entry-prevention model in one other direction, which to our knowledge has not yet been formalized; namely, we consider whether optimal contracts between buyers and sellers deter entry and whether they are suboptimal from a welfare point of view. It has been pointed out by many economists that contracts between buyers and sellers in intermediate-good industries may have significant entry-prevention effects and that such contracts may be bad from a welfare point of view.[3]

On the other hand, it is a widespread opinion among antitrust practitioners that contracts between buyers and sellers are socially efficient.[4] There have been a number of antitrust cases involving exclusive dealing contracts and often the decision reached by the judge has lead to considerable controversy. One famous case, *United States v. United Shoe Machinery Corporation* (1922), illustrates quite clearly the nature of the debate: the United Shoe Machinery Corporation controlled 85 percent of the shoe-machinery market and had developed a complex leasing system of its machines to shoe manufacturers, a leasing system against which, it was thought, other machinery manufacturers would have difficulty competing. The judge ruled that these leasing contracts were in violation of the Sherman Act; his decision has been repeatedly criticized by leading antitrust experts (see Richard Posner, 1976, and Robert Bork, 1978). The main argument against the decision has been expressed by Posner: "The point I particularly want to emphasize is that the customers of United would be unlikely to participate in a campaign to strengthen United's monopoly position without insisting on being compensated for the loss of alternative and less costly

*Department of Economics, Harvard University, Cambridge, MA 02138, and University of California, Berkeley, CA 94720, respectively. We are greatly indebted to Jean Tirole for helping us formulate the model. We also thank Jerry Green and Oliver Hart for their useful suggestions and kind encouragement. We have been most fortunate to benefit from many helpful discussions with Dilip Abreu, Richard Caves, Nancy Gallini, Andreu Mas-Colell, and Eric Maskin.

[1] See, for example, the seminal contributions by Michael Spence (1977) and Avinash Dixit (1979, 1980).

[2] For a recent survey, see Drew Fudenberg and Jean Tirole (1986).

[3] Spence (p. 544), for example, briefly mentioned contracts as a method for impeding entry; see also Oliver Williamson (1979). Furthermore, there is a literature on barriers to entry and vertical integration that is relevant to our discussion, since most of the time what vertical integration achieves in this literature can also be done through an appropriate contract. (See Roger Blair and David Kaserman, 1983.)

[4] This position has been forcefully defended by Robert Bork (1978), for example.

(because competitive) sources of supply" (p. 203). Exactly the same point is made by Bork (p. 140), who concludes that when we find exclusive dealing contracts in practice, then these contracts could not have been signed for entry-deterrence reasons.

Both Posner and Bork are right in pointing out that the buyer is better off when there is entry and that he (she) will tend to reject exclusive dealing contracts that reduce the likelihood of entry unless the seller compensates him (her) by offering an advantageous deal. Nevertheless, we show that contracts between buyers and sellers will be signed for entry-prevention purposes.

When the buyer and the seller sign a contract, they have a monopoly power over the entrant. They can jointly determine what fee the entrant must pay in order to be able to trade with the buyer; that is to say, if the buyer signs an exclusive contract with the seller and then trades with the entrant, he must pay damages to the seller. Thus he will only trade with the entrant if the latter charges a price which is lower than the seller's price minus the damages he pays to the seller. These damages, which are determined in the original contract (liquidated damages), act as an entry fee the entrant must pay to the seller. We show that the buyer and the seller set this entry fee in the same way that a monopoly would set its price, when it cannot observe the willingness to pay of its customers. Thus, the main reason for signing exclusive contracts, in our model, is to extract some of the surplus an entrant would get if he entered the seller's market.

These contracts introduce a social cost, for they sometimes block the entry of firms that may be more efficient than the incumbent seller. Entry is blocked because the contract imposes an entry cost on potential competitors. This cost takes two different forms: an entrant must either wait until contracts expire, or induce the customers to break their contract with the incumbent by paying their liquidated damages.

The waiting cost is larger, other things being equal, the longer the contract. We are thus led to study the question of the optimal length of the contract. It is a well-known principle in economics that if agents engage in mutually advantageous trade, it is in their best interest to sign the longest possible contract. A long-term contract can always replicate what a sequence of short-term contracts achieves.

This principle, however, sharply contrasts empirical evidence: In practice most contracts are of an explicit finite duration. Many economists have been puzzled by this obvious discrepancy between the theory and empirical evidence, and several authors have attempted to provide an explanation for why contracts are of a finite duration; most notably Oliver Williamson (1975, 1979) and Milton Harris and Bengt Holmström (1983).

We argue here that looking only at the length of a contract is misleading. What is important is to what extent a contract of a given length locks the parties into a relationship. Thus we are led to make the distinction between the *nominal length* of the contract (the length that is specified in the contract) and the *effective length* of the contract (the actual length that the parties expect the relationship to last at the time of signing). Liquidated damages constitute an implicit measure of the effective length of the contract.

The paper is organized as follows: Section I looks at optimal contracts between a single buyer and the incumbent seller, when both parties have the same information about the likelihood of entry. Section II analyzes optimal contracts when there is asymmetric information about the probability of entry. Section III deals with optimal contracts when there are several buyers. Finally, Section IV offers some concluding comments.

I. Optimal Contracts Between One Buyer and the Incumbent Seller

We consider a two-period model, where a single producer supplies one unit to a buyer. The latter has a reservation price, $P=1$, and buys at most one unit. The seller faces a threat of entry, which is modeled as follows: At the time of contracting the seller's unit cost is $c=\frac{1}{2}$, while the entrant's cost of producing the same homogenous good is not known. For simplicity we assume that the entrant's cost, c_e, is uniformly distributed in

[0, 1].[5] Furthermore, if entry occurs and no contract has been signed between the incumbent and the buyer, both suppliers compete in prices, so that the Bertrand equilibrium price is given by $P = \max\{\frac{1}{2}, c_e\}$. When there is no entry, the potential entrant makes zero profits. Thus entry will only occur if $c_e \leq \frac{1}{2}$ and the probability of entry is given by

$$(1) \qquad \phi = Pr\left(c_e \leq \tfrac{1}{2}\right) = \tfrac{1}{2}.$$

We attempt here to model in the simplest way the view of the world where there are many investors at each period of time who try to invest their funds in the markets where they hope to get the highest returns. The distribution of profits across markets, however, changes stochastically over time. Therefore entry into a given market may also be stochastic. In this story it is implicitly assumed that investors do not have an unlimited access to funds and/or that there are diminishing returns to managing more investment projects. If neither of these assumptions hold, then investment will take place until the marginal return on the last investment project is equal to the interest rate. Many good reasons have been given for why investors only have a limited access to funds (see for example, Joseph Stiglitz and Andrew Weiss, 1981, or Williamson, 1971).

The timing of the game is as follows: At date 1 the incumbent seller and the buyer negotiate a contract, then entry either takes place or does not. Finally at date 2, there is production and trade.[6] We assume that the entrant's cost, c_e, is *not observable* but the parties to the contract know the distribution function of c_e. Therefore, contracts contingent on c_e cannot be written.[7]

If no contract is signed at date 1, the buyer's expected payoff is given by

$$(2) \qquad (1-\phi)\cdot 0 + \phi \cdot \tfrac{1}{2} = \tfrac{1}{2}\cdot\tfrac{1}{2} = \tfrac{1}{4}.$$

That is, with probability $(1-\phi)$ there is no entry and the seller sets the price equal to one. Hence, the buyer gets no surplus. With probability ϕ, entry occurs and Bertrand competition drives the price down to the incumbent's unit cost $c = \frac{1}{2}$. Now, Posner's point simply was that any contract that is acceptable to the buyer must give him an expected surplus of at least $\frac{1}{4}$ (assuming that the buyer is risk neutral). We shall show that even though the seller faces this constraint, there are gains to signing long-term contracts and in preventing entry.

The buyer and the incumbent seller could conceivably sign very complicated contracts even in this simple setting. For example, the price specified in the contract may be contingent on the event of entry or even contingent on the entrant's offer.[8] We shall, however, restrict ourselves to simple contracts of the form $c = \{P, P_0\}$ and show that there is no loss of generality in considering only this type of contract. Here P is the price of the good when the buyer trades with the incumbent and P_0 is the price the buyer must

[5] The choice of a uniform distribution is entirely for the sake of computational simplicity. In our 1985 paper, we show that the qualitative results obtained here are valid for any continuous density $f(x)$ with a support such that the lower bound is finite and that contains the interval $[0\ \frac{1}{2}]$.

[6] When production takes place before entry, the analysis is slightly modified. When the buyer switches to the entrant, the incumbent must now incur a loss of $c = \frac{1}{2}$. Thus the Bertrand equilibrium in the post-entry game now is $P = c_e$, so that entry will be precluded (since the entrant always makes nonpositive profits). To avoid an outcome where *ex post* competition (after entry) drives out *ex ante* competition (see Partha Dasgupta and Stiglitz, 1984), we then need to assume that the entrant sometimes makes losses when he does not enter into the incumbent's market. In other words, the entrant sometimes has a negative opportunity cost (see our earlier paper).

[7] In general, what matters is not the actual unit cost of the entrant but his opportunity cost of not entering. If one takes this interpretation, then nonobservability of the entrant's opportunity cost is a mild assumption.

[8] One often observes contracts where a retailer provides a minimum price warranty of the form: "If the buyer is offered a lower price by another retailer for the same good, within t periods, he can then claim back the difference between the high and the low price." These are examples of contracts which are contingent on the entrant's offer. Of course, if such contracts are written then entry is precluded (since the entrant makes zero profits). See our discussion of these contracts in Section IV.

pay if he does not trade with the incumbent. In other words, P_0 represents *liquidated damages*.

When a contract $c = \{P, P_0\}$ is signed, the buyer gets a surplus of $1 - P$ if there is no entry. Furthermore, if there is entry, he will only switch to the entrant if the latter offers a surplus of at least $1 - P$. We shall assume that when the buyer is indifferent between switching and not switching, he trades with the entrant. Thus in the post-entry equilibrium, the buyer also gets a surplus of $1 - P$. Then a contract $c = \{P, P_0\}$ is acceptable to the buyer only if

(3) $$1 - P \geq \tfrac{1}{4}.$$

Next, an entrant can only attract the buyer if he sets a price $\tilde{P}$, such that

(4) $$\tilde{P} \leq P - P_0$$

(in equilibrium the entrant sets, $\tilde{P} = P - P_0$). And entry only occurs if the entrant makes positive profits:

(5) $$\tilde{P} - c_e \geq 0.$$

Thus, when a contract $c = \{P, P_0\}$ is signed the probability of entry becomes

(6) $$\phi' = \max\{0; P - P_0\}.$$

The incumbent now faces the following program:

(7) $$\max_{P,\,P_0} \phi' \cdot P_0 + (1 - \phi')(P - c),$$

subject to $\quad 1 - P \geq \tfrac{1}{4}.$

It is straightforward to verify that the optimal contract is then given by $c = \{\tfrac{3}{4}; \tfrac{1}{2}\}$.

There are several conclusions to be drawn. First, the incumbent's expected payoff of signing the contract $c = \{\tfrac{3}{4}, \tfrac{1}{2}\}$ is given by $\pi = \tfrac{1}{16} + \tfrac{1}{4}$. If he had not signed a contract, or if he had signed a contract that completely blocks entry, his expected payoff would be $\tfrac{1}{4}$. Hence he is strictly better off signing this contract and the buyer is not worse off.

Second, when $c = \{\tfrac{3}{4}, \tfrac{1}{2}\}$ is signed, the probability of entry is $\phi' = \tfrac{3}{4} - \tfrac{1}{2} = \tfrac{1}{4}$. Thus the optimal contract prevents entry to some extent but does not preclude entry completely. The contract $c = \{P, P_0\}$ changes the entry game in a subtle way. On the one hand, it sets a large entry fee, P_0, to the entrant. This reduces the likelihood of entry. But $P_0 = \tfrac{1}{2}$, does not completely eliminate entry, since the contract commits the incumbent to set a price $P = \tfrac{3}{4}$. Thus all entrants with costs $c_e \leq \tfrac{1}{4}$ will find it profitable to enter. Furthermore, even if the incumbent had the opportunity of lowering the price P below $\tfrac{3}{4}$ in the post-entry game, he would not want to do this. *The incumbent is strictly better off when the buyer switches to the entrant* in the post-entry game, for then he gets a surplus of $\tfrac{1}{2}$ compared with a maximum surplus of $P - c = \tfrac{1}{4}$, if he retained the buyer.

By signing a contract, the incumbent and the buyer form a coalition which acts like a nondiscriminating monopolist with respect to the entrant. The coalition sets P_0 like a monopolist sets its price when it cannot discriminate between buyers with different willingnesses to pay.[9] If c_e were observable, the contract could specify P_0 as a function of c_e and the coalition would be able to extract all of the entrant's surplus ($P_0 = \tfrac{1}{2} - c_e$).

The idea that the incumbent and the buyer can get together and extract some of the entrant's rent is very general. It does not depend, for instance, on the assumption that the seller sets the contract. Peter Diamond and Eric Maskin (1979) have obtained a similar result in the context of a model of search with breach of contract, where neither the buyer nor the seller has the power of making take-it-or-leave-it offers. Rather, Diamond and Maskin assume that the outcome of the bargaining game between a buyer and a seller is given by the Nash-bargaining solution.

[9]An interesting feature of the optimal contract is that if the probability of entry ϕ increases, then the optimal price P_0 may decrease. For example if the incumbent's unit cost is k then $\phi = k$ and $P_0^* = 1 - k(1-k) - k/2$. Thus $dP_0^*/dk < 0$ for $k < \tfrac{3}{4}$.

Given that the incumbent and the buyer can only act as nondiscriminating monopolists, with respect to potential entrants, the optimal contract introduces a *social cost*, for it sometimes blocks the entry of a firm with a lower cost of production than the incumbent. When an optimal contract is signed, entrants with costs $c_e \in [\frac{1}{4}; \frac{1}{2}]$ do not enter.

To close this section we explain why the buyer and the seller can restrict themselves to simple contracts, $c = \{P, P_0\}$. The buyer and the seller can form a coalition whose value is $\frac{1}{2}$ when they do not allow entry into the market (the buyer's reservation price is one and the incumbent's cost is $c = \frac{1}{2}$). They can raise their payoff by allowing entry and making the entrant pay a fee, which in general will be a function of the entrant's cost, c_e. But the entrant's cost is private information so that the coalition faces a revelation of information problem. Now, a direct mechanism would specify a transfer from the entrant to the coalition, which is a function of the entrant's cost report: $t(c_e)$. This function $t(c_e)$ must satisfy the incentive-compatibility (IC) constraints: for all $c_e \in [0,1]$,

$$(IC) \quad \pi(c_e) - t(c_e) \geq \pi(c_e) - t(\hat{c}_e) \quad \text{for all } \hat{c}_e \in [0,1].$$

(Where $\pi(c_e)$ is the entrant's rent when his cost is c_e.) The IC constraints imply that $t(c_e) = t$ for all $c_e \in [0,1]$. In other words, the entry fee is independent of the entrant's cost.

Next, the entrant's rent is given by the difference between the incumbent's cost and his cost, c_e (i.e., $\pi(c_e) = \frac{1}{2} - c_e$). The coalition chooses t to maximize:

$$t \cdot Pr(\pi(c_e) \geq t) = t \cdot Pr(\tfrac{1}{2} - c_e \geq t) = t(\tfrac{1}{2} - t).$$

Then the optimal transfer is $t^* = \frac{1}{4}$ and the expected surplus raised is $\frac{1}{16}$. Notice that the optimal contract $c = \{P = \frac{3}{4};\ P_0 = \frac{1}{2}\}$ also raises a surplus of $\frac{1}{16}$ from the entrant. We can now appeal to the revelation principle (Dasgupta, Peter Hammond, and Maskin, 1979), which says that no indirect mechanism does better than the best direct mechanism. That is, no other contract exists that raises a higher surplus than $\frac{1}{16}$. Therefore there is no loss in restricting the contracts to be of the form $c = \{P, P_0\}$.[10]

II. Asymmetric Information About the Probability of Entry

In Section I it was assumed that both the incumbent and the buyer know the true probability of entry. This is not always realistic and one would expect that often the incumbent is better informed about the possibility of entry than the buyer. For example, if the incumbent is a high-tech firm and is the only one to have the know-how to produce a given intermediate good, then it is likely to be much better informed than its customers about the ability of a potential competitor in acquiring this know-how and thus produce the intermediate good. Hence, in this section we assume that the incumbent has some private information about the likelihood of entry.[11]

Asymmetric information has important consequences for the determination of the optimal nominal length of the contract. Under symmetric information, there is no incentive for writing a contract of finite nominal length. On the contrary, the incumbent always gains by locking the buyer into a contract in every period, for then an entrant cannot avoid paying the entry fee by entering at a time when the buyer is not bound by a contract to the incumbent. Under asymmetric information, on the other hand, the seller may wish to sign a contract of finite nominal length in order to signal to the buyer that entry is unlikely. Of course, the seller could also signal his information by

[10] In the above discussion we have restricted ourselves to deterministic mechanisms. Since all agents are assumed to be risk neutral, there is no loss of generality in considering only deterministic mechanisms (see Maskin, 1981).

[11] One can think of situations where the buyer is better informed about the probability of entry. Then we have a classic self-selection problem and all the results obtained in this section would also apply to this case.

offering a contract with lower liquidated damages, P_0. Such a contract would reduce the buyer's switching cost and could only profitably be offered by a seller facing a low probability of entry. We show however, that under certain conditions, signaling through the length of the contract is strictly better than signaling through liquidated damages.

To keep the analysis simple, we shall assume that the probability of entry is either "high" or "low." The incumbent knows the true probability but the buyer does not. Furthermore, as in Section I, the incumbent makes the contract offer. The situation described here is akin to an "informed Principal" problem (see Roger Myerson, 1983, and Maskin and Jean Tirole, 1985).

As in Section I, we shall assume that the entrant's costs are uniformly distributed on $[0,1]$. The incumbent's cost, on the other hand, is either $c=\frac{1}{2}$ or $c=k$, where $0<k<\frac{1}{2}$. Then the probability of entry is low when $c=k$ and it is high when $c=\frac{1}{2}$, since when $c=k$, we have

$$\underline{\phi} \equiv Pr(c_e \leq k) = k < \tfrac{1}{2}, \tag{8}$$

and when $c=\frac{1}{2}$, we have

$$\bar{\phi} \equiv Pr(c_e \leq \tfrac{1}{2}) = \tfrac{1}{2}. \tag{9}$$

The buyer's prior beliefs about the incumbent's costs are given by $m = Pr(c=k)$.

Under asymmetric information, it is no longer true that the seller can restrict himself with no loss to simple contracts, $c=\{P, P_0\}$. In fact, we show in our earlier paper that the incumbent seller can achieve the symmetric information optimal outcome by offering contracts of the form $c=\{P, P^e, P_0\}$ where P_0 is defined as in the previous section, P is the price the buyer pays if he trades with the incumbent and entry did not occur and P^e is the price the buyer pays if he trades with the incumbent and entry took place. Alternatively, when the incumbent only offers contracts of the form $c=\{P, P_0\}$, he can never attain the symmetric information optimal outcome. Thus simple contracts $c=\{P, P_0\}$ are suboptimal under asymmetric information. Thus, if the more general contracts $c=\{P, P^e, P_0\}$ are feasible asymmetric information puts no restrictions on the nominal length of the contract.

We give the following argument for why such contracts may not be feasible: First, "entry" may be a very complicated event to describe, when a firm can enter with a nonhomogeneous good. The incumbent must then decide what commodities qualify as "entrants" and, even if a list of such commodities can be defined, an entrant would have an incentive to produce a good which is not on that list whenever $P > P^e$. Alternatively, if $P^e > P$, there would be an incentive for the incumbent to claim that entry has occurred whenever there is an ambiguity about the event of entry. In short, the event of entry may be difficult to observe, let alone to verify.

Second, when $P > P^e$, the buyer could bribe someone to "enter" only to force the incumbent to lower his price. Vice versa, when $P < P^e$, the incumbent may want to bribe someone to enter.

When only simple contracts $c=\{P, P_0\}$ are feasible, asymmetric information can put restrictions on both the liquidated damages P_0, and the length of the contract. In the present model, contract length is somewhat artificially defined since production and trade take place only once. It should however be clear from what follows that the conclusions reached here carry over to a model with N periods of production and trade ($N \geq 2$) where entry can take place in any of these N periods.

Here we compare the asymmetric information-contracting solution with the no-contracting solution and show that when the difference between high and low costs is sufficiently large, the low-cost incumbent is better off not signing a contract and leaving options open until the entry decision is taken by the potential competitor. In a model with N periods, this result would be modified and the low-cost incumbent would be better off signing a *shorter* contract than the high-cost incumbent.

When the seller makes a contract offer $c=\{P, P_0\}$, he conveys information about his type, so that the buyer's beliefs change.

Let the buyer's posterior beliefs be

$$(10) \qquad \beta(c) = Pr(\phi = \bar{\phi}/c).$$

The buyer will only accept the contract if

$$(11) \quad 1 - P \geq \beta(c)\bar{\phi}/2 + (1-\beta(c))\underline{\phi}(1-k)$$

From (8) and (9) we can rewrite (11) as

$$(12) \quad 1 - P \geq (\beta(c)/4) + (1-\beta(c))k(1-k)$$

When the incumbent signs a contract $c = \{P, P_0\}$, the probability of entry is given by

$$(13) \qquad Pr(c_e \leq P - P_0) = P - P_0.$$

Thus, the incumbent's payoff when he is respectively of type $\bar{\phi}$ or $\underline{\phi}$ is given by

(14)

$$V(c,\bar{\phi}) = (P - P_0)(P_0 - P + \tfrac{1}{2}) + P - \tfrac{1}{2}$$

$$V(c,\underline{\phi}) = (P - P_0)(P_0 - P + k) + P - k$$

for $P > P_0$, (otherwise $V(c,\bar{\phi}) = P - \frac{1}{2}$ and $V(c,\underline{\phi}) = P - k$). It is straightforward to verify that the Spence-Mirrlees condition is satisfied:

$$(15) \quad d/dk[-\partial V/\partial P/\partial V/\partial P_0] < 0.$$

In other words, it is more costly for an incumbent facing a higher probability of entry to lower P_0 than it is for an incumbent facing a lower probability of entry. Given condition (12) we can draw Figure 1 where $\bar{c}^* = \{P = \frac{3}{4};\ P_0 = \frac{1}{2}\}$ is the optimal symmetric information contract when $\phi = \bar{\phi}$. Notice that this contract will always be accepted by the buyer since the right-hand side in (12) is increasing in β and when $\beta = 1$ (12) becomes

$$(16) \qquad 1 - P \geq \tfrac{1}{4}.$$

In addition, the contract $\bar{c}^*$ is the best contract for the high-cost incumbent, among the class of contracts which generate beliefs $\beta(c) = 1$. It is common in signaling models to obtain a plethora of equilibria and our model is no exception to this rule. Any pair of contracts $(c, \bar{c}^*)$ where c is such that $P = 1 - k(1-k)$ and $0 \leq P_0 \leq P_0^*$ (see Figure 1) constitutes a separating equilibrium. Furthermore, any point in the shaded area in the diagram may be a pooling or semiseparating equilibrium of the signaling game. Following David Kreps (1984), however, we can refine the Bayesian equilibrium concept by using dominance and stability arguments and thus single out the best separating equilibrium $(c^{**}, \bar{c}^*)$ where c^{**} is defined as $c^{**} = \{P = 1 - k(1-k);\ P_0 = P_0^*\}$. How is P_0^* determined? It is the solution to the equation

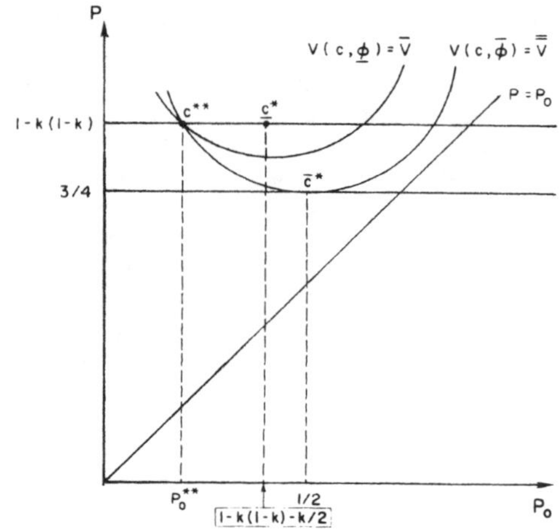

FIGURE 1

$$V(c^{**},\bar{\phi}) = V(\bar{c}^*,\bar{\phi}),$$

which can be rewritten as

$$(17) \quad (P - P_0)(P_0 - P + \tfrac{1}{2}) + P - \tfrac{1}{2} = \tfrac{1}{16} + \tfrac{1}{4}$$

where $P = 1 - k(1-k)$.

Now P_0^* is the smaller root of this quadratic equation (see Figure 1) and is given by

$$(18)\quad P_0^* = \left(\left(2P - \tfrac{1}{2}\right) - \sqrt{4P-3}\,\right)/2.$$

How does the optimal contract for the low-cost incumbent under asymmetric information compare with the optimal symmetric information contract given by $\underline{c}^* = \{P = 1 - k(1-k);\ P_0 = (2P-k)/2\}$?

The optimal contract under asymmetric information, c^{**} specifies the same price P as c^*, but it specifies lower liquidated damages: $P_0^* < P_0$. It is straightforward to compute that $P_0^* < P_0$ reduces to

$$(19)\qquad 1 + 4k^2 > 5k - \tfrac{1}{2}.$$

And for all $0 < k < \frac{1}{2}$ this inequality is verified.

Intuitively, the incumbent with low costs signals his type by offering to reduce liquidated damages below the first-best level. His information is credibly transmitted since it is too costly for the high-cost incumbent to reduce P_0 to that level and thereby induce too much entry.

We now show that for small k, the low-cost incumbent is better off not signing a contract than signing c^{**}. If the low-cost seller does not sign a contract, his expected profits are given by

$$(20)\qquad (1-\underline{\phi})(1-k) = (1-k)^2.$$

If he signs c^{**} he gets

$$(21)\quad V(c^{**}, \underline{\phi}) = (P - P_0^*)(k - (P - P_0^*)) + P - k,$$

where $\quad P = 1 - k(1-k)$

and $\quad P - P_0^* = \frac{1}{4} + \frac{1}{2}\sqrt{4(1-k(1-k))-3}\,.$

It remains to show that for small k, we have

$$(22)\quad \left[\tfrac{1}{4} + \tfrac{1}{2}\sqrt{4(1-k(1-k))-3}\,\right]k - \left[\tfrac{1}{4} + \tfrac{1}{2}\sqrt{4(1-k(1-k))-3}\,\right]^2 + 1 - k(1-k) - k \le (1-k)^2$$

And (22) reduces to

$$(23)\quad k \le \tfrac{1}{4} + \tfrac{1}{2}\sqrt{4(1-k(1-k))-3}$$

which is clearly verified for small k. Also, for k close to $\frac{1}{2}$, (23) is not satisfied. We summarize the above discussion in the following proposition:

PROPOSITION 1: *Under asymmetric information about the probability of entry (or equivalently about the incumbent's costs), the optimal contracting solution is such that*

(a) *the high-cost incumbent signs the optimal symmetric information contract* $\bar{c}^* = \{P = \frac{3}{4};\ P_0 = \frac{1}{2}\}$.

(b) *the low-cost incumbent either signs the second-best contract*

$$c^{**} = \left\{ P = 1 - k(1-k);\quad P_0^* = P - \tfrac{1}{4} - \tfrac{1}{2}\sqrt{4P-3}\,\right\}$$

(when k is close to $\frac{1}{2}$) or does not sign a long-term contract at all (when k is close to zero).

(c) c^{**} *is characterized by the property that liquidated damages (P_0^*) are lower than in the optimal symmetric information contract,*

$$\underline{c}^* = \{P = 1 - k(1-k);\ P_0 = P - (k/2)\}.$$

One can explain Proposition 1(b) as follows. As k becomes smaller the price $P = 1 - k(1-k)$ rises, which makes it more attractive for the high-cost firm to mimic the low-cost firm's behavior. In order to discourage the high-cost firm from cheating, the low-cost firm must therefore increase the gap $P - P_0 = [\frac{1}{4} + \frac{1}{2}(4(1-k(1-k))-3)^{1/2}]$. But this is equivalent to raising the probability of entry after a contract has been signed (see equation (13)). There comes a point where $\phi' = P - P_0 \ge \underline{\phi} = k$; that is, by raising $P - P_0$, the low-cost firm raises the *ex post probability of entry* (ϕ') above the *ex ante probability of entry* ($\underline{\phi}$) (see (23)). This essentially involves subsidizing some inefficient entrants to enter the market. The incumbent then gets a negative transfer from the entrant. He can do strictly better by not offering any transfer (i.e., by not signing a contract at all).

We have thus established that the *nominal* length of the contract may serve as a signal of the probability of entry. This result confirms the following basic intuition:

The buyer reasons as follows when he is offered a contract: "If the incumbent wants to sign a contract of a long duration he must be worried about entry, so that I infer from this that the probability of entry is high and I will only accept to sign this contract if he charges a low price. If, on the other hand, the incumbent offers a short-term contract, he reveals that he is not much preoccupied about entry, so that I will be willing to accept a higher price."

The result obtained in Proposition 1(c) implies that the social cost is smaller in the asymmetric information case than in the symmetric information case. That is, liquidated damages (P_0^*) are smaller in c^{**} than in $\underline{c}^*$; therefore fewer efficient firms will be kept out of the market. It is worth emphasizing this point, since one usually thinks of asymmetric information as a constraint that prevents agents from reaching a socially efficient outcome (a first-best optimum). This is a general theme in Agency theory (see Oliver Hart and Holmström, 1985). Here, on the contrary, asymmetric information about the incumbent's costs may actually force agents to choose the socially efficient outcome (whenever the condition in (23) is verified). *The informational asymmetry constrains the monopoly power of the incumbent and the buyer with respect to the entrant.* There is another interpretation of this result. Remember that the incumbent and the buyer are constrained in the first place by the informational asymmetry about the entrant's costs. Then, the conclusion reached here is that if there exists another informational asymmetry between the buyer and the incumbent (about the latter's cost) *the two informational constraints may cancel each other out.*

This is an important observation for agency theory. Informational constraints do not necessarily add up; they may cancel out.

III. Optimal Contracts with Several Buyers

One may wonder to what extent the results obtained in Sections I and II depend on the assumption that there is only one incumbent seller and one buyer? This section attempts to give a partial answer to this question. We compare in turn the situation where there is one buyer but several incumbent sellers, and the situation where there is one incumbent seller but several buyers. All the results established in Section I are valid in each case. Moreover, new interesting features are introduced in the latter situation, where a single incumbent negotiates with several buyers.

Consider first the situation where there are two or more identical sellers but only one buyer. Then, Bertrand competition essentially gives all the bargaining power to the buyer; he gets all of the surplus but the form of the optimal contract does not change. The buyer sets P_0 in the same way as the seller does, when the seller makes the contract offer.

The interesting situation is when there are several buyers and one seller. In this case, the entrant's profits depend on how many customers he can serve in the post-entry game. What is crucial, however, is how the size of the entrant's potential market affects the probability of entry. If the probability of entry is independent of the size of the market, then the case of several buyers reduces to the case of one buyer. In general, however, the size of the market will affect the probability of entry. For example, if the entrant must pay a fixed cost of entry, then his average cost is decreasing in the number of customers served and the probability of entry is in creasing in the number of customers.

In this latter case, when one buyer signs a long-term contract with the incumbent, he imposes a negative externality on all other buyers. By locking himself into a long-run relation with the seller, he reduces the size of the entrant's potential market so that, *ceteris paribus*, the probability of entry will be smaller. As a result, the other buyers will have to accept higher prices. We show that the incumbent can exploit this negative externality to extract more (possibly all) surplus out of each buyer. In some cases, the seller can impose the monopoly price ($P=1$) on each buyer, even though the *ex ante* probability of entry is arbitrarily close to one (*ex ante* refers to the no-contract situation). In addition, the seller can extract part of the entrant's surplus by choosing damages (P_0) appropriately, so that we get the paradoxical result that a seller facing a threat of entry may be better off than a natural monopoly. To reach this conclusion, we must push the logic of the game to its limits. This result is thus interesting mainly for illustrative purposes.

We will only consider the case of two buyers and one seller.[12] Both buyers are identical and have a reservation price $P=1$. The incumbent is as described in Section I. The entrant has the same unit costs as in Section I; in addition, he may face a fixed cost of entry, $F \geq 0$. We shall first consider the problem where F is strictly positive. Then, in the absence of any contract, the entrant's profit is given by

$$(24) \qquad \pi_e = 2\left(\tfrac{1}{2} - c_e\right) - F.$$

Thus, the *ex ante* probability of entry is given by

$$(25) \qquad \phi = Pr(\pi_e \geq 0) = (1-F)/2.$$

Suppose now that one of the buyers signs a contract with the incumbent where $P_0 = +\infty$. Then in the post-entry game, this buyer will never switch to the entrant. The latter can now hope to get at most:

$$(26) \qquad \hat{\pi}_e = \tfrac{1}{2} - c_e - F.$$

The other buyer therefore faces a lower likelihood of entry given by

$$(27) \qquad \hat{\phi} = Pr(\hat{\pi}_e \geq 0) = (1-2F)/2.$$

More generally, whenever one buyer signs a contract with the incumbent of the form $c = \{P, P_0\}$, the other buyer faces a new probability of entry given by

$$(28) \qquad \hat{\phi} = \max\left\{\frac{P - P_0 + \frac{1}{2} - F}{2}; \frac{1-2F}{2}\right\}.$$

We will analyze the negotiation game where the incumbent makes simultaneous contract offers to both buyers. The case where the incumbent makes sequential offers is considered in our earlier paper. There we establish that the timing of offers does not matter. The same outcome is obtained in the simultaneous offers case as in the sequential offers case.

The incumbent can without loss restrict the set of contracts to be of the form $c = \{P, P_0, P^r, P_0^r\}$, where

P = the price a buyer must pay if he trades with the incumbent and the other buyer has signed a long-term contract;

P_0 = the damages a buyer must pay if he switches to the entrant and the other buyer has signed a contract with the incumbent;

P^r = the price a buyer must pay if he trades with the incumbent and the other buyer did not sign a contract;

P_0^r = the damages a buyer must pay if he trades with the entrant and the other buyer did not sign a contract with the incumbent.

It is implicitly assumed here that all contracts are publicly observable. This is a strong assumption. In practice, all contracts are not observable. As a result, one can never be certain when a contract is observed, whether there does not exist a hidden contract which cancels the effects of the observed contract. In our model, however, the incumbent has an incentive to publicize all of his contracts, as will become clear below. Thus, hidden contracts are not a problem.

When the seller makes a contract offer $c = \{P, P_0, P^r, P_0^r\}$ to each buyer, B_1 and B_2, the latter play a noncooperative game where they have two pure strategies: "accept" and "reject." The payoff matrix of this game is represented in Table 1. By choosing P^r and P_0^r appropriately, the incumbent can ensure that $\hat{\phi} = (1-2F)/2$.

[12] We deal with the generalization to n buyers ($n \geq 2$) in our earlier paper.

TABLE 1— B_1

	Accept		Reject	
Accept	$1-P$	$1-P$	$1-p^r$	$\hat{\phi}/2$
Reject	$\hat{\phi}/2$	$1-p^r$	$\phi/2$	$\phi/2$

Essentially, this involves choosing P_0^r large enough so that the buyer who accepted a contract will not switch to the entrant. Now, accept is a (weakly) dominant strategy when

$$(29)\qquad 1-P \geq \hat{\phi}/2 = (1-2F)/4;$$

$$(30)\qquad 1-P^r > \phi/2.$$

When the incumbent offers a contract to both buyers such that (29) and (30) are satisfied (and such that $\hat{\phi} = (1-2F)/2$), the unique Nash equilibrium is for both buyers to accept the contract offer. As a result, both buyers receive a strictly lower payoff in equilibrium than if they both rejected the contract, since $\hat{\phi} < \phi$.

Thus when there are several buyers contracting with the incumbent, there is another reason why rational buyers are willing to perpetuate the monopoly position of the seller. As Steven Salop puts it, contracts "...are valued by each buyer individually even while they create an external cost to all other buyers" (1986, p. 273). He calls this situation a "*free-rider effect in reverse*" (emphasis added).

In addition to this effect, the seller can set P_0 appropriately so as to extract the maximum expected surplus from the entrant. To summarize, in this simple model with simultaneous offers, the set of optimal contracts is given by

$$(31)\qquad c^* = \left\{ P = 1 - \frac{(1-2F)}{4}; \quad P_0 = P - \frac{F+1}{4}; \quad P^r < 1 - \frac{\phi}{2};\ P_0^r > P^r + \tfrac{1}{2} + F \right\}.$$

And at the optimum the incumbent's expected payoff is given by

$$(32)\qquad \pi = \left(2(P-P_0) - F\right)\left(2\left(P_0 - P + \tfrac{1}{2}\right)\right) + 2\left(P - \tfrac{1}{2}\right) = \frac{(1-F)^2}{2} + 1 - \frac{(1-2F)}{2}.$$

Suppose now that $F \geq \frac{1}{2}$, then $\hat{\phi} = 0$ and the incumbent is able to impose the monopoly price ($P = 1$) on the buyer. His expected payoff at the optimum is then given by

$$(33)\qquad \pi = \left((1-F)^2/2\right) + 1.$$

Thus the incumbent does strictly better than a natural monopoly, since he can also extract some of the potential entrant's surplus. On the other hand, when $F = 0$, we have $\hat{\phi} = \phi = \frac{1}{2}$, and the "free-rider effect in reverse" disappears, so that the two buyers case reduces to a one-buyer case, where the customer purchases two units rather than one. In other words, when the probability of entry is independent of the size of the market, competition among buyers does not matter.

Thus the principles established in the one buyer-one seller case remain valid when we allow for either more than one buyer or more than one seller. The analysis is somewhat incomplete since we did not deal with the several buyers-several sellers case. The results obtained in Section I carry through to this more general model (see Diamond-Maskin). As far as the results in this section are concerned, it is likely that sellers will not be able to exploit to the same extent the free-rider effect in reverse.

IV. Conclusion

The principles formalized in this paper are very general. What is basically required for contracts to constitute a barrier to entry is that post-entry profits for the incumbent in the absence of any contract be lower than pre-entry profits (and vice versa for consumers). In addition, it is necessary that the incumbent cannot discriminate between entrants of various levels of efficiency. This is a rather mild assumption if one interprets the entrant's cost as an opportunity cost of entry as in our earlier paper. Throughout the paper we interpreted P_0 to be "liquidated damages," but P_0 may also represent down payments, deposits, collateral, future discounts, and benefits, etc. Thus, the analysis developed here has potentially a wide range of applicability.

Casual empiricism suggests that "endogenous switching costs" for customers are a widespread phenomenon. In the housing market, for example, advance deposits in rental contracts can be interpreted as serving this function (there are, of course, also moral hazard reasons for requiring deposits). Paul Klemperer (1986) provides a number of examples of endogenous switching costs, like frequent flyer programs, trading stamps, deferred rebates by shipping firms, etc. Also, fixed fees in franchise contracts may be used to extract some rent from a potential competitor. The contract between Automatic Radio Manufacturing Co. and Hazeltine Research (see *Automatic Radio Manufacturing Co. v. Hazeltine Research Inc.*, 1950) is a good example. Automatic Radio had to pay a fixed fee irrespective of whether it exploited the patents licensed by Hazeltine. Any new licensor therefore faced an entry barrier equal to the amount of this fee. Another striking example is the case of Bell Laboratories when it invented the transistor. There were other research institutes competing with Bell Laboratories. In order to preempt them, Bell Labs offered to publicize the technology to any potential licensee, in exchange for a fixed fee of $25,000. This fee served the same function as P_0, in the contract above. Moreover Bell Lab's strategy was to become the industry standard. Thus any individual licensee would have to take into account the additional switching cost of not being standardized (see E. Braun and S. Macdonald, 1978). Our analysis provides a rationale for the practices described here and explains why rational customers cooperate with firms in these anticompetitive practices. Unfortunately, the variety and potential complexity of these contractual clauses makes the task for antitrust authorities very difficult.

A rapidly growing literature on exogenous switching costs is related to our present study (see Klemperer for a recent thorough exposition). The welfare conclusions obtained in this research are radically different from ours. For example, in Klemperer, entry may be socially inefficient because consumers dissipate the gains from entry (in terms of lower prices and higher output) by incurring the socially wasteful switching costs. In our model, the social cost comes from insufficient entry; when entry occurs it is always welfare improving. Salop also studies the effect of various clauses, such as the "meeting the competition clause" or the "clause of the most favored nation" on competition. His emphasis is more on cartel coordination than entry prevention. In our model a "meeting the competition clause" would preclude entry since the entrant could never undercut the incumbent. *We have shown, however, that it is optimal not to eliminate entry completely*. Therefore, such clauses will never be adopted for entry-deterrence purposes; they may however be useful to facilitate cartel coordination, as Salop shows, since they increase the cost of price cutting.

Our theory of contract length is a substantial departure from existing theories. Most explanations have emphasized the idea that contract length is determined as a tradeoff between recontracting costs and the costs associated with the incompleteness of the contract (see Williamson, 1975, 1985; Ronald Dye, 1985a; Jo Anna Gray, 1976). A notable exception is Harris and Holmström. In practice, uncertainty about the future and the cost of writing complete contracts are without doubt important elements in the determination of contract length. The difficulty from a theoretical perspective is however that uncertainty about the future and "transaction costs" are notoriously vague categories. If contracts are to be incomplete what contingencies should the parties leave out of the contract? This is a very difficult question which has only received partial answers (see Dye, 1985b, and Hart-Holmström). Explanations of contract length based on contractual incompleteness crucially depend on how one answers this question (see Dye, 1985b). In this paper we have sidestepped the difficulty to provide a story based on asymmetric information. We believe that signaling aspects are important in the determination of contract length and view our explanation as complementary to the existing theories.

Recently, Benjamin Hermalin (1986) has developed another theory of contract length based on asymmetric information. He considers a competitive labor market where initially workers have private information about productivity but where in a later stage this information becomes public (for example, through output observations). He shows that by varying contract length, it is impossible for firms to *profitably* screen out low-productivity workers from high-productivity workers. Ideally, a firm wants to retain only high-productivity workers, but long-term contracts are most attractive to low-productivity workers. Thus, by screening out workers, the firm achieves the opposite of what it wants: it offers long contracts to low-productivity workers and short contracts to high-productivity workers. In equilibrium, either firms offer only short-term contracts, or they offer "trivial" long-term contracts that replicate the outcome achieved with short-term contracts. In our model, on the contrary, signaling (or screening) works. Moreover, when it is optimal for the low-cost incumbent to sign a short-term contract, there does not exist an alternative trivial long-term contract. One can view our explanation and Hermalin's as dual: in his model the high-productivity sellers do not want to be locked in a long-term contract; here it is the buyer who does not want to forego future opportunities.

REFERENCES

Aghion, Philippe and Bolton, Patrick, "Entry-Prevention through Contracts with Customers," unpublished, 1985.

Blair, Roger D. and Kaserman, David L., *Law and Economics of Vertical Integration and Control*, New York: Academic Press, 1983.

Bork, Robert H., *The Antitrust Paradox*, New York: Basic Books, 1978.

Braun, E. and Macdonald, S., *Revolution in Miniature: The History and Impact of Semiconductor Electronics*, New York: Cambridge University Press, 1978.

Caves, Richard, E., "Vertical Restraints in Manufacturer-Distributor Relations: Incidence and Economic Effects," mimeo., Harvard University, 1984.

Dasgupta, Partha and Stiglitz, Joseph, "Sunk Costs and Competition," mimeo., Princeton University, 1984.

______, Hammond, Peter and Maskin, Eric, "The Implementation of Social Choice Rules: Some General Results on Incentive Compatability," *Review of Economic Studies*, April 1979, *46*, 185–206.

Diamond, Peter A. and Maskin, Eric, "An Equilibrium Analysis of Search and Breach of Contract, I: Steady States," *Bell Journal of Economics*, Spring 1979, *10*, 282–316.

Dixit, Avinash, "A Model of Duopoly Suggesting a Theory of Entry-Barriers," *Bell Journal of Economics*, Spring 1979, *10*, 20–32.

______, "The Role of Investment in Entry Deterrence," *Economic Journal*, March 1980, *90*, 95–106.

Dye, Ronald, (1985a)"Costly Contract Contingencies," *International Economic Review*, February 1985, *26*, 233–50.

______, (1985b)"Optimal Length of Labor Contracts," *International Economic Review*, February 1985, *26*, 251–70.

Fudenberg, Drew and Tirole, Jean, "Dynamic Models of Oligopoly," in J. Lesourne and H. Sonnenschein, eds., *Fundamentals of Pure and Applied Economics*, New York: Harwood Academic Press, 1986.

Gray, Jo Anna, "Wage Indexation: A Macroeconomic Approach," *Journal of Monetary Economics*, April 1976, *2*, 221–35.

Harris, Milton and Holmström, Bengt, "On the Duration of Agreements," mimeo., IMSSS, Stanford University, 1983.

Hart, Oliver and Holmström, Bengt, "The Theory of Contracts," in T. Bewley, ed., *Advances in Economic Theory*, New York: Cambridge University Press, 1985.

______ and Moore, John, "Incomplete Contracts and Renegotiation," mimeo., MIT 1985.

Hermalin, Benjamin, "Adverse Selection and Contract Length," mimeo., MIT, 1986.

Klemperer, Paul, "Markets with Consumer Switching Costs," unpublished doctoral dissertation, Graduate School of Business, Stanford University, 1986.

Kreps, David M., "Signaling Games and Stable Equilibrium," mimeo., Stanford University, 1984.

Maskin, Eric, "Randomization in Incentive Problems," mimeo., 1981.

______ **and Tirole, Jean,** "Principals with Private Information, II: Dependent Values," lecture notes, 1985.

Myerson, Roger B., "Mechanism Design by an Informed Principal," *Econometrica*, November, 1983, *51*, 1767–97.

Posner, Richard A., *Antitrust Law: An Economic Perspective*, Chicago: University of Chicago Press, 1976.

Salop, Steven, "Practices that (credibly) Facilitate Oligopoly Coordination," in J. Stiglitz and F. Mathewson, eds., *New Developments in the Analysis of Market Structure*, Cambridge: MIT Press, 1986.

Spence, A. Michael, "Entry, Capacity, Investment and Oligopolistic Pricing," *Bell Journal of Economics*, Autumn 1977, *8*, 534–44.

Stiglitz, Joseph and Weiss, Andrew, "Credit Rationing in Markets with Imperfect Information," *American Economic Review*, June 1981, *71*, 393–409.

Williamson, Oliver E., "The Vertical Integration of Production: Market Failure Considerations," *American Economic Review*, March 1971, *61*, 112–23.

______, *Markets and Hierarchies: Analysis and Antitrust Implications*, New York: Free Press, 1975.

______, "Assessing Vertical Market Restrictions: Antitrust Ramifications of the Transaction-Cost Approach," *University of Pennsylvania Law Review*, April 1979, *127*, 953–93.

______, *The Economic Institutions of Capitalism*, New York: Free Press, 1985.

Automatic Radio Manufacturing Co. v. Hazeltine Research Inc., 339 U.S. 827, 834, 1950.

United States v. United Shoe Machinery Corporation, 258 U.S. 451, 1922.

[22]

ARE VERTICAL RESTRAINTS PRO- OR ANTICOMPETITIVE? LESSONS FROM *INTERSTATE CIRCUIT**

DAVID A. BUTZ
University of Michigan

and

ANDREW N. KLEIT
Pennsylvania State University

ABSTRACT

At the heart of antitrust law is the prohibition on horizontal collusion. To enforce this prohibition, the law must accurately define what collusion entails. One of the most controversial areas in antitrust is the issue of vertical restraints. In the last 20 years, economists have come up with any number of pro- and anticompetitive rationales for such restraints. Given this, perhaps one of the most important antitrust cases is *Interstate Circuit v. United States,* a case that combines issues of horizontal collusion and vertical restraints. A review of the facts shows that collusion cannot be properly inferred from the behavior of the parties involved and that the relevant vertical restraints had efficiency-enhancing properties. We then use Interstate Circuit's behavior to generate a theory of vertical restraints that not only explains the events in the case but also addresses an important controversy in the vertical restraints literature.

> [A distributor] could compete successfully only by granting exclusive licenses to Interstate and injuring subsequent run houses by refusing them license—a course clearly lawful,—or by doing the less drastic thing of agreeing to protect the good will of the pictures by putting necessary and not severely burdensome restrictions upon subsequent run exhibitors, which I think equally lawful. [Dissent of Justice Roberts (joined by Justices McReynolds and Butler), *Interstate Circuit v. United States*, 306 U.S. 208, 240 (1939)]

I. INTRODUCTION

AT the heart of antitrust law is the prohibition on collusion. To enforce this prohibition, the law must accurately define what collusion entails. Such definitions invite controversy, especially in settings where firms with potentially competing interests must cooperate to transact at all. For this reason, the debate over agreements between vertically related firms has been contentious, as antitrust scholars can offer up any number of pro- and anticompetitive rationales for any given vertical restraint. One of the most significant cases in this debate is

* We are grateful for helpful comments from Paul Clyde, Andrew Hansson, John Lopatka, Jim Meehan, Tim Sass, the editor, and an anonymous referee.

[*Journal of Law and Economics,* vol. XLIV (April 2001)]

Interstate Circuit v. United States.[1] *Interstate Circuit* has been cited literally hundreds of times in legal decisions over the past 20 years, and it has helped to determine both the course of collusion law and the academic arguments over the competitive consequences of vertical restraints. Here we show that a careful review of the facts in this case generates fundamental insights for our understanding of both collusion and vertical contracting. In addition, we use the facts of the case to motivate a model that enhances the relevancy of Lester Telser's[2] pathbreaking approach to vertical restraints.

Interstate Circuit now stands for two important propositions in antitrust law. First, it sets out an important precedent for the legal definition of conspiracy. The teachings of the case give instruction on how to infer collusion, using terms similar to modern game-theoretic notions of unilateral versus joint action. Second, it is a cornerstone of the theory of "raising rivals' costs," expounded by Thomas Krattenmaker and Steven Salop.[3] While raising rivals' costs enjoys a certain popularity among theorists, its empirical applications appear limited, with *Interstate Circuit* now the most significant case cited by Krattenmaker and Salop that has not been discounted.[4]

At one level, the facts in *Interstate Circuit* are straightforward. Interstate Circuit, the monopoly first-run movie theater (FRT) in several Texas cities in the 1930s, entered into contracts with movie distributors, after Interstate Circuit requested (or perhaps insisted) that the distributors do so. The contracts set the admission price of the distributors' films when they were presented at subsequent-run theaters (SRTs). Yet what is not apparent from these facts is why Interstate Circuit chose this legally suspect contract when, as the Supreme Court dissent above noted, other legal and effective alternatives were available.

This article uses legal briefs and court decisions to revisit the facts in *Interstate Circuit.* It challenges the notion that collusion can be inferred from the actions of the parties involved in this case, and it presents a new and more consistent analysis of the relevant vertical restraints. In doing so it reinvigorates Telser's[5] explanation for resale price maintenance (RPM). Telser argues that RPM stifles price competition in order to persuade retailers, and specifically discounters, to engage in more nonprice competition.[6] Telser's explanation has been criticized in the literature because (i) there is scant empirical evidence that RPM encourages

[1] 306 U.S. 208 (1939).

[2] Lester G. Telser, Why Should Manufacturers Want Fair Trade? 3 J. Law & Econ. 86 (1960).

[3] Thomas G. Krattenmaker & Steven C. Salop, Anticompetitive Exclusion: Raising Rivals' Costs to Achieve Power over Price, 96 Yale L. J. 209 (1986).

[4] See John E. Lopatka & Andrew N. Kleit, The Mystery of *Lorain Journal* and the Quest for Foreclosure in Antitrust, 73 Texas L. Rev. 1255, 1260–61 (1995), for a literature review.

[5] Telser, *supra* note 2.

[6] Economics, law and economics, and antitrust texts generally interpret Telser's story as implying that competition forces discounters to react to RPM by supplying more services. See, for example, B. Peter Pashigian, Price Theory and Applications 497 (1995); Dennis W. Carlton & Jeffrey M. Perloff, Modern Industrial Organization 530 (1994); 8 Phillip E. Areeda, Antitrust Law 151–52 (1989); and Richard A. Posner, Economic Analysis of the Law 275 (3d ed. 1986).

discounters to supply more services, (ii) manufacturers have no assurance that by stopping price competition they can get discounters to provide the specific point-of-sale services that manufacturers want, and (iii) discounters may enjoy the high margins that RPM creates without providing any additional services.[7]

To many of his critics, Telser's difficulties derive not from his intuitive free-rider story but rather from his description of how RPM bolsters services at discount outlets. In contrast, the model described here shows that when retailers are heterogeneous, a few retailers (FRTs in the case of *Interstate Circuit*) may have a comparative advantage at providing most of the promotional effort for all of the manufacturer's outlets. In this case, RPM serves not to force less efficient outlets (SRTs) to supply effort that they are not well positioned to provide but rather to prevent them from appropriating the quasi rents of the nondiscount outlets that do provide that effort. The result is that nondiscount outlets provide more promotional effort. Thus, higher prices at SRTs encouraged Interstate Circuit to promote films more aggressively, for the simple reason that it was better able to generate and appropriate the returns from such promotions. The model shows that Telser's free-rider argument stands on its own, with or without the prediction that discounters provide more services. This model is thus immune to the criticisms leveled at Telser's original story.

Section II describes of the motion picture industry and explains the importance of *Interstate Circuit* in the law and economics of antitrust. It then outlines the explicit and implicit assumptions in the theory of the case. Section III reviews the firms at issue and the legal history of the case. Section IV analyzes the underlying assumptions of the anticompetitive theories of *Interstate Circuit* and compares them to the facts of the case. Given that these theories do not explain Interstate Circuit's actions, Section V proposes an economic model to explain the relevant behavior. Section VI discusses the broader implications of our model in the context of the ongoing debate over vertical restraints. A conclusion follows.

II. Background

This section sketches out some institutional detail behind the *Interstate Circuit* case.

A. *Motion Picture Distribution and Exhibition*

From its outset, the film industry was concentrated and vertically integrated. By 1931, the five largest producer-distributors (Paramount, Fox, Warner Brothers, Loew's, and Radio-Keith-Orpheum) controlled 2,371 theaters, only about one-eighth of the total nationwide but the great majority of first-run theaters in large cities.[8] Paramount alone controlled 971 theaters. In many cities, one or two theater

[7] Perhaps the most pointed criticism in the economics literature comes from Benjamin Klein & Kevin M. Murphy, Vertical Restraints as Contract Enforcement Mechanisms, 31 J. Law & Econ. 265 (1988).

[8] Michael Conant, Antitrust in the Motion Picture Industry: Economic and Legal Analysis 26 (1960).

"circuits" monopolized the first-run exhibition market. Individual producer-distributors also dominated particular geographic regions, so, for example, Loew's controlled many circuits in the eastern United States, while Fox was strong in the Midwest.[9] Reciprocal "swap-booking" rights were established, giving one producer-distributor access in cities where it had monopoly affiliates in exchange for similar access in other areas.[10]

This high concentration was at least partly due to scale economies. On one level, large theaters operated at a lower cost per seat than small ones, especially in first-run venues requiring up-to-date facilities. More important, theater circuits with many films and outlets of varying sizes and locations allocated capacity more efficiently than a lone independent theater with only a few films. Circuits continuously updated demand forecasts, refreshed their offerings, determined opportunity costs, and then matched films with the optimal venues. The process yielded relatively high and efficient capacity utilization.[11]

Advertising economies derived from similar considerations. The cost of a metropolitan newspaper or radio advertisement was the same whether the exhibitor showed a film at several local theaters or only one. Large circuits negotiated for more favorable advertising rates, and they reallocated advertising dollars quickly as demand changed, focusing resources where advertising had the most impact. As the discussion in Section V makes clear, regular showings of feature films, downtown showcase theaters, trailers, and other promotional efforts leveraged all-important word of mouth to maximum effect and created large positive externalities for a circuit's many outlets.

Distributors earned revenues by charging theaters rental fees. In first-run exhibition, producer-distributors often indexed these fees to ticket revenues, while fixed rental fees were more typical in second-run exhibition. A film's life cycle resembled many other low-marginal-cost products that depreciate quickly. To maximize revenues, distributors established exclusive zones and "clearances" between runs so that films were not exhibited in cheap theaters too soon after showing in FRTs. Michael Conant[12] explains:

> The objective of the distributor in the establishment of the run, clearance, and zoning schedules is to maximize total revenue from all screenings. The division of the total local market for a film over time and over space into numerous submarkets allows the charging of different admission prices for each run of a film. Highest admission prices can be

[9] *Id.* at 51.

[10] Ralph Cassady, Jr., Some Economic Aspects of Motion Picture Production and Marketing, 6 J. Bus. 121 (1933).

[11] Conant, *supra* note 8, at 154–77, offers a detailed description of the geographic and temporal aspects of exhibition in Chicago. From 1920 to 1946, this market was monopolized by a Paramount subsidiary, Balaban and Katz Corporation, which operated a highly sophisticated 11-run system of release. In each run the circuit had venues of different sizes. For example, in the "Loop First Run," a film could be exhibited at any one of nine different downtown theaters, ranging in size from 980 to 3,852 seats.

[12] *Id.* at 59.

charged on first and early runs because a segment of the public prefers to view films immediately or soon after release. Large-scale advertising, both national and local, is designed to increase this preference.

. . . In general, the higher the admission price in any run, the longer the clearance necessary to cause people to attend the run and not wait for some later run with lower admission. Likewise, the larger the zone of protection from a rival showing of the same film, the more patrons will attend that run in the protected theater. There is thus a complex interdependence between run, clearance, zone, and admission price.

This view was the norm among industry experts.[13] All else equal, FRT exhibitors wanted long clearances, for example, while SRTs wanted to set lower prices than would maximize joint revenues. Industry experts recognized the legitimate use of runs, clearances, zones, and RPM to mediate these conflicts and thereby extract maximum total revenue from each film. Yet there was also a strong undercurrent of opinion that restraints could be abused. These sentiments heightened when producer-distributors acted "against" independent theater owners at the behest of a local FRT monopoly, as was the case in *Interstate Circuit.*

This potential dual purpose for RPM lies at the heart of this article. Did RPM serve primarily to enable producer-distributors to form a horizontal cartel to maximize total industry profits, or did it instead facilitate collusion vertically among different runs, thereby maximizing individual producer-distributor profits film by film? Of course, the purposes are not mutually exclusive. Our thesis is that these restraints played a significant role in mediating competition vertically among different runs and that they also helped to elicit promotional effort, which was critical to the success of any film. The effect was to increase the amount, quality, and impact of promotional effort for each film.

B. The Legacy of Interstate Circuit

Interstate Circuit has come to stand for two important propositions in antitrust law. The first proposition revolves around the legal rule by which collusion can be inferred. In his seminal article on collusive agreements, Donald Turner[14]

[13] The most important films first appeared in downtown showcase theaters or other "A" venues before moving to outlying "B" FRTs (where other films began) and then to subsequent runs. *Id.* at 154–77. Daniel Bertrand, The Motion Picture Industry: A Pattern of Control 40 (1941), and others detailed well-established patterns of zones and clearances and described the need for ticket prices to fall gradually from one run to the next so that subsequent-run theaters did not erode the larger revenues available from earlier runs. Even critics of the "excessive vertical restraints" acknowledged their legitimate uses. Statements such as that of Simon N. Whitney, Antitrust Policies and the Motion Picture Industry, in The American Movie Industry: The Business of Motion Pictures 168 (Gorham Kindem ed. 1982) are typical: "[T]he small exhibitor himself usually concedes that a reasonable clearance is justified to protect the larger investment made in first-run theaters. If the big theaters closed, and all patrons paid only 'neighborhood' prices, there would be insufficient revenue to induce production of expensive features of the sort that draw well at the box office." As another example, Cassady, *supra* note 10, devoted his article to allegedly anticompetitive industry practices but never mentions minimum ticket prices.

[14] Donald Turner, The Definition of Agreement under the Sherman Act: Conscious Parallelism and Refusals to Deal, 75 Harv. L. Rev. 655 (1962). A discussion of Turner's piece appears in John E. Lopatka, Solving the Oligopoly Problem: Turner's Try, 41 Antitrust Bull. 843 (1997).

TABLE 1

PAYOFFS TO DISTRIBUTORS

INDIVIDUAL PRODUCER-DISTRIBUTOR	INTERSTATE CIRCUIT	
	Deal	Boycott
Comply	1, 2	0, X
Deal	2, 1	0, X

focuses on *Interstate Circuit* to argue that collusion may be inferred whenever the actions of market participants taken together are inconsistent with those participants' individual welfare. For example, in a price-fixing cartel, given that all other firms charge supracompetitive prices, it would be profit maximizing for any one firm to lower its price. Therefore, any individual firm that does not do so must be colluding. In game-theoretic terms, collusion exists if an outcome is not a noncooperative (for example, Nash) equilibrium.

Consider the interests of any one distribution company involved in *Interstate Circuit.* Turner deduces that Interstate Circuit threatened not to deal with any distributors that did not agree to its terms. He then asserts that if all other distributors (or even a large minority) reject Interstate Circuit's demands, then it is individually rational for this one distributor to do the same. It is not in this distributor's interest to comply, and Interstate Circuit's threat is not credible. In Table 1, Interstate Circuit's payoff if the distributor complies (profit = 2) exceeds its payoff if the distributor refuses (profit = 1), and according to Turner this payoff exceeds the profits Interstate Circuit receives if it boycotts the distributor (profit = $X < 1$). Interstate Circuit's dominant strategy is to deal with the distributor, and knowing this, the individual distributor refuses to comply. Interstate Circuit must obtain films from somewhere, and so it cannot coerce distributors into imposing minimum prices on subsequent-run theaters. Because distributors would not have accepted Interstate Circuit's terms unilaterally, says Turner, we can infer collusion from their acceptance of these terms. We will suggest, however, that the value of X in Table 1 is a function of how the other distributors responded to Interstate Circuit's threats.

The second proposition arises from Krattenmaker and Salop, who use *Interstate Circuit* to underpin a theory of raising rivals' costs. According to their analysis, the distributors wished to collude to force subsequent-run theaters to raise their prices above competitive levels, but the distributors could not effectively enforce a cartel price among themselves. They therefore recruited Interstate Circuit as the "cartel ringmaster" to impose minimum prices and then to police the arrangement. With price competition ruled out, subsequent-run theaters had to resort to more costly means to attract customers. Krattenmaker and Salop describe the cartel ringmaster technique as "aptly illustrated by *Interstate Circuit.*"[15]

[15] Krattenmaker & Salop, *supra* note 3, at 238.

Other sources also find *Interstate Circuit* to be an important case. For example, William Kovacic[16] writes, "The foundation of modern judicial efforts to define the elements of a section 1 agreement can be traced from four Supreme Court decisions . . . beginning in 1939 with *Interstate Circuit v. U.S.*" As David Kaserman and John Mayo[17] describe it, "The decision in *Interstate Circuit* confirms the proposition that when a group of competitors enters into a series of similar but separate agreements with competitors or others, one can reasonably infer that the agreements resulted from collusion." Simon Whitney[18] says, "The Court's decision became the foundation for the doctrine—destined to reach prominence fifteen years later—that 'conscious parallelism of action' is illegal."

Together, the anticompetitive theories of *Interstate Circuit* make five assumptions. They are

a) that Interstate Circuit threatened not to deal with the distributors who balked at its pricing policy—required for Turner's analysis that Interstate Circuit's threat was not credible;
b) that there was sufficient business in the subsequent-run market in order for the distributors to be willing to risk alienating Interstate Circuit—required for Turner's analysis that the distributors would reject the proposed conditions because complying would cost them too much money in the second-run market;
c) that the observed response to Interstate Circuit's (alleged) threatened refusal to deal required collusion among the distributors—necessary for Turner's conclusion that collusion occurred;
d) that the distributors needed Interstate Circuit to impose and maintain minimum ticket prices in the subsequent-run market—necessary for the Kratenmaker/Salop cartel ringmaster theory; and
e) that there was no legitimate efficiency motivation for Interstate Circuit's behavior—necessary for both anticompetitive theories.

We suggest that each of these assumptions is incorrect. We discuss our rationale below.

III. The Defendants, the Plaintiff(s), and the Legal Proceedings

Interstate Circuit was the monopoly first-run movie theater in several Texas cities, including Dallas, Houston,[19] San Antonio, Forth Worth, Austin, and Gal-

[16] William E. Kovacic, The Identification and Proof of Horizontal Agreements under the Antitrust Laws, 38 Antitrust Bull. 5, 22 (1993).

[17] David Kaserman & John Mayo, Government and Business 204 (1995).

[18] Whitney, *supra* note 13, at 169.

[19] The District Court Brief for the United States to the Supreme Court [hereafter District Court Brief] indicates (at 7) that Interstate Circuit had competition for first-run showings from Metro-Goldwyn-Mayer in Houston.

veston.[20] It became the monopoly by buying up its bankrupt competitors at the height of the Depression. By 1935, Paramount had acquired a 50 percent ownership stake in Interstate Circuit.[21] Interstate Circuit charged 40 cents or more for adult admission for first-run showings after 6:00 P.M., and it also operated second- and subsequent-run theaters in all of these cities. "Numerous other persons, firms, and corporations" also operated second and subsequent-run theaters in these cities.[22] In total, Interstate Circuit had 43 theaters.[23]

In July of 1934, Interstate Circuit sent an identical letter to each of eight major movie distributors[24] saying that it would behave in a certain fashion if the distributors did not require their films to be shown at a price of at least 25 cents in subsequent-run theaters. (The letter is reprinted in the Appendix.) According to the second page of the Stipulated Facts, these eight distributors accounted for between 65 and 75 percent of the "feature picture" releases in the 1934–36 time period.[25] The distributors acceded to Interstate Circuit's letter, and the restraints were in force for the 1934–35, 1935–36, and 1936–37 movie seasons.

The legal events began when a subsequent-run theater brought a private antitrust case against Interstate Circuit (and only Interstate Circuit), filed under Texas state law, claiming the contracts were anticompetitive. In an unpublished decision, a state district court refused to issue a temporary injunction against the contracts. An appeals court decision dated August 6, 1935, *Glass v. Hoblitzelle*[26] upheld the initial decision. The U.S. Justice Department then sued both Interstate Circuit and the eight distributors, in a petition dated December 15, 1936, and won an injunction against the contracts at issue in a September 25, 1937, decision. The defendants appealed to the Supreme Court. (Under the Expediting Act, the appeal went straight from the district court to the Supreme Court.)

Initially, on April 25, 1938, the Supreme Court remanded the case back to the district court on Equity Rule 70½, asking for a statement of facts from the court.[27] The district court then recounted the facts it had found, consistent with its original decision. In a decision dated February 13, 1939, the Supreme Court voted 6–3 to uphold the decision finding Interstate Circuit and the distributors

[20] Texas Consolidated, an affiliate of Interstate Circuit and the monopoly FRT in several smaller Texas cities, was also named as a defendant in the suit.

[21] See *Variety*, February 29, 1936, at 6. We are unable to determine the exact time of the acquisition.

[22] 20 F. Supp. 868, 870.

[23] District Court Brief, at 7.

[24] The eight distributors were Columbia, Twentieth Century Fox, Metro-Goldwyn-Mayer, Paramount, RKO, United Artists, Universal, and Vitigraph.

[25] The number of release by firm/year are listed in Stipulated Facts at 3. Individual pictures released by distributor are listed in the appendix to the Stipulated Facts.

[26] 83 S.W.2d 796 (Tex. Civ. App. 1935). R. Z. Glass was the owner of the second-run theater that was the plaintiff.

[27] Equity Rule 70½ required a formal statement of facts from the district court. Justices Stone and Black dissented, arguing that there was sufficient information in the decision to allow for appellate review, while Justice Cardozo did not participate.

liable for conspiracy, even though there was no direct evidence that any conspiracy took place.

IV. Analyzing the Assumptions behind *Interstate Circuit*

In this section, we analyze, one by one, the five key assumptions behind the anticompetitive theories of *Interstate Circuit.*

A. *What Was Interstate Circuit's Threat?*

The first legacy of *Interstate Circuit* is that we can infer collusion among distributors, because otherwise individual distributors (acting in their own best interests) would have insisted that subsequent-run theaters be allowed to charge lower prices. This argument presumes that Interstate Circuit, acting alone, did not have the leverage to compel distributors to impose a minimum price. Its threat to terminate uncooperative distributors has been deemed not credible and, thus, insufficient to induce compliance.

Yet Interstate Circuit undoubtedly had various threats available to it that fell short of terminating distributors outright. Among other options, it could have moved uncooperative distributors' films to less desirable first-run theaters, altered show times, curtailed promotional effort, or lowered its own first-run price. Turner's argument makes sense, therefore, only if these alternative threats were also not credible or if they did not impose potential costs on distributors that warranted them giving up whatever benefits they derived from allowing subsequent-run theaters to charge low prices.

On the assumption that Interstate Circuit employed its most effective threat, it therefore makes sense to revisit the communications it had with its distributors. We believe outside analysts have misunderstood the exact nature of Interstate Circuit's threat. Interstate Circuit sent a brief letter to the distributors on April 25, 1934. It sent a more detailed letter on July 11, 1934, in which it threatened to change Interstate Circuit's policies if the individual distributors did not require subsequent-run theaters to charge at least 25 cents for showing feature films. The traditional interpretation of that threat[28] is that Interstate Circuit would refuse to deal with any distributor that allowed subsequent-run theaters to charge less than 25 cents. Along these lines, the original Justice Department petition to the district court stated that the threat was that if the distributors did not agree to the terms, "the exhibitor defendants would purchase no more product from said distributor defendants."

Yet much evidence suggests otherwise. The district court decision[29] states that Interstate Circuit threatened that it "would no longer attempt to maintain a night adult admission price of 40 cents or more" unless the distributors required that the subsequent-run movie houses charged at least 25 cents for admission. In its

[28] See, for example, Turner *supra* note 14, at 696.

[29] 20 F. Supp. 868, 871.

brief to the Supreme Court,[30] the Justice Department, contrary to its previous position, stated that the letter implied that Interstate Circuit "would insist that any picture shown first run at an Interstate theater at an admission price of 40 cents or more must not be exhibited in subsequent runs at less than 25 cents." The state appeals court also viewed the threat this way.[31] (The Supreme Court does not characterize what Interstate Circuit's threat was.)

A natural reading of the letter in question (see the Appendix) is that Interstate Circuit threatened not to deal with any distributor that did not meet its terms.[32] A second reading, however, may suggest that the district court's interpretation was correct. In particular, the fourth paragraph of the letter reads as follows: "In the event that a distributor sees fit to sell his product to subsequent runs in violation of this request, it definitely means that we cannot negotiate for his product to be exhibited in our 'A' theaters at top admission prices." This language is more consistent with a discussion of the venue and price level than a possible refusal to deal.

In their brief to the Supreme Court, the joint appellants[33] termed the threat yet another way: "If the distributor would not agree to impose the restrictions, Interstate Circuit could not afford to play the feature pictures of that distributor in its Class 'A' theaters, at which admission prices of 40¢ and 50¢, but that it would be forced to exhibit such pictures in its lower-class first-run theaters, to which admission prices of 25¢ and 35¢ were charged, thus decreasing the first-run rentals of the distributor. The minimum film rental for its Class 'A' theaters in Dallas was $1500 [per week], for its other first-run theaters in Dallas from $150 to $400. No threat of cessation of business with any noncomplying distributor was made."

Exactly how a threat to lower admission prices would be effective was explained by Karl Hoblitzelle, Interstate Circuit's president, to the district court. The Justice Department brief to the Supreme Court[34] states, "As Hoblitzelle testified, Interstate might have met the competition by lowering admission prices in its first run theaters. This decrease in admission prices would have lowered

[30] Justice Department Brief to the Supreme Court, at 8 [hereafter Justice Department Brief].

[31] The state appeals court (83 S.W.2d 796, 797) termed the threat this way, "[t]hat appellees [Interstate Circuit] threatened said major producing and distributing companies to discontinue taking their motion picture films for exhibition unless the latter in their contracts with the owners and operators of second-run theaters, including appellant, would obligate them to charge an admission price of at least 25 cents for all pictures *for which* appellees charge on first run an admission of at least 40 cents" (emphasis added).

[32] Apparently, this 40-cent price applied only to Interstate Circuit theaters. The discussion at the end of the letter dealt with Texas Consolidated theaters in the Rio Grande Valley.

[33] Joint Brief of Interstate Circuit *et al.* to the Supreme Court [hereafter Defendants' Joint Brief]. At the Supreme Court, Interstate Circuit and the distributors filed joint briefs.

[34] Justice Department Brief, at 62.

its license fee payments, which are generally based upon a percentage of the gross."[35]

Understanding the nature of the threat is crucial to any anticompetitive theory of *Interstate Circuit*. Certainly, if Interstate Circuit threatened not to deal with distributors who did not raise their subsequent-run prices, and if it carried out this threat, then it might find itself in the costly position of not having any feature films to show. On the other hand, a threat to lower its first-run price (or to exhibit films in less desirable "B" first-run theaters) may be far more credible. Such a statement may not be a threat at all, but merely an explanation of the profit-maximizing response to competition from subsequent-run theaters charging 15 cents admission for feature films. Indeed, it was accepted wisdom in the industry that the price level between runs was effectively dictated by the length of the clearance, which suggests that Interstate Circuit was simply pointing out well-established precedents to the distributors.[36] In particular, other evidence indicates that Interstate Circuit laid down explicit rules making the clearance period a function of the second-run price.[37]

Finally, the producer-distributors threatened by Interstate Circuit were not without recourse. Just as Interstate Circuit was affiliated with Paramount, other monopoly FRT circuits around the country were affiliated with rival producer-distributors. In an industry practice called "swap booking," the major producer-distributors relied upon reciprocal exhibition rights to gain access to FRTs in cities where they had none of their own.[38] To avoid jeopardizing Paramount's access to FRTs in other cities, Interstate Circuit would presumably have wanted to restrain its threats as much as possible.

B. *Was the Subsequent-Run Business Worth the Risk to Distributors' First-Run Profits?*

Whatever threat Interstate Circuit wielded against its distributors, those distributors must have weighed the potential costs incurred if Interstate Circuit

[35] Defendants' Joint Brief, at 6, also indicates that distributor revenues were based on a percentage of gross receipts.

[36] See Conant, *supra* note 8, ch. 3. While describing exhibition in Chicago, Conant sums up by saying (at 160), "[T]he system of spatial and temporal price discrimination, such as a zone-and-run system of film releases, could maximize profits only with fixed relations between admission prices in different runs." He also outlines (at 160–63) the contractual features of minimum prices.

[37] Independent theater owner H. A. Cole later testified at a congressional hearing (Hearings before the Committee on Interstate and Foreign Commerce, House of Representatives, pursuant to S. 280, 76th Cong., 3d Sess., pt. 1, at 387 (1940); reprinted in Bertrand, *supra* note 13, at 46): "I have here the clearance schedule for the Interstate Circuit in Texas. . . . It lays down the rules they expect to have followed, regarding the clearance of their theaters. . . . If you will notice, there is a provision that a neighborhood theater in Dallas . . . which charges 25 cents, shall wait 90 days after the downtown first run, before it can get its picture. . . . If the charge is 20 cents, it must wait 120 days. So there is the place where the control of prices comes in, because if I am running the 25-cent theater and elect or choose to reduce my admission price to 20 cents, I automatically force myself back 30 days further in clearance."

[38] Cassady, *supra* note 10, at 121.

carried out its threat against the benefits of allowing subsequent-run theaters to charge low prices. Refusal to comply with Interstate Circuit's demands would make sense only if the expected profits in the subsequent-run market exceeded the expected costs of refusal to comply (that is, the probability that Interstate Circuit would carry out its threat times the loss of first-run profits). For the distributors to rebuff Interstate Circuit, the subsequent-run profits must have been sufficient to warrant the risk of losing revenues from the first-run market.

Yet first-run feature film profits likely dwarfed subsequent-run profits. The Stipulated Facts[39] indicate that 70–75 percent of distributors' revenues came from first-run showings. We suspect, however, that much of the subsequent-run license revenues came from "B" movies, newsreels, short films, and cartoons. Feature film admission revenues were much greater for first-run theaters than for subsequent runs. The Justice Department reported that Interstate Circuit gained $1,077,820 in revenue in its cities, while revenues from all other operators in those cities were $69,595, a ratio of 15 to 1.[40] The Stipulated Facts also indicate that first-run license fees ran between $1,500 and $5,000 per picture, compared to $20–$30 for subsequent runs. Distributors would have been reluctant to risk their much larger first-run profits by refusing to comply with Interstate Circuit's demands. In this context, we believe it would not be surprising if distributors cooperated with Interstate Circuit, even without conspiring among themselves.

C. Could Distributor Collusion Be Inferred from the Response to Interstate Circuit's Letter?

The Justice Department's case analysis[41] closely resembled Turner's later analysis: "[I]f substantially all the distributors agreed to impose the same restrictions, each would benefit, whereas if substantially all did not so agree, the distributors imposing restriction would lay themselves open to serious injury and damage through the loss of business and customer good will." In its memorandum to the district court after the initial Supreme Court remand, the Justice Department stated, "[I]t is obvious that none of these distributors would have dared to impose these new, unusual, and extremely unpopular restrictions without knowing that each of its fellow distributors was about to do likewise."

Even if Interstate Circuit's restrictions were new and unpopular (an issue taken up elsewhere in this article), and even if it threatened to terminate distributors that did not adopt them, there is a second overlooked equilibrium consistent with the perceived facts in the case. Consider one hypothetical distributor and assume that all other distributors accepted Interstate Circuit's terms. While Interstate Circuit might have been unwilling to terminate all eight distributors, it might

[39] Stipulated Facts, at 4.

[40] For Texas Consolidated theaters, the revenues were $594,864 to $47,928, a ratio of 12 to 1 (District Court Brief, at 8). It is unclear how the Interstate Circuit and Texas Consolidated subsequent-run theaters were included in these calculations.

[41] *Id.* at 25.

have refused to deal with one or two, since it would have had other supply sources. In the context of Table 1, this suggests that $2 > X > 1$, making a threat to terminate the lone uncooperative distributor credible. If X is indeed in this range, the equilibrium to the game is (Comply, Deal). Thus, the resulting equilibrium could be the result of unilateral actions. As the joint appellants (Interstate Circuit and the distributors together) in their Supreme Court brief[42] asserted, "[I]t would have been against the financial interest of any complying distributor to refuse Interstate Circuit's request because the income of that distributor would have been reduced if its Class "A" pictures were subsequently shown [at subsequent-run theaters] in the same city at less than 25¢ admission."

Which equilibrium is more plausible? Modern game theory points out that it is hard to predict which of multiple Nash equilibria are likely to prevail.[43] The outcome where all distributors comply with Interstate Circuit's demands may be at least intuitively more likely, however, if some distributors adopted the policy unilaterally. Certainly, the more distributors who adopted the 25-cent policy unilaterally, the more credible any threatened refusal to deal becomes.

Relevant to this question, Interstate Circuit asserted that the distributors were not especially unhappy about the policy. Interstate Circuit[44] quotes United Artists as saying, "This is what you are asking us to do. You are wrong. We are asking you to do it. That is exactly United Artists' policy. We are not going to have the very fine highly specialized pictures United Artists makes double billed at cheap prices, and we are certainly going to demand high film rentals and a greater admissions price so we can participate to a greater extent."

In addition, the distributors also argued that many of them supported the restrictions. Their appeal for error to the district court[45] asserted that four distributors (United Artists, MGM, Paramount, and Vitigraph) agreed immediately, while only one distributor (Universal) was hostile. The joint appellants' Supreme Court brief[46] asserted that United Artists already had adopted the 25-cent policy before any letter from Interstate Circuit. The Justice Department[47] indicates that Paramount agreed to the restriction even prior to the July 11 letter. The distributors' appeal for error[48] also argued that MGM had already included such restrictions in its contracts with Interstate Circuit. Thus, there is substantial reason to believe that all of the distributors adopting the 25-cent policy would have been a Nash equilibrium in response to a threatened refusal to deal.

Even if Interstate Circuit's terms were new and unpopular, do any facts favor

[42] Joint Defendant's Brief, at 46.

[43] See, for example, Eric Rasmusen, Games and Information: An Introduction to Game Theory 35–37 (1990).

[44] Interstate Circuit Statement of Facts to the District Court, at 28.

[45] *Id.* at 4.

[46] *Id.* at 15.

[47] Justice Department Brief, at 10, n.6.

[48] *Id.* at 5.

the Justice Department/Turner equilibrium? On the claim that there was a distributor conspiracy, the district court merely stated,[49] "[T]he conviction is inescapable that there was such an agreement." Yet the only evidence the court cited was that Interstate Circuit's final contracts with the eight distributors were essentially identical.[50] As discussed above, there was no direct evidence of a conspiracy. Indeed, the Justice Department asserted the reverse, that there was nothing in the record to show that a conspiracy did not take place.[51]

D. *Were Distributors Unable to Impose Minimum Ticket Prices without Interstate Circuit's Help?*

The Krattenmaker and Salop argument that Interstate Circuit helped to run a distributor cartel assumes that distributors could not have proceeded without Interstate Circuit's help. Yet under the protection of the National Industrial Recovery Act (NIRA), then in effect, the distributors had imposed minimum prices on subsequent-run theaters even before Interstate Circuit took action. As the district court Special Findings of Fact[52] stated, "Prior to the 1934–35 season, the licensing contracts of the distributor defendants generally provided for a minimum admission price of 15 cents, although in some cases the minimum was 10 cents." As the Justice Department[53] conceded, "It is true that the distributors' contracts with subsequent run exhibitors generally provided for a minimum admission price of 15 cents." Justice Stone's decision for the Supreme Court[54] stated, "The distributor appellants had generally provided in their license contracts for a min-

[49] 20 F. Supp. 868, 874.

[50] It would not be surprising for the distributors to agree on nearly identical terms whether RPM was the product of collusion or a tool for greater efficiency. This test does not distinguish between the two hypotheses. Moreover, we suspect that the nondiscriminatory treatment of the distributors may have been heavily influenced by the practice of "swap booking," discussed above.

[51] Justice Department Brief, at 18–19. The Justice Department also pointed to the failure of the managers of Interstate Circuit and the superior officials of the distributors from outside the state of Texas to testify as evidence in and of itself of a conspiracy. The Texas officials of the distributors testified that they simply sent Interstate Circuit's request to New York and made no decisions on their own. Thus, any horizontal collusion would have occurred in New York. The Supreme Court ruled, following on the district court decisions, that the failure of these officials to deny that collusion occurred could aid in establishing grounds to infer that collusion did occur. Yet the defendants contended that original district court trial did not deal with issues of distributor collusion. Instead, the trial dealt with the relationship between Interstate Circuit and the distributors: "There is no allegation that the distributor defendants agreed or conspired among themselves to enter into such agreements with the exhibitor defendants or to impose the restrictions upon subsequent run licenses." (Joint Defendants' Brief, at 20.) Indeed, the original Justice Department petition to the district court (at 9–10) speaks of a "conspiracy" between the exhibitors and the distributors, but not of any conspiracy among the distributors themselves. We are unable to locate a record of the district court proceedings and thus cannot independently verify this claim. But we see no reason to believe that the Supreme Court attempted such verification, and we know from reviewing the Supreme Court brief that the Justice Department did not directly contradict the defendants' position on this issue.

[52] District court Special Findings of Fact, at 4.

[53] Justice Department Brief, at 11–12.

[54] 306 U.S. 208, 218 (1939).

imum admission price of 10 or 15 cents, and three of them had included restricting double billing." The state appeals court[55] also noted the prior existence of price maintenance under the NIRA, and as the discussion in Section IV*C* above makes clear, at least one and possibly three distributors set 25-cent minimum prices before Interstate Circuit acted. The industry literature often mentions RPM,[56] and minimum prices were enforced in many cities. Indeed, Daniel Bertrand says, "It is the universal practice for the distributor to stipulate in each exhibition contract the minimum admission price at which films may be shown."[57]

One interpretation of these facts is that individual distributors had a unilateral interest in limiting price competition and that RPM therefore had nothing to do with collusion. The model in Section V offers two motives for such unilateral efforts: (i) individual distributors wanted to stop subsequent-run theaters from dissipating the quasi rents stemming from their differentiated products, and (ii) these distributors sought to prevent subsequent-run theaters from free riding on Interstate Circuit's promotional efforts.

On the other hand, a second possibility is that these early efforts to impose RPM merely confirm that distributors had tried but failed to establish an effective distributor cartel on their own. Distributors may have had modest success, but they needed Interstate Circuit's help to raise minimum prices to the joint profit-maximizing level of 25 cents. Yet even if we accept this version of events, the tenor of the arguments changes. Individual distributors were clearly not opposed to minimum prices, and Interstate Circuit did not have the difficult assignment of raising prices from a competitive level to the cartel price. What then is required is an explanation of why Interstate Circuit would act to create market power upstream, thus generating the potential of a double marginalization problem.

E. Were There Any Efficiencies from Interstate Circuit's Behavior?

The preceding discussion highlights four flaws in the argument that collusion could be inferred from the actions the distributors took in Interstate Circuit. Given this, if these vertical restraints did not stem from collusion among distributors, then what was Interstate Circuit's motive? To address this question, consider a related query raised in Justice Robert's dissent: why did Interstate Circuit engage in the behavior that it did, when it could have easily, and legally, harmed the subsequent-run theaters much more effectively? Interstate Circuit negotiated how long the subsequent-run theaters would have to wait to show the first-run film, the "clearance" period, and as Justice Roberts indicated, Interstate

[55] 83 S.W.2d 796, 802.

[56] For example, Conant, *supra* note 8, at 162–63.

[57] Bertrand, *supra* note 13, at 41.

Circuit could have insisted upon longer clearances without provoking an antitrust challenge.[58]

Why were (and are) clearances used in this industry? The answer is simple. A theater owner requires the exclusive right to a property for a certain period of time to prevent lower-priced subsequent-run operators (or today, distributors of videocassettes) from free riding on the FRT's promotional effort. As the joint appellants put it to the Supreme Court,[59]

> The success of Interstate Circuit and of each of the distributor defendants necessarily depends upon successful first run exhibition. The success of first run exhibition in turn depends not merely upon the quality of the picture shown, but upon the attractiveness, comfort, and seating of the theater in which it is shown. . . . This is particularly true when the first run theater not only pays fifty times the rental on each picture but shows it on a single bill for a whole week and spends approximately $1000 a week on advertising which redounds to the benefit of the subsequent run exhibitors, who have practically no advertising costs.

The state appeals court decision also highlights the importance of advertising. The court indicated that FRTs on average spent $600 per week on advertising. The court also stated, "[A]pellant [the subsequent-run theater operator, Glass] conceded that he would reap a material benefit from the advertisement given a picture by class A theaters that was subsequently exhibited by him."[60]

Moreover, for our purposes promotional effort encompasses far more than advertising monies. Through their investments in modern facilities, showcase theaters, and high-quality equipment, and by their scheduling of feature films, FRTs' promotional efforts were critical to the success of any picture. Theatergoers could not easily judge the quality of any picture beforehand, and so they relied heavily on trailers, radio and newspaper advertisements, and especially word of mouth. A primary responsibility for theater circuits was to keep films moving appropriately through successive runs to take full advantage of the films' ephemeral commercial potential. Large first-run venues ensured that popular films would have adequate seating at the outset, while smaller neighborhood FRTs provided an outlet for the films immediately thereafter. Thus, promotional effort should be interpreted to include the generation of valuable word of mouth.

Section V offers a simple model explaining both how a minimum resale price protected Interstate Circuit's investments in promotional effort and why it was superior to a longer clearance period.

[58] The state appeals court (83 S.W.2d 796, 797) indicated that Interstate Circuit's contracts included a clearance clause prohibiting films from being shown in subsequent-run theaters until 75 days after they had been shown in first-run theaters. The Justice Department (Justice Department Brief, at 58–59) indicated that the typical clearance period was 45 days, though United Artists had 75 days.

[59] Joint Defendants' Brief, at 9–10.

[60] 83 S.W.2d 796, 799–800.

V. Efficiencies from Vertical Arrangements

In this section we present an efficiency argument for Interstate Circuit's behavior. Telser and Benjamin Klein and Kevin Murphy,[61] among others, argue that vertical restraints such as those that occurred in *Interstate Circuit* may arise because of externalities between firms. In *Interstate Circuit*, the case record shows that SRTs were free riding on the promotional efforts of the FRT. The contracts Interstate Circuit signed with the distributors may have eased this problem.[62] This section presents an economic model explaining how these contracts could have alleviated the free-rider problem. The section also discusses why the contracts used may have been more efficient than alternative, legal contractual forms.

A. *The Model*

A new film is exhibited for two periods ($t = 1, 2$). During the first period, the film shows at a monopoly first-run theater. During the second, it shows at a monopoly second-run theater.[63] Marginal costs are zero. Demand at the FRT is given by $Q_1 = Q_1(P, S, e, t)$, where Q_1 is the number of tickets sold at the FRT, P is the FRT's price, S is the SRT's price, e is first-period promotional effort measured in dollars expended, and t is the time that elapses between the first and second periods (the "clearance period"). Assume that $\partial Q_1/\partial P < 0$, $\partial Q_1/\partial S > 0$, $\partial Q_1/\partial e > 0$, and $\partial Q_1/\partial t > 0$. In words, the FRT sells more tickets when it lowers its own price, when the SRT raises its price, when promotional effort increases, or when the clearance period is extended. Let $R_1(P, S, e, t) = PQ_1$ denote the FRT's revenues.

Demand at the SRT is given by $Q_2 = Q_2(P, S, e, t)$, where Q_2 is the number of tickets sold by the SRT, and $\partial Q_2/\partial P > 0$, $\partial Q_2/\partial S < 0$, $\partial Q_2/\partial e < 0$, and $\partial Q_2/\partial t < 0$.[64] The SRT sells more tickets when it lowers its own price, when the FRT raises its price, when the FRT's effort increases, or when the clearance period is reduced. Second-period effort is set without loss of generality to zero, because the FRT has a strong comparative advantage at promotion. (Note that second-period effort could be introduced without altering the model's results.) Intuitively, this advantage arises because first-period promotional effort increases demand in both periods and because first-period customers themselves

[61] Telser, *supra* note 2; Klein & Murphy, *supra* note 7.

[62] Consistent with this, the district court noted (20 F. Supp. at 872) "that a cheap second or subsequent run destroys the earning capacity of the first run house, and therefore interferes with the return to the film producer." Similarly, defendants (Joint Defendants' Brief, at 11) said that "cheap subsequent runs price admissions and double featuring of Class A pictures were destroying Interstate Circuit's first run earning capacity."

[63] Here the second-run theater market is treated as a monopoly for modeling convenience. If this market were modeled competitively (as was actually the case), then price competition would lead to even deeper discounts in the SRT market than is reflected in the results that follow.

[64] To ensure a unique interior solution to the maximization problem, we need some straightforward assumptions about cross-partial derivatives for Q_1 and Q_2. These are left unstated here.

promote the film to second-period customers through word-of-mouth recommendations. Let $R_2(P, S, e, t) = SQ_2$ denote the SRT's revenues.

B. *The Benchmark*

As a benchmark, consider the joint profit-maximizing choice of these variables. Let F_1 and F_2 denote the fixed rental fees paid by the FRT and the SRT, respectively, to the film's owner.[65] The two theaters' combined profits are denoted by Π, where

$$\Pi = R_1(P, S, e, t) + R_2(P, S, e, t) - e - F_1 - F_2. \quad (1)$$

Taking the first-order conditions for each of the decision variables gives the following results:

$$\partial\Pi/\partial P = \partial R_1/\partial P + \partial R_2/\partial P = 0, \quad (2a)$$

$$\partial\Pi/\partial S = \partial R_1/\partial S + \partial R_2/\partial S = 0, \quad (2b)$$

$$\partial\Pi/\partial e = \partial R_1/\partial e + \partial R_2/\partial e - 1 = 0, \quad (2c)$$

and

$$\partial\Pi/\partial t = \partial R_1/\partial t + \partial R_2/\partial t = 0. \quad (2d)$$

In equations (2a), (2b), and (2d) there is a trade-off between the interests of the two venues. When the first-order conditions are met, lowering P or increasing t raises revenues at the FRT but at the expense of reduced revenues for the SRT, and increasing S benefits the SRT but hurts the FRT. The first-order conditions indicate that joint profits are maximized when these variables adjust such that on the margin the benefits to one venue exactly offset the harm done to the other. Finally, equation (2c) indicates that promotional expenditures should be set such that on the margin one additional dollar of promotion generates one additional dollar of total revenue at the two outlets. Denote the joint profit-maximizing values for these four variables as P^*, S^*, e^*, and t^*, and let $\Pi^* = R_1(P^*, S^*, e^*, t^*) + R_2(P^*, S^*, e^*, t^*) - e^* - F_1 - F_2$.

C. *Independently Owned and Operated Theaters*

The interests of the two independent theater owners do not align with these joint profit-maximizing outcomes. The FRT's and SRT's profits, respectively, are

[65] In practice, FRT rental fees were indexed to revenues, which implies that $F_1 = F_0 + \lambda R_1$, where $\lambda < 1$ is the producer-distributor's fractional share. This specification aggravates the basic problem, since the FRT pays for all effort, suffers free riding from the SRT, and keeps only a fraction $1 - \lambda$ of the remaining incremental revenues. To focus solely on SRT free riding, we use a fixed rental fee for both venues.

$$\Pi_1 = R_1(P, S, e, t) - e - F_1, \tag{3a}$$

and

$$\Pi_2 = R_2(P, S, e, t) - F_2. \tag{3b}$$

Assume for now that the distributor sets $t = t^*$, ensuring that the clearance period is no obstacle to the joint profit-maximizing outcome. Assume, as well, that the equilibrium is Nash. Then the FRT sets P and e to satisfy the following first-order conditions:

$$\partial\Pi_1/\partial P = \partial R_1/\partial P = 0, \tag{4a}$$

and

$$\partial\Pi_1/\partial e = \partial R_1/\partial e - 1 = 0. \tag{4b}$$

Similarly, the SRT chooses S to satisfy

$$\partial\Pi_2/\partial S = \partial R_2/\partial S = 0. \tag{4c}$$

Comparing equations (3a) and (3b) and equations (4a), (4b), and (4c) reveals that rivalry between the two theaters dissipates quasi rents. Each theater sets its price without regard to the other's revenues. Comparing equation (4b) to (2c) also reveals that the FRT ignores the positive externality its promotional effort creates for the SRT, and consequently it spends too little promoting the film. Resale price maintenance mitigates this conflict.

In particular, low prices at the SRT aggravate the promotional externality whenever $\partial^2 R_1/\partial e\, \partial S > 0$. In words, the FRT's returns to effort fall whenever the SRT lowers its price. By promoting the film more, the FRT may persuade more people to see the film, but if the SRT's price is low, the FRT never sees these customers. They flock to the SRT instead. If the FRT anticipates this prospect, it balks at promotion and demand falls. What might be a relatively modest promotional externality when prices are set at joint profit-maximizing levels becomes more serious once the SRT discounts its price to lure away the FRT's customers.

Consider a numerical example.[66] Holding the clearance fixed, suppose $Q_F = 48.75 + .25(eS)^{1/2} - P$. Thus, by construction, demand is linear in the FRT's own price and changes in either promotional effort or the SRT's price shift demand. Moreover, the terms e and S interact: a change in S alters the marginal benefit to the FRT from more effort. (Formally, $\partial(\partial R_1/\partial e)/\partial S > 0$.) The FRT's first-order conditions are

$$\partial\Pi_1/\partial P = 48.75 + .25(eS)^{1/2} - 2P = 0$$

and

[66] To make this example resemble the facts in *Interstate Circuit*, assume that A is denominated in dollars, P in cents, and Q_F in hundreds of tickets.

$$\partial\Pi/\partial e = .125P(e)^{-1/2}(S)^{1/2} - 1 = 0.$$

If the SRT sets its price $S = 25$, then the FRT maximizes profits by setting $P = 40$ and $e = 625$. In this case, $Q = 40$ and FRT profits equal 975 (before subtracting the rental fee). On the other hand, if the SRT sets its price $S = 15$, then the FRT maximizes profits by setting P equal to 32 and e equal to 238. In this case, $Q = 32$ and profits equal 776. Intuitively, if the SRT lowers its price from $S = 25$ to $S = 15$, it shifts the FRT's demand curve in toward the origin (as customers defect to the SRT) and reduces the FRT's promotional incentives.

This example shows how the FRT reacts to the SRT's lower price. The FRT reduces its reliance on promotional effort as a means to lure customers to its theater (effort falls by more than half) and instead focuses on price (which drops from 40 to 32). The reason is that while such effort may persuade consumers to see the film, many of those who are persuaded go to the SRT, lured by the low price there. In this context, Interstate Circuit's "threat" to lower the first-run price below 40 cents is entirely logical.

The film's owner can reduce this free-rider problem by imposing minimum prices on both the FRT and the SRT of $P = P^*$ and $S = S^*$, respectively. By doing so it can both encourage the FRT to put forth more effort and prevent quasi rent–dissipating price competition between the venues. Having also set $t = t^*$, the distributor is then free to focus on the residual problems it may face with the aforementioned promotional externality (for example, through co-operative advertising allowances or other subsidies). The film's owner has the incentive to take these actions because higher theater profits translate into higher rental fees.

Of course, there is no reason the film's owner must take the initiative in imposing the restraint. The impetus for minimum prices could come from the FRT. The point is that these actions are unilateral in any sense related to antitrust policy—the film's owner and the FRT have independent incentives to push for minimum prices whether or not they receive the support of an organized distributor cartel.

D. *How Does Retail Price Maintenance Affect Ticket Prices and Consumer Welfare?*

This numerical example illustrates the ambiguous welfare effects of the vertical restraints modeled here. Holding the clearance fixed, a reduction in the SRT's price shifts the FRT's focus toward price and away from promotional effort. In equilibrium, consumers pay less but have less reliable information on each film. In practice, of course, the clearance is not fixed, and if minimum prices are foreclosed, the most obvious alternative is a longer clearance period, as Justice Roberts suggested in his dissent. If SRTs charge low ticket prices, a distributor can extend t beyond t^*,[67] thereby reducing the quasi rent–dissipating price competition between the venues and the free riding by the SRT on the FRT's promotional effort. Yet by construction, joint profits fall short of Π^*. Assuming that the film's owner and the FRT each bear some repercussions, it follows that both prefer minimum ticket prices to longer clearance, and given the ephemeral commercial value of individual films, minimum ticket prices appear to be a more efficient means to segment markets.

If distributors are intent on protecting the much larger first-run market, as it is reasonable to suspect, then long clearance periods would also negate much of the competitive impact of lower prices at SRTs. Thus, FRTs would have no cause to lower their prices markedly. Second-run theaters would charge less, but their patrons would have to wait longer to see films. The change in quality-adjusted price is ambiguous.

E. *The Aftermath of Antitrust Intervention in the Motion Picture Industry*

What happened after the Supreme Court affirmed the decision in *Interstate Circuit*? Unfortunately, this was just one of many antitrust cases in the film industry during this period, and it is clear that most distributors continued imposing minimum ticket prices through the early 1940s. Moreover, the United States entered into World War II within 2 years of the decision, and television became commercially viable shortly after the war. As such, isolating the effects of this one case in any convincing way would be very difficult.

Having said this, though, there is an experiment some years later that sheds much light on the import of these restraints. In 1942, a private independent theater owner on Chicago's South Side filed suit against Balaban and Katz, the Paramount-affiliated monopoly first-run theater circuit in Chicago, along with another exhibitor, RKO Pictures, and the five major producer-distributors.[68] The suit alleged that defendants conspired to maintain a rigid system of exhibition (known nationwide as "the Chicago system of release"), that they used an illegal minimum price-fixing scheme, and that they discriminated unlawfully against the independent theater by refusing to allow it to bid or to negotiate for an earlier playing position than it had been granted. The jury decided for the plaintiff. The damage award was overturned on appeal but was ultimately affirmed by the Supreme Court. In late 1947, the defendants were enjoined from imposing clearances of any length between downtown (Loop) first-run and subsequent-run theaters (or extending the first run), and they were prohibited from setting minimum prices on subsequent runs. These stipulations, along with the aftershocks of the *Paramount* case,[69] ended the Chicago system of release. They also elim-

[67] Interstate Circuit demoted discounters' films to B theaters, which effectively adjusted the clearance.

[68] Bigelow v. RKO Pictures, 150 F. 2d 877 (C.C.A. 7, 1945), rev'd, 327 U.S. 251 (1946).

[69] United States v. Paramount Pictures, 334 U.S. 131 (1948).

inated any protection for Balaban and Katz or the distributors from discounting in subsequent runs.

The events that followed[70] illustrate the importance of the vertical restraints described here:

> The result . . . was a much faster play-off of films through the city's theaters. By 1950, instead of two theaters, one north and one south, playing any single picture on first neighborhood run, as under the old Chicago system of release, Paramount now released to 16. Instead of 4 to 6 theaters showing the picture on second neighborhood run, . . . Paramount now had as many as 30. Each of the other distributors established similar zoning plans. . . . Consequently, most pictures had completed their runs in five to seven weeks instead of the seventeen or more required under the old system. Advertising, especially word-of-mouth advertising, had much less time to be effective. This accelerated the drop in admissions that was due primarily to the rivalry of television.

Balaban and Katz often petitioned the court to relax these measures, arguing specifically, as Conant reports, that "such quick run-off . . . prevented exhibitors from receiving the full benefit of advertising, especially word-of-mouth advertising of early run patrons."[71] While consumers may have paid less during first runs (we do not know how first-run prices changed), they had fewer opportunities to see films in later runs (at lower prices) and had less reliable word-of-mouth information.

VI. Generalizing the Model

In our model, if producer-distributors can impose minimum prices, then some customers frequent the high-price/high-quality FRT and others patronize the low-price/low-quality SRT. Minimum prices do not eliminate price differences between outlets. On the contrary, SRTs depend upon discounts to attract customers who want lower prices and are willing to suffer lower quality in return. Our explanation predicts that minimum prices institutionalize modest price differences between the distribution channels.

This is a distinguishing feature of our explanation. Historically, the literature has assumed that manufacturers set their price floors so high that they eliminate all, or nearly all, price differentials across outlets. The objective in doing so is to create cartel profits or to shift retailers' focus to no-price competition. Robert Pitofsky, for example, says definitively, "The one point that emerges clearly in any debate concerning the *per se* rule is that minimum vertical price agreements lead to higher, and usually uniform, resale prices."[72] In restating his own special services story, Telser says that after RPM is adopted, "[o]ne retailer cannot free load on another, and each obtains an incentive to supply the special services

[70] As described by Conant, *supra* note 8, at 169.

[71] *Id.* at 174.

[72] Robert Pitofsky, In Defense of Discounters: The No-Frills Case for a *Per Se* Rule against Vertical Price Fixing, 71 Geo. Law J. 1487, 1488 (1983).

jointly with the physical product because only in this way can they sell the product."[73] This statement clearly presumes that RPM wipes out price differentials between retailers.

In this context, relatively low price floors would be difficult to reconcile with many of the pro- and anticompetitive explanations for RPM. If full-service stores charge one dollar for a particular branded item, while discounters charge 70 cents, and if the manufacturer then imposes a minimum resale price of 75 cents, what are we to conclude? If this is either an attempt to collude or a method to compel discounters to compete aggressively on point-of-sale services, it would seem a feeble effort.

We do not aspire in this short space to test our hypothesis rigorously, but we believe it worthwhile to make the point that this is not a settled empirical issue. Unfortunately, any attempt to resolve the question is complicated by the fact that RPM is presently per se illegal. As such, our only modern data on RPM arise out of antitrust litigation.[74] Such data are likely biased, because litigation is most likely in instances where manufacturers force discounters to raise their resale prices markedly. Potential litigants are less apt to notice or care if manufacturers impose low price floors. It may be easy to overlook the manufacturer that discreetly imposes a 75 cent minimum price on discounters that previously charged 70 cents; it is harder to miss a manufacturer that forces them to charge one dollar.

What is needed is evidence from a time and place where manufacturers could impose RPM without fear of prosecution. Fortunately, the same economic forces in the 1930s that enabled film producers to impose minimum ticket prices on second-run theaters also contributed to the "fair trade" movement that allowed manufacturers to set minimum resale prices on their drugstore brands. In the late 1930s, 42 states passed such fair-trade laws. These laws, together with the Miller-Tydings Act of 1937, empowered manufacturers to impose minimum prices. Many exploited the opportunity to do so.

H. J. Ostlund and C. R. Vickland[75] compiled an extraordinary but heretofore neglected data set examining the impact of fair trade. These authors conducted a nationwide survey of leading items in retail drugstores in 1939. They focused on those "well-known, fast-selling, trade-marked items which had been placed under fair trade contracts—items of the type frequently advertised at cut prices." They included only items that were under fair-trade contracts in all 42 fair-trade states, and they omitted some brands because of data collection difficulties. They sent report forms to all drugstores in fair-trade states except those in Alabama. The response rates among all but the smallest stores exceeded 30 percent.

[73] Lester G. Telser, Why Should Manufacturers Want Fair Trade II? 33 J. Law & Econ. 409, 410 (1990).

[74] As in Pauline M. Ippolito, Resale Price Maintenance: Empirical Evidence from Litigation, 34 J. Law & Econ. 263 (1991).

[75] H. J. Ostlund & C. R. Vickland, Fair Trade and the Retail Drug Store (1940).

Ostlund and Vickland's data show that chain stores often (but not always) charged significantly less than independent drugstores and that manufacturers routinely set low minimum resale prices. In six of 50 cases, manufacturers actually set their minimum prices below the average chain store price. In an additional 14 cases, manufacturers used their minimum prices to close less than one-fourth of the gap between the average prices of the two respective types of drugstores.[76] There were only three instances where manufacturers set their minimum resale prices above the average independent drugstore price and only 10 cases total where manufacturers closed even one-half of this price gap.

One product examined, Lady Esther Face Cream, offers a vivid example. Independent stores on average charged 49.9–51.1 cents for this brand (depending upon store size), while chain stores averaged 36 cents. When given the opportunity to impose a minimum price, the manufacturer chose 39 cents. It is clear that this price floor neither created a cartel nor forced chain stores to engage in substantial incremental service competition. It left in place the dual distribution channel, with one clientele getting high service levels at independent drugstores while the other clientele got lower prices but fewer amenities at the chain stores. Moreover, some manufacturers enforced their minimum prices very selectively.

This evidence corroborates the hypothesis that manufacturers wanted to accommodate different types of outlets serving different clienteles. As long as they could use zoning and RPM to keep the markets separate, there is no reason to infer that they were unhappy with the chain stores' low service levels.[77]

Our model generalizes beyond drugstores. Indeed, ephemeral goods such as fashion apparel provide an even closer fit with our story. We have in mind dealers who play a promotional and capacity management role resembling Interstate Circuit's. Just as movie chains must select portfolios of films, apparel retailers must forecast which products customers will prefer and in what combinations and quantities. They then manage their offerings, with prospective blockbuster items exhibited in the choicest "showcase" spots within their stores at the outset and then rotated to less visible space as demand tapers off, lowering prices gradually over the 6 weeks to 2 months that any given item is displayed. Retailers exploit positive externalities within their stores: when one product is displayed well, it generates higher sales for the items around it. Full-service retailers' efforts

[76] Ostlund and Vickland, *id.*, report average prices for five categories of independent drug stores, based on annual revenues. The calculations here use stores with annual sales between $10,000 and $20,000 (which seem to account for the greatest annual revenues) as a benchmark, but the conclusions would not change if other categories were used instead. Independent stores with annual sales exceeding $50,000 had slightly lower prices and would yield modestly different results, but they were few in number.

[77] We do not dismiss the possibility that there were multiple motives for RPM. Consider Lanteen, with an independent store average price of 83.4–83.8 cents and an average chain price of 80.2 cents. Once could argue that the 79-cent minimum price might have served only to shift deep discounters' focus toward service competition. But this argument effectively concedes our point: there was no intent to force the remaining chain stores to stop discounting below the independent store price or to force deep discounters to match the services offered at independent drugstores.

to sell specific items also increase demand for the same brands at discount outlets. Discounters offer low prices and low quality; they benefit from full-service stores' promotions but provide few of their own; and as long as they do not lower their prices too much or too quickly, their discounts have little adverse impact on full-service retailers. The manufacturer earns maximum profit from having two distribution channels coexisting, and by subsidizing full-service stores' effort, it ensures that this effort is joint profit maximizing. The manufacturer wants only to exercise control over the timing and extent of discounts. Relatively low price floors serve this purpose.

This insight—that price floors need not be high to have their desired effect—actually turns popular RPM anticompetitive arguments on their heads. William Comanor argues that RPM forces many customers to pay for point-of-sale services that they do not want: "Furthermore, there remains the inherent problem with vertical restraints that all distributors will sell at the same final price, so that there are not benefits in the form of increased sales from reducing distribution costs. Consumers are not provided with the choice between high-priced, high-quality-conscious outlets and low-priced, less imposing distribution facilities."[78] Pitofsky[79] and others make similar claims, all of which presume that manufacturers always use RPM to create uniform resale prices and homogeneous services. Yet in our framework the motivation for RPM is precisely the opposite! The manufacturer's objective is to provide incentives for full-service outlets (rather than discounters) to put forth additional effort. Resale price maintenance serves this purpose. Its effect is to increase the difference in point-of-sale services offered by the two retailer types. Customers can then buy the product with or without these services, as they see fit. Moreover, while resale price differences may narrow when RPM is introduced (if full-service retailers raise their resale prices by less than discounters do), they are not eliminated.

Furthermore, in our model, the discounter has low costs precisely because it is inefficient. It is excused from supplying promotional effort because such effort has little impact on demand. By the time films reach subsequent-run theaters, there is typically only limited commercial potential left to promote. Each dollar spent by FRTs on promotional effort has far greater impact, and so it makes sense for FRTs to bear the promotional burden, presumably in return for lower rental fees, advertising subsidies, or other remuneration from producer-distributors. Without RPM, though, SRTs might be forced to undertake more of their own promotions (because longer clearances diminish the impact of the FRT's promotional effort), shifting this activity from the efficient FRT to the relatively inefficient SRT. Prohibiting RPM can thus actually force discounters to provide too much promotional effort and incur higher costs.

It is also worth noting that in our model the manufacturer has few other options

[78] William S. Comanor, Vertical Arrangements and Antitrust Analysis, 62 N.Y.U. L. Rev. 1153, 1159 (1987).

[79] Pitofsky, *supra* note 72.

for remedying its free-rider problems. It cannot contract with the discounter to provide additional promotional effort, because that is not the goal, and absent RPM, it has no cause to subsidize the full-service outlet's effort. As long as the discounter uses low prices to lure away a large fraction of the customers this promotional effort generates, the manufacturer has no more incentive than the full-service retailer to pay for this effort. In short, the problem is that the discounter's price is too low and has nothing to do with its lack of promotional effort. Those who advocate keeping RPM per se illegal often assert that there are alternative means to solve Telser-style free-rider problems. In our model, this is not the case.

VII. Conclusions

Interstate Circuit has left an important legacy in antitrust law and economics. A review of the case, however, reveals that the crucial assumptions behind this legacy are flawed. First, Interstate Circuit did not threaten to terminate uncooperative distributors. Its contract provisions were not new, unusual, or unpopular. Second, distributors made relatively small sums in the subsequent-run market, making it implausible that they would have opposed Interstate Circuit's efforts to raise minimum subsequent-run prices. Third, the behavior of the distributors can be described as a Nash equilibrium, and therefore it is inappropriate to infer collusive behavior from it. Fourth, distributors routinely imposed minimum ticket prices unilaterally, before Interstate Circuit took action. Finally, the pricing restraint on second-run theaters could have acted both to foreclose quasi rent–dissipating price competition and to protect investments in promotional effort from free riders.

While it is possible that Interstate Circuit was motivated more by a unilateral interest in foreclosing rivalry from subsequent-run theaters than any concern over free riding, we think this unlikely. Had this been Interstate Circuit's primary objective, it could have taken a more direct, effective, and legally defensible approach by insisting on a longer clearance period, as Justice Roberts's dissent implies.

In broader terms, we can use our analysis to examine the legacy of *Interstate Circuit* with respect to the definition of collusion and to our understanding of the empirical importance of "raising rivals' costs." With respect to the definition of collusion, it is certainly true that non-Nash behavior is a necessary condition for deducing collusion. But this article shows that deducing collusive behavior requires both an understanding of the relevant game and an understanding of all possible Nash equilibria.

Finally, we propose a variation on Telser's seminal free-rider story that is immune from the usual criticisms. Here the goal of RPM is neither to establish a uniform resale price across all outlets nor to compel discounters to supply additional point-of-sale services. The objective is simply to prevent discounters from luring away customers that full-service outlets have worked hard to cultivate. Using Depression-era data, we show that manufacturers often set relatively low price floors. These manufacturers were determined only to limit, rather than extinguish, discounting. By narrowing (but not eliminating) the differential between discounters' and full-service stores' resale prices, manufacturers provide incentives for full-service stores to increase services. Thus, in contrast to the claims of Comanor, RPM can act to increase, rather than decrease, product differentiation and customer choice across outlets.

We suggest that these lessons have great relevance for contemporary antitrust policy. Indeed, the fact situation and inference of collusion in *Interstate Circuit* is remarkably similar to that of a prominent contemporary matter, *Toys "R" Us*,[80] where the Federal Trade Commission (FTC) relied heavily on *Interstate Circuit* in its opinion. In this matter, each of eight major toy producers entered into exclusive dealing arrangements with the retailer Toys "R" Us, upon the assumption that the other producers had agreed to exclusive dealing. The FTC found this interdependency sufficient to determine that horizontal collusion had occurred. But by the analysis above, given that the other major manufacturers had agreed to exclusive dealing, it would be in an individual producer's interest also to agree and protect its access to Toys "R" Us. No horizontal collusion is required for this outcome.

With respect to raising rivals' costs, Krattenmaker and Salop cite several major antitrust cases to support their theory. Of these cases, only *Interstate Circuit* has not previously been rebutted. With this article, therefore, this last remaining case is shown not to apply. On the contrary, by insisting upon minimum prices on subsequent-run theaters, Interstate Circuit held itself out as willing to provide more promotional effort that benefited subsequent-run theaters. There is no indication that subsequent-run theaters suffered higher advertising costs or had to undertake any other costly measures after minimum prices were imposed.

APPENDIX

Letter from Interstate Circuit to the Eight Movie Distributors

July 11, 1934

Messrs.: J. B. Dugger, Herbert MacIntyre, Sol Sachs, C. E. Hilgers, Leroy Bickel, J. B. Underwood, E. S. Olsmyth, Doak Roberts.

GENTLEMEN: On April 25th, the writer notified you that in purchasing product for the coming season 34–35, it would be necessary for all distributors to take into consideration in the sale of subsequent runs that Interstate Circuit, Inc., will not agree to purchase produce to be exhibited in its "A" theaters at a price of 40¢ or more for night admission, unless distributors agree that in selling their product to subsequent runs, that this "A" product will never be exhibited at any other time or in any other theater at a smaller admission price than 25¢ for adults in the evening.

In addition to this pricing restriction, we also request that on "A" pictures which are

[80] Toys "R" Us v. F.T.C., 221 F.3d 928 (7th Cir. 2000).

exhibited at a night admission price of 40¢ or more—they shall never be exhibited in conjunction with another feature picture under the so-called policy of double-features.

At this time the writer desires to again remind you of these restrictions due to the fact that there may be some delay in consummating all our feature film deals for the coming season, and it is imperative that in your negotiations that you afford us this clearance.

In the event that a distributor sees fit to sell his product to subsequent runs in violation of this request, it definitely means that we cannot negotiate for his product to be exhibited in our "A" theaters at top admission prices.

We naturally, in purchasing subsequent runs from the distributors in certain of our cities, must necessarily eliminate double featuring and maintain the maximum 25¢ admission price, which we are willing to do.

Right at this time the writer wishes to call your attention to the Rio Grande Valley situation. We must insist that all pictures exhibited in our "A" theaters at a maximum night admission price of 35¢ must also be restricted to subsequent runs in the Valley at 25¢. Regardless of the number of days which may intervene, we feel that in exploiting and selling the distributors' product, that subsequent runs should be restricted to at least a 25¢ admission scale.

The writer will appreciate your acknowledging your complete understanding of this letter.

R. J. O'Donell
General Manager
Interstate Circuit Theaters and Texas Consolidated Theaters

Bibliography

Areeda, Phillip E. *Antitrust Law.* Vol. 8. Boston: Little, Brown & Company, 1989.

Bertrand, Daniel. *The Motion Picture Industry: A Pattern of Control.* Washington, D.C.: U.S. Government Printing Office, 1941.

Carlton, Dennis W., and Perloff, Jeffrey M. *Modern Industrial Organization.* 2d ed. New York: Addison-Wesley, 1994.

Cassady, Ralph, Jr. "Some Economic Aspects of Motion Picture Production and Marketing." *Journal of Business* 6 (1933): 113–31.

Comanor, William S. "Vertical Arrangements and Antitrust Analysis." *New York University Law Review* 62 (1987): 1153–65.

Conant, Michael. *Antitrust in the Motion Picture Industry: Economic and Legal Analysis.* Berkeley: University of California Press, 1960.

Ippolito, Pauline M. "Resale Price Maintenance: Empirical Evidence from Litigation." *Journal of Law and Economics* 34 (1991): 263–301.

Kaserman, David, and Mayo, John. *Government and Business.* New York: Dryden, 1995.

Klein, Benjamin, and Murphy, Kevin M. "Vertical Restraints as Contract Enforcement Mechanisms." *Journal of Law and Economics* 31 (1988): 265–97.

Kovacic, William E. "The Identification and Proof of Horizontal Agreements under the Antitrust Laws." *Antitrust Bulletin* 37 (1993): 5–81.

Krattenmaker, Thomas G., and Salop, Steven C. "Anticompetitive Exclusion:

Raising Rivals' Costs to Achieve Power over Price." *Yale Law Journal* 96 (1986): 209–93.

Lopatka, John E. "Solving the Oligopoly Problem: Turner's Try." *Antitrust Bulletin* 41 (1997): 843–908.

Lopatka, John E., and Kleit, Andrew N. "The Mystery of *Lorain Journal* and the Quest for Foreclosure in Antitrust." *Texas Law Review* 73 (1995): 1255–1306.

Ostlund, H. J., and Vickland, C. R. *Fair Trade and the Retail Drug Store.* Minneapolis: Druggists' Research Bureau, 1940.

Pashigian, B. Peter. *Price Theory and Applications.* New York: McGraw-Hill, 1995.

Pitofsky, Robert. "In Defense of Discounters: The No-Frills Case for a *Per Se* Rule against Vertical Price Fixing." *Georgetown Law Journal* 71 (1983): 1487–95.

Posner, Richard A. *Economic Analysis of the Law.* 3d ed. Boston: Little, Brown & Company, 1986.

Rasmusen, Eric. *Games and Information: An Introduction to Game Theory.* Cambridge, Mass.: Basil Blackwell, 1990.

Telser, Lester G. "Why Should Manufacturers Want Fair Trade?" *Journal of Law and Economics* 3 (1960): 86–105.

Telser, Lester G. "Why Should Manufacturers Want Fair Trade II?" *Journal of Law and Economics* 33 (1990): 409–17.

Turner, Donald F. "The Definition of Agreement under the Sherman Act: Conscious Parallelism and Refusals to Deal." *Harvard Law Review* 75 (1962): 655–743.

Whitney, Simon N. "Antitrust Policies and the Motion Picture Industry," In *The American Movie Industry: The Business of Motion Pictures,* edited by Gorham Kindem, pp. 168–92. Carbondale: Southern Illinois University Press, 1982.

Part VII
Network Externalities

[23]

Network Externalities, Competition, and Compatibility

By MICHAEL L. KATZ AND CARL SHAPIRO*

There are many products for which the utility that a user derives from consumption of the good increases with the number of other agents consuming the good. There are several possible sources of these positive consumption externalities.[1]

1) The consumption externalities may be generated through a direct physical effect of the number of purchasers on the quality of the product. The utility that a consumer derives from purchasing a telephone, for example, clearly depends on the number of other households or businesses that have joined the telephone network. These network externalities are present for other communications technologies as well, including Telex, data networks, and over-the-phone facsimilie equipment.

2) There may be indirect effects that give rise to consumption externalities. For example, an agent purchasing a personal computer will be concerned with the number of other agents purchasing similar hardware because the amount and variety of software that will be supplied for use with a given computer will be an increasing function of the number of hardware units that have been sold. This hardware-software paradigm also applies to video games, video players and recorders, and phonograph equipment.

3) Positive consumption externalities arise for a durable good when the quality and availability of postpurchase service for the good depend on the experience and size of the service network, which may in turn vary with the number of units of the good that have been sold. In the automobile market, for example, foreign manufacturers' sales initially were retarded by consumers' awareness of the less experienced and thinner service networks that existed for new or less popular brands.

In all of these cases, the utility that a given user derives from the good depends upon the number of other users who are in the same "network" as is he or she. The scope of the network that gives rise to the consumption externalities will vary across markets. In some cases, such as the automobile example, the sales of only one firm will constitute the relevant network. In other cases, the relevant network will comprise the outputs of all firms producing the good. For example, the number of stereo phonographs of any one brand is not a determinant of the supply of records that a consumer can play on his or her stereo. In still other markets, the network may comprise the products of a coalition of firms that is a subset of the entire market, as in the case of computers, where some groups of manufacturers adopt common operating systems.

The central feature of the market that determines the scope of the relevant network is whether the products of different firms may be used together. For communications networks, the question is one of whether consumers using one firm's facilities can contact consumers who subscribe to the services of other firms. If two firms' systems are interlinked, or compatible, then the aggregate number of subscribers to the two systems constitutes the appropriate network. If the systems are incompatible, such as Telex and cable, then the size of an individual

*Department of Economics and Woodrow Wilson School, respectively, Princeton University, Princeton, NJ 08544. We thank the anonymous referees for helpful suggestions. We also thank seminar participants at Princeton, Columbia, Queens, the Federal Trade Commission, and MIT for comments. This material is based upon work supported by the National Science Foundation under grants nos. SES-820942 and SES-82-07377.

[1] In addition to the sources of consumption externalities mentioned in this paper, there are a number of more subtle ones. These include: (*i*) the fact that product information is more easily available for more popular brands; (*ii*) the role of market share as a signal of product quality; and (*iii*) purely psychological, bandwagon effects.

system is the proper network measure for users of that system.

Similarly, for hardware-software markets, the issue is whether software produced for use on one brand of hardware may be run on another brand of hardware. If two brands of hardware can use the same software, then the hardware brands are said to be compatible. The relevant network is the set of users who have compatible brands of hardware. In the personal computer market, the CPM operating system has been designed to allow several brands of computers to use common programs. In the case of quadraphonic audio discs, on the other hand, the records made for one type of player cannot be used on a player that uses a different quadraphonic technology. Here, unlike the case of stereos, the relevant network for a given brand of equipment comprises the set of brands that use the same technology, not the entire market.

For the durables example, the relevant network is the set of brands that require the same parts of servicing skills. If a particular model of automobile has customized parts or requires specialized repair skills, then an owner of the model will find a thinner, and probably more expensive, service system. This smaller network will reduce his or her initial willingness to pay for the model.

Despite the significance of markets in which network externalities are present, relatively little work has been done in this area. The analysis done so far has been set in a monopoly context and has focussed on communications networks. Shmuel Oren and Stephen Smith (1981) is a recent reference to this literature. As the examples above make clear, it is important to extend the study of network externalities to an oligopolistic setting.

In this paper, we develop a simple, static model of oligopoly to analyze markets in which consumption externalities are present. We examine two basic sets of issues. First, we study the effect of consumption externalities on competition and the form of the market equilibrium. When network externalities exist, consumers must form expectations regarding the size of competing networks. We use a notion of rational, or fulfilled expectations, equilibrium. Our basic findings are that consumption externalities give rise to demand-side economies of scale, which will vary with consumer expectations. As a result, multiple fulfilled expectations equilibria may exist for a given set of cost and utility functions. For some sets of expectations only one firm will produce output, while for other sets of expectations there will be several firms in the market. These equilibria verify the following intuition: if consumers expect a seller to be dominant, then consumers will be willing to pay more for the firm's product, and it will, in fact, be dominant.

The second area that we explore is the compatibility decision. Typically, firms can choose whether to manufacture compatible products, and thus can determine whether individual firm or aggregate market sales are the relevant ones in the evaluation of the consumption externalities. An important question, therefore, is whether firms will have proper incentives to produce compatible goods or services.

Gerald Brock (1975) and Robert Kurdle (1975) have done interesting case studies of compatibility decisions in the U.S. mainframe computer and farm machinery industries, respectively. Neither, however, develops a model of equilibrium in which to analyze firms' compatibility incentives. Using our model, we compare the private and social incentives to produce compatible products. We find that firms with good reputations or large existing networks will tend to be against compatibility, even when welfare is increased by the move to compatibility. In contrast, firms with small networks or weak reputations will tend to favor product compatibility, even in some cases where the social costs of compatibility outweigh the benefits. Viewing firms as a collective decision maker, we find that in our model the firms' joint incentives for product compatibility are lower than the social incentives.

The paper is organized as follows. In Section I, we present the model and define the equilibrium concept. The set of market equilibria is characterized in Section II. We examine the private and social incentives for compatibility in Section III, primarily under the assumptions that all of the costs of compatibility are fixed. There is a brief summary of our results and a discussion of the relevance of these results for public policy in Section IV. We outline an alternative approach to the formation of consumer expectations in the Appendix. It is shown that the equilibria are qualitatively similar if the firms are able to commit to given network sizes before consumers make their purchase decisions.

I. A Formal Model of Network Competition

A. *Consumers*

We look at a partial equilibrium oligopoly model in which there are no income effects and consumers act to maximize their surplus. A consumer buys at most one brand and purchases either one or no unit of any given brand.

The surplus that a consumer derives from buying a unit of the good depends on the number of other agents who join the network associated with that product. When the good is durable, an individual's consumption benefits will depend on the future size of the relevant network. Consumers will base their purchase decisions on *expected* network sizes. To capture this important feature of many markets with network externalities in our static, one-period model, we assume that consumers must make their purchase decisions before the actual network sizes are known. The timing is as follows. First, consumers form expectations about the size of the network with which each firm is associated. Second, the firms play an output game, taking consumers expectations as given. This game generates a set of prices. Consumers then make their purchase decisions by comparing their reservation prices (based on expected network sizes) with the prices set by the n firms, $i=1,\dots,n$.

We do not explicitly model the process through which consumers' expectations are formed. We will, however, impose the requirement that in equilibrium consumers' expectations are fulfilled. Let x_i^e denote the number of customers that a consumer expects firm i to have, and let y_i^e be the consumer's prediction of the size of the network with which firm i is associated. All consumers are assumed to have identical expectations of network sizes. When the brands are incompatible, each makes up its own network so $y_i^e = x_i^e$. When m firms' products are compatible, say brands 1 through m, then there is a single network for these brands and

$$y_i^e = \sum_{j=1}^{m} x_j^e \qquad \text{for } i=1,2,\dots,m.$$

Networks are assumed to be homogeneous in the sense that if two networks are of equal size, then all consumers view the two networks as perfect substitutes.

Consumers are assumed to be heterogeneous in their basic willingness to pay for the product, but homogeneous in their valuations of the network externality. Specifically, a consumer of type r has a willingness to pay $r + v(y^e)$ for a product with expected network size y^e. Without further loss of generality we can normalize r and $v(0)$ so that $v(0)=0$. We can interpret r as the consumer's basic willingness to pay for the good and $v(y)$ as the value he or she attaches to the consumption externality when the number of subscribers is y. The externality function is taken to be twice continuously differentiable, with $v'>0$, $v''<0$, and $\lim v'(y)=0$ as $y \to \infty$. The basic willingness to pay for the good, r, varies across consumers and is assumed to be uniformly distributed between minus infinity and A with density one.[2] We assume that A is positive.

Each agent purchases the brand that maximizes his or her surplus. Letting p_i denote the price charged for brand i, a consumer of type r chooses the brand for which

$$(1) \qquad r + v(y_i^e) - p_i$$

[2] The uniform density assumption amounts to assuming a linear demand curve for the product. We assume that the support of r has no finite lower limit in order to avoid having to consider corner solutions, where all consumers enter the market.

is largest. If (1) is negative for all i, then a type r consumer stays out of the market and purchases none of the brands.

B. *Firms*

Given the homogeneity of the products, two firms i and j will both have positive sales only if

$$(2) \qquad p_i - v(y_i^e) = p_j - v(y_j^e),$$

where $p_i - v(y_i^e)$ is the expected hedonic price of brand i, that is, the price adjusted for the network size. Equation (2) says that the hedonic prices must be equal when multiple firms have positive sales. Let ϕ denote the common value of the hedonic prices given in equation (2).

For a given value of ϕ, only those consumers for whom $r \geq \phi$ enter the market. Given the uniform distribution of r, there are $A - \phi$ such consumers. Thus, if the firms sell a total of $z \equiv \Sigma_{i=1}^n x_i$ units, then prices must be set such that $A - \phi = z$, or

$$(3) \qquad A + v(y_i^e) - p_i = z \qquad \text{for all } i \text{ such that } x_i > 0.$$

From equation (3) we see that firm i receives a price of

$$(4) \qquad p_i = A + v(y_i^e) - z.$$

The price that firm i receives depends on the expected size of its network, y_i^e, and on the total unit sales of the n firms, z.

There are two types of costs that must be modeled. First, there are costs of production. We assume that production costs are the same for all firms and that these costs take the form of a fixed cost, G, plus a constant per unit variable cost, g. That is, the cost to firm i of producing x units of output is $G + gx$. As long as the fixed costs are smaller than the firm's equilibrium revenues minus variable costs, the fixed costs have no effect on the equilibrium. To simplify the exposition, we assume that the fixed costs of production are equal to zero. Without loss of generality, we also take the variable costs of production to be equal to zero. Assuming that g is equal to zero is equivalent to redefining r to be the excess of the consumer's basic willingness to pay for the good over the constant per unit cost.[3]

There is a second type of cost that we must consider, the cost of the achieving compatibility. For most of the analysis we will assume that the costs of compatibility are fixed costs, that is, are independent of scale. This amounts to assuming that compatible products have the same marginal production costs as incompatible products. (We discuss the consequences of relaxing this assumption of Section III, Part D). The fixed cost of compatibility that we analyze could include costs of developing and designing a compatible product, the costs of negotiating to select a standard, and the costs of introducing a new, compatible product. Let F_i denote the fixed costs of compatibility incurred by firm i. Note that F_i need not be the same for all firms.

If all of the networks are incompatible, then $y_i^e = x_i^e$, and firm i earns profits equal to

$$(5) \qquad \pi_i = x_i(A - z + v(x_i^e))$$

when it has sales of x_i and total output is z.

When all n products are compatible, $y_i^e = \Sigma_{j=1}^n x_j^e \equiv z^e$, for all i. Therefore, when total output is z and firm i has sales of x_i, the firm's gross profits are

$$(6) \qquad \pi_i = x_i(A - z + v(z^e)),$$

from which we must subtract F_i to get profits net of the fixed costs of compatibility.

C. *Fulfilled Expectations Equilibrium*

Our equilibrium concept is that of fulfilled expectations Cournot equilibrium, where each firm chooses its output level under the assumptions that: (a) consumers' expecta-

[3] It is for this reason that negative values of r make sense; the redefined variable r measures the excess of a consumer's basic willingness to pay over the marginal production costs of an additional unit.

tions about the sizes of the networks, $(y_1^e, y_2^e, \ldots, y_n^e)$, are given; and (b) the actual output level of the other firms, $\Sigma_{j \neq i} x_j \equiv x_{-i}$, is fixed.

Assumption (b) is the standard Cournot assumption. For any fixed set of consumer expectations, the problem is equivalent to the standard linear demand Cournot model with constant marginal costs. Assumption (a) is relaxed in the Appendix, which considers the case in which the y_i^es are formed *after* the firms have selected their output levels. Differentiating equation (5) and rearranging terms, the first-order conditions $d\pi_i/dx_i = 0$ imply that the equilibrium sales levels $(x_1^*, x_2^*, \ldots, x_n^*)$ must satisfy

$$(7) \qquad x_i^* = A + v(y_i^e) - \sum_{j=1}^{n} x_j^* \qquad \text{for } i = 1, 2, \ldots, n.$$

Note that the right-hand side of equation (7) equals p_i.

For any given set of expectations, we can solve equation (7) simultaneously for the x_i^*s to obtain the unique Cournot equilibrium that corresponds to that set of expectations:

$$(8) \quad x_i^* = \left\{ A + nv(y_i^e) - \sum_{j \neq i} v(y_j^e) \right\} \Big/ (n+1) \qquad \text{for } i = 1, 2, \ldots, n.$$

The outcome is just the standard linear demand Cournot equilibrium where the differences in $v(y_i^e)$ are analogous to production cost differences. Equation (8) defines a function that maps expectations $(y_1^e, y_2^e, \ldots, y_n^e)$ into Cournot equilibrium network sizes $(y_1^*, y_2^*, \ldots, y_n^*)$ for a given pattern of compatibility. Let $\Gamma(y^e)$ denote this function.

In the absence of rationality constraints on consumer expectations, there is a Cournot equilibrium for any set of expectations. But for most sets of expectations, the expectations will not be fulfilled in the corresponding Cournot equilibrium; the actual network sizes are not equal to the expected ones. Although it is possible that (in the short run, at least) consumers could be mistaken about network sizes, it is useful to limit the set of possible equilibria by imposing the restriction that expected sales be equal to actual sales in equilibrium. Formally, our equilibrium notion is that of Fulfilled Expectations Cournot Equilibrium (*FECE*), where a *FECE* is an n-vector of network sizes $y^* = (y_1^*, y_2^*, \ldots, y_n^*)$, such that $y^* = \Gamma(y^*)$. If consumers expect the network sizes to be y^*, then in the corresponding Cournot equilibrium the network sizes will indeed equal y^*; consumers' expectations will be fulfilled.

D. *Welfare Formulae*

Given the cost and demand assumptions that we have made, profits and welfare can be written as functions of the firms' individual levels of output. By equation (7), in equilibrium, firm i's output level is equal to the price that firm receives. Thus, the ith firm's profits in equilibrium are $\pi_i = (x_i^*)^2$. We will denote aggregate profits by $\pi \equiv \pi_1 + \ldots + \pi_n$.

The surplus that a consumer derives from joining a network depends on the *actual* size of the network; in equilibrium, the actual size will equal that network's *expected* size. By equations (1) and (3), when market output is z, a type r consumer expects to derive surplus of $r + z - A$ from joining a network. Only those consumers for whom r is greater than $A - z$ join a network; the other consumers stay out of the market and derive no surplus. Integrating over all consumers who do enter the market, we obtain consumers' expected surplus

$$(9) \quad S(z) = \int_{A-z}^{A} (\rho + z - A)\, d\rho = z^2/2.$$

In any fulfilled expectations equilibrium, expected and actual consumers' surplus will be equal, and we can use equation (9) when discussing actual consumers' surplus.

We take the sum of producers' and consumers' surplus as our social welfare measure. Hence, in any fulfilled expectations

Cournot equilibrium, welfare (gross of the fixed costs of compatibility) is given by

$$(10) \quad W(x_1,\dots,x_n) = \pi(x_1,\dots,x_n) + S(x_1+\dots+x_n) = \sum_{i=1}^{n} x_i^2 + z^2/2.$$

II. The Characterization of Equilibria

In this section, we examine the structure of fulfilled expectations equilibria for compatible and incompatible products, respectively.

A. *Complete Compatibility*

Suppose that any two products are compatible with one another. Then there is a single network of expected size $z^e = \Sigma_{i=1}^{n} x_i^e$, and for all i, $y_i^e = z^e$. Equation (8) becomes

$$(11) \quad x_i^* = (A + v(z^e))/(n+1) \quad \text{for } i = 1,2,\dots,n.$$

If we impose the fulfilled expectations requirement that $z^e = x_1^* + \dots + x_n^*$ and sum equation (11) over all i, we obtain

$$(12) \quad z^c = (n/(n+1))(A + v(z^c)),$$

where z^c denotes the fulfilled expectations equilibrium value of total output when the products are compatible. Under our assumptions on $v(\cdot)$, equation (12) has a unique solution, as is clear from Figure 1. This unique compatible-products equilibrium is symmetric: $x_i^c = z_i^c/n$ for all i. We have shown:

PROPOSITION 1: *When all products are mutually compatible, there is a unique FECE. It is symmetric, and the aggregate level of output is given implicitly by equation* (12).

As the number of firms becomes increasingly large, the compatibility equilibrium converges to the perfectly competitive equilibrium; z^c approaches $A + v(z^c)$, and the hedonic price, $A + v(z^c) - z^c$, approaches the marginal cost level of zero.

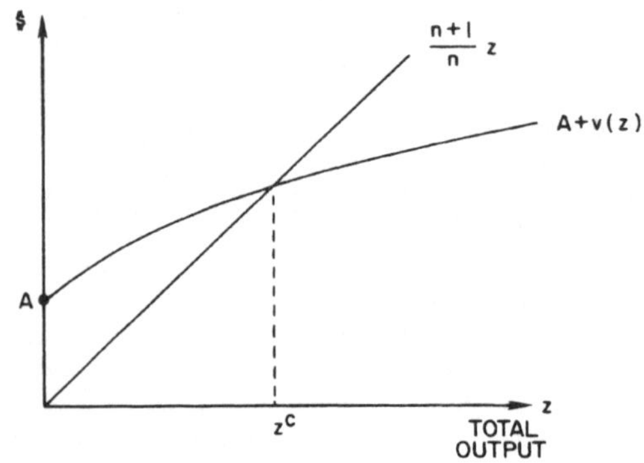

FIGURE 1. EQUILIBRIUM WITH COMPLETE COMPATIBILITY

B. *Complete Incompatibility*

Now we consider the case where any two brands are incompatible with one another so that $y_i^e = x_i^e$. In equilibrium, each firm i is optimizing given the actions of the other firms, x_j, $j \neq i$, and consumers' expectations, x_i^e. Using equation (7) in conjunction with the fulfilled expectations condition $x_i = x_i^e$, we have $x_i = A + v(x_i) - z$, or

$$(13) \quad \sum_{j \neq i} x_j = A + v(x_i) - 2x_i \quad \text{for } i = 1,2,\dots,n.$$

For a given value of x_{-i}, equation (13) can be solved for x_i. The graph of equation (13) is called firm i's *equilibrium reaction correspondence*. One possible shape of this correspondence is illustrated in Figure 2.[4]

The equilibrium reaction correspondence should not be confused with a standard reaction function. The latter merely states firm i's best response to the other firms, given consumer expectations. There will be a different reaction function for each set of expectations. The equilibrium reaction corre-

[4]It is also possible that firm i's reaction schedule is strictly downward sloping. This will occur if and only if $v'(0) < 2$.

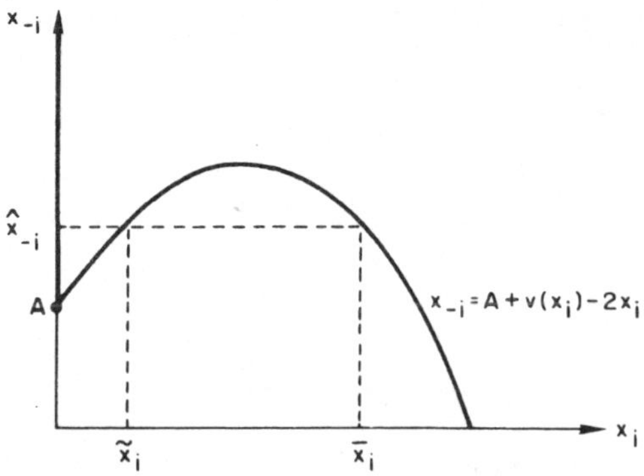

FIGURE 2. FIRM i'S EQUILIBRIUM REACTION CORRESPONDENCE

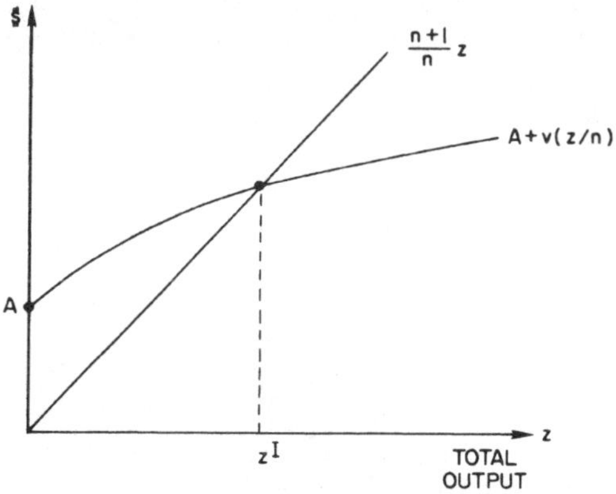

FIGURE 3. UNIQUE SYMMETRIC EQUILIBRIUM WITH COMPLETE INCOMPATIBILITY

spondence gives the set of points such that if the other firms played x_{-i} and consumers expected brand i to have a network size of x_i, then x_i would in fact be firm i's best response. Suppose the other firms set their output at $\hat{x}_{-i}$ in Figure 2. Then firm i's best response to $\hat{x}_{-i}$ would fulfill consumer expectations if these expectations were either $\tilde{x}_i$ or $\bar{x}_i$. Note that firm i treats consumer expectations as exogenous, and thus the firm does not choose between $\tilde{x}_i$ and $\bar{x}_i$.

In Figure 2, firm i's equilibrium reaction correspondence is drawn to include the x_{-i} axis for $x_{-i} > A$. This part of firm i's reaction schedule is not derived from equation (13), which only applies when $x_i > 0$. Instead it is derived from the corner condition, $d\pi_i/dx_i < 0$ at $x_i = 0$. When $x_i^e = x_i = 0$, $d\pi_i/dx_i = A - x_{-i}$, so it is optimal for firm i to set $x_i = 0$ if $x_i^e = 0$ and $x_{-i} > A$.

Having derived the firms' fulfilled expectations reaction schedules, we turn now to the characterization of equilibria. There are three types of equilibria that are possible when the networks of competing firms are incompatible: (*i*) symmetric oligopoly with n active firms; (*ii*) symmetric oligopoly with $k < n$ active firms, which we call natural oligopoly; and (*iii*) asymmetric oligopoly.

1. *Symmetric Oligopoly.*

PROPOSITION 2: *When each brand is incompatible with all* $(n-1)$ *of the other brands, there exists a unique symmetric equilibrium in which* $x_i = z^I/n$ *and aggregate sales,* z^I, *are given implicitly by*

$$(14) \quad ((n+1)/n)z^I = A + v(z^I/n).$$

PROOF:

Taking $x_i = z/n$ and adding up equation (13) for $i = 1,\ldots,n$, gives $(n-1)z = nA + nv(z/n) - 2z$. Rearranging yields equation (14), which has a unique solution, as Figure 3 illustrates.

2. *Natural Oligopoly (Not all Firms Active).* While a unique symmetric equilibrium always exists, there are asymmetric equilibria that exist for certain parameter values. Given the symmetry in the equilibrium response correspondences, such asymmetric equilibria always come in sets (where the elements of the set differ from each other only by the transposition of the firms' indices). One such type of equilibrium entails some firms exiting the market (i.e., producing no output) and the other firms behaving as oligopolists with a diminished number of competitors.

PROPOSITION 3: *A symmetric equilibrium with* k *active firms exists if and only if* $v(A/k) \geq A/k$.

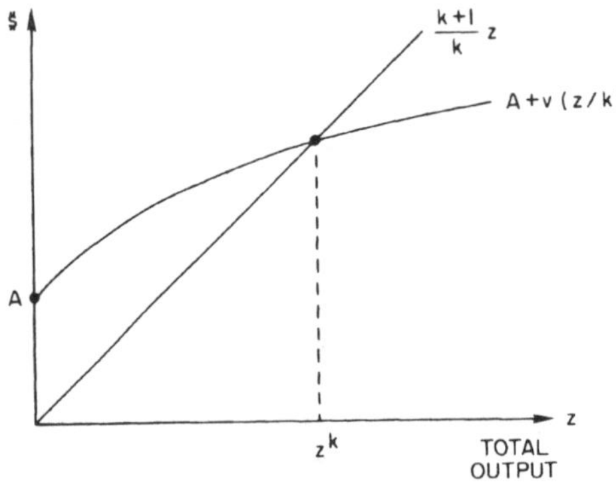

FIGURE 4. NATURAL OLIGOPOLY

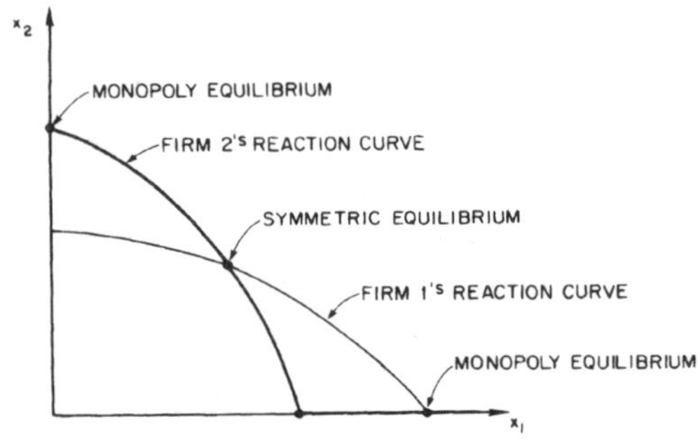

FIGURE 5. NATURAL MONOPOLY EQUILIBRIA

PROOF:

Suppose that k firms each produce $x_i = z/k$ units of output, and the remaining $n-k$ firms produce no output. Adding up equation (13) for the k active firms, we obtain $(k-1)z = kA + kv(z/k) - 2z$, or

$$((k+1)/k)z = A + v(z/k). \tag{15}$$

As Figure 4 illustrates, there will be a unique solution to equation (15). Let z^k denote this solution.

We must check that the remaining $n-k$ firms do not have incentives to produce positive output, that is, that $A + v(0) - z^k = A - z^k < 0$. Again from Figure 4, it is clear that $z^k \geq A$ iff $A + v(A/k) \geq ((k+1)/k)A$, or $v(A/k) \geq A/k$.

COROLLARY 3.1: *For any $k \leq n-1$, if a k-active-firm symmetric equilibrium exists, then a $(k+1)$-active-firm symmetric equilibrium exists.*

COROLLARY 3.2: *For any $k \leq n-1$, if a k-active-firm symmetric equilibrium exists, then $z^k < z^{k+1}$.*

Both corollaries follow from the concavity of $v(\cdot)$. Note that equilibrium with $k=1$ (the monopoly outcome) or some other low value of k is more likely to obtain when consumers' basic willingness to pay for the good is low (so that A is low) or when the network effects are strong (so that $v(A)$ is large for a given A).

Proposition 3 shows that the network externalities are similar to fixed costs in that they can lead to a limited number of active producers. The analogy between fixed costs and network externalities is not complete, however. This point is demonstrated by Corollary 3.1 and the fact that for the given set of demand conditions, an n-active-firm equilibrium exists for arbitrarily large n. In the case of fixed costs, one cannot squeeze an arbitrarily large number of active producers into the industry.

Figure 5 shows the reaction curves for a case in which a natural monopoly equilibrium exists. It is interesting to note that the monopolist's profits, may be *lower* than the profits of a duopolist in the 2-active-firms symmetric equilibrium. In other words, a monopoly may benefit from entry. This unusual result follows from the fulfilled expectations condition: a monopolist will exploit his position with high prices and consumers know this. Thus, consumers expect a smaller network and are willing to pay less for the good. If the monopolist could commit himself to higher sales he would be better off, but this commitment is not credible so long as he is the sole producer.[5]

3. *Asymmetric Oligopoly.* The third possible equilibrium configuration is one in which

[5] We consider the case where commitment is feasible in the Appendix.

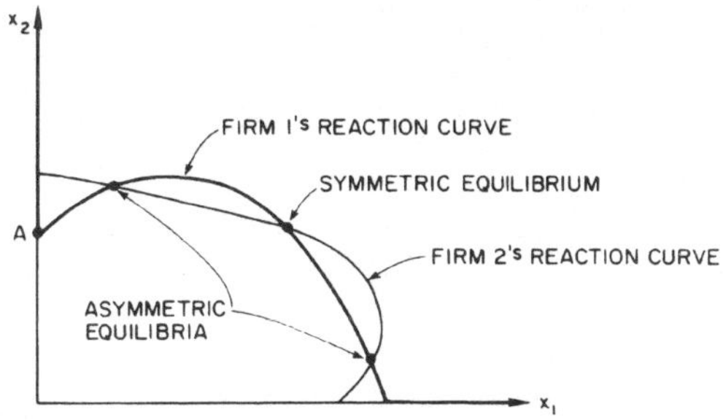

FIGURE 6. ASYMMETRIC DUOPOLY

$k \geq 2$ firms produce positive but unequal levels of output. We have constructed examples of such equilibria, although they are difficult to characterize in general. These asymmetric equilibria verify the intuition that a firm may be successful and enjoy a large market share simply because it is expected to by consumers.

One example of an asymmetric duopoly equilibrium is shown qualitatively in Figure 6. Despite a linear demand curve and a concave network valuation function $v(y)$, a variety of possibilities may arise. Figure 6 shows a situation in which asymmetric equilibria exist as well as symmetric and natural monopoly equilibria. In other cases, the only stable equilibria are asymmetric ones.

C. *Partial Compatibility*

When there are more than two firms, the extent of product compatibility may fall in between complete incompatibility and industrywide compatibility. Assuming that the compatibility relation is symmetric and transitive, the pattern of compatibility can be characterized by the set of compatibility groups, G^j $j=1,\dots,J$, where all of the brands within a given group are mutually compatible with each other and are incompatible with any nonmember brands.[6] Thus,

[6] The G^j, $j=1,\dots,J$, form a partition of the set $\{1,2,\dots,n\}$.

if firm i is in group G^j,

$$y_i = \sum_{k \in G^j} x_k \equiv y^j.$$

For a firm i in group j, the first-order condition is $x_i = A - z + v(y^j)$. Thus, all firms in a given group will choose the same level of output, x^j. Let m^j denote the number of firms in compatibility group j. Then, in equilibrium, for all $x^j > 0$ we must have

$$(16) \qquad x^j = A - z + v(m^j x^j).$$

Equation (16) has the same qualitative properties as our earlier equilibrium conditions, and similar types of equilibria will arise. Here, we will not characterize these equilibria directly. In the next subsection, however, we will compare the equilibria that obtain under different degrees of compatibility.

D. *The Output Effects of Compatibility Changes*

In analyzing compatibility, it is important to understand the effects of an increase in compatibility on the equilibrium levels of output. What happens to output levels if two compatibility groups "merge" to form a new group where all of the brands in the post-merger group are compatible with one another?

PROPOSITION 4: *The level of total output is greater under industrywide compatibility than in any equilibrium with less than complete compatibility.*

PROOF:

For all firms with positive levels of output, $x_i = A + v(y_i) - z$. Adding up over all firms and rearranging gives us $(n+1)z = nA + \Sigma v(y_i)$, as illustrated in Figure 7. Under complete compatibility, $y_i = z$ for all firms. Absent complete compatibility, $y_i < z$ for at least one firm. Thus, the curve $nA + nv(z)$ lies above $nA + \Sigma v(y_i)$ where the y_i's are

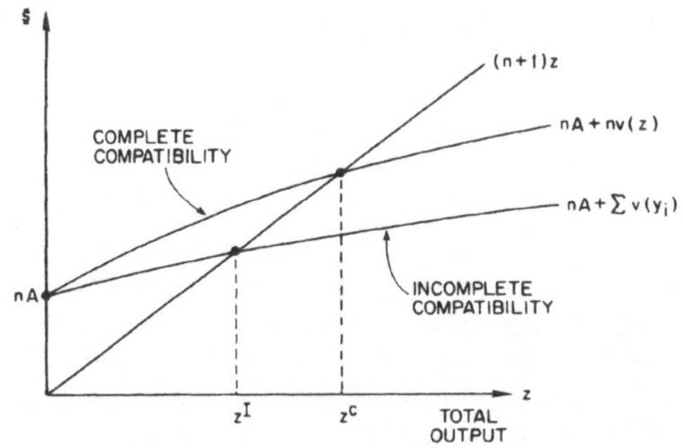

FIGURE 7. COMPLETE VS. INCOMPLETE COMPATIBILITY

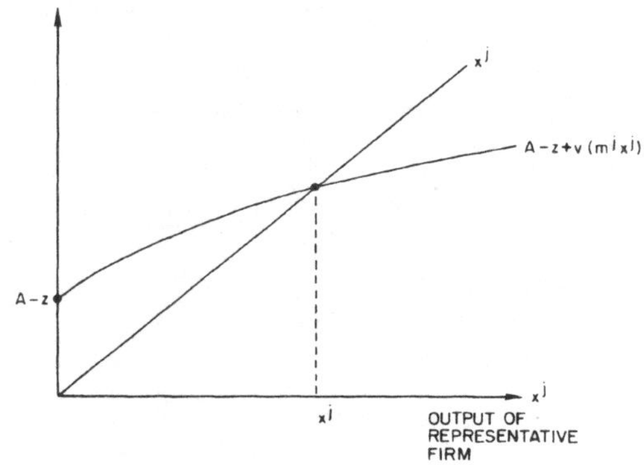

FIGURE 8. EQUILIBRIUM OUTPUT OF A FIRM IN COALITION j

determined under incomplete compatibility. Referring to Figure 7, we see that the equilibrium level of z is greater under industry-wide compatibility.

When the move to increased compatibility does not result in *complete* compatibility, total output need not rise. The following proposition, however, states a sufficient condition for industry output to increase.

PROPOSITION 5: *Suppose that two groups of firms make their products mutually compatible. If premerger total output is less than A, then in any postmerger equilibrium*: (a) *the average output of the firms in the merging coalitions will rise*; (b) *the output of any firm not in the merging coalitions will fall*; *and* (c) *industry output will rise.*

PROOF:

Let $\hat{x}^j$ denote the premerger output level of a firm in coalition j and $\hat{z}$ denote premerger total output. By equation (16), $\hat{x}^j = A - \hat{z} + v(m^j\hat{x}^j)$. Figure 8 illustrates this condition, where we have made use of the fact that industry output is less than A.

Label the compatibility groups that merge as 1 and 2. Let $\tilde{x}^j$ and $\tilde{z}$ denote the *post*-merger output levels analogous to the $\hat{x}^j$ and $\hat{z}$. If total output falls, then for $j \geq 3$, $A - \tilde{z} + v(m^jx^j)$ will lie everywhere above $A - \hat{z} + v(m^jx^j)$, and from Figure 8 we see that x^j will increase (i.e., $\tilde{x}^j > \hat{x}^j$). By similar arguments, $\tilde{z} = \hat{z}$ implies $\tilde{x}^j = \hat{x}^j$ for $j \geq 3$ and $\tilde{z} > \hat{z}$ implies $\tilde{x}^j < \hat{x}^j$ for $j \geq 3$.

Now, consider the firms in the merged coalitions. For these firms (i.e., $j = 1,2$), $A - z + v(m^jx^j) < A - z + v(m^1x^1 + m^2x^2)$ as long as x^1 and x^2 are positive. The effect of compatibility is to shift up the $A - z + v$ curve when viewed as a function of x^j (as in Figure 8). The effect of z on this curve is the same as for $j \geq 3$. Therefore if $\tilde{z} \leq \hat{z}$, then $\tilde{x}^j > \hat{x}^j$ for $j = 1,2$.

Suppose that $\tilde{z} \leq \hat{z}$. Then $\tilde{x}^j \geq \hat{x}^j$ for all j, with strict inequality for $j = 1,2$. But $z = \Sigma m^jx^j$, so we have a contradiction. Therefore, industry output rises due to the increased compatibility; $\tilde{z} > \hat{z}$. We already have shown that an increase in industry output implies that firms not in the merging coalitions produce less; $\tilde{z} > \hat{z}$ implies $\tilde{x}^j < \hat{x}^j$ for $j \geq 3$. Thus, it must be the case that the firms in the merging coalitions produce more: $m^1\tilde{x}^1 + m^2\tilde{x}^2 > m^1\hat{x}^1 + m^2\hat{x}^2$.

Note that Proposition 5 does *not* state that the new level of per firm output for the enlarged coalition will be larger than both $\hat{x}^1$ and $\hat{x}^2$; it states only that the new level of output will be larger than their mean. Note also that by Proposition 4, if total output under complete compatibility, z^c, is less than A, then $z < A$ in *any* equilibrium. From equation (12), $z^c < A$ if $v(A) < A/n$. So,

$v(A) < A/n$ is sufficient for $\hat{z} < A$, the hypothesis of Proposition 5.

When industry output in the premerger equilibrium equals or exceeds A, an increase in compatibility may be accompanied by a reduction in both industry output and the average level of output of the firms in the merging coalitions. To see this point, consider the following example. There are n firms, $v(A) \geq A$, and initially there is complete incompatibility. By Proposition 2, there exists a unique symmetric equilibrium in which all n firms are active. By Proposition 3, there exist n natural monopoly equilibria, each of which entails the natural monopolist producing A or more units of output. The natural monopolist's output level is less than that of the industry in the n-active-firm symmetric equilibrium (Corollary 3.2).

Suppose that the industry initially is in the n-active-firm symmetric equilibrium, and that some, but not all, of the firms form a compatibility coalition. The natural monopoly equilibria where a nonmerging firm is the natural monopolist will remain equilibria after the merger. Thus, while the premerger equilibrium entailed all firms active, the postmerger equilibrium could be one in which all but one firm shuts down. As we have just stated, industry output falls in this case. Moreover, the firms who formed the compatibility coalition are among those who were active in the premerger equilibrium, but are inactive in the postmerger equilibrium.

III. The Private and Social Incentives for Network Compatibility

To this point, we have treated the compatibility of the products as an exogenous characteristic of the market. In most markets where network externalities are important, the compatibility of the products will be the result of explicit decisions by the firms. When the network externalities are large, the choice of whether to make the products compatible will be one of the most important dimensions of market performance.

There are many cases in which firms will disagree on the desirability of making their products compatible; the move to compatibility may increase the profits of some firms while lowering the profits of others. Thus, we must be careful to specify the mechanism by which compatibility is achieved and whether side payments among firms are feasible.

It is useful to think of there being two basic technologies by which compatibility can be achieved. First, compatibility may arise through the *joint adoption of a product standard*, where a given set of firms must act together to make their products compatible with one another. The CPM operating system for personal computers and the broadcast television standards are two examples. Second, compatibility can be achieved through the *construction of an adapter*, where a single firm can act unilaterally to make its product compatible with those of another firm or group of firms. In the 1960's, for example, Honeywell developed a program that would allow its mainframe computers to run programs initially written for IBM hardware.[7] At present, there is intense competition, both in the market and in the courts, as the video game manufacturers such as Coleco develop adapters that allow their hardware to run the video game programs of competing firms. In other cases there need not be a physical adapter; one firm can adopt another network's specifications for its product design.

When the firms cannot make side payments among one another and when the compatibility mechanism is a product standard, the products of a given set of firms will be made compatible if and only if *all* of these firms would earn greater profits as a result. In contrast, when the compatibility mechanism is an adapter, and side payments are infeasible, the products of two firms will be made compatible if *either* firm would find the move to be profitable.

When side payments are feasible, the firms will make their products compatible if and only if the change in the profits of firms within the set that can make side payments to one another exceeds the joint costs of compatibility.

[7]See Brock, p. 78.

We will examine several cases that vary in terms of the compatibility technology and feasibility of side payments. In analyzing the private incentives for compatibility, we will look at each firm's change in profits, $\Delta\pi_i = \pi_i^c - \pi_i^I$, and the change in their joint profits $\Delta\pi = \Sigma_{i=1}^n \Delta\pi_i$, and we compare these with the costs of compatibility. For most of this section we will take these costs to be purely fixed costs. The social incentives for compatibility are given by $\Delta W = W^c - W^I$. We denote the change in consumers' surplus by $\Delta S = S^c - S^I$.

A. *The Incentive when Side Payments among All Firms are Feasible*

If side payments among all firms are feasible, then a set of side payments could be constructed so that all firms' profits would be increased individually if and only if compatibility would raise joint profits; the private incentives are given by the change in industrywide profits under either compatibility technology.[8] The change in social welfare, $\Delta W = \Delta\pi + \Delta S$, so the social and private incentives will diverge when the move to compatibility changes the level of consumers' surplus. Since $S(z) = z^2/2$, consumers' surplus will go up if and only if output does. By Proposition 4, we know that output and, hence, consumers' surplus will rise with the move to full compatibility. Thus, if $\Delta\pi > 0$, then $\Delta W = \Delta\pi + \Delta S > 0$.

PROPOSITION 6: *When compatibility costs are purely fixed costs, any move to complete compatibility that raises industry profits is socially beneficial.*

Proposition 6 states that firms' incentives for compatibility are not socially excessive. In fact, they may be inadequate. Since $\Delta S > 0$, $\Delta W > \Delta\pi$. If the industrywide costs of compatibility, F, satisfy $\Delta\pi < F < \Delta W$, then the private firms will fail to adopt a socially desirable system of compatibility. The reason is that the firms cannot appropriate all the benefits of compatibility.[9]

PROPOSITION 7: *Even when arbitrary side payments among all firms are feasible, profit-maximizing firms may fail to achieve complete compatibility in cases where complete compatibility is socially optimal.*

A similar pair of results can be derived from Proposition 5 for markets in which the initial equilibrium entails $z < A$ and compatibility is increased (although not necessarily to industrywide compatibility). This result too relies on the fact that the move to increased compatibility raises total output under the stated conditions.

B. *The Adoption of an Industry Standard*

When the compatibility mechanism is the adoption of an industry standard, the firms must jointly decide to make their networks compatible. Any firm can veto the move to compatibility. Therefore, if no side payments are feasible, the standard will be adopted if and only if all firms joining the standard benefit from its creation. If we assume that firm i bears a cost F_i to adopt the standard and that side payments are infeasible, then adoption will occur if and only if $\Delta\pi_i > F_i$ for all adopters of the standard.

Suppose that side payments are feasible only when made among firms achieving compatibility. Such side payments might take the form of licensing fees or compensation for the expenses of making the products compatible, for example. In this case, a sufficient condition for achieving compatibility with a standards technology is that the joint profits of the firms achieving compatibility rise.

[8] Instead of payments made in return for not achieving compatibility, we might see expenditures on legal proceedings aimed at blocking the move to compatibility.

[9] This result is analogous to the fact that a monopolist may be unable to earn a positive profit by providing a socially useful product if there are fixed costs and he or she cannot perfectly price discriminate.

It is clear that, when the compatibility technology is a standard, allowing cost sharing will raise the likelihood of the firms choosing compatibility. If each firm prefers adoption of the standard ($\Delta\pi_i > F_i$ for all i), then the firms in aggregate will ($\Sigma\Delta\pi_i > \Sigma F_i$), while the converse is not true. Thus, we can strengthen Proposition 6:

PROPOSITION 8: *The private standardization rule is more stringent when cost sharing is infeasible than when it is feasible. The set of cases in which the firms fail to adopt a socially beneficial standard is therefore larger. It remains true that any privately profitable industrywide standard is desirable.*

To see the effect of cost sharing, suppose that there are only two firms in the industry. The compatibility equilibrium is symmetric, so the firm with the smaller incentive to adopt a standard is the one with initially higher profits, that is, the initially larger producer, say firm 1. If the initial equilibrium is symmetric and $F_1 = F_2 = F$, then $\Delta\pi_1 - F = \Delta\pi_2 - F$ and the presence or absence of cost sharing or other side payments is irrelevant. If the initial equilibrium is asymmetric, however, the condition for standardization, $\Delta\pi_1 > F$ is *strictly* more stringent than the adoption condition with side payments, $\Delta\pi > 2F$. The problem is that the larger firm will lose market share to its smaller rival as a result of standardization. If it can unilaterally block standardization, it may do so, despite the fact that its rival and consumers would benefit. Permitting cost sharing and other side payments will help alleviate the problem of insufficient private adoption incentives for moves to complete compatibility.

When the compatibility increase is to less than complete compatibility, private incentives may be excessive, and such cost sharing may exacerbate the problem. There are two reasons why private incentives may be excessive. First, when the increase is to less-than-complete compatibility, total output and consumers' surplus may fall, so that $\Delta\pi > \Delta W$. Second, there will be some firms that are not members of the groups making their products compatible. As shown in the proof of Proposition 5, these firms may produce less output and thus have lower profits in the new equilibrium. Absent side payments from these firms, the firms considering compatibility will not take the losses of other firms ($\Sigma_{j \neq i}\Delta\pi_j < 0$) into account. The social incentives, however, depend on the profits of all firms; $\Delta W = \Delta\pi_i + \Sigma_{j \neq i}\Delta\pi_j + \Delta S$.

PROPOSITION 9: *When the increase in compatibility leads to less-than-industrywide compatibility, the private incentives to standardize may be excessive.*

C. *The Construction of an Adapter*

In the adapter case, a firm unilaterally can act to make its product compatible with those of another network. In contrast with the adoption of an industry standard, if side payments to block compatibility are not feasible, then the adapter will be constructed as long as at least one firm earns increased profits from compatibility. When the compatibility mechanism is an adapter, the most reasonable assumption about the costs of compatibility is that the firm that constructs the adapter is the only one to bear the cost, F. Thus, firm i's private incentive to construct an adapter is $\Delta\pi_i - F$, while the social incentive is $\Delta\pi_i + \Sigma_{j \neq i}\Delta\pi_j + \Delta S - F$. The difference, $\Delta\pi_{-i} + \Delta S$, may in general be either positive or negative, implying that firm i's incentives to construct an adapter may be too low or too high from a social welfare point of view.

To see how the private and social incentives differ, suppose there are only two firms. Since the smaller firm in the initial equilibrium has the most to gain by the move to a symmetric equilibrium with compatibility, we need look only at the incentives of a firm with an initial market share of not more than 50 percent—firm 2, say. Since $\Delta\pi_2 > \Delta\pi_1$, the private decision will be to become compatible if and only if $\Delta\pi_2 > F$.[10] Compatibility is

[10] We are ignoring the possibility that the firms play a waiting game in which each hopes (in vain) that the

socially optimal if and only if $\Delta W > F$. The divergence between the social and private incentives is given by $\Delta W - \Delta\pi_2 = \Delta\pi_1 + \Delta S$. By Proposition 4, we know that $\Delta S > 0$; the fact that consumers enjoy some of the benefits of compatibility tends to make the private incentives too low. On the other hand, it is not true in general that $\Delta\pi_1 > 0$, so we cannot conclude in general that the private adoption decision is too conservative.

One case in which the private adoption incentives are too low is when the initial equilibrium is symmetric. In that case, $\Delta\pi_1 = \Delta\pi_2$, so that if $\Delta\pi_i > 0$ for one firm, then the change in profits is positive for the other firm as well. As a result, $\Delta W > \Delta\pi_i$ whenever $\Delta\pi_i > 0$, and we have

PROPOSITION 10: *Suppose there are only two firms (or coalitions). If the incompatibility equilibrium is symmetric and there are no side payments, then the private incentives to construct an adapter are too low.*

When there are only two coalitions, permitting side payments to share the costs of the adapter would promote efficiency when the incompatibility equilibrium is symmetric. The adapting coalition confers benefits both on its rival, which free rides on compatibility, and on consumers. Side payments can help solve the free-riding problem, but (by Proposition 6) still leave the firms with insufficient incentives.

When the incompatibility equilibrium is asymmetric, it is possible that the initially larger firm (which does not build the adapter) loses so much market share when the smaller firm builds an adapter that its profits fall, that is, $\Delta\pi_1 < 0$. If this effect dominates the increase in consumers' surplus, that is, if $\Delta\pi_1 + \Delta S < 0$, then $\Delta W < \Delta\pi_2$ and firm 2's compatibility incentives are excessive. The increase in firm 2's market share at the expense of firm 1 is a private gain for which there is no corresponding social benefit.

other will build an adapter even though each would privately benefit from building the adapter itself.

PROPOSITION 11: *Suppose there are only two coalitions. A coalition with an incompatibility market share of less than 50 percent may have socially excessive incentives to construct an adapter.*

This result is most likely to obtain when the incompatibility equilibrium entails one coalition having a very small market share, as in the monopoly equilibrium.

When the means of achieving compatibility is the construction of an adapter, one firm may attempt to make the networks compatible even though the other firms would prefer that the networks remain incompatible. In such cases, the latter firms may be willing to make expenditures to block compatibility, perhaps through legal channels (currently, there are numerous court cases involving video game and personal computer compatibility). It is not possible to say in general whether such expenditures promote or diminish efficiency. In some cases, $\Delta\pi_1 < 0$, $\Delta\pi_2 > F$, and $\Delta W < F$ as noted in Proposition 11, and firm 1's ability to block the adapter will raise efficiency (if the blocking costs themselves are not too high). In other cases, $\Delta\pi_1 < 0$, $\Delta\pi_2 > F$, and $\Delta W > F$, so blocking the adapter would reduce social welfare, even if the blocking costs are zero. For a given cost and demand structure, one can determine whether ΔW exceeds F or not, but it is not possible to determine this relationship simply on the basis of $\Delta\pi_2$ exceeding F.

D. *Extensions and Generalizations*

We have made some restrictive assumptions in order to simplify our analysis of the incentives for network compatibility. It is useful to put the results that we have obtained into perspective by discussing the general nature of the divergence between the social and private incentives to achieve compatibility. Essentially, there are two sources of distortion. In making its compatibility decision, each firm ignores the effects that this move will have on: 1) the level of consumers' surplus; and 2) the profits of the other firms.

Consider the first effect. When the move to compatibility raises consumers' surplus, the firms' incentives tend to be too low. Conversely, when the move to compatibility lowers consumers' surplus, the firms are biased towards compatibility. The change in consumers' surplus can itself be decomposed into two components: (a) the change due to the shift in the level of total output; and (b) the change that arises when the marginal consumer values the network externality differently than does the average consumer.

(a) The level of consumers' surplus is an increasing function of the level of total output. When the only costs of compatibility are fixed, we showed that the move to complete compatibility raises output and, hence, consumers' surplus. In this case, $\Delta\pi$ is less than ΔW. Once we relax the assumption that the move to compatibility has no impact on marginal costs, however, output may be lower with complete compatibility than without. The adoption of an industry standard or the construction of an adapter will necessitate the redesign of some or all of the products, which may lead to shifts in the variable costs of production (either upwards or downwards). Whereas the fixed costs of compatibility do not affect the equilibrium output level, changes in marginal costs do. In particular, when the increase in marginal costs is sufficiently large relative to the network effects, total output will be lower under complete compatibility than under incompatibility. In these cases, consumers' surplus will fall as a result of the move to complete compatibility and $\Delta\pi$ is greater than ΔW—the firms' joint incentive are excessive.[11]

(b) The level of consumers' surplus also depends on the relationship between the marginal and inframarginal consumers' valuations of the good. For a given level of output, the firms must set prices low enough to attract the marginal consumer. The lower is the marginal consumer's valuation relative to the average consumer's valuation, the larger will be consumers' surplus.

In our model, all consumers value the network externality equally, and all consumers' valuations of the good rise equally when compatibility is achieved. Thus, for a fixed level of output, the firms can raise prices by just this amount and consumers' surplus is unaffected. More generally, consumers may differ in their valuations of the network externality. If the network externality is stronger for the marginal consumer, then the move to compatibility will raise his or her willingness to pay for the good by more than that of the average consumer. For a given level of output, the firms will be able to raise the price by more than the increase in the average consumer's willingness to pay for the product. Consumers' surplus will fall, and the joint private incentives will tend to be greater than the social incentives. Of course, if the network externality is smaller for the marginal consumer, then the bias will run in the other direction.[12]

The change in consumers' surplus puts a wedge between the change in joint profits and the change in total welfare. When side payments are not feasible, the decision to achieve compatibility depends on the individual profit levels of the firms, and there is a second wedge. The change in profits may be positive for some firms and negative for others. As we have shown, the relationship between the changes in firms' profits will depend on two factors. First, it will depend on their relative changes in market shares

[11] In fact, when compatibility raises producers' marginal costs, the firms may use the move to compatibility *solely* as a coordinating device to reduce their joint output (i.e., they may have incentives to make their products compatible even if there are no network externalities). This result is an example of the general theory of cost-based facilitating practices (see Steven Salop and David Scheffman, 1983; Katz and Harvey Rosen, 1985; and Jesus Seade, 1983): in an oligopoly, all firms may benefit from jointly increasing their costs because it induces them to reduce their collective output, which may raise their revenues by more than the increase in costs.

[12] It is straightforward, but messy, to extend our model in this direction. There is nothing about this particular problem that is intrinsic to networks. For discussion of the general inability of prices to convey information about the preferences of inframarginal consumers, see A. Michael Spence (1975) and the references cited therein.

and revenues in moving to compatibility. When one group of firms gains market share and profits at the expense of another, the first group will be biased towards compatibility and the latter will be biased away from it. Second, the relationship will depend on the relative costs of compatibility that the producers incur. When the costs of compatibility fall more heavily on some firms than on others, there is a free-rider problem that tends to bias the firms away from compatibility.[13]

IV. Conclusion

We have developed a simple model to capture what we believe is a very significant element of competition in several important markets. Despite this simplicity, some general points emerge. First, the structure of the equilibria in our model confirms the importance of consumers' expectations in markets where network externalities are present. We have subjected expectations to a rationality constraint, but the expectations formation process remains an important element of the market to model explicitly. Given the possibility of multiple equilibria when products are incompatible, firms' reputations may play a major role in determining which equilibrium actually obtains. For example, the existence of a strong reputation for being a market share leader may explain IBM's rapid rise to preeminence in the personal computer market. It would also be useful to consider firms' expenditures to influence consumers' expectations, such as precommitments to a given level of software.

Turning to the compatibility decisions, although we would not want to draw policy conclusions at such an early stage in the analysis, our model does point to areas in which public policy can have an important impact. We have shown that the private decision will depend crucially on the decision locus (whether firms can act unilaterally or if consensus is required) and on the feasibility of side payments. Public policy can influence both of these features. Patent and copyright laws are a significant determinant of whether the compatibility technology is better modeled as the joint adoption of an industry standard (when patents are strictly and broadly enforced), or as the unilateral construction of an adapter (when they are loosely enforced or narrowly applied). From Proposition 1, we know that if the costs of adapting are negligible, and there are no other entry barriers, the market will be perfectly competitive.[14]

Allowing firms to make side payments also may influence the likelihood of compatibility being adopted—upwards when the technology is an industry standard, and either upwards or downwards when the compatibility technology is an adapter. The discussion in Section III, Part D, also points out the need for policymakers to scrutinize the form of the side payments or royalties. Per unit charges may have the effect of implicit cartels by inducing outputs contractions. Finally, public policy can affect the costs of compatibility. Antitrust exemptions that allow industry groups to get together may lower the costs of achieving compatibility and thus make it more likely.

The model here is only a beginning. Explicitly dynamic, multiperiod models are needed to shed additional light on the behavior of markets in which network externalities are important. We hope that this paper will encourage further research in the area of network competition and public policy towards compatibility.

Appendix

In the text, we have examined a model where a firm's announcement of its planned level of output has no effect on consumer expectations. This model can be viewed as

[13] Here we are assuming that when the compatibility technology is an adapter, the costs fall more heavily on the adapting firm.

[14] This outcome may not be the socially optimal one. Absent the ability to earn rents from its network size (through incompatibility), a firm may not have incentives to make the investments necessary to obtain the network. The issues are exactly analogous to those encountered in the analysis of optimal patent policy.

one in which the firms are unable to commit themselves, so that only the output levels of the *FECE* are credible announcements. In this Appendix, we consider the opposite polar case in which firms *can* commit to announced output levels before consumers make their purchase decisions. Firm i commits itself to output level x_i and consumers make their purchase decisions by looking at $v(y_i) - p_i$ across all brands. Firm i chooses its level of output taking the output level of the other firms as given. Thus, we have a standard Cournot equilibrium with demand-side economies of scale.

Given total output z and firm output x_i, firm i has profits of

$$x_i\{A + v(y_i) - z\}.$$

Differentiating with respect to x_i, the first order conditions are

$$\text{(A1)} \quad A + v(y_i) - 2x_i - \sum_{j \neq i} x_j + x_i v'(y_i) = 0 \qquad \text{for } i = 1, 2, \ldots, n.$$

The only difference between equation (A1) and our earlier first-order condition is the addition of the term $x_i v'(y_i)$. This term captures the fact that firm i can directly influence consumers' expectations regarding its network size. $x_i v'(y_i)$ is positive, so that firm i's reaction curve will shift upwards in comparison with the earlier equilibrium reaction correspondence.

The analysis is essentially unchanged from that in the text; we simply substitute $v(y_i) + x_i v'(y_i)$ for $v(y_i)$ in firm i's reaction function. Some additional assumptions on v are necessary to ensure that this substitute function is itself concave. In the case of complete incompatibility ($y_i = x_i$ for all i), and a constant elasticity network externality function $v(x) = \beta x^{\alpha}$, we simply replace $v(x) = \beta x^{\alpha}$ by $v(x) + xv'(x) = \gamma x^{\alpha}$, where $\gamma = (1+\alpha)\beta$.

Qualitatively, the "commitment" equilibria differ from those analyzed in the text in the following ways. 1) Each firm's reaction correspondence becomes a reaction function, since it can "choose" x_i^e as well as x_i (see the discussion of Figure 2 in Section II, Part B). 2) Equilibrium entails greater output, as each firm accounts for the $x_i v'(y_i)$ term, which shifts its reaction curve outwards. 3) No longer can a firm make greater profits in the $k+1$-active-firm equilibrium than in the k-firm equilibrium.

REFERENCES

Brock, Gerald, "Competition, Standards, and Self-Regulation in the Computer Industry," in R. E. Caves and M. J. Roberts, eds., *Regulating the Product: Quality and Variety*, Cambridge: Ballinger, 1975.

Katz, Michael L., and Rosen, Harvey S., "Tax Analysis in an Oligopoly Model," *Public Finance Quarterly*, January 1985, *13*, 3–20.

Kurdle, Robert T., "Regulation and Self-Regulation in the Farm Machinery Industry," in R. E. Caves and M. J. Roberts, eds., *Regulating the Price: Quality and Variety*, Cambridge: Ballinger, 1975.

Oren, Shmuel S. and Smith, Stephen A., "Critical Mass and Tariff Structure in Electronic Communications Markets," *Bell Journal of Economics*, Autumn 1981, *12*, 467–86.

Salop, Steven and Scheffman, David, "Raising Rivals' Costs," *American Economic Review Proceedings*, May 1983, *73*, 267–71.

Seade, Jesus, "Prices, Profits and Taxes in Oligopoly," unpublished draft, University of Warwick, 1983.

Spence, A. Michael, "Monopoly, Quality, and Regulation," *Bell Journal of Economics*, Autumn 1975, *6*, 417–29.

[24]

Clio and the Economics of QWERTY

By PAUL A. DAVID*

Cicero demands of historians, first, that we tell true stories. I intend fully to perform my duty on this occasion, by giving you a homely piece of narrative economic history in which "one damn thing follows another." The main point of the story will become plain enough: it is sometimes not possible to uncover the logic (or illogic) of the world around us except by understanding how it got that way. A *path-dependent* sequence of economic changes is one of which important influences upon the eventual outcome can be exerted by temporally remote events, including happenings dominated by chance elements rather than systematic forces. Stochastic processes like that do not converge automatically to a fixed-point distribution of outcomes, and are called *non-ergodic*. In such circumstances "historical accidents" can neither be ignored, nor neatly quarantined for the purpose of economic analysis; the dynamic process itself takes on an *essentially historical* character. Standing alone, my story will be simply illustrative and does not establish how much of the world works this way. That is an open empirical issue and I would be presumptuous to claim to have settled it, or to instruct you in what to do about it. Let us just hope the tale proves mildly diverting for those waiting to be told if and why the study of economic history is a necessity in the making of economists.

*Department of Economics, Encina Hall, Stanford University, Stanford, CA 94305. Support provided for this research, under a grant to the Technological Innovation Program of the Center for Economic Policy Research, Stanford University, is gratefully acknowledged. Douglas Puffert supplied able research assistance. Some, but not the whole, of my indebtedness to Brian Arthur's views on QWERTY and QWERTY-like subjects is recorded in the References. I bear full responsibility for errors of fact and interpretation, as well as for the peculiar opinions abbreviated herein. A fuller version with complete references, entitled "Understanding the Economics of QWERTY or Is History Necessary?," is available on request.

I. The Story of QWERTY

Why does the topmost row of letters on your personal computer keyboard spell out QWERTYUIOP, rather than something else? We know that nothing in the engineering of computer terminals requires the awkward keyboard layout known today as "QWERTY," and we all are old enough to remember that QWERTY somehow has been handed down to us from the Age of Typewriters. Clearly nobody has been persuaded by the exhortations to discard QWERTY, which apostles of DSK (the Dvorak Simplified Keyboard) were issuing in trade publications such as *Computers and Automation* during the early 1970's. Why not? Devotees of the keyboard arrangement patented in 1932 by August Dvorak and W. L. Dealey have long held most of the world's records for speed typing. Moreover, during the 1940's U.S. Navy experiments had shown that the increased efficiency obtained with DSK would amortize the cost of retraining a group of typists within the first ten days of their subsequent full-time employment. Dvorak's death in 1975 released him from forty years of frustration with the world's stubborn rejection of his contribution; it came too soon for him to be solaced by the Apple IIC computer's built-in switch, which instantly converts its keyboard from QWERTY to virtual DSK, or to be further aggravated by doubts that the switch would not often be flicked.

If as Apple advertising copy now says, DSK "lets you type 20–40% faster," why did this superior design meet essentially the same rejection as the previous seven improvements on the QWERTY typewriter keyboard that were patented in the United States and Britain during the years 1909–24? Was it the result of customary, nonrational behavior by countless individuals socialized to carry on an antiquated technological tradition? Or, as Dvorak himself once suggested, had there been a conspiracy among the members of the typewriter oligopoly to suppress an invention which they feared would so increase typewriter efficiency as ultimately to curtail the demand for their products? Or perhaps we should turn instead to the other popular "Devil Theory," and ask if political regulation and interference with the workings of a "free market" has been the cause of inefficient keyboard regimentation? Maybe it's all to be blamed on the public school system, like everything else that's awry?

You can already sense that these will not be the most promising lines along which to search for an economic understanding of QWERTY's present dominance. The agents engaged in production and purchase decisions in today's keyboard market are not the prisoners of custom, conspiracy, or state control. But while they are, as we now say, perfectly "free to choose," their behavior, nevertheless, is held fast in the grip of events long forgotten and shaped by circumstances in which neither they nor their interests figured. Like the great men of whom Tolstoy wrote in *War and Peace*, "(e) very action of theirs, that seems to them an act of their own free will, is in an historical sense not free at all, but in bondage to the whole course of previous history..." (Bk. IX, ch. 1).

This is a short story, however. So it begins only little more than a century ago, with the fifty-second man to invent the typewriter. Christopher Latham Sholes was a Milwaukee, Wisconsin printer by trade, and a mechanical tinkerer by inclination. Helped by his friends, Carlos Glidden and Samuel W. Soule, he had built a primitive writing machine for which a patent application was filed in October 1867. Many defects in the working of Sholes' "Type Writer" stood in the way of its immediate commercial introduction. Because the printing point was located underneath the paper carriage, it was quite invisible to the operator. "Non-visibility" remained an unfortunate feature of this and other up-stroke machines long after the flat paper carriage of the original design had been supplanted by arrangements closely resembling the modern continuous roller-platen. Consequently, the tendency of the typebars to clash and jam if struck in rapid succession was a particularly serious defect. When a typebar stuck at or near the printing point, every succeeding stroke merely hammered the same impression onto the paper, resulting in a string of repeated letters that would be discovered only when the typist bothered to raise the carriage to inspect what had been printed.

Urged onward by the bullying optimism of James Densmore, the promoter-venture capitalist whom he had taken into the partnership in 1867, Sholes struggled for the next six years to perfect "the machine." From the inventor's trial-and-error rearrangements of the original model's alphabetical key ordering, in an effort to reduce the frequency of typebar clashes, there emerged a four-row, upper case keyboard approaching the modern QWERTY standard. In March 1873, Densmore succeeded in placing the manufacturing rights for the substantially transformed Sholes-Glidden "Type Writer" with E. Remington and Sons, the famous arms makers. Within the next few months QWERTY's evolution was virtually completed by Remington's mechanics. Their many modifications included some fine-tuning of the keyboard design in the course of which the "*R*" wound up in the place previously allotted to the period mark "." Thus were assembled into one row all the letters which a salesman would need to impress customers, by rapidly pecking out the brand name: TYPE WRITER

Despite this sales gimmick, the early commercial fortunes of the machine, with which chance had linked QWERTY's destiny remained terrifyingly precarious. The economic downturn of the 1870's was not the best of times in which to launch a novel piece of office equipment costing $125, and by 1878, when Remington brought out its Improved Model Two (equipped with carriage shift key), the whole enterprise was teetering on the edge of bankruptcy. Consequently, even though sales began to pick up pace with the lifting of the depression and annual typewriter production climbed to 1200 units in 1881, the market position which QWERTY had acquired during the course of its early career was far from deeply entrenched; the entire stock of QWERTY-embodying machines in the United States could not have much exceeded 5000 when the decade of the 1880's opened.

Nor was its future much protected by any compelling technological necessities. For, there were ways to make a typewriter without the up-stroke typebar mechanism that had called forth the QWERTY adaptation, and rival designs were appearing on the American scene. Not only were there typebar machines with "down-stroke" and "front-stroke" actions that afforded a visible printing point; the problem of typebar clashes could be circumvented by dispensing with typebars entirely, as young Thomas Edison had done in his 1872 patent for an electric print-wheel device which later became the basis for teletype machines. Lucien Stephen Crandall, the inventor of the second typewriter to reach the American market (in 1879) arranged the type on a cylindrical sleeve: the sleeve was made to revolve to the required letter and come down onto the printing-point, locking in place for correct alignment. (So much for the "revolutionary" character of the IBM 72/82's "golf ball" design.) Freed from the legacy of typebars, commercially successful typewriters such as the Hammond and the Blickensderfer first sported a keyboard arrangement which was more sensible than QWERTY. Then so-called "Ideal" keyboard placed the sequence DHIATENSOR in the home row, these being ten letters with which one may compose over 70 percent of the words in the English language.

The typewriter boom beginning in the 1880's thus witnessed a rapid proliferation of competitive designs, manufacturing companies, and keyboard arrangements rivalling the Sholes-Remington QWERTY. Yet, by the middle of the next decade, just when it had become evident that any micro-technological rationale for QWERTY's dominance was being removed by the progress of typewriter engineering, the U.S. industry was rapidly moving towards the standard of an upright front-stroke machine with a four-row QWERTY keyboard that was referred to as "the Universal." During the period 1895–1905, the main producers of non-typebar machines fell into line by offering "the Universal" as an option in place of the Ideal keyboard.

II. Basic QWERTY-Nomics

To understand what had happened in the fateful interval of the 1890's, the economist must attend to the fact that typewriters were beginning to take their place as an element of a larger, rather complex system of production that was technically interrelated. In addition to the manufacturers and buyers of typewriting machines, this system involved typewriter operators and the variety of organizations (both private and public) that undertook to train people in such skills. Still more critical to the outcome was the fact that, in contrast to the hardware subsystems of which QWERTY or other keyboards were a part, the larger system of production was nobody's design. Rather like the proverbial Topsy, and much else in the history of economies besides, it "jes' growed."

The advent of "touch" typing, a distinct advance over the four-finger hunt-and-peck method, came late in the 1880's and was critical, because this innovation was from its inception adapted to the Remington's QWERTY keyboard. Touch typing gave rise to three features of the evolving production system which were crucially important in causing QWERTY to become "locked in" as the dominant keyboard arrangement. These features were *technical interrelatedness*, *economies of scale*, and *quasi-irreversibility* of investment. They constitute the basic ingredients of what might be called QWERTY-nomics.

Technical interrelatedness, or the need for system compatibility between keyboard "hardware" and the "software" represented by the touch typist's memory of a particular arrangement of the keys, meant that the expected present value of a typewriter as an instrument of production was dependent upon the availability of compatible software created by typists' decisions as to the kind of keyboard they should learn. Prior to the growth of the personal market for typewriters, the purchasers of the hardware typically were business firms and therefore distinct from the owners of typing skills. Few incentives existed at the time, or later, for any one business to invest in providing its employees with a form of general human capital which so readily could be taken elsewhere. (Notice that it was the wartime U.S. Navy, not your typical employer, that undertook the experiment of retraining typists on the Dvorak keyboard.) Nevertheless the purchase by a potential employer of a QWERTY keyboard conveyed a positive pecuniary externality to compatibly trained touch typists. To the degree to which this increased the likelihood that subsequent typists would choose to learn QWERTY, in preference to another method for which the stock of compatible hardware would not be so large, the overall user costs of a typewriting system based upon QWERTY (or any specific keyboard) would tend to *decrease* as it gained in acceptance relative to other systems. Essentially symmetrical conditions obtained in the market for instruction in touch typing.

These decreasing cost conditions—or *system scale economies*—had a number of consequences, among which undoubtedly the most important was the tendency for the process of intersystem competition to lead towards de facto standardization through the predominance of a single keyboard design. For analytical purposes, the matter can be simplified in the following way: suppose that buyers of typewriters uniformly were without inherent preferences concerning keyboards, and cared only about how the stock of touch typists was distributed among alternative specific keyboard styles. Suppose typists, on the other hand, were heterogeneous in their preferences for learning QWERTY-based "touch," as opposed to other methods, but attentive also to the way the stock of machines was distributed according to keyboard styles. Then imagine the members of this heterogenous population deciding in random order what kind of typing training to acquire. It may be seen that, with unbounded decreasing costs of selection, each stochastic decision in favor of QWERTY would raise the probability (but not guarantee) that the next selector would favor QWERTY. From the viewpoint of the formal theory of stochastic processes, what we are looking at now is equivalent to a generalized "Polya urn scheme." In a simple scheme of that kind, an urn containing balls of various colors is sampled with replacement, and every drawing of a ball of a specified color results in a second ball of the same color being returned to the urn; the probabilities that balls of specified colors will be added are therefore increasing (linear) functions of the proportions in which the respective colors are represented within the urn. A recent theorem due to W. Brian Arthur et al. (1983; 1985) allows us to say that when a generalized form of such a process (characterized by unbounded increasing returns) is extended indefinitely, the proportional share of one of the colors will, with probability one, converge to unity.

There may be many eligible candidates for supremacy, and from an *ex ante* vantage point we cannot say with corresponding certainty which among the contending colors—or rival keyboard arrangements—will be the one to gain eventual dominance. That part of the story is likely to be governed by "historical accidents," which is to say, by the particular sequencing of choices made close to the beginning of the process. It is there that essentially random, transient factors are most likely to exert great leverage, as has been shown neatly by Arthur's (1983) model of the dynamics of technological competition under increasing returns. Intuition suggests that if choices were made in a forward-looking way, rather than myopically on the basis of comparisons among the currently prevailing costs of different systems, the final outcome could be influenced strongly by expectations. A particular system could triumph over rivals merely because the purchasers of the software (and/or the hardware) expected that it would do so. This intuition seems to be supported by recent formal analyses by Michael Katz and Carl Shapiro (1983), and Ward Hanson (1984), of markets where purchasers of rival products benefit from externalities conditional upon the size of the compatible system or "network" with which they thereby become joined. Although the initial lead acquired by QWERTY through its association with the Remington was quantitatively very slender, when magnified by expectations it may well have been quite sufficient to guarantee that the industry eventually would lock in to a de facto QWERTY standard.

The occurrence of this "lock in" as early as the mid-1890's does appear to have owed something also to the high costs of software "conversion" and the resulting *quasi-irreversibility of investments* in specific touch-typing skills. Thus, as far as keyboard conversion costs were concerned, an important asymmetry had appeared between the software and the hardware components of the evolving system: the costs of typewriter software conversion were going up, whereas the costs of typewriter hardware conversion were coming down. While the novel, non-typebar technologies developed during the 1880's were freeing the keyboard from technical bondage to QWERTY, typewriter makers were by the same token freed from fixed-cost bondage to any particular keyboard arrangement. Non-QWERTY typewriter manufacturers seeking to expand market share could cheaply switch to achieve compatibility with the already existing stock of QWERTY-programmed typists, who could not. This, then, was a situation in which the precise details of timing in the developmental sequence had made it privately profitable in the short run to adapt machines to the habits of men (or to women, as was increasingly the case) rather than the other way around. And things have been that way ever since.

III. Message

In place of a moral, I want to leave you with a message of faith and qualified hope. The story of QWERTY is a rather intriguing one for economists. Despite the presence of the sort of externalities that standard static analysis tells us would interfere with the achievement of the socially optimal degree of system compatibility, competition in the absence of perfect futures markets drove the industry prematurely into standardization *on the wrong system*—where decentralized decision making subsequently has sufficed to hold it. Outcomes of this kind are not so exotic. For such things to happen seems only too possible in the presence of strong technical interrelatedness, scale economies, and irreversibilities due to learning and habituation. They come as no surprise to readers prepared by Thorstein Veblen's classic passages in *Germany and the Industrial Revolution* (1915), on the problem of Britain's undersized railway wagons and "the penalties of taking the lead" (see pp. 126–27); they may be painfully familiar to students who have been obliged to assimilate the details of deservedly less-renowned scribblings (see my 1971, 1975 studies) about the obstacles which ridge-and-furrow placed in the path of British farm mechanization, and the influence of remote events in nineteenth-century U.S. factor price history upon the subsequently emerging bias towards Hicks' labor-saving improvements in the production technology of certain branches of manufacturing.

I believe there are many more QWERTY worlds lying out there in the past, on the very edges of the modern economic analyst's tidy universe; worlds we do not yet fully perceive or understand, but whose influence, like that of dark stars, extends nonetheless to shape the visible orbits of our contemporary economic affairs. Most of the time I feel sure that the absorbing delights and quiet terrors of exploring QWERTY worlds will suffice to draw adventurous economists into the systematic study of essentially historical dynamic processes, and so will seduce them into the ways of economic history, and a better grasp of their subject.

REFERENCES

Arthur, W. Brian, "On Competing Technologies and Historical Small Events: The Dynamics of Choice Under Increasing Returns," Technological Innovation Program Workshop Paper, Department of Economics, Stanford University, November 1983.

Arthur, W. Brian, Ermoliev, Yuri M. and Kaniovski, Yuri M., "On Generalized Urn Schemes of the Polya Kind," *Kibernetika*, No. 1, 1983, *19*, 49–56 (translated from the Russian in *Cybernetics*, 1983, *19*, 61–71).

______, ______, **and** ______, "Strong Laws for a Class of Path-Dependent Urn Processes," in *Proceedings of the International Conference on Stochastic Optimization, Kiev*, Munich: Springer-Verlag, 1985.

David, Paul A., "The Landscape and the Machine: Technical Interrelatedness, Land Tenure and the Mechanization of the Corn Harvest in Victorian Britain," in D. N.

McCloskey, ed., *Essays on a Mature Economy: Britain after 1840*, London: Methuen, 1971, ch. 5.

______, *Technical Choice, Innovation and Economic Growth: Essays on American and British Experience in the Nineteenth Century*, New York: Cambridge University Press, 1975.

Hanson, Ward A., "Bandwagons and Orphans: Dynamic Pricing of Competing Technological Systems Subject to Decreasing Costs," Technological Innovation Program Workshop Paper, Department of Economics, Stanford University, January, 1984.

Katz, Michael L. and Shapiro, Carl, "Network Externalities, Competition, and Compatibility," Woodrow Wilson School Discussion Paper in Economics No. 54, Princeton University, September, 1983.

Veblen, Thorstein, *Imperial Germany and the Industrial Revolution*, New York: MacMillan, 1915.

[25]

THE FABLE OF THE KEYS*

S. J. LIEBOWITZ and STEPHEN E. MARGOLIS
North Carolina State University

I. Introduction

The term "standard" can refer to any social convention (standards of conduct, legal standards), but it most often refers to conventions that require exact uniformity (standards of measurement, computer-operating systems). Current efforts to control the development of high-resolution television, multitasking computer-operating systems, and videotaping formats have heightened interest in standards.

The economic literature on standards has focused recently on the possibility of market failure with respect to the choice of a standard. In its strongest form, the argument is essentially this: an established standard can persist over a challenger, even where all users prefer a world dominated by the challenger, if users are unable to coordinate their choices. For example, each of us might prefer to have Beta-format videocassette recorders as long as prerecorded Beta tapes continue to be produced, but individually we do not buy Beta machines because we don't think enough others will buy Beta machines to sustain the prerecorded tape supply. I don't buy a Beta format machine because I think that you won't; you don't buy one because you think that I won't. In the end, we both turn out to be correct, but we are both worse off than we might have been. This, of course, is a catch-22 that we might suppose to be common in the economy. There will be no cars until there are gas stations; there will be no gas stations until there are cars. Without some way out of this conundrum, joyriding can never become a favorite activity of teenagers.[1]

* Earlier drafts benefited from seminars at Clemson University and North Carolina State University, and we would like to thank the participants at those seminars. We would also like to thank James Buchanan, Dan Klein, Bill Landes, Nancy Margolis, Craig Newmark, John Palmer, Gregory Rehmke, George Stigler, and Wally Thurman for their suggestions.

[1] This trap is treated more seriously in the literature on standards than in other economics literature. This reflects a supposition that foresight, integration, or appropriation are more

[*Journal of Law & Economics*, vol. XXXIII (April 1990)]

The logic of these economic traps and conundrums is impeccable as far as it goes, but we would do well to consider that these traps are sometimes escaped in the market. Obviously, gas stations and automobiles do exist, so participants in the market must use some technique to unravel such conundrums. If this catch-22 is to warrant our attention as an empirical issue, at a minimum we would hope to see at least one real-world example of it. In the economics literature on standards,[2] the popular real-world example of this market failure is the standard Qwerty typewriter keyboard[3] and its competition with the rival Dvorak keyboard.[4] This example is noted frequently in newspaper and magazine reports, seems to be generally accepted as true, and was brought to economists' attention by the papers of Paul David.[5] According to the popular story, the keyboard invented by August Dvorak, a professor of education at the University of Washington, is vastly superior to the Qwerty keyboard developed by Christopher Sholes that is now in common use. We are to believe that, although the Dvorak keyboard is vastly superior to Qwerty, virtually no one trains on Dvorak because there are too few Dvorak machines, and there are virtually no Dvorak machines because there are too few Dvorak typists.

This article examines the history, economics, and ergonomics of the typewriter keyboard. We show that David's version of the history of the market's rejection of Dvorak does not report the true history, and we present evidence that the continued use of Qwerty is efficient given the current understanding of keyboard design. We conclude that the example of the Dvorak keyboard is what beehives and lighthouses were for earlier

difficult in the case of standards. The current literature fails to explain why these "externalities" are particularly relevant for standards. We will have more to say about this in forthcoming work.

[2] See, for example, Joseph Farrell & Garth Saloner, Standardization, Compatibility, and Innovation, 16 Rand J. Econ. 70 (1985); Michael L. Katz & Carl C. Shapiro, Network Externalities, Competition, and Compatibility, 75 Am. Econ. Rev. 424 (1985); and Jean Tirole, The Theory of Industrial Organization (1988).

[3] "Qwerty" stands for arrangement of letters in the upper lefthand portion of the keyboard below the numbers. This keyboard is also known as the Sholes, or Universal, keyboard.

[4] This is also sometimes known as the DSK keyboard, for Dvorak Simplified Keyboard (or the simplified keyboard). As explained below, the letters are arranged in a different order.

[5] Paul A. David, Clio and the Economics of QWERTY, 75 Am. Econ. Rev. 332 (1985); and Paul A. David, Understanding the Economics of QWERTY: The Necessity of History, in Economic History and the Modern Economist (William N. Parker ed. 1986).

market-failure fables. It is an example of market failure that will not withstand rigorous examination of the historical record.[6]

II. Some Economics of Standards

Some standards change over time without being impaired as social conventions. Languages, for example, evolve over time, adding words and practices that are useful and winnowing features that have lost their purpose. Other standards are inherently inflexible. Given current technologies, it won't do, for example, for broadcast frequencies to drift the way that orchestral tuning has. A taste for a slightly larger centimeter really can't be accommodated by a sequence of independent decisions the way that increased use of contractions in academic writing can. Obviously, if standards can evolve at low cost, they would be expected to evolve into the forms that are most efficient (in the eyes of those adopting the standards). Conversely, an inappropriate standard is most likely to have some permanence where evolution is costly.

In a recent article on standards, Joseph Farrell and Garth Saloner[7] present a formal exploration of the difficulties associated with changing from one standard to another. They construct hypothetical circumstances that might lead to market failure with respect to standards. To refer to the condition in which a superior standard is not adopted, they coin the phrase "excess inertia." Excess inertia is a type of externality: each nonadopter of the new standard imposes costs on every other potential user of the new standard. In the case of excess inertia, the new standard can be clearly superior to the old standard, and the sum of the private costs of switching to the new standard can be less than the sum of the private benefits, and yet the switch does not occur. This is to be differentiated from the far more common invention of new standards superior to the old, but for which the costs of switching are too high to make the switch practicable. Users of the old standard may regret their choice of that standard, but their continued use of the old standard is not inefficient; would it not be foolish to lay all regrets at the doorstep of externalities?

Farrell and Saloner's construct is useful because it shows the theoretical possibility of a market failure and also demonstrates the role of information. There is no possibility of excess inertia in their model if all partici-

[6] See Ronald H. Coase, The Lighthouse in Economics, 17 J. Law & Econ. 357 (1974); and Steven N. Cheung, The Fable of the Bees: An Economic Investigation, 16 J. Law & Econ. 11 (1973). Our debt is obvious.

[7] Farrell & Saloner, *supra* note 2.

pants can communicate perfectly. In this regard, standards are not unlike other externalities in that costs of transacting are essential. Thus, standards can be understood within the framework that Coase offered decades ago.[8]

By their nature, this model and others like it must ignore many factors in the markets they explore. Adherence to an inferior standard in the presence of a superior one represents a loss of some sort; such a loss implies a profit opportunity for someone who can figure out a means of internalizing the externality and appropriating some of the value made available from changing to the superior standard. Furthermore, institutional factors such as head starts from being first on the market, patent and copyright law, brand names, tie-in sales, discounts, and so on, can also lead to appropriation possibilities (read "profit opportunities") for entrepreneurs, and with these opportunities we expect to see activity set in motion to internalize the externalities. The greater the gap in performance between two standards, the greater are these profit opportunities, and the more likely that a move to the efficient standard will take place. As a result, a clear example of excess inertia is apt to be very hard to find. Observable instances in which a dramatically inferior standard prevails are likely to be short-lived, imposed by authority, or fictional.

The creator of a standard is a natural candidate to internalize the externality.[9] If a standard can be "owned," the advantage of the standard can be appropriated, at least in part, by the owner. Dvorak, for example, patented his keyboard. An owner with the prospect of appropriating substantial benefits from a new standard would have an incentive to share some of the costs of switching to a new standard. This incentive gives rise to a variety of internalizing tactics. Manufacturers of new products sometimes offer substantial discounts to early adopters, offer guarantees of

[8] Ronald H. Coase, The Problem of Social Cost, 3 J. Law & Econ. 1 (1960). Of course, inertia is not necessarily inefficient. Some delay in settling on a standard will mean that relatively more is known about the associated technology and the standards themselves by the time most users commit to a technology. Recall the well-known discussion of Harold Demsetz, Information and Efficiency: Another Viewpoint, 12 J. Law & Econ. 1 (1969), on the nature of efficiency. If a God can costlessly cause the adoption of the correct standard, any inertia is excessive (inefficient) in comparison. But it seems ill advised to hold this up as a serious benchmark. Excessive inertia should be defined relative to some achievable result. Further, some reservation in committing to standards will allow their creators to optimize standards rather than rushing them to the market to be first. If the first available standard were always adopted, then standards, like patents, might generate losses from the rush to be first. Creators might rush their standards to market, even where waiting would produce a better and more profitable product.

[9] We may ask ourselves why new standards are created if not with the idea of some pecuniary reward. One would hardly expect nonobvious and costly standards to proliferate like manna from heaven.

satisfaction, or make products available on a rental basis. Sometimes manufacturers offer rebates to buyers who turn in equipment based on old standards, thus discriminating in price between those who have already made investments in a standard and those who have not. Internalizing tactics can be very simple: some public utilities once supplied light bulbs, and some UHF television stations still offer free UHF indoor antennas. In many industries, firms provide subsidized or free training to assure an adequate supply of operators. Typewriter manufacturers were an important source of trained typists for at least the first fifty years of that technology.[10]

Another internalizing tactic is convertibility. Suppliers of new-generation computers occasionally offer a service to convert files to new formats. Cable-television companies have offered hardware and services to adapt old televisions to new antenna systems for an interim period. Of interest in the present context, for a time before and after the Second World War, typewriter manufacturers offered to convert Qwerty typewriters to Dvorak for a very small fee.[11]

All of these tactics tend to unravel the apparent trap of an inefficient standard, but there are additional conditions that can contribute to the ascendancy of the efficient standard. An important one is the growth of the activity that uses the standard. If a market is growing rapidly, the number of users who have made commitments to any standard is small relative to the number of future users. Sales of audiocassette players were barely hindered by their incompatibility with the reel-to-reel or eight-track players that preceded them. Sales of sixteen-bit computers were scarcely hampered by their incompatibility with the disks or operating systems of eight-bit computers.

Another factor that must be addressed is the initial competition among rival standards. If standards are chosen largely through the influence of those who are able to internalize the value of standards, we would expect, in Darwinian fashion, the prevailing standard to be the fittest economic competitor. Previous keyboard histories have acknowledged the presence of rivals, but they seem to view competition as a process leading to results indistguishable from pure chance.

Consideration of the many complicating factors present in the market

[10] David, Understanding, *supra* 5. Additionally, see Herkimer County Historical Society, The Story of the Typewriter: 1873–1923 (1923), which notes that in the early 1920s a single typewriter company was placing 100,000 typists a year.

[11] Arthur Foulke, Mr. Typewriter: A Biography of Christopher Latham Sholes 106 (1961), which notes: "Present old keyboard machines may be converted to the simplified (Dvorak) keyboard in local typewriter shops. It is now available on any typewriter. And it costs as little as $5 to convert a Standard to a simplified keyboard."

suggests that market failure in standards is not as compelling as many of the abstract models seem to suggest. Theoretical abstraction presents candidates for what might be important, but only emprical verification can determine if these abstract models have anything to do with reality.

III. The Case for the Superiority of the Dvorak Keyboard

Paul David[12] introduces economists to the conventional story of the development and persistence of the current standard keyboard, known as the Universal, or Qwerty, keyboard. The key features of that story are as follows. The operative patent for the typewriter was awarded in 1868 to Christopher Latham Sholes, who continued to develop the machine for several years. Among the problems that Sholes and his associates addressed was the jamming of the type bars when certain combinations of keys were struck in very close succession. As a partial solution to this problem, Sholes arranged his keyboard so that the keys most likely to be struck in close succession were approaching the type point from opposite sides of the machine. Since Qwerty was designed to accomplish this now obsolete mechanical requirement, maximizing speed was not an explicit objective. Some authors even claim that the keyboard is actually configured to minimize speed since decreasing speed would have been one way to avoid the jamming of the typewriter. At the time, however, a two-finger hunt-and-peck method was contemplated, so the keyboard speed envisioned was quite different from touch-typing speeds.

The rights to the Sholes patent were sold to E. Remington & Sons in early 1873. The Remingtons added further mechanical improvements and began commercial production in late 1873.

A watershed event in the received version of the Qwerty story is a typing contest held in Cincinnati on July 25, 1888. Frank McGurrin, a court stenographer from Salt Lake City, who was apparently the first to memorize the keyboard and use touch-typing, won a decisive victory over Louis Taub. Taub used the hunt-and-peck method on a Caligraph, a machine that used seventy-two keys to provide upper- and lower-case letters. According to popular history, the event established once and for all that the Remington typewriter, with its Qwerty keyboard, was technically superior. More important, the contest created an interest in touch-typing, an interest directed at the Qwerty arrangement. Reportedly, no one else at that time had skills that could even approach McGurrin's, so there was no possibility of countering the claim that the Remington keyboard arrangement was efficient. McGurrin participated in typing contests and

[12] David, Clio and the Economics of QWERTY, *supra* note 5.

demonstrations throughout the country and became something of a celebrity. His choice of the Remington keyboard, which may well have been arbitrary, contributed to the establishment of the standard. So it was, according to the popular telling, that a keyboard designed to solve a short-lived mechanical problem became the standard used daily by millions of typists.[13]

In 1936, August Dvorak patented the Dvorak Simplified Keyboard (DSK), claiming that it dramatically reduced the finger movement necessary for typing by balancing the load between hands and loading the stronger fingers more heavily. Its inventors claimed advantages of greater speed, reduced fatigue, and easier learning. These claims have been accepted by most commentators, including David, who refers, without citation, to experiments done by the U.S. Navy that "had shown that the increased efficiency obtained with the DSK would amortize the cost of retraining a group of typists within ten days of their subsequent full-time employment."[14] In spite of its claimed advantages, the Dvorak keyboard has never found much acceptance.

This story is the basis of the claim that the current use of the Qwerty keyboard is a market failure. The claim continues that a beginning typist will not choose to train in Dvorak because Dvorak machines are likely to be difficult to find, and offices will not equip with Dvorak machines because there is no available pool of typists.

This is an ideal example. The number of dimensions of performance are few, and in these dimensions the Dvorak keyboard appears overwhelmingly superior. These very attributes, however, imply that the forces to adopt this superior standard should also be very strong. It is the failure of these forces to prevail that warrants our critical examination.

IV. The Myth of Dvorak

Farrell and Saloner mention the typewriter keyboard as a clear example of market failure.[15] So, too, does the textbook by Tirole.[16] Both

[13] This history follows David, Clio and the Economics of QWERTY, *supra* note 5, but also see Wilfred A. Beeching, A Century of the Typewriter (1974), as an example of an account with the features and emphasis described here.

[14] David, Clio, *supra* note 5, at 332. If true, this would be quite remarkable. A converted Sholes typist will be typing so much faster that whatever the training cost, it is repaid every ten days. Counting only working days, this would imply that the investment in retraining repays itself approximately twenty-three times in a year. Does this seem even remotely possible? Do firms typically ignore investments with returns in the range of 2,200 percent?

[15] Farrell & Saloner, *supra* note 2.

[16] Tirole, *supra* note 2, at 405, states: "Many observers believe that the Dvorak keyboard is superior to this [Qwerty] standard, even when retraining costs are taken into account.

works cite David's article as the authority on this subject. Yet there are many aspects of the Qwerty-versus-Dvorak fable that do not survive scrutiny. First, the claim that Dvorak is a better keyboard is supported only by evidence that is both scant and suspect. Second, studies in the ergonomics literature find no significant advantage for Dvorak that can be deemed scientifically reliable. Third, the competition among producers of typewriters, out of which the standard emerged, was far more vigorous than is commonly reported. Fourth, there were far more typing contests than just the single Cincinnati contest. These contests provided ample opportunity to demonstrate the superiority of alternative keyboard arrangements. That Qwerty survived significant challenges early in the history of typewriting demonstrates that it is at least among the reasonably fit, even if not the fittest that can be imagined.

A. *Gaps in the Evidence for Dvorak*

Like most of the historians of the typewriter,[17] David seems to assume that Dvorak is decisively superior to Qwerty. He never questions this assertion, and he consistently refers to the Qwerty standard as inferior. His most tantalizing evidence is his undocumented account of the U.S. Navy experiments. After recounting the claims of the Navy study, he adds "If as Apple advertising copy says, DSK 'lets you type 20 to 40% faster' why did this superior design meet essentially the same resistance as the previous seven improvements on the Qwerty typewriter keyboard?"[18]

Why indeed? The survival of Qwerty is surprising to economists only in the presence of a demonstrably superior rival. David uses Qwerty's survival to demonstrate the nature of path dependency, the importance of history for economists, and the inevitable oversimplification of reality imposed by theory. Several theorists use his historical evidence to claim empirical relevance for their versions of market failure. But on what foundation does all this depend? All we get from David is an undocumented assertion and some advertising copy.

However, it would be foolish for a firm to build this alternative keyboard and for secretaries to switch to it individually." Under some circumstances it might have been foolish for secretaries and firms to act in this manner. But this type of behavior hardly seems foolish in many real-world situations. For example, large organizations (federal, state, and local governments, Fortune 500 companies, etc., often have tens of thousands of employees, and these organizations could undertake the training if the costs really are compensated in a short time. See notes 11 and 14 *supra*.

[17] For example, see Beeching, *supra* note 13, or Foulke, *supra* note 11.

[18] David, Understanding, *supra* note 5, at 34.

The view that Dvorak is superior is widely held. This view can be traced to a few key sources. A book published by Dvorak and several coauthors in 1936 included some of Dvorak's own scientific inquiry.[19] Dvorak and his coauthors compared the typing speed achieved in four different and completely separate experiments, conducted by various researchers for various purposes.[20] One of these experiments examined the typing speed on the Dvorak keyboard, and three examined typing speed on the Qwerty keyboard. The authors claimed that these studies established that students learn Dvorak faster than they learn Qwerty. A serious criticism of their methodology is that the various studies that they compared used students of different ages and abilities (for example, students learning Dvorak in grades 7 and 8 at the University of Chicago Lab School were compared with students in conventional high schools), in different school systems taking different tests, and in classes that met for different periods of time. Still more serious is that they did not stipulate whether their choice of studies was a random sample or the full population of available studies. So their study really establishes only that it is possible to find studies in which students learning to type on Qwerty keyboards appear to have progressed less rapidly in terms of calendar time than Dvorak's students did on his keyboard. Even in this Dvorak study, however, the evidence is mixed as to whether students, as they progress, retain an advantage when using the Dvorak keyboard since the differences seem to diminish as typing speed increases.

In general, it is desirable to have independent evaluation, and here the objectivity of Dvorak and his coauthors seems particularly open to question. Their book is more in the vein of an inspirational tract than a scientific work. Consider the following (taken from their chapter about relative keyboard performances):

> The bare recital to you of a few simple facts should suffice to indict the available spatial pattern that is so complacently entitled the "universal" [Qwerty] keyboard. Since when was the "universe" lopsided? The facts will not be stressed, since you may finally surmount most of the ensuing handicaps of this [Qwerty] keyboard.
>
> Just enough facts will be paraded to lend you double assurance that for many of the errors that you will inevitably make and for much of the discouraging delay you will experience in longed-for speed gains, you are not to blame. If you grow indignant over the beginner's role of "innocent victim," remember that a little emotion heightens determination.[21]

[19] August Dvorak, Nellie L. Merrick, William L. Dealy, & Gertrude C. Ford, Typewriting Behavior (1936).

[20] *Id.* at 226.

[21] *Id.* at 210.

Analysis of the present keyboard is so destructive that an improved arrangement is a modern imperative. Isn't it obvious that faster, more accurate, less fatiguing typing can be attained in much less learning time provided a simplified keyboard is taught?[22]

The Navy study, which seems to have been the basis for some of the more extravagant claims of Dvorak advocates, is also flawed. Arthur Foulke, Sholes's biographer, and a believer in the superiority of the Dvorak keyboard, points out several discrepancies in the reports coming out of the Navy studies. He cites an Associated Press report of October 7, 1943, to the effect that a new typewriter keyboard allowed typists to "zip along at 180 words per minute" but then adds "However, the Navy Department, in a letter to the author October 14, 1943 by Lieutenant Commander W. Marvin McCarthy said that it had no record of and did not conduct such a speed test, and denied having made an official announcement to that effect."[23] Foulke also reports a ***Business Week*** story of October 16, 1943, that reports a speed of 108, not 180, words per minute.

We were able to obtain, with difficulty, a copy of the 1944 Navy report.[24] The report does not state who conducted the study. It consists of two parts, the first based on an experiment conducted in July 1944 and the second based on an experiment conducted in October of that year. The report's foreword states that two prior experiments had been conducted but that "the first two groups were not truly fair tests." We are not told the results of the early tests.

The first of the reported experiments consisted of the retraining of fourteen Navy typists on newly overhauled Dvorak keyboards for two hours a day. We are not told how the subjects were chosen, but it does not appear to be based on a random process. At least twelve of these individ-

[22] *Id.* at 217.

[23] Foulke, *supra* note 11, at 103.

[24] We tried to have the Navy supply us with a copy when our own research librarians could not find it. The Navy research librarian had no more success, even though she checked the Navy records, the Martin Luther King Library, the Library of Congress, the National Archives, the National Technical Communication Service, etc. We were finally able to locate a copy held by an organization, Dvorak International, and would like to thank its director, Virginia Russell, for her assistance. She believes that they obtained their copy from the Underwood Company. We would be more sanguine about the question of the document's history had it been available in a public archive. The copy we received was A Practical Experiment in Simplified Keyboard Retraining—a Report on the Retraining of Fourteen Standard Keyboard Typists on the Simplified Keyboard and a Comparison of Typist Improvement from Training on the Standard Keyboard and Retraining on the Simplified Keyboard, Navy Department, Division of Shore Establishments and Civilian Personnel, Department of Services, Training Section, Washington, D.C. (July and October 1944).

uals had previously been Qwerty typists, with an average speed of thirty-two words per minute, although the Navy defined competence as fifty words per minute. The typists had IQs that averaged 98 and dexterity skills with an average percentile of 65. The study reports that it took fifty-two hours for typists to catch up to their old speed. After completing an average of eighty-three hours on the new keyboard, typing speed had increased to an average of fifty-six net words per minute compared to their original thirty-two words per minute, a 75 percent increase.

The second experiment consisted of the retraining of eighteen typists on the Qwerty keyboard. It is not clear how these typists were picked or even if members of this group were aware that they were part of an experiment. We are not told whether this training was performed in the same manner as the first experiment (the Navy retrained people from time to time and this may just have been one of these groups). The participants' IQs and dexerity skills are not reported. It is difficult to have any sense whether this group is a reasonable control for the first group. The initial typing scores for this group averaged twenty-nine words per minute, but these scores were not measured identically to those from the first experiment. The report states that because three typists had net scores of zero words per minute initially, the beginning and ending speeds were calculated as the average of the first four typing tests and the average of the last four typing tests. In contrast, the initial experiment using Dvorak simply used the first and last test scores. This truncation of the reported values reduced the measured increase in typing speed on the Qwerty keyboard by a substantial margin.[25]

The measured increase in net typing speed for Qwerty retraining was from twenty-nine to thirty-seven words per minute (28 percent) after an average of 158 hours of training, considerably less than the increase that occurred with the Dvorak keyboard.

[25] It is not an innocuous change. We are told that three Qwerty typists initially scored zero on the typing test but that their scores rose to twenty-nine, thirteen, and sixteen within four days (at 20). We are also told that several other typists had similar improvements in the first four days. These improvements are dismissed as mere testing effects that the researchers wish to eliminate. But the researchers made no effort to eliminate the analogous testing effect for the Dvorak typists. Truncating the measurements to the average of the first four days reduces the reported speed increases for the three typists with zero initial speed by at least thirteen, twelve, and fourteen. Assuming the existence of two other typists with similar size-testing effects, removing this testing effect would reduce the reported speed improvements by 3.6 words per minute, lowering the gain from 46 percent to 28 percent. The effect of the truncation at the end of the measuring period cannot be determined with any accuracy, but there is no testing effect to be removed at this stage of the experiment after many tests have been taken. While the apparent effect of these measurement techniques is significant, the indisputable problem is that they were not applied equally to the Qwerty and Dvorak typists.

The Navy study concludes that training in Dvorak is much more effective than retraining in Qwerty. But the experimental design leaves too many questions for this to be an acceptable finding. Do these results hold for typists with normal typing skills or only for those far below average? Were the results for the first group just a regression to the mean for a group of underperforminig typists? How much did the Navy studies underestimate the value of increased Qwerty retraining due to the inconsistent measurement? Were the two groups given similar training? Were the Qwerty typewriters overhauled, as were the Dvorak typewriters? There are many possible biases in this study. All, suspiciously, seem to be in favor of the Dvorak design.

The authors of the Navy study do seem to have their minds made up concerning the superiority of Dvorak. In discussing the background of the Dvorak keyboard and prior to introducing the results of the study, the report claims: "Indisputably, it is obvious that the Simplified Keyboard is easier to master than the Standard Keyboard."[26] Later they refer to Qwerty as an "ox" and Dvorak as a "jeep" and add: "no amount of goading the oxen can materially change the end result."[27]

There are other problems of credibility with these Navy studies having to do with potential conflicts of interest. Foulke[28] identifies Dvorak as Lieutenant Commander August Dvorak, the Navy's top expert in the analysis of time and motion studies during World War II. Earle Strong, a professor at Pennsylvania State University and a one-time chairman of the Office Machine Section of the Amercian Standards Association, reports that the 1944 Navy experiment and some Treasury department experiments performed in 1946 were conducted by Dr. Dvorak.[29] We also

[26] Navy, *supra* note 24, at 2.

[27] *Id.* at 23.

[28] *Supra* note 11, at 103.

[29] Earle P. Strong, A Comparative Experiment in Simplified Keyboard Retraining and Standard Keyboard Supplementary Training (U.S. General Services Administration 1956). However, Yamada, trying to refute criticisms of Dvorak's keyboard, claims that Dvorak did not conduct these studies, he only provided the typewriters. See Hisao Yamada, A Historical Study of Typewriters and Typing Methods: From the Position of Planning Japanese Parallels, 2. J. Information Processing 175 (1980). He admits that Dvorak was in the Navy and in Washington when the studies were conducted but denies any linkage. We do not know whom to believe, but we are skeptical that Dvorak would not have had a large influence on these tests, based on the strong circumstantial evidence and given Foulke's identification of Dvorak as the Navy's top expert on such matters. Interestingly, Yamada accuses Strong of being biased against the Dvorak keyboard (at 188). He also impugns Strong's character. He accuses Strong of refusing to provide other (unnamed) researchers with his data. He also implies that Strong stole money from Dvorak because in 1941, when Strong was a supporter of Dvorak's keyboard, he supposedly accepted payment from Dvorak to conduct a study of the DSK keyboard without ever reporting his results to him.

know that Dvorak had a financial stake in this keyboard. He owned the patent on the keyboard and had received at least $130,000 from the Carnegie Commission for Education for the studies performed while he was at the University of Washington.[30]

But there is more to this story than the weakness of the evidence reported by the Navy, or Dvorak, or his followers. A 1956 General Services Administration study by Earle Strong, which was influential in its time, provides the most compelling evidence against the Dvorak keyboard.[31] This study is ignored in David's history for economists and is similarly ignored in other histories directed at general audiences. Strong conducted a carefully controlled experiment designed to examine the costs and benefits of switching to Dvorak. He concluded that retraining typists on Dvorak had no advantages over retraining on Qwerty.

In the first phase of Strong's experiment, ten government typists were retrained on the Dvorak keyboard. It took well over twenty-five days of four-hour-a-day training for these typists to catch up to their old Qwerty speed. (Compare this to the claim David makes about the Navy study's results that the full retraining costs were recovered in ten days.) When the typists had finally caught up to their old speed, Strong began the second phase of the experiment. The newly trained Dvorak typists continued training, and a group of ten Qwerty typists began a parallel program to improve their skills. In this second phase, the Dvorak typists progressed less quickly with further Dvorak training than did Qwerty typists training on Qwerty keyboards. Thus Strong concluded that Dvorak training would never be able to amortize its costs. He recommended that the government provide further training in the Qwerty keyboard, for Qwerty typists. The information provided by this study was largely responsible for putting Dvorak to rest as a serious alternative to Qwerty for those firms and government agencies responsible for choosing typewriters.[32]

Strong's study does leave some questions unanswered. Because it uses experienced typists, it cannot tell us whether beginning Dvorak typists could be trained more quickly than beginning Qwerty typists. Further, although one implication of Strong's study is that the ultimate speed

[30] Yamada, *supra* note 29.

[31] Strong, *supra* note 29.

[32] At the time of Strong's experiment, Dvorak had attracted a good deal of attention. At least one trade group had taken the position that, pending confirmation from the Strong study, it would adopt Dvorak as its new standard. See U.S. Plans to Test New Typewriter, New York Times, November 11, 1955; Revolution in the Office, New York Times, November 30, 1955; Key Changes Debated, New York Times, June 18, 1956; U.S. Balks at Teaching Old Typists New Keys, New York Times, July 2, 1956; and Peter White, Pyfgcrl vs. Qwertyuiop, New York Times, January 22, 1956, at 18.

achieved would be greater for Qwerty typists than for Dvorak typists (since the Qwerty group was increasing the gap over the Dvorak group in the second phase of the experiment), we cannot be sure that an experiment with beginning typists would provide the same results.[33]

Nevertheless, Strong's study must be taken seriously. It attempts to control the quality of the two groups of typists and the instruction they receive. It directly addresses the claims that came out of the Navy studies, which consider the costs and benefits of retraining. It directly parallels the decision that a real firm or a real government agency might face: is it worthwhile to retrain its present typists? The alleged market failure of the Qwerty keyboard as represented by Farrell and Saloner's excess inertia is that all firms would change to a new standard if only they could each be assured that the others would change. If we accept Strong's findings, it is not a failure to communicate that keeps firms from retraining its typists or keeps typists from incurring their own retraining costs. If Strong's study is correct, it is efficient for current typists not to switch to Dvorak.

Current proponents of Dvorak have a different view when they assess why the keyboard has not been more successful. Hisao Yamada, an advocate of Dvorak who is attempting to influence Japanese keyboard development, gives a wide-ranging interpretation to the Dvorak keyboard's failure. He blames the Depression, bad business decisions by Dvorak, World War II, and the Strong report. He goes on to say,

> There were always those who questioned the claims made by DSK followers. Their reasons are also manifold. Some suspected the superiority of the instructions by DSK advocates to be responsible, because they were all holders of advanced degree(s); such a credential of instructors is also apt to cause the Hawthorne effect. Others maintain that all training experiments, except the GSA one as noted, were conducted by the DSK followers, and that the statistical control of experiments [was] not well exercised. This may be a valid point. It does not take too long to realize, however, that it is a major financial undertaking to organize such an experiment to the satisfaction of statisticians. . . . The fact that those critics were also reluctant to come forth in support of such experiment[s] . . . may indicate that the true reason of their criticism lies elsewhere.[34]

This is one nasty disagreement.[35]

Nevertheless, Yamada as much as admits that experimental findings

[33] In fact, both the Navy and General Service Administration studies found that the best typists took the longest to catch up to their old speed and showed the smallest percentage improvement with retraining.

[34] Yamada, *supra* note 29, at 189.

[35] Also see note 29 *supra*.

reported by Dvorak and his supporters cannot be assigned much credibility and that the most compelling claims cited by Yamada for DSK's superiority come from Dvorak's own work. Much of the other evidence Yamada uses to support his views of DSK's superiority actually can be used to make a case against Dvorak. Yamada refers to a 1952 Australian post office study that showed no advantages for DSK when it was first conducted. It was only after adjustments were made in the test procedure (to remove "psychological impediments" to superior performance) that DSK did better.[36] He cites a 1973 study based on six typists at Western Electric, where, after 104 hours of training on DSK, typists were 2.6 percent faster than they had been on Qwerty.[37] Similarly, Yamada reports that, in a 1978 study at Oregon State University, after 100 hours of training, typists were up to 97.6 percent of their old Qwerty speed.[38] Both of these retraining times are similar to those reported by Strong and not to those in the Navy study. Yamada, however, thinks the studies themselves support Dvorak.[39] But unlike the Strong study, neither of these studies included parallel retraining on Qwerty keyboards. As the Strong study points out, even experienced Qwerty typists increase their speed on Qwerty if they are given additional training. Even if that problem is ignored, the possible advantages of Dvorak are all much weaker than those reported from the Navy study.

B. Evidence from the Ergonomics Literature

The most recent studies of the relative merits of keyboards are found in the ergonomics literature. These studies provide evidence that the advantages of the Dvorak is either small or nonexistent. For example, A. Miller and J. C. Thomas conclude that "the fact remains, however, that no alternative has shown a realistically significant advantage over the Qwerty for general purpose typing."[40] In two studies based on analysis of hand-and-finger motions, R. F. Nickells, Jr., finds that Dvorak is 6.2

[36] Yamada, *supra* note 29, at 185.

[37] *Id.* at 188.

[38] *Id.*

[39] Yamada interprets the Oregon study to support the Dvorak keyboard. To do so, he fits an exponential function to the Oregon data and notes that the limit of the function as hours of training goes to infinity is 17 percent greater than the typist's initial Qwerty speed. This function is extremely flat, however, and even modest gains appear well outside the range of the data. A 10 percent gain, for example, would be projected to occur only after 165 hours of training.

[40] A. Miller & J. C. Thomas, Behavioral Issues in the Use of Interactive Systems, 9 Int. J. of Man-Machine Stud. 509 (1977).

percent faster than Qwerty,[41] and R. Kinkhead finds only a 2.3 percent advantage for Dvorak.[42] Simulation studies by Donald Norman and David Rumelhart find similar results:

> In our studies . . . we examined novices typing on several different arrangements of alphabetically organized keyboards, the Sholes [Qwerty] keyboard, and a randomly organized keyboard (to control against prior knowledge of Sholes). There were essentially no differences among the alphabetic and random keyboards. Novices type slightly faster on the Sholes keyboard, probably reflecting prior experience with it. We studied expert typists by using our simulation model. Here, we looked at the Sholes and Dvorak layouts, as well as several alphabetically arranged keyboards. The simulation showed that the alphabetically organized keyboards were between 2% and 9% slower than the Sholes keyboard, and the Dvorak keyboard was only about 5% faster than the Sholes. These figures correspond well to other experimental studies that compared the Dvorak and Sholes keyboards and to the computations of Card, Moran, and Newell . . . for comparing these keyboards. . . . For the expert typist, the layout of keys makes surprisingly little difference. There seems no reason to choose Sholes, Dvorak, or alphabetically organized keyboards over one another on the basis of typing speed. It is possible to make a bad keyboard layout, however, and two of the arrangements that we studied can be ruled out.[43]

These ergonomic studies are particularly interesting because the claimed advantage of the Dvorak keyboard has been based historically on the claimed ergonomic advantages in reduced finger movement. Norman and Rummelhart's discussion offers clues to why Dvorak does not provide as much of an advantage as its proponents have claimed. They argue,

> For optimal typing speed, keyboards should be designed so that:
> A. The loads on the right and left hands are equalized.
> B. The load on the home (middle) row is maximized.
> C. The frequency of alternating hand sequences is maximized and the frequency of same-finger typing is minimized.
>
> The Dvorak keyboard does a good job on these variables, especially A and B; 67% of the typing is done on the home row and the left-right hand balance is 47–53%. Although the Sholes (Qwerty) keyboard fails at conditions A and B (most typing is done on the top row and the balance between the two hands is 57% and 43%), the policy to put successively typed keys as far apart as possible favors factor C, thus leading to relatively rapid typing.[44]

[41] Cited in Hisao Yamada, Certain Problems Associated with the Design of Input Keyboards for Japanese Writing, in Cognitive Aspects of Skilled Typewriting 336 (William E. Cooper ed. 1983).

[42] Cited in *id.* at 365.

[43] Donald A. Norman and David E. Rumelhart, Studies of Typing from the LNR Research Group, in Cognitive Aspects of Skilled Typewriting 45, 51 (William E. Cooper ed. 1983).

[44] *Id.*

The explanation for Norman and Rummelhart's factor C is that during a keystroke, the idle hand prepares for its next keystroke. Thus Sholes's decision to solve a mechanical problem through careful keyboard arrangement may have inadvertently satisfied a fairly important requirement for efficient typing.

The consistent finding in the ergonomic studies is that the results imply no clear advantage for Dvorak. These studies are not explicitly statistical, yet their negative claim seems analogous to the scientific caution that one exercises when measured differences are small relative to unexplained variance. We read these authors as saying that, in light of the imprecision of method, scientific caution precludes rejection of the hypothesis that Dvorak and Qwerty are equivalent. At the very least, the studies indicate that the speed advantage of Dvorak is not anything like the 20–40 percent that is claimed in the Apple advertising copy that David cites. Moreover, the studies suggest that there may be no advantage with the Dvorak keyboard for ordinary typing by skilled typists. It appears that the principles by which Dvorak "rationalized" the keyboard may not have fully captured the actions of experienced typists largely because typing appears to be a fairly complex activity.

A final word on all of this comes from Frank McGurrin, the world's first known touch-typist:

> Let an operator take a new sentence and see how fast he can write it. Then, after practicing the sentence, time himself again, and he will find he can write it much faster; and further practice on the particular sentence will increase the speed on it to nearly or quite double that on the new matter. Now let the operator take another new sentence, and he will find his speed has dropped back to about what it was before he commenced practicing the first sentence. Why is this? The fingers are capable of the same rapidity. It is because the mind is not so familiar with the keys.[45]

Of course, performance in any physical activity can presumably be improved with practice. But the limitations of typing speed, in McGurrin's experiment, appear to have something to do with a mental or, at least, neurological skill and fairly little to do with the limitations on the speeds at which the fingers can complete their required motions.

C. Typewriter Competition

The Sholes typewriter was not invented from whole cloth. Yamada reports that there were fifty-one inventors of prior typewriters, including

[45] George C. Mares, The History of the Typewriter (1909).

some earlier commercially produced typewriters. He states: "Examination of these material(s) reveal that almost all ideas incorporated into Sholes' machines, if not all, were at one time or another already used by his predecessors."[46]

Remington's early commercial rivals were numerous, offered substantial variations on the typewriter, and in some cases enjoyed moderate success. There were plenty of competitors after the Sholes machine came to market. The largest and most important of these rivals were the Hall, Caligraph, and Crandall machines. The Yost, another double-keyboard machine, manufactured by an early collaborator of Sholes, used a different inking system and was known particularly for its attractive type. According to production data assembled by Yamada,[47] the machines were close rivals, and they each sold in large numbers. Franz Xavier Wagner, who also worked on the 1873 Remington typewriter, developed a machine that made the type fully visible as it was being typed. This machine was offered to, but rejected by, the Union Typewriter Company, the company formed by the 1893 merger of Remington with six other typewriter manufacturers.[48] In 1895, Wagner joined John T. Underwood to produce his machine. Their company, which later became Underwood, enjoyed rapid growth, producing two hundred typewriters per week by 1898.[49] Wagner's offer to Union also resulted in the spin-off from Union of L. C. Smith, who introduced a visible-type machine in 1904.[50] This firm was the forerunner of the Smith-Corona company.

Two manufacturers offered their own versions of an ideal keyboard: Hammond in 1893 and Blickensderfer in 1889.[51] Each of these machines survived for a time, and each had certain mechanical advantages. Blickensderfer later produced what may have been the first portable and the first electric typewriters. Hammond later produced the Varityper, a standard office type-composing machine that was the antecedent of today's desktop publishing. The alternative keyboard machines produced by these manufacturers came early enough that typewriters and, more important, touch-typing were still not very popular. The Blickensderfer ap-

[46] Yamada, *supra* note 41, at 177.

[47] *Id.* at 181.

[48] Beeching, *supra* note 13, at 165.

[49] *Id.* at 214.

[50] *Id.* at 165.

[51] David, Understanding, *supra* note 5, at 38. Also see Beeching, *supra* note 13, at 40, 199. Yamada, *supra* note 29, at 184, in discussing the Hammond keyboard arrangement states: "This 'ideal' arrangement was far better than Qwerty, but it did not take root because by then Remington Schools were already turning out a large number of Qwerty typists every year." In 1893, Blickensderfer offered a portable typewriter with the Hammond keyboard.

peared within a year of the famous Cincinnati contest that first publicized touch-typing.

In the 1880s and 1890s typewriters were generally sold to offices not already staffed with typists or into markets in which typists were not readily available. Since the sale of a new machine usually meant training a new typist, a manufacturer that chose to compete using an alternative keyboard had an opportunity. As late as 1923, typewriter manufacturers operated placement services for typists and were an important source of operators. In the earliest days, typewriter salesmen provided much of the limited training available to typists.[52] Since almost every sale required the training of a typist, a typewriter manufacturer that offered a different keyboard was not particularly disadvantaged. Manufacturers internalized training costs in such an environment, so a keyboard that allowed more rapid training might have been particularly attractive.

Offering alternative keyboards was not a terribly expensive tactic. The Blickensderfer used a type-bar configuration similar in principle to the IBM Selectric type ball and, so, could easily offer many different configurations. The others could create alternative keyboard arrangements by simply soldering the type to different bars and attaching the keys to different levers. So apparently the problem of implementing the conversion was not what kept the manufacturers from changing keyboards.

The rival keyboards did ultimately fail, of course.[53] But the Qwerty keyboard cannot have been so well established at the time the rival keyboards were first offered that they were rejected because they were nonstandard. Manufacturers of typewriters sought and promoted any technical feature that might give them an advantage in the market. Certainly shorter training and greater speed would have been an attractive selling point for a typewriter with an alternative keyboard. Neither can it be said that the rival keyboards were doomed by inferior mechanical characteristics because these companies went on to produce successful and innovative, though Qwerty-based, typing machines. Thus we cannot attribute our inheritance of the Qwerty keyboard to a lack of alternative keyboards

[52] Herkimer County Historical Society, *supra* note 10, at 78.

[53] We should also take note of the fact that the Qwerty keyboard, although invented in the United States, has become the dominant keyboard throughout the world. Foreign countries, when introduced to typewriters, need not have adopted this keyboard if superior alternatives existed since there would not yet have been any typists trained on Qwerty. Yet all other keyboard designs fell before the Qwerty juggernaut. In France and some other countries, the keyboard is slightly different than the Qwerty keyboard used in the United States. The major difference is that the top left-hand keys are Azerty (that is also what these keyboard designs are called) and several letters are transposed, but most of the keys are identical.

or the chance association of this keyboard arrangement with the only mechanically adequate typewriter.

D. Typing Competitions

Typing competitions provided another test of the Qwerty keyboard. These competitions are somewhat underplayed in the conventional history. David's history mentions only the Cincinnati contest. Wilfred Beeching's history, which has been very influential, also mentions only the Cincinnati contest and attaches great importance to it: "Suddenly, to their horror, it dawned upon both the Remington Company and the Caligraph company officials, torn between pride and despair, that whoever won was likely to put the other out of business!" Beeching refers to the contest as having established the four-bank keyboard of the Remington machine "once and for all."[54]

In fact, typing contests and demonstrations of speed were fairly common during this period. They involved many different machines, with various manufacturers claiming to hold the speed record.

Under the headline "Wonderful Typing," the *New York Times*[55] reported on a typing demonstration given the previous day in Brooklyn by a Mr. Thomas Osborne of Rochester, New York. The *Times* reported that Mr. Osborne "holds the championship for fast typing, having accomplished 126 words a minute at Toronto August 13 last." In the Brooklyn demonstration he typed 142 words per minute in a five-minute test, 179 words per minute in a single minute, and 198 words per minute for 30 seconds. He was accompanied by a Mr. George McBride, who typed 129 words per minute blindfolded. Both men used the non-Qwerty Caligraph machine. The *Times* offered that "the Caligraph people have chosen a very pleasant and effective way of proving not only the superior speed of their machine, but the falsity of reports widely published that writing blindfolded was not feasible on that instrument."[56] Note that this was just months after McGurrin's Cincinnati victory.

There were other contests and a good number of victories for McGurrin and Remington. On August 2, 1888, the *Times*[57] reported a New York contest won by McGurrin with a speed of 95.8 words per minute in a five-minute dictation. In light of the received history, according to which McGurrin is the only person to have memorized the keyboard, it is inter-

[54] Beeching, *supra* note 13, at 41.

[55] New York Times, February 28, 1889, at 8.

[56] *Id.*

[57] *Id.* at 2.

esting to note the strong performance of his rivals. Miss May Orr typed 95.2 words per minute, and M. C. Grant typed 93.8 words per minute. Again, on January 9, 1889, the *Times*[58] reported a McGurrin victory under the headline "Remington Still Leads the List."

We should probably avoid the temptation to compare the Caligraph speed with the Remington speeds, given the likely absence of any serious attempts at standardizing the tests. Nevertheless, it appears that the issue of speed was not so readily conceded as is reported in Beeching's history. Typists other than McGurrin could touch-type, and machines other than Remington were competitive. History has largely ignored events that did not build toward the eventual domination by Qwerty. This focus may be reasonable for the history of the Remington Company or the Qwerty keyboard. But if we are interested in whether the Qwerty keyboard's existence can be attributed to more than happenstance or an inventor's whim, these events do matter.

V. Conclusions

The trap constituted by an obsolete standard may be quite fragile. Because real-world situations present opportunites for agents to profit from changing to a superior standard, we cannot simply rely on an abstract model to conclude that an inferior standard has persisted. Such a claim demands empirical examination.

As an empirical example of market failure, the typewriter keyboard has much appeal. The objective of the keyboard is fairly straightforward: to get words onto the recording medium. There are no conflicting objectives to complicate the interpretation of performance. But the evidence in the standard history of Qwerty versus Dvorak is flawed and incomplete. First, the claims for the superiority of the Dvorak keyboard are suspect. The most dramatic claims are traceable to Dvorak himself, and the best-documented experiments, as well as recent ergonomic studies, suggest little or no advantage for the Dvorak keyboard.[59]

[58] *Id.*

[59] See text at notes 30–43.

There are several versions of the claim that a switch to Dvorak would not be worthwhile. The strongest, which we do not make, is that Qwerty is proven to be the best imaginable keyboard. Neither can we claim that Dvorak is proven to be inferior to Qwerty. Our claim is that there is no scientifically acceptable evidence that Dvorak offers any real advantage over Qwerty. Because of this claim, our assessment of a market failure in this case is rather simple. It might have been more complicated. For example, if Dvorak were found to be superior, it might still be the case that the total social benefits are less than the cost of switching. In that case, we could look for market failure only in the process that started us on the Qwerty keyboard (if the alternative were available at the beginning). Or we might

Second, by ignoring the vitality and variety of the rivals to the Remington machine with its Qwerty keyboard, the received history implies that Sholes's and McGurrin's choices, made largely as matters of immediate expediency, established the standard without ever being tested. More careful reading of historical accounts and checks of original sources reveal a different picture: there were touch-typists other than McGurrin; there were competing claims of speed records; and Remington was not so well established that a keyboard offering significant advantages could not have gained a foothold. If the fable is to carry lessons about the workings of markets, we need to know more than just who won. The victory of the tortoise is a different story without the hare.

There is more to this disagreement than a difference in the evidence that was revealed by our search of the historical record. Our reading of this history reflects a more fundamental difference in views of how markets, and social systems more generally, function. David's overriding point is that economic theory must be informed by events in the world. On that we could not agree more strongly. But ironically, or perhaps inevitably, David's interpretation of the historical record is dominated by his own implicit model of markets, a model that seems to underlie much economic thinking. In that model, an exogenous set of goods is offered for sale at a price, take it or leave it. There is little or no role for entrepreneurs. There generally are no guarantees, no rental markets, no mergers, no loss-leader pricing, no advertising, no marketing research. When such complicating institutions are acknowledged, they are incorporated into the model piecemeal. And they are most often introduced to show their potential to create inefficiencies, not to show how an excess of benefit over cost may constitute an opportunity for private gain.

In the world created by such a sterile model of competition, it is not surprising that accidents have considerable permanence. In such a world, embarking on some wrong path provides little chance to jump to an alternative path. The individual benefits of correcting a mistake are too small to make correction worthwhile, and there are no agents who might profit by devising some means of capturing a part of the aggregate benefits of correction.

It is also not surprising that in such a world there are a lot of accidents. Consumers are given very little discretion to avoid starts down wrong

have concluded that Dvorak is better and that all parties could be made better off if we could costlessly command both a switch and any necessary redistribution. Such a finding would constitute a market failure in the sense of mainstream welfare economics. Of course, this circumstance still might not constitute a market failure in the sense of Demsetz, which requires consideration of the costs of feasible institutions that could effect the change.

paths. A model may assume that consumers have foresight or even that they are perfectly rational, but always in a very limited sense. For example, in the model of Farrell and Saloner, consumers can predict very well the equilibrium among the two candidate standards. But they are attributed no ability to anticipate the existence of some future, better standard. We are not led to ask how the incumbent standard achieved its status; as in David's telling, "It jes' growed."

But at some moment, users must commit resources to a standard or wait. At this moment, they have clear incentives to examine the characteristics of competing standards. They must suffer the consequences of a decision to wait, to discard obsolete equipment or skills, or to continue to function with an inferior standard. Thus, they have a clear incentive to consider what lies down alternative paths. Though their ability to anticipate future events may not be perfect, there is no reason to assume that it is bad relative to any other observers.

Finally, it is consistent that, in a world in which mistakes are frequent and permanent, "scientific approaches" cannot help but make big improvements to market outcomes. In such a world, there is ample room for enlightened reasoning, personified by university professors, to improve on the consequences of myriad independent decisions. What credence can possibly be given to a keyboard that has nothing to accredit it but the trials of a group of mechanics and its adoption by millions of typists? If we use only sterilized models of markets, or ignore the vitality of the rivalry that confronts institutions, we should not be surprised that the historical interpreations that result are not graced with the truth that Cicero asks of historians.

Bibliogrphy

Beeching, Wilfred. *A Century of the Typewriter.* New York: St. Martin's Press, 1974.

Cheung, Steven N. S. "The Fable of the Bees: An Economic Investigation." *Journal of Law and Economics* 16 (April 1973): 11–33.

Coase, Ronald H. "The Problem of Social Cost." *Journal of Law and Economics* 3 (October 1960): 1–44.

Coase, Ronald H. "The Lighthouse in Economics." *Journal of Law and Economics* 17 (October 1974): 357–76.

David, Paul A. "Clio and the Economics of QWERTY." *American Economic Review* 75 (May 1985): 332–37.

David, Paul A. "Understanding the Economics of QWERTY: The Necessity of History." In *Economic History and the Modern Economist,* edited by W. N. Parker. New York: Basil Blackwell, 1986.

Demsetz, Harold. "Information and Efficiency: Another Viewpoint." *Journal of Law and Economics* 12 (April 1969): 1–22.

Dvorak, August; Merrick, Nellie L.; Dealey, William L.; and Ford, Gertrude C. *Typewriting Behavior*. New York: American Book Co., 1936.

Farrell, Joseph, and Saloner, Garth. "Standardization, Compatibility, and Innovation." *Rand Journal* 16 (Spring 1985): 70–83.

Foulke, Arthur. *Mr. Typewriter: A Biography of Christopher Latham Sholes*. Boston: Christopher Publishing, 1961.

Herkimer County Historical Society. *The Story of the Typewriter: 1873–1923*. New York: Andrew H. Kellogg, 1923.

Katz, Michael L., and Shapiro, Carl. "Network Externalities, Competition, and Compatibility." *American Economic Review* 75 (June 1985): 425–40.

Kinkhead, R. "Typing Speed, Keying Rates, and Optimal Keyboard Layouts." *Proceedings of the Human Factors Society* 19 (1975), pp. 159–61.

Landes, William M., and Posner, Richard A. "Trademark Law: An Economic Perspective." *Journal of Law and Economics* 30 (October 1987): 265–309.

Liebowitz, S. J. "Tie-in Sales and Price Discrimination." *Economic Inquiry* 21 (July 1983): 387–99.

Liebowitz, S. J. "Copying and Indirect Appropriability: Photocopying of Journals." *Journal of Political Economy* 93 (October1985): 945–57.

Mandeville, Bernard M. *The Fable of the Bees*. New York: Capricorn Books, 1962.

Mares, George C. *The History of the Typewriter*. London: Guilbert Pitman, 1909.

Margolis, Stephen E. "Two Definitions of Efficiency in Law and Economics." *Journal of Legal Studies* 16 (July 1987): 471–82.

Miller, L. A., and Thomas, J. C. "Behavioral Issues in the Use of Interactive Systems." *International Journal of Man-Machine Studies* 9 (1977): 509–36.

Navy Department. *A Practical Experiment in Simplified Keyboard Retraining—a Report on the Retraining of Fourteen Standard Keyboard Typists on the Simplified Keyboard and a Comparison of Typist Improvement from Training on the Standard Keyboard and Retraining on the Simplified Keyboard*. Department of Services, Training Section. Washington, D.C.: Navy Department, Division of Shore Establishments and Civilian Personnel, July 1944 and October 1944.

New York Times. "Typewriters Contest for a Prize." August 2, 1888.

New York Times. "Remington Still Leads the List." January 9, 1889.

New York Times. "Wonderful Typing." February 28, 1889.

New York Times. "Revolution in the Office." November 11, 1955.

New Yort Times. "U.S. Plans to Test New Typewriter." November 11, 1955.

New York Times. "Pyfgcrl vs. Qwertyuiop." January 22, 1956.

New York Times. "Key Changes Debated." June 18, 1956.

New York Times. "U.S. Balks at Teaching Old Typists New Keys." July 2, 1956.

Norman, Donald A., and Rumelhart, David E. "Studies of Typing from the LNR Research Group." In *Cognitive Aspects of Skilled Typewriting*, edited by William E. Cooper. New York: Springer-Verlag, 1983.

Strong, Earle P. *A Comparative Experiment in Simplified Keyboard Retraining and Standard Keyboard Supplementary Training*. Washington, D.C.: U.S. General Services Administration, 1956.

Tirole, Jean. *The Theory of Industrial Organization*. Cambridge: MIT Press, 1988.

Yamada, Hisao. "A Historical Study of Typewriters and Typing Methods: From the Positon of Planning Japanese Parallels." *Journal of Information Processing* 2 (1980): 175–202.

Yamada, Hisao. "Certain Problems Associated with the Design of Input Keyboards for Japanese Writing." In *Cognitive Aspects of Skilled Typewriting*, edited by William E. Cooper. New York: Springer-Verlag, 1983.

Part VIII
Antitrust, Regulation, and Bureaucracy

[26]

USE OF ANTITRUST TO SUBVERT COMPETITION*

WILLIAM J. BAUMOL *and* *JANUSZ A. ORDOVER*
Princeton and New York Universities *New York University*

The day after Congress passed the changes in the clean air legislation which substantially tightened emissions standards the Japanese automakers called an emergency meeting of their engineers. On the same day the carmakers in Detroit called an emergency meeting of their lawyers. [JOKE CIRCULATING AT THE TIME]

THERE is a specter that haunts our antitrust institutions. Its threat is that, far from serving as the bulwark of competition, these institutions will become the most powerful instrument in the hands of those who wish to subvert it. More than that, it threatens to draw great quantities of resources into the struggle to prevent effective competition, thereby more than offsetting the contributions to economic efficiency promised by antitrust activities. This is a specter that may well dwarf any other source of concern about the antitrust processes. We ignore it at our peril and would do well to take steps to exorcise it.

The problem is not an easy one. In a sense it is inherent in the very nature of the antitrust process. There is no doubt, for example, that mergers can sometimes inhibit or undermine competition and that predatory pricing can sometimes serve as an instrument of monopolization. But then, because of that, a merger that promises to introduce efficiencies that make it necessary for other firms in the industry to try harder is vulnerable to challenge by those rivals, who will claim that it is anticompetitive. Similarly, a firm that by virtue of superior efficiency or economies of scale or scope is able to offer prices low enough to make its competitors uncomfortable is all too likely to find itself accused of predation. Such attempts

* We thank the C. V. Starr Center for Applied Economics at New York University for assistance in the preparation of this paper. Professor Ordover's research has been financed in part by the National Science Foundation. We also thank W. Baxter, J. Miller, and the other participants at the Conference for helpful comments. E. F. Glynn of the FTC vastly improved our discussion of antitrust in Japan and in the EEC Member States.

[*Journal of Law & Economics*, vol. XXVIII (May 1985)]

to use the law as an instrument for the subversion of competition do not confine themselves to private lawsuits. All too often the enterprise seeking to erect a protective umbrella about itself will be tempted to try to subvert the antitrust authorities, Congress, and even the president's office as partners in its purpose. One suspects that the costs in terms of the efficiency of the firm and the economy that is subject to this sort of attack are high. One knows that the costs in terms of the time of management, lawyers, economists, and others absorbed in the litigation process itself are enormous. And it is almost all economic waste.

I. Protectionism as Rent Seeking

Few observers will deny that some firms succumb to the temptation to seek governmental protection from the unpleasantness of effective competition. The blatant attempts by some steel and auto firms to have foreign imports restricted, the transparent purpose underlying a number of private antitrust suits, among other examples, can leave little doubt that the phenomenon is a reality. Yet, at least in some discussions, the volume of such protectionist activity is viewed as fortuitous, explainable largely in terms of cultural characteristics, political climate, and other influences beyond the purview of economic analysis. For example, American litigiousness is sometimes contrasted with Japanese distaste for direct confrontation as an explanation of the differences in the volume of private suits in the two countries.

Economic theory nonetheless has a good deal to say about the matter. The theory of rent seeking contributed by James Buchanan and extended to a variety of legal issues by Richard Posner tells us just how much protectionist effort one can expect in any particular set of circumstances. To summarize the argument very briefly, rent is defined by economists as any earnings by the supplier of an activity that exceed the minimum amount necessary to elicit the services of that supplier. Any supercompetitive (monopoly) profits of a firm are a rent. The theory of rent seeking tells us that where entrepreneurs are free to spend money in an attempt to gain control of such a source of rent, that is, when entry into a rent-seeking activity is completely free, when rent seeking is perfectly competitive or at least perfectly contestable, the resources devoted to the attempt will reach just the amount necessary to consume the entire rent. Rent seekers suing one another to gain control of a source of monopoly profit will spend so much on lawyers, consultants, and so on, that they will dissipate the entire expected monopoly profit in the process. That is just a corollary of the theorem that under perfect competition (excess) profits must be zero. In the circumstances posited, the struggle for the monopoly profits is a perfectly competitive process (or, at least, one that is perfectly contestable).

The result may seem to constitute a mere transfer of wealth from the monopolist to lawyers and economists, but it is much worse than that. In the process the latter are led to devote considerable (and valuable) time in a way that yields no socially valuable product. In other words, here rent seeking transforms into pure waste a quantity of resources equal in value to the rent that is sought.

The search for protection, which is the subject of this paper, is rent seeking (or rent preserving), as we now show. But it is not necessarily competitive, and so the analysis requires some modification. Envision the following scenario. Firm A offers generous salaries to its management, and firm B, with a leaner compensation package, undercuts A's prices, thereby eliminating the rents constituted by the overcompetitive salaries. A can hope to force B to cease and desist and perhaps even to collect treble damages from B by suing it for predatory pricing. What quantity of resources will A devote to this purpose?

First we note that even if other firms in the industry are hurt by A's pricing behavior, there is no competitive pressure driving A to use up its entire expected gain in its rent-preserving outlays. To see what will occur, let us first assume that A is the only firm affected by B's prices and then consider the case where several enterprises have their rents threatened.

Where A alone is involved, and assuming that its chances of achieving its protectionist goal increase monotonically with the quantity of resources it devotes to the purpose, then, as usual, profit maximization requires it to spend on its litigation effort up to the point where an additional dollar in outlay increases the expected rent yield by no more than $1.00. This may well leave firm A with a considerable expected gain from the undertaking. But it is also likely to involve a very substantial total outlay, that is, a very large amount of waste.

Where several other firms C, D, and E will benefit along with A if B is forced to end its "unfair competition," each of them will find it profitable to spend some money to increase the probability of victory. The joint profit-maximizing outlay will be greater, in general, than when only A's rents are at stake, since the marginal expected yield to the group as a whole must be at least as great as the marginal yield to A alone. However, in the absence of effective collusion, the behavior of the group may well not be (joint) profit maximizing, and it may involve outlays by the group lower than those that maximize their joint profits. This is so because an externality (free-rider) issue is involved. Any increment in probability of success against B achieved by an increase in A's expenditure will also benefit firms C, D, and E. As a result, when the marginal net benefit of such outlays to firm A reaches zero, its marginal benefit to the group of firms will still be positive. It follows that the total rent-seeking expenditure of the group can be expected to be less than that which maximizes their combined expected rent return.[1] The group's outlay will almost certainly be at least as large as the largest of the outlays of any one of the four rent-seeking firms would have been had it been the only competitor of B. To see this, it would have paid, say, firm C to spend X dollars in litigation if A and D were not spending anything for the purpose. If C finds that A and D together are spending only $X - \Delta$ for the purpose, then surely it will pay C to obtain the same probability of success as it would have in isolation since now it only costs him $\Delta < X$ dollars to do so. The Slutsky theorem for the firm not subject to a budget constraint tells us that this must be so because what is involved is a reduction in the price of increased probability of success in the rent-seeking undertaking.

We conclude from all this that while protectionist activity is a form of rent seeking, its expected benefits to the rent seeker are not likely to be dissipated completely in wasteful litigation expenditure. But the theory suggests nevertheless that the expenditures may typically be very substantial and that the social costs stemming from such direct waste may well prove very high.[2]

This is by no means the only type of social cost of protectionism. There are at least two other sorts of cost: monopolistic resource misallocation, and disincentives for internal operating efficiency for the individual firms, which may prove far more serious. The nature of the first of these is obvious to anyone familiar with welfare economics. After all, the immediate purpose of the protectionist activity is to subvert the forces of competition, and if the effort succeeds, it will lead to pricing and other decisions that are different, perhaps very different, from those that would emerge under competition. It follows that resources can be expected to be misallocated, as is always true under unregulated monopoly in a market that is not contestable.

[1] We cannot be certain of this since it depends on the concavity-convexity properties of the pertinent relationships. The presence of externalities themselves is likely to cause problems on that score. On this see William J. Baumol & David F. Bradford, Detrimental Externalities and Non-Convexity of the Production Set, 40 Economica 160 (n.s. 1972); or William J. Baumol & Wallace E. Oates, The Theory of Environmental Policy (1975), at ch. 8.

[2] The astonishing outlays by major firms on the antitrust litigations in which they have been involved confirms that these expenditures can indeed be substantial. For example, Alan A. Fisher & Robert H. Lande, Efficiency Considerations in Merger Enforcement, 71 Calif. L. Rev. 1580, 1673 (1983) estimate that Du Pont, Seagram, and Mobil spent about $13.5 million in private legal fees to acquire Conoco. In addition, they estimate at 1673 n.308 that an average merger antitrust case costs anywhere between $700,000 and $1.4 million. To this one must add costs incurred by the DOJ, or the FCC, and the courts.

The second social cost takes the form of inefficiency in the protected firm. First, if a company is insulated from competition, the pressures that would otherwise force it to operate with maximal efficiency are simply removed.[3] It is freer than it otherwise would be to engage in nepotism and sloppy supervision, to display excessive caution in risky decisions, and to avoid innovations that require management to exert itself. In short, protectionist activity frees the firm to engage in the degree of inefficiency that suits the proclivities and abilities of its management.

The third social cost of protectionism is its effect on the immediate objectives, and hence the organization, of the firm. If such rent seeking is the easier way to increase its profits or to achieve other managerial objectives, the firm's energies will be directed toward preparation for its litigative ventures, which will receive priority over efforts to increase productivity or to improve the product line. Engineers will become relatively less numerous in the ranks of top management, and lawyers will assume a correspondingly larger share.[4]

In sum, the social costs of rent-seeking protectionism can be very high (though we have no estimate of their magnitude). Indeed, if it is true that productivity growth in the United States is suffering from a serious longer-term malaise, it is not implausible that the incentives for firms to undertake the sort of rent seeking we are discussing has played a role that is not negligible.

We repeat that the antitrust and regulatory institutions have shown

[3] Some sense of magnitude of the expenditures that insulation from competition can elicit is suggested by the surprising size of the cut in wage and salary outlays in aviation that followed airline deregulation.

[4] A simple model making use of the Slutsky theorem readily confirms that if the antitrust laws increase the expected returns to litigation, they will also increase the firm's outlays on lawyers and other inputs that contribute to the probability of success in such litigation. A very elementary model for the purpose maximizes the profit function.

$$\Pi^*(\mathbf{Z}, x) = \Pi(Z) + vr - x \tag{1}$$

subject to

$$r = f(x), f'(x) > 0, \tag{2}$$

where $\mathbf{Z}$ = the vector of the firm's inputs and outputs, x = its litigation-related expenditure, r = its probability of victory in litigation, v = its expected increase in profit as a result of victory, $f(x)$ = probability of litigative success as a function of the firm's expenditure on litigation, and $\Pi(Z)$ = the firm's profit from its normal production activities in the absence of litigation.

We may regard r, the probability of success, as an additional output of the firm and v as the per unit return to an increase in the value of r. Then, if the sufficient conditions for the Slutsky theorem are satisfied, we know that we must have $\partial r/\partial v > 0$. That is, if the availability of the antitrust rules increases the payoff to litigative rent-seeking activity, the profit-maximizing firm will act to increase the probability of success in this arena. But by (2), in order to do so it must increase x, so that we have our result, $\partial x/\partial v > 0$.

themselves to be sources of substantial incentives and opportunities for such rent-seeking activity. Whenever a competitor becomes too successful or too efficient, whenever his competition threatens to become sufficiently effective to disturb the quiet and easy life his rival is leading, the latter will be tempted to sue on the grounds that the competition is "unfair." Every successful enterprise comes to expect almost as a routine phenomenon that it will sooner or later find itself the defendant in a multiplicity of cases. It is an enchanted topsy-turvy world in which vigorous competition is made to seem anticompetitive and in which "fair competition" comes to mean no competition at all.

The runners-up, the firms that despair of succeeding through superior efficiency or more attractive products, use different instruments in seeking protection from rivals. The antitrust laws are not always useful as means to handicap competition from abroad, but they are apparently a prime instrument for the creation of impediments to effective competition by American rivals. The reason the antitrust laws can be used in this way is clear. The borderline between measures that are legitimate competitive moves and those that are destructive instruments of monopolization is often difficult to define even in principle (witness, for example, the intricacies of the concept of predatory innovation). Moreover, whatever the criteria adopted, in practice they rarely lend themselves to clear-cut evidence and unambiguous conclusions. The runner-up firm then finds itself with the opportunity to claim that almost any successful program by a rival is "anticompetitive" and that it constitutes monopolization. Antitrust, whose objective is the preservation of competition, by its very nature lends itself to use as a means to undermine effective competition. This is not merely ironic. It is very dangerous for the workings of our economy.

II. Antitrust Provisions That Encourage Protectionism

We cannot hope to provide an exhaustive list of the antitrust institutions that lend themselves to the purposes of the protectionist. We simply offer several illustrations. We discuss the treble-damages provisions, vagueness of criteria of predation and other types of unfairness of competition, and excessive severity of tests of anticompetitiveness.

Treble Damages[5]

The availability of trebled damages payments to the plaintiff has several arguments in its favor. First, there is evidence that in antitrust suits pri-

[5] See Kenneth G. Elzinga and William Breit, Private Antitrust Enforcement: The New Learning, in this issue, and Frank H. Easterbrook, Detrebling Antitrust Damages, in this issue, for an extensive discussion of the social costs and benefits of the trebling of damages.

vate plaintiffs have a relatively low probability of winning their cases.[6] If private antitrust suits are considered desirable in at least some cases, the plaintiffs must be offered an expected return at least equal to the heavy litigation costs they are likely to incur. While treble damages do not generally increase the probability of victory (and may well decrease it by forcing the defendant to expend larger resources to protect his interests), they almost certainly increase the expected award to a plaintiff. Second, in some cases (such as successful price fixing), in addition to the culprit's ill-gotten gains, his victims suffer a deadweight loss in the form of distorted relative purchase quantities which the courts do not recognize in their damage calculations. A multiplied damage payment then serves as very rough compensation for such deadweight losses, though any resemblance between the two magnitudes is certain to be purely coincidental. Third, no doubt some violators of the antitrust laws escape unscathed and sometimes are not even brought to trial, let alone convicted and punished. Optimal deterrence requires such firms to face ex ante a probable punishment that does fit the crime. This means that the higher the probability that any particular violator of the law will get away with it, the higher must be the fine exacted from those who are brought to justice.

All of these arguments are legitimate so far as they go, but they neglect the other side of the matter. From the point of view of society, escalated damages awards also increase the probable payoff to protectionist activity. The runner-up who hopes to impose legal obstacles on the vigorous competitive efforts of his all-too-successful rival is offered the prospect of also acquiring a substantial amount of funding in the process. It has even been charged that runners-up have been known to start such suits in the hope of acquiring the funding that the capital market denied them.

Trebled damages also increase the amounts it pays both defendant and plaintiff to expend in combating the case, for such damages increase the pool of rents to be disputed. And, as usual, the waste of economic resources elicited can be expected to be proportional to the size of the available rents. It is noteworthy that, as in the case of rivalrous advertising, such enhanced outlays on a legal battle will tend to cancel one another, at least in part. They will benefit neither the plaintiff nor the defendant, while raising the cost to society.

All in all, the case against trebled damages is far from clear-cut. Yet the fact that they provide a direct incentive for protectionist activity suggests that the issue requires reconsideration. We will return to this subject

[6] See Richard A. Posner, A Statistical Study of Antitrust Enforcement, 13 J. Law & Econ. 365 (1970); National Economic Research Associates, Statistical Analysis of Private Antitrust Enforcement, Final Report (1979).

later, when we discuss policy appropriate for the phenomenon of protectionist misuse of antitrust institutions.

Vagueness of Antitrust Criteria

Knowledgeable students of antitrust issues often are impressed with the difficulty of determining and defining in a manner that is universally applicable the borderline between acceptable and unacceptable behavior. Scherer's attack on the famous Areeda-Turner article is a classic illustration, carefully cataloguing a variety of circumstances under which almost any reasonable but explicitly defined standard of predatory pricing can be expected to condone activities that are anticompetitive or to condemn activities that are innocent or even benign.[7] No categorical rule can fully encompass intentions, antecedent and subsequent circumstances and developments, interdependence with actions other than those under immediate consideration, and the host of other pertinent considerations. Such a point of view would seem to lead toward heavy reliance on the good judgment of the courts, toward a universal reign of some form of rule of reason. It leaves matters subject to vague and general guidelines derived from the obscure admonitions of the pertinent law and the available precedents, and beyond that it gives the courts the duty of deciding matters case by case, on the basis of individual judgment and in light of attendant circumstances.

Here is not the place to examine all the likely consequences of such a procedure or to consider the implications of wide range in capability and economic sophistication that one encounters among judges. Rather, our concern here is that obscurity and ambiguity are convenient tools for those enterprises on the prowl for opportunities to hobble competition. As we know, it is not always necessary to win cases in order to blunt a rival's competitive weapons. Harassment by lawsuit or even the threat of harassment can be a marvelous stimulus to timidity on the part of competitors. The potential defendant who cannot judge in advance with any reasonable degree of certainty whether its behavior will afterward be deemed illegal is particularly vulnerable to guerrilla warfare and intimidation into the sort of gentlemanly competitive behavior that is the antithesis of true competition.

Thus, to continue with our example, whatever one may think of the Areeda-Turner test (and we do consider it to constitute a major infusion of

[7] F. M. Scherer, Comment on Areeda and Turner, 89 Harv. L. Rev. 869 (1976). Phillip Areeda and Donald F. Turner, Predatory Pricing and Related Practices under Section 2 of the Sherman Act, 88 Harv. L. Rev. 697 (1975).

logic into the arena), it seems to us certainly to have made a critical and beneficial contribution simply by reducing vagueness in the criterion of predation in pricing. This makes protectionist misuse of the antitrust laws much less easy.

Severity of the Tests of Anticompetitiveness

A third phenomenon that facilitates protectionist efforts is reliance on rules increasing the range of private activities subject to condemnation as "anticompetitive." Here, too, the Areeda-Turner contribution provides an excellent illustration. The long debate between advocates of fully distributed cost tests of anticompetitiveness in pricing and advocates of incremental or marginal costs for this purpose has a straightforward interpretation in terms of our discussion. Though we are not disinterested observers of this debate, we are reasonably confident that it is not bias alone that leads us to interpret advocacy of the fully distributed cost approach as a systematic protectionist onslaught. We believe the evidence strongly supports the thesis that it is a standard put forward almost exclusively by firms that were unlikely to compete successfully on the merits of their performance alone. They advocate their costing approach as a device to limit the price-cutting opportunities of rivals rendered more efficient by economies of scale or scope, by superior management, or by other legitimate sources of superiority. This is surely attested to by the frequency of cases in which full distribution has been used to argue that some prices are unacceptably low, when the pricing behavior that should most be feared by guardians of the public interest in the presence of market power is overcharging, not underpricing.

Thus, rules that make vigorous competition dangerous clearly foster protectionism. That point is obvious enough. What is perhaps only a bit less obvious is that protectionists are not prone to wait passively for such overrestrictive rules to fall into their laps. Rather, a central element in their strategy is persistent expenditure of money and effort to change the rules in ways that favor their cause, and resistance to any attempt to reduce impediments to effective competition. When an agency such as the FTC proposes to hold hearings on the advisability of revision of one of its rules that may be suspected of discouraging competition, those who stand to bear the brunt of any enhanced competitive pressures can be expected to resist energetically.

In sum, it seems plausible that rules defining unacceptable competitive practices that lean toward potential plaintiffs are a major source of encouragement to protectionist efforts. The presence of such rules is not happenstance. They are often attributable to the deliberate efforts of those who stand to gain by using the antitrust mechanism to emasculate competition.

The preceding paragraphs are intended to suggest that the search for protection from competition by runner-up firms, and the use of antitrust institutions for the purpose, is encouraged by a number of attributes of those institutions themselves. We do not mean to apportion blame or even to claim that any one group can be said to be at fault. Our purpose is to look for strategic points that lend themselves to modification and that are therefore appropriate foci for ameliorative policy—a subject to which we will return presently.

It must, however, be pointed out that even if antitrust rules were modified to make them less susceptible to rent-seeking activities described here, such activities might not disappear or even decline materially. More likely, firms might merely divert their rent-seeking resources to other political and legal arenas.

III. Case Examples of Strategic Uses of Antitrust

The purpose of this section is to illustrate by means of a few actual cases the protectionist uses of antitrust and associated forms of government intervention such as regulation. Our examples involve mergers and joint ventures, as well as monopolization cases.

A. The GM-Toyota Joint Venture

The GM-Toyota joint venture illustrates clearly the strategic role of antitrust litigation. Here, it is Chrysler and Ford, the horizontal competitors of the joint venturers, that have pressed the Federal Trade Commission to reject the joint venture on the ground that it will restrain competition in the automobile market in general and in the subcompact segment of the market in particular. Recently the FTC approved the joint venture. Undeterred, Chrysler has been pressing a private antitrust action in an attempt to accomplish what it failed to do at the FTC.

This sort of opposition is predictable, and in a manner that is rather ironic it can signal clearly the likely effects of the joint venture. If the enterprise were in fact likely to acquire monopoly power and charge excessive prices, other U.S. auto firms undoubtedly would benefit from the resulting protective umbrella, which would enable them to raise their prices as well. If this is the probable outcome, then those rivals can be expected to view the joint venture with equanimity and silent acquiescence. But if the joint venture really is likely to introduce economies or improve product quality, it is sure to make life harder for the domestic rivals of the participants who will then have to run correspondingly faster in order to stand still.[8] Paradoxically, then and only then, when the joint venture is really beneficial, can those rivals be relied on to denounce the undertaking as "anticompetitive."[9] That is exactly the response of Chrysler and Ford, who have presented themselves here as defenders of consumers' interests even though before other forums they have not hesitated to argue for blatantly protectionist measures such as higher trade barriers. Once again, consistency has given way to expediency.

B. MCI v. AT & T: The Economics of Price Inflexibility[10]

MCI was perhaps the first firm to challenge AT & T's monopoly in the long-distance telecommunications market. Beginning in 1963, MCI embarked on an extensive investment program in microwave transmission facilities. Because of its (and the FCC's) policy of "universal service" or "nationwide averaging," AT & T's relative rates along different routes did not correspond closely to relative costs, with service along sparsely used routes comparatively underpriced. This was a clear invitation for "cream skimming" entry. Understandably, MCI at least initially attempted to specialize in serving the high-density routes in which AT & T earned more substantial profit margins.

MCI's moves to enter these routes predictably led to an attempt by AT & T to adjust its relative rates to correspond more closely to costs. MCI alleged that these responses were anticompetitive. Litigation ensued.[11] Of course, MCI's initial entry primarily into AT & T's more profitable routes is unobjectionable. The benefits of competition depend on the willingness of entrants to seek out profitable opportunities. What is far more questionable is MCI's attempt to use antitrust litigation as a means to restrain AT & T's ability to respond to competitive incursions. It was charged that by adjusting its prices on different routes to correspond more closely to

[8] Admittedly, it is possible that the joint venture will make GM a more formidable competitor not because of any gains in economic efficiency but merely because it will make it easier for GM to satisfy the asinine Company Average Fuel Efficiency (CAFE) regulations.

[9] Steven Salop suggested to one of us that a merger of joint venture may be a part of a strategy employed by the merging partners, or co-venturers, to elevate the rivals' costs and thereby harm competition. We doubt that "predatory" mergers or joint ventures are a frequent occurrence. In such a rare instance, the rival would have to assume the standard of proof of a potential anticompetitive effect that is appropriate for monopolization cases, rather than that which is appropriate for a merger case.

[10] We are not disinterested discussants of this case. Both of us have carried out work for AT & T. One of us not only served as a witness for AT & T in the MCI case but also recommended the type of price response to MCI's entry that AT & T later adopted.

[11] MCI Communications Corp. v. AT & T, 369 F. Supp. 1004 (E. D. Pa. 1973) vacated and remanded, 496 F.2d 214 (3d Cir. 1974); MCI Communications Corp. v. AT & T, 462 F. Supp. 1072 (N. D. Ill. 1978), rev'd, 708 F.2d 1081 (7th Cir. 1983).

costs, even on routes where competition had not yet appeared, AT & T was launching "preemptive strikes." One can imagine what would have been said if instead AT & T had reduced prices *only* on the routes where MCI had opened for business.

MCI insisted during the trial and in its appellate brief that a "full-cost" approach should be used to calculate AT & T's costs and to perform the tests of predatoriness.[12] Indeed, according to MCI, citing Dr. William Melody's testimony, many "economists advocate the use of fully distributed costs as the proper test for below-cost predatory pricing in the telecommunications industry."[13]

There is no need to dwell here on the inefficiencies that result from the use of fully allocated costs as constraints on the price responses of regulated and unregulated firms. It suffices to note that insistence that such costs are the appropriate price floors invites socially inefficient entry that is elicited not by genuine cost advantages and productive efficiencies but by false profitability signals. There is no doubt that potential and actual entrants (such as MCI) have a strong incentive to rigidify the price responses open to an incumbent who is confronted with newly emerging competition. It seems clear that the staunchest advocates of full-cost pricing have been firms anxious to hobble their disquietingly effective rivals.

C. *Strategic Uses of Antitrust in Takeover Cases*

The targets of tender offers frequently initiate antitrust suits against their unwanted suitors. The critical issues are whether the targets should be allowed to institute injunction proceedings or whether instead the enforcement of merger statutes should be left to the government and to customers who are likely to be injured if the merger brings competition to an end, elevates prices, and causes resource misallocation. The issue is not straightforward. While the incentive for management to bring an antitrust case need not coincide with the interests of the consumers,[14] it is nevertheless true that the management of the target is probably better informed than any other group about the likely consequences of the acquisition for future competition.

There is no question that a target's management, bent on derailing the tender offer, has a potent weapon in the antitrust laws. The two most

[12] Brief of Appellees, MCI Communications Corp. and MCI Telecommunications Corp. (March 5, 1981), at 112.

[13] *Id.* at 113–14. The court of appeals disagreed and decided against MCI on most points.

[14] This point is made in Frank H. Easterbrook & Daniel R. Fischel, Antitrust Suits by Targets of Tender Offers, 80 Michigan L. Rev. 1155 (1982).

recent instances in which highly lucrative offers were defeated with the aid of the antitrust laws were *Grumman Corp. v. LTV Corp.*[15] and *Marathon Oil Co. v. Mobil Corp.*[16] The latter case illustrates the problem clearly. Marathon's management possessed extensive, firsthand information about the scope of its geographic operations and about the marketing of gasoline to independents, which was at issue in the antitrust proceedings. On the other hand, Marathon's management hardly shared the interests of the automobile owners in cheap and plentiful gasoline.[17] Indeed, if the target's management were truly guided by shareholders' interests, it ought to sell the company to the bidder likely to obtain the highest profit from the transaction.[18] But when such enhanced profits result from the elevation of market power in the postmerger market, the interests of the consumers and of the target's stockholders clash directly.

IV. Alternative Enforcement Procedures: Japan and the EEC

In this section we briefly compare antitrust procedures in the United States with those of our major trading partners: Japan and the EEC. We do not claim any expertise on the antitrust laws of other countries. However, expertise is not required in light of our limited objective—to explore how other countries have held in check the use of antitrust litigation as a strategic weapon in the hands of competitors. (Of course, none of the discussion is meant to imply that the antitrust policies in other countries constitute ideal models for the United States that should recommend themselves to American scholars and policymakers.)

A. *Japan*[19]

Japan has dealt with the problem of strategic use or abuse of the antitrust laws by largely consolidating enforcement in its Fair Trade Commission (JFTC). In Japan a person injured by acts in violation of the antimonopoly laws has a right to sue for damages under Section 709 of the Civil Code. And any person injured by conduct found illegal by the JFTC has a right, under Section 25 of the Antimonopoly Act, to recover dam-

[15] 665 F.2d 10 (2d Cir. 1981).

[16] 669 F.2d 378 (6th Cir. 1982).

[17] In fact, if the management had wanted to trigger an auction for Marathon by impeding Mobil's actions, it might have been implying that it was expecting another oil company as the next suitor.

[18] That is, if the target's managers can somehow share in these incremental profits.

[19] Information in this section is culled from notes by Matsushita; see M. Matsushita, Informal Notes for the Conference on Japan's Antimonopoly Legislation and Doing Business with Japan, Japan Society (January 5, 1978).

ages.[20] Yet as of 1983 only five damage suits had been filed under Section 25. The reasons for the reluctance of private Japanese plaintiffs to seek damages in court are not easy to determine. We think that the national distaste for litigation cannot explain it fully. In particular, the fact that damages are not readily awarded in Japan and that plaintiffs can sue under Section 25 only if the JFTC has found the conduct complained of to be illegal surely discourages private actions for damages.[21]

Japan's FTC is basically an administrative agency with some quasi-judicial powers. Its judicial powers are exercised only rarely. According to the Japanese antitrust expert M. Matsushita of Sophia University, only four antitrust criminal cases have occurred in the past thirty years of antitrust enforcement. The main channel through which the JFTC shapes competition is informal. The JFTC may issue "warnings" that are usually respected. In addition, the JFTC provides "guidance" that helps the companies to avoid conflict with the antitrust laws, especially in international contracts.

When the JFTC brings a formal action, it usually ends with the company (or companies) accepting the JFTC's recommendation decision. Available estimates indicate that some 90 percent of these recommendations are accepted. Those that are not accepted usually are resolved during trial through consent decisions that embody the proposals of the respondent.

Private complaints are filed with the JFTC. The JFTC must then investigate but need not take an enforcement action. However, according to the Japanese experts, frequently investigation alone suffices to induce the investigated firm (or firms) to stop the activity that has been challenged.

[20] Hiroshi Iyori & Akinori Uesugi, The Antimonopoly Laws of Japan 127 (2d ed. 1983). We are grateful to Edward Glynn of the FTC for correcting our earlier discussion of private enforcement in Japan.

[21] Economists are usually loath to seek explanations in alleged differences in "national character" to explain the Japanese record. Arguments based on national character are difficult to test and are, in any event, treacherous, as the following illustrative story suggests: "An Australian expert, invited by the Japanese government, had this to say in his Report, as excerpted in the *Japan Times* of August 18th 1915: 'Japan commercially, I regret to say, does not bear the best reputation for executing business. Inferior goods, irregularity and indifferent shipments have caused no end of worry . . . My impression as to your cheap labour was soon disillusioned when I saw your people at work. No doubt they are lowly paid, but the return is equally so; to see your men at work made me feel that you are a very satisfied easy-going race who reckon time is no object. When I spoke to some managers they informed me that it was impossible to change the habits of national heritage . . . First class managers . . . are required to wake things up and get out of the go-as-you-please style that seems universal at present.' " Cited in J. N. Bhagwati, Development Economics: What Have We Learnt (mimeographed, Columbia Univ. 1984), at 27.

Thus, here there does remain some scope for strategic use of the JFTC investigatory powers.

Yet the incentives for the allegedly harmed petitioners to use this process are limited. They receive no financial recompense for any harm they have suffered. Their only benefit derives from the JFTC's ability to require cessation of the allegedly anticompetitive activity. The incentive to use the JFTC for protection from competition is thereby weakened, especially if the cost of filing the complaint is high.

It is noteworthy that in a few cases complaining parties have attempted to sue the JFTC for the failure to act on their complaints. However, appellate authorities have ruled that only respondents can appeal a JFTC decision and have thereby severely restricted the complainants' standing to sue.

In sum, in Japan antitrust enforcement is placed almost exclusively in the hands of its JFTC, which relies heavily on informal mechanisms such as warnings and reviews. The strategic use of the antitrust mechanism is circumscribed because the parties who claim they were harmed must first convince the JFTC to act and cannot appeal from the JFTC decisions.

One may well feel that this arrangement goes too far and that its protection of anticompetitive activities is excessive. However, it does certainly help to check the litigiousness of business firms and their use of antitrust as a means to restrain effective competition.

B. The EEC Member States

It would add unduly to the length of this paper, and strain the information at our disposal, to analyze the vulnerability to strategic abuse of the national laws on competition where they exist in the EEC countries. It is safe to say, however, that the incentives for abuse probably are significantly weaker in the EEC member states than they are in the United States, at least for the following reasons. First, in the EEC member states the plaintiff who wins a case is not entitled to treble damages. Second, in the EEC member states contingent fee arrangements with lawyers do not exist in antitrust cases. Third, discovery procedures are less developed in Europe than they are in the United States, which may make it more difficult for a plaintiff to obtain the "incriminating" evidence with which to fuel rent-seeking anticompetitive activities.[22] Fourth, in the EEC mem-

[22] However, as Edward Glynn has noted, extensive "discovery" available under American law can at times also be used to "bludgeon" a financially weak plaintiff into dropping his case.

ber states the right to trial by jury in money damage cases is not available. Fifth, in Britain especially an unsuccessful plaintiff must bear the defendant's costs.[23] And, finally, in Europe some aspects of the competition law, for example merger statutes, fall only within the purview of governmental bodies. This greatly reduces the opportunity for strategic use of these laws.

Having said all this, we must emphasize one important continuing development in the EEC member states that bears directly on the issues raised in this paper. It has by now become fairly well established through judicial authority that "actions for injunctions and for compensation may be brought in national courts by plaintiffs claiming to suffer loss as a result of infringements of Articles 85–86 and 90 EEC Treaty. . . . This confirms that Articles 85–86 are laws for the protection of individual interests and *not* merely laws for the protection of the public interest or the community."[24] Thus, for example, rivals now can avail themselves of EEC statutes on competition if they can claim to have been affected in their intracommunity business activities by allegedly anticompetitive actions of a dominant firm.

This extension of the enforcement of the EEC competition statutes in general, and of Article 86 in particular, opens an opportunity for strategic use of the statutes. The leading United Kingdom case that has established that plaintiffs can, in fact, sue shows that the EEC competition statutes can be used to retard rather than promote allocative efficiency.[25] In that case, the plaintiff was purchasing most of its "bulk butter" from the Milk Marketing Board (which apparently had a dominant position in the relevant market) for resale to a single purchaser in the Netherlands. At some point the defendant changed its marketing strategy and decided to sell its bulk butter to four distributors in England and Wales. The plaintiff was instructed to purchase its butter requirements from the designated distributors. Allegedly, this would have rendered its resale activities unprofitable. The plaintiff sued and asked for injunctive relief. The relief was not granted. Nevertheless, the case set a precedent for future suits.

The preceding sequence will be familiar to the American students of

[23] We note, however, that the effects of fee shifting on litigation incentives are not as clear as one might expect. See Steven Shavell, Suit, Settlement and Trial: A Theoretical Analysis under Alternative Methods for the Allocation of Legal Costs, 11 J. Legal Stud. 55 (1982); and Janusz A. Ordover & Ariel Rubinstein, A Sequential Concession Game with Asymmetric Information (mimeographed, C. V. Starr Center for Applied Economics, New York Univ., July 1984).

[24] John Temple Lang, Enforcement in National Courts of Community Competition Rules on Enterprises, Notes for Lecture, Brussels (March 1983).

[25] Garden Cottage Foods, Ltd. v. Milk Marketing Board (1983) 2 ALL ER 770.

antitrust. Vertical relations between a manufacturer and his dealers have been a subject of frequent litigation, often of doubtful merit. It appears that now, by involving Article 86, dealers in the EEC may have acquired an important weapon with which to attack the distribution arrangements of their suppliers.[26] This has occurred at a time when, in the United States, various commentators have suggested that per se legality be granted to such arrangements. Time will tell whether competitors in the EEC will use the statute against one another.

V. What Is to Be Done?

There are no easy and costless remedies for the abuse of antitrust by those who use it for protection from competition. The difficulty is inherent in the problem, for anything that is done to make it harder for plaintiffs to use our antitrust institutions anticompetitively automatically also makes it easier for others to get away with acts of monopolization. This trade-off is apparently unavoidable, because anything that makes conviction of the defendant more likely necessarily makes suits more attractive to plaintiffs in pursuit of protection from effective competition. The Japanese, as we have seen, have largely solved the problem of protectionism, but only by virtual prohibition of initiatives by the victims of monopolistic behavior. In dealing with the shortcomings of our antitrust institutions that are the subject of this paper, we must be careful not to undermine the antitrust laws themselves.

The most obvious remedial change is a restriction of the sort of circumstances to which treble damages apply. One should consider both the use of a multiple smaller than three, at least in those types of cases, such as predatory pricing, in which rent-seeking protectionist activity seems to abound, and in some types of cases one might even consider restriction of the amount of the award to the magnitude of the damage actually shown to have been sustained.

Such proposals are not new, but we do have a new wrinkle to suggest. The choice of multiplicand in damages payments faces at least two conflicting goals. Given the possibly low probability of discovery of an antitrust violation and of conviction on the charge, optimal deterrence clearly calls for a multiplicand greater than unity, and on that score trebling of damages may perhaps not be too bad an approximation to the optimum.

[26] In the United Kingdom, such practices are also examined in the Restrictive Practices Court in which there is "a great deal of wasted time particularly with economists swearing against each other—canceling each other out!" As was observed extrajudicially by Advocate-General Warner of the Court of Justice of the European Communities, in Enterprise Law of the 80's 235 (F. M. Rowe, F. G. Jacobs, & M. R. Joelson eds. 1980).

On the other hand, if this encourages rent seeking we may want, on this score, a much smaller damages award.

Environmental economics has shown how an analogous problem can be dealt with. There, deterrence policy can use the polluter pays principle as an effective instrument. But if that payment is used to compensate the polluter's victims on the basis of the amount of damage they suffer, a moral hazard problem arises—for it undermines the incentive for potential victims to seek pollution-avoiding locations or to take other measures to protect themselves from damages. Indeed, it can be proved that *any* such compensation to utility-maximizing victims will reduce their pollution-deterrent resource outlays below the socially optimal level. The solution implicitly advocated by economists for pollution policy is simple. The polluter should indeed pay, but the payments should be collected by government, at least in part, and should not go to the victims. In that way the payment scheme is provided with two parameter values—the price the polluter is charged, and the amount that victims are compensated. These parameter values can then be chosen so as to elicit both the optimal reduction of polluter emissions and the optimal self-defensive effort by the victim.

In private antitrust suits a similar solution is at least worth considering. That is, the defendant who is found guilty might continue to pay three times (or some other multiple of) the estimated damages. But the plaintiff can be made eligible to a smaller multiple (and perhaps even a multiple less than unity) of that damages figure. The difference would then go into the public treasury as a tax on violators of the antitrust laws. Once again, this provides two distinct parameters (the defendant's multiple and the plaintiff's multiple) to the designers of public policy who can select their values separately so as to provide the proper incentive for deterrence of violations while at the same time offering an appropriate disincentive for rent-seeking protectionism.

One may want to take a further step in this direction. Mere accusation and trial subjects the defendant firm to enormous expenses and even greater ex ante risks of an expensive adverse decision, even if it transpires ex post on the basis of convincing evidence that it is completely innocent. The possibility of required compensation to the defendant for these damages caused by the plaintiff might well discourage frivolous and mischievous suits, including those undertaken in the hope that an out-of-court settlement will prevent the latter from having to reveal the weakness of his case. Thus, the third remedy we propose for consideration is liability of the plaintiff for costs incurred by the defendant in the event of acquittal.

A fourth line of defense against protectionism is the adoption of clearer criteria of unacceptable behavior, such as the predation tests proposed by Areeda and Turner or those we have suggested.[27] For reasons already discussed, vagueness in the standards of unacceptable behavior plays into the hands of those who would use the antitrust laws as anticompetitive weapons.

Fifth, one may well consider it desirable, for similar reasons, to inhibit, if not necessarily prohibit, the ability of the management of a company that is a takeover target to bring an antitrust suit against the unwanted acquirer.[28]

Here it should be emphasized that we do not want to immunize mergers or acquisitions from the antitrust laws. Rather, we suggest the possibility that (only) those most likely to misuse the process for protectionist purposes be limited in their ability to bring private suits against the transaction on antitrust grounds. Others, including the pertinent government agencies, should clearly remain free to do so.

All of these suggestions are offered very tentatively and with great hesitation. They are mostly untried, and our lack of competence in the law surely raises questions about their workability, their consistency with other legal rules, and perhaps even (in some cases) their constitutionality.

We end by repeating an earlier caveat. It is not by accident that every one of our very tentative proposals incurs some social cost in that it reduces to some degree the available deterrents to monopolistic behavior. This is unavoidable, because any measure that offers some promise of dealing effectively with the problem discussed in this paper must necessarily involve some reduction in the incentive to bring litigation and hence must weaken to a degree the position of the potential plaintiff. It seems clear to us that *some* move in this direction is urgent if antitrust and regulation are to be prevented from becoming major impediments to competitiveness, efficiency, and productivity growth in the U.S. economy. The question is not whether some such moves are justified. The issue, rather, is how substantial those moves should be—how great a modification constitutes a social optimum in the trade-off between the two competing perils to true competition—excessive weakening of the deterrents to monopolization and excessive facilitation of attempts to subvert effective competition through protectionist misuse of our antitrust institutions.

[27] William J. Baumol, Quasi Permanence of Price Reduction, 89 Yale L. J. 1 (1979); Janusz A. Ordover & Robert D. Willig, An Economic Definition of Predation: Pricing and Product Innovation, 91 Yale L. J. 8 (1981).

[28] In a recent case, the U.S. District Court for the Central District of California ruled that the target of a tender offer lacks standing to seek a preliminary injunction to halt the acquisition as a violation of the Clayton Act. Carter Hawley Hale Stores, Inc. v. The Limited, Inc., 587 F. Supp. 246 (C. D. Cal. 1984).

[27]

Is the theory behind *U.S. v. AT&T* applicable today?

BY TIMOTHY J. BRENNAN*

I. Introduction

Ever since it was announced in 1982 and enacted in 1984, the Modified Final Judgment (MFJ) adopted to settle the Department of Justice's 8-year antitrust suit against AT&T has been the subject of intense scrutiny and debate among lawyers, economists, policy makers, industry participants, and the public at large. Decisions by the Department of Justice and the courts narrowed the

* Policy Sciences Graduate Program and Department of Economics, University of Maryland, Baltimore, MD.

AUTHOR'S NOTE: *This article was written while the author was a Gilbert White Fellow at Resources for the Future; RFF's support is gratefully appreciated. The author also has consulted with the Antitrust Division of the Department of Justice on telecommunications policy matters. Nothing here represents the position of RFF, the Department of Justice, or any of their officials or personnel. The author appreciates very much the comments of Robert Thorpe, Molly Macauley, David Loomis, Arthur McGrath, and participants in the 14th Annual Rutgers Advanced Workshop in Regulation and Public Utility Economics. All opinions and errors remain the author's responsibility.*

scope of these restrictions, only to intensify the decibel level from their proponents, who asserted greater vulnerability to assorted anticompetitive threats, and their opponents, primarily the regional Bell operating companies (RBOCs). Technological changes, primarily through the digitization of wireline networks, explosion in data communications, development of switched wireless systems, and plunging prices for complementary computers and multimedia equipment have made the telephone industry even more prominent. Among the policy responses, as I write, include court petitions from some of the RBOCs to vacate the MFJ and legislative proposals to eliminate the line-of-business restrictions.

Lost in the rush to reform is the idea that there were some reasons to force AT&T to divest its local telephone operations. These reasons may have been primarily theoretical, backed by interpretations of AT&T's predivestiture conduct rather than econometric evidence that keeping local telephone exchange companies from operating in other related markets would improve economic performance. One can debate whether these reasons caused the divestiture, or whether they served as an intellectual rationale for a political and legal decision. Nevertheless, unless one adopts a completely deterministic view of the policy process, there is some merit in asking the forgotten question: If the divestiture made sense in 1984, why would it not make sense in 1995?

The heated rhetoric surrounding this question is one compelling motivation for a systematic assessment of whether the "old" theory currently applies. Moreover, the conventional indicators of whether antitrust complaints are justified are mixed in this situation. The so-called first theorem of antitrust—If a competitor complains about X, X must be good—is not helpful. The telephone companies whose practices are currently circumscribed by the MFJ stand as both input suppliers and as potential competitors to the complaining firms.

It may be useful to look at the leading examples. The economist's instinct would be to treat AT&T's or MCI's opposition to allowing local telephone companies to provide interexchange service as yet another example of using antitrust, regulation, and the political process to attempt to insulate oneself from competition. A similar conclusion would follow from observing the opposition of the cable industry to moves to rescind legislative obstacles to telephone delivery of video services. However, both long-distance telephone companies and cable companies currently rely on local telephone company services to be able to provide their services. Long-distance companies usually require local telephone company connections providers to originate calls, and almost always need those connections to complete calls. Cable companies have traditionally used telephone company poles or conduits to spread their distribution and feeder cables out to reach homes. As such, these firms are, according to the "old" theory, as potentially vulnerable to the exercise of monopoly power by regulated local telephone companies *qua* input supplier in economically bad ways as they may be vulnerable to those companies *qua* competitor in good ways.

This review of the current debate begins with a restatement of that theory, laid out in detail in the pages of the *Antitrust Bulletin* around 7 years ago.[1] Despite the attention given to the AT&T's divestiture of its local telephone operations and the concomitant line of business restrictions the MFJ placed on the divested holding companies, the mechanics of the theory, especially the role of regulation, are insufficiently appreciated. In reviewing the grounds for the divestiture, four crucial factors become apparent—the nature of regulation, the degree of market power, the effectiveness of injunctive relief, and the size of economies of scope. Assuming that these factors justified the divestiture in 1984—a perhaps controversial assumption, but one not currently under much dispute—the legal question will turn on whether circumstances regarding these factors have changed sufficiently in the last 10 years to warrant effective repeal of the divestiture by allowing local telephone companies to reintegrate back into long-distance service and newly diversify into video programming.

---

[1] Brennan, *Why Regulated Firms Should Be Kept Out of Unregulated Markets: Understanding the Divestiture in* U.S. v. AT&T, 32 ANTITRUST BULL. 747 (1987).

Fortunately, the policy debate has produced considerable economic documentation that addresses the "changed circumstances" question. Seeking vacation of the MFJ, some RBOCs sponsored a collection of forty-seven supporting affidavits, from fifty-six leading economists and telecommunications policy experts.[2] Examining those affidavits should provide some insight into the strength of the theoretical and empirical case for unfettering the RBOCs, and perhaps offer some advice as to the remaining question Congress, the FCC, and the courts need to answer before deciding whether and under what circumstances this unfettering should take place.

II. The "old" theory, to the present day

Despite all of the academic, legal, and political attention devoted to *U.S. v. AT&T* and the MFJ, the economic rationale for the case remains widely misunderstood. There are two things the case was clearly *not* about, nor should have been. The first was that AT&T was an example of the proposition that size should be a per se antitrust violation. It is worth remembering that at the same 1982 press conference at which the Department of Justice announced the resolution of its 8-year-long case against AT&T via the divestiture of the local operating companies, it dropped its 13-year-old case against IBM, stating that the latter case was "without merit." A second candidate, recently appearing in press commentary inspired in part by the rise of Microsoft and the demise of IBM in the computer industry, is that some big firms would be better off leaner and meaner. Advocates of this rationale suggest that IBM would have been better off had antitrust been used to break it up. Leaving aside whether such a remedy would

[2] *Motion of Bell Atlantic Corporation, Bell South Corporation, Nynex Corporation, and Southwestern Bell Corporation to Vacate the Decree*, Appendix, U.S. v. Western Electric Co. Inc., and American Telephone and Telegraph Co., Civil Action 82-0192, U.S. Dist. Court (D. C.), July 6, 1994 (hereafter, RBOC Affidavits). The purpose of citing these affidavits is neither to criticize them nor to offer them as representative of expert consensus, but only to use them as an authoritative source of potential changed circumstances that would justify eliminating the MFJ.

have been legal given the evidence at hand, it is probably not good policy for the government to decide which firms should be restructured to make them more responsive to future technological changes.

A more serious yet still incorrect rationale for the divestiture in *U.S. v. AT&T* is that vertical integration by monopolies is inherently bad, because of the propensity to "leverage" market power from the monopolized market into erstwhile competitive markets. Advances in the analysis of vertical integration have at least suggested some situations in which it may exacerbate market power. However, leveraging theories then and now still have to overcome the well-known argument that if a firm has a monopoly in one market, particularly one which provides an input on a "fixed proportions" (i.e., unit for unit) basis to downstream suppliers, it can already capture all of the monopoly profits that could be extracted after vertically integrating. If so, the only reasons to integrate vertically would be to realize cost reductions or other operating efficiencies that, while increasing profits, represent gains to the economy as a whole.

The justification for breaking up AT&T was, in fact, wholly consistent with the so-called "Chicago school" viewpoint that vertical integration and restraints are somewhere between benign and beyond the ability of government to determine which, if any, are malignant. William Baxter, the Reagan-appointed Assistant Attorney General who pledged to litigate *U.S. v. AT&T* "to the eyeballs" and engineered the divestiture, is not known for his populist or protectionist inclinations. The key factor that differentiated AT&T from IBM and other monopolists for whom multimarket activities have been the subject of antitrust scrutiny is not that it was big or potentially mismanaged. Possession of market power was a necessary condition, to be sure, but market power alone would not have been sufficient to justify requirements that AT&T divest its local operating companies, and that those divested companies by and large be prevented from manufacturing equipment or marketing information or long-distance telephone services.

Rather, the crucial differentiating factor was that its monopolies in local telephone services were regulated, in particular, in such a way that rates for local telephone service were based on the imputed costs of providing those services. In different ways, the incentive for AT&T to continue as a multimarket firm, and to engage in the conduct for which it was accused, was to evade those regulatory constraints on the exercise of its market power in local telephone service. Since it could not directly extract monopoly profits through high prices to telephone subscribers and high interconnection charges to long-distance companies, it allegedly looked to indirect means of extracting those profits through affiliated subsidiaries operating in markets for long-distance service and telephone equipment.

The two tactics for regulatory evasion are a litany familiar to many telecommunications and antitrust lawyers, economists, and policy observers, even if there may be some confusion about the specifics.

A. Discrimination

The first of these tactics is known in the telecommunications community as "discrimination." In more traditional antitrust parlance, it might be better regarded as a Sherman section 2 monopolization case, via a tie-in or control over an "essential facility." The story begins with the premise that AT&T's local telephone service was not only an important product on its own, but is a necessary adjunct or complement for the provision of a number of ancillary services. Among the most crucial examples of this were:

> A manufacturer of telephone switches and software, transmission lines, or sophisticated "customer premises equipment" (CPE), i.e., business and residential telephones and routing systems, may require information necessary to make one's products compatible with the local telephone service standards and technology.
>
> Suppliers of "information services," i.e., data storage, processing and retrieval services including electronic mail and on-line databases, need timely and relatively noise-free connections to local telephone networks in order to deliver their services to consumers. These providers might also need technical specifications on how the local telephone

networks themselves switch, packetize, and transmit data, in order to optimize the speed and precision of their information services.

Most notably, providers of "interexchange services," i.e., long-distance calling, generally have facilities that can route and transmit calls among metropolitan areas. To actually connect residences or offices, the interexchange carriers (IXCs) have to connect to local telephone networks.

During the time AT&T's conduct was under scrutiny in the antitrust litigation, information services still existed more on the drawing board than in the market. With regard to equipment, especially CPE, AT&T had attempted to use the regulatory process first to bar entry outright, and then later to force its CPE competitors to install costly and generally nonfunctional "protective connecting arrangements."[3] AT&T's "protect the network" defense was hardly obvious and sometimes implausible, particularly in its opposition to the marketing of a $10 plastic device one could place on a telephone handset to make one's conversations quieter and less intrusive to those nearby.[4] The most notorious examples of discrimination, however, involved denials, delays, and then degradation in the local telephone network connections AT&T provided to MCI and other IXCs competing with its long-distance service.[5] More blatant examples of using the regulatory process to "raise rivals' costs"[6] probably could not be found.

[3] A good summary of this history is in BROCK, TELECOMMUNICATION POLICY FOR THE INFORMATION AGE 79–101 (1994).

[4] *Id.* at 81.

[5] United States v. AT&T, 524 F. Supp. 1336, 1348–52 (D.D.C. 1981); Brock & Evans, *Predation: A Critique of the Government's Case in U.S. v. AT&T, in* BREAKING UP BELL: ESSAYS ON INDUSTRIAL ORGANIZATION AND REGULATION 41, 49 (David Evans, ed., 1982); Noll & Owen, *The Anticompetitive Uses of Regulation: United States v. AT&T, in* THE ANTITRUST REVOLUTION 290, 304–06 (Lawrence White & John Kwoka, eds., 1992).

[6] Noll & Owen, *supra* note 5, at 305. This phrase is taken from the now popular heading for a collection of theories covering practices by which a firm can increase its market power through strategies designed to limit the ability of its competitors to compete. *See, e.g.*, Krattenmaker & Salop, *Anticompetitive Exclusion: Raising Rivals' Costs to Achieve*

Telecommunications policy researchers and practitioners have come to refer to this family of cases as "discrimination," because AT&T typically treated its affiliated equipment and long-distance services more favorably than they treated unaffiliated competitors in those markets. In effect, however, the discriminatory episodes were tying arrangements in which AT&T would essentially allow customers to use their monopoly local telephone exchange services only if they also used AT&T's CPE and long-distance services. At first glance, these tie-ins conform to traditional "leveraging" Sherman section 2 theories used to warrant concerns with tying arrangements, where market power in a monopoly was apparently used to monopolize complementary markets.[7] In *U.S. v. AT&T*, the tying monopoly was in local service, and the tied goods were CPE and interexchange service.

As such, however, a traditional tie-in theory of the case would have to overcome the objection that a tie-in is unnecessary to exercise market power that it could not already exercise from the monopoly already possessed over the tying good.[8] Depending upon one's perspective on antitrust policy, this objection is at least a nuisance, if not an insurmountable objection to proceeding with a case.[9] In *U.S. v. AT&T* and the related private cases, how-

Power Over Price, 96 YALE L. J. 209 (1986). Whether this theory is a productive addition to the antitrust policy maker's toolkit in unregulated contexts is a matter of some dispute. *See, e.g.*, Brennan, *Understanding "Raising Rivals' Costs"*, 33 ANTITRUST BULL. 95 (1988); Coate & Kleit, *Exclusion, Collusion, or Confusion?: The Underpinnings of Raising Rivals' Costs*, 16 RESEARCH L. ECON. 73 (1994).

[7] POSNER, ANTITRUST LAW: AN ECONOMIC PERSPECTIVE 171–72 (1976).

[8] *Id.* at 173. Tie-in sales may allow a monopolist to extract more profit via that market power by enabling it price discriminate, but the effects on equity and efficiency from such price discrimination are difficult to predict in general. CARLTON & PERLOFF, MODERN INDUSTRIAL ORGANIZATION 468–79 (1990). A recent game-theoretic rationale for tie-ins is that they may enable a firm to commit *not* to reduce output in the tied product market, because doing so would force it to forego profits in the tying product market. This commitment could deter entry in the tied product market. Whinston, *Tying, Foreclosure, and Exclusion*, 80 AMER. ECON. REV. 837 (1990).

[9] BORK, THE ANTITRUST PARADOX 365–66 (1978).

ever, the plaintiffs could meet this general objection because state and federal regulation of local telephone rates prevented AT&T from exercising its erstwhile monopoly power in local telephone markets. Without that regulation, AT&T would not have needed to monopolize interexchange service or CPE to maximize profits. It could have charged interexchange carriers monopoly access fees to originate and terminate calls, and it could have directly charged end-users high monthly dial-tone charges rather than maintain high equipment prices. Moreover, in principle it could charge even higher local service fees if complementary markets in CPE and interexchange became more competitive, with more efficient providers. Access and dial-tone regulation provided the economic incentive for AT&T to maintain its presence in those other markets, exercise its local exchange market power indirectly by discriminating against vertical competitors, and exploiting that advantage by charging higher prices for its affiliated services. The direct purpose of the tie-in is regulatory evasion; its manifestation is downstream monopolization.[10]

B. *Cross-subsidization*

The role of regulation is even more intimately connected with the second type of tactic motivating the divestiture and line-of-business restrictions: cross-subsidization. The gist of the cross-subsidization theory is creatively self-serving accounting.[11] Under

---

[10] The regulatory evasion theories depend on the premise that the other markets in complementary services are not tightly regulated. While the FCC set interstate long-distance rates and state regulators set CPE charges, both of those were considerably above marginal cost. Consequently, AT&T would have the incentive to use its local exchange to inhibit competition in those markets, keeping those profit margins for itself. Brennan, *supra* note 1, at 773–75. Whether AT&T was justified in excluding competition, in order to preserve publicly mandated subsidies of local exchange service and deter inefficient entrants who could compete only because they would not have to pay those subsidies, was and continues to be controversial. BROCK, *supra* note 3, at 143.

[11] This distinguishes "cross-subsidization" as understood by telecommunications and antitrust analysts from the understanding in some economic contexts, where it is an indicator of misaligned pricing.

(*footnote 11 continued*)

traditional regulation, the rates for the regulated services such as local telephone subscription are, at least in theory, based on the regulated firm's costs for providing those services. If such a telephone company diversifies into other markets that use similar types of labor, resources (including financial capital), equipment, and technologies, such as long-distance service, it could increase its profits by assigning the expense of those similar inputs to the regulated account. If its regulator treats those misallocated expenses as if they were spent on providing local telephone service, it will pass along those costs to the customers in the form of higher telephone rates. As far as the accounts are concerned, the firm will show earnings for telephone service equal only to the normal rate of return. It would get its profits from the unregulated enterprises, for which it had in effect charged some of the expenses to local telephone customers. While the profits show up in the unregulated markets, and thus, may appear to be the result of monopolization of those markets, they essentially are the direct result of exercising monopoly power over local telephony.[12]

As with discrimination, the incentives and consequences of cross-subsidization may still be widely misunderstood, because of a failure to recognize the importance of regulation. Just as discrimination could be viewed at first glance as an application of a traditional but problematic "leveraging" tie-in theory, so too could cross-subsidization be described as an application of a traditional but problematic "deep pocket" predation theory, in which a wealthy telephone company uses its profits to support below-cost pricing, to drive competitors out of its other markets. The standard argument against the "deep pocket" theory of predation is

The specific concern is whether prices are below "incremental" costs for some services and above "stand alone" costs for others. Faulhaber, *Cross-Subsidization: Pricing in Public Enterprises*, 65 AMER. ECON. REV. 966 (1975). In this antitrust context, the concerns are less sophisticated and, as we see below, need not necessarily imply that prices are "predatory" in some markets, at least in the Areeda-Turner sense of being below incremental costs.

[12] The formal theory underlying this concern with cross-subsidization is in Brennan, *Cross-Subsidization and Cost Misallocation by Regulated Monopolists*, 2 J. REG. ECON. 37 (1990).

that the gross depth of the pocket does not affect the net profits of predation. If predation is profitable, a small firm should be able to do it. If it is unprofitable, as many would expect, the absolute size of the predator will not matter.[13] Furthermore, a firm will not raise its price in its monopoly market just to fund predation in other markets; it presumably is already charging a price that generates maximum profits from its monopoly. If the firm is regulated so that the price in its monopoly market is based on reported costs, it then has a specific incentive to misallocate unregulated business costs to the regulated sector. Cost-based regulation may create a causal connection between output in the unregulated market and price in the regulated market that is generally absent in completely unregulated contexts.

For this reason, the prospect of cross-subsidization can make credible a threat to predate that would generally be not worth making in unregulated situations. However, cross-subsidization can be harmful without any adverse effect on price in the unregulated market. The regulated firm may be able to shift costs to the regulated side, raising rates there, without necessarily changing competitive conditions elsewhere. For example, suppose that a telephone company could cross-subsidize some of the up-front fixed costs associated with marketing of electronic databases. If the cross-subsidy does not affect marginal costs, it will not lead the telephone company to increase its sales in the database market. Whether the relationship between it and other database providers is competitive or oligopolistic, overall market price and output would be unaffected by the cross-subsidy. Its only manifestation would be on the telephone company's database profits, which would reflect, dollar-for-dollar, the results from raising rates in the regulated market.

---

13 As with almost any theoretical claim in industrial organization, one can find exceptions. TIROLE, THE THEORY OF INDUSTRIAL ORGANIZATION 379 (1989) argues that bankruptcy risk may make small firms less able to borrow. If so, large firms may have an incentive to cut price, keep the firms small, and prevent borrowing that would enable those small firms to compete in later periods.

C. *Relief, remedy, and repeal*

Regulators, legislators, and other policy makers were generally aware of at least the potential for competitive abuses following from discrimination and cross-subsidization. During the time the Justice Department was investigating and litigating against AT&T, these agencies offered to ease the concerns by imposing additional regulation of AT&T's internal operations to prevent these practices. The Antitrust Division, particularly after William Baxter became Assistant Attorney General, sought the more draconian approach of forcing AT&T to divest its regulated local monopolies. After divestiture, the local monopolies would be stripped of the incentive and ability to evade regulation and inhibit competition in ancillary markets. A local telephone company has no reason to discriminate against unaffiliated long-distance carriers or equipment manufacturers if it is itself not in those markets, since it would have no way to take advantage of that discrimination. Similarly, there would be no costs from unregulated operations to cover local telephone rate increases if there were no regulated operations. Realizing that its alternatives were intrusive internal regulation, continued restriction of its unregulated operations, and the likelihood that it would lose the case, AT&T found it impossible to refuse the Justice Department's offer to end the case in exchange for divestiture.[14]

Despite whatever successes the divestiture has had in encouraging competition in equipment, long-distance and information services markets, the residue that haunts us to the present day is that the principles warranting the break-up of AT&T into regulated monopoly and competitive components also warranted preventing the divested local telephone companies from reentering AT&T's long-distance and equipment markets, as well as the then nascent markets in information services. Accordingly, the MFJ imposed the notorious line-of-business restrictions on the RBOCs. Sensing their controversial nature, the court modified the Justice Department's proposal in a number of significant ways, allowing

[14] AT&T was also able to shed restrictions stemming from the original 1956 decree that kept it from providing anything other than communications services. U.S. v. AT&T, 552 F. Supp. 131, 226 (D.D.C. 1982).

the RBOCs to sell CPE and directory advertising (Yellow Pages), requiring triennial reviews of the restrictions, and instituting a process by which the MFJ restrictions would be waived if the RBOCs could show that diversification would not harm competition in the markets they would be entering.

During the first triennial review in 1987, the Justice Department proposed lifting all of the line-of-business restrictions except that on interexchange service. The interexchange ban should be lifted if state regulators stripped the RBOCs of their exclusive franchises to provide telephone service. Among many of the most important arguments in favor of this apparent reversal were that the burdens of MFJ enforcement, technological restructuring of telephone networks, and the high level of competition in the ancillary markets.[15] In addition, the Department, following the focus of the MFJ on competition in the entered markets, expressed the view that increased telephone rates caused by cross-subsidization were a regulatory problem, not an antitrust concern. In 1991, the court rejected the Department's arguments, citing a lack of competition in local telephony and a series of perceived abuses of their monopoly position. It retained the bans on manufacturing and interexchange service, and reluctantly lifted the ban on information services only because neither AT&T nor the Department supported its continuation.[16] The present legal, regulatory, and legislative controversies are the legacy of that decision.

III. From where we stood to where we stand

The present compelling issue is the extent to which the rationale for the 1984 divestiture and the MFJ's line-of-business

---

[15] Huber, The Geodesic Network (1987). The Huber Report served as the factual foundation for the Department's reevaluation of the MFJ.

[16] AT&T, by this time a user rather than supplier of local telephone services, and as a potential victim of either RBOC discrimination and cross-subsidization or RBOC competition, opposed the Department's proposals for the elimination of the restrictions on manufacturing and interexchange services.

restrictions applies to the RBOCs in 1995. Reviewing that rationale, particularly the role that regulation plays, suggests four crucial questions:

> *Incentive*: Does the extent and nature of regulation continue to give local telephone companies an incentive to exploit their market power through diversification into other lines of business?
>
> *Ability*: Would local telephone companies have the market power necessary to be able to carry out discrimination and cross-subsidization tactics?
>
> *Monitoring*: Even if local telephone companies have this ability and incentive, do state and federal regulators, including antitrust authorities, have the means and motivation to detect and prevent anticompetitive conduct through diversified affiliates?
>
> *Efficiencies*: Are there benefits from allowing local telephone companies to diversify that outweigh the risks of harms from unpoliced discrimination or cross-subsidization?

Examining these questions in an absolute sense is difficult, if not intractable. A somewhat easier task, and one more relevant to practical legal and regulatory standards, is to see what circumstances may have changed since 1984 that would lead one to answer these questions differently in 1995.

A. *Incentive*

If the anticompetitive incentive to diversify is a by-product of the regulation of local telephone service, changes in the incentive to diversify should depend on changes in the level or method of that regulation. One major change has been the widespread consideration and implementation of forms of "incentive regulation," such as price caps. Despite the many names and nuances, the defining idea of incentive regulation schemes that differentiates them from traditional rate-of-return regulation, is that the price the regulated firm can charge for its services is independent of the costs over which it has discretion. Under traditional regulation, rates are (in theory) set in such a way as to generate just enough revenue to cover the costs of providing the service. When rate-of-return regulation works according to design, a firm has no incentive to control expenses in the short run or to reduce them in the long run through innovation. Any reduction in cost would bring about a reduction in price, stripping the firm of any profit it would receive from cutting cost.

The "incentive" in incentive regulation comes from the inference that if a regulated firm cannot raise rates if costs go up, and if it will not have to cut rates if its costs fall, then it will keep at the margin any profits it makes if it cuts costs. Consumers share in the expected productivity gains from *ex ante* imposition of productivity-related rate decreases, but these decreases are, in principle, divorced from actual reductions in costs, to preserve the incentive to economize.[17] Moves away from cost-of-service regulation to direct price controls or incentive regulation would reduce or eliminate incentives to cross-subsidize unregulated services, by taking away ratepayer funding of unregulated operations.[18] Regulated rates would not be raised to cover misallocated costs of those services. Over thirty states are considering or implementing some forms of incentive regulation of local telephone companies.[19]

---

[17] Kwoka, *Productivity and Price Caps in Telecommunications*, *in* PRICE CAPS AND INCENTIVE REGULATION IN TELECOMMUNICATIONS 77 (Michael Einhorn, ed., 1991). There is some evidence from intrastate long-distance markets that incentive regulation leads to lower prices. *See* Mathios & Rogers, *The Impact of Alternative Forms of State Regulation of AT&T on Direct Dial Long Distance Telephone Rates*, 20 RAND J. ECON. 437 (1989). A question, difficult to answer through econometric testing, is whether an observed relationship between lower rates and incentive regulation reflects the effect of the incentive regulation on costs and prices, or whether state regulatory expectations on the intensity of competition lead it to adopt less rigorous forms of regulation. If the latter is the case, imposing incentive regulation where regulators have chosen not to do so might not lead to reduced prices, despite the observed correlation between the two.

[18] Brennan, *supra* note 12. RBOC Affidavits by Arrow & Carlton at ¶ 20; Crew & Kleindorfer at ¶ 13; Milgrom & Roberts at ¶ 49; Perloff & Karp at ¶ 125–26; and Sappington at ¶ 30.

[19] RBOC Affidavits by Arrow & Carlton at appendix 2.1–2.2; Mitchell & Vogelsang at ¶ 70; Wilk at appendix 2.

The effectiveness of price caps requires a public commitment to divorce regulated rates from prices, which is difficult and unlikely for the government to achieve.[20] If the regulated firms appear to be making a great deal of money because of the cost-cutting incentives created by price caps, there will be considerable political pressure to force a reduction in prices and, perhaps, a return to cost-based regulation. The imposition of federal regulation of cable rates in 1992, as a response to the price and profit increases that followed the 1984 congressional preemption of price controls built into local cable franchise contracts, is a useful example of this tendency. In the other direction, a regulated firm that loses money when costs fail to fall as much as was anticipated or allowed for in advance, will be expected to exert political pressure to raise its rates.

Not only might we expect political institutions to be responsive,[21] but legal standards guaranteeing the opportunity to earn a "just and reasonable" return on investments[22] reflect judicial dispositions to protect the firms as well. Such dispositions appropriately reflect the need to make the government honor its commitments to regulated firms that having installed expensive plants and equipment, are vulnerable to postconstruction regulatory decisions to set prices so low that only operating costs, not those capital investments, are covered. In any event, if legal constraint or political pressure continues to tie costs to rates, moves to incentive regulation may be little more than rate-of-return regulation with a time lag between the change in costs and the change in rates. While lengthening the lag between cost and rate changes

20 *See* Brennan, *Regulating by 'Capping' Prices*, 1 J. REG. ECON. 133, 142 (1989); Baron, *Information, Incentives, and Commitment in Regulatory Mechanisms: Regulatory Innovation in Telecommunications, in* PRICE CAPS AND INCENTIVE REGULATION IN TELECOMMUNICATIONS 47 (Michael Einhorn, ed., 1991).

21 Peltzman, *Toward a More General Theory of Regulation*, 19 J. LAW ECON. 211 (1976).

22 Federal Power Commission v. Hope Natural Gas, 320 U.S. 591 (1944).

provides less incentive to cross-subsidize, it does not eliminate that incentive altogether.

It is also important to note that while price caps or incentive regulation can eliminate the incentive to cross-subsidize, it does nothing about the incentive to discriminate against unaffiliated competitors in unregulated markets. The latter incentive comes about because effective discrimination would tie purchase of the unregulated service to purchase of the regulated service. This tactic would allow the firm to add the otherwise prohibited monopoly premium for the regulated service to the price of the unregulated service. Discrimination prevents competitors in the unregulated market from unraveling the tie by giving consumers the opportunity to avoid it. Incentive regulation combats cross-subsidization only because that tactic depends not only on the fact of regulation but on its form, particularly, the policy that changes in reported costs affect changes in rates.[23]

The inability of price caps to eliminate the incentive to discriminate, and the difficulty of making commitments, suggests that the real way to eliminate the need to restrict lines-of-business to prevent evasion of regulation is simple: eliminate the regulation. While there is some discussion of deregulating the local exchange, such moves appear not to be widespread.[24] This is unfortunate, not only because it fails to remove the clear cause of the incentive for anticompetitive diversification, but because it implies that local exchange companies may retain the market

---

[23] A variant on the cost misallocation story is that a regulated firm could vertically integrate upstream, and sell inputs to itself at inflated prices, causing regulated rates to rise, with the attendant profits realized on the books of the upstream subsidiary. Since this tactic also requires cost-based regulation to be effective, incentive regulation would combat it as well. *See* RBOC Affidavit by Fisher, at ¶ 25.

[24] The RBOC Affidavit by Perloff & Karl raises the issue, but mentions only discussion of the issue in California (¶ 126–28). Appendices 2.1 and 2.2 of the RBOC Affidavit by Arrow & Carlton indicate that only Nebraska has adopted a general deregulatory policy; Indiana and South Dakota have deregulated small telephone companies, with less than 6000 or 10,000 lines, respectively.

power necessary for giving them the ability to discriminate or cross-subsidize. To that question we now turn.

B. Ability

Regulation would not matter if local telephone companies faced competition. If long-distance companies could connect to any number of local exchange companies (LECs) to originate and complete calls, the regulated incumbent could not create a market advantage for its affiliated interexchange carrier by delay or degrading interconnections. The interexchange competitors would look elsewhere for access. If consumers could choose among local exchange competitors for telephone service, a regulated incumbent could not pass along rate increases constructed with the help of misallocated costs. Consumers would evade the cross-subsidization by turning to other carriers who did not try to raise prices, preventing not only higher local rates but eliminating the threat that cross-subsidization would be used to fund predation.

An important and yet to be fully appreciated development since the 1984 divestiture is that technological change and unbundling of local telephone services has apparently created separate service markets within the "local exchange" rubric, with potentially different competitive and regulatory circumstances.[25] The "old" theory rationalizing the divestiture and the line-of-business restrictions by and large treated local exchange service as a monolith. In fact, the component parts of that local exchange service all may constitute separate markets, with separate competitive conditions. Among the potential separate or separable markets, with potential competitors listed, are the following:

> "*Local loops*," i.e., connections from customer premises to a switch that allows calls to be routed throughout the local exchange area, including to points of connection with long-distance carriers. The telephone company currently provides these connections primarily with copper wires. Cable television cable, cellular radio-telephones, and planned wireless "personal communications systems" are actual or potential competitors in some degree.

25 *See, e.g.*, RBOC Affidavit by Mitchell & Vogelsang at ¶ 3.

Bulk transport, i.e., unswitched private-line transmission capacity between two points. Telephone companies provide this service either on a contractual special construction basis or by committing capacity of their local networks to insure that these connections are not congested with other telephone traffic. The most notable examples of such a service involve direct connections between high volume users, e.g., large companies or office buildings, and interexchange carriers. Fiber-optic technology has opened up this bulk transport market to so-called competitive access providers (CAPs[26]), saving their customers or the need to pay local telephone company charges for this service.[27]

Local switching networks that collect and route traffic throughout the local exchange. A limited amount of switching capacity has faced competition for some time, in that multiline business users can substitute an on-site switch for the local network switch for calls within the firm's premises. In a somewhat similar manner, a cellular telephone company's switches can route calls among its subscribers without going through the local exchange. The fiber-optic lines CAPs provide to central business districts could be used for routing calls in those areas.[28] Last, and perhaps most important, these technologies may render cable networks convertible into switched networks, despite the fact that cable networks are typically designed to send signals in one direction from a single central point.

There may be other separate markets relating to billing, operator services, and other enhancements to local service, such as switch-based voice mail or call-forwarding.

Not all of these markets appear to be equally competitive. Bulk transport appears to be the most competitive; loops and networks less so. Moreover, the ability to enter and compete in some or all of these markets depends on thorny interconnection price and policy issues that state and federal regulators have only begun to confront, much less resolve. However, the possibility that local

---

26 Not to be confused with "price caps."

27 RBOC Affidavits by Hausman at ¶ 14, Mitchell & Vogelsang at ¶ 12; and Brock, *supra* note 3, at 247–54.

28 An interesting related development is that the capacity of fiber-optic lines may be so great that one could design networks so all calls go through all lines to all locations, where on-site signal identifiers pull out only those calls intended for that destination. Such a network would provide the equivalent of switched service without the switches.

exchange service combines separate markets means that the role of regulation and the extent of market power need to be considered on a market-by-market basis. In particular, evidence of "market power" need not imply that the line-of-business restrictions are justified, nor does evidence of "competition" imply that the restrictions are unjustifiable.

Consider the interexchange service question, and assume that bulk transport is competitive while local loop and switching markets remain regulated monopolies. Suppose first that control over bulk transport is necessary to carry out discrimination, or that the only interexchange costs that could be falsely represented are those similar to costs incurred in the provision of bulk transport. If so, continued regulated monopoly over local loops becomes irrelevant, since the LEC would no longer have the relevant market power necessary to discriminate or cross-subsidize. However, suppose that costs could be shifted onto the loop or switching sectors, or that loops and switched service provision might be denied or delayed to interexchange carriers or their customers. In this case, competition in the bulk transport market is irrelevant; the ability to discriminate or cross-subsidize persists. In general, competition in some markets may not warrant lifting of restrictions if the crucial markets will remain regulated monopolies for the foreseeable future. Unlike 1984, when local exchange service appeared to be a permanently regulated impregnable monopoly, resolution of this issue requires a much more careful analysis of exactly how a local telephone company could discriminate and cross-subsidize, and whether those tactics are susceptible to regulatory monitoring and prevention.

C. Monitoring

Continued regulation-created incentives to vertically integrate and discriminate and cross-subsidize, and continued power in relevant regulated local exchange markets that creates the ability to disadvantage competitors and to pass through costs to consumers, do not warrant antitrust-related concern if the regulators are able to monitor and police RBOCs to prevent such conduct. The underlying premise of the divestiture was that regulators were unwilling or unable to deter discrimination or control cross-subsidization during the decades when AT&T's allegedly was acting anticompetitively. The question, therefore, is whether the situation has changed. This involves two separate inquiries as to whether that ability or willingness has changed.

Since cross-subsidization is essentially an exercise in misallocating cost, improved ability to counteract it would involve better accounting techniques. Since the divestiture, the FCC and some of the states have imposed more detailed cost reporting rules.[29] The courts have cast doubt on whether these improvements are a material change, vacating and remanding the FCC's 1987 *Computer III* rules, in part because the FCC did not explain why it had changed its conclusion in its 1980 *Computer II* proceeding that accounting controls were ineffective.[30] Moreover, accounting controls will not work if networks are designed in such a way as to maximize the costs that are shared and fundamentally impossible to attribute specifically to either the regulated or unregulated service. If these shared costs are charged to the regulated side, we can get cross-subsidization, despite accounting "safeguards" insuring that no postdesign costs attributable to the unregulated sector are misallocated to the regulated side of the business.[31]

There may be more cause for optimism regarding discrimination. The FCC's *Computer III* proceeding also initiated a set of rulemakings leading to prescriptions that local telephone companies provide unbundled "open network architecture" and "comparably efficient interconnection" arrangements. These rules would ostensibly allow unaffiliated competitors in local exchange markets or downstream telecommunications services to get the same treatment the telephone companies give their own affiliates, with-

---

[29] Brock, *supra* note 3 at 227. *See also* RBOC Affidavits by Farmer at ¶ 8–11, 25–31; Rivera, Firestone & Halprin at ¶ 66, 72, 80; Sappington at ¶ 37; Wilk at ¶ 18.

[30] California v. FCC, 905 F.2d 1217 (9th Cir., 1990).

[31] Brennan, *supra* note 12, at 42–44; Baseman, *Open Entry and Cross-Subsidization in Regulated Markets*, *in* Studies in Public Regulation 329 (Gary Fromm, ed., 1981).

out forcing competitors to purchase service they do not need.[32] These reforms have faced some skepticism.[33] Moreover, rules that mandate equal treatment leave a telephone company free to "discriminate" to some degree against firms with technologies and services that would work better with a different type of connection than a phone company gives itself.[34]

A second reason to be more hopeful with discrimination is grounded in the belief that regulators have been effective at monitoring discrimination since the divestiture. The two prominent contexts in which regulators have shown their ability are the "equal access" requirements between interexchange carriers and the RBOCs, and the interconnection of cellular carriers to local networks.[35] In neither case, however, is the analogy perfect. Equal access for interexchange carriers may have been effective and easy to enforce just because the MFJ's restrictions eliminated any incentive the RBOCs might have had to discriminate.[36] Whether enforcement would be equally effective if the RBOCs had an

---

32 Brock, *supra* note 3 at 224–26. *See also* RBOC Affidavits by Sappington at ¶ 15–16.

33 AFTER THE BREAK-UP: ASSESSING THE NEW POST AT&T DIVESTITURE ERA 56 (commentary by William McGowan), 165 (commentary by Nina Cornell), 345 (commentary by Dale Hatfield) (Cole ed., 1991).

34 Brennan, *Divestiture Policy Considerations in an Information Services World*, 13 TELECOM. POLICY 243, 251 (1989). Ironically, a potential virtue of these unbundling rules is that they may force RBOCs to adopt standardized technologies that would prevent designing systems in such a way to create artificially shared costs of providing regulated and unregulated services that might be shifted to the regulated sector. *Id.* at 252.

35 RBOC Affidavits by Arrow & Carlton at ¶ 29; Hausman at ¶ 21; Rivera, Firestone & Halprin at ¶ 30, 44.

36 In theory, equal access regulation should be unnecessary. The two practical reasons for requiring it are first that as long as local telephone service is regulated to just cover costs, local telephone companies have no affirmative profit motive to insure that everyone is efficiently connected. More specifically, there was concern at the time of the divestiture that the RBOCs would honor old family ties and continue to favor AT&T despite the divestiture. This latter concern appears to have proven quite unwarranted.

incentive to favor an affiliate is another question.[37] The cellular experience speaks more readily to that issue, but the fact that regulators structured the cellular industry with only two suppliers per market, with limited spectral capacity, raises some doubts as to how competitive the industry would really be. If the gains from duopoly are sufficiently great, there may have been little reason for local telephone companies to resist antidiscrimination requirements, especially if engaging in discrimination in this market, and getting caught, might lead the government to extend restrictions on their entry into other markets.

Recent efforts to formulate and enforce antidiscrimination and proper cost allocations rules suggest that whether regulators are more *inclined* to monitor may be more important than whether regulators are better *able* to monitor. The *U.S. v. AT&T* history is instructive. Cross-subsidization was never detected as such. Instead, AT&T was accused of "pricing without regard to cost," i.e., acting *as if* it could cover any losses from undercutting competitors by shifting costs to its regulated monopolies. The alleged discrimination against competing CPE and long-distance providers was open and notorious; the main dispute was about whether the conduct was excused by FCC regulation, or a manipulation of it. In either case, a key factor was that the regulators were not particularly sensitive to the need for vigilance to protect competition in ancillary markets. Now that such competition is active rather than merely anticipated, and now that anticompetitive abuses are more widely understood, the threat of regulation and enforcement of unbundling rules may be a more credible and effective deterrent to monopolistic conduct.[38]

---

[37] A pricing issue related to discrimination is whether the RBOC would give interconnection access discounts to its affiliated long-distance carrier. Even if the RBOC is nominally required to charge its affiliated interexchange carrier the same access fee it charges its unaffiliated competitors, it may act as if it is charging itself only the marginal cost of providing access, unless its interexchange carrier is acting as an independent profit center. Without that independent accountability, a telephone company may have no reason to regard a fee it charges to its affiliated interexchange carrier as a cost.

[38] A related argument is that a benefit of the divestiture was the creation of seven local telephone companies. Regulators might be able to

If attentive regulators can thwart overt discrimination and apparent predation, then anticompetitive conduct depends on nearly paradoxical circumstances.[39] For discrimination to be effective, consumers must recognize its effect, otherwise they will not pay a premium for service from the favored affiliate, and the unaffiliated providers will not be put at a competitive disadvantage. However, for discrimination to be successful, the regulators must not be able to recognize it. A similar "between a rock and a hard place" argument applies to cross-subsidization. Regulators must be sufficiently diligent to pass costs on to ratepayers, but insufficiently diligent or able to ascertain whether those costs were actually employed in the provision of the regulated service.[40] It may be optimistic to conclude that the regulators can monitor discrimination and cross-subsidization to eliminate any risk of monopolistic abuses, but the nearly open invitation to engage in such abuses facing AT&T from the early 1950s to the late 1970s is no longer on the table.

D. Efficiencies

The line-of-business restrictions impose two possible categories of economic losses in the telecommunications industry and the economy at large. The first is that they may prevent the RBOCs from realizing economies of scope between local exchange services and equipment manufacturing or interexchange

regulate better if they can compare the performance of the firm they are regulating to those that they are not. Whether such "benchmarking" causes movement toward more efficient performance or regression to an inefficient mean is difficult to predict. The similarities across the RBOCs in their incentives and abilities as described above may outweigh differences among them that their regulators can exploit.

[39] The following arguments if from FAULHABER, TELECOMMUNICATIONS IN TRANSITION 118–120 (1987); *see also* Brennan, *supra* note 34, at 247–49.

[40] Some commentators point out that political pressures would also discourage regulators from shifting costs in such a way as to raise local telephone rates. *See, e.g.*, RBOC Affidavits by Wilk at ¶ 17. Of course, this was true prior to the divestiture, and it did not seem to deter "pricing without regard to cost."

service. The second, and more interesting cost, is that keeping the RBOCs out of ancillary monopoly or oligopoly markets may make those markets less competitive than they otherwise would be.[41]

While the *U.S. v. AT&T* litigation never officially reached the "relief" stage, when the pros and cons of the divestiture would have been contested, economies of scope issues were paramount at the time. These included contentions regarding the efficiencies from complete network management, "one-stop" shopping, common switches and lines for both local and long-distance service, and complementarities in research and development. One of the mottoes of AT&T during the litigation was "If it ain't broke, don't fix it." However, as William Baxter put it in an interview 5 years after the divestiture, "The decree [MFJ] implicitly made a wager that the regulatory distortions of those portions of the economy, which could have been workably competitive, yielded social losses in excess of the magnitude of economies of scope that would be sacrificed by this approach."[42] Current claims of scope economies by and large make arguments that would have applied to the "sacrifice" side of Baxter's balance at the time of the divestiture. They may suggest that breaking up AT&T was a mistake in the first place, but they offer little guidance to courts or policy makers having to ascertain whether 1995 is sufficiently different from 1984 to warrant a change in policy.

A much more interesting possible changed circumstance involves whether the expectation that the markets from which the RBOCs were banned have become as "workably competitive" as Mr. Baxter and the advocates of divestiture anticipated. The greatest controversy has been whether the long-distance market is competitive, dominated by AT&T's price leadership,[43] or a tacitly

---

[41] The identification of these losses and estimations of their magnitude relative to the gains from preventing cross-subsidization are examined in Brennan & Palmer, *Comparing the Costs and Benefits of Diversification by Regulated Firms*, 6 J. REG. ECON. 115 (1994).

[42] Cole, *supra* note 33, at 30.

[43] RBOC Affidavit by Hausman at ¶ 7, 34; Schmalensee at ¶ 4, 13; Taylor at ¶ 8.

colluding cartel.[44] The key piece of evidence seems to be that prices in the long-distance market, net of interconnection payments to local telephone companies, seem, if they fell at all, not to have fallen as fast since the divestiture as they did prior to the divestiture.[45]

As with almost any other empirical question in economics, ferreting out the signal from the noise is not easy. Since AT&T was, at least nominally, a rate-of-return regulated firm in long-distance as well as local markets, with a depreciating rate base on which to reap earnings and with growing demand, one would expect that its long-distance rates at the time of the break-up might have been near the competitive level and declining. Moreover, the breadth of service offerings and discount packages interexchange carriers make available to business and residential customers implies that identifying a "price" of long-distance service to compare with interconnection fees may be tricky, to say the least. Any benefits of RBOC entry into proscribed markets depends crucially on whether they will be net additions to the market, rather than as replacements for either current competitors or for other firms who would have entered in their stead.[46] Finally, any benefits of RBOC entry may depend not just on its entry, but whether that entry reduces AT&T's role as a price leader or disrupts any tacit collusion. Such benefits cannot be guaranteed.

IV. The ephemeral bottom line

Any prescriptive theory in economics is only as good as its assumptions are valid. Consequently, confidence in prescribing that local telephone companies remain out of ancillary markets would have to be weaker now than in 1984, but still not compellingly so. Regulatory reform may reduce the incentive to cross-

---

44 RBOC Affidavit by MacAvoy at ¶ 39.

45 RBOC Affidavit by Schmalensee at ¶ 10, table 1; Taylor at ¶ 18.

46 Brennan & Palmer, *supra* note 41, at 131–34; even if there is net entry, diversification is likely to reduce net economic benefits unless there were three or fewer firms in the entered market.

subsidize, but failure to deregulate still perpetuates the incentive to discriminate. The disaggregation of local exchange service into separate product markets, with competition primarily in bulk transport and connection to interexchange carriers, offers some hope that the ability to exercise market power via discrimination or cross-subsidization may have fallen in the last decade. However, competition in the full panoply of local services is certainly not yet strong enough to have persuaded state and federal governments to deregulate local service. Experience in monitoring telephone company conduct and efforts to devise new accounting controls may be less relevant or significant than the perception that the regulatory atmosphere is far less conducive to anticompetitive consequences than it was prior to *U.S. v. AT&T*. Any remaining risk of anticompetitive conduct might be worth taking if it would increase competition in other markets. The evidence of competition in interexchange service is apparently not universally persuasive, but it is difficult to tell whether it is sufficiently oligopolistic to justify vacating the MFJ.

A final consideration may suffice to sway many of us sitting on the fence. If telecommunications industry participants believe that the MFJ's days are probably numbered, that in and of itself might be a good reason to drop it. Policies, such as the line-of-business restrictions, that affect long-run business and investment plans are effective only to the degree that the government can credibly commit to them. Public commitment to particular policies, regulations and laws is not impossible; our monetary and commercial systems rely on it. In this instance, however, it is hard to argue that the government is guaranteeing that the restrictions in the MFJ will be maintained. Doubts began when Judge Greene allowed the RBOCs to provide CPE and introduced the triennial review and waiver process, and were greatly exacerbated by the Justice Department's support of repealing most of those restrictions by 1987. Since then, there has been perpetual discussion of regulatory or legislative efforts to take the MFJ out of the hands of the antitrust courts.

If credible commitment to continue the line-of-business restrictions is absent, the present state of affairs may be the worst of all possible worlds. Continuing to implement the MFJ restrictions deters entry by the RBOCs, while the expectation of future revocation may deter entry by RBOC competitors, out of fear that the RBOCs are either more efficient competitors or prepared to reenact in a more subtle manner the anticompetitive scenarios that led to the divestiture in the first place. Consequently, the current compromised environment could well be the least competitive of all. The ideal solution might be for the government to reestablish a credible commitment to maintain the MFJ. If that is impossible, and certainly if it is unwise, the best solution may be to go to the other extreme and vacate the MFJ altogether.

Whether the validity of the theory itself of the credibility of the government's commitment should be the factor determining the MFJ's survival, legal, political, and economic resolution of the controversy will be determined by an analysis of that theories assumptions. Identifying the key issues—incentive, ability, monitoring effectiveness, and countervailing efficiencies—and the facts that might determine how they have changed since the 1984 divestiture should help lead to better telecommunications policy making as we near the 21st century.

[28]

BUREAUCRACY AND POLITICS IN FTC MERGER CHALLENGES*

MALCOLM B. COATE,
Federal Trade Commission

RICHARD S. HIGGINS,
Capital Economics

and

FRED S. MC CHESNEY
Emory University

I. Introduction

SINCE Stigler's article on the economic theory of regulation,[1] public interest views of regulation increasingly have yielded to self-interest explanations. That is, well-organized private groups purchase regulatory favors in the political marketplace, benefiting both themselves and politician-sellers at the expense of less well-organized groups. However, one form of government regulation, antitrust, has largely escaped characteri-

* Our analysis and conclusions are our own and do not necessarily reflect the views of our respective institutions. Helpful comments were received during presentations of an earlier draft of this article at Claremont McKenna College, Clemson University, Emory University, George Mason University, Yale University, and the 1988 annual meeting of the Southern Economic Association. We acknowledge with gratitude helpful comments from Peter Aranson, George Benston, Roger Blair, David Haddock, Kathleen McChesney, Timothy Muris, Paul Pautler, John Siegfried, Rodney Smith, Robert Tollison, and Bruce Yandle; and research assistance from Alan Eberhart and Nancy Cole. Research on this article began when McChesney was John M. Olin Fellow in Law and Economics at the University of Chicago Law School. He thanks the John M. Olin Foundation for its support.

We have reluctantly agreed to recite the following, written by the FTC's Office of General Counsel:

This paper was prepared using nonpublic information from Federal Trade Commission internal files. Access to this information was available to Messrs. Higgins and Coate because they were employees of the Commission, and it was made available to Mr. McChesney because he was a consultant to the FTC Bureau of Economics. The Commission's Bureau of Economics has major disagreements with the methodology, analysis, inferences, and conclusions contained in this paper, and neither the Commission nor any of its members has authorized or endorsed its creation or publication. The FTC General Counsel determined that precluding publication would not be in the public interest and authorized its publication under secs. 5.12 and 5.21 of the FTC Rules of Practice, 16 C.F.R. secs. 5.12 and 5.21.

[1] George J. Stigler, The Theory of Economic Regulation, 2 Bell J. Econ. 3 (1971).

[*Journal of Law & Economics*, vol. XXXIII (October 1990)]

zation as a political, interest-group bargain. "Antitrust is one of the few remaining areas in which it is commonly assumed that government operates in the public interest."[2] Stigler himself believes antitrust a rare instance of benevolent regulation.[3] Some have tested this claim by examining the cases brought by antitrust authorities but found little evidence that public interest (social welfare) considerations drive antitrust enforcement. However, the alternative hypothesis, that antitrust is a politically driven, private-interest sort of regulation, has also been tested and found to be largely unsupported.

This article joins the debate by examining decisions of the Federal Trade Commission (FTC) to challenge horizontal mergers, using nonpublic data from that agency's files. The FTC does not purport to base its enforcement of merger law on the public interest variables identified by previous authors; rather, the commission's merger enforcement policy focuses on variables specified in the Department of Justice's merger guidelines. All other things equal, the guidelines predictably would play a role in agency determinations to challenge a merger, a hypothesis tested here using the internal FTC data.

Our data also elucidate the separate roles played by FTC lawyers and economists in influencing FTC decisions to challenge mergers. Several studies of the FTC have advanced—but never tested—hypotheses about these two groups within the agency. Lawyers supposedly have greater incentives to initiate cases than do economists, but both lawyers and economists are said to affect agency decisions whether to file a complaint. Those and related hypotheses are also tested here.

Finally, we model antitrust enforcement by the FTC as also influenced, ceteris paribus, by pressure from Congress. This pressure reflects demands from management and labor of companies at risk from reorganization through mergers and takeovers. Although mergers and takeovers are socially beneficial overall, the configuration of winners and losers confronts a politician with asymmetric benefits and costs. Individual share-

[2] William F. Shughart II & Robert D. Tollison, The Positive Economics of Antitrust Policy: A Survey Article, 5 Int'l Rev. of Law & Econ. 39, 53 (1985).

[3] Stigler calls the Sherman Act "a public interest law . . . in the same sense in which I think having private property, enforcement of contract, and suppression of crime are public-interest phenomena . . . I like the Sherman Act." Thomas Hazlett, Interview with George Stigler, Reason, Jan. 1984, at 46. See also George J. Stigler, The Economic Effects of the Antitrust Laws, 9 J. Law & Econ. 225 (1966). For similarly benign views of the intent (though not effect) of antitrust law, see Robert Bork, The Antitrust Paradox 50–71 (1978). For further discussion of the tenacity of the public interest view of antitrust, see Robert E. McCormick, The Strategic Use of Regulation: A Review of the Literature, in The Political Economy of Regulation: Private Interests in the Regulatory Process 26 (Robert A. Rogowsky & Bruce Yandle eds. 1984).

holders who gain are weakly organized and scattered throughout the country; institutional shareholders are too numerous and well diversified to have strong incentives to organize. Management and labor that may lose their jobs or be transferred are better organized and more concentrated in a particular politician's district. An antitrust regime can be useful to a politician in the same way that antitakeover legislation is, avoiding the risk that resources and votes will exit a politician's jurisdiction following completion of a merger.

Section II briefly reviews previous attempts to explain antitrust, then presents an alternative model of bureaucratically and politically directed antitrust enforcement. The FTC is modeled as responsive to (i) the merger guidelines, (ii) internal agreement or disagreement between its own lawyers and economists, and (iii) pressure from politicians seeking to block mergers. Section III tests the model by examining FTC decisions whether to challenge a proposed merger between 1982 and 1986. The model is shown to explain considerably more of antitrust enforcement than has been possible heretofore. High values for the variables identified in the merger guidelines almost guarantee a merger challenge. In addition, congressional pressure on the FTC to block mergers is found to increase significantly the likelihood that the commission will do so.

II. Determinants of Antitrust Enforcement

A. *Previous Inquiries*

Statistical examination of antitrust enforcement began with Posner.[4] Building on Posner's data, Long, Schramm, and Tollison (L-S-T) developed a cross-industry model of welfare loss potentially caused by antitrust infractions and examined whether the Justice Department brought more cases in industries where amounts of potential welfare loss were greater.[5] They found that welfare loss "played a minor role in explaining antitrust activity. . . . Much of the explanation of antitrust activity clearly lies outside our model."[6]

Subsequent work to explain antitrust enforcement in social welfare (public interest) terms has aimed at improving the L-S-T model. Siegfried, for example, ran the L-S-T tests using more disaggregated data and a

[4] Richard A. Posner, A Statistical Study of Antitrust Enforcement, 13 J. Law & Econ. 365 (1970).

[5] William F. Long, Richard Schramm, & Robert Tollison, The Economic Determinants of Antitrust Activity, 16 J. Law & Econ. 351 (1973).

[6] *Id.* at 361–62.

larger sample.[7] However, his results were not qualitatively different from the L-S-T results, and they generally explained even less of the Antitrust Division's enforcement activities. When Siegfried altered various L-S-T assumptions, his model's explanatory power fell even further, leading him to conclude that "economic variables have little influence on the Antitrust Division."[8] Asch noted difficulties in using industry data of any sort, since antitrust cases are filed against firms, not entire industries.[9] Other than the need to focus more on micro (firm) levels of enforcement, however, Asch advanced no particular hypothesis about antitrust. Indeed, he concluded that the "appropriate interpretation" of his empirical results was "not entirely clear," even "puzzling."[10]

Thus, in attempts to predict antitrust enforcement ex ante, the "public interest hypothesis has not been supported by empirical work."[11] As an alternative, antitrust has been modeled as an interest-group process akin to other economic regulation, whereby antitrust is used to benefit well-organized private interests. A priori, the hypothesis is appealing: as attested by current judicial regulation of the telephone industry, antitrust often results in de facto regulatory regimes administered by government agencies and the courts.[12] Thus, some studies attempted to locate the

[7] John J. Siegfried, The Determinants of Antitrust Activity, 17 J. Law & Econ. 559 (1975).

[8] *Id.* at 573. Overall, Siegfried concluded that "government is more interested in questions concerning the division of the economic pie than in increasing its total size. . . . [T]here is apparently *no* consideration of economic benefits in the decision process for allocating antitrust cases." *Id.* at 563, 567 (emphasis in original).

[9] Peter Asch, The Determinants and Effects of Antitrust Activity, 17 J. Law & Econ. 575 (1975).

[10] *Id.* at 579.

[11] Bruce Yandle, Antitrust Actions and the Budgeting Process, 59 Pub. Choice 263 (1988). Studies of particular areas of enforcement likewise find that antitrust does not increase, and often reduces, economic welfare. Government price-fixing cases apparently target ineffective cartels, rather than successful ones that cause significant economic damage. Howard P. Marvel, Jeffrey M. Netter, & Anthony M. Robinson, Price Fixing and Civil Damages: An Economic Analysis, 40 Stan. L. Rev. 561 (1988). Firms successfuly charged by the government with price-fixing have had lower rates of profitability than a random sample of firms. Peter Asch & Joseph J. Seneca, Is Collusion Profitable? 58 Rev. Econ. & Stat. 1 (1976). Likewise, mergers challenged by the government are generally not anticompetitive. See, for example, B. Espen Eckbo & Peggy Wier, Antimerger Policy under the Hart-Scott-Rodino Act: A Reexamination of the Market Power Hypothesis, 28 J. Law & Econ. 119 (1985). Noteworthy also is the considerable evidence that the remedies awarded the government in successful antitrust cases seem not to have achieved stated welfare goals. For example, George A. Hay & Daniel Kelley, An Empirical Survey of Price-Fixing Conspiracies, 17 J. Law & Econ. 13 (1974); Kenneth Elzinga, The Antimerger Law: Pyrrhic Victories, 12 J. Law & Econ. 43 (1969); Robert A. Rogowsky, The Pyrrhic Victories of Section 7: A Political Economy Approach, in Public Choice and Regulation: A View from Inside the Federal Trade Commission (Robert J. Mackay, James C. Miller III, & Bruce Yandle eds. 1987).

[12] For example, Frank Easterbrook, The Limits of Antitrust, 63 Tex. L. Rev. 1, 35 n.72 (1984) (citations omitted): "Many antitrust suits are regulatory. The Department of Justice

private beneficiaries of antitrust, whose influence (via the political process) could explain the origin and enforcement of the antitrust statutes. Such attempts, notably those of Stigler and of Baxter, also have failed empirically.[13]

B. A Bureaucratic-Political Model of Antitrust Enforcement

1. Bureaucratic Factors

There are several likely reasons for the prior models' inability to explain antitrust enforcement. First, prior inquiries have ignored the criteria that the antitrust agencies themselves specify as determining their case selection. With mergers, for example, the Department of Justice and the FTC have officially adhered to written merger guidelines for the past twenty years.[14] The more recent guidelines (issued on June 14, 1982, and revised in 1984) define various factors that will increase the likelihood of an antitrust challenge to a merger, including the degree of and change in market concentration (measured by the Herfindahl-Hirschman Index [HHI]), the existence of significant barriers to entry, the likelihood of successful collusion for reasons other than barriers to entry, and the possibility that one firm may be failing. Prior models have not included the merger guidelines criteria as determining antitrust enforcement, perhaps because antitrust enforcers' measures of these variables have not generally been available.[15] Our access to internal FTC case files permits

used antitrust suits to establish district courts as regulatory agencies over industries in which the Antitrust Division was persuaded that competition was 'unworkable,' but in which the political process had not acted. Approximately 53 antitrust decrees entered through 1979 are regulatory in character. This substantially exceeds the number of industries regulated by statute." See also E. Thomas Sullivan, The Antitrust Division as a Regulatory Agency: An Enforcement Policy in Transition, 64 Wash. U. L. Q. 997 (1986).

[13] George J. Stigler, The Origin of the Sherman Act, 14 J. Legal Stud. 1, 8 (1985). Stigler tested the hypotheses that agrarian and small-business interests account for the origins of federal antitrust law but reported a "failure to find strong evidence for any explanation for the passage of the Sherman Act." Baxter hypothesized that two groups in particular, private antitrust lawyers and smaller firms, stand to gain from greater antitrust enforcement. William F. Baxter, The Political Economy of Antitrust, in The Political Economy of Antitrust (Robert D. Tollison ed. 1980). Discriminating tests of his hypotheses were difficult to identify, and the data Baxter did present were inconclusive.

[14] U.S. Dep't of Justice merger guidelines, May 30, 1968. The guidelines were amended in 1982 and 1984. For the text of the 1968, 1982, and 1984 guidelines, plus the FTC's statement that it would give "considerable weight" to Justice's 1982 guidelines, see Section of Antitrust Law, Am. Bar Ass'n, Horizontal Mergers: Law and Policy 264–336 (1986).

[15] But see Robert A. Rogowsky, The Justice Department's Merger Guidelines: A Study in the Application of the Rule, 6 Res. L. & Econ. 135 (1984). Rogowsky examined the extent to which the Antitrust Division has followed its merger guidelines, finding that from 1968 to 1981 over 20 percent of the merger cases filed by the government fell below the defined threshold of concentration. Rogowsky did not, however, specify or test a model of enforcement action.

us, however, to determine whether these factors increase the chances of FTC enforcement action.

A second reason for the weak explanatory power of previous models, especially the private-interest models, has been their failure to model the agency decision in terms of the incentives of particular agency personnel. Lawyers and economists face different incentives to bring cases. Attorneys are said to favor more litigation than do economists because court challenges increase lawyers' human capital as litigators and thus raise their subsequent returns in private practice.[16] Even in the shorter run, heading a major investigation is required for FTC lawyers to advance to higher government employment grades (which also increase salaries); no such requirement applies to economists. The influence of economists at the FTC has grown considerably, particularly as economists have been named as commissioners and (once) even as chairman of the commission.[17] Economists tend to stay longer at the agency instead of using federal experience to build capital for subsequent private employment.

Conflicting incentives will lead to disagreement between lawyers and economists about whether to bring cases, and disagreements will reduce the likelihood of merger challenges. One would hypothesize that the FTC brings more cases when both lawyers and economists agree that the magnitudes of the various factors set out in the merger guidelines have reached worrisome levels. Disagreement among agency personnel as to the desirability of a particular merger challenge, in contrast, probably will reduce the likelihood that a case will be brought.

2. Political Factors

There is another reason for the largely unsuccessful attempts at explaining antitrust enforcement from an interest-group perspective. Those efforts have generally considered only private industries possibly served by antitrust. The likely private beneficiaries from antitrust may, however,

[16] "The principal attraction of Commission service to lawyers who wish to use it as a steppingstone to private practice lies in the opportunities it affords to gain trial experience. . . . It is the experience of trying cases, the more the better, not the social payoff from the litigation, that improves the professional skills and earning prospects of FTC lawyers." Richard A. Posner, The Federal Trade Commission, 37 U. Chi. L. Rev. 47, 86 (1969). Every other study of the FTC agrees. For example, Kenneth W. Clarkson & Timothy J. Muris, Commission Performance, Incentives, and Behavior, in The Federal Trade Commission since 1970: Economic Regulation and Bureaucratic Behavior 300 (Clarkson & Muris eds. 1981). The same incentives are said to motivate antitrust lawyers at the Justice Department. For example, Suzanne Weaver, The Decision to Prosecute: Organization and Public Policy in the Antitrust Division 38–41 (1977).

[17] For example, Robert A. Katzmann, Regulatory Bureaucracy: The Federal Trade Commission and Antitrust Policy 52–53 (1980).

cut across particular industries. Examination of the private winners and losers from mergers, plus the interests of politicians themselves, suggests that merger enforcement would be politically driven by the same groups favoring restriction on corporate takeovers generally.

In a merger, the wealth of shareholders in both firms increases.[18] Even the threat of a merger will benefit shareholders of potential target firms if management seeks to operate more efficiently to avoid a takeover. Small shareholders who gain ordinarily are not organized and are geographically dispersed; their small individual holdings give them little incentive to be active politically. Likewise, larger institutional shareholders are too numerous, dispersed, and well diversified to have strong incentives to organize. But with gains to shareholders often come losses to two more concentrated groups, firms' current management and labor. Jobs may be eliminated and offices may be closed or moved, as a result either of the merger or of reorganization to fend off takeover threats. This means that the merger (or threat of merger) of a firm in politicians' home districts or states confronts them (and their management and labor constituents) with concentrated expected costs, while the expected benefits are spread among shareholders nationwide. Imperiled home-district management and labor will value political help to stop the merger; failure to stop it not only will mean the district loses wealth, but politicians may lose votes as jobs are transferred.

Of course, the districts where jobs and offices ultimately are located will benefit, so other politicians may have an incentive to favor a merger. But the particular districts that benefit are more difficult to perceive (more uncertain) ex ante, so potential labor and management beneficiaries have less incentive to press for the merger. Thus, the value of the probable loss to the current district is typically greater than the value of the possible gain to another. The expected costs to losing politicians outweigh the gains to winning politicians, ceteris paribus. To politicians who stand to lose, an antitrust challenge can be beneficial in defeating the attempted merger altogether; at a minimum it will slow down completion of the merger, increasing the likelihood that the parties themselves will call off the proposed arrangement.

In effect, the antitrust system works like private and public antitakeover devices, although the similarities have not been fully appreciated. Privately, target managements can file antitrust actions to repel hostile bidders; they can acquire assets preemptively to increase concen-

[18] See generally Michael Jensen & Richard Ruback, The Market for Corporate Control: The Scientific Evidence, 11 J. Fin. Econ. 5, 9–16 (1983), which recites the empirical evidence.

tration levels and so elicit a governmental antitrust challenge to the proposed takeover.[19] Under either strategy, antitrust is a close substitute for other private devices (for example, poison pills) to fend off bids.

The public system of antitrust enforcement also works like antitakeover statutes, which have been shown to decrease the number of successful takeovers.[20] The Hart-Scott-Rodino (H-S-R) procedure of premerger notification requires that merger partners notify federal antitrust authorities of their proposed merger, then wait for government clearance before completing any deal.[21] In essence, therefore, the H-S-R system works like the Williams Act, the principal federal statute regulating takeovers, which requires notification of the Securities and Exchange Commission (SEC) and a mandatory waiting period before tender offers can be completed.[22]

Political considerations alone will not determine agency decisions. Antitrust enforcers purport to follow the government's merger guidelines in deciding what mergers to challenge, and these also should affect bureaucratic choices. At the margin, however, political demands for enforcement will increase the bureaucratic supply of mergers challenged. There is considerable anecdotal evidence that the FTC commissioners do at times bring pressure for more cases.[23] The principal implication of the

[19] For example, Panter v. Marshal Field & Co., 646 F.2d 271 (7th Cir.), cert. denied, 102 S. Ct. 658 (1981). See Gregg A. Jarrell, The Wealth Effects of Litigation by Targets: Do Interests Diverge in a Merge? 28 J. Law & Econ. 151 (1985).

[20] Gregg A. Jarrell & Michael Bradley, The Economic Effects of Federal and State Regulations of Cash Tender Offers, 23 J. Law & Econ. 371 (1980).

[21] The Hart-Scott-Rodino Antitrust Improvements Act of 1976 is codified at 18 U.S.C. sec. 18a *et seq.*

[22] Just as legislators have proposed extending the Williams Act waiting period, they have also sought to extend H-S-R waiting periods before mergers can be completed. See, for example, H.R. 586 100th Cong. 1st Sess. (Jan. 8, 1987). That bill would require an "economic impact statement" for mergers. It would require (i) notice whether the proposed merger would result in the sale or closing of any facility or termination of its operations, (ii) an estimate of the number of jobs that would be lost, and (iii) an estimate of revenue that would be lost "by each governmental entity in the geographical jurisdiction." H.R. 586, 100th Cong., 1st Sess. sec. 4(b) (2) (1987).

[23] In May 1987, the FTC commissioners met to "decide the fate" of the Bureau of Competition director, who was accused of bringing too few cases. "Here Comes the Pendulum," FTC: Watch, May 29, 1987, at 1. "The meeting was scheduled far enough in advance that [BC Director] Zuckerman had time to visit all the Commissioners . . . and promise to get the bureau up to speed. According to knowledgeable agency officials, Zuckerman's promises to the Commissioners will require the Competition Bureau to bring on the order of thirty (30) cases in the next six months, an output which would be prodigious by recent standards." *Id.* at 2. It was subsequently reported that the budget for merger surveillance and thus the number of investigations had increased considerably. "A little direct intervention by the Commissioners," it was concluded, "goes a long way." "Mergers," FTC: Watch, June 26, 1987, at 5.

model presented here is that in bringing such pressure, the FTC commissioners respond to politicians' demand for more antitrust cases. This model of antitrust has implications for a more general debate. Many social scientists, including some economists, view administrative agencies as operating with few effective constraints imposed by legislators: this view characterizes many prior studies of the Federal Trade Commission.[24] Others argue along the lines of the present hypothesis: that the benefits to politicians of controlling bureaucratic agencies are worth the costs.[25] In the end, the issue is an empirical one.

III. Empirical Evidence

To test the bureaucratic-political model of merger enforcement, we reviewed the internal records associated with all H-S-R "second requests" concerning horizontal mergers issued by the Federal Trade Commission between June 14, 1982 (the date of the new merger guidelines) and January 1, 1987. Second requests obtain the data necessary to evaluate potentially anticompetitive transactions.[26] The sample includes seventy commission decisions.[27] In forty-three cases, the merger was allowed to

[24] For example, Katzmann, *supra* note 17; Clarkson & Muris, *supra* note 16.

[25] For general discussions and empirical tests, see Barry R. Weingast & Mark J. Moran, Bureaucratic Discretion or Congressional Control? Regulatory Policymaking by the Federal Trade Commission, 91 J. Pol. Econ. 800 (1983); William F. Shughart II, Robert D. Tollison, & Brian L. Goff, Bureaucratic Structure and Congressional Control, 52 So. Econ. J. 962 (1982); Roger L. Faith, Donald R. Leavens, & Robert D. Tollison, Antitrust Pork Barrel, 25 J. Law & Econ. 329 (1982). See also William E. Kovacic, The Federal Trade Commission and Congressional Oversight of Antitrust Enforcement: A Historical Perspective, in Mackay, Miller, & Yandle eds., *supra* note 11, at 65 (FTC's antitrust enforcement "consistent with, and responsive to, congressional policy preferences"); Posner, *supra* note 16, at 82–85 (discussing ways politicians can use the FTC to benefit their constituents).

[26] For a description of the Hart-Scott-Rodino procedures, including issuance of "second requests," see, for example, Heublein, Inc. v. FTC, 539 F.Supp. 123, 124–25 (D.D.C. 1982). Following a second request, the FTC staff can dispose of a matter in several ways. The investigation may be closed, based on the staff's concurrence in a recommendation to close, which is subject to reversal by the commission. Alternatively, there may be a recommendation to the commission that a complaint be issued. In this case, the commission votes either to issue a complaint or to close the investigation.

[27] The seventy cases were drawn from the total of 109 H-S-R second requests issued between June 14, 1982, and January 1, 1987. Investigations were dropped from the sample if the merger was vertical (ten cases); the attempted merger was abandoned when the second request was issued, so the FTC's case file lacked information on the relevant variables (eight cases); the transaction was a joint venture, rather than a merger (four cases); the merger received early approval, presumably because the merger raised no serious competitive issues, so the FTC's case file contained insufficient information to be included in the sample (nine cases); the cases had been closed before sufficient information had been included in the files (three cases); or the HHI fell below the lower bound (1000) stated in the guidelines for a challenge (five cases).

proceed without interference; in the other twenty-seven cases (including those in which the merger was allowed to proceed only following some agreement with the FTC, such as a negotiated divestiture) the commission issued a complaint. Of the twenty-seven complaints issued, the FTC has not lost a case.[28]

A. *Explanatory Variables*

1. Merger Guidelines Variables

The five FTC commissioners vote whether to challenge a merger on the basis of information in formal staff memoranda, which usually are submitted separately by the lawyers of the Bureau of Competition (BC) and the economists of the Bureau of Economics (BE). The files for the seventy proposed mergers prepared for the commission's decisions reveal what each staff believes to characterize the relevant legal and economic considerations about each proposed merger. To distinguish the relative influence of lawyers' and economists' views on the decision to challenge, we identified the separate views of BC and BE as to the principal criteria included in the merger guidelines.[29]

For each merger, we first noted lawyers' and economists' calculations of the HHI in the relevant industry and the change in the index from the proposed merger. The calculations were translated into two binary variables. The first, for BC, equals one for those mergers where the lawyers argued that the industry HHI exceeded 1800 (making the industry "highly concentrated" under the guidelines) and that the merger would cause at least a fifty-point HHI increase (and so would be deemed "a matter of significant competitive concern" under the guidelines). The second variable, for BE, equals one for cases where the economists argued the HHI was below 1800 or the increase would be less than fifty points. (For mergers involving diversified firms, and so different HHI's for different markets, the highest HHI was used.) Thus, a particular case could have both variables equal to one only if the two bureaus disagreed. Disagreements occur, often when the economists and lawyers define the relevant

[28] Of the twenty-seven complaints issued, twenty-six cases were completed at the time of this writing; in the last one, an administrative ruling in favor of the FTC was still on appeal. As noted, the twenty-seven complaints include cases where the merger was allowed to proceed only subject to some agreement with the commission (such as a divestiture) since complaints must be filed in such cases.

[29] In cases when the director of the Bureau of Competition disagreed with his staff and sided with the Bureau of Economics, the staff position was used here as BC's position on the merger.

market differently.[30] (As would be predicted, this usually happened because lawyers argued for narrower markets than did economists.)

For other variables identified as relevant in the merger guidelines, a similar procedure was followed. For barriers to entry, binary variables for the BC and BE determinations were included. The BC barrier-to-entry variable was coded one when the lawyers claimed significant entry could not occur for at least two years, the period specified in the merger guidelines. The BE barrier variable was assigned the value one when BE found that entry would easily occur within two years. Positive values for both variables again signal disagreement. Ease of collusion was handled the same way, with a dichotomous variable for each bureau. A value of one for the BC variable indicated that the lawyers thought collusion relatively easy, while a one for BE meant the economists thought the opposite. (Zeros for the barrier-to-entry or collusion variables in some cases indicate that the bureau simply did not address the issue.) Finally, where the failing-firm doctrine was cited by BC as applicable, a failing-firm variable was coded one. Ordinarily, the commission views application of the doctrine as a purely legal issue.

2. Political Variables

To measure the effect of politics on each proposed merger, we used two variables. The first provides a proxy for political effect by measuring the amount of news coverage given the merger. Bigger mergers generate greater news coverage. The larger the merger, the more likely it is to result in job losses, plant closings or relocations, revenue losses to local jurisdictions, and thus the likelier it will be to encounter political resistance. Our measure of news coverage, as an indirect measure of the political pressure stemming from a proposed merger, is the count of the number of articles that mentioned the merger in the *Wall Street Journal* prior to the FTC's decision. Predictably, the commission will respond to pressure brought by better-organized labor and management groups, meaning it will challenge mergers generating more publicity.

Restricting the citations variable to articles before the FTC's merger decision reduces concerns over any problem of simultaneity between the number of articles and the decision whether to challenge the merger; the decision would increase the number of citations afterward. To be sure simultaneity was avoided, the equation was also estimated with the natural logarithm of the total merger bid price substituted for the citation

[30] For the seventy cases in the sample, the two bureaus disagreed about the definition of the relevant market sixteen times.

count. Bid price would perform like citations, capturing the potential loss of wealth and jobs in the districts affected and so the expected cost to politicians of letting the merger proceed. Higher bid prices therefore would increase the probability of the FTC's voting to challenge the merger. However, because the FTC vote would not affect the bid price, there is no simultaneity problem.

Political pressure is included more directly in the model by a twelve-month moving average, centered on the FTC's second request date, of the number of times commissioners or senior (politically appointed) FTC staff were called before congressional committees to testify on their antitrust enforcement records. Calling commissioners and staff to defend their antitrust records is a technique that politicians use frequently to increase amounts of antitrust enforcement. The FTC commissioners and staff prepare "case counts" to show that they are active in investigating cases and filing an acceptable number of complaints. Politicians berate commission witnesses when they deem the number of cases brought too low.[31] Individual congressmen and senators even advocate particular enforcement actions.[32] The debate in 1984 over amending the Export Administration Act to ban oil company mergers for five years shows the link between merger enforcement and political interest in local industries. The debate principally concerned job losses in the jurisdictions affected.[33] The budget process also reflects congressional desires for more antitrust cases. Antitrust agency budgets are allocated according to the enforcement zeal shown; passage of the Hart-Scott-Rodino Act in 1976 in particular caused a significant increase in antitrust budgets.[34]

[31] See, for example, Katzmann, *supra* note 17, at 146, discussing FTC testimony before its appropriations subcommittee: "[One] yardstick that the subcommittee uses in judging how well the commission is performing has to do with case-load statistics."

[32] *Id.* at 147–60.

[33] Yandle summarizes congressional concerns:

> The plan for the amendment had been triggered by the 1984 merger attempt of Texaco and Getty Oil Company, which would have been the largest merger in the nation's history. In the unfolding discussion, the senators first expressed grave concern about the inevitable monopoly power . . . [and then about] specific details associated with the FTC's antitrust review of the Texaco-Getty merger and the effects of the merger on plant operations in their states. For example, Senator Lautenberg raised as an issue Texaco's Eagle Point refinery in [West Deptford], New Jersey, indicating that 500 jobs and $1.8 million in local tax revenues were at risk. Senator Dole commented on the potential closing of a refinery in [El] Dorado, Kansas, where 1,000 jobs were at stake. He then indicated that he would "be meeting with officials of Texaco and others who may be able to shed more light on this."

Yandle, *supra* note 11, at 272.

[34] *Id.* at 271 (table 3).

B. The Regression Model

We defined a binary dependent variable, VOTE, equal to one when the commission voted a complaint in a case (including cases of divestiture or other negotiated changes in the merging parties' original agreement) and zero when it allowed the merger to proceed as the parties originally agreed. Given the binary dependent variable, we used the Probit model,

$$\text{PROB[VOTE} = 1] = F[aX],$$

where F is the normal distribution function and aX is a linear combination of the explanatory variables. Table 1 lists the independent variables, their means and standard deviations, and their predicted signs in the regression model.[35]

The parameter estimates for each explanatory variable are presented in Table 2. All variables have the predicted signs. The coefficients of all but the failing-firm variable are significant at the 10 percent level; most are significant at the 5 percent level. Overall, the model easily passes the chi-square likelihood ratio test, indicating that the explanatory variables significantly influence the probability of a complaint. We note in particular that the pseudo-R^2 computed from the likelihood statistic suggests that the model explains about half the variance in the dependent variable,[36] much more than previous studies of antitrust enforcement have been able to explain.

[35] The variable for congressional appearances, the effect of which is tested here, includes only hearings in which antitrust (rather than the FTC's consumer protection functions) was the subject. The means and standard deviations of BEBARLO and BECOLLO are identical, but this is coincidence. BECOLLO measures BE's assessment of the ease of collusion for reasons other than barriers to entry; the evaluation of entry barriers is captured by BEBARLO. The Pearson coefficient of correlation between the two variables (.11) is insignificant. Indeed, the correlations between the different merger guidelines variables for each bureau are generally insignificant. For the Bureau of Competition, the correlation coefficients are:

	BCHERFHI	BCBARHI
BCHERFHI		
BCBARHI	.02	
BCCOLHI	.18	.28

The coefficients for the Bureau of Economics are:

	BEHERFLO	BEBARLO
BEHERFLO		
BEBARLO	.04	
BECOLHI	−.02	.11

Thus the data indicate that the individual variables identified by the merger guidelines are evaluated on their own separate merits.

[36] R. Carter Hill, George G. Judge, William E. Griffith, Helmut Lutkepohl, & Tsoung-Chao Lee, The Theory and Practice of Econometrics 767 (1985).

TABLE 1

SUMMARY AND PREDICTED SIGN OF REGRESSION MODEL INDEPENDENT VARIABLES

Name	Definition	Mean	Standard Deviation	Predicted Sign
BCHERFHI	One if BC claims HHI > 1800 and change > 50, zero otherwise.	.714	.455	+
BEHERFLO	One if BE claims that HHI < 1800 or change < 50, zero otherwise.	.429	.498	−
BCBARHI	One if BC claims barriers to entry high, zero otherwise.	.814	.392	+
BEBARLO	One if BE claims barriers to entry low, zero otherwise.	.343	.478	−
BCCOLHI	One if BC claims industry conducive to collusion, zero otherwise.	.443	.500	+
BECOLLO	One if BE claims industry not conducive to collusion, zero otherwise.	.343	.478	−
FAILFIRM	One if BC claims failing-firm doctrine applicable, zero otherwise.	.057	.234	−
CITES	Number of articles mentioning merger in *Wall Street Journal* before FTC decision	2.57	4.84	+
HEARINGS	Twelve-month moving average of FTC or political staff testimony before Congress.	5.83	3.61	+

1. Political Influences

The coefficient estimates for the two variables measuring political pressure, CITES and HEARINGS, lead us to conclude that the commission does respond to political considerations, ceteris paribus. A chi-square test shows that the two variables are jointly significant at the 1 percent level. Using the point estimates of the regression coefficients and evaluating the derivative of the normal distribution function at the mean values of the independent variables, we can calculate the marginal effects of the political variables on the probability that the commission will vote to seek a complaint. The marginal *Wall Street Journal* story raises the probability of a challenge 4.7 percentage points, and one additional congressional hearing raises the probability of a merger challenge by 4.2 percentage points. Thus, commission decisions are significantly influenced by political concerns. Reestimating the equation with the log of the total merger bid price substituted for CITES yields results qualitatively the same as those in Table 2; all coefficients retain the same signs, and all that are

TABLE 2

PROBIT REGRESSION PARAMETERS

Variable	Coefficient
BCHERFHI	1.11**
	(1.53)
BEHERFLO	−.962**
	(−1.65)
BCBARHI	1.84*
	(1.85)
BEBARLO	−.880**
	(−1.58)
BCCOLHI	1.65*
	(3.16)
BECOLLO	−.880*
	(−1.83)
FAILFIRM	−4.33
	(−.01)
CITES	.169*
	(1.82)
HEARINGS	.151*
	(1.71)
Constant	−4.01*
	(−2.47)
Likelihood ratio test	46.3*
Pseudo-R^2	.497

NOTE.—*t*-statistics are in parentheses.
* Significant at the .05 level.
** Significant at the .10 level.

statistically significant remain so except the HHI variables, whose significance falls to just below 10 percent.[37]

The political variables may understate the FTC's overall susceptibility

[37] The estimated equation (with the absolute value of *t*-statistics in parentheses) was the following:

$$\text{VOTE} = \underset{(2.44)}{-3.96} + \underset{(1.21)}{.832}\,(\text{BCHERFHI}) - \underset{(1.27)}{.717}\,(\text{BEHERFLO}) + \underset{(1.65)}{1.39}\,(\text{BCBARHI})$$
$$-\underset{(1.71)}{.957}\,(\text{BEBARLO}) + \underset{(2.85)}{1.42}\,(\text{BCCOLHI}) - \underset{(1.92)}{.916}\,(\text{BECOLLO})$$
$$-\underset{(.01)}{4.47}\,(\text{FAILFIRM}) + \underset{(1.51)}{.234}\,(\text{PRICE}) + \underset{(1.57)}{.130}\,(\text{HEARINGS}) + u,$$

with PRICE (in millions of dollars) representing the logarithm of the merger bid price. (PRICE has a mean of 4.98 and standard deviation of 1.69.)

to political considerations. The sample does not include attempts to merge that would have occurred but for parties' perception that merger would be unacceptable politically. Data availability and measurement difficulties also preclude inclusion of a full set of political variables, so some of the unexplained variation in the dependent variable may have a political basis. Moreover, if Congress influences the bureaucratic decision to challenge mergers after development of the merger guidelines, it would also influence the bureaucratic decisions reflected in the guidelines themselves. If antitrust enforcers were to announce enforcement criteria promising fewer cases than Congress found acceptable, enforcers would be made to alter the guidelines. Mindful of this possibility, officials would adjust the criteria: for example, congressional influence would cause concentration ratios triggering second requests to be set lower than would otherwise be the case. The tests here cannot capture any political influence that affected the guidelines themselves.

Finally, BC staff legal analysis may itself include responses to political pressure. That is, factual findings presented to the commission may already reflect political choices made at the subcommission level. To test this hypothesis, we modeled the BC staff recommendation as a function of the two political variables and of BE's reading of the economic variables. The political variables were individually and jointly insignificant, however.[38] Thus, commission responsiveness to political influences appears to reside at the level of the commissioners themselves, not at the staff level.

2. Bureaucratic Influence

Merger Guidelines Variables. The evidence on bureaucratically interpreted guidelines factors also supports our hypotheses. A claim by BC that the HHI, difficulty of entry, or ease of collusion is worrisome would increase the likelihood of commission action, ceteris paribus. Likewise,

[38] The estimated equation (with the absolute value of t-statistics in parentheses) was the following:

$$\underset{}{\text{BCCHOICE}} = \underset{(1.56)}{.627} - \underset{(2.72)}{1.04}\,(\text{BEHERFLO}) - \underset{(2.26)}{.831}\,(\text{BEBARLO}) - \underset{(.32)}{.113}\,(\text{BECOLLO})$$

$$-\underset{(.01)}{5.75}\,(\text{FAILFIRM}) + \underset{(.81)}{.0321}\,(\text{CITES}) + \underset{(.78)}{.0426}\,(\text{HEARINGS}) + u,$$

where BCCHOICE is the choice of the Bureau of Competition to favor the FTC's challenging the merger (BCCHOICE = 1) or allowing the merger to proceed (BCCHOICE = 0). While the political variables have no significant influence on BC's choice, BE's evaluation of the concentration index (BEHERFLO) and of the possible existence of barriers of entry (BEBARLO) are highly significant predictors of BC's decision.

BE claims that the HHI, ease of entry, or difficulty of collusion do not justify challenging a merger would reduce the likelihood that the commission would vote to challenge. A chi-square test indicates that the three economic variables as interpreted by BC are jointly significant at the 1 percent level, as are the same variables as interpreted by BE.

With the political variables held constant at their means, the equation as estimated in Table 2 can be used to estimate more precisely the relative importance of the merger guidelines criteria. When BC and BE agree that the HHI, entry barriers, and likelihood of collusion are all high, there is a 97 percent probability that the FTC will challenge a merger.[39] If both bureaus agree that entry barriers and likelihood of collusion are high, but that the HHI is not high, the probability of a challenge falls to 43 percent. The HHI is apparently the least important of the three guidelines factors, however. If the bureaus agree that entry barriers are low while the two other factors are high, the probability of a challenge falls to 21 percent. If the likelihood of collusion is agreed to be low even when the other two factors are thought to be high, the probability of a challenge is only 27 percent. The role of concentration ratios in FTC thinking, at least during the period studied, appears smaller than other considerations.[40]

Table 2 also shows, however, that within the two bureaus the three merger guidelines variables may be of equal importance. Although there is no reason a priori to believe that all factors would count equally, little empirical difference appears in the size of the coefficients for the HHI, entry barriers, and ease of collusion as the FTC economists reckon them. Only the coefficient for BC evaluation of the HHI is appreciably less (1.11) than those for entry barriers (1.84) and ease of collusion (1.65), and this result is not statistically significant.

A chi-square test indicates that one cannot reject the null hypothesis that within each bureau all guidelines factors are weighted equally. The same test shows, however, that the factors are weighted differently between the two bureaus.[41] It will prove useful below to reestimate the

[39] The probability is computed by first finding the value of the linear expression estimated in Table 2 at the mean values of the political variables and then incorporating the different assumptions about the BC and BE evaluations of the merger guideline factors (HHI, entry barriers, and likelihood of collusion). The failing-firm variable, insignificant in Table 2, is assumed to be zero. Next, based on a standardized-normal distribution table, the probability corresponding to the particular value of the linear expression is recorded. The same procedure is used to derive other probabilities discussed here based on Table 2. The reader can calculate probabilities of a merger challenge for merger guideline assumptions not discussed by using the data in Table 2 and a standardized-normal table.

[40] The differences are suggestive but not statistically significant; the confidence intervals surrounding the point estimates contain the other point estimates.

[41] To test this hypothesis, the equation was estimated with only one composite variable. The computed chi-square test statistic was 3.06.

equation shown in Table 2 on the assumption that each bureau weights the three guidelines factors the same. Two composite variables, BC and BE, were constructed to measure the sum of each bureau's dummies for the three merger guidelines factors. The reestimated model (with absolute t-values in parentheses) is

$$\begin{aligned} \text{VOTE} = & \underset{(3.21)}{-4.17} + \underset{(3.65)}{1.56}\,(\text{BC}) - \underset{(2.93)}{.85}\,(\text{BE}) - \underset{(.01)}{4.52}\,(\text{FAILFIRM}) \\ & + \underset{(2.19)}{.158}\,(\text{CITES}) + \underset{(2.00)}{.164}\,(\text{HEARINGS}) + u, \end{aligned}$$

with the likelihood ratio test equal to 45.6 and the pseudo-R^2 equalling .489. Qualitatively, the results are identical to those in Table 2.

Lawyers versus Economists. While lawyers and economists both are influential in the decision whether to challenge a merger, lawyers' influence appears to dominate. As shown in Table 2, the absolute size of the BC coefficients for the HHI, entry barriers, and ease of collusion is greater than the BE coefficients for those variables. The reestimated model above shows that the composite BC variable is greater in absolute value than the composite BE variable. Based on the coefficients from the reestimated model, Table 3 shows more precisely the different effects of BE and BC evaluations of factors identified in the merger guidelines as anticompetitive. The table shows the probabilities that a merger will be challenged, under alternative BC and BE evaluations of the number of troublesome guidelines factors. For example, if the two bureaus agree that only one factor is a problem, the probability of a challenge is only .002; if they agree that two of the three factors are problematic, the likelihood of a challenge rises to .295; if both bureaus agree that all three factors present potential problems, the probability of a challenge is .969.

Table 3 is particularly interesting in measuring the effects of bureau disagreement. When the two groups disagree, BC apparently has a greater effect on a particular decision than BE.[42] If BC alleges that three guidelines factors are problematic when BE claims only two are worrisome, the

[42] The data here do not capture any influence that BE has on the BC factual analysis. (Casual empiricism suggests that BC has little effect on the BE analysis.) During an investigation, economists critique the BC staff analysis. These questions may persuade BC either to close the case before or shortly after a second request (in which event the case would not be in the sample) or to adjust their opinion in the final memorandum (changing disagreement to agreement on a key guidelines factor). Thus, our results may underestimate the net effect of economists at the FTC. The results reported in note 38, *supra*, indicate that BE's evaluations of guidelines factors are significant predictors of BC's decision whether to advocate challenging a merger.

TABLE 3

PROBABILITY OF FTC MERGER CHALLENGE AS A FUNCTION OF BC AND BE MERGER GUIDELINES EVALUATIONS

NUMBER OF FACTORS ALLEGED POTENTIALLY ANTICOMPETITIVE BY:

		Bureau of Competition			
		0	1	2	3
Bureau of Economics	0	*	*	.013	.249
	1	*	.002	.083	.568
	2	*	.018	.295	.847
	3	.003	.106	.623	.969

* Less than .001.

likelihood of a challenge is .847; in the reverse situation, however, when BE claims that three factors are problematic while BC alleges that only two factors are worrisome, the likelihood of suit is only .623. If BC claims that all factors are at worrisome levels when BE says that none are, the probability of a challenge is .249. If BE claims that all factors are problematic when BC says that none are, the probability of a challenge is only .003. In short, lawyers' evaluation of the variables identified in the merger guidelines has a greater effect than does the evaluation by economists.

IV. CONCLUSION

In deciding whether to challenge or allow a merger, the Federal Trade Commission relies on a number of criteria, including the various criteria specified in the Department of Justice merger guidelines. With data from the commission's own files, we show that the evaluations of agency lawyers and economists concerning the Herfindahl-Hirschman Index, ease of entry, and likelihood of collusion all perform as one would predict, and all significantly influence commission decisions.

Moreover, access to the internal data permits examination of the respective roles of attorneys and economists. A disagreement between economists and lawyers about whether to challenge a merger is not a "fair fight." Lawyers have greater influence with the commission over the decision.

Finally, we hypothesize that the process is also driven by the desires of politicians to stop mergers. Merger challenges, like antitakeover legislation, prevent the exit of resources and votes from a politician's jurisdiction and, thus, allow the politician to respond to organized labor and management interests that seek to prevent the changes caused by mergers. As we show in statistical tests, greater political pressure does cause the FTC to challenge more mergers.[43]

In the end, therefore, a constellation of identifiable interests benefits from the FTC's stopping mergers. Politicians, their organized constituents opposed to mergers, and agency attorneys are apparently among the principal beneficiaries. Overall, the merger guidelines are applied with an upward bias, resulting in a greater propensity to challenge mergers in the marginal case. Greater appreciation of the ways that antitrust works and, in particular, of the role of politics in the process should begin to dispel the notion that antitrust can be viewed as driven solely by congressional and bureaucratic concerns for competition.

[43] Inferences justified by the results here are of course limited to the period under study, 1982–86. We note, however, that antitrust in the Reagan administration has supposedly been driven more by truly economic concerns, a position apparently justified by the data. See Warren P. Preston & John M. Connor, Federal Antitrust Activity under the Reagan Administration: New Evidence (unpublished manuscript, Univ. South Carolina 1987). If, as shown here, politics plays an important role in antitrust enforcement even when economic welfare is a more dominant concern, the influence of politics must have been even greater prior to the 1982 merger guidelines.

[29]

FIGHT, FOLD OR SETTLE?: MODELLING THE REACTION TO FTC MERGER CHALLENGES

MALCOLM B. COATE, ANDREW N. KLEIT, and RENE BUSTAMANTE*

This paper models the reaction of firms to Federal Trade Commission (FTC) decisions which seek to block proposed horizontal mergers. We find that firms' responses to the FTC's decisions depend on a number of factors, but only weakly on the structural merits of the FTC's challenge. For a large number of the FTC's merger challenges, we find that firms have strong incentives to settle with the Commission, regardless of the relevant competitive concerns. Therefore, in these matters the FTC appears to have powers more like a regulatory agency than a prosecutor.

I. INTRODUCTION

Scholars studying law and economics have identified four stages through which every legal dispute moves. The first stage involves an alleged injury which leads to the legal dispute. Second, the injured party decides whether to advance a claim. Once a claim is advanced, the plaintiff and defendant may negotiate to settle the claim. If the negotiation fails, the dispute moves to litigation. By subdividing the legal process into these four stages, it is possible to study the interaction at any one stage in greater detail.

This paper models the third stage of this process in an antitrust setting, the interaction between the Federal Trade Commission (FTC) and private parties interested in consummating horizontal mergers that may adversely affect competition. The FTC must decide whether to advance a claim against the merger and seek to block the transaction. If such a claim is made, the merging parties may "fight," forcing a resolution of the dispute through litigation by moving forward with the transaction. They may also "fold," abandoning the transaction, or "settle," entering into an agreement with the government to resolve the issues underlying the merger challenge. This decision to fight, fold or settle is somewhat more complicated than the standard settle or litigate question because the prospective nature of the alleged competitive injury gives the defendant an opportunity to abandon the transaction before the injury occurs.

Our basic hypotheses with respect to this process are that firms' decisions depend not only on the competitive merits of the FTC's case, but, perhaps more importantly, on the political, conglomerate and financial nature of the relevant transaction and how the nature of the case fits into the merger review process. Section II presents the background for the analysis by discussing the institutional structure of the FTC, explaining the merger review process, and then presenting an overview of a firm's options when faced with a

* Federal Trade Commission, Louisiana State University, Federal Express. This article is based on non-public data obtained from Federal Trade Commission internal files. The Commission's General Counsel has authorized publication of such data in aggregated form under Commission Rule 4.11(g), 16 C.F.R. 4.11(g). The analysis and conclusions presented herein are those of the authors, and do not purport to represent the views of the Commission or of any individual Commissioner, or the official position of any Commission Bureau. We would like to thank James Hughes, Ron Johnson, Pauline Ippolito, Don McFetridge, Philip Nelson, Tim Sass, Mark Williams, and two anonymous referees for helpful comments on this paper. Marybeth Theriot also provided helpful editorial assistance.

Economic Inquiry
(ISSN 0095-2583)
Vol. XXXIII, October 1995, 537–551

decision by the FTC to block a merger. Section III models the decision faced by firms, defines the equations to be estimated, and surveys the data set of FTC merger challenges. A multinomial logit model of a firm's fight, fold or settle decision is estimated in section IV, followed by an interpretation of the results and an application of the model using both historical data and information from mergers proposed during fiscal 1992 and 1993. We find that the level of the competitive overlap associated with the relevant transaction is an important determinant of firms' fight, fold or settle decisions. In particular, if the competitive overlap involves a small percentage of the transaction, firms generally prefer to reach a negotiated settlement with the Commission. In such cases, the settlement decision appears unaffected by the underlying merits of the FTC's legal position. In other cases, the merits of the case may play a role in the firm's litigation decision. We also find that the potential efficiencies offered by the merger affect the firms' decision-making process, with firms more likely to fight and less likely to settle if the merger is expected to generate efficiencies.

II. ISSUES IN MERGER ENFORCEMENT

Background on the Federal Trade Commission

The FTC is a government agency charged, along with the Antitrust Division of the Department of Justice, with enforcing the antitrust laws. Much of the antitrust casework involves the evaluation of the competitive effects of proposed horizontal mergers.[1] To interdict a proposed merger, the FTC must obtain a preliminary injunction from a federal district court, with possible review from the relevant court of appeals. If the court declines to issue the injunction, the firms are free to merge, though the FTC can initiate a lengthy court process to attempt to obtain a permanent injunction against the merger.

Commission decisions are made by a majority vote of the five Commissioners, each of whom are appointed by the President and confirmed by the Senate for terms of up to seven years. In each matter, the Commissioners usually receive separate memoranda from both the staff and senior management of both the Bureau of Competition (the lawyers' bureau) and Bureau of Economics (the economists' bureau) to assist in their decision-making process. The parties also have an opportunity to present their positions to the Commissioners through submissions and meetings.

Overview of the Merger Review Process

A legal dispute over a horizontal merger fits into the standard law and economics framework, although the prospective nature of the competitive injury requires a slight modification of the model. Firms propose mergers based on their respective interests. A small fraction of proposed mergers, if consummated, may threaten competition and present a risk of antitrust injury. If the firms recognize the potential injury, they have the option to abandon the transaction. Parties, however, may have a difficult time a priori knowing how the FTC will react to their proposed transaction. (See Johnson and Parkman [1991].) Little is generally known about the decision of firms to advance a potentially anticompetitive merger because of the secrecy of the merger negotiation process.

If the firms choose to proceed, the Hart-Scott-Rodino Act would, in most cases, require them to notify the government of the proposed transaction and observe a

1. The FTC's merger enforcement also includes cases against consummated horizontal mergers, vertical transactions and conglomerate mergers when issues of potential competition exist. Such cases, however, are relatively rare and therefore do not present the opportunity for systematic analysis.

thirty-day waiting period.[2] If the merger raises competitive concerns, the government can issue a request for additional information and further delay the process. At the end of the investigation, the government will either challenge the transaction or close the investigation. Coate, Higgins and McChesney [1990] have found that the FTC's decision to move against a merger depends on both political considerations and case-specific facts. The Commission is more likely to challenge the transaction if the Herfindahl index is over the Merger Guidelines' threshold of 1800, if barriers to entry exist, or if other factors make the market conducive to anticompetitive behavior.[3] Data generated by both the Bureau of Competition and Bureau of Economics are statistically significant in explaining the FTC's decision.

If the government decides to challenge the transaction, the parties have three choices.[4] They can "fight" by moving forward and forcing the government to obtain a court order to block the transaction, can "fold" and abandon the transaction, or "settle" by entering into a consent agreement with the government to spin off assets to eliminate the competitive concern.

The final stage in the horizontal merger enforcement process is litigation. Recent studies by Coate [1992] and Kleit and Coate [1993] of federal judicial merger decisions made after the issuance of the 1982 Merger Guidelines have found that to prevail in a merger case, the government must show high concentration in the market, as measured by the relevant Herfindahl statistic, and barriers to entry in the relevant market. Even in these cases, if the Herfindahl is not well over 1800, evidence on structural factors conducive to competition can rebut the presumption from a high Herfindahl. Thus, it appears that the merits of a case have a significant impact on the outcome of litigation.

In private litigation, the four stages of the process would be interdependent (Perloff and Rubinfeld [1988]). Here, the interdependence hinges on the ability of the FTC to exploit the peculiarities of the legal process that may lead firms not to fight the FTC, regardless of the merits of the case. For example, litigation against the FTC may force the firm to incur opportunity costs if the firm forgoes a settlement that would bring the process to a quick resolution. In effect, aspects of the transaction unrelated to the competitive concerns can be held "hostage" by the FTC. This situation would not occur in a textbook example of an anticompetitive merger involving two firms competing to sell a product in a highly concentrated market, because that scenario leaves no assets to hold hostage. In the modern world of conglomerate firms, however, a merger may involve both competitive overlaps and wide areas where the firms are not related at all. In such acquisitions, the firms would desire to consummate the

2. Transactions are covered if a firm with assets or net sales of $100 million or more acquires an ownership interest in a firm with assets or net sales of at least $10 million, or a firm with assets or net sales of $10 million or more acquires a firm with assets or net sales of at least $100 million (15 U.S.C. sec. 18A(a) (2)). Reporting requirements are triggered if, as a result of the transaction, the acquiring firm would hold at least 15 percent of the stock in the target or more than $15 million of the target's voting securities (15 U.S.C. sec. 18A(a) (3)). For further details, see Johnson and Parkman [1991]. The government often learns of small uncovered transactions through the news media or informal channels. An investigation may then result, although the government lacks the formal waiting period requirements. Because the legal cost of defending a small transaction can easily dwarf the efficiency benefits, firms in this situation almost always cooperate with the government's investigation.

3. For a model of Canadian merger enforcement policy, see Khemani and Shapiro [1993]. They find that high market shares and barriers to entry make enforcement more likely, while import penetration makes enforcement less likely.

4. The actual negotiation process may begin before the Commission has taken a formal vote to move against a merger. A vote, however, must be taken to issue a complaint against a transaction and accept a consent for public comment. While the Commission can reject consents after the public comment period, this rarely occurs. Minor changes, however, may be made to account for technical problems overlooked in the initial negotiations.

noncontested portion of the merger quickly and deal with the contested portion later.

There is, however, no simple legal mechanism currently available to allow a partial acquisition to occur. The FTC has the ability to hold up the entire acquisition while seeking a preliminary injunction to block a relatively small aspect of the deal. (See Kolasky, Proger, and Englert [1985, 52].) In such situations, a firm may have a strong incentive to reach a settlement with the Commission, spin off the contested assets, and allow the remainder of the transaction to proceed. Thus, we suggest that, in a number of cases, firms would desire to settle with the FTC on the Commission's terms, even if the merits of the Commission's case are weak. (See a similar discussion along these lines in Posner [1972].) Here we seek to test this hypothesis by focusing on the share of the transaction linked to competitive concerns. We will test whether the firm's decision responds to this competitive overlap variable.

In addition, by modelling the effect of the share of the transaction linked to competitive concerns and the value of the transaction not subject to the competitive concerns, we can use the model to predict which cases would end in litigation if the FTC allowed the innocuous parts of the transaction to proceed unchallenged. If a number of such cases are found, the FTC would appear to behave more as a regulatory commission rather than as a prosecutor subject to judicial review under a "preponderance of the evidence" standard. Moreover, if various other factors, such as the value of the transaction and the size of the acquiring firm (see discussions below), enter into the decision, we can also net out these effects to allow the litigation decision to turn on the merits of the case. Again, if the model predicts a number of cases would end in litigation but for these considerations, we would suggest that the FTC functions as a regulatory agency, substituting its evaluation of the competitive merits of a transaction in place of what the caselaw would imply.

Finally, abstracting from the "hostage" issue, enforcement decisions can also be based on non-systematic factors, such as politics or incentives of FTC staffers. Thus, the FTC may desire to accept less stringent settlements to both increase its number of successful cases and to prevent potentially embarrassing losses in federal court. On the other hand, the FTC's complicated internal procedures may prevent it from taking such actions. (See McCubbins, Noll, and Weingast [1987].) Below we will test to see if evidence suggests that parties can enter into less stringent settlements with the Commission if the Commission's case is weak. We also test to determine if the general political climate affects a firm's decision-making process.

III. MODELLING THE FIGHT VS. FOLD VS. SETTLE PROCESS

Modelling the Utilities of the Choices

When faced with an FTC merger challenge, a firm has a choice of either fighting, folding, or settling. Along the lines of Landes [1971], it will choose the option that offers it the highest expected utility (profit). Therefore, it is necessary for us to model the expected utilities of each option. Arbitrarily, we assume that the relative level of utility from folding is zero.

The utility from fighting depends on a number of factors. Let **X** represent a vector of independent variables affecting the benefits of fighting and **Y** represent a vector of independent variables affecting the costs of fighting. This makes the utility of fighting

$$(1) \quad U(Fighting) = F(\mathbf{X}) - G(\mathbf{Y}) + \varepsilon_1 .$$

The benefits of fighting will be a function of a number of factors. Conceptually, the benefits depend on the probability of winning in court, which is a function of the merits of the case. Benefits will also depend on the profits from realizing the acquisition. The benefits of the acquisition will have two parts, the anticompetitive benefits (which will also be a function of the merits of the case), and the available efficiencies from the transaction.[5]

The costs of fighting also have several components. The most obvious is the actual cost of litigation in federal court. Further costs arise because the FTC has a policy of always following a preliminary injunction case with a complaint to its own administrative law system. (See Lopatka and Mongoven, forthcoming.) These proceedings can take years, with hearings before an administrative law judge, an appeal to the FTC sitting as a court, and then (if the FTC rules for its own staff and against the merger) an appeal to a federal circuit court. We suggest, however, that these costs can be viewed as relatively constant across firms. The interest a firm has in incurring these costs, however, appears to depend on the general efficiencies associated with the transaction, a factor likely linked to the overall value of the transaction.

Fighting may also affect the firm's reputation with respect to the government. Large firms may expect more interactions with government regulators than small firms. Thus, their behavior in any one interaction should take into account potential effects on later interactions. For example, a large firm could be more likely to litigate to establish a reputation for toughness along the lines of Milgrom and Roberts [1982]. On the other hand, the large firm could be less likely to litigate to avoid causing problems with future government encounters.

In addition to the direct costs of litigation, a firm must contend with the opportunity costs associated with delaying the transaction. These costs could be avoided if the firm abandons the transaction and refiles for only the competitively neutral aspect of the deal. It may be difficult to isolate the competitive problems in some deals, but this opportunity cost will not exist for all transactions and will likely be a function of the conglomerate aspects of the relevant deal.

Similarly, the utility of settling can be specified as

$$U(Settle) = H(\mathbf{Z}) - K(\mathbf{W}) + \varepsilon_2, \quad (2)$$

where **Z** represents a vector of benefits of settling and **W** represents a vector of costs of settling. We see the benefits of settling as being related to the value of the acquisition excluding the assets to be divested. Moreover, both the benefits and the costs of a settlement are likely to be a function of the available efficiencies. Although divestitures are likely to require the firm to give up most efficiencies, it is possible that a settlement can be crafted to retain some of the efficiencies. On the other hand, the purchase price may implicitly include the value of a significant portion of the efficiencies, so a divestiture would be costly to the firm. Other costs of the settlement depend on the burden of complying with the FTC's order. FTC settlements, with their procedures for divestiture and "hold separate" provisions, impose both legal and operational costs on firms. It is possible, however, that the FTC may offer less costly settlements to firms where the merits of the FTC's case are weaker. Thus, the cost of settlement could be negatively related to the merits of the FTC's position.

5. It is unlikely that courts recognized efficiencies as much of an antitrust defense during our period of study. Even if efficiencies were thought to have a significant impact on the outcome of the case, the 1984 Guidelines stated that the defense should be based on "clear and convincing" evidence. Appeals Court Judge and former Assistant Attorney General for Antitrust Ginsburg [1991, 97] has called reaching this standard "well-nigh impossible." Further, even if defendants can meet this level of proof, only efficiencies in the relevant anticompetitive market may count. See also *FTC v. University Health, Inc.*, 938 F.2d 1206 (11th Cir. 1991).

Data and Specification

We reviewed all seventy-eight of the Commission's attempts to enjoin horizontal transactions for fiscal years 1984 to 1991. The memos presented a wealth of background data such as the sales of the acquiring firm, the acquired entity and the parent company, the price of the transaction, the magnitude of the competitive overlap, measures of the potential anticompetitive effect of the acquisition and the date of the acquisition. We include those cases in which the parties have offered a settlement, but exclude the transactions that were abandoned before Commission action.[6] Cases were deleted from the sample when the merger involved a partial stock acquisition (one case), when the Commission did not have sufficient notice to complete a full investigation before moving to enjoin the merger in court (two cases) or when the transaction was characterized as a joint venture (three cases). This left a total of seventy-two cases in which the Commission voted for a complaint against a prospective merger.

To represent the value of the transaction, we use the variable *VALUE*, which is the estimated acquisition price of the transaction (in 1982 dollars using the GDP deflator) taken from the Bureau of Competition's memos. To model the ability of the FTC to hold up non-contested portions of the acquisition, we calculate the overlap figure (*OVERLAP*) by estimating the percentage of the deal subject to the competitive concerns, usually by dividing the sales in the market(s) under investigation by the total sales of the target entity.[7] When sales data were not available, we used other proxies such as the ratio of the number of stores in the geographic market(s) of concern to the total number of stores sold. We also calculate a variable *SETTLE VALUE* = (1 − *OVERLAP*)*VALUE*, which is equal to the value of the uncontested part of the transaction that potentially could be held up by the Commission. Reputation effects associated with the size of the acquiring firm are modelled with *SALES* defined as the total sales of the acquiring firm, measured in 1982 dollars.

Each memo also contained an analysis of the basic facts of the case, such as the Herfindahl index, ease of entry and competitive effects (e.g., ability to exploit market power). The Bureau of Economics data showed much more variance than the Bureau of Competition data. Generally, the Bureau of Competition's memos noted the Herfindahl was high, barriers to entry were present and anticompetitive behavior was possible.[8]

The Bureau of Economics's memos were significantly different, with some case evaluations having relatively low Herfindahls, other case discussions noting no barriers to entry and still other case reviews finding no theory of anticompetitive effects. We believe that the Bureau of Economics's data represent the best available proxy for the competitive potential of the merger. We will measure the merits of

6. By checking the records on second requests issued, FTC enforcement actions and agency files, we found that very few transactions were abandoned after the staff arrived at an enforcement recommendation, but before the Commission decision. In some of these cases, withdrawn deals were refiled later and the Commission moved to enjoin the transaction.

7. All the overlaps subject to merger challenge are counted in the overlap variable, because the Commission tends to obtain full settlements. It would make little sense for a party to settle one overlap, merely to go through a trial on the merits of other overlaps.

8. This observation does not imply that the Bureau of Competition's analyses are biased. The sample of seventy-two cases were all recommended by the Bureau of Competition's staff, so one may expect the bureau's staff would believe that they are all meritorious cases. Numerous other investigations were closed, with the bureau's analysis showing low Herfindahls, low barriers or no anticompetitive story. For a further discussion, see Coate, Higgins, and McChesney [1990] and Coate and McChesney [1992].

the FTC's case with the variable *STRUCTURE*, which is equal to the Bureau of Economics's estimate of the post-acquisition Herfindahl index multiplied by a dummy variable which takes on the value one if the bureau's staff found barriers to entry in the relevant market and equal to zero if the Bureau of Economics found no barriers. In the few cases involving multiple overlaps, the data from the most anticompetitive overlap is recorded. Thus, the *STRUCTURE* variable measures both the firm's probability of winning in court (negatively related to the probability of fighting) and the potential anticompetitive gains from the acquisition (positively related).

A number of the memoranda also contained limited information on merger-related efficiencies. Although these analyses did not always generate a clear recommendation as to the relevance or the level of efficiencies, we believe it is reasonable to measure the strength of the efficiency concerns by a variable, *EFFICIENCIES*, equal to the number of pages dedicated to dealing with the efficiency question in both the Bureau of Economics's and Bureau of Competition's analyses.[9] In effect, the strength of the parties' efficiency defense is measured by the number of pages in the staff memos needed to fully explain these issues to the Commission. It is also important to note that lengthy efficiency discussions in the staff memos are in very large part a response to the parties' efficiency claims. Finally, the FTC (and Department of Justice) policy of requiring evidence to support efficiency claims gives parties incentives to make presentations when they have such evidence and not to make such presentations when they do not. (Another way of viewing this variable would be to consider it a measure of how seriously the Commission's staff took the parties' efficiency arguments.)

To measure unspecified efficiencies, which we model as proportional to the size of the transaction, we use the variable *VALUE*. This in turn implies that larger transactions will have larger efficiencies associated with them, which in turn implies that parties with larger acquisitions are more likely to incur the transactions costs necessary to fight the Commission. We also include in our specification a variable, *TIME*, equal to the number of months after the first case in the sample when the FTC made its relevant enforcement decision. (The first case in the sample is January 1984.)

The final variable attempts to measure the political considerations facing a firm. We use a political index variable, *POLITICS*, which averages the percentage of Democratic representatives in the House and Senate after the biannual elections. As Congress becomes more Democratic, we expect firms to bear higher costs from resisting enforcement action, hence litigation is less likely. It may be that the more Democratics in Congress, the more likely a firm is to face retribution from the legislature as a result of resisting the FTC.

The theoretical benefit model thus includes both the structural and efficiency variables. Adding the time index yields

$$(3) \qquad F(X) = \alpha_0 + \alpha_1 STRUCTURE + \alpha_2 EFFICIENCIES + \alpha_3 VALUE + \alpha_4 TIME.$$

For the costs of fighting, we assume *SALES* proxies the effect of reputation costs. In addition, we use *OVERLAP* to proxy the probability that the opportunity costs of delay must be considered, because the deal can be restructured to avoid the competitive concerns. As *OVERLAP* approaches one, the probability of restructuring the deal falls to zero and the opportunity costs of delay become moot. The

9. We found no evidence that staff or management at the Commission engages in explicit trade-offs of anticompetitive and efficiency effects of mergers, contrary to the analysis of Comanor and White [1992].

political variable *POLITICS* is also included to reflect the possibility that the firms' perception of costs is affected by the political environment. Again adding a time parameter, the costs of litigation are

$$(4) \quad G(Y) = \alpha_5 + \alpha_6 SALES + \alpha_7 OVERLAP + \alpha_8 POLITICS + \alpha_9 TIME.$$

Let $\alpha_{10} = \alpha_0 - \alpha_5$ and $\alpha_{11} = \alpha_4 - \alpha_9$. Equation (1) now becomes

$$(5) \quad U(Fight) = \alpha_{10} + \alpha_1 STRUCTURE + \alpha_2 EFFICIENCIES + \alpha_3 VALUE - \alpha_6 SALES - \alpha_7 OVERLAP - \alpha_8 POLITICS + \alpha_{11} TIME + \varepsilon_1$$

with the signs on α_2, α_3 and $-\alpha_7$ expected to be positive, the sign on $-\alpha_8$ expected to be negative and no priors for the other coefficients.

For the benefit of settling, we first take into account the value of the firm that would be obtained through acquisition after a (potential) divestiture of the offending assets, *SETTLE VALUE*. We also consider any efficiencies that might be available, using our *EFFICIENCIES* variable as discussed above, as well as the impact of *TIME*. This generates

$$(6) \quad H(Z) = \beta_0 + \beta_1 SETTLE\ VALUE + \beta_2 EFFICIENCIES + \beta_3 TIME.$$

We view the cost of settling as having two attributes, the stringency of the FTC settlement and the efficiencies taken away by the settlement. We suggest that the weaker the merits of the FTC's case (as measured by *STRUCTURE*), the less costly the settlement required by the Commission. Also, the cost of the settlement could depend on political factors, although we hesitate to predict a sign. The cost of settling may also be a function of time. This generates

$$(7) \quad K(W) = \beta_4 + \beta_5 STRUCTURE + \beta_6 EFFICIENCIES + \beta_7 POLITICS + \beta_8 TIME.$$

Let $\beta_9 = \beta_0 - \beta_4$, $\beta_{10} = \beta_2 - \beta_6$, $\beta_{11} = \beta_3 - \beta_8$, all three unsigned. The utility of settling now becomes

$$(8) \quad U(Settle) = \beta_9 + \beta_1 SETTLE\ VALUE + \beta_{10} EFFICIENCIES - \beta_5 STRUCTURE - \beta_7 POLITICS + \beta_{11} TIME + \varepsilon_2,$$

with β_1 expected to have a positive sign, $-\beta_5$ taking on a negative sign and β_7 unsigned.

Let us now assume that the error terms are distributed logistically and that independence of irrelevant alternatives holds. Let

$$A = \alpha_{10} + \alpha_1 STRUCTURE + \alpha_2 EFFICIENCIES + \alpha_3 VALUE + \alpha_6 SALES + \alpha_7 OVERLAP + \alpha_8 POLITICS + \alpha_{11} TIME,$$

and

$$B = \beta_9 + \beta_1 SETTLE\ VALUE + \beta_{10} EFFICIENCIES + \beta_5 STRUCTURE + \beta_7 POLITICS + \beta_{11} TIME.$$

This implies that the probability of fighting, settling, and folding respectively equal

(9) $$P_1 = e^A / (1 + e^A + e^B)$$

(10) $$P_2 = e^B / (1 + e^A + e^B),$$

(11) $$P_3 = 1 - P_1 - P_2.$$

Using standard methods of maximum likelihood and multinomial logit analysis, we can now estimate the parameters in equations (5) and (8).

We first examine the data before presenting the regression results. Table I presents the average values of the variables for the given fight, fold or settle outcome. The average *OVERLAP* was 82.7 percent in the litigated cases, 62.7 percent in the abandoned cases and only 17.3 percent in the settled cases. In particular, overlaps of 10 percent or less almost always (94 percent in the sample) result in settlements, while overlaps of up to 30 percent usually (77 percent) end in settlements. On the other hand, large overlaps of over 50 percent almost always (94 percent) lead to either litigation or the abandonment of the deal. Similarly, the mean of the page-based efficiency variable is 22.5 pages for the litigated cases, but only 11.5 for the abandoned cases and 5.3 for the settled cases. Both the differences in the average overlap and efficiencies are statistically significant. Also of interest is the price of the transaction (*VALUE*) and the value of the acquisition not related to the competitive overlap (*SETTLE VALUE*). Both numbers are relatively low for the litigated and abandoned cases, and significantly higher for the settled transactions. Finally, the average size of the acquiring firm (*SALES*) is significantly higher if the transaction ends in a settlement rather than litigation.

IV. ESTIMATION OF THE MODEL

Presentation of the Results

Table II presents the estimated results of our econometric model. The first column defines the fight vs. fold equation, while the second column identifies the settle vs. fight equation.[10] As implied above in equations (5) and (8), coefficients on *VALUE*, *OVERLAP* and *SALES* are only estimated for the fight equation, while a coefficient on *SETTLE VALUE* is only estimated for the settle equation.[11]

There is marginal evidence in Table II that, on net, the merits of a case affect the fight vs. fold decision, as the t-statistic on *STRUCTURE* equals only 1.59.[12] Thus, the statistical analysis gives only weak support to the hypothesis that the opportunity to succeed on the merits outweighs

10. If the FTC used *OVERLAP* as a proxy for the probability of an easy settlement and allowed this factor to influence its enforcement decision, we would have to adjust for sample selection bias with respect to the cases where the parties chose to settle. (Under this scenario, the low overlap cases would be overrepresented in the sample.) Following Hughes and Snyder [1989] we test for this problem by estimating a bivariate probit model, with one equation for the FTC enforcement decision (with a model similar to Coate, Higgins and McChesney [1990]) and the other for the firm's decision to settle (with a model similar to the one in this paper). (See Snyder [1990, 451–2] for a similar approach in a setting with two available choices.) The coefficient relating the error terms of the two equations is insignificant, with a t-statistic of –0.32, indicating no relationship between the equations. Moreover, unlike results reported in Hughes and Snyder, the coefficients generated by the bivariate estimation process are almost identical to the coefficients generated by independent univariate probits for the coefficients that were significantly different from zero. Thus, we are unable to reject the null hypotheses of no sample selection bias in the data. A test of the means of the *OVERLAP* variable tends to confirm this result, as no statistical difference is observed between the mean value of *OVERLAP* from the sample of closed cases and the mean value from the sample of enforcement actions.

11. A logarithmic transformation was applied to the *VALUE*, *SALES* and *EFFICIENCY* variables before the model was estimated.

12. Models not reported here with different merits variables have lower t-statistics on these variables. We also ran models with $STRUCTURE^2$, but failed to obtain a significant coefficient for that variable.

TABLE I
Variables Means by Fight, Fold and Settle Status
(Standard Deviations In Parentheses)

Variable	Fight N=13	Fold N=30	Settle N=29	Overall N=72
OVERLAP[123]	82.69 (26.54)	62.73 (32.33)	17.34 (20.65)	48.06 (37.55)
EFFICIENCIES[123]	22.42 (19.15)	11.51 (11.95)	5.328 (6.776)	10.99 (13.23)
STRUCTURE	2985 (2313)	3766 (2396)	3527 (3861)	3529 (3034)
VALUE[23]	134.0 (203.2)	88.95 (117.7)	1969 (4385)	854.5 (2906)
SETTLE VALUE[23]	24.36 (64.59)	36.53 (74.92)	1780 (4131)	736.5 (2735)
SALES[2]	2598 (4123)	5266 (7743)	7592 (1184)	5721 (8944)
TIME	44.23 (29.3)	55.63 (23.15)	51.62 (27.8)	51.96 (26.19)
POLITICS	55.45 (2.41)	56.57 (1.99)	56.28 (2.09)	56.25 (2.12)

[1] indicates that the mean of the variable for fight outcomes is statistically different from the mean for fold outcomes at the 10 percent level, [2] indicates that the mean of the variable for fight outcomes is statistically different from the mean for settle outcomes at the 10 percent level, and [3] indicates that the mean of the variable for fold outcomes is statistically different from the mean for settle outcomes at the 10 percent level.

the incentive to capture anticompetitive profits related to a high structural index in litigation decisions. We also found no evidence that the Commission offers less burdensome settlements when it is pursuing a weaker case on the merits, as the t-statistic on the merits variable in the settle vs. fold equation is only 0.06.

Other control variables have the anticipated effects. The level of efficiencies has the predicted effects on fighting relative to folding, with higher efficiencies making fighting more likely. In addition, the presence of efficiencies also makes settling less likely relative to folding.[13] A higher overlap variable increases the odds on litigation vs. folding. The time variable has no

13. We test for the independence of irrelevant alternatives by estimating the parameters without either the fight or settle cases along the lines of Hausman and McFadden [1984]. In either situation, the coefficient estimates were almost identical, with Hausman statistics of 1.34 and 0.0002, respectively. Neither statistic is significant, indicating that the hypothesis of equal coefficients cannot be rejected. For a more complete robustness analysis of a related model see Coate, Kleit, and Bustamante [1993]. The results in that paper generally carry over to the slightly different specification presented here.

TABLE II
Multinomial Logit Model

	Fight vs. Fold Equation	Settle vs. Fold Equation
VALUE	.8575 (1.64)	–
OVERLAP	.05083** (2.26)	–
SALES	–1.280** (–2.04)	–
SETTLE VALUE	–	1.260** (3.45)
EFFICIENCIES	1.901** (2.37)	–1.112** (–2.24)
STRUCTURE	–.0005153 (–1.59)	.00000806 (0.06)
TIME	.08136 (1.50)	.02290 (0.68)
POLITICS	–1.244** (–1.95)	.1081 (0.27)
Constant	–.9498 (–0.24)	–5.086** (–2.11)

Pseudo R-square: 0.5598 Log Likelihood: –32.97

t-statistics in parentheses, * indicates significance at the 10 percent level and ** indicates a 5 percent level, using two-tailed tests. The Pseudo R-square is calculated by taking one minus the log likelihood of the equation divided by the log likelihood estimated using only the constant terms.

significant impact on the odds of settlement and only a very weak effect on the odds of litigation. The level of a firm's sales is negatively related to the fight vs. fold decision, indicating that large firms seek to generate a reputation for "good behavior" with the government. The settle value of the transaction (after adjustment for divestiture) also serves to increase the probability of a settlement, while the value of the transaction has a weakly positive impact on the ratio of probability of litigation to folding. Finally, the political index significantly reduces the likelihood of litigation relative to folding, while having no effect on the probability of a settlement.

Given these results, we can conclude that the size of the overlap (and the derived level of *SETTLE VALUE*) affects decisions, with firms involved in deals with small overlaps almost certain to settle and firms involved in deals with large overlaps more likely to fight. Efficiencies are also important. If efficiencies are relatively large, the firm is more likely to fight to

TABLE III
Prediction Table for Historical Data

		Predicted Outcome				
		Fight	**Fold**	**Settle**	**Total**	**% Correct**
Actual	Fight	10	2	1	13	77
Outcome	Fold	3	24	3	30	80
	Settle	0	3	26	29	90
Total		13	29	30	72	83

save the proposed merger. Settlements are also affected by efficiencies, with firms tending to abandon, rather than settle, transactions with larger efficiencies. The merits of a case appear to play a relatively small role in the litigation decision. The value of the transaction also plays a role in the decision, with large deals tending to be more likely to end in litigation. Likewise, political considerations affect the litigation decision, with firms less likely to litigate in periods of strong Democratic political control.

Application of the Model: Predictions vs. Actual Outcomes

Table III examines how well the model predicted the actual outcome of the merger cases. Fitted values were computed for each data point and the result with the largest probability is taken as the predicted outcome.[14] The model predicts correctly 77 percent of the cases that end in litigation, 90 percent of the settlements and 80 percent of the abandoned mergers. Overall, the model predicts 83 percent of the cases correctly.

14. The smallest highest predicted value in the data set was 44.2 percent.

Of the twelve cases where the model did not predict the actual outcome, three cases (one of which was a fight) had actual outcomes with probabilities over 40 percent. In two other cases, the third highest probability represented the actual choice. The first involved an unusual settlement mechanism, and the second involved a case that ended in litigation under peculiar circumstances. In the seven remaining cases, one represented a situation in which the parties chose fighting (predicted probability 17 percent) over folding (82 percent), three were cases where folding (24 percent, 23 percent and 28 percent) were chosen over settling (76 percent, 77 percent and 72 percent), two involved folding (31 percent and 16 percent) over fighting (69 percent and 84 percent) and in one case the parties decided to settle (12 percent) instead of fold (87 percent).

Application of the Model: Sensitivity

Some indication of the impact of particular variables can be gained by reviewing what effects they have on the probability of each outcome, given our basic model of Table II. For example, assuming a case has the attributes described by the mean of the estimated sample, the basic model shows that firms will fold with a 55.6 percent probability, settle with a 42.8 percent probability, and fight with only a 1.6 percent probability.[15] Holding all other variables constant and raising the overlap variable one standard deviation to 85.6 percent (with the accompanying change in *SETTLE VALUE*) generates an 18.3 percent increase in the probability of folding to 73.9 percent, a 30.9 percent decrease in the settle rate to 11.9 percent, and an 12.6 percent rise in the fight probability to 14.2 percent. Similarly, holding all other variables constant and reducing the overlap variable one standard deviation to 10.5 percent reduces the fold probability 15.9 percent to 39.7 percent, raises the settle rate 17.4 percent to 60.2 percent, and lowers the fight rate 1.5 percent to an unlikely 0.1 percent.

Changing the level of efficiencies has similar, but smaller effects. Raising the efficiency variable one standard deviation while holding all other variables at their sample means generates an increase in the fold rate to 69.1 percent, a decrease in the settle rate to 16.8 percent, and an increase in the fight rate to 14.1 percent. Lowering the efficiency variable to zero reduces the probability of folding to 12.8 percent, raises the settle rate to 87.3 percent, and lowers the fight rate to a tiny 0.01 percent.

Raising the *STRUCTURE* variable one standard deviation while holding all other variables at their sample means has little effect on outcomes, raising the probability of folding 0.2 percent, the probability of settling 1.0 percent, while reducing the chances of fighting 1.3 percent. Lowering the *STRUCTURE* variable 1.13 standard deviations (to 0, representing a case with no barriers to entry perceived by the Bureau of Economics's staff), however, has a slightly larger impact. In this scenario, the probability of folding falls 3.6 percent to 52 percent, the probability of settling declines 4.0 percent to 38.8 percent, while the probability of fighting rises 7.6 percent to 9.2 percent.

Changes in the political index (*POLITICS*) also affect the likely outcome. A one standard deviation increase in the political variable would increase the probability of a settlement to 49.1 percent, while lowering the likelihood of abandoning the transaction to 50.8 percent and almost eliminating the chance of litigation at 0.1 percent. On the other hand, a one standard deviation reduction in the political variable raises the likelihood of litigation to 19.8 percent with reductions to 49.7 percent for the fold rate and 30.5 percent for the settle rate.

Application of the Model: Predictions

One can also apply the model to proposed mergers to predict the likely response to a Commission merger challenge. In the two-year period immediately following September 1991 (the end of the data set for the regression in Table II), the Commission challenged twelve proposed horizontal transactions. Nine cases ended in settlements, with the parties selling off offending assets or technology. In six of these cases, the model predicted a probability of settlement of more than 90 percent, while in the others the settlement probability exceeded 50 percent. The model also correctly predicted the one abandoned merger, as well as both the cases that ended in litigation. Thus, the model has successfully predicted the outcomes of all of the FTC merger challenges for these two years.

Finally, as discussed above, the FTC does not allow firms to consummate part of an acquisition while litigating the remainder. The model, however, can predict

15. For a case that has attributes equal to the sample mean of those cases that folded, the model predicts an 80 percent chance of folding, with an 18 percent chance of a settlement and a 2 percent chance of litigation. For a case with attributes equal to the sample mean of those cases where the firms chose to settle, settling has a 98 percent chance of occurring, while folding is expected to occur with a 2 percent likelihood. Finally, for a case where the attributes are equal to that of the sample mean for the cases that ended in litigation, fighting is expected to occur with a 66 percent probability. Folding is the primary alternative with almost a 32 percent chance.

the outcome of the various cases if the FTC changed policies and allowed the consummation of the competitively neutral part of the transaction by lowering *VALUE* to the value of the contested part of the transaction, assigning *SETTLE VALUE* to zero (because there would be nothing left to settle) and replacing *OVERLAP* with 100 to reflect the fact that the remaining part of the deal would be subject to competitive concerns. Under these conditions, our results indicate that twenty of the cases in the data set would have been litigated, including eleven of the thirteen that actually were litigated and eight cases that were actually abandoned. Five of the twenty-four transactions correctly predicted to be abandoned would have ended in litigation without this "hostage" effect, while one of the twenty-six settlements would have gone to court. Thus, the model suggests that the Commission's refusal to allow partial acquisitions precluded a litigated outcome of six of the fifty successfully modelled cases.

In addition, it is also possible to exploit other hostage effects related to the size of the transaction. As our model shows, both small deals and transactions by large corporations are unlikely to be litigated. We can use our model to estimate the impact of these factors. For example, starting after the FTC allows the noncontroversial aspects of a transaction to settle, one can replace the actual value of the potentially anticompetitive transaction with the sample mean of $118 million for all cases with contested values under $118 million.[16] Calculating expected probabilities for each data point suggests that twenty-eight cases would end in litigation, including all of the thirteen actual litigations. Moreover, the model predicts that in these circumstances ten of the twenty-four folds and two of the twenty-six settlements predicted by the method used for Table III would go to litigation. The procedure can be taken one step further to minimize the reputation effect by setting the acquiring firm's sales to $100 million for all transactions assigned a value of $118 million which currently show sales over $100 million.[17] The model would then predict fifty-seven litigated cases, including all thirteen actual litigations. Transactions would rarely fold, with only one of the twenty-four abandoned cases and eleven of the twenty-six settlements predicted in Table III now being dropped before litigation. Thus, when taken together, the three "hostage" effects tend to induce firms to either drop or settle the competitive problems when faced with FTC action.

V. CONCLUSION

The results of this study have clear implications for our understanding of antitrust policy. The econometric model shows that firms are very unlikely to litigate when the overlap is small, the value of the transaction is low and/or the acquiring firm is large. These conditions encompass a significant number of FTC cases. Thus, it appears that the nature of the merger process, not the merits of individual cases, is the driving force in the outcomes of these cases. Therefore, the FTC (and likely its sister agency, the Department of Justice) must be seen in large part as a regulator, not a law enforcer, because there is no viable independent review of a large number of its bureaucratic decisions. To retain a judicial standard in antitrust cases, the decision makers must therefore act as courts and assign the litigation staff the burden of proof when making enforcement decisions.

16. This is calculated as the difference between the average value for the overall transaction and the mean settle value, both taken from Table I.

17. This number is chosen arbitrarily to be similar to the $118 million value of the transaction used in the analysis. One could use a larger figure for sales and find fewer firms litigate their cases.

The model also sheds light on the firm's decision-making process. The significance of the efficiency variable appears to suggest that some mergers are efficiency motivated, because firms are more willing to incur litigation costs to complete a transaction when efficiencies are high. Similarly, firms appear less willing to enter into settlements in markets where significant efficiencies are likely to be available. The structure of the market may have an effect, with firms more willing to litigate weak cases, though the evidence did not strongly confirm this result. Finally, political considerations also appear to have some influence on the firm's fight, fold or settle decision.

REFERENCES

Coate, Malcolm B. "Economics, the Guidelines and the Evolution of Merger Policy." *Antitrust Bulletin*, Winter 1992, 997–1024.

Coate, Malcolm B., Richard S. Higgins, and Fred S. McChesney. "Bureaucracy and Politics in FTC Merger Challenges." *Journal of Law and Economics*, October 1990, 463–82.

Coate, Malcolm B., Andrew N. Kleit, and Rene Bustamante. "Fight, Fold, or Settle?: Modelling the Reaction to FTC Merger Challenges." Federal Trade Commission Working Paper No. 200, February 1993.

Coate, Malcolm B., and Fred McChesney. "Empirical Evidence on FTC Enforcement of the Merger Guidelines." *Economic Inquiry*, April 1992, 277–293.

Comanor, William S., and Lawrence J. White. "Market Power or Efficiency?: A Review of Antitrust Standards." *Review of Industrial Organization*, 7(2), 1992, 105–16.

Ginsburg, Douglas H. "Antitrust as Antimonopoly." *Regulation*, Summer 1991, 91–100.

Hausman, Jerry, and Daniel McFadden. "Specification Test for the Multinomial Logit Model." *Econometrica*, September 1984, 1219–40.

Hughes, James, and Edward Snyder. "Policy Analysis of Medical Malpractice Reforms: What Can We Learn From Claims Data?" *Journal of Business and Economic Statistics*, October 1989, 423–30.

Johnson, Ronald, and Allen Parkman. "Premerger Notification and the Incentive to Merge and Litigate." *Journal of Law, Economics & Organization*, April 1991, 145–62.

Khemani, R. S., and D. M. Shapiro. "An Empirical Analysis of Canadian Merger Policy." *Journal of Industrial Economics*, June 1993, 161–77.

Kleit, Andrew N., and Malcolm B. Coate. "Are Judges Leading Economic Theory? Sunk Costs, the Threat of Entry and the Competitive Process." *Southern Economic Journal*, July 1993, 103–18.

Kolasky, William J., Jr., Phillip A. Proger, and Roy T. Englert. "Anticompetitive Mergers: Prevention and Cure," in *Antitrust and Regulation*, edited by Franklin M. Fisher. Cambridge, Mass.: MIT Press, 1985, 49–84.

Landes, William M. "An Economic Analysis of the Courts." *Journal of Law and Economics*, April 1971, 61–108.

Lopatka, John E., and James F. Mongoven. "After Preliminary Relief in Merger Cases is Denied, What Then?" *Research in Law and Economics*, 17, 1995 forthcoming.

McCubbins, Matthew D., Roger G. Noll, and Barry R. Weingast. "Administrative Procedures as Instruments of Political Control." *Journal of Law, Economics, and Organization*, Fall 1987, 243–77.

Milgrom, Paul, and John Roberts. "Predation, Reputation, and Entry Deterrence." *Journal of Economic Theory*, 27(2), 1982, 280–312.

Perloff, Jeffrey M., and Daniel L. Rubinfeld. "Settlements in Private Antitrust Litigation," in *Private Antitrust Litigation: New Evidence, New Learning*, edited by Lawrence White. Cambridge, Mass.: MIT Press, 1988.

Posner, Richard A. "The Behavior of Administrative Agencies." *Journal of Legal Studies*, June 1972, 305–47.

Snyder, Edward A. "The Effect of Higher Criminal Penalties on Antitrust Enforcement." *Journal of Law and Economics*, October 1990, 439–62.

U.S. Department of Justice. "Department of Justice and Federal Trade Commission Horizontal Merger Guidelines." *Antitrust Trade and Regulation Report*, No. 1559, April 2, 1992.

Name Index